"THE GOLDMAN BOOK TELLS ALL."
Baltimore Sun

"The best yet on Elvis...More fascinating than the myriad eccentricities of the Sun King, though, is Goldman's portrait of Presley's renowned manager, Colonel Tom Parker...No one has ever chipped away so successfully at Parker's favorite fairy tale—that he is the king of the flimflam men."

Playboy

"Fascinating...frequently brilliant...Goldman has uncovered an extraordinary amount of fresh material about his subject."

Houston Post

"A WHOLE NEW ELVIS"
Washington Post

"Startling new conclusions about Presley... fascinating....It is, without doubt, the most illuminating book extant on the former king of rock 'n' roll."

Pittsburgh Post-Gazette

"The analysis of Presley's music is really quite brilliant, especially when he comes to explaining its sources, its techniques, and the reasons for its appeal...A convincing profile of Presley's deep characterological faults...An impressive amount of digging, what with his having conducted more than 600 interviews and turned up hard news on Presley's drug habits, on his financial misarrangements with Colonel Parker, on the Colonel's mysterious Dutch origins, on the unusual call Presley paid President Nixon while 'high as a kite' on drugs and fired with zeal to stamp out drug abuse, and on the precise circumstances surrounding Presley's death."

Christopher Lehman-Haupt, *The New York Times*

"A grim riveting replay of the success trauma that finally shredded one of the most exuberant talents of our time."

Cosmopolitan

ELVIS

ALBERT GOLDMAN

AVON
PUBLISHERS OF BARD, CAMELOT, DISCUS AND FLARE BOOKS

AVON BOOKS
A division of
The Hearst Corporation
959 Eighth Avenue
New York, New York 10019

For Barry Berkman,
a faithful friend through many trials

Contents

Acknowledgments

IN A WORK entailing so many sources and informants as this biography, it is virtually impossible to acknowledge every contribution. Certain individuals and organizations were so helpful, however, that they deserve especial thanks. John A. Whisler, of the Memphis–Shelby County Public Library, made available the unpublished manuscript of his exhaustive bibliography of writings about Elvis Presley. Philip W. McMullin, president, Institute of Family Research, contributed his organization's genealogical research into the Pressley Family. Dirk Vellenga of *De Stem*, Breda, Holland, provided all the information about Colonel Parker's Dutch origin. James K. Caughley furnished in addition to his oral testimony excerpts from his diary and the unpublished manuscript of his recollections of Elvis. The contributions of the following individuals lie for the most part in the area designated by the rubric following each group of names.

Richard E. Davis, Lamar and Nora Fike, Alan Fortas, Dave Hebler, Marty Lacker, Jerry Schilling, Gene Smith, Red and Pat West, Sonny and Judy West (the Guys and the Wives); Betty McCann, Billie Wardlow Mooneyham, Dixie Locke Emmons, Debra Paget, Natalie Wood, Joan Blackman, Anita Wood Brewer, Gloria Mowel Stratton, Heidi Heissen Busley, Frances Forbes, Connie Stevens, Barbara Leigh, Linda Thompson, Ginger Alden (Elvis's women friends); Mary Jane Lyon, Floyd Presley, Vester Presley, Christine Roberts, Truitt Smith, Doshia Steele (the Presleys and the Smiths); James and Eula Dell Ausborn, Ernest Bowen (WELO); Mrs. Billie Boyd, Trellis Leeman Burch, the Reverend W. Frank Smith (Tupelo); Coach Rube Boyce, Buzzy Forbes, Mrs. Jeanette Fruchter, Farley Guy, Bernard and Guy Lansky, Mrs. William Morris (Memphis, early years); Cecil and James Blackwood,

Jake Hess, Joe Mascheo, J. D. Sumner, Charles Wolf (gospel); Warden Steve Hargett, Tom Gregory, Charles Marx, Larry Phillips (Parchman); Maurice Hulbert, B. B. King, Robert Thomas, Rufus Thomas (WDIA); Tillman Franks, David Houston, Horace Logan, John Prime *(Louisiana Hayride);* Ray Brown, Jack Clement, Frankie Connors, D. J. Fontana, Bill Justis, Stanley Kesler, Wink Martindale, Scotty Moore, Robert, Helen and Sonny Neal, Jim Stewart (Sun years); Eddy Arnold, Whitey Ford, Bitsy Mott, Father Rohling, Carl Sedlmeyer, Jr., Jimmy Rogers Snow (Colonel Parker's early career); Jean Aberbach, Chet Atkins, Mae Boren Axton, Freddy Bienstock, Bo Diddley, Al Dvorin, Bones Howe, George Johnstone, Gordon Stoker, Ben Wiseman (early recording and stage career); Pandro Berman, Marcia Borie, Bill Campbell, Raphael Campos, Jack Cummings, Bill Dakota, Richard Egan, Frank Faylen, Virginia Grant, Katherine Hereford, Carolyn Jones, Hal Kanter, Jerry Katzman, Nancy Sinatra Lambert, Marlyn Mason, Mary Ann Mobley, Gene Nelson, Willy Nichols, Jeremy Slate, Deborah Walley (Hollywood); Eddie Fadal, Sgt. William H. Norwood, Rex and Elisabeth Mansfield, Walter Schweinsmann (Army); Sister Loyola Fox, Currie Grant, Milan LeFevre, Sister M. Adrian Mully, Mike Stone (Priscilla); Chris Bearde, Bill Bellew, Steve Binder, Bob Finkel, Tom Sarnoff (Singer Special); Emilio Muscelli, Joe Guercio, Dr. Elias Ghanem, Nick Naff, Terry Riesner, Dr. Max Shapiro, Sol Schwartz, Alex Shoofey (Las Vegas); John Corcoran, Ed Parker, Kang Ree, Bill Wallace (karate); Jack Adams, Flo and Gloria Demeno, Gill Gilleland, Ed Hookstratten, Mary Jenkins, Jackie Kahane, Harry Levitch, Dr. David Meyer, Bill Morris, Dee Presley, Billy and David Stanley, Charlie Thompson, Sam Thompson, Dr. Spencer Thornton (final years); Dr. Michel Janis (autopsy procedure); Sid Bernstein; Paul Klein (programming chief, NBC); Rocco Laginestra (formerly president, RCA Victor); Blanchard E. Tual (Colonel Parker as manager); Prof. Carole Berkin, Jerry Carrigan, Prof. Charles W. Crawford, Shelby Foote, Joe Lewis, Doc Pomus, Gloria Stavers (general background); Paul Dougher, Paul Dowling, Nick Hunter, John Lumsdaine, Sylvia Chase, Susan Braudy (films, records, tapes, transcripts); Anne Pitrone, Leslie Meredith (editorial assistants); Harry Hall (researcher); Barbara Hohol (typist); Joe Schoenfeld (cicerone); Rene Lachicotte (factotum).

Finally, I wish to thank Kevin Eggers, who first conceived this project; Lamar Fike, who was my guide to the Presley circle and who conducted a number of valuable interviews; Milton Glaser, who designed the spiritual portrait of the young Elvis on the hardcover dust jacket; Edgar J. Scherick, who bought the movie rights; and most of all Gladys Justin Carr, who was not only my forbearing and helpful editor but on occasion my savior.

Fame, after all, is no more than the quintessence of all the misunderstandings collecting round a new name.

Rilke on Rodin

ELVIS

Prologue: The Royal American

THOUGH democracy is ostensibly the opposite of monarchy, the mass culture that is American democracy has betrayed in every age a deep atavistic yearning for royalty. From the days of "King" Andrew Jackson to those of the "Kingfish," Huey Long; from the era of the Robber Barons to the age of the movie "kings" and "queens"; from the first black demagogues, Marcus Garvey and Father Divine, to the "Prophet," Elijah Muhammed; from the earliest Mafia chieftains to the bowing, kneeling and hand-kissing of *The Godfather;* from the regal F.D.R. to the "Imperial Presidency" of President John F. Kennedy to the Great Pretender, Richard Nixon (who ordered the White House police costumed in the Graustarkian uniforms of European palace guards), Americans have fulfilled their craving for royalty and the trappings of royalty in so many ways that the impulse to set up kings and worship them must be reckoned one of the basic features of the national character. In this long history of infatuation with self-anointed but indubitably powerful and charismatic sovereigns, no figure looms larger than Elvis Aaron Presley.

Elvis received his title, King of Rock 'n' Roll, as early in life and with the same sense of divine right as any

1

hereditary monarch. For many years, however, he comported himself less like a king than a prince: one of those
spoiled Arab princelings who throw around their money
and recruit their harems in Hollywood or St. Tropez, until
the sad day comes when they are summoned home to assume their duties as chief of the tribe. Though he was
acclaimed in the fifties, it was not until the seventies that
the King finally laid claim to his royal prerogatives, the
tardiness of his coronation being balanced by its extravagance. Indeed, once Elvis felt the crown upon his brows,
he could never get enough of the perquisites of royalty,
each new claim to princely prerogative or assertion of
kingly privilege leading immediately to an even more audacious feat of self-aggrandizement. As King Elvis contrived his costumes and elaborated his rituals, as he enlarged his court and extended his largesse, as he viewed
himself even more fixedly as a man with a vast if ill-
defined mission, his subjects responded by according him
more and more of the honor and glory owing to a king.
The immense crowds that gathered everywhere he appeared, the fanatical devotion, amounting to worship, with
which he was adored, the mad passion to make contact
with the royal body—a mania he sought to gratify by
tossing sweat-stained scarves to the people—make it obvious that his regal posturings were as much a fulfillment
of his public's deepest longings as they were expressions
of his own megalomania.

An American king, Elvis saw his empire extend around
the globe, until it comprised even the remotest regions,
the most exotic peoples. In fact, he inspired even greater
enthusiasm and awe in other countries than he did at
home because foreigners did not recognize any faults in
his title, any limits to his vaunted powers or any rival
claimants to his throne. Consequently, the exalted status
which Elvis enjoyed the world around varied only as local
customs vary in the treatment of such an extraordinary
being. If the English celebrated him with racy pop journalism, as they do their own royal family, the Germans
feted him by founding learned journals and publishing
Festschriften packed with historical minutiae. If the Russians denounced him as a symbol of the corrupt and cor-

rupting culture of the West, the oriental nations acclaimed him as the ideal figure of that American civilization they are so eager to emulate and assimilate. Not since the great days of Charlie Chaplin has any solo performer attained such universal popularity. At the time of his death in 1977, Elvis Presley's was the second most commonly reproduced image in the world. The first was Mickey Mouse.

Implicit in the image of the King was always the suggestion of the Messiah. Though Elvis was wont to say, "There is but one King," even the fact that he felt obliged to make the disclaimer is revealing. It illustrates, once again, the profound harmony that existed between Elvis's deepest, most gratifying self-image—in this case as a divinely appointed Messenger, Master or Chosen One—and the yearnings of his public: those millions of faith-starved souls perpetually in search of a cult or a charismatic figure who can gratify their yearning for spiritual enlargement and fulfillment. Ironically, Elvis was just such a person himself. His own original disciple, he was the first to identify his sudden and overwhelming success as a product of divine, not merely mortal favor. Having recognized himself as one of those awesome beings who appear only once in a millennium to give a wholly new inspiration to their civilization, it was only a matter of time until he began to allow this illumination to show forth in his public manner and dress. Indeed, nothing is more apparent in Elvis's final phase than the religious aura in which he sought to cloak himself, straining after even the most extravagant effects, up to and including transfiguration.

In this climactic period, he chose as his entrance theme the apocalyptic opening bars of Richard Strauss's *Also Sprach Zarathustra,* a music that invested the King's appearance with an air of sublimity, as of the arrival of the Superman from outer space. Striding onstage in a vast coliseum holding as many as eighty thousand souls, he would stand for a moment, caught in the intersecting beams of the great Zeppelin searchlights, allowing the masses to drink in the majesty of his appearance. Clad always in white, studded and gauded with flashing jewels

and metals, he gleamed as if lit from within by some preternatural radiance.

The famous costume, which commenced its evolution
as little more than a stunning male negligee, had been
elaborated through countless subsequent designs into a
regalia. The originally abstract decorative patterns had
come to focus in boldly totemic images: an orange and
black tiger, a gold and blue peacock, a Mayan stone calendar, an Aztec pyramid, a triadic rainbow—every costume the King wore was fraught with meaning for his
devotees. Finally, on the occasion of his greatest appearance, on the Satellite Show—the televised performance
destined for an audience equivalent to half the population
of the entire world—Elvis demanded and received the full
regalia. From that time forth, he wore a high Napoleonic
collar; a short but voluminous Elizabethan cape; a broad,
massively buckled gladiator's belt; and on his chest stood
rampant a crimson, gold and azure eagle. Behold! His
Royal and Imperial American Highness!

The private life of the Rock King conformed as closely
to the royal model as did his public presence. Around his
throne flocked all the familiar types found in every court:
fawning lackeys, fearless bodyguards, jealous minions,
feeble-minded fools, earnest petitioners, impoverished
kinsmen, grasping tradesmen and even grieving mothers,
bringing their sick children to be healed by the King's
touch. King Elvis had his bustling majordomo, his privi-
leged jester, his court musicians, his conscience-soothing
confessor, his minister of the exchequer, his household
physician and his royal goldsmith, who traveled everywhere with the King, carrying boxes of costly baubles
which his master would distribute to favorites or to
strangers, according to his whim. Needless to say, the King
had countless concubines: poor but beautiful girls of compliant temper, dazzled by his princely glamour and mu-
nificence. Also, in every period, there was one woman, the
declared mistress, as she would have been called at the
court of Louis XIV, who was recognized as the special
favorite and treated with appropriate respect. Above all,
the Rock King, like many a famous monarch, had a sinister
chief minister, a scheming grand vizier, well armed with

palace spies and an infallible sense of the King's weak-
nesses, who spent his life enriching himself at the King's
expense, while manipulating his master like a puppet.

To comprehend the phenomenon that was Elvis Presley,
therefore, one must be prepared to take the concept of
kingship not only literally but extravagantly, to its furthest possible reach. One must bring to bear upon this
bizarre but representative American not only the knowledge of kings and courts found in Saint-Simon's memoirs
of the Sun King but the more primitive notions of solar
deities found in Frazer's *The Golden Bough*. One must be
prepared to recognize in the life-style of a southern hillbilly showbiz celebrity those archaic customs of the seventeenth-century French court, the *couchée* and the *levée*,
for even such trivial and quotidian acts as getting in or
out of bed became highly formularized rituals at the court
of the Rock King. Indeed, it would be no exaggeration to
say that, as with his most ancient and primitive proto-
types, the life of King Elvis consisted of nothing but rit-
ualized routine. The clearest evidence of this condition
is the fact that on those exceedingly rare occasions when
Elvis did something spontaneous, he threw his entire entourage into a panic. Kings are cardinal figures, upon
whom their worlds turn; they must not behave erratically.

Elvis compared himself frequently with the president
of the United States. He declared that if he so desired he
could himself be the president. Considering the sort of
person that Elvis became in later life, this is a startling
idea. Yet, nothing that has happened in recent times mil-
itates against the notion of a famous entertainer becoming
the leader of the American people. It did not require the
election of Ronald Reagan to demonstrate that at this point
in their history, Americans feel most fulfilled by leaders
who are, or at least resemble, movie stars. Authority in
our society has devolved upon players. Why not, then, in
a future time, instead of movie stars, rock stars? No less
an expert than Richard Nixon assured Elvis that he had
the power over people's imaginations that would enable
him to obtain high office.

In truth, Elvis aspired to an office higher than that
occupied by any president. He viewed himself as one who

ruled the world by virtue of a unique power conferred
directly and exclusively upon him by the Most High. Like
Baron Corvo, Elvis Presley fancied himself a glamorous
latter-day pope: a prince, a potentate, a pontiff; a figure
of costly robes and cumbersome ceremonies; a human icon
carried about on the shoulders of lesser beings and set up
in public places to shed his spiritual effulgence upon the
faithful, before being restored to his throne in that strange
palace that is more a sanctuary than a seat of power, more
the shrine of a cult than the capital of a kingdom.

If the idea of kingship defines Elvis in his glory, it is
no less apt for characterizing Elvis in his fatal decline. In
his last years, the Rock King became the Fisher King.
Unmanned by a mysterious wound, presiding over a shadowy court that flitted all about the country, King Elvis
seemed fit only to rule a wasteland, the perfect emblem
for the midseventies. The more debilitated Elvis became,
the more he craved the refuge of his palace. At every opportunity, he would fly back to Graceland and shut himself
up inside it for weeks, sometimes months. Though great
numbers of the faithful besieged the gates and were even
conducted like pilgrims about the grounds, the mansion
itself presented a forbidding appearance, its windows
sealed, its doors guarded. Indeed, if there were any place
in America to which the word could be applied, one would
have declared that Graceland was taboo.

The first step in revealing Elvis Presley is to violate
that taboo. Though his house is still barred to the public,
still sending forth almost palpable waves of resistance, the
best way to commence the account of the most enigmatic
of all our popular kings, the most obscured and distorted
by the power of myth, is to break the spell that hovers
over his seat and track him to his innermost retreat.

So let us imagine ourselves back in the final years of
the King's reign, in possession of the supreme privilege
of the royal entrée. Let us pass through the Music Gate
and ascend the winding driveway to the top of the wooded
knoll on which stands the famous house, more legendary
than any house in America save the White House. Being
forearmed with the knowledge of true Elfans, we will
choose the date of our visitation in accordance with the

royal calendar. It was a long-established rule, reflected in all his business arrangements, that the King must lie at home upon Christmas. When we approach the mansion, the month will be January and the time will be night, the only proper time to visit the court of the Rock King.

Chapter 1

The King's Palace,
the King's Pleasure

THOUGH the holidays are long past, Graceland looks still like a picture on a Christmas card. The classic colonial façade, with its towering white columns and pilasters, is aglow with jewel lights, rose, amethyst and emerald. The templelike pediment is outlined in pale blue fire. This same eerie electric aura runs like St. Elmo's fire along the eaves, zigzags up and down the gables and shimmies down the drainpipes to the ground. Here it pales beside the brilliance of a rank of Christmas trees that have been transformed into cones of ruby, topaz, carnelian and aquamarine incandescence.

Prominently displayed on the front lawn is an elaborate crèche. The stable is a full-scale adobe house strewn with straw. Life-sized are the figures of Joseph and Mary, the kneeling shepherds and Magi, the lambs and ewes, as well as the winged annunciatory angel hovering over the roof beam. Real, too, is the cradle in which the infant Jesus sleeps.

When you step through the ten-foot oak door and enter the house, you stop and stare in amazement. Having just come from the contemplation of the tenderest scene in the Holy Bible, imagine the shock of finding yourself in a *whorehouse!* Yet there is no other way to describe the

9

drawing room of Graceland except to say that it appears
to have been lifted from some turn-of-the-century bordello
down in the French Quarter of New Orleans. Lulu White
or the Countess Willie Piazza might have contrived this
plushy parlor for the entertainment of Gyp the Blood. The
room is a gaudy mélange of red velour and gilded tassels,
Louis XV furniture and porcelain bric-a-brac, all informed
by the kind of taste that delights in a ceramic temple
d'amour housing a miniature Venus de Milo with an elec-
trically simulated waterfall cascading over her naked
shoulders.

Looking a little closer, you realize that the old madams
of the French Quarter would have been horrified at the
quality of the hangings and furniture at Graceland. They
decorated their sporting houses with magnificent pieces
crafted in Europe, upholstered them in the finest reps and
damasks, laid costly Persian carpets on their floors and
hung imposing oil paintings on their walls. Though it cost
a lot of money to fill up Graceland with the things that
appealed to Elvis Presley, nothing in the house is worth
a dime.

Take that fake fireplace that blocks with its companion
bookcases (filled with phony leather bindings) the two big
windows that should offer a commanding view of the front
lawn. This hokey facsimile looks like it was bought at the
auction of some bankrupt road company of *East Lynne*. Or
consider the Louis Quinze furniture strewn about the parlor. Every piece is elaborately carved and gilded, escutch-
eoned and cabrioleted; but it's not only fake (Louis XV's
upholsterers didn't go in for sectional sofas), it's that
dreadful fake antique that Italian gangsters dote on: garish, preposterous, uncomfortable and cheating wherever
it can, as in the substitution of velour for velvet. Or look
at the real fireplace of white marble that stands against
the back wall of the room, obviously innocent of use. It,
too, has been flanked not with bookcases but with a great
spread of smoked-glass mirror threaded with gold seams.
The whole ensemble is crowned with an electric clock inside a three-foot sunburst that looks like someone took an
ostrich egg and smashed it against the glass.

The entrance to the adjoining music room is flanked by

two tall, broad windows adorned with painted peacocks. Marvelously campy as are these bits of stained glass, they can't hold a candle to the bizarre chamber they frame. In this mad room, King Elvis's obsession with royal red reaches an intensity that makes you gag. Not so much a room as a crimson cocoon, every inch of it is swathed in red satin drapes, portieres, valences and braided ropes. As weird as anything in Edgar Allan Poe, the effect is that of stepping into the auricle of an immense heart. At the center of this king-sized valentine is the crowning touch: a concert grand piano that appears to have been dipped in liquid gold.

The entrance to the next room is blocked by a tall folding screen covered with mirrored glass. Screens and other masking devices abound at Graceland because Gladys and Vernon, Elvis's parents, imbued him with the old hillbilly superstition: Never close up windows or doors. Through this folding looking glass lies one of Elvis's favorite spots, the trophy room. A pop archeologist would find the excavation of this site a satisfying occupation. No part of Graceland was subject to more visions and revisions.

Originally, this room was a patio adjoining the dressing rooms for the outdoor pool. On hot Nilotic nights, Elvis and the Guys (known to the media as the "Memphis Mafia") would sit here cutting the ripe red hearts out of iced watermelons and vying to see who could eat the most. As they consumed this sweet satisfying pap, they would spit the pits out on the ground as Sweetpea, Gladys's Pomeranian, pranced about in the black hail.

In the late sixties, Elvis decided to build a forty-foot room over the patio to house his slot car racecourse. On a huge raised platform, a figure-eight track was laid out, in whose grooves could be fitted expensive scale-model replicas of Ferraris, Maseratis, Lotuses and Porsches. By means of an electric drive system, you could race these little cars around the tracks and up and down inclines at great speeds, which Elvis sought constantly to increase by means of continual improvements in the cars' motors. Manipulating the pistol-grip controls, you could make the cars skid, spin out and crash. It was a grand if costly game, and the Guys enjoyed it enormously.

Like all of Elvis's toys, the slot cars soon lost their charm. One day the track was banished to the attic, where it was stored alongside cartons of old teddy bears, discarded guitars and gilt lamps from the house on Audubon Avenue. Elvis never allowed anything to be cast out of Graceland except human beings. Once an object, no matter how trivial, came into his possession, it remained with him for the rest of his life.

Commencing in the Royal Period, the slot car room became the trophy room. Elvis pushed back the end wall twenty feet to make a chamber fit for a pharaoh's tomb. Then he filled it with gold. He ranked his fifty-three gold records along one wall, like patents of nobility. Against the opposite wall, he piled up, like the offerings before a shrine, a great heap of gold loving cups, gold statuettes and gold tablets. The effect is less that of a trophy case than of the display case of a trophy manufacturer.

The showcase effect is even more pronounced in the center of the room, which is occupied by a set of old-fashioned department store counters, under whose glass tops or stuffed inside storage drawers and cupboards lie an immense profusion of plaques, medals, certificates and scrapbooks received from professional organizations, charities and fan clubs. Like any true sovereign, King Elvis never forgets that all his wealth and power are derived from his subjects. No matter what they offer him, whether it be a huge stuffed animal or a little crocheted doily, he not only keeps the gift but puts it on display.

The oddest feature of the trophy room is the soda fountain that stands in one corner, one of two at Graceland, the other one being downstairs in the poolroom. Soda fountains and jukeboxes are symbolic objects for fifties rock heroes, no more to be wondered at than the old binnacle in the den of a steamship captain or the pair of crossed sabers on the wall of a retired general. What is disconcerting about this domestic altar is its formica meanness. Yet it would be out of character for Elvis to own a handsome old green marble counter with mottled glass lamps and quaint seltzer pulls because Elvis detests everything antique with the heartfelt disgust of a real forward-looking American of his generation. Like so many of his kind, he gloats over the spectacle of the wrecking ball bashing down the walls of historic Memphis. In fact, he likes to get into the driver's seat of a bulldozer and smash down old buildings himself. As he says: "When I wuz growin' up in Tupelo, I lived with enough fuckin' antiques to do me for a lifetime." That is why everything about the King must be spanking new, from his Louis XV furniture to his late model Seeburg jukebox—so drab compared to a dazzling peacock Wurlitzer.

On the left-hand side of the entrance hall is the dining room. In the center of the crimson carpet is a large quadrangle of black marble tiles on which is set the table: an eight-foot oval of mirrored glass on an ebonized and fluted wooden pedestal. Round the table in great state stand ten tall, ladder-backed Louis XIV chairs with tufted velour seats. They appear to have been drawn up for King Elvis and the Nine Worthies. (When Elvis dines with the Guys, he often jokes about Jesus breaking bread with his disciples. They respond by singing the old hymn, "What a Friend We Have in Jesus," substituting "Elvis" for "Jesus.") Above the table hangs a brass Louis XIV chandelier with two tiers of scrolled candlearms fitted with glass lusters. At each corner of the room, like bumpers on a game board, are tall diagonal bric-a-brac cabinets or chrome-plated étagères crammed with statuettes, vases, jars, boxes, plaques, goblets, ewers, compotes, porringers, shells, cloches, etc., *viz:*

    ceramic statuette of a grey poodle
    ceramic statuette of a nude girl with perched bird
    pair of Portuguese glazed pottery drug jars
    five specimens of butterflies in plastic cases
    artificial floral bouquet under a glass cloche
    two glass bowls with bouquet of black and white
        feathers
    model of 1932 antique radio
    ceramic statuette of a trumpeting elephant

Wherever Elvis goes in his travels, he indulges his middle-aged woman's passion for knickknacks, curios and chatzkahs. A domestic appraiser once remarked that Elvis appeared to have furnished Graceland largely from roadside stands.

A familiar feature of a number of the world's greatest palaces is a room decorated in an exotic style, inspired, perhaps, by the culture of one of the ruler's most remote or colorful provinces. Graceland possesses such a room; indeed, of all the public rooms in the mansion, it is the King's favorite. The den is an addition to the original building, created by enlarging and enclosing a back porch that ran along the entire rear wall. The room looks like Elvis scooped up the setting for one of his Hawaiian movies and brought it home inside a sixty-foot walnut hope chest. You reach the den by going through the kitchen, which is all white formica, walnut paneling and Kitchen-Aid stainless steel, with a couple of oddly feminine touches, like the calico carpeting and the hanging lampshades painted with fruits and vegetables. Entering the den, the first thing that strikes you is a towering statue of the god Tiki, confronting the visitor with outstretched arms holding an empty bowl. Obviously not an ashtray nor an hors d'oeuvre tray nor a place to drop your calling card, this empty basin is a puzzler. In any case, the statue serves to proclaim the room's provenance.

The style of the den could be characterized as Polynesian Primitive or Ugh! The decorator divided its sixty-foot length with another of those hinged screens that one finds all over Graceland. This one is composed of huge panels of stressed, stained pine perforated in long spermatozoid scrolls cut in the wood with a chain saw. On the side of the screen opposite that dominated by the figure of Tiki is a seating area focused upon an early-model Advent video projector.

Here, as Elvis watches his favorite football teams or boxing matches with the Guys, he enjoys the full flavor of the Polynesian Primitive. The huge sofa and the pair of oversized armchairs are carved out of the same dark coarse pine as the room divider and upholstered with thick, dark artificial fur. As the chairs have huge pawlike armrests, the impression created by this curious suite is rather like the Three Bears watching TV. This animalistic sofa is also Elvis's favorite downstairs dining spot. Like so many boy-men, he dislikes the formality of table service. Whenever possible, he has his meals served to him here on the cocktail table, a huge slab of boldly grained wood cut out of the crotch of a cypress tree and surfaced with what appears to be about a quarter-inch layer of lustrous polyurethane.

The most impressive feature of the den is the wall behind the TV, which is straight out of the lobby of a Waikiki Beach resort hotel. Constructed of layers of rough-cut fieldstone, it has been arranged artfully like a natural cataract and equipped with pipes and a pumping system so that a constant stream of soothing water flows down over the jutting rocks, catching as it falls the colors cast by the lamps concealed in the ceiling. What more perfect object of contemplation could be imagined for a man who is perpetually stoned?

As was often the case with palaces when they were inhabited by kings and not just exhibited as monuments, the grandeur of the principal building at Graceland conceals the meanness of the dependents' quarters. Though you often read awestruck descriptions of Graceland's imposing façade, you never see a word about the trailers and mobile homes up on the hill behind the house, where reside Elvis's poor hillbilly relations and caretakers. These number Aunt Nashville and her husband, Earl Pritchett; Elvis's cousin, Billy Smith, and his attractive wife, Jo; and Elvis's nurse, Tish Henley, and her husband, Tommy, a deputy sheriff. These folk comprise just a fraction of the extensive staff of Graceland. In addition to the people who live on the grounds, Elvis always keeps a couple of his men domiciled in the mansion. A garage adjoining the dining room has been converted into a full-scale apartment in which have lived first Marty Lacker, the foreman, and his family; then, Sonny West, the chief bodyguard, and his family. Charlie Hodge, the most symbiotically attached of Elvis's men, has lived continuously by his master's side since they were discharged from the army in 1960. Charlie has an apartment, well adapted to his gnomelike character, down in the basement. Graceland's housekeeper, Aunt Delta Mae—a big, bossy, iron-haired woman, often heard shouting, "Lord, I can't do a thing with these damned niggers!"—lives in what had been formerly Gladys's

and Vernon's room at the back of the ground floor, which
she shares now with her mother, Minnie Mae.

To this cadre must be added all the people who work
at Graceland but live elsewhere. Elvis's father and his
second wife, Dee, and her three boys by her first marriage
live at the back of the property on an adjacent street in
an attractive house with a gambrel roof. The gatekeepers,
led by Vernon's brother, Vester, number enough men to
mount a twenty-four-hour guard seven days a week at the
Music Gate. Other members of the staff include the valets,
Gee Gee Gambill and "Hamburger James" Caughley; the
four or five black maids or cooks; the yardmen, who attend
to the horses in the stable and the cars and other motor
vehicles in the garage, as well as performing the various
chores demanded by the thirteen and a half acre estate;
and the office staff, which works behind the mansion in
what was once the smokehouse. Finally, one must add all
the rest of the Guys, who, whether they make their homes
in Memphis, like Red West, Joe Esposito and Larry Geller,
or in some other city, like Lamar Fike in Nashville or
Jerry Schilling in Los Angeles, are often on the property.
Altogether, Graceland embraces an enormous extended
family in the classic southern plantation tradition.

Southern, too, is the mood of Graceland: that slumber-
ous, monotonous, somnambulistic atmosphere in which
people pad noiselessly about performing long-accustomed
tasks while engaging in endless small talk and gossip. It
is Elvis himself who sounds the low *Om* that is the keynote
of this drowsy domestic symphony. The moment he returns
from an engagement, he retreats to his upstairs apartment
and remains there for long periods, virtually incommu-
nicado.

The King's bedchamber is the most bizarre room in the
hillbilly palace. The walls are padded and tufted with but-
ton-studded strips of black artificial suede. The crimson
carpet covers not only the floor but rises at the foot of the
bed like a red wave, atop which rides an enormous color
TV set. Confronting the bed are two big windows that
overlook the front lawn. Sealed with the same black up-
holstery that covers the walls, they are crowned with gold
valences and hung with floor-length crimson drapes, pro-

ducing a somberly surrealistic image, like a painting by Magritte. The space between the windows is filled with a mirror, which reflects the bed.

What a bed! An immense slab, nine by nine, a double king size, it has a mortuary headboard of black quilted Naugahide, with a built-in plastic back angle and retractable armrests of speckled metal, like the skeletons of those padded "husbands" beloved of suburban matrons. To one side is an easel supporting a large photograph of Elvis's mother; on the other a sepia-toned portrait of Jesus Christ. Back in the corners of the room crouch big round seats covered with white fake fur like enormous bunnies.

As in a funeral parlor, the light in this inner sanctum is always dim, supplied by cove lamps that illuminate the ceiling but produce below only a murky subaqueous gloaming. The air is chilled, the temperature being driven down during the hot Memphis summer by powerful refrigeration units that groan night and day to keep the King from sweating. The odor of the room is sometimes fetid, the stink of a Bowery flophouse full of dirty old men incontinent of their urine and feces. The most grotesque object in this Cave of Morphia, this black and crimson womb, this padded cell, is the King.

Propped up like a big fat woman recovering from some operation on her reproductive organs, Elvis bears a startling resemblance to the picture of his mother which he contemplates so fixedly for hours at a time. His crown of blue-black hair, showing lots of grey at the roots, reflects his mother's hair. His creaseless moon-shaped face matches her expressionless facial mask. The greatest similarity is in the bee-stung eyes, especially the dusky tint of the skin about the eyes, as if both of them wore the identical shade of mascara.

Elvis's immense bulk is owing entirely to the eating habits that he developed as a child under his mother's loving care. He gorges himself with food at every time of day or night. Concealed in his clothes closet is a full-sized refrigerator kept stocked with snacks for those abrupt and unpredictable attacks of the "munchies" that beset speed freaks. Sometimes he seeks to curb the ill effects of his between-meal noshing by stocking his box entirely with

yogurt. This tactic avails him nothing, because after lap-
ping up a couple of containers of sweet, luridly colored pap,
instead of feeling his appetite sated, he experiences the
deep arousal of true hunger. Then, nothing can stop his
compulsive gobbling, until he has emptied twenty or thirty
of the waxy boxes. Or, suppose he confines himself to
healthful fruit: some fine ripe honeydew melons. Drawn
like a great bear to the honey in the heart of the melon,
he'll cut into and scoop out the oozing pulp in a trice, not
stopping until he has put away six or eight of the massive
fruits. Or if his sweet tooth is really aching, he will ring
up his valet, Hamburger James, at three in the morning
and send him out to buy at some all-night market a
hundred dollars worth of popsicles. As the rest of the world
is brewing coffee and frying eggs, James will be toting up
to his master's lair a huge bowl of Eskimo Pies, Fudge-
sicles, Dreamsicles and Nutty Buddys. Next afternoon, the
bowl will be back in the kitchen full of dry, stained sticks.

What Elvis craves most of all are those warm, home-
cooked rural southern meals that his mother used to lay
on the table. To assure himself that he can enjoy this kind
of mess whenever he pleases, he staffs the kitchen at
Graceland around the clock. The clock is, in fact, the first
thing in Elvis's mind when he awakes from his erratic
slumbers and casts his first addled look at the TV, which
is never turned off but always turned down to the point
of near inaudibility, a generator of soothing white noise.
Ringing up the kitchen, he will demand the time of day.
"Four o'clock, Boss," sings out the day cook, Mary Jenkins.
Elvis, as besotted as Falstaff behind the arras, rejoins:
"In the morning or the afternoon?"

Actually, he has no need of a telephone to order his
meals. He could ring a bell and achieve the same result
because he eats precisely the same meal every day. His
favorite feed consists of a pound of King Cotton bacon,
fried to a crisp, a quadruple order of mashed potatoes,
brimming with "thickenin' gravy"; a large portion of sauerkraut; a dish of crowder peas; and a stack of sliced tomatoes. Piling the sauerkraut and peas atop the potatoes,
he stirs these soft foods into a thick viscous paste. Then
spooning up this mush with one hand, with the other he

grasps the solid foods, eating always with his bare fingers. Though he seizes his bacon strips or pork chops without utensils, he seeks to keep his fingers as clean as possible, holding his pinky erect in the air, like Chaucer's dainty Prioress, who "no wet her fingers in her sauce deep." When the King drinks from his cup, he will twist it around so that his lips touch the rim above the handle, a part never soiled by contact with another person's lips. Should you make the mistake of trying to taste something from Elvis's dish, he will sputter with rage and slap your hand away. Touching anything on the Rock King's plate constitutes as shocking a breach of etiquette at Graceland as it would at Versailles if a courtier were to have snatched one of the Sun King's ortolons from under his long Bourbon nose.

Elvis, when he eats, pays no more attention to his food than would a child. Chattering, laughing and toying with his food, distracted one moment by the TV, the next by the phone, he piddles and paddles in his plate until the meal grows cold and has to be removed and replaced by another warm meal. In this manner, he contrives to eat a sizable portion of two or even three meals at a time. This distracted but compulsive eating is the sole cause of the mysterious, much debated "disease" that blew him up at the end of his life to his final weight: 255 pounds.

Once he has filled his belly, it's time for the King to lie back again and recreate his soul. Gazing up at the ceiling, covered with squares of avocado-gold Naugahide, while steeped in the mindless euphoria of opiates, Elvis must often have felt he was staring into the cloud with the golden lining. His condition suggests those lines from Shakespeare adopted by T. S. Eliot as the epigraph for "Gerontian":

> Thou hast nor youth nor age
> But as it were an after dinner sleep
> Dreaming of both.

Elvis is never alone during his long retreats. He has never been alone for more than a few moments in his entire life. Now, especially, is it necessary that he be companioned twenty-four hours a day lest he die from an

overdose or one of those queer accidents that are always
befalling drug addicts. The King's gentlemen of the bedchamber must perform many services. The first and foremost is the ritual of the injection.

Unlike most drug addicts, Elvis never takes a shot in
the mainline. He associates intravenous injections with
the despised character of the "junkie," a type he would like
to see rounded up en masse and committed to lifelong
imprisonment in concentration camps. So all his liquid
drugs are administered intramuscularly by skin popping.
Years of being stuck four or five times a day have made
Elvis's flesh resemble a pincushion. If a tiny drop of dye
had been injected with every shot he has received, he
would now resemble the Tattooed Lady in the circus. When
it's time for his Dilaudid or Demerol or speed, the cham-
berlain must go up and down the back of his body or behind
the legs or even into the armpits or between the toes to
find a bit of skin that has not been punctured.

Once the injection has been administered, the King has
to be watched carefully to make sure that he doesn't gag
on his own saliva or strangle on a bit of food. Times without
number his men have saved his life by thrusting their
hands down his gullet and pulling out a half-masticated
cheeseburger or a deadly peach pit. When Elvis has to
urinate or move his bowels, he must be carried to the
bathroom. If only one man is on duty, he will use a fire-
man's lift. Otherwise, the King will be too feeble to negotiate the distance and too unsteady to risk standing over
the toilet, where he could easily fall down and brain himself. Carrying him to the bathroom is no problem: All the
King's men are powerful churls. The difficulty resides in
knowing when he has to relieve himself. When he sinks
deeply into his hibernation, barely breaking consciousness
twice in twenty-four hours, he voids unwittingly like an
infant or a senile old man. At one point, he fouled himself
so often that thick towels were pinned around his buttocks
like great man-sized diapers.

Another danger lies in the fact that the King craves
company that will not merely guard but participate in his
strange subliminal existence. Like all junkies, he likes to
feel that everyone is sharing in his sin so that the burden

of guilt may be borne more lightly. Consequently, he has taken in his later years to employing young men who have the same longing to get high and stay high for weeks at a time. Actually, it makes life much easier for Elvis's male nurses if they're always stoned, for otherwise the boredom of the duty would be intolerable. Elvis does talk to his men from time to time, but it is such a mumbling, dopey and inconsequent soliloquy that nothing could be more annoying than being compelled to listen to this gibberish. Yet there is no avoiding Elvis's blithering because, like the Ancient Mariner, he lays hold on his listener by the arm, thus preventing his escape, while with his free hand he conducts his monologue as if it were music, slurring and stumbling, with eyes tight shut, often falling into the stammer that plagued him as a youth. At such times his frustration becomes so acute from his inability to free his tongue that the attendant is forced to slap his master's face smartly. Then the King continues his incoherent discourse, groping for the lost threads of thought, until, finally, he runs down to a long head-drooping, slack-jawed pause and blissfully nods out.

Another distraction offered to the body servants is occasional permission to invite to the King's bedchamber young women as dates. Elvis cannot bear to be seen in his ruinous condition, but he enjoys spending long hours in his large, well-appointed bathroom, where he has a comfortable reading chair. As he holds before his uncertain gaze a book of religious teachings or some science fiction novel, he sometimes detects through the door sounds that can only be construed one way. The guard has taken his young woman to bed, Elvis's bed, and is enjoying her now while his master waits patiently for the summons to return to his freshly warmed mattress grave.

When the King craves entertainment, he has a number of ways of enjoying himself in his deep drug trances. Above his bed are suspended a couple of color TV sets, rigged as they might be for a man suffering from total paralysis. Elvis, who is suffering only from partial paralysis, finds this overhead position unsatisfactory. Generally, he trains his wavering attention on the mammoth screen at the foot of his bed. On its surface he watches through droopy-lidded

eyes and with many lapses of consciousness all his favorite
films on videotapes. He may enjoy the *Great Fights of the
Century* or brood over the Kennedy assassination footage
or imagine himself Clint Eastwood in *Dirty Harry* or feel
a little trickle of purely mental lust ogling his Danish
porno films, which show buxom wenches being fucked by
horses, donkeys and boars. Best of all he loves to laugh at
the antics of Monty Python and his merry men. The gro-
tesquerie, the goofy put-ons, the physical extravagance,
just the sheer childish nonsensicalness of these films appeal enormously to Elvis's sense of humor, his deepest but
least recognized trait of mind.

It must not be thought that during his weeks and sometimes months of withdrawal from the world that the King
has no awareness of the life about him. He can tune into
any room or examine the fans at the Music Gate by means
of remote-controlled cameras that are planted all over
Graceland and feed back to a monitor beside Elvis's bed.
It is a common experience in this strange house to be in
the midst of a conversation and notice suddenly that the
camera on the ceiling has panned around and is focused
directly on your face. The King is watching!

If Elvis is in a sentimental mood, he will call, like Old
King Cole, for his fiddlers. His favorite record is a series
of recitations by the aging Charles Boyer set against a
background of Hollywood strings. Elvis is especially fond
of Boyer's rendition of "Where Does Love Go?" As the easy-
listening violins play an effortless waltz, threaded with
the reedy sound of the Parisian squeezebox, the soft, husky
voice of the famous actor asks, with many thoughtful
pauses and inquisitive intonations:

> *Eef the hart ees the place whaar lahve comes from,*
> *Than whaare does lahve go whan eet dies?*
> *Back een the hart whar eet came from,*
> *Ohr tarn eento tears in thee eyes?*

After a couple of verses filled with such poignant reflections, a chorus of fresh maidens' voices bursts out of the
quadraphonic speakers. On astro-strings the music soars
into that stratosphere that sorts so well with transconti-

nental flights and those other flights inspired by drugs. Thus high on silken wings, gazing into a golden haze, sustained gently at every point on his body, as if floating in a big black tub, with ears and soul full of romantic sentiments and soaring violins, the King of Rock 'n' Roll must be pictured, taking his royal ease.

The only thing that can rouse Elvis from his deep drug potations is the need to go back on the road. Never at any time in the later years did King and court assemble at Graceland except on the eve of a tour. After all the years, Elvis's veterans have changed in appearance nearly as much as their bloated boss. Red West, Elvis's oldest companion, once as delicate-featured as a girl, is now a haggard, goat-faced man who looks mean even when he's sound asleep. Sonny West has become a huge, shaggy mountain man, handsome with broad cheekbones and dark eyes, but running to flesh. Lamar Fike, from being a bird-eyed fat boy with a gleaming Tony Curtis haircut, has ballooned into an immense Sidney Greenstreet type, with a sarcastic and saturnine expression affixed to his face. Approaching the awesome and alarming weight of four hundred pounds, he will soon have to undergo a dangerous, life-shortening operation that will cut enough centimeters out of his gut to rush his food through his body before it can turn to fat. Only Joe Esposito, the crew chief, looks about the same as he did when he joined the outfit. "Diamond Joe" still affects the look of a sharp, flashy "Italian gangster." Only he's gotten terribly uptight. Sometimes, he breaks out in fever blisters all over his swarthy, jowly face from the sheer stress of his job, which has shifted from being road manager to acting as Elvis's chief keeper. It's an incredibly demanding existence, symbolized by the beeper Joe wears now on his belt, as if he were a medical doctor or an emergency repairman.

Getting Elvis back into his harness after he has spent two or three weeks lost in the "dark backward and abysm" of opiates is a difficult and exasperating labor. On the eve of a tour, the star's intimates resemble Dr. Frankenstein's laboratory assistants struggling to animate the recumbent monster. Short of a jolt of heaven-sent electricity, nothing can restore the King to life. That is why Elvis, like his

prototype, Buck Rogers—who never went anywhere in
either his rocketship or his earth-borer without the bald,
gnomish Dr. Huer—would not think of venturing forth
into the wilds of Rapid City, South Dakota, or Eugene,
Oregon, without having at his side his white-haired, low-
keyed, methodically proficient personal physician, Dr.
George Nichopolous.

Even when he has been revived by the doctor's medicines and hauled to his feet like a fallen statue by his
mistress, Linda Thompson, and his feeble old father, Vernon, Elvis is hardly in a condition to do two weeks of one-
night stands or make up for all the shows he has blown
at Las Vegas. Imagine how he feels on such nights when
he drags himself to the glaring, bulb-studded mirror in his
bathroom, where he examines himself with the practiced
eye of a great star and a supreme narcissist. Always there
was a part of him that was like those famous female models
who, when they study themselves in a glass, see not the
ravishing image that beguiles the world but a mass of
glaring faults that grow worse every year with age. Elvis
always hated his "chicken" neck (disguised generally with
a high collar) and his "gantlin'" legs, which he was forced
to expose in all those dumb beach movies. Even as a poor
lad working in a factory he had found the money to mask
the gap between his front teeth with a cap (which is the
reason no photograph taken before his eighteenth year
shows him smiling). He suffers always from the sense that
he is too short, which is why in every item of footwear he
owns, from a boot to a bedroom slipper, there is a half-inch
lift. Even his fabled hair troubles him because, like his
father's great healthy crop, it has turned almost completely grey. Recently, he has had a discreet facelift. Now
all these problems appear trivial in comparison to the hideous image he presents in the mirror.

He could be the Pillsbury Doughboy, so fat and puffy
and pillow-stuffed does he appear. From the rear, he
doesn't look so bad: He still has narrow "quarters" and
flaring shoulders. When he faces front, or worse, turns in
profile, the effect is appalling. He looks exactly like one
of those barrel-shaped good ole buddies who spend their
lives riding high above an eighteen-wheeler—the kind

who say with comic wistfulness: "Been a long time since ah could look down an' see mah pecker!" So huge has Elvis grown that none of his famous costumes will fit him. More than a score of these splendid garments hang in his wardrobe room, all of them decorated with beads from Czechoslovakia and semiprecious stones from Brazil, outfits that cost ten thousand dollars apiece—and none of them will zip shut over his mountainous belly!

As costume after costume is fetched forth by the frowning flunkies, there is bound to come a moment when the notorious Presley temper flares. Suddenly, Elvis "flashes"— and a costly gold Piaget embellished with fire opals explodes against the bathroom wall. Instantly, poor old Vernon is down on his creaky knees, trying to retrieve the pieces. Elvis sneers at the shattered watch and rumbles, "Let it go, Daddy—it's jes' money!"

Now Linda is trimming Elvis's forelock because he wouldn't see the hairdresser who came every day for a week. She's also trying to jolly her sullen lover into a better humor with her usual little quips and coquetries when he flinches or she slips, something goes amiss, and with a roar of rage Elvis seizes his lock and confirms his worst fears—she has cut off far too much! Joe Esposito has to come rushing to the rescue, inspecting the damage and calming Elvis and explaining exactly how they'll make it good when they get to Las Vegas—if only they can get there! All evening Joe has been running upstairs and downstairs, phoning out to Memphis Aero to change the flight time and trying to ease Elvis forward without appearing to push because, at the slightest sign of coercion, Elvis will throw another temper tantrum and the whole party will be further delayed.

Meanwhile, downstairs, all the Guys are lobbed out in the den watching a midnight movie. They drove down from the nearby Howard Johnson's motel in their rented cars at eight o'clock; now, it's one in the morning and still no sign of Elvis. Finally, a phone rings in the kitchen. The word comes from on high: "Boss is ready!" Instantly, the Guys shoot out of their chairs and rush to the vestibule to receive their King, their gold insignia, a lightning bolt crowned with the letters TCB ("Takin' Care o' Business") glittering on their chests. As they stare at Elvis descending the long, steep staircase, they are astonished at his latest traveling costume.

He's wearing a red terry-cloth robe with a monk's hood from which protrude the bottoms of his black nylon pajamas and his patent leather boots. His head is enveloped completely in the cowl, save for the face and eyes, which are screened by tinted aviator glasses with the initials EP worked across the bridge. Two bulges on either hip show that he's packing his pearl-handled Patton .45s. (Inside his left boot is a two-shot Derringer.) Like some ancient bellman, he's carrying in his hand a large makeup kit, shaped like a tiny chest of drawers, in which he keeps his money, his credit cards and his drugs.

No sooner does he reach the bottommost step than he turns wordlessly to enter his grandmother's room. The old lady is a strange, weird-looking creature: a tall skinny scarecrow with a wizened little face always covered up with sunglasses, the senile bride of the Murnau Nosferatu. She will be lying back in her La-Z-Boy® chair watching TV or be bent over her organ, which sends low churchy vibes through the house late at night. "Ah gotta go to work, Dodger!" sings out Elvis, as he kneels ponderously beside the old woman and pats her on the back. "If you need anythin', you jes' call me at the hotel. Ah'll call you every day, so don't worry about nuthin'." Minnie Mae smiles blindly and says, "You take care now, sonny boy. Dontcha work yeseff into a sickness." Then, as he kisses her on the forehead, she reaches a long emaciated arm around his neck and returns his embrace.

Back again in the vestibule, Elvis shouts as if he were still in army bivouac, "Move it! Let's go!" Joe echoes the order, "Hit it! Let's roll!" Instantly, the front door flies open. Sonny, riding shotgun in the limo, ducks out and opens the car's rear door. Elvis marches straight down the hall; then, just as he's about to step across the threshold, he breaks his stride for a second to reach down and snatch something off the hall table. Always when he leaves home, he makes that last nervous grab for a book, a walking stick, a long, silvery police flashlight. Then he's out the door, down the steps and into the limo.

What a limo! It's the biggest Mercedes made, a huge six-door stretchout in midnight blue, dubbed by its makers *Der Grosse Pullman*. Curtained all round for privacy and equipped with a bar, TV and radio-phone, it's the last word in four-wheel luxury. As Elvis and Linda settle back on the thick red cushions, covering themselves with a fox fur rug, Red drives down the curving road to the Music Gate. A gaggle of fans sets up a shout in the cold night air as the big car pauses at the highway, then turns sharply right to disappear into the night. No sooner does it clear the gate than the long line of cars parked along the stone wall of the estate suddenly springs to life. These are fans who have been sitting out here in the chill for hours just to enjoy the pleasure of following Elvis to the airport. Now they take off in pursuit. This impromptu motorcade has been anticipated, like every other detail of Elvis's carefully guarded life. A second, smaller Mercedes has now caught up with *Der Grosse Pullman* to act as a buffer between Elvis and his followers.

During the ten minutes it takes to reach the airport, Linda tries to make conversation while Elvis sulks. On the other side of the glass partition that divides the passenger from the driver's compartment, Sonny is on the phone calling the airport tower and informing it that Elvis is approaching. As soon as the tower gets the word, it flashes the news to the security guards at the private gate and to the crew of the *Lisa Marie* out on the strip. When Captain Elwood Davis receives the message, he reaches up to his serried instrument panel and flips a switch marked "Logo." Eighty feet behind him, two bright flood-lights suddenly illuminate the towering tail of the air-plane. Like a great white sail it stands out against the night sky emblazoned with the gold lightning bolt crowned with TCB and topped off with an American flag.

Elvis likes to boast that he is the only entertainer ever to own for his personal use a four-engine jet airliner. He acquired the big plane to mark his fortieth birthday, his original intention being to fly about the world in an exact replica of *Air Force One*. When he discovered that the cheapest Boeing 707 on the market was $888,000 and that customizing it to suit his tastes would bring the cost up

to a million and a half dollars, he yielded to reality to the
extent of purchasing a plane that was fifteen feet shorter:
a Convair 880 that had carried ninety-six passengers when
it was owned by Delta Airlines. When you run your eye
along the great white hull of the royal coach, you're reminded instantly of *Air Force One* because the plane bears
the same broad red and blue band from nose to tail. Elvis
was chagrined by the fact that he could not have the glittering silver hull of the presidential plane. He compen-
sated for this and other such frustrations by fashioning
the interior far more luxuriously than would any head of
state, save perhaps an oil sheik.

What Elvis demanded for his travels was a flying hotel
suite. The forward cabin is a very plushy, oddly effeminate
club room, furnished with two long curving bench sofas
covered with fat cushions of crushed velour, one aquamarine, the other chocolate brown. The plush aqua carpet
catches the light from the arched ceiling, which is padded
with canary yellow vinyl. Along both sides of the cabin
run continuous bands of short drapes, like café curtains,
made of fabric dyed like bull's-eyes of blue, orange and
brown stained glass. The club room contains also some
card tables, leather lounge chairs, TV monitors and a fif-
teen-thousand-dollar quadraphonic sound system.

Behind this room is the dining-conference room, which
is furnished with six huge leather spaceman chairs ranged
along either side of a surfboard-shaped Danish modern
table with a green leather surface and a teak rim. Meals
served on this spiffy board are framed with silverware
bearing Elvis's personal monogram. The room also boasts
a communications center, including a skyphone that can
be used to make calls anywhere in the world.

The most important compartment is, of course, the bedroom. Elvis insisted that it be located at the rear of the
fuselage so that he could embark or disembark without
having to show himself to the people in the main cabin.
This demand conflicted with his other imperative: that the
room be very quiet, the quietest spot in any plane being
forward, not aft of the engines. As for decor, Elvis wanted
an airborne version of his bed-and-bath suite at Graceland.
Like the Boy in the Bubble, he had come to feel that he

could not survive outside his artificially contrived personal environment.

The bedroom of the *Lisa Marie* is decorated entirely in shades of restful blue: royal blue for the carpeting, which runs up to the windowsills; pale blue for the huge velvet bedspread; royal blue again for the suede headboard. At one end of the bed is the TV monitor, ready to display the antics of the Monty Python troupe. Just beyond the TV installation is the dressing room, with its large plate-glass mirror bordered with theatrical lightbulbs. Finally, there is the bathroom, which gathers together in a final flourish the whole *esthétique d'Elvis*.

Picture a plastic bathroom counter in a shade of brilliant lapis lazuli with a canary yellow sink. Atop the sink is an ornately patterned, gold-plated nozzle and faucet fixture, whose handles are real lapis, à la Sherle Wagner. *Voilà!* With this assemblage of precious metal, semiprecious stone and cheap plastic, combined ostentatiously but unimaginatively into the sort of private fixture dear to the heart of a Palm Springs matron (or a rich old queen), you have the epitome of the King's taste.

The moment Elvis arrives beside the plane, the crew goes into action. The baggage has been loaded long since, the flight plan brought up to date. The moment the cabin is sealed, the firing sequence is initiated. One engine after another is ignited and brought up to full power to test its airworthiness. Then, when all the engines have been checked out, the fifth jet engine, the auxiliary power unit (employed in place of those massive trucks the airlines use), is switched off and raised on steel cables into the forward baggage compartment. All buttoned up and ready for flight, the copilot calls the tower: "This is eight-eighty Echo Pappa waiting for taxi and take-off instructions." "Eight-eighty Echo Pappa," replies the tower, "you're cleared for runway eighteen left. Taxi and go into position and hold." After idling at the end of the runway, while a dozen or more French-built Federal Express jets go aloft, the *Lisa Marie* is cleared for take-off, thunders down the runway and lifts into the air.

The big plane soars majestically across the country carrying the King lobbed out in his queen-sized bed with all his men in the forward cabin playing hearts or watching in-flight movies or eating cheeseburgers prepared in the galley's microwave ovens. As the King voyages high above his demesnes, the air controllers send greetings to the great man. At the end of each dry, professionally phrased message, indicating which controller has received the plane on his radar screen, there is always a final enthusiastic personal message for this plane: "Give 'em hell, Echo Pappa!...Wish I were with you, eight-eighty!...Tell Elvis we love 'im! Now, I'm gonna hand you off to Denver Center on one-oh-eight point seven. Have a good evening!" All across America, invisible heralds hail the King as he advances on his royal progress.

Chapter 2

The View from
the Imperial Suite

THE *Lisa Marie* lands just before dawn at Las Vegas and taxis to the Hughes Air Terminal, a private facility immune to gawkers. The Las Vegas Hilton has been alerted by skyphone and advised of the ETA. The moment the plane comes to a stop, it is surrounded by black limousines and a stake-bed truck for the luggage. Everyone leaves the plane before Elvis, who is the last to board and the last to disembark. Finally, he comes down the stairs, gripping the rail firmly, looking like the Mad Monk or the ruler of one of those remote and exotic kingdoms who is given every year his weight in gold. No sooner does the door slam shut on Elvis's limousine than the machine lurches forward and starts racing for the hotel as if it were as ambulance. When it nears the immense building, standing on the valley bottom like a rocket city straining for release, the car makes a sharp turn to avoid the main entrance and pulls up at a freight-loading area in the back. The King enters the hotel near the kitchen, and after threading a maze of industrial passageways, reaches the service elevator that will carry him up thirty floors to the penthouse.

Entering the Imperial Suite at dawn, Elvis and his

31

party could behold one of the greatest sights of Las Vegas.
The designer of this lavish and dramatically situated
apartment arranged it for just such trumpet-blowing moments. As you enter, you pass through three successive
foyers, which open wider, wider, wider, until suddenly
you're standing at the top of a couple of very broad stairs
that lead down into an enormous sunken living room, extending from side to side about sixty feet. Directly opposite
you is a wall of glass through which you gaze due east at
the mountains, flaring at this hour with spectacular colors.
Instinctively, you walk across the room, open wide the
French windows and step out onto the roof of the hotel,
the highest point in the entire valley. Into your nostrils
flows the crisp clear desert air, as you glut yourself on the
flaming colors in the sky.

Nothing like this ever happened when Elvis Presley
arrived at dawn atop the Las Vegas Hilton. Had anyone
been so bold as to open the drapes that hung along the
wall to allow the morning light and air into the room, he
would have been fired on the spot. Like Count Dracula
retreating to his coffin, Elvis entered his apartment intent
not on the vital signs of light and warmth but demanding
the darkness and the chill of a tomb.

You may be sure he found it, for he never arrived at
any hotel without having had his rooms prepared for him
by an advance party that would have included one of his
valets. In Las Vegas this team arrives from Elvis's home
in Los Angeles with a truckload of stage costumes and
other paraphernalia promptly on the stroke of noon the
afternoon preceding Elvis's appearance. This is the earliest moment they can gain admission to the suite, which
has been occupied up to that hour by the star of the preceding show or some other bigwig. Now with the help of
the hotel staff, they come off the service elevator, past the
uniformed security man who sits always at a table outside
the Imperial Suite, checking every visitor's identification.
Elvis's men have already received their plastic I.D. badges
bearing their pictures, numbers and party designation.

They come with an immense load of luggage: no less
than fifty-two pieces. The most conspicuous items are the
"rollers," black fibreboard cases on little wheels that open

up like old-fashioned steamer trunks, providing hanging space for costumes on one side and six drawers for folding wear on the other side. Seven of these rollers will be taken downstairs later in the day to Elvis's dressing room, where the costumes will be hung up and the other gear set out. Now, the task is to prepare Elvis's bedroom and bathroom according to the master plan, which is set out in three notebooks carried by one of the assistant valets.

The master bedroom has a king-sized bed on a dais. At its left foot on a swiveling pedestal is the TV set. To this instrument the men immediately attach a videotape unit so that Elvis can enjoy his favorite bits of sex and violence. Next, they remove from specially constructed boxes Elvis's religious library: two hundred and fifty volumes dealing primarily with the occult. His favorites, like *The Impersonal Life* or *The Autobiography of a Yogi,* he carries by the dozens so that he can lay them like tracts on prospective proselytes. Next to his bed are laid his closest companions, the Bible and the *Physician's Desk Reference* (to drugs). He will also want the latest issues of *The Watchtower* and the publications of the Self-Realization Fellowship, along with the current numbers of all the karate magazines: *Black Belt, Fighting Stars, Inside Kung-Fu.*

Once the books have been arranged, the next item of importance is the hi-fi system and Elvis's record collection. His taste in music has never altered in twenty years. He's still listening to the Golden Gate Quartet, the Harmonizing Four and all those rich, black, burbling barreltones: Billy Eckstine, Roy Hamilton, Arthur Prysock and Brook Benton. Nowadays, though, he is drifting back to the country music that he first heard as a child. That is why the valets set the radio dial to the local country station.

Next, the exercycle must be brought up from the storage room and set up in the bedroom. The humidifiers and air purifiers must be installed to guard against "Vegas throat." The little refrigerator stocked with Mountain Valley spring water. A bowl of fruit is placed within reach. The last touch is the proper positioning of Elvis's trophy from the Junior Chamber of Commerce as one of the Ten Outstanding Young Men in America. Elvis is very proud of this award and when he gazes at it, he sometimes recollects his embarrassed, almost strangled little speech of acknowledgment: "I, I, I'd like you folks to know that I was the hero of the comic book. I saw movies and I was the hero of the movie. So every dream I ever dreamed has come true a hundred times."

The next job is stocking Elvis's bathroom. It is the subject of one entire notebook. Among the more revealing items are the great variety of powerful laxatives and Fleet enemas. Like all junkies, Elvis suffers from a paralyzed colon. Opiates immobilize the striate muscles that produce defecation. The abnormally large doses of laxatives that he must take to rouse his numbed gut force his body to the opposite extreme. Sometimes, he loses control of his bowels completely. Many a morning, it is necessary to strip the bed before the housekeeper arrives, lest the gossip spread through the hotel that "Elvis Presley shits in his bed." Hamburger James is always bustling out of the Imperial Suite with some unspeakable object in his hand. If it isn't a load of king-sized sheets stained with urine or feces, it's a bath towel wrapped around a cache of spent plastic syringes. James is a sly fellow. He has learned to take an elevator to a floor far from the penthouse, where, espying an unattended trash truck, he can dump his incriminating bundle and then make off again without anybody being the wiser.

The packing lists call for at least two hair dryers; a dozen professional beautician's brushes with black plastic handles and white plastic bristles and two dozen combs. There is also Prell Shampoo for Dyed Hair and a hair spray called Presto. Elvis's other toiletries are nothing special. He brushes his teeth a couple of times a day with Colgate. He sprays himself with Brut. If he wants a close shave, he uses a Wilkinson straight razor; otherwise, he employs an electric razor.

One item need not be stocked in quantity: soap. Elvis's brand is Neutrogena but he rarely bathes. Lamar says Elvis takes a "whore's bath"—a quick negligent wipe of the armpits and the crotch. He may not even do that much. Priscilla was so disgusted by Elvis's lack of personal cleanliness that when she renovated their last home on Monovale Road, she had his shower stall rigged with three spray nozzles: one for the head, one for the torso and one for the lower extremities. It was a good idea, but Elvis objected. Taking showers was dangerous. How many times had he slipped and fallen!

Once the bedroom and bathroom have been prepared, the crew goes to work on the wardrobe closets. They unpack Elvis's street clothes, never worn in the street, of course, but carried for those times when he has to get out of bed and face strangers. Since he saw *Superfly*, he's been dressing like a black pimp. From his old friends, Lansky Brothers, he has bought a dozen frock coats and vests, jivey planter's hats and cravats, in a whole rainbow of colors, all cut from the crushed velvet that has become his favorite fabric.

Never a man to take less than the most, Elvis buys two pairs of pants with every suit, as if he feared he might wear one out, and matching shirts by the dozen. His boots are San Remos or Verdis, all patent leather in white, black or blue, size 11D, with dancer's soles and heels (crisscross black rubber treads). Under the boots he wears calf-length socks in matching colors. Elvis is five feet, eleven inches tall, but with a half-inch lift and an inch or inch-and-a-half heel, he appears to be well over six feet.

The two items he gives away from the stage—his flamboyantly colored scarves and his flashy rings—he carries by the gross. Originally the scarves were authentic items of wardrobe. Then, Elvis realized that it was foolish to throw anything of value to the fans. So he ordered a load of gaudy rags from a little tailor in Vegas, which he distributes now with princely gestures. The rings that people are always fighting to get he buys from Schwartz and Ableser, a jewelry shop in Beverly Hills where Elvis likes to hang out. He buys a lot of cheap junk, such as Tiger's Eyes, that flash in the stage lights like real gems. The fans assume that the rings must be valuable because Elvis is wearing them. Actually, they're just the tawdry prizes that come with this particular box of Cracker Jack.

Elvis's real jewelry is in his makeup kit. The moment he arrives in the suite, he hands this treasure chest to his valet, who places it on the right-hand side of the bed, within easy reach. The case is arranged in the same strict

order that characterizes everything in Elvis's periphery.
The top drawer contains his various pills, tablets, spansules and pulvules. There are round white Quaaludes
stamped "Rorer 714"; shiny "Black Beauty" Biphetamines;
garnet-colored Placidyls in round 100- or 200-milligram
capsules and elongated 500-miligram spansules; chalky
Demerols; heart-shaped Dexedrines; and deadly little tablets of Dilaudid in innocent ice-cream colors—green, gold,
lavender and yellow—each with the number of milligrams
stamped on it, ranging from one to four. Each cylindrical
plastic vial containing these drugs bears a label reading:
"Caution: A federal law prohibits the transfer of this drug
to any patient other than the patient for whom it was
prescribed." The names on these labels (unbeknownst to
them) are Lamar Fike, Red West, Sonny West, James
Caughley and Lisa Marie Presley. Elvis's syringes and
injectable drugs are carried in a smaller, auxiliary case.

The second drawer is filled with jewelry, including his
diamond horseshoe ring, his diamond-studded wedding
band and his kenpo karate ring, a fat red ruby. Also in
this compartment is his wallet, which is usually empty.
Another wallet contains his driver's license, credit cards
and union cards. The prize item in this drawer is the gold-
and-blue enamel shield that Elvis received when he was
appointed by Richard Nixon an agent of the Bureau of
Narcotics and Dangerous Drugs. There it lies just below
all those illegally prescribed pills.

The next drawer holds a spare tooth cap, a tube of Blis-
tex (for cold sores), a nail file and a button of eye shadow.
The bottom drawer may contain as many as four expensive
watches of various designs.

The moment Elvis reaches his bedroom, he divests himself of his robe, takes off the two .45s he is carrying in
holsters and places them on the table beside his pillow.
Then, he sits down and allows the valet to remove his
boots and extract the two-shot over-and-under Derringer.
Next, he takes a handful of sleeping pills and washes them
down with a long swig of mineral water straight from the
bottle. The moment Elvis seems comfortably disposed in
bed, Hamburger James wheels in the cart on which he has
been keeping warm the King's cheeseburgers. Placing a

towel for a tablecloth across the bedspread, James serves the meal. The cheeseburgers are done to a hard, friable texture. Elvis is disposed to choke on his food and often has to be whacked on the back. By the time he has finished eating, he should be ready to nod out. Tonight, the disruption in his routine produced by the trip excites his habitual insomnia. It is Linda's job to soothe and coax and smooth him down until he submits to sleep.

As Elvis lies against the pillow with his left arm thrown across his eyes, Linda sits at the edge of the bed reading in a low soft voice from Kahlil Gibran's *The Prophet*. Elvis's favorite passages are those that deal with love and marriage:

> *Then Amitra spoke again and said, And what of*
> *Marriage, master?*
> *And he answered saying:*
> *You were born together, and together you shall be*
> *forevermore.*
> *But let there be spaces in your togetherness,*
> *And let the winds of heaven dance between you.*
> *Love one another but make not a bond of love.*
> *Sing and dance together and be joyous, but let each one*
> *of you be alone.*

As Linda reads, she casts glances at Elvis from time to time. She's hoping she'll see some sign that he's growing drowsy. At one point, he's so still, she pauses, looking at him carefully and almost holding her breath. Suddenly, he starts awake and says in a querulous little boy's voice, "Mommy, I have to go to the bathroom!" "All right," says Linda, in a soothing maternal tone, "Mommy will take you." Then, she half holds and half hauls Elvis as he labors to disengage himself from the sheets. Linda is a big strong girl, like a female athlete. She gets one of Elvis's arms over her shoulder and walks him step by shuffling step to the bathroom. Then she supports him as he urinates into the toilet.

Now they are back in the bedroom and Linda is opening

the Bible to read to Elvis his favorite passage, Corinthians:
I, 13. When they first met, she had these verses inscribed
on a plaque which he could keep next to his bed. Elvis's
Bible is well worn and heavily underscored. She finds the
chapter quickly and commences reading the famous words:
"Though I speak with the tongues of men and of angels,
and have not charity, I am become as sounding brass or
a tinkling cymbal." Elvis lies back with a blissful expression on his face, like a child hearing his favorite bedtime
story. He has every word memorized and may even mum-
ble in unison with her at times. Especially he enjoys the
last part, commencing: "When I was a child, I spake as a
child: but when I became a man, I put away childish
things."

"Mommy," Elvis whines as soon as the reading concludes, "I need more of my sleeping medications." Linda
is growing a little exasperated at this point. This refusal
to sleep, this demand for more pills, it's the pattern that
always precedes one of Elvis's bad spells, which conclude
invariably with an overdose and a big panic. She's been
with him enough years to know the dangers of giving
in to his sick demands. So when he says to her in that
sad little boy voice, "I need more sleeping medication—
I'm awake," she replies firmly, "Honey, you are *not*
awake. You're asleep. Just close your eyes and you'll go
right to sleep." He's very cranky tonight. "No!" he insists.
"I'm wide awake now! I need some more sleeping medication."

This is always the way they carry on because ostensibly
Linda controls the pills, and he loves to wheedle them out
of her. She is not about to give in because she can see that
he is deliberately hanging onto the edge of consciousness
and could easily fall asleep if he would just let go. She
denies him again and again; he protests, whines, pleads,
and even stirs as if to reach for the bottle himself. Finally,
she can bear it no more. An anger, a deep resentment that
she hardly knew she harbored, suddenly forces itself out
through her lips.

Standing upright and staring down at him reproach-
fully, she says: "Do you want to die that badly? Why put

yourself through this torture? Why don't you take one of those guns there and blow out your brains? Just do it quickly and don't make the people who love you suffer by watching you kill yourself inch by inch." It's an astounding statement. Nobody ever talks to Elvis like that. Even she never talks to him like that. The words just popped out of her mouth as if someone else were saying them through her.

For a moment, he stares at her in astonishment. Then he starts to giggle and gurgle like a baby. Half closing his eyes, he snickers and murmurs in baby-talk, "Okay, Mommy. Aw'll go sleepy." Amazed to see him back down for once, she returns to her soothing mother voice and murmurs: "Just lie there and close your eyes, Baby Bunt-in'—and hush!"

At about the same time that Elvis is losing conscious-ness, twenty-six stories below him Colonel Parker is wak-ing up and preparing for a busy day. The Colonel has a year-round suite of three rooms at the end of a wing on the fourth floor; one of his many perks from the hotel. As you walk down the corridor, the first sign you see of the Colonel's presence is two huge replicas of Nipper, the RCA dog, mounting guard. Then, the walls exchange their nor-mal appearance for that of a board fence around a con-struction site. They are heavily placarded and postered all over with pictures of Elvis—the spoor of the Abominable Snowman. When you enter the Colonel's private quarters, you are assailed by a barrage of the same visual static. The rooms resemble a junk shop. They are crammed with chatzkahs, bric-a-brac, curios, mementos and gimmicks from floor to ceiling. There are statues of elephants, huge teddy bears, trick store items and relics of old promotion campaigns. On a shelf near the door is an ancient pro-motion kit for *Tickle Me:* a packet of twenty-five chicken feathers in all sizes and colors ranging from pinfeathers to turkey quills, and a furry purple caterpillar with silvery

cut-glass eyes and a lolling red tongue. When you stroke
it with your finger, it curls up or wriggles or turns som-
ersaults.

The walls are covered with photographs of the Colonel
and Elvis. There is the famous early shot of the Colonel
seated in his shirtsleeves at a typewriter with the young
Elvis curling his lip: Colonel is batting out a snappy press
release by the hunt and hit method. Next to it is the standard Hollywood picture of the famous pair, seated side by
side in director's chairs, puffing happily on long cigars.
Next to that is one of the shots used years ago on a Christmas card: Elvis gotten up in a cute little suit on one side
of a towering tree and on the other side a rotund Santa,
none other than Kris Kringle Parker. The Colonel's favorite pictures of himself show him in full military uniform: either as a slender young man in the Smokey the
Bear hat, crumpled cotton khakis and leather "leggins"
of an American soldier between the great wars or in jowly
middle age wearing the elaborately swathed, sashed, and
tasseled uniform of a Southern colonel in the Civil War.

Looking about these eccentrically decorated rooms,
which the Colonel has redecorated at the hotel's expense
every time he has a run of bad luck at the tables, you
discern great stashes of loot tucked away under every
counter and in every corner. Cases of fine wine, boxes of
Cuban cigars, cartons of slab bacon from Early's Honey
Stand in Franklin, Tennessee, crates of Mountain Valley
water, which Colonel calls his "Arkansas champagne."
The apartment resembles an eccentric millionaire's fallout
shelter. Everywhere you look, you see the things that businesses give their best customers as gifts and favors: heavy
crystal ashtrays, elaborate carving sets, silver gilt goblets,
executive clocks, numerous RCA appliances in the latest
models—radios, phonographs, color TVs. There is so much
plunder piled up in these rooms that you make your way
through them with difficulty.

The Colonel is a man who believes in mixing business
with pleasure; in fact, business is his pleasure. On a morning like this, he may have invited to breakfast a couple
of men from the hotel's publicity department. They will
be served a prodigious meal: the finest fruits, all out of

season and every piece perfectly ripe (once the Colonel had a young man fired from the kitchen staff because he sent up some bananas that weren't fit to eat); costly rib eye steaks topped with fried eggs; imported cheeses; country ham and bacon; hot biscuits and coffee cake. A waiter will stand at the table all through the meal lifting the silver covers on the dishes and piling up the plates. Colonel will drink cup after cup of scalding hot coffee that would make another man scream with pain. If the old man is in a good mood, he may even take a flaming match and lower it down his throat. Then, he lights up one of his immense Montecristo's and sucks in the joy of perfect contentment. When the meal has concluded, at least half the expensive food will be carted back to the kitchen as garbage. The Colonel, like Elvis, is a heroic consumer, a great waster and squanderer, an exemplar of that age now past when every successful, self-made American felt a deep and satisfying compulsion to piss it all away.

At nine o'clock sharp, the Colonel's aide-de-camp will report for duty. He's always some immaculately dressed young robot who is loaned to the Colonel by the hotel as a go-fer. One of the world's greatest freeloaders, the Colonel is not content just with meals, rooms, offices, transportation and lavish gifts, he's also very keen on getting his pounds of flesh. For years a whole succession of attractive young men from RCA, MGM and the William Morris Agency have toiled as the Colonel's lackeys.

The Colonel is a master of busywork; all day long he piles up lists of urgent chores that require the attention of many men to perform. It is vital to the Colonel's *amour-propre* that he always be rapping out commands, shouting, *"Mister* Diskin!" or *"Mister* Parkhill," like Charles Laughton in *Mutiny on the Bounty*. Then he sends them off on some damn fool task. In fact, one of his favorite expressions after he delivers an order is, "That's a command!" You always expect his men to reply, "Aye, aye, sir!" and swing a smart salute.

Once the aide has reported for duty, the Colonel is ready to hold his first meeting of the day with his staff. The Colonel can never have enough of meetings, those invaluable occasions when he can lecture his men or think

out loud or reminisce about the good old days in the carnival. Meetings are the Colonel's way of holding court, and
he has his retinue, no less faithful and obedient than
Elvis's Guys. Tom Diskin, who started out with the Colonel
way back in the days before Elvis, is still on deck. Diskin
is a very intelligent man, a fact belied by a life spent
echoing every statement by his boss, "That's right, Colonel!" Mr. Diskin has both gained and lost a lot through
his years of faithful service. He's been very liberally paid—
the Colonel believes in binding his men to him with hoops
of gold; on the other hand, the Colonel has driven Diskin
so hard over the years that his nerves have cost him a
good portion of his stomach.

George Parkhill is another of the Colonel's veterans.
Parkhill is a big man, over six feet tall and scaling about
two hundred forty pounds. A sharp dresser, adorned always in fancy jewelry and wearing Bally shoes, he gives
the impression of having come from people with money.
At one time he was a VP at RCA; then the Colonel took
him on and has kept him ever since, although the two
have had some bad fallings-out produced by Parkhill's intolerance for the Colonel's unending bullshit. Like other
members of this group, Parkhill has a florid complexion.

The Colonel's secretary, Jim O'Brien, like George Parkhill, has never married. Very devoted to his master and
very efficient in his job, he has been with the Colonel since
the late fifties. Colonel picked him up from Jean Aberbach
of Hill and Range, another man who always prefers men
to women as secretaries. The only woman who has ever
been a member of the Colonel's entourage is Lou Ann
Miller, who was originally a secretary for the hotel's former general manager, Alex Shoofey. Miss Miller is a tall,
attractive spinster in her midthirties, always neatly
dressed in skirts and blouses with a minimum of jewelry,
somewhat perfunctory in manner but very solicitous of the
Colonel's needs. She's the type of woman who identifies
completely with her boss. The Colonel gives her plenty to
do: virtually round-the-clock demands. Rest assured, however, that there has never been anything improper about
their relationship. Colonel Parker is a man who has never
been known to look at any woman save his wife, Marie.

Colonel's staff has completed much of its work by the time Elvis opens. In fact, with Elvis's semiannual appearances in Las Vegas reduced to two weeks from the customary four, demand for tickets to his shows has reached such a pitch that one wonders just how important it is that Colonel Parker and a half-dozen aides labor day in, day out, preparing tacky ads, vulgar radio pitches and corny souvenirs to turn on the fans.

Once the Colonel's staff has helped itself to coffee and settled down at the long table, Colonel will start issuing orders. "George, have you got the album covers ready? If you don't, why don't you call Mel Ilberman and if Mel hasn't got 'em, call Pat Kellegher and if he hasn't got 'em, find out what's happenin'!" As Parkhill starts to answer, objecting, "Well, I don't know..." Colonel cuts him off with a curt, "I don't wanna hear 'don't know'—find out now!" Fixing his hard blue eyes next on Tom Diskin, the old man asks: "Now, Mr. Diskin, when's Mr. Rocco comin' in?" (Colonel has never learned how to pronounce the name of RCA Records' president, Rocco Laginestra.) "Make sure now that Mr. Rocco is taken care of." Between each sharply worded command, the Colonel takes a puff on his big dark cigar and a draught of coffee. Really, there's nothing much to do: The ritual of business far exceeds its substance.

Finally, he figures he's discharged his obligation to appear busy. "O.K., that's enough!" he barks. "Now, everybody, let's go to the office. We'll work there for a while, and then we'll go on from there. Now, let's go!" With that, he claps his hands loudly, like a kindergarten teacher demanding attention, and storms out the door of the suite to his office across the hall. There he sinks down at once at a desk and places a call to his home in Palm Springs. Getting his wife on the line, he engages in a little homey banter. "How are you honey? How you doin'? Cats O.K.? Everythin' is fine here. I'll be home on Friday. I'm bringing some fresh catfish. We'll have a fry downstairs." The Colonel is always careful not to inquire too carefully about his wife's health because she'll tell him how she feels—*bad!* The Guys call her "the most miserable woman on earth." Her favorite expression is "I hate it!" She is ailing but not yet invalid. Once in a while she still gets herself together to visit her husband in Vegas. She may even play a little 21, but if she loses, she's liable to throw the cards in the dealer's face.

Once the obligatory morning call to the house has been made, the Colonel will declare, "I think we better go down to my casino office." That's the signal to commence the day's gambling. Arriving at the back of the casino, cigar smoke pouring from his mouth, walking very fast with his cane in hand, looking neither left nor right, the Colonel, you'd swear, is heading for an important appointment. God forbid anyone obstructs his progress or dares to touch him on the arm! The old man will go berserk with rage and raise his cane threateningly. After a short stop at the casino manager's office to exchange pleasantries, the Colonel will say, apropos of nothing, "Well, okay, I'm goin' out to my other office"; then he will make his way through the jungle of slot machines on his way to the wheel. He may toss some money into the slots as he proceeds; if he hits, one of his men will stop to collect the silver. Once the Colonel reaches the table and greets the dealer, he completely shuts out the rest of the world. It makes no difference whether he is playing on a cold table or surrounded by a crowd of people: He is alone with his obsession. "Red'll be my color today. Gimme a stack o' red!" he snaps at the croupier, who is wearing a white styrofoam boater with a red ribbon around the crown stamped in gilt letters, "ELVIS." Obediently, the man slides an enormous stack of chips across the board.

As Colonel Parker starts his morning play, in a little room near the entrance to the showroom, the hotel's maitre d' is poring over his huge pasteboard seating charts. Emilio is a nice, plump, smiling, middle-aged Italian, who talks as if he had a mouth full of marbles. At this time of day he does not wear his frilly blue jabot shirt or his custom-tailored tuxedo or his costly studs and cuff links. He is attired in a dark English blazer and looks quite scholarly with his half-glasses sliding down his nose. As the switchboard operators in the adjoining office receive frantic calls for tickets for the severely rationed performances, Emilio ponders deeply the problem of accommodating such a demand. Elvis's appearances at the hotel are regarded by the maitre d' as the greatest and most challenging moments of his career. At the same time, he is exercised by the thought of how much money these two weeks will put in his pocket and those of his men, all of whom are sworn to pool their gratuities and then receive shares that are calculated carefully in terms of rank, seniority and various other considerations. Though no one but Emilio will ever know precisely how much money is entailed in such operations, a little basic arithmetic produces some startling results. If one computes the tips for one night, figuring two thousand couples, with the average tip twenty dollars—ten dollars to the captain who seats them and ten dollars to the waiter who serves them—the bottom line is twenty thousand dollars. As hundreds of people will pay anything to obtain admission to the shows and as everyone wants seats as close to the stage as possible, it may be assumed that considerably more than the minimum gratuity will be received: say, thirty thousand dollars a night for fourteen nights straight or over a half million dollars in tips. As all this money is in cash, in small bills, it's clear that Emilio is looking at a very good thing through his half-glasses.

As the maitre d' wrestles with the problem of the giant 747 that has just landed with a couple hundred wealthy Japanese or the question of where to put Cary Grant or what to do about the fire marshal, who keeps threatening to enforce the legal seating limit, Hamburger James is at the mail desk in the lobby collecting all the letters that have arrived addressed to Elvis or members of his group. Sorting through the lot swiftly, he divides the fan mail, which will be returned to the office at Graceland, from the personal mail. The latter he divides again between that destined for the Guys and Elvis's personal mail, which is given to Joe. Joe decides what letters should be given to Elvis just as he decides what reviews Elvis should read, what callers Elvis should receive and what news of the group Elvis should hear.

James takes the elevator to the thirtieth floor, where he receives from the security guard the key to the front door. Letting himself into the hushed apartment, he walks across the living room and opens the drapes slightly, al-

lowing a subdued light to enter the room. Next, he turns
on the big color TV that faces the sofa, being careful to
keep the volume very low. There must no more be jarring
sounds than there are garish lights. Finally, he goes to
the gilt-trimmed white bar, where he takes a champagne
glass and fills it with eighteen brightly colored vitamin
pills, including A, B12, C, D and E.

At that moment, he hears the bell at the service entrance, whose ring signals the arrival of room service with
Elvis's breakfast, ordered always the preceding night. Entering the big bare kitchen, James opens the door and
helps the waiter roll the cart down the two steps into the
sunken living room and across the carpeted floor to the
wrought iron, glass-topped coffee table where Elvis takes
his meals. Lifting the covers to make sure the order has
been filled precisely and verifying that the flame is burning inside the warming oven, James signs the check and
tips the waiter.

Now he goes back to the bar, where there is a direct
line to Elvis's room and presses the button. After a long
pause, Linda's voice comes on the line. "Tell E," says
James, "that his breakfast is here." Then he hangs up and
moves quickly toward the coffee table. Taking a cloth from
the cart, he covers the table; then, he sets it with silverware, Saltines, butter patties, sliced tomatoes, a bottle of
Mountain Valley water and the glass full of vitamins.

Elvis emerges from his bedroom looking very groggy
and wobbly. He braces himself against the wall for a moment; then, he steers a cautious course across the living
room to the sofa. His hair is down in his face. He wears
blue pajamas under a dark blue bathrobe. His boots are
unzippered and in his hand is a gleaming .45, which he
plants beside his plate. As James prepares to serve the
meal, Elvis picks up the glass full of vitamins and downs
it at a gulp. He prides himself on his ability to swallow
any number of pills at once. Then he takes the bottle of
mineral water and drains it.

James serves the meal noiselessly. No speech is permitted before the second cup of coffee. He pours the first
cup, steaming hot and extra strong. Then he places before
his master his invariable order for breakfast: a six-egg

Spanish omelet, twenty strips of crackling crisp bacon, an order of hash browned potatoes and a pitcher of fresh-squeezed orange juice. Elvis's first question is: "Where are the Guys?"

"Joe went out to the airport to git Lisa. Sonny is talkin' to the security dudes. Ole Red is laid up in his bed."

"Tell him to get his ass up here," growls Elvis, who is not to be trifled with when he awakens.

As James bustles across to the phone at the bar, Linda appears in her negligee. She's bright and cheery in the "morning." Giving Elvis a kiss on the forehead, she settles down at his side on the sofa.

Linda and Elvis have had some strange experiences here. One of the best remembered is the night in February 1974, when, after the first show, they came back to the penthouse to relax and watch television. Linda went into her bathroom and was sitting on the commode when, suddenly, she heard an explosion and saw, simultaneously, a hole appear in the roll of toilet paper next to her knee and a mirror on the other side of the bathroom explode into shards of glass. Pulling herself together and rushing out into the living room, along with several of the Guys, she discovered Elvis lolling on the sofa facing the common wall with the bathroom holding in his hand a still-smoking Savage .22 pistol. He had taken a shot at a light fixture, missed his aim and put the bullet clear through the wall and nearly into Linda's leg.

Elvis often relieves his boredom or vents his anger by picking up the gun that always lies near his hand and either pointing it at the cause of his displeasure or firing it. That is why his valets check his weapons constantly to make sure the first chamber is always empty. If they had not taken this precaution, certain people now living would be dead and Elvis Presley would be alive but behind bars. Elvis's favorite target is any television set that offends him with a malfunction or a bad program. Once Elvis fired into a TV and the bullet ricocheted and hit Dr. Nick above the heart. Just a spent bullet. Nothing to be alarmed about. That is also Elvis's attitude when somebody questions the wisdom of his firing the pistol into the ceiling of the penthouse. "If this is really the penthouse," he drawls, "there ain't nuthin' above us that *could* get hurt!" How's that for logic? The one funny part about this bit is the way the Guys cover for their boss by buying all the TVs he blows out, saying that Elvis has taken such a liking to the set that he can't bear to leave without it. You can always judge what Elvis's mood has been on a tour by counting the number of mechanical corpses being schlepped off the plane at Memphis.

About three in the afternoon, Elvis goes downstairs to rehearse with the orchestra. He hates to rehearse. He hates to even be here in Vegas. In fact, there is no part of Elvis's career that he still enjoys. He has done it all so many times in so many places to so many ga-ga audiences that the whole business fills him with disgust. People whisper that he's suffering from a serious illness. They're right! It's called terminal boredom.

When he arrives onstage, the cyclorama is up, exposing the brick walls and pipes behind the stage. The electricians are up on tall ladders adjusting the lights. The carpenters are assembling the platforms for the orchestra. Elvis makes the rounds, greeting the principals: the conductor, Joe Guercio; the drummer, Ronnie Tutt; the lead guitarist, James Burton; and J. D. Sumner of the Stamps Quartet.

Guercio is a nervous, fast-talking dude who wears tinted aviator glasses and gives off an aura of breathless showbiz ring-a-ding-ding. A mediocre musician, he left the highly competitive New York studio world to labor at Las Vegas. Eager to please, he's very deferential toward any star. As Elvis's show never changes from one year to the next, there isn't much to discuss. Maybe the conductor has come up with some little gimmick to give the show a slight air of originality, like doing the *2001* theme in the disco version popularized by Deodato. Elvis winces at the word "disco," as if Guercio had said "tampon." Still, Elvis has spent a lifetime listening to half-assed ideas like this and trying to make them work. He agrees to give the new version a try. Guercio, delighted to have had an idea accepted, turns around eagerly to the band and goes into the new ta-ta-tum, ta-ta-tum *2001*. Elvis listens, casting mocking glances at Red, as if to say, "Ain't this a crock!"

The whole thing is ridiculous; but when it's over, he agrees to try it that night.

Now they start going through the other tunes. They play the arrangements by heart, and Elvis blows out the lyrics in half voice, sitting on a stool with his mineral water beside him in a silver ice bucket. From time to time he interpolates dirty lyrics. He laughs at every little goof and goofs on himself, mocking his own style of singing. When they get to the big production number, which is the only good thing that Elvis has added to the show in years, a medley called "American Trilogy," Lamar and the hotel's lighting man come out on the stage and explain that they're going to throw some projections onto a screen that will drop in behind Elvis during the piece. Unfortunately, they can't demonstrate the effect just now because the projector operator hasn't arrived; but if it doesn't work out, they can always cut it. Again, Elvis is instinctively suspicious but he agrees. It's his day to be big about things. He mustn't get the engagement off on the wrong foot. Suddenly, in the middle of the next number, he bolts from the stage, with a couple of the Guys taking off with him. He's not sick or upset. He just figures he's had enough of this crap. It's time to get back upstairs and get a taste of his favorite honey.

While the rehearsal has been proceeding on the stage, beneath the stage that diligent mole, Hamburger James, has been burrowing into cabinets, closets and wardrobe drawers, unpacking, with the aid of an assistant, the seven rollers that he has brought down from the Imperial Suite. The star's dressing room at the International is on the same lavish scale as are all the accommodations in this gargantuan establishment. Not a room but a suite, this subterranean flat comprises a large lounge, equipped with a bar and furnished for either relaxing between shows or holding those informal receptions for VIPs after the show which allow both the famous entertainer and his famous guests a moment of exclusive communion. Off the lounge is the dressing room proper, equipped with all the customary facilities and two bathrooms. Adjacent to the dressing room is a tiring room, with a bed for those who crave rest and a piano for those who wish to warm up before the performance, as Elvis did in his more vigorous days, gathering the vocal quartet around him to sing gospel songs before going onstage.

As Hamburger James removes each costume from its case, he examines it carefully for tears or stains or stuck zippers, which require the application of his ever-ready graphite squirter. At the same time that he is rubbing scuff marks off white boots with a rubber eraser, on the subterranean shopping mall, Linda is trying on a white kid frontier suit with fabulous fringes at Suzie Cream Cheese. A floor above the mall, in the hotel's lobby and in the casino and the maze of public rooms that spread from the Keno parlor in all directions, like a major New York subway station, everywhere you look, you see Elvis posters, Elvis banners, Elvis, Elvis, Elvis. Silver-sequined guitars, giant pink teddy bears, yellow hound dogs, white boaters with red ribbons emblazoned "Elvis": As the Guys say, "You can't take a crap without looking up and seeing Elvis." The Colonel has converted the entire hotel into a giant snow job.

There will be but one show tonight: a dinner show that commences at eight with the meal and then offers an hour and a half of entertainment, commencing at ten. Admission is by invitation only, which means the house will be composed almost entirely of friends and well-wishers, most of them invited by Colonel Parker. The real grind does not start until tomorrow. Elvis has one night to work into the harness. At this point in his career, there is always the distinct possibility that he will not go the distance.

When Elvis gets back upstairs, he is greeted by Priscilla and little Lisa, who runs gleefully into her father's outstretched arms. The child lives with her divorced mother in an apartment at the Marina del Rey in Los Angeles, but she often sees her father either on the West Coast or in Memphis. Nothing pleases her more than spending time with Daddy because he spoils her outrageously. Elvis and Priscilla hold diametrically opposed views on child-rearing. She is a great believer in discipline and character-building. He feels that the primary value of success lies in being able to do exactly as you please and granting the same privilege to those you love. Lisa is being reared, therefore, in a totally schizophrenic manner, subject one moment to firmly enforced rules and order, released the next to run wild and imitate all the bad examples set by her father. Priscilla has balanced on a tightrope for years, trying on the one hand to preserve an atmosphere of good-humored cooperation between herself and Elvis, while, on the other hand, attempting to maintain some control over her daughter when she visits her father.

Priscilla looks much more beautiful now that she has gotten away from Elvis. Freed from the obligation to dress, make up and wear her hair in the vulgar styles that Elvis demanded, Priscilla has reverted to her natural appearance as an exquisite and tremulously feminine little creature accoutered in the latest and most sophisticated fashions. In this respect as in every other she stands in total contrast to Linda, who is not especially beautiful but who has a much bigger, bolder and more stagy appearance and the exhibitionistic personality of a real southern belle.

Elvis puts on an air of affectionate familiarity with Priscilla in public, but he makes her terribly nervous and apprehensive, as well he might, after years of alternating threats of physical violence with abject pleas for her return. Sometimes when he's really stoned, he'll dial up her number and when she answers, he'll just sit there speechless holding the receiver in his hand. Though Elvis hasn't loved Priscilla in years, he can never recover from the mortal wound his pride received when he learned that she had taken a lover.

It pleases him, however, to think that Priscilla and Lisa will be in the audience when he walks out on stage. Whatever his faults as a human being, he is still the King when he stands before his public. That is the way he likes everyone to see him and think of him. So he insists always that on opening nights Lisa be flown to Las Vegas, even if it's necessary that she go back home the very next morning, so that she will see her famous daddy in all his glory.

By 6:30, the faithful Hamburger James is back downstairs, preparing himself for the big event of the day: dressing his master for the stage. Since James has been gone, there have been many deliveries and visits to Elvis's dress-

ing room by porters, maids and bellmen. A big red banner
emblazoned with gold letters has been stretched across
one wall of the lounge, shouting: "Welcome Back to a
Wonderful Stay." Huge wreaths of red roses stand about,
as for a funeral, bearing cards from Conrad and Barron
Hilton, Rocco Laginestra and other big shots. More interesting are the cards from the staff: the greetings from
waiters in the showroom, maids who clean the penthouse,
casino managers and pit bosses, all of whom look to Elvis
to boost their income dramatically by his appearances.

James has seen all these tributes so many times before,
he pays them scant regard. His concern is first the bar,
which he is pleased to see has been freshly stocked for
visiting VIPs and equipped with a hot plate on which
James will prepare the tea with honey that Elvis drinks
to prepare his throat before he goes on stage. James fills
up the humidifiers with water and switches them on.
Checks to see that there are towels in the bathroom—not
that Elvis will take a shower but he must be rubbed dry
when he comes offstage drenched in sweat.

By the time James has everything in readiness, he
hears the familiar voice of Colonel Parker, who is entering
the suite with Tom Diskin. James bustles out and pours
the two men cups of coffee at the bar. Colonel quizzes
James about Elvis and receives vague answers. James is
in awe of the Colonel, a man he assumes to have nearly
divine powers; but the valet is not one of the Colonel's
snitches, like Joe Esposito or Charlie Hodge. By the time
the Colonel has poured the cup of hot coffee down his
asbestos throat, there is a racket in the hall signifying the
arrival of Elvis.

The King's progress from one suite on the roof of the
hotel to another suite in its basement is one of the most
ritualistic performances of his ceremonial day. Though no
one will see Elvis come downstairs but the hotel staff, he
dresses always for the occasion as if he were going out on
a date. In fact, it's the only time in the day when he does
dress properly, with a jacket and a scarf and all his fancy
jewelry. As he prepares himself to sally forth, all the Guys
gather in the main foyer of the suite, chattering nervously
in anticipation of the moment when Elvis will appear.

Then, suddenly, he is among them, perfectly dressed and groomed and smelling of Brut.

Striding vigorously, as if determined to go somewhere in a hurry and set something straight, Elvis comes out of his wing with nary a sunshaded glance to left or right. Instantly, all the Guys close about him, like Secret Service agents guarding the president. The service door to the Imperial Suite swings open. The security man on duty presses down on the transmitting button of his walkie-talkie and reports to his control center: "Fourteen is in progress. He has just taken Elevator Nine and..." The freight elevator is operated by another uniformed guard, who twists his key and closes the door. As the car drops to the second floor, all the Guys start chatting Elvis up like football players at a pep rally. They joke, they jolly, they pour on the good vibes. One thing they never do—touch him. Elvis stands in their midst, clad in black, masked by his shades, his hair perfectly styled and locked in place, looking as if he had been quick frozen.

When the elevator door opens on the bare concrete, fluorescent-smeared service corridors of the second floor, the hotel's main floor, another security guard is standing by to report Elvis's arrival at his station. It is about a three-minute walk through the maze of passages that lead eventually to the dressing room. In the old days, Elvis used to charge along these corridors with the same momentum with which he left the penthouse. Then, as the drugs took hold of him, his pace slackened, his step faltered. Finally, his equilibrium got so bad that somebody got the bright idea of providing Elvis with a golf cart to drive through the passageways. Now, without a moment's hesitation, Elvis hops inside the machine, which is ready to roll, and looking straight ahead, as if it were the most natural thing in the world, he starts driving through the hallways at the back of the hotel, surrounded by jogging henchmen and uniformed guards, past steaming kitchens and rattling pantries, past a big plate-glass window that lets in upon the employee's cafeteria, where, in response to the cheers of the workers, he raises his hand mechanically, like any ruler waving from any open car to his people.

When Elvis reaches the hydraulic elevator that com-
municates between the showroom stage and the dressing
rooms directly below, the two guards accompanying him
report his position again to central control. It is the static-
ridden voice of the guard's walkie-talkie that the alert
ears of Hamburger James catch now, as he darts into the
hall to take up his station.

As Elvis walks into the lounge, he gives the makeup
case he has been carrying to James and greets the Colonel
and Diskin. "Step into my office, son," says the Colonel,
gesturing toward the inner room. Colonel always closets
himself with Elvis before a show. He will have some little
item to report: what celebrities will be in the house or who
wants to have his picture taken with Elvis. Actually, all
the Colonel is interested in doing is giving his property
the once-over. The old man lives in constant fear now that
Elvis will collapse or cop out or do something erratic onstage that will cause a scandal. Elvis knows he's being
examined. Like any junkie, he's a practiced actor, adroit
at deceiving the squares and making them believe that
he's straight. He doesn't wear those sunglasses night and
day for nothing. After a very brief exchange, during which
Colonel does all the talking, the old man leaves. Now
James enters the room with an assistant to commence the
ritual of dressing the King.

All Elvis has to do to prepare himself for the stage is
to remove his street clothes and don a jump suit. You
would think one assistant could handle the job. In fact, it
requires the efforts of many men to prepare Elvis for exhibition. As soon as the King has stripped down to his thin
white dancing briefs, no different really from a pair of
women's panties, and sits down on his chair—an act that
flexes as many tubes of flesh about his midriff as has the
Michelin Man—he asks nervously: "Where's Elias?" Though
he is traveling with his personal physician, whose black
medical bag is stuffed with goodies, Elvis likes to maintain
a close working relationship with his local doctor. Dr. Elias
Ghanem arrives so punctually after his presence is inquired after that he appears to have been summoned up
like a genie. He even looks a little like Sabu, with his
swarthy skin and dark eyes and boyish features. He and

Elvis closet themselves briefly in the bathroom, where the doctor gives Elvis his preshow injection; then, the door opens and Elvis resumes dressing, as the doctor ducks out of the dressing room.

As Elvis sprawls in his chair with outstretched legs, waiting to feel the effect of the shot he has just received, Hamburger James busies himself about his master's knees. First, the valet takes a couple of huge Band-Aids and sticks them on the kneecaps; then, he slips over Elvis's feet and draws up his legs those elastic bandages that athletes wear on their joints. The purpose of all these dressings is to cushion the shock in case Elvis is inspired to go down on one knee in one of his Al Jolson salutes to the house. When you weigh over two hundred pounds, falling on one knee can be a shocking, even a shattering, experience. Next, James takes Elvis's hands, one at a time, with their long, thin, spatulate fingers, and wraps about the fingers ordinary-sized Band-Aids that will protect Elvis's skin from the fingernails of the women who clutch at him. The bandages will also prevent his rings from sliding off; they are not sized for his hands because he intends to give them away.

Once the protective padding has been affixed, it's time to cope with the natural padding, the huge belly that makes Elvis look as though he has swallowed a watermelon. As Elvis gets to his feet, aided by James's assistant, the valet wraps his master in a white corset. They don't call it a corset: The word is "brace." It's a surgical-looking garment that gathers the flesh in front and secures it from behind with a web of laces. Naturally, it is not a good thing for a singer to be laced into a gut sling that will restrict his breathing, especially when he's short of breath from other causes, as is Elvis. These days, however, nobody ever judges or even thinks of Elvis Presley as a singer. The sole criterion for his performances is his physical appearance, measured entirely by his weight. A good performance is one, for which you'd have to go back several years, in which he appears slender and youthful; a bad appearance is one in which he looks and acts so obese and dopey that everyone is embarrassed.

Now, laced into his corset, Elvis is shown the few cos-

tumes that still fit. He chooses for this evening an outfit
embroidered with the crowned head of King Tutankha-
men. Next, they have to get him into it. While James
hunkers at his master's feet, ready to slip the leg over his
foot, James's assistant offers his shoulder for support. Elvis
chicken-legs his way into the garment and stands free for
a moment while James runs the zipper up to the sternum.
Once the massive, ten-thousand-dollar, solid gold gladiator's belt is fastened around the waist, another device for
hiding the star's girth, the costuming is complete.

Charlie Hodge arrives now to give Elvis's hair the final
touches. When the famous coif, so well trained that with
one shake of the head it falls into place, has been arranged
and secured with hair spray, James pops up to give Elvis
a farewell squirt of Brut. Finally, the last gentlman of the
dressing chamber, Joe Esposito, appears to make his token
contribution to Elvis's dress. Joe takes one of the brightly
colored scarves that James is holding and arranges the
cloth carefully about Elvis's neck. Meantime, James has
folded neatly the dozen scarves that Elvis will cast into
the audience that night in a climactic ceremony suggestive
of the distribution of the eucharist. Elvis will proceed from
one side of the stage to the other shadowed by little Charlie, who will deftly loop each scarf about Elvis's neck,
where it will lie for a couple of seconds receiving the charismatic charge of the King's body. Then, like a perfunctory
old priest, Elvis will snatch off the scarf in a reflexive and
self-absorbed manner, all the time singing into a hand
mike, and throw the orange or golden cloth into the sea
of outstretched arms and hands.

The overhead P.A. announces now that the comedian
is in the final five minutes of his routine. James takes the
lavishly decorated cape from the wardrobe and secures it
at the back of Elvis's high Napoleonic collar. "How do I
look?" asks Elvis, staring into the mirror, as if he were
addressing his other self. As his men chorus, "Great, Boss!"
he turns abruptly toward the door, signaling that the investment is complete.

As Elvis is ushered to the wings at stage left by Red
and Sonny, who show the way with red flashlights, he is
beginning to feel the clarifying effect of his last injection.

It will take him a couple of numbers before he hits his stride, but by the time the show is underway, he will feel a furnace burning inside his body and the sweat will start to pour out of him. Even so, he has abused his body so badly for so many years that no matter what the drug or the dose he takes, he can no longer recover his natural manic energy.

His stage movements these days are sluggish and constrained, his speech is often slurred, his once-remarkable memory fails him and his voice is very uneven. So often does he crack on the high notes that measures have been taken to disguise his failures. The back-up singers are miked so that when Elvis reaches for a high note and misses, one of the men behind him will hit the note and in the resulting mix, controlled by the sound technician, the audience will not be able to detect that the ringing note they hear did not come from Elvis, standing there with his mouth open and his arms flung dramatically apart.

On this night, everything goes wrong from the start. As the orchestra takes off into the new version of the 2001 theme, Elvis suddenly realizes that he doesn't know exactly where to make his entrance. Elvis always makes a no-bullshit entrance, walking right on without an introduction and collaring the mike like a man who means business. Usually, all he has to do is start across the stage and there is an ovation. Tonight, when he steps out on the boards, he realizes that his timing is off. He isn't getting the sort of hand he should receive. As he goes into his opening numbers, he is bugged by the thought that nothing is working out properly. The ensembles are ragged, his voice is rough, the stage monitors aren't loud enough so that he can really hear himself. Though he keeps on smiling and singing, a terrible rage is starting to seethe inside his breast.

Usually, the high point of the show is "American Trilogy." This flag-waver symbolizes everything that Elvis has become in his maturity. The number starts off with a wistful performance of "Dixie," Elvis singing lone and bluesy, with a drummer-boy snare in the background. On the words, "I was born early one frosty morn," his voice rises keenly because the line reminds him of his own birth one bitterly cold morning back in Mississippi. He sings it now as if that time were a thousand years ago and he a grieving exile from his homeland. Then, the music slides into "The Battle Hymn of the Republic," the drums beating strongly and the brass taking stentorian snorts into the deeps or cresting high on silver foam, as the massed voices behind Elvis create the impression of a great host advancing. Suddenly, though, the mood shifts again; and at this moment, the last great moment of his musical career, he sings in a voice of deep poignancy a few lines from an old black spiritual titled "All My Trials." Achieving a sudden, hushed intimacy with his vast audience, he croons as a mother to her child, "Now, hush little darlin', don't you cry. You know your daddy's bound to die." That line sends chills down many a listener's back. It is one of those unconscious prophecies that great performers sometimes make from the stage. For one instant it raises the level of this crass and blowsy show to where Elvis should have always stood, with the men and women of soul. Soon, though, the "Battle Hymn" returns, the noise and theatrics mount up to a great rabble-rousing climax and that one little spark of beauty and sincerity is lost in the tawdry blaze of a showroom spectacular.

This night is cursed from beginning to end. Instead of the show reaching its full emotional climax with "American Trilogy," the whole performance collapses during this number into a complete fiasco. Just as Elvis is getting into his wistful, nostalgic recollection of "Dixie," down from the overhead, with an audible whirring of machinery, comes a round projection screen. Elvis spins around to greet the portent and exclaims with the hand mike close to his lips: "What's that! The moon comin' down?" Then as the slides start to flash on the orb, they prove to be horribly embarrassing pictures for a southerner: shots of slaves being auctioned on the block and cruel overseers walking about with whips. As the "Battle Hymn" commences, the Lincoln Memorial appears on the screen, followed by stagy movie footage of the Civil War. "Good night!" exclaims Elvis. "Maybe I oughta get a pointer and...'Next, class, we have...'" Finally, somebody orders the screen hauled up again, and the number ends to confused applause and laughter.

By the time Elvis comes offstage, he is ready to kill. Brushing past everyone in the wings and charging down the stairs to the dressing room, he sends a string of curses sailing after him that alarms the Guys. No one can calm him, no one can console him. Only the timely appearance of Dr. Nichopolous, bringing balm for the star's wounds, can soothe the raging Elvis. That night there is no party, no receiving of congratulations from celebrity guests, no hanging out with the Guys. Elvis goes back to his room to sulk and brood and vow that never again will he play "this fuck'n Vegas!"

About six in the morning, aroused by a subtle, unconscious prompting, Linda awakes and rolls over in bed to check on Elvis. Instantly, she realizes that something is wrong. His breath is coming with unnatural slowness and with long, rasping, rattling noises that make him sound like a man who is drowning. Putting her hand on his face, she is shocked to feel that it is ice cold. Switching on the bed lamp, she sees immediately that he is unwell because his skin, always pale, has now an ashen, deadly hue.

"Elvis! Honey! Wake up!" she urges, eager to assure herself that this is nothing serious. Elvis replies only with another of his long, gagging breaths, which seem to come only with great effort and at long intervals. "Elvis!" she snaps with alarm. *"Wake up!"* He makes no response at all. Now, she steels herself to do something that she detests but which she knows she must do. She slaps Elvis's face smartly with her open hand. He just lies there as if she had never touched him.

Now, Linda is terrified. She picks up the phone and dials Joe's room. Joe comes on the wire groggy and thick-voiced. The instant he gets the message, his voice changes. "Hold on," he barks. "I'm calling Nick, and I'll be up there myself in a minute."

Joe and the doctor arrive at practically the same moment. Dr. Nichopolous is wearing an undershirt and slacks. In his hand is a black medical bag. He takes one look at Elvis and asks Linda to leave the room. Then, he and Joe go to work.

"Well, Marcus Welby," cracks Joe, "why don't you give him a shot? What are you waiting for?"

Nick, who has been holding Elvis's pulse and is now listening to his heart with a stethoscope, looks up with an expression of melancholy resignation imprinted on his face. "Sometimes it's not as easy as you think," he sighs. "Here, help me get him into that chair."

Chapter 3

Redneck Roots

THE TENNESSEE hills are not designated as such on any map. The phrase is a local appellation used by the folk of several counties in the northeast corner of Mississippi for the subsiding southwestern margin of the Appalachians. Forming a strong natural barrier to the flow of people from east to west, these mountains captured many migrant settlers, who found in isolated valleys or upland meadows the promise of security, privacy and sustenance enough to maintain life. So detached from the world did these people become that eventually they appeared like survivors from a much earlier age. A race of Rip Van Winkles, when they awoke in the twentieth century they discovered that the world had long since forgotten their folkways, which derived from the seventeenth century. Mountain men, hillbillies, they constituted a distinctive breed of southern yeomanry, closely related to their cousins in the hills of the Carolinas. In Mississippi, especially, they were an odd lot because they represented the state's least characteristic area, a spur of piedmont stuck in the flank of a region of rolling black prairies or table-flat delta lands or hot coastal plains taking the sluggish wash of the Gulf of Mexico.

To the northerner cooped up in his immense cities and prey to strange fancies about the "real America," people like

61

these hill folk are synonymous with the great modern dream of "roots." They are imagined as holding fast to their turf like European peasants, who in some instances have occupied the same spot of ground for nine hundred years. As for the hillbillies, nothing could be further from the truth. A more deracinated and restless race could not be imagined. Though some of them maintained the same regional ambit through a number of generations, typically they moved every year. Migrant farm laborers or sharecroppers, with no real stake in the soil, they were seekers after better situations. As there are rarely any better situations for people incapable of standing still and improving their own lot, the hill folk wandered endlessly without ever finding anyplace where they could strike roots and settle down permanently.

Just as the hillbillies had no real awareness of the present, they had no grasp on the past. As Lord Raglan demonstrated in a classic argument, history is almost entirely a function of literacy. Given a population that cannot read or write, history becomes myth. Though the folk may live like fossils of a distant past, they have no recollection of that past, even when it bears on their nearest blood relations. When an interviewer told Vernon Presley that he bore an old English name, he replied with honest surprise: "I never heard tell of any of my kinfolk coming over from anywhere." Then, reflecting further, he allowed: "I guess it must have been a long way back. We just seem always to have been here. And it's the same with Gladys's family, the Smiths."

Elvis Presley, a lot better educated than his nearly illiterate father, never had the vaguest idea of who his people were until just before he died. Then, he received from a genealogical research organization in Salt Lake City an elaborate family tree, which traced the Presleys back nine generations to the "emigrant," the first man of the line who came to America. He proved, not surprisingly, to be an Anglo-Irishman, named David Pressley.[1] Nothing is really

---

[1]Because Elvis's ancestors were illiterate, there was no settled spelling for their name, but the traditional spelling, "Pressley," conveys the correct pronunciation, whereas "Presley" leads to the common error of pronouncing the name "Prezley."

known of this man or his son, Andrew Pressley, Senior, except that they landed, apparently, at New Bern, North Carolina, in the 1740s and were soon granted extensive tracts
of probably quite worthless lands along the Rocky River,
then the boundary between the Carolinas. It is not until we
reach the third generation of the family in this country that
we get a little flash of individual identity around the figure
of Andrew Pressley, Junior.

Assuming that Andrew wasn't lying when he turned
up in front of a pension board many years after the Rev-
olutionary War and claimed to have served two hitches as
a "summer soldier"; assuming further that on his second
hitch this blacksmith from Rowan County, North Carolina, remained with the other 150 militiamen in his battalion, who were stationed in the center of the front rank
at the Battle of Eutah Springs, South Carolina, the last
major engagement of the War of Independence fought in
the South: assuming all this and accepting his sworn testimony that "he received several [musket] balls through
his garments," it would follow that Andrew Pressley, Junior, was a minor American hero. For of one thing we can
be sure: His volunteer unit fought with great bravery on
that hot morning in the year 1781.

After skirmishing up a dirt road through a piney wood
near the Santee River, the militiamen burst onto an eight-
acre farm clearing and saw drawn up before them, ready
for battle, two thousand Redcoats. Instead of hugging the
cover of the woods, the militia made straight for the British. "It was with equal astonishment," wrote an eyewitness
after the battle, "that both sides contemplated these men
steadily and without faltering, advance with shouts and
exhortations into the hottest of the enemy fire, unaffected
by the continual fall of their comrades around them." The
militia were overwhelmed eventually by a British bayonet
charge; but they had won the first honors of the day, which
concluded with the English retreating on Charleston, from
which they never again emerged until the war's end.

When the skimpy documents of those early times allow
us next a glimpse of Elvis's ancestors, we discover not a
patriot or hero but a coward, deserter and bigamist. In
1861, Dunnan Pressley, Junior, married Martha Jane

Wesson at Fulton, Mississippi, the seat of Itawamba County. This district in the northeast corner of the state had been opened to settlement in 1832 by a treaty with the Indians, the Chickasaw Cession. Dunnan was drawn to the region, most likely, as were many other veterans of the Mexican war, by the search for cheap land. In those days, the going price for an acre of richly timbered soil was twenty-five cents. To a poor settler, children were another vital resource. Dunnan produced two children with his new wife in quick succession: Rosalinda and Rosella. The latter, born in 1862, was Elvis Presley's great-grandmother.

Just a couple of months before Gettysburg, in 1863, Dunnan returned to the wars, enlisting in Ham's Regiment of Mississippi Cavalry. No longer the naive young Tennessee volunteer he had been in the Mexican War, Dunnan was intent this time on fraud. Obtaining the rank of corporal and a three-hundred-dollar bounty for his horse, he no sooner joined his unit than he was listed on its rolls as a deserter. Then, a couple of months later, he joined and deserted Davenport's Battalion in precisely the same manner, taking the bounty and then taking French leave. Now, having twice deserted the cause for which he had sworn to fight, he rounded off the job of shucking his responsibilities by abandoning his wife and infant daughters.

The manner of Dunnan's departure was preserved for over a century in the memories of his descendants. His granddaughter, Mrs. Robie Stacy, recalled in 1977: "My mother told me that when she and her sister were just little babies, their grandparents had taken them to church one Sunday and when they came back, their father, Dunnan, was gone. He went back to his other wife and child."

Dunnan drifted west in his declining years through Arkansas to Missouri, where he died in 1900, petitioning to the end for an increase of his soldier's pension because of incapacitation owing to: "irsepulas and rheamtism weak eyes and dafness in the right ear and gravil or disease of the kidness." Meantime, his abandoned daughter, Rosella, grew to be a very strange and mysterious woman. Commencing at the age of nineteen and continuing over a period of twenty-eight years, she bore at least nine illegitimate children. Never once did she identify her lover or make any claim on him—or them.

Rosella supported her brood by working as a wandering farmhand. Her life can be viewed as a sustained act of protest against her mother's fate. Instead of marrying and risking the pain and humiliation of abandonment, she never married. Yet she did not relinquish the primary role of woman in her world; indeed, she sustained it more fully than many and entirely through her own resources. She found her compensation, however, in never having to share her children's love with any man, even to the slight extent of permitting her children to imagine their absent and unknown father. On this last point, she was firm as a rock: "I can't remember anyone ever talking about who our father was," recalls Mrs. Doshia Steele, one of the surviving daughters of Rosella, in 1980 a tiny little woman of ninety-three, who lives to this day not far from her mother's last home on the old McDaniel Farm near Fulton. "It was a big mystery when we were children. My mother just didn't talk about it."

Like the Pressleys, Gladys's family, the Smiths, originated in the Carolinas and moved westward over a span of several generations. Elvis's great-great-grandfather, John Smith, is listed in the census of Atlanta in 1850. In 1874, his son, Obe Smith, married a widow from Alabama, Ann Mansel, and established the family in northeastern Mississippi in the area of Saltillo, just north of Tupelo. The second-born of this union was Robert Lee Smith, Elvis's grandfather. "Bob" Lee's marriage to Octavia Lavinia "Doll" Mansell was perhaps the most significant alliance in Elvis's genealogy, for there is strong reason to believe that husband and wife were first cousins, a potentially dangerous mating combination. Genetics may explain why the children of Bob Lee's brothers and sisters turned out well, whereas Bob and Doll produced children who exhibited an abnormally high incidence of addiction to drugs and alcohol, emotional disorders and premature death. Particularly was this true of the male side of the family.

Consider Gladys Smith's three brothers: Tracy was born deaf and dumb; Travis died in his thirties; Johnny died at

the age of forty-six (as did Gladys). Both Travis and
Johnny were heavy drinkers and dangerously violent
when drunk, given to brandishing knives and guns. This
same pattern is just as clearly marked in the next generation. Four men carried the name Smith in this group:
Junior and Gene, the children of Lavelle Smith; and Bobby
and Billy, the sons of Travis Smith. The oldest boy in each
of these families came to an early and violent death: Junior
died of a convulsion before he was thirty, after a life darkened by homicidal madness; Bobby committed suicide a
few years later by swallowing arsenic. Finally one comes
to Elvis, whom we see now as possibly the victim of a fatal
hereditary disposition.

No emotional blight affected Bob Smith; he was a merry
man, and his daughter, Gladys, resembled in youth her
frolicsome father. Though Gladys sank deep into depression in later years, her basic disposition was always fun-
loving, even a little manic, like that of her famous son.
"She laughed and joked all the time. Jolly—just as jolly
as could be," recalls Gladys's cousin, Mrs. Mary Lyons,
who knew Gladys in her teens. "She wanted everybody to
be happy, everybody to be enjoying themselves. Dancing—
she was always skipping around trying to dance. When
she was in the house, she'd be apunching one of us in the
ribs." All of this sounds exactly like Elvis.

When Gladys was nineteen or twenty, her father, who
had already gone blind, began to fail. The family decided
to change its survival strategy. In the past, they had been
sharecroppers and migrant workers. "If a place didn't
suit," recollects Truitt Smith, another cousin, "they'd move
on. Generally, it didn't suit." Now, they decided to take
advantage of the development of the garment industry at
Tupelo, which had become during the early thirties one
of the model towns of the "New South," that melding of
the agricultural and the industrial so strongly supported
by the New Deal.

The Smiths took a house in East Tupelo so that the
unmarried girls in the family would have easy access to
work. Gladys obtained employment at the Tupelo Garment
Company, working twelve hours a day, five or six days a
week. It was piecework, stitching shirts together at a sew-

ing machine. An efficient operator could earn thirteen dollars a week, which was considerably more than the wages of an agricultural laborer.

East Tupelo in the early thirties consisted of a score of dingy white frame bungalows arranged on a grid of muddy rock roads where the old Saltillo Road leads north off the highway from Birmingham to Tupelo. Situated where the last foothill melts into the plain, the hamlet looks out across a broad and swampy bottom, threaded by the Mud River and crossed by the highway levee, to the city of Tupelo, with which at the time it had no affiliation.

East Tupelo was full of Pressleys: so many, in fact, that at one time twenty-six children at the local school bore the name. Jessie Pressley, Elvis's grandfather, had come first, followed by his brothers, Noah and Calhoun. Jessie had quit school at eleven to go to work. In 1913, at the age of seventeen, he married Minnie Mae Hood, a tall, homely girl from a solid local family. At first, they farmed for shares some land in Clay Community, just west of Fulton. It was here that their two boys, Vester and Vernon, were born. When the owner of their farm sold the land after the war, the Pressleys moved to East Tupelo. Now the family was enlarged by the birth of three daughters: Delta Mae, Gladys Earlene and Nashville Lorene. By this time, Minnie Mae had come to hate her young husband.

Jessie was actually a very likable fellow; his problem was that, like his famous grandson, he was not the sort of man who should have married. His younger brother, Calhoun, once offered a good characterization of Jessie:

> For most of his life Jessie drifted from one job to another all over Mississippi, Kentucky, Missouri. He was a sharecropper in the summer and a lumberjack in the winter. Jessie worked hard and played hard. He was an honest man, but he enjoyed drinking whiskey and was often involved in drunken bar brawls. As a result, Jessie spent many a night sobering up in jail.
>
> He was a slim, handsome man about six feet tall with black hair. I reckon Elvis inherited his looks from Jessie. He was also a dapper dresser. Clothes

were one of the most important things in his life. We used to call him "the lawyer" because he dressed so smart. He loved fine clothes. His favorite suit was a tailor-made brown one with pearl buttons. He saved up for months until he had enough money to buy it—twenty-four dollars. He paraded around town like a peacock, with his head in the air and a cane in his hand. Owning expensive clothes was his only ambition in life. He hated poverty and he didn't want people to know he was poor. He felt that if he wore a tailor-made suit, people would look up to him.

Calhoun Pressley makes it appear that Jessie's penchant for fine clothes and drink were just idiosyncrasies that affected him alone. In fact, they caused his family great suffering. The family sometimes went without food because Jessie had squandered on drink the money they needed to subsist. When he went far afield in search of work, months would elapse without any word from him or any remittance. The effect this waywardness had on his children is not hard to imagine. Vester and Vernon received virtually no education. At the age of forty, Vernon could barely sign his name.

When Gladys met Vernon, she was already a woman: twenty years of age, making a good living, and very much in command of her life. She was attractive, almost pretty, with dark hair parted at the side and pulled tight around her head, and large dark eyes under strong brows with a shadowy tint to the surrounding skin. This distinctive dark coloring Gladys got from her mother, Doll, who had a dusky complexion. Vernon, on the other hand, was very blond, with the distinctive features of the Presley men: the long muscular neck, the bony hard face, the keen little eyes—the Grant Wood American Gothic look. Just a typical country younker at sixteen, Vernon must have fallen at once under the sway of Gladys, who was not only older but a much stronger personality. Gladys was a worker; Vernon was a shirker. Gladys was an ebullient extrovert; Vernon was always uptight and distrustful. Most important, Gladys possessed some intelligence and imagination;

whereas Vernon was always a dullard and a donkey, a boy destined to spend a lifetime trying to become a man.

Their marriage, everyone agrees, was a love match. It was also, most likely, a somewhat impulsive act. "We should have been in school, but we eloped," Gladys told a reporter in 1956. "We didn't elope very far," added Vernon. "We just went down the road to Verona and got married." In fact, they were not married in Verona, which is five miles south of Tupelo in Lee County, but in Pontotoc, which is twenty miles west of Tupelo in Pontotoc County, the area in which Gladys was born. Embarrassed, evidently by the disparity in their ages, they falsified the figures on the marriage license. She claimed to be nineteen, though she was twenty-one; he added five years to his age, claiming to be twenty-two. Having achieved what they regarded as a proper balance of ages, they became man and wife on June 17, 1933.

Vernon and Gladys moved in at first with the Jessie Pressleys. Vernon was working for a well-known dairy farmer and cattle and hog broker named Orville S. Bean. Bean made a business of loaning money to people to build their own homes, the houses becoming his property until he had received his principal and interest through monthly rent payments. When Gladys became pregnant in the spring of 1934, Vernon took a $180 loan from Bean and, with the aid of his father and brother, built a two-room cabin on a lot owned by his father next door to the Presley house on North Saltillo Road. This is the famous "birthplace" and an eloquent example of the transfiguring power of the Presley Myth.

The house which attracts as many as a million visitors a year bears today a totally different aspect than it did when Elvis Presley was born. The local ladies who are the keepers of this shrine were horrified by the shanty's original appearance and took great pains to transform it into the cute little doll house which it should have been according to the Myth. They painted the bare grey boards gleaming white. They papered the rough wooden walls with primrose-patterned wallpaper. They hung dimity curtains at the windows. They filled the cramped interior with a clutter of objects which the Presleys never had the money to purchase: a sewing machine, a baby's high chair, solid pieces of furniture and electric appliances, such as a fan and a radio. Then, they hung a swing on the tiny front porch and landscaped the grounds. When they were finished with their foolish labors, they had effected the typical substitution of fantasy for history that is the essence of Elvis Presley's story.

Chapter 4

The Little Family

LONG BEFORE Gladys came to term, she became convinced that she was carrying twins. So strong was her belief that she and Vernon chose names for the unborn children, whom she was likewise sure would both be boys. The boys' first names were taken from the male side of the family: "Jessie" was chosen in honor of Vernon's father; "Elvis" was a tribute to Vernon, being his middle name. The twins' middle names were selected with great care to make them rhyme both to the ear and the eye, thus proclaiming Gladys's ultimate intuition: that these babies would be not merely fraternal but *identical* twins.

To attain the mirror effect she was seeking, she distorted the spelling of the twins' names, either deliberately or inadvertently through ignorance: "Elvis Aron" was spelled with a single "a" and "Jessie Garon" with an "o" instead of the customary "i." Further signs of ingenuity are the equivalent number of syllables in each name and the balance struck by matching one Old Testament name, Jessie or Aron, with one ancient English name, Elvis or Garon. The final twist in the name knot attached the boys to their father by giving them all one name that rhymed: viz., Aron, Garon, Vernon. It was not, however, the connection with the father but the link with the other twin that was permanent. Gladys wanted to assure that throughout his entire future life Elvis Aron, for example, could never hear, speak or read his own name, without hearing in his mind its faint chiming echo—Jessie Garon.[1]

All these loving refinements in the selection and adjustment of names for identical twins who exist only in the imagination of an expectant mother attest to an extraordinarily high degree of prenatal fantasy. Though events were to confirm Gladys's prediction to a surprising degree, they could just as well have turned out otherwise. By anticipating the future not only so vividly but so extravagantly and with such complete disregard for probability, Gladys declared herself a woman impatient with reality and prone to paint over the ordinary face of things with fantastical forms and colors reflecting her own hopes and fears. This turn of mind was highly characteristic of all three members of the little family.

Elvis, for example, got the idea in later years, when he was absorbed in the study of the occult, that he might be a divinely appointed Master, Messenger or Messiah, put on earth to perform some momentous mission. Nothing could dissuade him from this belief and everything that he observed about himself, whether it were a little crease on his palm in the shape of a cross or a fancied likeness between his face and the image in a religious painting, confirmed him in his conviction that he was the "One." Significantly, it was in the circumstances of his birth that he found the strongest confirmation of his divine calling.

Vernon confided to Elvis that he had known the exact moment of his son's conception because at that instant he had blacked out. Though there were other, more rational, ways of interpreting this momentary loss of consciousness, Elvis insisted on seeing it in terms of his grand obsession. It was a clear sign, he argued, that at the critical moment, his father's body had become the vehicle for a higher being. Thus, like the heroes of mythology, Elvis came to believe that the man he called "Daddy" was no more his father

[1]"Elvis" was spelled in seventeenth-century England "Helwiss" or "Helwys," which indicates its derivation from "Heloise." "Aron" was changed legally by Elvis in later years to "Aaron."

than was Joseph the father of Jesus. Further confirmation
of this weird notion was the story Vernon told of going out
into the backyard on the night of the birth and being
astonished to see the heavens ringed around with a blue
light. This recollection thrilled Elvis because blue was a
color he had long identified with himself and to which he
attributed supernatural significance.

As these few examples suggest, the Presleys are not
sober witnesses to their own history. Time and again they
twisted the anticipation or recollection of events into the
gratifying forms of wish fulfillment. This is the first reason
why the Presley Myth is so unsound as biography. The
second, more important, reason is the eagerness with
which people everywhere translate the quirky squiggle of
real happenings into the smooth, regular patterns of mythology. Myth, after all, is what we believe naturally.
History is what we must painfully learn and struggle to
remember. The conflict of myth and history is particularly
evident in the story of Elvis's birth.

According to the Myth, Elvis Presley was the first born
of identical twins (the mythic hero is always the first
child), the second twin being dead upon birth. It is highly
characteristic of the mentality of Elvis Presley's millions
of fans and numerous hagiographers that none of them
ever thought to verify this story by seeking out the appropriate records. Not until 1980 was the truth about Elvis's birth revealed, when Mrs. Sara Potter, the daughter
of the attending physician, Dr. William Robert Hunt, discovered an entry in her father's record books that set the
matter in a true light.

Dr. Hunt was an old-time country physician who maintained an office over Riley's Jewelry Store on Tupelo's
Main Street. By the time he retired in the fifties, he had
supervised the birth of 1,854 babies. This figure is significant because it suggests the doctor's penchant for careful
bookkeeping. For every year of his practice, going back to
his first year, 1913, the doctor kept a "baby book" in which
he entered the circumstances of each "labor case." Thanks
to the baby book for 1935, we know now the basic facts of
Elvis's birth, facts of which Elvis himself remained ignorant throughout his life, he having been one of the first

of those millions who have been deceived by Gladys's and
Vernon's curious propensity for making unaccountable
alterations in their family history.

On the night of January 7–8, a bitterly cold night in
northern Mississippi, Dr. Hunt attended Gladys Presley
at home. Most likely, he was seeing her for the first time.
He noted in his book that at 4:00 A.M. Mrs. Presley was
delivered of a stillborn son. Then, at 4:35, she had a second
delivery, another son, who survived. On the birth certificate, he spelled the surviving baby's name "Evis Aaron,"
which is undoubtedly the way it was pronounced. He noted
that the father was a white, eighteen-year-old laborer. In
his baby book, he recorded that the family was unable to
pay the fifteen-dollar fee, but that he collected the money
eventually from "welfare." Thus was born the King.

According to the Presley Myth, Gladys's prediction was
fulfilled: The two boys to whom she gave birth were identical twins. As will soon be obvious, this idea had enormous
importance in Elvis's life. Yet, can it be regarded as a fact?
Elvis claimed that he bore the sign of an identical twin
visibly on his body in the form of an odd webbing which
stretched between the second and third toes of his right
foot. Needless to say, such an anomaly indicates nothing
about twinship, the idea being simply an old Negro superstition. Actually, there is no evidence whatsoever that
Elvis's twin was an identical sibling. The random odds are
three to one against such an occurrence, and the only way
of determining the fact in infancy is through laboratory
tests.

These rational considerations were, of course, very remote from the mental world of the Presleys. Once Gladys's
hunch that she was carrying twins was confirmed by the
event, it would have taken a lot more than scientific argument to persuade her that she was mistaken in her
insistence that the twins were identical. The conviction
that preceded the birth persisted after the birth to give
rise to many other unfounded ideas. Gladys was not simply
ignorant: She was highly superstitious, a hillbilly Cas-
sandra, given to prophetic dreams and weird intuitions,
quick to identify chance happenings as signs and omens—
all traits of mind which she imparted to her son. What

were the mental constructions that she built upon the death of the twin?

We know that she grieved profoundly for Jessie Garon. He was laid out in a tiny coffin in the living room and buried in an unmarked grave in nearby Princeville Cemetery. His death cast a deep shadow over the birth of Elvis, who, psychologically speaking, was born under a bad sign. The birth, which had been anticipated as a welcome access of life, double life at that, produced in a fact a double death: Not only did Jessie Garon perish but Gladys was informed by the doctor—or concluded herself—that she could never again bear children. Perhaps this is why her grief for the lost twin proved to be an affliction without a term. Soon, she had transformed the dead infant into a spooky presence about the house.

One of the first things that Elvis Presley learned at his mother's knee was that he had a dead brother identical to him in every respect. He heard his mother talk about this brother constantly, invoking him by name, just as if Jessie Garon had once enjoyed the life that Elvis was leading now. His mother told him that the personality of the dead twin was transferred to the living twin, thus planting in his mind the notion of metempsychosis, which blossomed years later in the conviction that he was a reembodied Master who had lived in ancient times. She also taught him that Jessie Garon was an angel up in heaven with whom Elvis could commune through prayer. Often mother and son went to the cemetery to visit the dead Jessie's grave. At the age of four or five, Elvis began to hear his brother's voice, enjoining him to do good deeds and lead a good life. In fine, as Elvis grew up, he had beside him always a phantom double, a secret sharer, a veritable *Doppelgänger*. This spirit brother is one of the most important characters in the life of Elvis Presley, for from adolescence onward, Elvis exhibited with increasing clarity all the signs of a split personality. His behavior patterned itself into two sharply opposed selves, which embodied two radically different fantasy systems, one inspired by an extravagant notion of goodness, the other by a no less exaggerated idea of evil. Every feature of Elvis's

subsequent life and career bears the unmistakable stamp
of this dichotomy.

As a child Elvis aspired to be a saint on earth. At the
age of nine, for example, he received the baptism of the
spirit, a sacrament of the Pentecostal church. This occasion
filled him so with the spirit of Christian charity that he
took his only possessions, a handful of comic books, and
gave them away to the neighbor children. Subsequently,
his parents bought him a tricycle, a costly gift for people
so poor. Elvis gave the tricycle away not once but several
times, until finally his parents were compelled to allow
the gift to stand. Nothing was more basic to Elvis Presley,
therefore, than a passionate desire to be good and do good.
One can see this impulse asserting itself with increasing
urgency all through his life up to the very end. On the
other hand, this yearning to be a living saint was countered by an equally powerful compulsion which drove him
in the opposite direction and made him often a diabolic
figure: not just a man who does wrong but who seduces
others into the path of sin and relishes their fall. This Bad
Elvis also gained in power as the years passed and often
threatened dire deeds, which were averted often only at
the last moment by the intervention of other people or by
the awakening of Elvis's better self.

Two years after Elvis was born, Gladys witnessed the
lingering death of her mother from tuberculosis. Doll was
laid to rest beside her husband in an unmarked grave in
the pastoral cemetery beside the little frame church at
Springhill, not far from Saltillo. Gladys, once so cheerful
and ebullient, so eager to dance and make others dance,
was being clouded over by repeated sorrows. First, the
death of her father, then the death of Jessie Garon, now
the death of her mother: one misfortune piled atop the
other. One worse thing was shortly to befall her and complete the revolution in her personality. She was to see her
handsome young husband, the sole support of herself and
Elvis, taken off to prison.

No one at this late date recalls distinctly the details of
the crime. Vernon, Travis Smith (Gladys's twenty-three-
year-old brother) and a certain Lether Gable were charged
with forging a check on Orville S. Bean. Evidently, Vernon

sold a hog to his employer for four dollars and was paid
by check. Then Vernon and his friends conceived the crazy
notion of altering the figure on the check so that it read
forty dollars. Nobody can explain why these young men
acted in this manner or how they hoped to escape detection.

An accusation was lodged, and the evidence was laid
before a grand jury. On November 17, 1937, the *Tupelo
Journal* reported that "three men, Travis Smith, Luther
[*sic*] Gable and Vernon Pressley [were] indicted for forgery
and placed under bonds of $500." Initially, all three en-
tered pleas of not guilty. Then, in the time between the
indictment and the trial, intense efforts were made by the
families of the young men to persuade Orville Bean to
withdraw his charges. Noah Presley, who was a close
friend of Bean, offered twice the amount of the money that
had been stolen. Bean proved vindictive. He was determined to prosecute the men to the limits of the law. The
offense was a felony. Despite the smallness of the sum, the
penalty was severe.

When the circuit court met for its May session, the case
of the three young men appeared on the docket. Their
choice was to stand trial, with conviction virtually assured
and a harsh sentence in prospect, or to change their plea
to guilty and throw themselves on the mercy of the court.
The final disposition of the case appears in the minutes
for the ninth day of the sitting, May 25, 1938, when, in
a brief interruption of the proceedings, the presiding judge,
Thomas J. Johnston, announced the sentences for all those
cases that had been concluded. Under docket number 9756,
"State *vs*. Travis Smith, Lether Gable and Vernon Presley," the following notice appears:

"Plea of not guilty entered on a former day this day
withdrawn and Defendants at this time issue a plea of
guilty to a charge of forgery: upon such plea it is OR-
DERED AND ADJUDGED by the Court that the defendants for their said offense be and each is hereby sentenced
to serve a term of three (3) years in the State penitentiary,
and they are hereby remanded to the custody of the sheriff
for safekeeping in the county jail until called for by the
proper officer or agent for transportation and delivery to
said institution."

"Said institution" meant only one thing: *Parchman*. A
dread name. A name that cries the blues. An American
concentration camp pitched in the heart of the Mississippi
Delta. Parchman meant laboring from sunup to sundown
six days a week under the searing Delta sun. Parchman
meant the "long lines": rows of men in blue-and-white
striped pajamas, laboring along the cotton furrows or in
the chain gangs beside the highways under the shotgun
of a trustee mounted on a horse. Parchman meant that if
a man did not deliver his two hundred pounds of cotton
a day, or if he were guilty of some other offense, he would
be disciplined with "Black Annie," an eight-foot leather
belt that was laid across the prisoner's back under the
stern eye of the warden.

When the sheriff's van drove Vernon Presley and his
mates down the legendary Highway 61 in the first week
of June 1938, the cotton couldn't have been more than six
inches high. Cotton was the soul of the Delta and the real
reason for Parchman. Cotton demanded the kind and
quantity of labor once supplied by African slave gangs.
When the slaves were freed, some shrewd old men in Jackson decided to replace them with prisoners. Thus Parchman became one of the greatest plantations in the South:
twenty thousand acres in extent, at some points thirty-
five miles across. One half of the land was planted in
cotton; one half in corn, cane and all the garden crops
necessary for the sustenance of two thousand inmates.
Almost totally self-sufficient, the prison colony was farmed
under the supervision of a local planter at a handsome
profit for nearly half a century.

Eighty percent of Parchman's population was black,
which meant eight of the ten camps were black. First of-
fenders were supposed to be kept apart from hardened
criminals, but this ideal could not always be realized. Just
four years before Vernon's incarceration, as the result of
an extensive reform of the penal statute, a medical staff
had been added to the prison, which hitherto had had none.
There was also a recreation officer and a camp musician—
none other than the famous blues singer, Bukka White.
His crime? Murder. Place of arrest? A recording studio in
Chicago. In May 1939, White was recorded at Parchman

by Alan Lomax. His song had a certain grim appropriateness: It was titled "Sic 'Em Dogs on Down."

How long Vernon served is open to question. The last five months of his three-year sentence were commuted by the governor, probably for good behavior. His official date of discharge was January 4, 1941. No sooner did he plead guilty than Orville Bean turned mother and child out of their house. They moved next door with Vernon's parents, and Gladys went to work as a seamstress and laundress. By the time Vernon was released, the whole economy of the country was being transformed by the war boom. Vernon told the compiler of a "fanzine" in 1956 that he spent the war years working in a defense plant in Memphis, returning home only on weekends. (As a felon he was draft-exempt.) His prolonged absence had a profound effect on Elvis's development.

Nearly always alone with his mother from the age of thirty months to eleven years, Elvis became a classic mama's boy. Neighbors and relatives of the Presleys recall distinctly the details of Gladys's behavior with Elvis: how she "worshipped" the child; how she never let him out of her sight; how she escorted him to school and back every day; how she would panic and start shouting if she couldn't find him; how she forbade him to go swimming or do anything that might possibly endanger him; how she would attack any child with whom Elvis got into a fight.

The most suggestive feature of the relationship of mother and son is their extreme physical intimacy. Elvis slept in the same bed with Gladys until he was at the threshold of puberty. His most characteristic gesture of affection for his mother was petting her, particularly on a lump of flesh that rose at the base of her neck atop the spine. His nickname for his mother was also suggestive of years of childish petting and patting: He called Gladys, "Satnin'." This name, like all the affectionate terms in which mother and son conversed, was a treasured relic of Elvis's baby prattle. Other such words were "sooties" for "footies" and "Butch" for "milch." So elaborate and private did this affectional language grow that in later years strangers watching Elvis "petting on" his mother and communing with her in baby talk got the impression that

mother and son "spoke the secret language of some weird
religious cult."

Constantly in his mother's company, Elvis was no less
constantly urged to open his mind and reveal to his mother
all his thoughts and feelings. So accustomed did Elvis grow
to sharing his inner life with his mother, so dependent did
he become on her judgment and advice, that in later years
he thought nothing of waking her up in the middle of the
night if he had some problem on his mind which kept him
awake. There can be no question that the extraordinary
introversion that characterizes Elvis throughout his adult
life, his extreme reluctance to confide in anyone or reveal
his inner thoughts, is explainable by the fact that he believed there was only one person in the world who could
understand and guide him. When he lost his mother, he
closed up like a clam.

Another way in which the bonds between mother and
son were strengthened was through the pampering and
coddling which characterized the relationship. Though the
Presleys were desperately poor when Elvis was a child,
money was found to buy him expensive gifts, like a bicycle
or a guitar. Elvis was stuffed with scarce food and even
provided with silver table utensils, like a little prince. He
was a lonely little prince, however. One of the most important features of his upbringing was the fact that he was
kept apart from his relatives, from the local children and
from the world in general. In affect, he was reared to be
a recluse.

Though too little evidence of Gladys's character has
been preserved to allow one to speak with confidence of
her inner being, there were many reasons for her to pro-
long and intensify her relationship with Elvis far beyond
what is normal for mother and child. The principal reason
was that she had no other person to love. Her mother and
father were dead; toward her sisters and brothers she displayed an ambivalent attitude. Indeed, so detached did
Gladys become from her kin that people said in later years
that she had been reared as an orphan. Vernon had proven
himself an ineffectual boy-man rather than a capable husband and father. At the critical moment in the marriage,
he had made a foolish and fateful error, which shifted the

entire responsibility for caring for Elvis onto Gladys's shoulders. So Gladys concentrated all her love on her son.

Vernon's habitual absences did not serve to make his presence at home any more welcome. Quite the contrary: Vernon had a highly disturbing effect on Elvis. In later years, Vernon recalled that every time he did something against which Elvis had been warned by Gladys, the child would exhibit the most extreme anxiety. "When we went swimming," Vernon chuckled, "Elvis would have fits if he saw me dive. He was so afraid something would happen to me." Fires were commonplace among the wooden shanties of East Tupelo. Gladys recounted Elvis's behavior when he saw his father running in and out of a house trying to save the furniture: "Elvis was so sure his daddy was going to get hurt that he screamed and cried. I had to hold him to keep him from running in after Vernon. So I said sharp, 'Elvis, you just stop that. He's all right. Your daddy knows what he's doing.' He quieted right down." (You can bet he did when he heard his mother's masterful voice.) These stories show the child's keen fear of death and his terror at the prospect of his father's death, an eventuality that had been given an especial reality by Vernon's imprisonment and long absences.

Elvis's apprehensiveness about Vernon is mirrored by Vernon's fears for Elvis. The story most frequently repeated among Presley intimates concerns the night that Vernon awoke from a nightmare convinced that his own house was afire. Without a moment's hesitation, he scooped up Elvis and tried to throw him out the window. You couldn't find a clearer projection of how many an adoring father feels unconsciously about the intrusive presence of his infant son. After all, before Elvis came along, the immature Vernon was Gladys's baby.

According to the Myth, the Presleys were a deeply religious family. They attended a little country church, where they sang often as a trio: mother, father and tiny son. It was a church of the First Assembly of God, a fundamentalist church, a Pentecostal church; hence, a church of the most earthy and impassioned religious expression, where Negro hymn singing alternated with outbursts of speaking in tongues and dancing in the spirit. Here, Elvis first imbibed the deep soul of the South. Here, he witnessed revival meetings that implanted forever in his mind the image of that charismatic stage figure, the itinerant preacher: part minister, part entertainer; part saint, part demoniac. Here, more than anywhere, Elvis was shaped by the profound forces that eventually burst out again on the vast stage of the Rock Age. So teaches the Myth.

Imagine, having heard this gospel for a quarter of a century, how it must feel to pick up a phone one day in New York City and call a number in Verona, Mississippi, which is answered by a youthful-sounding voice: that of the Reverend W. Frank Smith, who became minister of the First Assembly of God Church in East Tupelo in the year 1944. Reverend Smith, being a real preacher and not the figment of some rock writer's imagination, is quite astounded at the reputation of his church and its service, as well as by the reputed behavior of those once-familiar members of his congregation, the Vernon Presleys. He remembers them and that time quite clearly. Indeed, his life having had a firm consistency, leading him today in much the same paths as when he took up his ministry, he recollects that early time with ease. To sum up his testimony, he scorns the Myth as a lie. He contradicts it down to the finest detail. He cannot imagine how such preposterous notions were ever believed by anyone.

The legendary church was not some country tabernacle, with peaked roof, tiny steeple and tall pointy windows. It was simply a one-story house, no different in kind from any other in that community of four-room bungalows. The congregation comprised about twenty-five members. The service began at eleven and lasted for an hour. The congregation, standing in its places and clapping time, would sing such familiar hymns as "I'll Fly Away" or "When the Roll Is Called Up Yonder." These hymns would be accompanied by the piano, and Reverend Smith made it a practice to bring his guitar and strum along with the singing.

The services were always decorous. Though the members were free to shout "Amen!" or "Praise God!" there was no speaking in tongues or overtly emotional behavior. Reverend Smith preached always the message of Jesus. He might grow heated in his tone, but he does not consider

himself a demonstrative preacher. He would remain close
to his pulpit and employ only the conventional gestures
of emphasis. Traveling evangelists would appear sometimes at the church, but they were never of the extravagant, spellbinding variety. Nothing they did could be characterized as dancing or "cutting up." Once a month, there
would be a testimony service. Several members of the congregation would get up and make little avowals. A member
might say: "Well, I wanna thank the Lord for savin' *me*.
And bringin' *me* to the church."

Reverend Smith does not recollect that the Presleys
ever distinguished themselves in any way by their singing,
either individually or by performing as a family trio. There
were people in the congregation who sang solos, but Vernon and Gladys were not among them. Vernon's cousin,
Sayles Pressley, was the principal singer. He had organized an amateur gospel quartet and sometimes led the
congregation in its hymn singing. The minister recollects
teaching Elvis a few guitar runs and noticing that the boy
had an instruction book for his instrument. Music was not
among the worldly delights banned by the Assembly of
God; nonetheless, the church was highly puritanical. The
members were forbidden to go to movies or dances, to drink
alcohol or smoke tobacco.

During my conversations with the Reverend Smith, he
asserted repeatedly that he did not see any source for Elvis's singing or performing style in the practices of the
little church in East Tupelo, though he did believe that
later, in Memphis, Elvis came under influences, including
gospel performers, who might have decisively affected his
imagination. But the Elvis Presley known to fame was not
shaped in a country church.

Elvis's real inspiration came from the first from the
radio. In the forties, powerful transmitters in Nashville
and Memphis began to beam all sorts of music into the
area of Tupelo. As soon as Elvis obtained access to a receiver, his musical education commenced. The first product of this education was a prize-winning performance,
which the boy gave at the age of eleven, singing a song
he had learned off the air.

The occasion on which Elvis Presley first got up on a

public stage and sang a tune was Children's Day at the
annual Mississippi-Alabama Fair and Dairy Show. The
song he chose embodied, most likely, his deepest emotions:
It was the Red Foley hit, "Old Shep," a very old-fashioned,
highly sentimental ballad in which the singer recalls with
keen nostalgia a dead pet dog. The melancholy reverie
that is the substance of this song strikes one at first as an
incongruous theme for an eleven-year-old boy; but when
one reflects on Elvis's upbringing, with the ghost of Jessie
always at his side, the selection and his success in rendering it makes perfect sense. That day he won second
prize. First prize was awarded to six-year-old Becky Harris, who sang a sexy, bluesy number called "Sentimental
Journey" that would have been far more appropriate than
"Old Shep" to the Elvis Presley known to fame.

In 1946, the Presleys moved into Tupelo and Vernon
got a job driving a truck for the wholesale grocery firm of
L. P. McCarty. Though Elvis is always associated with
Tupelo, he lived in the city less than three years. According
to the Myth, these years were spent in a horrid black slum,
known by the pungently Dickensian name of Shakerag.
Though the ordeal of living in a black slum is something
every true fan is supposed to grieve over, at the same
time—by the paradox of *felix culpa,* the fortunate fall—
this descent to the depths is regarded as the source of
Elvis's extraordinary mastery of the black musical idiom,
to say nothing of all the jivey dance steps he cut. As always,
the Myth is mistaken. Elvis did live in a slum, but it was
not the notorious black slum in the northwest quarter of
the city; it was on the east side of town, on Commerce
Street, where the shopping mall stands today. The family
did not remain long at this address; they moved several
times, their next house being in Mobile Alley, a narrow
lane that ran at right angles to the railroad tracks near
the fairgrounds. Finally, they wound up in the northeast
quarter, near the slaughterhouse, on North Green Street.
All of these neighborhoods were white; all were poor and
ugly. They were no worse, however, than living in a two-
room shack in East Tupelo. At the time, Vernon was earning $22.50 a week, which was doubtless a lot more than
he ever received from the tight-fisted Orville Bean.

No sooner had Elvis won a prize singing a country song than he met a real-life country musician, Tupelo's only native entertainer, Mississippi Slim. Slim (whose real name was Carvel Lee Ausborn) had a kid brother, James, who was in the same class as Elvis at Milham Junior High. In the company of this brother, Elvis began to visit the local radio station, WELO, which was virtually across the street from the house in Mobile Alley. Every Saturday morning Mississippi Slim would broadcast in front of a tiny audience. Watching performers working in radio studios became from this time forth an important feature of Elvis's life. As the radio studio was no different from the recording studio, Elvis was already familiarizing himself as a twelve- or thirteen-year-old boy with what was soon to become one of his two major theaters of creative expression.

Otherwise, Elvis was a classic autodidact. He never studied music. He never sat in with other musicians. His access to clubs and jamming joints was nil. His strange fantasylike approach to performing owed a lot to mere ignorance and inexperience. Apart from his early and rather superficial acquaintance with Mississippi Slim, one would be hard put to name even one other secular musician with whom the young Elvis Presley was acquainted until he had actually begun recording and performing professionally.

In September 1948, the Presleys packed up their few belongings in a decrepit 1937 Plymouth and took off for Memphis. Elvis said in later years that they were broke and that Vernon was hoping to find a job in the big city. The move—made abruptly after the school year had commenced and surrounded subsequently with a cloud of secrecy—suggests some fresh misfortune was about to descend upon the family, which they averted by flight. The Tupelo police told the compilers of *All About Elvis* that Vernon Presley had been caught selling moonshine and was given two weeks to get out of town.

The automobile in which the Presleys made their escape had a very stiff and balky accelerator. Its operation was generally assigned to Elvis so that his father could concentrate on the driving. So we must picture the little family on that fateful day, proceeding up Route 78, the morning sun behind them, driving through rolling country, the highway festooned fantastically for miles with great growths of kudzu weeds, with the little blond Elvis, dressed in overalls, giving the old heap the gas, while Vernon steers and applies the brake and Gladys sits surrounded with her little pile of worldly goods, staring glumly out the window.

Chapter 5

Portrait of the Artist as a Young Punk

In THE customary accounts of Elvis Presley's life, the journey of the little family to Memphis always ends with an ominous roll on the kettle drums. Expelled from the bucolic world of Tupelo, these poor innocents are depicted as being swallowed up in the hell of the big city. Even worse, they are glimpsed being sucked down to the bottommost ring of the inferno—the public housing projects. *The projects!* Just the naked word is enough to summon up fearful images: sinister asphalt playgrounds, looming concrete monoliths, steel elevator doors that close like traps on their prey. Like so much else in the legend of Elvis, this impression is totally false.

The Lauderdale Courts is a drab little pile of red brick buildings constructed during the New Deal and reflecting in its austere but idealistic design the influence of the New Towns in England. The "big" building is but three stories high and bent in a sprung C configuration. The Presleys resided on the first floor at the right hand side of the main entrance in apartment 328. Across a broad front lawn, edged with neatly trimmed shrubs and shaded with trees, were the other buildings: a pair of two-story structures and a row of garden apartments with good-sized gardens.

The basic image in Elvis's day was of an island of sensible but severe-looking suburban housing set in a sea of decaying gingerbread tenements.

Far from being a bad deal, the Courts were the Presley's lucky strike. They moved in May 1, 1949, after having spent a wretched winter in a roach-infested old house, where they had to cook on a hot plate in their single room and share a common bathroom. For this slum lodging, they were charged with the same rent, $35 a month, which they paid now to the Memphis Housing Authority for a two-bedroom flat with all the modern facilities. Yet the Presleys never had a good word for the Courts. Their biggest complaint was the requirement that every tenant declare his income. Rent was pegged to salary according to the formula: one month's rent equals one week's salary. Vernon had gotten a job on the loading platform of United Paint, not many blocks distant, which paid, with the customary four hours overtime, $38.50 a week. Now, twice a year, he had to go to his boss and get him to write the Housing Authority, telling it exactly how much he was earning. If you earned more than three thousand dollars a year, you had to move. Vernon bitched about that one for the rest of his life. He would sit up in the hillbilly palace at Graceland, surrounded by every luxury, shaking his head gravely and sighing, "They just wouldn't let you get ahead."

Vernon's real problem was that he had a wife who rarely worked, a son too young to work and a mother who had no intentions of seeking her first job at the age of fifty-four. Minnie Mae had moved in with Vernon as soon as he got his new apartment. She had been divorced by Jessie in 1947, after thirty-four years of marriage. Vernon said always said that his father had deserted his mother, but the truth was precisely the opposite.

A tacit policy consigned to this particular housing unit all the war widows and divorced or abandoned mothers. These women, knowing nothing of relief checks, had to be the men. They worked long hours for low pay in sewing factories, cafeterias and hospitals. Their children worked, too. Consequently, there was no rowdiness, no dissipation, no crime. The apartments were kept immaculately clean

because every so often a keen-eyed lady would appear unannounced at your door to peer inside your stove or cast
an appraising glance at the hardwood floors, which had
to be kept gleaming. Public assistance southern style, the
Lauderdale Courts were a far cry from the welfare jungle
of the North.

By the time the Presleys moved into their new home,
Elvis had nearly completed the ninth grade at L. C. Humes
High School on Manassas Street, about a twenty-minute
walk from the project past the loading platform where
Vernon labored with a painter's cap on his head. Gladys
continued her practice of walking Elvis to and from school,
but the first day the boy was so alarmed by his new environment that he ducked out of the building and ran all
the way home. Humes was a lot larger than the schools
to which Elvis was accustomed. A big red brick building
with "gothic" trim, it was dedicated to turning out "com-
merical" and "vocational" graduates. Most of the 1,600
kids majored in drafting, home economics or secretarial
skills. Of all the dumb activities in this dumb working-
class school about the dumbest was shop: Elvis Presley's
major.

Every day, like a prisoner in some old-fashioned penitentiary, Elvis would arrive in a workshop full of obso-
lescent power tools and don a long dark apron. Then, he
would go to a storeroom presided over by a student trustee
and ask for his "project." Out would come a carving board
or a salad bowl or some other infantile object upon which
he was expected to labor for the next hour. As he stood at
his bench sanding or planing or polishing, along would
come the shop teacher, Mr. Widdop. Like any other shop
teacher, he's a dour old dude with a couple of clip-on pencils
on the bib of his apron or in the breast pocket of his work
coat. As he inspects Elvis's project, he lays an angle on it
to make sure that it's "square" or a level to make sure
that it's "true." Then, he takes out a hard, sharp carpen-
ter's pencil and scores lines in the wood, indicating where
more work remains to be done. Poor Elvis looks down on
the surface and realizes what hard labor it will be just to
sand off those damn pencil marks. As the shop teacher
accompanies his desecration of the project with brusque

comments, Elvis keeps murmuring like a depressed but
obedient darkie, "Yessir, yessir!"

For the rest, we haven't the slightest idea what Elvis
did at Humes until his last two years. He appears to have
entered the school like a drop of water disappearing into
the ocean or a lump of lead sinking to its bottom. Painfully
shy and totally self-effacing, he was one of those kids who
are always found head down in the back row of the classroom. His social invisibility was paralleled by his academic
mediocrity. Early and late, in grade school at Tupelo and
in high school at Memphis, he was your typical C student.
Though sometimes he did a little better in his favorite
subject, English, or brought home bad grades, which were
caused, most likely, by too much after-school work, he was
best characterized by the word, mediocre.

Gladys did not permit Elvis to play out of her sight
until he was fifteen. Even then, his whole world outside
of school and church was confined to a circle of a few blocks.
Yet, because these blocks were in the heart of the city,
they were rich in recreational facilities. In the immediate
vicinity were a swimming pool, a movie house, a record
store hangout, several ice cream parlors, Ellis Auditorium
(Memphis's largest hall), an Odd Fellows' lodge with a
poolroom and St. Mary's Church, which had dances for
kids, as well as a USO, where the local girls could dance
with servicemen under strict chaperonage. After school,
the boys played football, sometimes challenging the
"culleds," who lived across the way near St. Joseph's Hospital.

The greatest fun all year came in June when the Cotton
Carnival filled Main Street with fancy floats with pretty
girls all dolled up as for Mardi Gras. Along historic Front
Street, where the cotton factors had their offices overlooking the steep cobblestoned embankment leading down to
the Mississippi dockside, a great red-and-white carnival
would erect its midway and set up its mechanical rides.
The carnival was always one of Elvis's favorite recreations,
especially those booths where you can win a teddy bear
by toppling wooden bottles with a well-aimed baseball.

When Elvis was fifteen, he started going steady. The
girl was a skinny little tomboy named Betty McMann, who

lived on the third floor. Though the pair spent a lot of time together for a year, they couldn't afford anything more expensive than a Dutch treat on Saturday afternoon at the Suzore No. Two, a narrow little rerun house with wooden seats and faded prints of horror films, where you could see two features and a string of serials for fifteen cents. Betty would have much preferred to go dancing at St. Mary's. She worked hard many an afternoon in her living room trying to teach the embarrassed and awkward Elvis how to do the two-step. The lessons were not successful. Indeed, it is one of the ironies of Elvis's life that, famous as a figure of corybantic ecstasy, he was never able to dance with a girl. Elvis was one of those people who can dance only by themselves.

In the evenings, when the weather was warm, Elvis would come out on the front stoop after supper and entertain the neighbors by singing and playing his guitar. Everyone enjoyed his performances and encouraged him to sing, but he was so shy that he would never commence his performance until it grew dark. (At parties, he would insist that all the lights be extinguished.) Once he was satisfied that he was invisible, he would chord the instrument softly and sing sentimental country songs, one of his favorites being the Eddy Arnold tune, "Won't You Tell Me Molly Darling?" Some nights, he changed the girl's name to "Billie," a gesture designed to please his second girlfriend, thirteen-year-old Billie Wardlow.

A big-boned country lass, tall, pretty, vivacious, with a thick rural accent learned in Mississippi, Billie inspired Elvis to offer her such amusing gifts as a box of chocolate-covered cherries and a skinny gold bracelet with a pendant heart. Unlike Betty McMann, who wanted to go dancing but settled for the movies, Billie Wardlow would not accept less than the best. She insisted on going to the USO and cavorting with the servicemen. This soon ended her relationship with Elvis, who, never having had to share anything, was the least likely boy on earth to share his girl's attentions with another boy. When the moment of parting came, Elvis got big tears in his eyes. "Billie," he cried, "I was gonna ask you to marry me!" Then, looking at her hard, he added, "If you ever tell anybody I cried over you,

I'll never talk to you again!" On that note, the brief romance ended.

Elvis was now sixteen. Never again during his school years did he become involved with a girl. Instead, he became involved in a profound emotional crisis that transformed him from a silly little country boy running around in a plaid shirt and farmer jeans to the "weird kid with the sideburns"—and the adolescent hero of an age of adolescents.

The onset of Elvis's emotional crisis was signaled by the appearance of recurrent nightmares. These dreams were so powerful that they resembled states of absolute possession or even the condition of being spellbound. Night after night, as Elvis lay sleeping on the sofa in the living room, he would imagine he was being attacked by a mob of angry men. They would circle him ominously as he hurled at them defiant challenges. Then a violent struggle would commence. Elvis would cry out in his sleep and lay about him fiercely. Sometimes, he would leap out of bed and whirl the bedclothes about his head, under the impression that he was swinging a heavy chain. Or he would be wakened violently by an agonizing jolt of pain as he smashed his fist into a wall or tore off a toenail kicking against the sheet. If he did not awaken, he might rise from bed in a cold sweat, with eyes open but glazed, and make for the nearest door or window.

Once when he came to consciousness, he found himself standing out in the hall of the building, naked except for his Jockey briefs. Evidently, he had fled his attackers by slipping out of the door of his apartment and mounting the stairs toward the third floor, where both Betty and Billie lived. Aghast at finding himself exposed in public, he was about to run for shelter when he was stopped cold by the sound of people entering the building downstairs. With a flash of horror, he realized that he was caught. Listening desperately to the voices, he recognized one of them as that of a girl who lived on the second floor. Scampering up to the third floor on bare feet, he was able to avoid the humiliation by cowering there on the landing while the girl kissed her date goodnight.

Any ordinary family of that day who observed their

child exhibiting such startling symptoms would have
taken him straight to a doctor. The Presleys were not an
ordinary family: They were hillbillies, on familiar terms
with the weird. They associated Elvis's behavior with his
father's nightmares and decided that this was an hereditary affliction, something that simply had to be borne.

The primary image presented by Elvis's nightmares is
the familiar paranoid delusion of the one against the
many. This image may have been born of fantasy or it may
have been inspired by reality, for at the time that Elvis
began to suffer these nightmares—the critical period of
his sixteenth year—he was involved at school in scenes
of persecution that were not much different from those
that flashed on his mind while asleep. Though it is impossible to say which came first, the dream or the reality,
the issue is not of any ultimate importance because Elvis's
persecution was as much a product of his strange personality as were his dreams.

The cause of Elvis's troubles at school was, significantly, the first unmistakable expression of his genius. On
a summer's day in the year 1951, Elvis Presley decided to
crown himself with the world's most celebrated hairstyle.
This momentous decision was arrived at only after years
of earnest experimentation. Elvis recognized early, apparently, that his strength lay in his hair: his dirty blond,
baby-fine locks. Billie Wardlow remembers going downstairs once after school to visit with Gladys and discovering
that Elvis's mother had given him a kinky, curly permanent. Another time, Billie screamed with shock when
Elvis appeared in a Mohawk, a single strip of hair running
down the center of the skull. Now, all these experiments
were about to conclude in the making of a masterpiece.

Like an artist rendering deliberately and confidently
a finished sketch, Elvis went not to a barbership but to a
local beautyshop and ordered the astonished operator to
fashion his hair into a classic Duck's Ass. He had already
allowed his sideburns to grow down his pimply, Clearasil-
daubed cheeks as far as his ear lobes. He also sought at
this historic moment to raise a mustache because the ultimate purpose of all these efforts was simply to make him
look older. Informed by the beautician that his hair grew

"every which way," Elvis bought his first little round tin
of Royal Crown Pomade, a really potent grease used by
the local Negroes to fix their conks. Elvis applied so much
of this gook to his hair that it turned several shades darker
and acquired such a lustrous sheen that it appeared glazed.

Next, he required a change of clothes. Over to Beale
Street he goes, not many blocks distant, heading for the
store patronized by the local black pimps and players: Lansky Brothers. Bernie Lansky is out in front of the shop,
as usual, hustling the trade. A jive-talking Jew of a type
familiar in every black ghetto, Lansky smiles and makes
his pitch: "Hey, man, what you need today?" Elvis drifts
around the tables, piled high under glaring fluorescent
lights with gabardine slacks and shirts in brilliant hues.
He picks out a pair of shiny black pants with a colored
inset along the seam, lime green or lemon yellow. (His
trademark pink-and-black combinations date from his
twentieth year.) The pants are pegged at the ankles, ballooned at the knees, pleated at the waist, which rises in
a four-inch band to just under the bottommost rib. A
skinny suede belt is threaded through the dropped loops
and the buckle whipped around to ride above the left hip.
A loud "gab" shirt with a rolled "Mr. B" (Billy Eckstine)
collar worn turned up, and the metamorphosis is complete.
Elvis is proto-Punk.

This act of self-creation marks the true beginning of
Elvis Presley's career as a pop culture hero. Though he's
still years away from rock music and the Sun Studio, he's
already very close to the classic Presley image. The image
precedes the talent, as it was destined likewise to outlive
the talent, becoming an imperishable pop eidolon.

Elvis's image derives directly from the style that was
popular after World War II in the working-class neighborhoods of New York. Thousands of young men dressed
and looked and carried themselves much like Elvis Presley
when he was still in bib overalls. The real question about
the Presley look is not where did it come from but how
could a little cracker boy in the slums of Memphis get hip
to it? A good clue is provided by the name which Elvis
gave to his legendary hairstyle. Instead of calling it, as
everyone else did, a Duck's Ass, Duck's Tail, Duck's Wings

or D.A., Elvis referred to his famous comb as the "Tony
Curtis Cut."

In 1949, Tony Curtis made his second appearance on
the screen in *City Across the River,* a movie version of
Irving Shulman's *The Amboy Dukes,* a pop novel about a
Jewish youth gang in Brooklyn. Assuming that Elvis saw
this film, it was bound to make a deep impression on him.
Set in a slum no different essentially from Elvis's scabrous
neighborhood, its characters lower-class vocational high
school boys with parents similar to Vernon and Gladys,
the film turns on the accidental murder by the boys of
their shop teacher. The character portrayed by Tony Curtis—who wears a gleaming, flawlessly shaped D.A. with
a teasing forelock—is a charming and slightly girlish sort
of "bubie" boy, who is good with his fists but very sweet,
and speaks in a singsong pattern that sounds like baby
talk. If ever a film was designed to speak to a young man's
condition and temperament, this was the picture for Elvis
Presley.

When Elvis turned up at Humes in the fall of 1951
looking like Tony Curtis, he discovered a great truth: Private dreams carried into public places can turn into ter-
rifying, humiliating nightmares. The tough working-class
kids turned on Elvis as if he had been Tiny Tim. They
baited, mocked and jeered him. They said he looked "like
a squirrel jes' come down outta the trees." Soon it was open
season on squirrels.

No matter how much the kids tortured him, Elvis refused to relinquish his strange image. This refusal to back
down and conform has been glorified for a quarter century
as the defiant act of a rock rebel. One of the cardinal
features of the mythic Elvis is the idea that he was a guy
who wouldn't let the world push him around. Not troubling
anyone else, just enjoying his own dream, he would never
provoke a fight; but if someone put him down, even if they
looked at him the wrong way, you dig?, he would turn into
a real ass-kicking redneck mother! This idea is enshrined
elaborately, for instance, in the classic hagiography of rock
saints, *Rock Dreams,* a volume of imaginary portraits of
rock stars and their milieus by the Belgian artist Guy
Peellaert.

Turning to the page that evokes the high-school Elvis, we gaze upon a handsome and serene young man with a weight-lifter's torso, leaning casually against a lamppost in downtown Memphis with the dreamy expression of Lord Byron leaning against a broken column. Behind the saint lurks an obscenely fat and ugly biker, clad in leather jacket and military cap, holding in one ham-hock hand a can of beer. He is staring with a derisive grin at the back of Elvis's head, which we know is coiffed in a ravishing D.A. The dramatic implications of the encounter are spelled out in the legend, composed by the British pop critic, Nik Cohn (the man who wrote the story on which *Saturday Night Fever* was based): "Outside the poolhall, standing in the sun, I was minding my own business and combing my hair, when along came a carhop [*sic*] and called me dirty names. First the length of my hair, then the cut of my clothes, and then the way I curled my lip. He stared into my eyes and spat on my blue suede shoes. Right there on the pavement, with one foot in the gutter, I cut him all to pieces." There you have the mythical Elvis Presley, king of the streets.

Now, let us lay beside this devotional picture a candid shot of the real sixteen-year-old Elvis at Humes. The source this time is *Elvis—What Happened?* and the speaker is Elvis's lifelong friend and companion, Red West. Red is a senior at the time, a tough, aggressive, football-playing poor boy, whose ribs are visibly deformed from rickets, a disease produced by not having enough money or enough brains to eat right. Red walks into the boys' room and discovers that he has stumbled upon a squirrel-hunting party.

> The place was full of smoke; you could hardly see in front of you for all the smoke. But I could see far enough to notice that old "E" was in a whole heap of trouble again. About four or five guys had him in there, and they were holding him and pushing him up against the wall and then grabbing him from behind. They were yelling and laughing and wising off at him and his hair. They decided that they were gonna cut his hair.
> I knew the guys who were hassling Elvis. They

were on the football squad. When I saw Elvis's face, it just triggered something inside me. I mean, they weren't really bad guys; they weren't gonna kill him or anything but there was a look of real fear on his face. He was looking like a frightened little animal. I just couldn't stand seeing it. When you're very poor, you tend to let everyone look after their own troubles; but that face of Elvis—I can see it to this day. I saw that face like that many times later. It always had the same effect on me. Just churned up something inside me. It's a child's face and it asks for help.

"Now look," I said to this bunch: "this ain't gonna do anyone any good. There ain't no need for this. If he likes his hair that way, well, no sense in hassling him. Now, if you cut his hair, you're gonna have to cut my hair, too; and that's gonna develop into something else."

Red was Mister Bad Ass. The other boys backed off.

This scene shows that Elvis's famed rebellion was nothing of the kind. Elvis didn't set out consciously to break any rules or violate any taboos or provoke either his peers or his superiors. He was inspired by a movie to make himself over into an image that he found esthetically and imaginatively fulfilling. Obviously, he was not prepared to fight for his right to maintain his pose. His fearful and supplicating attitude is conveyed very well in Red West's description. It is exactly the attitude of a kid who has been attacked in a manner that he did not anticipate and cannot repel. His only emotion is fear; his only thought to escape.

If Elvis is not a figure of youthful rebellion, an ass-kicking redneck spoiling to take on the world, what are we to make of his stubbornly defiant behavior? Assuming that he was too naive to anticipate what would happen to him when he turned up at school looking like a freak, why didn't he wise up and protect himself from further persecution by wearing his hair like all the other boys with their crew cuts and flattops? Why did he continue to behave like a homosexual who struts in drag down some mean street knowing full well that his provocative appearance invites abuse and injury?

If you ask the homosexual why he takes such risks, he is liable to reply by turning the question around and demanding to know why his appearance should make other men react so violently. This turn of mind was also highly characteristic of Elvis Presley. When he became famous doing an act that was denounced by virtually every adult that witnessed it as a male burlesque show, Elvis denied heatedly that there was anything improper in his performance. What was wrong, he kept asking, with all these crazy old types who said he was dirty?

One could dismiss such professions of innocence as hypocritical lies, the phony excuses of a performer who knows exactly in what his appeal consists but is too smart ever to admit the truth. When you examine Elvis's life in detail, however, you find countless instances of contradictory behavior that appear to spring out of a personality that was unconsciously dichotomous. He's like the character of the rich drunk in Chaplin's *City Lights* whose behavior at night is in total contradiction to the way he acts during the day.

What happened to Elvis when he adopted his famous image was a second birth, whose pangs were those violent and painful nightmares. Out of this birth emerged a second, hitherto repressed personality, which stood in total contradiction to the cute little mama's boy who was the furthest thing in the world from a street punk. The model this new personality was formed upon was that nightmare figure of the fifties—the juvenile delinquent.

At first, this new bad-assed Elvis is little more than a shell: a haircomb and a costume inhabited by a shy, self-doubting, self-effacing kid. Eventually, though, this shell begins to fill with the man it proclaims. *Sartor resartus.* Clothes make the man. Five years later, Elvis has become the tough punk that he set out unconsciously to emulate as a boy. He's pretty good with his fists, and he's already started pulling guns on people. The first gun he pulls, on a marine in Memphis, is, significantly, a starter's pistol that fires nothing but blanks. By the end of his life, Elvis will own every deadly weapon in the modern small arms arsenal and will be a seventh-degree black belt in karate. His last film project will star him as a karate instructor who is really an undercover narc. When the film writer asked Elvis for his ideas about the character, Elvis snarled: "I want to be the baddest motherfucker there is!" It takes time to grow a second self, but the start of this process is visible from the moment Elvis adopts his famous look.

It must not be thought that once the Bad Elvis started to emerge the Good Elvis began to recede. Quite the contrary: Both characters developed apace, alternating, like the faces on a turning coin. Thus, at the very moment when Elvis was carefully modeling himself upon the image of the slick, sinister, big-city hoodlum, he was also struggling determinedly to become a football hero and was joining the ROTC, whose neat military uniform he wore with great pride. Even more mind-boggling was his announcement that his ultimate ambition was to become a Tennessee State Highway Patrolman. Cops and crooks, good guys and bad guys: Elvis would play both these parts all the rest of his life and always in full costume.

Between the extremes of Elvis the Good and Elvis the Bad there now began to emerge the amorphous figure of Elvis the entertainer. Until his last year in high school, Elvis reserved his playing and singing for his neighbors at the Courts. Having mustered the courage to brave the bullies in the school, he now found the strength to overcome the even greater threat posed by an audience of strangers. The credit for luring him into the open goes to his homeroom teacher, Miss Mildred Scrivener.

"I never knew Elvis could sing," recollected Miss Scrivener in later years, "until someone in my class said Elvis should bring his guitar to our homeroom picnic. Elvis did bring his guitar, and while everybody else was running around doing what young people do, Elvis sat quietly by himself playing and singing to the few who gathered around him. Slowly, other students began to come to him. There was something about his plaintive singing which drew them like a magnet." When Miss Scrivener was put in charge of the annual variety show, she asked Elvis to appear—along with thirty other kids. The arrangement was simple: Each youngster would perform a single piece.

The one who received the most applause would then be declared the winner and perform an encore as his reward.

The night of the show, there was an unaccustomed air of tension backstage at Humes. Some of the kids were really eager to win and be acclaimed. As they went out onstage to sing their songs or play their pieces, they pushed themselves to the limits. It was precisely the sort of highly competitive situation that Elvis had been shying away from through all his years in this school. Tonight, however, he was standing on much surer ground than he had ever felt in the classroom or the shop or on the playing field. He knew his game. He appeared onstage wearing a solid red shirt, which he had borrowed for the occasion. He chose as his song the same piece with which he had won seven years before at the Tupelo fairgrounds: "Old Shep."

When he got into this familiar tearjerker, using his "plaintive" voice, he projected the pathos of the boy grieving over his dead dog so perfectly that even some of the teachers broke down and cried. The kids were amazed at how well Elvis sang. They gave him a tremendous hand. When they got through clapping and shouting, there wasn't much doubt about who would be declared the winner. Even then, Elvis could not believe that he had won. Miss Scrivener had to practically push him back onstage, urging, "It's you, Elvis! Go on out there and sing another song!" When he came off, he was walking on air. "I'll never forget the look on his face," the teacher exclaims when she recalls the moment. "They really liked me, Miss Scrivener," Elvis gasped. "They really liked me!"

Chapter 6

Quartette

ELVIS'S sixteenth year was his most decisive. This is the reason, most likely, why all the rest of his life he remained so much like a sixteen-year-old boy. He dreaded nothing more than a disturbance of the ideal pattern that he established at this time. Basic to the pattern was the perfect positioning of his polar twins. Elvis the Bad acquired the classic punk look and began his evolution toward that Snarling Darling who would become eventually the greatest hero of rock 'n' roll. Elvis the Good moved off at this time in precisely the opposite direction. He elected to become a lay priest, a gospel singer, a dancer before the Lord.

Elvis's discovery of the world of gospel took place one night in this same year at Ellis Auditorium, where he went to attend an all-night sing. This was a very odd thing for a teenager to do, but it must always be borne in mind that Elvis Presley was a very odd teenager. The show he witnessed had a profound effect upon him. Chances are it was the first real show he had ever seen. As a sing is one of those parochial institutions endemic to the South, it is necessary before we go any further to describe in some detail the scene that would have greeted the naive and impressionable youngster.

For days before the event, he would have been hearing

101

the ballyhoo for the sing on the radio. The phrase "all-night" must have been especially titillating for a kid who went to bed normally at ten o'clock. Actually, this traditional epithet was just typical American hyperbole. The shows were four-hour concerts, beginning at eight and concluding at midnight: not all night by any means but a very late hour for God-fearing folk. The audience would have numbered several thousand people. Such entertainments were very popular at the time in Memphis, which, in the early fifties, had become the national headquarters for white gospel. As for the composition of the crowd, we have a neat characterization of it from the mouth of Elvis's favorite gospel singer, Jake Hess: "There's church people that don't go to movies; they go to sings for entertainment. There's people that don't go to church; the sing is their church. Then, there's John Q. Public: the people that just like male quartet." Even Zarathustra couldn't say it better.

The bill for the sing would have numbered five quartets. So stereotyped was gospel at this time in the form of the vocal foursome that the commonest designation for the music was "quartet," spelled often "quartette," in conformity with that characteristic southern predilection for the archaic. In truth, there was nothing venerable about quartette but the hokey spelling of its name. A more crassly commercial type of entertainment could hardly be imagined. For years the presiding spirits of the gospel world have been shrewd businessmen, like the founder of the quartet idiom, James D. Vaughan, and his successor, Virgil Oliver "V. O." Stamps, publishers of religious music who used gospel quartets as traveling salesmen, assigning them territories, equipping them with touring cars and paying them a percentage on all the songbooks which they sold at sings, singing conventions or through their local broadcasts, which were generally sponsored by flour companies.

It was in this manner that the most famous of all gospel quartets, the Blackwood Brothers, weathered the Depression and matured their skills until they achieved widespread popularity in the early fifties. The Blackwoods— James, Doyle, Roy and R. W.— were the sons of a sharecropper in Chocktaw County, Mississippi. While singing

on the radio in Jackson, Mississippi, they were discovered
by V. O. Stamps, who recruited them for his singing sales
organization and consigned them for the next ten years
to the blizzards and heat waves of Shenandoah, Iowa. Now,
in 1951, they are local celebrities in Memphis, heard every
day at noon on the radio and the hosts for the monthly
sings at the Auditorium.

The Blackwoods' closest rivals are a much more flam-
boyant group that soon became Elvis's favorites: Hovie
Lister and the Statesmen, whose lead singer is the great
Jake Hess. The other quartets might have included the
Sunshine Boys, from Florida, whose bass is J. D. Sumner
(who in later years led Elvis's backup quartet); the Speer
Family, from Atlanta (who appear on Elvis's first RCA
records); the Stamps Quartet from Dallas; or the original
Jordanaires (not the pop group that accompanied Elvis but
a group of young Missourians who were the greatest white
exponents of the traditional Negro spiritual style). In the
treasured next-to-closing spot would appear the hometown
favorites, the Blackwood Brothers.

The staging for these performances is of the simplest:
The act curtain is closed when one enters the house, and
a bit of scenery representing a stone balustrade or some
equally unlikely object has been erected along the curtain
line. A couple of old-fashioned standing mikes, such as you
would see in a broadcasting studio, are stuck up in the
middle of the stage, their cables running conspicuously
across the floor. A grand piano, "the only appropriate accompanying instrument," according to V. O. Stamps, is
parked on a steel dolly to the right of the mikes.

Though the stage setting might be called minimal or
austere, you certainly wouldn't apply those words to the
costumes or the style of the performers. "Lurid," "garish"
or "Nigrah" would be more appropriate epithets for the
five performers who come charging out onstage this night,
without benefit of introduction, wound up to the intensity
of a black flash act. In fact, judging by their costumes, the
Statesmen could have just finished a highly successful
appearance with the annual Gospel Train show at the
Apollo Theater in Harlem. They're wearing heavily draped
double-breasted suits, redolent of zoot suits, made of raw

silk and dyed in a spectacular color of solid red, glinting
with iridescent sparklers. Their hair, which if combed
straight forward would fall below their chins, is soaked
with pillow-staining VO5 and teased up into Chinese pom-
padours that are impossibly high. As their beefy piano
player, MC and honcho, Hovie Lister, squats hastily on
the revolving stool and starts thumping out a fast um-
chick, um-chick rhythm, this jive-assed quartet divides
like a pack of smartly smacked pool balls, and, each pair
seizing a mike, they streak off into one of their patented
flag-wavers, "It Will All Be Over," an insanely cheery and
eupeptic paean to death.

"It will all be over...the journey here will end...a new
day will begin...we'll join the choir of angels singing out
the victory song"—racing along at breakneck speed, the
quartet suddenly falls silent as the bass, the towering "Big
Chief" Weatherington, an organ-pipe of a man, goes into
a growling ostinato, a locomotive wheel of sound, repeating
with nimble tongue endlessly: "Just-a-little-while, just-a-
little-while, just-a-little-while." When he's established his
hypnotic drone, the other voices come charging in on top
of the wheel:

> Just a little while to stay here.
> Just a little while to wait,
> Just a little while to labor,
> In the path that's always straight.

Meantime, the audience—they're a little slow, after all,
this is the first number—has finally gotten over its shock
at this musical Blitzkrieg and is shouting its approval.
Now Big Chief and the other voices go into a fast antiphon,
like banging a ball up against a wall:

> BASS: And we will shout!
> TRIO: Hallelujah!
> BASS: And we will sing!
> TRIO: Hallelujah!

Now they've got the audience on the ropes. It's time to
"turn them out," give them the coup de grace. Suddenly,

the individual voices, entering one after another at progressively higher pitches, pile up into a spectacular vocal pyramid, like circus tumblers.

> *Just a little while!*...
> *Just a little while!*...
> *Just a little while!*...

Then the bass does a vocal nose dive down in the hurricane cellar, producing a chord that spans three octaves. But they're still not through! Just when the crowd is tensing to acclaim them with shouts and applause, they take off again, after this false cadence, and start a series of upward transpositions. Now each time they sing a verse, they step off from a higher position on the scale. Up once they go; up again they go; the third time, they're way up in the attic and the tempo is quickening when suddenly—would you believe this?—the high tenor takes off in a Nigrah shouting style that brings down the house. They're singing, "Sweeping through the pearly gates," and going like Ben Hur, and this dude is echoing back the phrases from on high in falsetto, like some big old mammy in a Sanctified church. Before the audience can recover, the quartet goes into a riff straight out of the book of some old swing band, repeats it a few times in perfect harmony; then, with a startling chord pulled out of their mouths like bubble gum, they suddenly pop and stop!

As the applause dies down, old Hovie gets up and collars a mike and thanks the folks right hearty in that cornpone accent they so love to hear. Pausing for a second, as if to take thought, he offers a little confession:

"While the boys was singin' that song, mah mind turned to a favorite subject of every man, woman, boy and girl—*love!*" There's an audible gasp from the house: "He can't be meanin'...ah mean to say...wha's that he?..." No, it's O.K.! He means the *other* kinda love! "Love is a great word," old Hovie intones like a preacher. Then gettin' up into that Pentecostal pulpit tone, he gives it to all those doubting Thomases, right between the eyes: "God-gave-his-only-begotten-son-and-his-only-begotten-son-gave-his-life-on-Calv'ry!"

There! That should hold 'em. Now he just rounds it off nice: "That was a love that supersedes all love that man has ever known. [How 'bout that "supersedes"? There's some language for ya! Right outta the good book!] It's love that give me the joy an' the heppiness in mah heart. And it's the LOVE! [pause] that makes me free tahnight! *Listen!*"

Now, the "boys" go into "It's Wonderful to Know He Is Mine." This is one of Jake Hess's show-forth tunes. Everybody knows Jake: He's that little dude there with the eyes that keep poppin' open like a baby doll's (Jake says he does that for the people in the back rows) and the little hands that work like puppeteers' fingers. Hell! He looks like a cute little puppet himself with that big nutcracker mouth on him. What a voice! So clear, so clean, so sh-har-ply ar-tic-u-la-ted. He sounds like he's vocalizing the syllabification in the spelling book. Now, he's going into his specialty: the recitation. "When Ai-eh yam disc-cour-raged": He's really punchin' out those syllables now. Funny, if he were anyone else, you'd say he sounded like one of those high-pitched faggots—you know the kind that talk so affected with a clothespin on their nose? "Or Ai yam fi-illed with glooooom." Oh, boy, he can really color a note: shade it real dark. "Gaw-od se-ends his a-ngel to-oo see-eek in ma-ah roo-oom." He's really got everybody transfixed with this thing he does with the words. Singers say he got it from Billy Eckstine.

Though Jake's an eccentric, he's no clown. He's the greatest stylist in the business. When the Quartet gets into one of their I-love-you-Jesus vocal valentines, Jake sings with such refinement of tone and dynamics, such startling attacks and swooning melismata, that he virtually reduces the whole house to tears.

Somewhere in that house is Elvis Presley, who is soaking all this up like his mother's thickenin' gravy. When the day comes for him to record "Hi want you, Hi need you, Hi luh-huh-huh-huv yew-hew!" he will reveal what these sings taught him. When he records gospel, he will simply steal the Statesmen's arrangements.

Christian sentiment, Christian joy, the hand-clappin', foot-stompin' enthusiasm of that ole-time religion, these are the staples of a gospel sing; but shoutin' and weepin' aren't the only sources of entertainment. Gospel shows produce a lot of laughs. Those who know the Lord and love the Lord and dwell with the Lord are comfortable in the Lord's presence. They can take their ease in Zion and laugh their asses off! That's J. D. Sumner's job: to get the people laughin'. Ole J.D., he come out walkin' with his Sunshine Boys: They all be wearin' black shoes and he got on red! Then, he starts talkin' to the people in that cold-cellar voice of his, tellin' them how it feels to be a new boy in town.

"We're stayin' over here at a *ho*-tel, and that girl they got runnin' the elevator—she must be new to the job. I come to get on the elevator this mornin', an' she jus' threw that thing in high gear and we went all the way to the bottom! We hit with a thud an' I let out a groan! She turned around to me and said, 'What's the matter? Did I stop too quick for you?' I said, 'Oh, no! I always wear mah britches down around mah ankles!'"

It doesn't take much to make these folks laugh. If they don't laugh enough to please J. D., he's got this other thing he's famous for doing. It's called the Gooney Bird. J. D.'s a big tall man, as dignified as a cigar store Indian. When he wants a laugh, however, he'll suddenly throw his arms up in the air with his coattails in his hands and go to jumpin' and hoppin' around the stage like a big crazy buzzard flittin' around a dead varmint on the highway.

When intermission comes, the folks have a chance to get a cold Coke and buy the new songbooks and the glossy eight-by-tens of the quartets, which they can get autographed after the show. As the admission is only a quarter for kids and fifty cents for adults, the musicians must hustle for every extra buck. If they've got a little record company, as do the Blackwoods, they'll have somebody out in the lobby selling their big heavy 78s. LPs are kinda newfangled for this crowd.

The Blackwoods, who are local celebrities, get a tremendous hand when they walk out onstage dressed all in white. They're much more conservative than the Statesmen; in fact, for years they wore nothing but black. They stick pretty closely to the more traditional, Negro-influ-

enced gospel tunes in those tight seesaw rhythms that
lurch rather than rock. Their lead singer, the little
WASPy-looking James Blackwood, is no match for Jake
Hess, but the group is a very tightly meshed, neatly efficient machine for grinding out the old favorites. When
they want to get hot, they have a piano player who goes
into a flat-out boogie-woogie (which if his skin were black
would be called barrelhouse and be a shame before God!).
The bass singer runs scales on these boogie numbers using
his vocal chords as if they were a string bass. The fact is
that some of their hits, like "Peace in the Valley," were
written by black composers; but no matter how much of
the black style these white boys take, it always comes out
sounding as Caucasian as the Klan.

It isn't hard to imagine the effect of this show on the
young Elvis Presley. He would have been dazzled by the
costumes, hairstyles, jivey stage antics and virtuoso singing. He would have been astonished to see how the stuffy
old music of the church could be transformed into such
thrilling entertainment. He might even have felt that
strange stirring that passes through a man when he
catches his first glimpse of the world where he is destined
to spend his life. Though Elvis never became a conventional gospel singer, he did bring the gospel flavor and
tone to every sort of music he sang.

When the Blackwoods moved to Memphis in 1950, they
chose as their church the First Assembly of God. Their
baritone, R. W., enrolled his younger brother, Cecil, in the
same Sunday school class as Elvis. Therefore, in addition
to seeing the Blackwoods every month at the Auditorium
and watching them broadcast from the Hotel Peabody, he
also saw this famous group perform many times in his
church and soon became friendly with the younger brother
in the weekly scripture class. These personal associations
are important because Elvis was such a shy boy that if he
had not been so encouraged he might not have been able
to step over the line that divides the fan from the star. As
it was, he soon found himself backstage at the Auditorium
talking to the first professional musicians he had met since
his childhood acquaintance with Mississippi Slim in Tupelo.

The first gospel star to befriend the weird-looking kid with the side-burns was J. D. Sumner. J. D. recalls Elvis coming around so often and asking so many questions that he made a nuisance of himself. He also made himself such an accustomed presence that the first time he failed to appear, J. D. noticed his absence. Next time they met, the singer asked his most devoted fan what had kept him from the show. Elvis confessed that he couldn't raise the fifty cents for the ticket. After that, J. D. sneaked the boy in through the stage door, until Elvis got a job at the shows selling Cokes from an ice chest slung over his shoulder.

Once Elvis had discovered white gospel, it would have been natural for him to open his ears to black gospel, which was also broadcast every day on the radio in Memphis, a city renowned for its "shouting" churches. Black gospel exhibited a totally different character than white gospel. Instead of being a holy vaudeville full of straw-hat tunes, soft-shoe rhythms and J-E-L-L-O harmonies, black gospel was the bedrock of soul, "the forge and the flame" of black song. What's more, at this moment in its history it was undergoing the final degree of secularization that would make it soon the most vital component of the new R & B, which would become in turn the foundation for the new rock 'n' roll.

By turning his attention now to such immensely influential musicians as the Soul Stirrers (a quintet whose leader, R. H. Harris, was the model for Sam Cooke and Bobby "Blue" Bland); the Harmonizing Four (whose legendary bass, Jimmy Jones, Elvis discovered years later parking cars in North Carolina); the Swan Silvertones (perhaps the greatest of all black quartets); and such solo voices as Clara Ward (the model for Aretha Franklin) and Sister Rosetta Tharpe (a major influence on Dinah Washington and Little Richard), Elvis was not only cutting into the mainline of black vocal music but was doing so just at the moment when this whole buried world was about to burst onto the stage of national consciousness. Gospel soon inspired a wide range of pop music, extending from the "Sanctified" Ray Charles (whose big 1955 hit, "I Gotta Woman," was just a pop lyric pasted over "My Jesus Is All the World to Me") to the appearance of the greatest of all

R & B quartets, the Drifters, whose inspired lead singer, Clyde McPhatter, was originally a gospel singer, to the endless proliferation of do-wop groups ("do wop" is derived from the familiar gospel chant, "do Lord"), this juvenile fad being simply the reductio ad adolescence of a cappella gospel quartet.

When Elvis got out of high school in 1953, he wasn't thinking, as his yearbook pictured him, of "doing a bit of picking and singing" in a country and western club: His sights were trained on another goal entirely. He wanted to be a professional gospel singer. What's more, he almost reached this goal. Having befriended at church the son of the minister, Jimmy Hamill, and developed a good relationship with his Sunday school classmate, Cecil Blackwood, Elvis was hovering around a newly formed gospel quartet called the Songfellows. At first, he was just a hanger-on, a guy who would go along for the ride whenever the group got a gig. Then, one night when they were all in the car, one of the boys started praising Elvis, saying: "Why, he can imitate anyone—Jake Hess, Frank Sinatra, Dean Martin...." From that time forth, Elvis was often invited to sing with the group.

His first job working as a single was at the Eagle's Nest, in a motel, swimming pool and nightclub complex on the outskirts of town. The customary entertainment in this room was western swing music, the band of the moment being the Johnny Long Orchestra. Elvis performed in the lulls between the band's performances. He came onstage, as he does in *Jailhouse Rock,* trying to get the attention of a roomful of chattering men and women sitting at tables covered with red-checked cloths. Instead of singing a country and western tune, however, he would open his mouth and start belting out the current hits of Dean Martin! Can you dig it? "When the moon hits your eye like a big pizza pie—*that's* amore!" Twang, twang! Of all offbeat images of Elvis Presley, this little snapshot has got to be the most bizarre.

With nothing to encourage his dreams of a singing career except an occasional spot at the Eagle's Nest, where nobody listened to him, the eighteen-year-old Elvis Presley had little going for him. It was one of the dreariest periods of his life. Most of his waking hours were spent working on an assembly line. His uncles, Travis and Johnny, had been employed for years at Precision Tool, on McLemore and Kansas. When Elvis and Gene Smith finished with their schooling, the older men got the boys jobs at the factory. Precision Tool manufactured 90- and 101-millimeter shells for the army. Elvis's job was to insert three rods and twelve screws into the shell casing. He and Gene were the fastest men on the line. They worked from 7:00 in the morning till 3:30 in the afternoon. The pay was good for beginners: $1.65 an hour or sixty-six dollars a week. That was considerably more than Vernon Presley was earning after working for five years at United Paint. The only problem Elvis had on the job was caused by his long hair. The older men threatened to crop his head and Gene's. The boys offered at first to fight it out; then they thought better of it and went to the barber for a light trim.

In this same winter just before his nineteenth birthday, Elvis got a new job, which paid less money but pleased him much more: driving a truck for Crown Electric. Elvis had always been crazy about cars and other motor vehicles. No sooner did he get a driver's license at seventeen than he got his picture in the paper changing a tire in the citywide Road-E-O. (He came in second, "losing first place," as the school principal announced at assembly, "by a sideburn.") It wasn't just machines that excited him, it was the romance of being a truck driver.

With Elvis contributing his wages to the family, the fortunes of the Presleys finally began to mend. They had been forced to leave the Courts the previous winter because with Gladys working part-time as a nurse's aide and Elvis doing a variety of odd jobs, including a couple of punishing months working a full-time shift after school at MARL Metal, a kitchen furniture manufacturer (Elvis's job application raised a lot of laughs because at seventeen he claimed no less than five dependents), the Presleys' combined income inched up over the maximum allowed by the Housing Authority. They moved first to an apartment on Cypress Street, which was unsatisfactory. Then they moved again, to an old gingerbread frame house on Alabama Street, whose front porch faced their former building

at the Courts. The house was divided into a duplex. The
Presleys occupied the ground floor, with Gladys and Vernon sleeping in the only bedroom, Minnie Mae bunking
on a cot in the dining room, and Elvis crashing on the sofa
in the living room. The upstairs flat had been rented by
the house's owner, Mr. Dubrovner, the orthodox Jewish
ritual slaughterer, to Rabbi Alfred Fruchter, the orthodox
rabbi of a nearby *shul*.

The young rabbi and his wife, Jeanette, became friendly
with the Presleys and were often useful to them in small
ways. Mrs. Fruchter remembers loaning Gladys small
sums of money. She recalls how charming it was to see
Elvis come home on Friday and give his paycheck to his
mother. The Fruchters were also good people to have as
neighbors because they possessed two important devices
that the Presleys lacked: a telephone and a phonograph.
On a weekend, while Vernon and Elvis would stand out
in the street washing the green 1942 Lincoln Zephyr
coupe—which Vernon had bought for fifty dollars and
given to Elvis for his eighteenth birthday—Rabbi Fruchter would entertain himself by playing records of those
great, operatically-voiced cantors, Shlomo Kussevitsky
and Moyshe Oysher. In all the digging around for the roots
of the Presley sound, no one has ever considered the possibility that he was influenced by Jewish cantorial singing.

In February 1954, Elvis met Dixie Locke, the first girl
with whom he ever got involved in a serious relationship.
Dixie was just a kid at the time: a fifteen-year-old high
school sophomore. She had gone one night with a couple
of other girls to a high-school hangout called the Rainbow
Rollerdome. At some point in the evening, she spotted an
odd-looking boy whom she often saw at church. It was she
who approached Elvis. He was not in a condition to approach anyone because he had put on a pair of roller skates
without learning how to skate and was clinging anxiously
to the safety rail. As always he was spectacularly costumed. He had on a pink suit with a bolero jacket and a
black stripe down the pants leg—a carhop's outfit. When
Dixie introduced herself, Elvis engaged her in an intense
conversation that continued as he got her out of the roller

rink and into his car and over to Kay's Drive-In on Crump Boulevard.

Elvis poured out his whole story to Dixie. He told her that he came from desperately poor people: that his father was incapacitated for work with back trouble, that his mother was also ill, that he himself was unemployed and that even the old car he was driving was borrowed. It wasn't until he had brought Dixie to the door of her house in South Memphis that Elvis finally confessed that he had been fibbing, admitting that both he and his father had jobs and that the car was his own. Dixie assumed later that Elvis had been testing her: seeking to determine whether she would accept him at the very lowest figure. She may well have been right: Elvis was obsessed all his life with the thought that women wanted to "use" him. On the other hand, it may have been that he simply wanted pity and used the infantile device of feigned afflictions to make sure that he got the full measure of sympathy from this responsive young girl.

Dixie was not disposed to take the meeting as anything out of the ordinary, but to Elvis it represented a great new dawn of love and affection. Though neither he nor Dixie lived in homes that had telephones, he discovered that she could be reached through an aunt who had a phone and lived next door. Arranging for a date that very weekend, Elvis showed up at the Locke house wearing another of his bizarre costumes. With his long greasy hair and sideburns and pimply complexion all contributing to the highly negative impression he made on Dixie's father, a laborer at the Railway Express terminal, and her mother, both of whom were reluctant to allow their daughter to go off for the evening with such an obvious weirdo, Elvis came close to a humiliating rejection. Yet, by dint of numerous "Yes, sirs," and "No, ma'ams," those mechanical gestures of politeness that served Elvis so well throughout his life, the parents were brought around and the couple released to spend the rest of the evening in another prolonged talk.

Elvis, never the one to dillydally when he knew what he wanted, soon set the relationship on a routine course that would last until he started going out of town to work. Every weekend, he would bring home his paycheck and

give it to his mother or father, who would give him back
fifty cents or a dollar for his weekend date. If there was
enough money to put gas in the car, he would drive to
South Memphis, pick up Dixie and take her to the Suzore,
where they would see a cheap double feature. After the
show, they would go to Charlie's, a dim little shop across
the street, where an ancient man sold snacks and phonograph records. Elvis would get a Pepsi and Dixie a
NuGrape soda; then they would adjourn to a booth, where
Elvis would listen with a spellbound expression on his face
to recordings by black blues singers. His favorite record
was "Tomorrow Night" by Lonnie Johnson. When Dixie's
curfew came at eleven o'clock, Elvis would drive her home
or put her on the bus. The only variations in the routine
were the nights when they went to Riverside Park, the
little patch of green overlooking the Mississippi from the
bluff in front of Front Street, where they could sit on a
bench under the Confederate monuments and neck—until
they were rousted by the searchlight on a patrol car—or
the nights when they went out to a teen hangout near
McKellar Lake, where most kids danced to the juke box
but Dixie and Elvis didn't because Elvis couldn't. They
also went to a lot of all-night sings, Dixie sharing in Elvis's
tremendous enthusiasm for the music and especially for
Jake Hess. Dixie cannot remember Elvis ever voicing his
ambition to become a professional singer.

Dixie soon became acquainted with the other members
of the Presley family. She found the atmosphere of the
home depressing and disconcerting. Instead of the strong
father to whom she was accustomed, she discovered in the
Presley household a total inversion of the natural order.
The child was the head of the house, the mother came
second and the father was in the place occupied normally
by the son. The mother viewed their social position as that
of people at the very bottom of the barrel. Dixie now understood why Elvis would talk about her typical working-class
family as if they were "uptown." The other feature of the
Presley family that impressed Dixie was their extreme
reluctance to make friends or even visit other people.
Again, Dixie attributed this reclusiveness to Gladys, who

she realized wanted nothing better than to take Elvis and retreat to a desert island.

In the summer of 1954, Elvis's dream of joining the Songfellows finally became a reality owing to a horrible disaster that shocked the city of Memphis. The Blackwood Brothers had become extremely successful by this time, largely because of a recording contract with RCA, which produced an immediate hit, "The Man Upstairs." In June 1954, they had won first place on the *Arthur Godfrey Talent Scout Show,* which greatly increased the demand for their appearances all over the country. To squeeze their bookings closer together, they had started traveling by light airplanes, which they bought instead of chartered. Their baritone, R. W., got interested in flying and qualified as a pilot. Then, on the night of June 30, 1954, just before the quartet was about to perform at Clanton, Alabama, R. W. took off in the group's two-engine Beechcraft with the bass singer, Bill Lyles, and a local lad, to test the conditions for their departure later that night. When he tried to land on the short dirt strip, he crashed. The plane burst into flames and all three men were killed.

On July 2, the dead men were given a huge public funeral. Services were held at the Auditorium and Frank Clement, the governor of Tennessee, pronounced the eulogy. The Statesmen and the Speer Family sang. Thousands of grief-stricken people attended the ceremonies and watched the funeral cortege move solemnly through the streets of Memphis. Elvis was deeply affected by the disaster and spent a whole night sitting on a park bench with Dixie grieving.

James Blackwood announced that he would never sing again. Gradually, as he overcame his sorrow, he determined to re-form the group and continue his career. J. D. Sumner was hired to replace the dead bass singer. Then, a replacement was sought for R. W. Finally, it was decided that the most appropriate substitute would be his brother, Cecil.

Not two weeks after the crash, Cecil turned up one day at Elvis's house with important news. He announced that he was leaving the Songfellows for the Blackwoods. Now there would be an opening in the junior quartet. Elvis

could have his long-sought chance to become a professional
gospel singer.

Elvis listened to Cecil with obvious astonishment. Then
his expression changed to one of chagrin. "I can't do it!"
he snapped. "Why not?" demanded Cecil. Elvis paused for
a moment. Then, looking Cecil hard in the eye, expecting
perhaps a rebuke, he repeated, "I can't do it." This time
he added the surprising explanation, "I done signed a contract to sing the blues."

Chapter 7

Hoot 'n' Holler

THE BLUES that Elvis was about to record was not the country blues nor the city blues nor even the Memphis blues: It was rhythm and blues, the sound of the postwar black ghetto. In the year 1954, R & B was starting to spill out of the ghetto, but it still wasn't the kind of song with which most white singers were familiar. Nonetheless, the nineteen-year-old Elvis Presley showed himself highly knowledgeable regarding this and a number of other black styles, both current and past, secular and religious. How did Elvis learn to sing black?

The customary answer, that Elvis grew up with "all that" around him in Mississippi, is no longer tenable. As for the notion that the adolescent Elvis spent a lot of time hanging around the blues joints on Beale Street, all one has to do to test that idea is imagine how Gladys would react to such a pastime. Why, every weekend people got killed down on Beale (though the bodies were always conveyed to some other part of town, a practice that inspired the local proverb: "You never find a dead nigger on Beale!"). No, it is unthinkable that the boy who spent his weekends with a little high school girl going to the movies and listening to records at Charlie's would slip into the darkest and most dangerous part of the ghetto to hear somebody sing the blues. In fact, the real source of Elvis's

117

precocious knowledge of the blues was exactly the same
as that from which he had drawn his original inspiration
as a little country singer: the radio.[1]

Just one month after Elvis's arrival in town, in October
1948, the South's first black-oriented radio station went
on the air at Memphis. A feeble little 250-watter at sev-
enty-two kilocycles, it was just a shout at the bottom of
the dial. No radio station in history, however, has ever
exerted a greater impact on musical taste. A whole school
of subsequently famous performers grew up listening to
the station. What they got out of the experience was cer-

[1]A new book titled *Beale Black and Blue* by two Memphis
newspaper people contains the following assertions: 1) that Elvis
started hanging around the blues bars on Beale during his high
school years; 2) that he participated on at least one occasion in
an all-black amateur contest at the local vaudeville house, the
Palace Theater; 3) that he got his famous "wiggle" from a local
black entertainer named Charlie Burse at a joint called the Grey
Mule. The sources cited are Nat D. Williams (of whom more later)
and Robert Henry, a long-time Beale Street entertainment man.
Normally such sources would carry a lot of weight; however, in
this case there are many reasons for challenging the statements,
at least in the form in which they were made. First, Elvis's closest
intimates at the time, such as his cousin, Gene Smith (who accompanied Elvis to all his first little gigs), deny these stories
absolutely. Second, my own researches on Beale, which entailed
interviews with many old-timers, produced no comparable memories. Finally, in an article published in 1956—and quoted in
Beale Black and Blue—the same Nat D. Williams who is cited
now as saying that Elvis was a great favorite on Beale writes
that he cannot understand what Presley was doing at a Goodwill
Show sponsored by the local black radio station: "Why Elvis came
and how he got in the middle of such a concentrated kodachrome
crowd, one may never know." This is not the tone one would adopt
for a local favorite. Therefore it seems reasonable to conclude that
Mr. Williams and Mr. Henry, both elderly gentlemen today, may
have telescoped their memories of Elvis's later appearances on
Beale with the myth of his youthful adventures on that legendary
street. After all, he was still a boy of nineteen when he became
a local celebrity; how easy to think of him way back then as being
still a high-school amateur.

tainly as valuable as any Ph.D. ever granted in Afro-American Studies. Not only did they obtain unlimited "exposure" to both the secular and sacred music of black people, they also received a marvelous education in black humor and language through the raps and bits of their professors, who were the South's first black "personality jocks." As if all this weren't enough, a couple of these professors subsequently became famous practitioners of the arts they taught. They became, in fact, some of the biggest names in the last phase of urban blues and soul music. As nothing of substance has ever been published on the "Mother Station of the Negroes," let us tune in now on the story of how the blues was reborn at Memphis.

The establishment of the South's first black radio station was purely a case of do or die. In 1948, WDIA was a hapless little country music outlet teetering on the verge of bankruptcy. Faced with the decision whether to give up and get out or do something new and risky, the white owners of the station, Bert Ferguson and John R. Pepper, decided it was better to go black than go broke.

Now the owners were faced with the problem of finding the proper staff. Black announcers and DJs from the North could have been brought to Memphis, but how would they go over with the people down on the plantations? What's more, if you got some uppity nigger from the North, he might say something on the air that would make a stink. The best thing would be to find a good local man who could handle the job.

The first announcer recruited proved to be a perfect choice. Professor Nat D. Williams, known subsequently to generations of black Memphians as "Nat Dee," was a history teacher at Booker T. Washington High School. Though some feared he might be too highbrow for the common folk, the Professor's late-afternoon "drive-time" show, *Tan Town Jamboree,* became extremely popular because it featured all the latest R & B hits.

The next black jock to be hired had a showbiz background and was hip to the style of Negro DJ's in the North. In the age of re-bop, rhyming slang and jumped-up music, the idea was to talk fast-fast-fast, a verbal Blitzkrieg that blew the listener's mind. Listening to his new jock streak

down the track one day, Mr. Ferguson said, "Maurice, you
talk so fast, you oughta have a name that means speed.
From now on, you're gonna be 'Hot Rod' Hulbert." A few
weeks later, Hot Rod Hulbert was racing through a station
break when his tongue slipped and he identified himself
as "Hard Rod Hulbert." That got him a lot of attention.

Soon Hulbert was working a three-a-day schedule at
the badly under-manned station. Each show went on the
air at a different hour, was aimed at a different audience
and demanded a different mood and rap. Hulbert complied
by dividing himself into three different Rods. At eight in
the morning, following Nat Dee's sunrise show, *Tan Town
Coffee Club,* which was mostly R & B, "Maurice Hulbert,
Jr." would go on the air with his gospel show, *Tan Town
Jubilee.* As the driving beat and raucous shouting of the
Five Blind Boys, the Dixie Hummingbirds and the Mighty,
Mighty Clouds of Joy blared over the air, Hulbert would
come on like a black preacher up in the pulpit. Between
his pitches for hair-straightener and Dixie Peach Complexion Creme, he would read passages from the Bible in
a deep, inspiring scripture voice. He went over so well with
this act that he was invited to play Jesus in the annual
Christmas drama at the Auditorium.

At ten o'clock in the morning, Hulbert would shift
masks to do a program aimed at the housewives, maids
and laundresses: *Sweet Talkin' Time.* Now, he was "Maurice the Mood Man.": smooth, sexy, intimate. Reaching
down into his deepest, richest, most vibrato-throbbing
voice, he would talk to the girls in valentines:

> *You bring sunshine into my life,*
> *You make me forget the toil and strife.*
> *You take out of me the years*
> *I've struggled through with so much sorrow and tears!*
> *It was difficult to resist because—pause!*
> *You—pause!—were—pause!—temptation!*

With the last word, he'd drop the needle into a slick white
rendition of "Temptation," that classic erotic romantic ballad with its jungle-drum beguine break.

At three o'clock in the afternoon, "Hot Rod Hulbert"

made his first appearance of the day, talking like a chattering hipster teletype, going a mile a minute as the way-out MC of the *Sepia Swing Club*. This show was all up!-up!-up! Jokes and jive and patter picked up off the street. One day doing a fast blitzy commercial for E-Z Credit Layaway, his tongue, as he recalls, "got stuck in my eye teeth so bad I couldn't see." As the words of the commercial came tumbling out as a series of nonsense syllables, Hulbert snapped to the fact that he had invented a tongue twister. He wrote it all out—O-ble-doo-ba-blah-blah-blah-doo-*lay-a-way*—and discovered there were nineteen syllables in all. That gave him an inspiration: For nineteen days before Christmas he taught his radio listeners one new syllable a day, until they could riddle off the whole long preposterous bit, like a scat-singing jazz vocalist. So many people mastered the trick that everywhere you went in black Memphis, you heard the silly syllables.

We have no way of knowing how much of WDIA's programming Elvis Presley absorbed in the five years between his arrival in Memphis and his first efforts as a professional singer. We do have Elvis's testimony that he listened to the station constantly. What is more, no sooner did he become famous than he offered to lend his support to the station. There are a number of photographs of Elvis at WDIA's annual Goodwill Revue in December 1956. Apparently, the racial taboos of Memphis forbade Elvis's appearance on the show, but he was on hand to lend his support to the cause. There is also a picture from this time of Elvis shaking hands with WDIA's most famous disc jockey, Riley B. King, better known as B. B. King.

King was not long off the plantation when he arrived in West Memphis, Arkansas, where there was a local station, KWEM, that split its broadcast schedule between white country music and black blues. The presiding presences on the black segments were Sonny Boy Williamson, King's idol, and Chester Burnett, soon to become famous in Chicago as Howlin' Wolf. When Riley King heard there was a new black station in Memphis, he took a bus to the downtown Greyhound terminal and then walked three miles out to Union Avenue, reaching number 2074 in a pouring rain. King went on the air that very day and soon

was a regular on a show called *Pay Day*. Eventually, he
got a sponsor, a tonic called Pepticon. His show's theme
was a blues jingle:

> *Pepticon sure is good,*
> *Pepticon sure is good,*
> *Get it anywhere in your neighborhood.*

By the time the young singer had worked up to a staff job
on the *Heebie Jeebie Show,* he had expanded his name to
read "Beale Street Blues-Boy."

Programming all the best R & B music, the stuff with
the most soul, King spun the first records of Lloyd Price
and Fats Domino, as well as those of established stars like
Louis Jordan and Dinah Washington. If he found a side
that appealed to him by a white singer, like Frank Sinatra,
Bing Crosby or Frankie Laine, he would toss it into the
pot. Though WDIA programmed very little white music,
there were always some songs, like Johnny Ray's bizarre
hit, "Cry," that appealed to the black audience.

By 1951, B. B. King had built a reputation as a club
act and recording star. He was getting so many out-of-
town bookings that he had to give up his radio job. His
replacement was another black entertainer destined to
become nationally known: Rufus Thomas. A husky, bald-
headed, rubber-legged clown of a man, Thomas had joined
the Rabbit's Foot Minstrels way back in 1935. Over the
years he had amassed a great deal of showbiz experience.
As the MC of the weekly amateur night at the Palace
Theater on Beale, Thomas was still active on the stage,
though he made his living stoking the boilers at the Memphis Luggage Factory. His style as a DJ was superfly. To
open his midnight show, *Hoot and Holler,* he would shout:

> *I'm young and loose and full of juice!*
> *I got the goose so what's the use?*
> *We're bright and gay but we ain't got a dollar!*
> *Rufus is here—so let's hoot 'n' holler!*

By 1954, WDIA was making so much money with its
black programming policy that the whole operation was

refinanced and put on a big-time footing. From a feeble
little 250-watter, the station was switched overnight to a
mighty 50,000-watt transmitter that reached out for
hundreds of miles to gather into its net the huge black
population of the entire tristate area: Tennessee, Mississippi and Arkansas. Now, when you picked up an advertising, media marketing or music biz trade paper, you saw
ads that laid it right on the line. "America's Only 50,000-
Watt NEGRO Station Covers the Golden Market of
1,237,686 Negroes—nearly 10% of America's Total Negro
Population." Can you imagine the heat a statement like
that engendered in the loins of any red-blooded American
space buyer? Hey! It was heavy! Inevitably, it inspired the
owners of other Memphis stations to wonder whether there
might be some way, some trick of media miscegenation,
that might allow them to cut a slice of this rich black
devil's food cake. You couldn't sell the culleds unless you
spoke their language, of course. But what if you found
some good ole boy with a crazy line of jive like the nigger
pusenality jocks that could towahk that same shit! Hey!
You'd have yeseff sumpin', wouldncha, son? Well, that's
'zactly how Brother Dewey Phillips got his shot.

Dewey Phillips! What a natural-born freak! You think
city people are wild? You think all that off-the-wall jive
comes from the Harlem ghetto? No, mah boy, they's many
a crazy, likah drinkin', pill poppin' countrah boy that kin
get hissef jes' as racked-up 'n' ragged as the craziest coon
they ever treed on Beale Street. It's a damn shame that
we just can't take the paper on this page and stamp it in
a pressing plant like one of those little old pressed-paper
records to let you hear this good ole boy do his stuff. No
tricks of typography, no Tom Wolfe razzamatazz on the
top buttons of the typewriter—#*¢%&!!!—will ever sim-
ulate the sound that this nut made over the late-night,
deep-South radio circa 19 and 54.

Just picture yourself cruising around Memphis in the
premidnight hours, with your car radio tuned to WHBQ,
which broadcasts from the mezzanine of the Old Chisca
Hotel (Chickasaw, the Indians of the Memphis bluffs)
down on Main Street. You've just heard Howlin' Wolf practically masticate the mike with his big chops as he rasped,

"*Bay*—bee, wheredya spen' las' night?" Suddenly, the announcer's mike switches on, and another Arkansas voice, nearly as harsh and contorted, a white cracker voice that sounds like its owner is just recovering from having his face pushed through a windshield, comes on the air spewing words like a Stengun. "Dat-wuz-de-Wolf!" gushes the voice. "Now, it's ole Phillips, playin' da *Red, Hot 'n' Blues,* comin' threw HBQew in *Ho-*tel Chisko, on the magazine flowh. We cumin' atchoo cutahsey People's Fernitcher Company, 310 South Main, where ya jes' pay a little down an' pay for it while ya wearin' it out—or when they ketch up with ya! Ha! Thass more like it! It's awright! Nervous? Gitten' a divorce? It's OK. Jes' tell 'em Phillips sentcha! Now, anybody wannah buy a fur-lined mousetrap? No! Well, got one here by Sister Rosetta Tharpe—'Strange Thing's Are Happenin' Every Day!'" At that instant, out of the speaker blasts the red-hot trumpet voice of the inspired sister shouting biblical phrases in thrilling, flawlessly phrased jazz licks, echoed ritualistically by the stoic mezzo of Marie Knight, as the air waves crepitate with the rockin', rollickin' boogie-woogie beat of the lady herself, playing lime-tart acoustic guitar, like Scrapper Blackwell with Leroy Carr on a rompin' an' ravin' night in Naptown.

Dewey Phillips, that classic cornpone speed freak, was soon to play an important part in the unfolding of Elvis's fame as the first DJ ever to broadcast an Elvis Presley record. The maker of that record was also named Phillips, though there was no family relationship between the men. Sam Phillips, the proprietor of Sun Records, was Memphis's foremost independent record producer. Not your typical indie operator—a Jewish hustler from Big Town—Phillips was an earnest, cat-faced country boy from the Bible Belt, born and reared near the same little city that had produced W. C. Handy, Florence, Alabama. Instead of getting into the music business by running a record store or a nightclub in the ghetto, Phillips began his career in radio. His first job was spinning white gospel and country music discs at a station in nearby Muscle Shoals. Perhaps the most important difference between Phillips and other R & B producers was that he made to every record he cut a very tangible and absolutely indispensable contribution: Phillips was the recording engineer.

The creator of the "Sun Sound" learned the craft of recording music in the late forties while working as a station engineer at WREC in Memphis. One of his regular assignments was taping for subsequent broadcast over the CBS network the bands that played at the Skyway Room atop the Hotel Peabody. In 1950, Phillips decided to supplement his salary by establishing a professional recording service. The studio he constructed, largely with his own hands, has been restored recently as a landmark by Gray Line Tours. Located about a mile from Elvis's old home in the Lauderdale Courts, 706 Union Avenue is a narrow, deep, one-story building that looks about right for a neighborhood hardware store or painting supply shop. The façade is two tall display windows flanking a narrow door. Inside is a very small reception area that was once narrowed even more by desks on either side: one for Phillips and the other for his receptionist, secretary and woman-of-all-work, Marion Keisker.

Passing through another doorway into the main portion of the building, you find yourself in a good sized, thirty-by-eighteen-foot recording studio lined with white acoustic tile. Patterned after the typical radio station of the time, the room's only peculiarity was a dog-leg wall designed to break up the sound waves and improve the chamber's acoustics. Phillips used a maximum of eight Shure, RCA and Electrovoice mikes positioned on upright stands or hanging from booms. No baffles were employed and according to Phillips's technical assistant, Jack Clement, the principal source of the much-admired Sun Sound was simply leakage from one instrument into its neighbor's mike.

The back wall of the studio has a raised horizontal window behind which is the control booth. Here Phillips installed an RCA radio-style console with five input channels controlled by rotary "pots" or knobs. On either side of the console stood the Presto lathes for cutting custom discs: one for microgroove, the other for 78s. At the back of the booth were the tape recorders: two big bulky Ampex 350s. The famous "slapback" echo, the hallmark of Sun Records, was not produced by an echo chamber. A second mike was run from the soloist to a second tape recorder and this recording was overdubbed on the primary recording with a split-second delay. No other overdubbing was done. The recording procedure consisted simply of striking a balance between the mikes and then capturing the whole performance in a single take.

Memphis Recording Service advertised, "We Record Anything—Anywhere—Anytime." In practice, "anything" reduced to an endless series of weddings, funerals, conferences and public addresses. Phillips would cart his portable gear out to the job and take down the words of ceremony or business for nine dollars per LP side. If you came into the studio, you could make a 78 RPM record for just four dollars.

No sooner did Phillips complete his studio than he began to get some business of an entirely different kind. Independents in other parts of the country, Chess in Chicago and Modern in Los Angeles, for example, were very interested in obtaining recordings of unknown but promising performers in the Memphis area. The arrangement was that Phillips would engage the musicians and pay the cost of the session; then, if the results were what the out-of-town company was seeking, it would lease the master from Phillips and pay him so many cents per side sold. In this manner, the obscure radio engineer found himself making the first recordings of subsequently famous artists like B. B. King, Howlin' Wolf and Bobby "Blue" Bland. Not only did Phillips's recordings pass muster as viable commercial products: A couple of them astonished everyone by climbing to the very top of the R & B charts.

"Rocket 88," a honking, hard-driving paean to the lifestyle symbolized by the new rocket-tailed Oldsmobile 88, was put together by the then totally unknown Ike Turner, who was working as a DJ on a station in Jackson, Mississippi. Issued by Chess with the name of the singer, Jackie Brenston, on the label, the record not only rocketed to the Number One position but remained on the charts for seventeen weeks. Another side, called "Booted," featuring a mediocre singer named Roscoe Gordon, repeated the success of "Rocket 88" by reaching first place and hanging on the charts for thirteen weeks. These successes were enough to convince Sam Phillips that instead of just functioning as an engineer, he should become an independent record producer. Thus was born Sun Records, its logo a crowing red rooster standing on a fence haloed by a bright yellow rising sun.

Sun issued its first record on March 1, 1952. A screeching duet for alto saxes, it went nowhere. Several subsequent releases fared just as badly; eventually the whole first year of operation had to be written off as a loss. Though Phillips was working with first-rate black talent, such as the famous pioneer of the electric harmonica, Little Walter—soon to become one of the greatest stars of the Chicago blues style—Sun couldn't produce a hit.

In addition to the problems of making successful records, Phillips and his partners faced some steep business hurdles. Breaking into the record business has never been easy, while making out in the hucklebuck world of R & B had long challenged the resourcefulness of even the greatest hustlers. Hits were the name of the game. Without them, no indie could survive. One way to get a hit was to come up with a new gimmick. This is exactly what Rufus Thomas supplied when, almost a year to the day after the company's first release, he came into the office with a hot new idea.

Thomas had written an answer to a record that was rapidly climbing the charts: Willie Mae Thornton's "Hound Dog." Answer records were an old device in the R & B game: a great way to catch a free ride on the coattails of somebody else's hit. His answer, "Bearcat," was fine so far as the words went: Rufus threw Willie Mae's putdown of shiftless men right back in her teeth. The problem was they were stuck for a tune, always the item in shortest supply in the music business and especially hard to come by at Sun, which had no house composers or arrangers and was far away from the teeming brains in the Brill Building. As speed was vital if they were to cash in on a current hit, someone suggested that they rip off the original tune. Sam Phillips agreed. The record was cut the same day and rushed into production. It hit the charts and started to climb. On the strength of its success, Phillips landed a

series of distribution deals in key markets. Then, the funk
hit the fan.

"Hound Dog," written by Jerry Leiber and Mike Stoller
with Johnny Otis, had been issued by Peacock Records of
Houston, which was operated by a very tough and bellig-
erent black dude named Don Robey, who was notorious for
traveling around town with a couple of pistol-packing
bodyguards. Robey sued Phillips for violation of his copyright and BMI refused to license the "new" song. A judge
ruled in Robey's favor, but when the two producers started
thrashing out their problems, they decided it was better
to let the rip-off remain on the market making money they
could share than simply to kill the record. Phillips wound
up paying two cents per side to Robey and all court costs.

Having scored with one gimmick, it was time to look
for another. One day Phillips received a promising demonstration record from Nashville. It was a black vocal
group singing a song titled "Just Walkin' in the Rain,"
written by their lead singer, Johnny Bragg. The group's
name, the Prisonaires, was explained by the fact that they
were all serving time in the state penitentiary at Nashville. Working out a fast deal with the prison officials,
Phillips obtained the services of this vocal chain gang.
They arrived under heavy guard to give their "command"
performance. Strange to say, the record leaped to Number
Ten on the country music charts and was covered immediately by a number of pop singers, including the still
unknown Johnny Ray. Subsequently, the Prisonaires recorded a song of praise for Tennessee's music-loving Governor, Frank Clement ("Well, what about Frank Clement?
He's a mighty, mighty man o' god!"), and won their release
from the slammer. The Prisonaires scored their hit in April
1953. After that Sun did not have another hit until Elvis
Presley broke through in the summer of 1954.

Elvis turned up at 706 Union Avenue for the first time
on a Saturday afternoon in the fall of 1953. According to
the Myth he came to cut a record as a birthday present for
his mother. As his mother's birthday was long past and
the Presleys had no phonograph, this story can be discounted as an early attempt to exploit Elvis's relationship
with Gladys. Elvis himself stated that he had no expec-

tations of a singing career at this time but was simply curious to hear how he sounded on record. The two tunes he cut that day were oldies by the Ink Spots, and it's indicative of Elvis's mimetic approach to recording that he sought to copy both the high, sweet tenor of Bill Kenney in the chorus and the deep resonant bass of Hoppy Jones in the talking bridge. Elvis described his guitar playing as sounding like "somebody beating on a bucket lid."

Though Elvis's performance was gauche, his voice triggered a strong association in the mind of Marion Keisker, who was alone that day at the studio. She recalled Sam Phillips saying repeatedly, "If I could find a white boy who could sing like a nigger, I could make a million dollars." Keisker wrote down Elvis's name and Rabbi Fruchter's phone number. Beside them she noted: "Good ballad singer. Hold."

Elvis got his big chance at Sun about nine months later when Phillips, eager to cut a new song but needing a high, soulful voice, gave in to Keisker's urgings and agreed to try "the kid with the sideburns." Elvis came panting into the studio, having run virtually the whole way from Alabama Street. After trying repeatedly to copy the demo record, he faced finally a disappointed and exasperated Sam Phillips, who demanded, "Well, what *can* you sing?" Elvis started pulling tunes out of the air, ranging through every style but with the emphasis falling on his hero, Dean Martin. When the audition ended, Elvis hadn't sold Phillips. The producer said Elvis needed "a lot of work." Elvis said that he would like "to get me a band."

As it happened, Phillips had a western swing band on tap called Doug Poindexter's Starlite Wranglers. The guitarist, Winfield Scott Moore, was an ambitious young fellow, fresh out of the service, recently married, working at his brother's cleaning plant but eager to make a career in the music business. Phillips put Elvis together with Scotty Moore and with his neighbor on Belz Street, Bill Black, an older musician, a burly clown who played string bass. As the three men began to work together, they discovered a common ground in their sense of time. As Black remarked in later years, "Rhythm was what Elvis went by."

Just before Phillips recorded Elvis Presley in the summer of 1954, he appears to have changed his recording strategy. He began to swing away from black artists and concentrate on white country singers. His real goal remained, however, finding a way to combine the feel of black music with the audience appeal that could be generated in the pop market only by a white singer.

Chapter 8

Solar Flair

On THE EVENING of July 6, 1954, the nineteen-year-old Elvis Presley arrived at 706 Union Avenue for his first professional recording session. After a day on which the temperature had reached 102 degrees, the tightly sealed, white-tiled studio was sweltering. At nightfall, a mist blanketed the city. Perhaps this soggy atmosphere accounts for the quality of Elvis's initial effort, a corny country ballad titled "I Love You Because."

On the first take, Elvis employs a specious tenor that slides from note to note with greasy insinuation, while the electric guitar runs tremolos up and down the strings, like wiggling water bugs. When Elvis reaches the talking bridge, his voice becomes expressionless, his sentiments unbelievable. Hollowly, he recites: "Ah love you...Ah love you, baby...because..."—*because it says so in this dumb song!*

In a later take, he *whistles* the introduction and omits the embarrassing recitation. This time, though, the tempo drags so badly that the song hovers on the verge of collapse. Sam Phillips could not have been feeling optimistic when he switched on the studio monitor and told the boys to take a break.

Before the session Phillips had suggested to Elvis that he do one of the songs of Arthur "Big Boy" Crudup (pro-

131

nounced Croodup), a pioneer of the Mississippi-Chicago
electric blues style. They had talked over all the Crudup
numbers that Elvis knew—"Cool Disposition," "Rock Me
Mama," "Hey Mama," "Everything's All Right"—and settled on "That's All Right Mama," Elvis's especial favorite.
Now, during the break, the fidgety Elvis started goofing
on this tune, trying to raise a laugh.

"Elvis just started clowning," recollects Scotty Moore.
"I joined in as soon as I found out what key we were in.
Then, the control room doors opened. Sam was in there
doin' somethin', and he came out and said: 'What are y'all
doin'?' Elvis said, 'I don' know—just goofin' off!' Sam said,
'Well, that sounds pretty good. Back up and see if you can
figure out what you're doin',' and let's put it on tape.' So
we kinda talked it over and figured out a little bit what
we were doin'. We ran it again, and of course, Sam is
listenin'. 'Bout the third or fourth time through, we just
cut it—and that was that! It was basically a rhythm record. It wasn't any great thing. It wasn't Sam tellin' him
what to do. Elvis was joking around, just doing what come
naturally, what he felt."

The record so modestly described by one of its makers
was, in fact, a remarkable feat of breathing in one cultural
atmosphere and breathing out another. When you play the
Presley side immediately after hearing the Crudup cut,
you can hardly believe that both singers are doing the
same tune. The difference is as great as that between Mick
Jagger and Aretha Franklin singing "I Can't Get No Satisfaction"; in fact, the difference is rather the same, the
later version in each case being what might be called the
eroticization of the original.

Crudup's old recording summons up the atmosphere of
the South Chicago blues bars during the days of go-man-
go jump jazz. The tempo is fast, the rhythm is tense, the
vocal delivery is as hard and straight as a hard, black
bowling ball rolling down a polished alley. Elvis's performance, by contrast, suggests a farm boy lying up in a
fragrant hayloft daydreaming of what he'd like to do with
that little mama who is giving him such a runaround. The
rhythm is relaxed and rural, the guitar chimes like a bell,
the atmosphere is vernal—a hillbilly *Frühlingstimmen!*

There is intensity, though, in the singing. Pitching his voice way up high, in a range that suggests ecstasy, Elvis phrases the lines so that they stretch and yearn and writhe like a boogaloo; then, when he reaches the refrain, "That's all right, mama, that's all right with me," he teases and taunts and releases the tension he has been building in a cadence that drifts down with sensuous little swells and diminuendos like a dancer boogeyin' down. The total effect can be summed up in one word—*sexy!*

Sam Phillips skillfully seconded this inspired interpretation by enhancing the high ecstatic voice with a subtle aura of quavering echo. It's worth noting that this was the first time Phillips ever employed this effect in recording a white singer. It was a stroke of genius—perhaps the most brilliant inspiration of this famous producer's career. Indeed, when you weigh the forces that contributed to Elvis Presley's breakthrough, Phillips's claim to importance appears completely justified. Not only did he give Elvis the right steer in directing him away from lugubrious ballads to the currently fashionable R & B material, but he attached to his new star's raw and untrained voice the electronic prosthesis that masked his vocal faults while it transformed—or should we say transfigured?—his vocal quality into the now legendary Presley sound.

The balance of this first session was spent in finding a song that would work as the B side of the Crudup tune. The solution that was arrived at entailed another transmogrification of a traditional style. Impelled by some profound and instinctive principle of cultural compensation, these southern boys and their bossman decided to make the flip side of their bid for fame a take-off from the other side of the southern racial barrier (or the other end of the state of Tennessee), a classic white-trash bluegrass song: Bill Monroe's "Blue Moon Over Kentucky."

Just as in the Crudup song Elvis stretched and writhed, as if under the spell of spring fever, so in this country classic, at the points where Monroe is snapping off his phrases like rattraps or shooting up abruptly into a yodeler's falsetto, Elvis is caressing the open-voweled rhymes— "on a moonlight *naiiiight,* stars were shinin' *braiiiight,*" in rising and falling glissandos, like a Neapolitan tenor.

(No wonder he came to have such an admiration for Mario Lanza!)

Having flourished his leek so triumphantly with the Crudup song, it was natural that Elvis should let out his mind a little further on this follow-up recording. If "That's All Right Mama" enjoys the honor of having been Elvis's breakthrough, his first great moment in the ring, "Blue Moon" enjoys the distinction of being the first side on which Elvis opens up his bag of tricks. The first and greatest trick is what has been called aptly Elvis's "vocal orchestration." This is the knack of using the voice to suggest all the instruments and effects that are lacking in the threadbare world of folk music. As a young man who had heard a vast amount of music but who had no greater musical resources than his vocal chords, his rhythm guitar and his tiny two-piece, semipro "band," Elvis Presley found himself in the familiar position of the musically inspired, musically initiated, but musically deprived all over the world. His solution to his problem was the classic solution, the solution that occurs instinctually to every muscial primitive—he made himself into a one-man band.

Now what do bands do when they open up a tune? They set the mood, establish the rhythm and build up the listener's expectations by playing an introduction. What happens in these introductions? Well, the band sets a riff, a simple rhythmic phrase bitten off from the first notes of the melody; then they play a flashy cadence and cut the mother loose! Which is just what the nineteen-year-old Elvis Presley did that hot night in the studio at Memphis with "Blue Moon." As Scotty and Bill and Elvis himself laid the rhythm, a Western swing rhythm, Elvis vocalized a riff built on the phrase, "Blue moon...Blue moon"; then, when he came to the cadence, he improvised a lick that will go down in history as the quintessential Presley getoff. Down the scale he tumbled in vigorous syncopation, singing, "you're Go-nah BRING-ah me BACK mah BABy to-NIGHT" while the reverb gave his voice a bizarre fun house echo. Only then, did he raise his voice to the "singing" level and deliver the song.

These naive artifices of the young Elvis Presley show him functioning as an instinctive composer. He's starting to apply all the things he learned during his curious apprenticeship to the gospel stage. Syllabifying the words—"you're go-nah bring-ah"—was, of course, the hallmark of Jake Hess's vocal style. Actually, it is an ancient practice that goes back to the very origins of American syncopated music in the ragtime era around the turn of the century. The classic example is that minstrellike song (parodied by T. S. Eliot in "Sweeney Agonistes"), "Under the Bamboo Tree," which is phrased: "If you like-ah me like I like-ah you," etc. Far from being an expression of the way-out new world of rock 'n' roll, this gimmick was hoary with eld. So were, if the truth be told, most of Elvis's characteristic mannerisms, including not only his favorite vocal tricks but his dance steps, catch phrases and stage postures. Remember that Elvis studied showbiz in the oldest schools in the nation: the all-night sing and black southern radio. His notion of what was hip was almost quaint.

Being "out" is sometimes better than being "in." Especially is this the case when you're destined to become the embodiment of a culture as profoundly regressive—in all senses of the word—as was rock 'n' roll. The motto of this music was never better articulated than in that song of the sixties that ran: "Gonna buy me a time machine and go to the turn of the century. Everything's happening at the turn of the century." Rock from the beginning was a throwback to an earlier and more naive kind of music than the commercial jazz or the Broadway show tunes that had dominated American consciousness during the thirties and forties. Year by year, step by step, rock delved back into the past until finally it created the climate for a full-scale revival of ragtime, the thing that was "happenin' at the turn of the century." So Elvis Presley's naive mimicry of the styles and sounds of preceding generations—the introductory riffs of the swing bands, the hubba-hubba rhythm vocalizing of the twenties, the cornball glottal stroke—stood him in good stead when it came time to reverse the course of American musical history and start driving with eyes firmly fixed on the rearview mirror.

The jazzing up of the country style coupled with the rusticating of the R & B idiom, itself derived from black rural roots, established a new genre in American music called rockabilly. No sooner had Elvis shaped the basic mold than into it poured the talents of a whole school of hitherto unknown performers, commencing with Carl Perkins, Johnny Cash, Jerry Lee Lewis and Roy Orbison (all Sun artists), and going on to include Buddy Holly, the Everly Brothers and the early Beatles; for as John Lennon remarked, "Before Elvis there was nothing."

To think of a nineteen- or twenty-year-old boy producing this sort of effect with his very first efforts as a professional is to recognize that the young Elvis was a pop genius. As Kant says, genius exists to allow nature to give new rules to art, its distinctive hallmark being originality. To comprehend the originality of an Elvis Presley, however, you have to recognize first that it derives in great degree from an apparently opposite principle: the instinct of mimicry.

The secret of Elvis's art lay not in an act of substantive creation but in a recasting of one traditional style in terms of another. To make such a transposition, you have to be stylistically sophisticated. You have to see all the familiar styles lying before you like so many spots of color on a painter's palette. Such sophistication would have taken many years to develop in the premedia world of popular music. Once, however, every American child started growing up with unlimited access to every kind of music provided by radio, any boy with a good ear and the necessary talent could get hip fast.

Elvis Presley was from his earliest years a marvelous mimic. This gift was fundamental to both his great success and his great failure as an artist. It enabled him on the one hand not only to pick up on the going thing but to do all sorts of tricks with the currently popular styles, including the basic trick of transmuting one style into its opposite. On the other hand, Elvis's mimetic aptitude exposed him to the temptation to turn into a commercial copycat.

During his Sun years, he used his talent to create a music that was essentially playful and parodistic. In approaching pop song in this spirit, he established the basic esthetic for rock 'n' roll. Rock is not, as is always said, simply an amalgam of blues, country, pop, etc. This is to define it by its sources and substances instead of its soul.

The music's essence lies in its attitude. That attitude first
comes to expression in Elvis, then in Little Richard and
then in the Beatles, to name the greatest performers in
the tradition. All of these singers are at bottom parodists.
They assume the identity provided by a particular style;
then, working behind this mask, they achieve the exhilarating freedom of the ventriloquist talking through his
zany dummy. Inevitably, they tend toward falsetto and
caricature. They may even wind up becoming parodies of
themselves, as did Elvis, Little Richard and John Lennon.
What's more, the degree of sophistication, allusion, and
fantasy in their work may vary greatly from the purely
instinctive sass of Little Richard to the much more calculated "styling" of Elvis to the sometimes brilliantly resourceful travesties of John Lennon, which shade into the
bizarre but compelling juxtapositions of surrealism. The
important thing is to recognize that the root of rock is in
the put-on and the take-off, the characteristic fusion of
enthusiasm and mockery that was almost universal in the
pop culture of the fifties: a slant on things that you find
as much in *Mad* or the routines of Sid Caesar or the comic
pornography of Terry Southern as you do in the funny
songs of Leiber and Stoller or the funny singing of Elvis
Presley.

On one of the rejected takes of "Blue Moon" that has
surfaced in recent years, you can hear Sam Phillips exclaiming through the studio monitor: "Hell, that's different! That's a pop song now, Little Vi! That's *good!*" How
good it was became apparent on the following Saturday
night, when Sam Phillips took a demo of his new record
over to Dewey Phillips at WHBQ. Dewey had premiered
other Sun releases; he was always willing to give the local
product a spin. Elvis's record posed a problem, however,
because Dewey programmed nothing but black singers. As
he and Sam Phillips were discussing this difficulty, Dewey
got the idea of calling in another, younger, DJ, who was
preparing his morning broadcast. This was Wink Martindale, later well known as a quiz show MC. Martindale
offers a good description of what happened on this famous
night.

"Dewey called me in after Sam brought the record down

to get my opinion. He played it for me. I thought the guy
was black. Sam said, 'No, he's not black. He's white. He
drives a truck for Crown Electric.' Then, he told the story
of how Elvis had come in to make a record for his mother's
birthday and so forth. He told me, 'We've been working
for a year and a half to get something commercial.' Dewey
had some hesitancy about playing the record because he
played nothing but race music. Finally, around nine-fifteen
or nine-thirty, he put it on the air. The results were incredible.

"You have to understand that Dewey always took a lot
of requests and even talked to people on the air. This was
before TV, and every kid in Memphis was listening to him.
This night the switchboard lit up like a Christmas tree.
Dewey would play 'Blue Moon Over Kentucky,' then turn
it over and play 'That's All Right Mama.' It was just those
two sides for the rest of the evening. Finally, Dewey said
to Sam, 'Get that guy down here!' Sam got in touch with
Elvis's mom."

Gladys Presley recalled in 1956 that Elvis "fixed the
radio that night and told us to leave it on that station.
Then he went to the movies. I guess he was just too nervous
to listen." When Phillips reached Gladys, Dewey Phillips
got on the line and yelled, "You just get that cottonpickin'
son of yours over here to the station. I want him on the
air." Gladys was thrilled. "I ran over and I hugged Vernon
and I suppose I cried a little bit. Then we both went looking
for Elvis."

Elvis had retreated with a friend to the dark security
of the Suzore 2. When he spied his mother going down the
aisle searching for him, he whispered: "Mama, what's happening?" "Plenty, son," said Gladys, "but it's all good."
Then Gladys and Vernon took the boys over to the radio
station on the mezzanine of the Chisca Hotel. When Elvis
came into the studio, Dewey Phillips barked: "Sit down.
I'm gone interview you." "Mr. Phillips," trembled Elvis,
"I don't know nuthin' bout bein' interviewed." "Just don't
say nuthin' dirty," snapped Phillips.

Many years later Phillips told a writer: "I asked him
where he went to high school. He said, 'Humes.' I wanted
to get that out because a lot of people listening had thought

he was colored. Finally, I said, 'All right, Elvis, thank you very much.' 'Aren't you gone interview me?' he asked. 'I already have,' I said. 'The mike's been open the whole time.' He broke out in a cold sweat."

The next month produced a flurry of developments in Elvis's catapulting career. Five thousand orders for the record were booked in the first week after it was played on the air. Officially released on July 19, by the end of the month it was Number Three on Memphis's country and western chart. Immediately a swarm of people approached Elvis to seek some financial advantage from the newly fledged performer. Sam Phillips advised Elvis to sign a ten percent deal with Scotty Moore as booking agent to discourage the sharks. Phillips also had the good idea of calling a local disc jockey named Bob Neal, who was promoting a country show at the Overton Park Shell, to ask if there was a spot on the program for Elvis. Neal asked what it would cost him. Phillips said Elvis would work for free just for the publicity. Neal countered that they better get him in the union and pay scale, which was virtually nothing. Phillips then got together with Joe Cuoghi, who owned Popular Tunes, a record store on Poplar Avenue, and they split the cost of an ad in the paper showing a cut of Elvis's head and advertising his appearance as if he were the star of the show and the headliner, Slim Whitman, were just an added attraction.

On the night of July 30, 1954, Elvis Presley made his real debut as a public performer. The Shell in Overton Park is a small acoustic mirror placed on a shallow but broad stage at the bottom of an amphitheater cut into a hillside and furnished with long benches. Elvis had his turn at the commencement of the program. Walking on-stage with Scotty Moore and Bill Black, he waited till Scotty had plugged in and then kicked off with "That's All Right Mama," giving the tune everything he had. No sooner did he start singing, than he began to hear a lot of shouting and screeching from the audience. Too obsessed with going over big to worry what was causing the noise, he kept on singing and banging his guitar till he got through the tune. Then, after the applause, he launched into "Blue Moon." Again, there was a lot of unexplained noise from the crowd. When Elvis finished this time, he discovered that he had stopped the show cold. The audience was demanding an encore. As Elvis huddled with the band, he demanded: "What's makin' 'em holler so much?" "It was your leg, man!" Scotty and Bill told him, laughing. "It was the way you were shakin' your left leg. That's what got 'em screamin'."

Chapter 9

The Hillbilly Cat

THE BIGGEST payoff Elvis received from his first hit was a shot at the most prestigious country music show in America: *Grand Ole Opry*. As with everything else in the career of Elvis Presley, this overnight hop to the top of the country jamboree circuit was an unprecedented short circuit of the usual laborious course which commenced typically on some little hillbilly station out in the sticks, then worked up to one of the popular regional shows, like the *Wheeling Jamboree* or the *Louisiana Hayride,* until, finally, the aspiring star reached the oldest and most successful program of them all, broadcast from the capital of country music, Nashville. What an audition for the *Opry* offered was a chance to become an *Opry* regular: one of the more than a hundred performers who appeared at least twenty times a year, receiving in addition to a fee of about forty dollars the right to use the name of the *Opry* in all their publicity and to be booked by the *Opry*'s Artist Service Bureau on the tours that played to millions of people every year.

Though the *Opry* represented the summit of aspiration for any true country act, it was a highly unsuitable showcase for Elvis Presley. During the course of its thirty-year history, the *Opry* had become a bastion of conservatism. Its audience was comprised of old people and kids, with nary a teenager in attendance. The program had a deliberately old-fashioned barn dance atmosphere that relied heavily on nostalgia for the good ole days. Only one black man had ever been a regular, and there was a strict taboo against the use of drums on the *Opry* stage. Booking Elvis Presley with his long hair, lurid clothes and rhythm and blues style into this house was like throwing him into the lion's den.

September 25, 1954, the date of Elvis's first and only performance on the show, was selected by Sam Phillips because it coincided with the release of Elvis's second record: "I Don't Care if the Sun Don't Shine" coupled with "Good Rockin' Tonight." On the morning of that memorable day, Elvis, Scotty, Bill, Sam Phillips and Marion Keisker piled into two cars and drove the two hundred miles from Memphis to Nashville, stopping finally in the alley behind the famous old Ryman Auditorium. A relic of the religious revivals of the late nineteenth century, the Ryman is a forbidding-looking brick and stone Romanesque structure suggesting a cross between a church and a prison. The fan-shaped interior is filled with steeply-raked curved wooden benches dimly lit by bullet-shaped painted-glass windows. Elvis, who had imagined the pantheon of country pops as a more resplendent place, spent the afternoon wandering around the quaint old building exclaiming: "You mean this is what I've been dreaming about all these years!"

Jim Denny, the truculent manager of the *Opry,* refused to allow Elvis to plug his new record. He insisted that the young singer perform the two songs that had already been successful. He also raised hell because Elvis hadn't brought his "full band"! The show divided then, as now, into half-hour segments, each one presided over by one of the reigning stars. Elvis was assigned to the portion MC'ed by the current hero of country music, Hank Snow. The feisty little Snow would soon learn to know Elvis only too well; at this time, he had never heard of him. When the time came to make the introduction, he snapped: "What's your name?" "Elvis Presley, sir," came the answer. "No," Snow snorted, "I mean what name do you sing under?"

Chet Atkins, destined soon to become the organizer of

Elvis's recording sessions at Nashville, caught his first glimpse of the new star that night. He was shocked by Elvis's appearance. "I couldn't get over that eye shadow he was wearing," recalls Atkins with a sly smile. "It was like seein' a couple of guys kissin' in Key West." Atkins remembers Elvis going over well with the audience. Unfortunately, he provoked the ire of the choleric Denny, who voiced his disgust bluntly. As soon as the show was over, Denny told Elvis: "We don't do that nigger music around here. If I were you, I'd go back to driving a truck."

All the way home to Memphis, he cried hot tears. Monday morning, he was right back where Denny said he should be: driving a truck for Crown Electric.

The disaster at Nashville was soon offset by a solid success on the *Opry*'s rival show, the *Louisiana Hayride.* In fact, Elvis could have begun his radio career with triumph instead of defeat if it hadn't been for Sam Phillips's failure of judgment in booking him on the *Opry.* The *Hayride* was the logical choice for Elvis because in its short six-year history it had proven itself just as open and receptive to new talent as the *Opry* had been closed and scornful toward novelty. The great Hank Williams had gotten his start on the *Hayride,* as had Webb Pierce, Slim Whitman, Jim Reeves, Faron Young and so many others that the show had been tagged "The Cradle of the Stars."

The *Hayride* was presented in the massive Shreveport Municipal Auditorium, which has a seating capacity of about 3500. The set for the broadcasts was a big painted drop depicting a barn and silo set against a country landscape and overhung by a huge spreading tree whose leaves were glued on a hanging border. On the front of the barn was painted in bold letters, "LOUISIANA HAYRIDE" and the call letters of the station that produced the show, KWKH. The format for the three-hour program was a succession of fifteen-minute sequences, each one featuring one of the regular performers on the show.

It was early in the program when the announcer, Frank Page, introduced Elvis. "Just a few weeks ago," he said, "a young man from Memphis, Tennessee, recorded a song on the Sun label; and, in just a matter of weeks, that record has skyrocketed right up the charts. It's really doing well all over the country. He's only nineteen years old. And he's a singer who's forging a new style. *Elvis Presley!* Let's give him a hand! [Applause] Elvis, are you geared up with your band to let us hear your songs?" Elvis was not only geared up but wired up. His voice, so high, so rural, so charged with nervous tension, raced along as he replied: "I'd like to say how happy we are to appear on the *Louisiana Hayride*. And we're gonna do a song for you—[to Page] you got anything else to say? We're gonna do a song for you we got on Sun Records that goes like this...." Then Elvis and his boys were off and running, shouting and strumming "That's All Right Mama."

So warm was their reception that Elvis and the Blue Moon Boys—as they were starting to call themselves— were invited back the following week and offered a one-year contract. The agreement stipulated that they would work a forty-eight-week session, with weekends off at the discretion of the management. Remuneration was "scale": eighteen dollars for the leader and twelve dollars for the sidemen. In other words, Elvis and his two men were expected to drive four hundred miles down from Memphis and four hundred miles back every weekend to spend the most valuable night of the week working on the *Hayride* for a grand total of fifty-four dollars!

The real compensation lay in the fact that Elvis would soon become a familiar name in the "territories"—Texas, Louisiana, Arkansas—where everyone listened to the *Hayride*. He would be able to pick up a lot of bookings in the area and also participate in the package shows that were constantly put together by various promoters who drew on the pool of talent that had been assembled by the *Hayride*. Eventually, Elvis would work every small town in the region, becoming especially popular in Texas, where he played a five-day tour at least once a month, opening, say, in Wichita Falls and playing one-nighters in Bryan, Conroe, Austin and Gonzales; or opening in Shreveport and moving west to Paris, San Marcos, Austin and Nacogdoches. It was no accident, therefore, that Elvis Presley's first fame was in this part of the country and that his first fan club was organized in Dallas.

Radio was the real foundation of Elvis's success. Radio

put him before a large listening public at a time when he had only a few records. Radio broadcast these records far beyond the limited advertising and distribution powers of Sun Records. Radio inspired local bookers to engage Elvis. Radio even spread Elvis's story by affording him a chance in every town he played to get on a local DJ show and give an interview. As we shall see soon, though Elvis came to fame in the age of television, it was always radio that did the basic work of spreading the Presley gospel.

All through the fall and winter of 1954–55, Elvis continued to record at Sun. It is unfortunate that we cannot accompany him through these legendary sessions, but there is no way to reconstruct his progress in detail. As so many of the songs display the same devices of performance, however, we are justified in taking them as a whole and discussing them as a consistent body of work. As such, they stand in marked contrast to the recordings Elvis made even in his first year with RCA. Indeed, it is widely felt today that the Sun records represent the best of Elvis Presley and that the moment he shifted to Victor, the quality of his work became markedly commercial. What then distinguishes the Sun records and makes them superior?

The first thing one has to say is that they are not all superior. The slow ballads, like "I Love You Because," "Harbor Lights," "Blue Moon," etc., are distinctly inferior not only to the rhythm tunes but to the ballads that Elvis recorded as early as 1957. The poise, the vocal control, even the quality of voice demanded by ballad singing were obviously resources that Elvis did not command at the commencement of his career. What we are talking about when we say that the Sun records are his best are only the rhythm songs.

What makes these performances so interesting is their extreme eccentricity. They are extremely playful, witty and inventive. Every tune is cast in a different mold, which usually has nothing to do with the original. Each song sets running through Elvis's mind a stream of musical associations that constitute a kind of fantasia inspired by the song. The basic appeal is, therefore, to the musical imagination. To characterize these performances in terms of

mere energy or rhythm or any ethno-musical quality is
wrong. The performances are densely detailed, quirky
with oddity, sometimes downright funny. The reason they
don't wear thin, as do Elvis's later and more famous recordings, is the same reason why jazz recordings hold the
attention through dozens of playings: The performances
are highly spontaneous and have the not easily exhausted
suggestiveness of brilliant sketchwork. Essentially, they
are play: the play of high spirits that sends ideas shooting
in every direction like sparks. They might even be considered the comic flip side to the even denser and more
suggestive blues fantasias of that other brilliant young
recording genius, Robert Johnson.

The clue to the esthetic of all these sunny sides is in
the false start that Elvis makes on "Milkcow Boogie." He
commences this song by singing in the style of an old
country bluesman, mimicking the tintype vocal quality,
phrasing and tempo. Then, after a few bars, he breaks off
abruptly and exclaims: "Hold it, fellas! That don't *move*
me. Let's get real, real gone for a change!" Then, they take
off again, doing a green-apple quickstep that transforms
the tune into a headlong rhythm song. Elvis rides the vocal
line like a bucking bronco, improvising freely as he dashes
along. What he is saying, in effect, is that the time has
come to jazz up the old blues. Yet, the truth is that twenty
years before he made this recording, jazz musicians were
performing the same trick with tunes that they would play
in conventional style and then swing. Twenty or thirty
years before swing, the trick would have been to rag the
tune. Back around the turn of the century, as Jelly Roll
Morton demonstrated on a classic Library of Congress recording, New Orleans musicians turned a French Qua-
drille into "Tiger Rag." In fine, what Elvis is doing in his
Sun records is repeating instinctively that process of making music new by recharging its rhythm that has characterized every stylistic revolution in the history of twentieth-century pops. This instinctive compliance with the
deepest pattern in our popular musical culture gives the
Sun sides an archetypal quality.

As to the distinction between the Sun records and those

Elvis made in his first years for RCA, the distinguishing difference is not vocal or technical or emotional: It is mental. Elvis is much more creative at the commencement of his career. He is much more lighthearted. He's having fun and coming up with an endless stream of amusing ideas. Instead of laboring to copy a hit by Little Richard or masticating a piece of musical bubblegum, he's sending up a lot of old or old-fashioned tunes that don't deserve to be treated seriously. This prevailing tone of high-spirited mockery explains also why he fails so completely with the ballads. Not only does he lack the poise and control they demand; he doesn't genuinely sympathize with them. He has to put on an act when he mouths these trashy complaints. It's hard to be a great crooner at the age of nineteen.

In November 1954, Elvis got a call from the promoter who had booked him on the Overton Shell show, Robert Neal Hobgood. Bob Neal was one of the best-known public personalities in Memphis and its environs. Broadcasting from the local country station, WMPS, he was on the air twice a day with two very popular shows. In the early, early bright, from five to eight A.M., he entertained the folks from two hundred miles around with hillbilly records, cornball jokes and ukelele solos on the *Bob Neal Farm Show*. At noon, he was back on the air for an hour with the *High Noon Roundup*, a show divided into fifteen-minute segments, including one that featured the Blackwood Brothers. There was a studio audience for this show. Seated among that little audience was often the young Elvis Presley, who during his lunch break would bop over to the station in the basement of the Peabody Hotel. In the afternoons and evenings, Neal would do what he called his "promotions." These were little country music shows which he staged within a hundred-mile radius of Memphis. The routine was invariable. In the late afternoon, Neal, his wife, Helen, and the oldest of his five children, Sonny, would take off in their Lincoln and drive down to, say, Hernando, Mississippi or Eldorado, Arkansas. There, at the local schoolhouse, they would meet two or three second- or third-string acts from *Grand Ole Opry*, who were eager to work any date just to gain the experience and exposure.

Helen would sell tickets at the door: fifty cents for children, one dollar for adults. Sonny would hawk glossy souvenir pictures of the "stars." Bob Neal would be the show's MC, warming up the house with the same corny patter and ukelele playing he did on the air. After the show was over, Neal would give the school its cut for the use of the auditorium, divide the rest of the take between himself and the other performers, then dive gratefully into the back seat of his car to get some sleep in anticipation of his show early the following morning.

As if this were not enough hustling for one man, Neal also ran a record store that bore his name on Main Street, next door to the Warner Theater, and operated a management agency at 160 Union Avenue called Memphis Promotions. It was while wearing his manager's hat that Neal called Elvis. Neal had been impressed by the young singer's success on the *Louisiana Hayride.* Now he wanted to know whether he was correct in assuming that Sam Phillips had Elvis tied up in the neat little business package. When he asked Elvis whether he had a manager, the answer was no. This was not quite accurate, of course, but Elvis was not going to pass up the chance to get a real professional manager just because he had a little deal going with Scotty. Elvis and Neal came to an agreement immediately and Scotty made no objections to the arrangement.

The deal was quite conventional. Bob Neal was to undertake all the duties of a personal manager: pushing records, booking dates, handling business arrangements. In return, he was to receive fifteen percent commission. He suggested also that the boys take twenty percent off the top and set it aside as a promotion fund. D. J. Fontana, the drummer Elvis had picked up on the *Hayride,* would continue receiving his hundred dollars a week in salary and Elvis, Scotty and Bill would divide the balance according to their usual split: fifty percent to Elvis; twenty-five percent each to Scotty and Bill. The term of the contract was one year. It was at this time, in November 1954, that Elvis finally quit his job at Crown Electric.

When Neal started calling up DJs to promote Elvis's records, he found that his new client did not fit the bill.

The country jocks said that Elvis sounded like a blues act. The R & B jocks said that Elvis sounded too country for their shows. Gradually, Neal realized that Elvis's records would not sell his talent. Elvis's personal appearances would have to create the demand for the records.

These appearances now became more frequent. Neal had the schoolhouse circuit down pat. He could book a lot of locations just on the strength of his own name. He could advertise the shows on his radio programs. He had a lot of acts who would open the shows for fifty dollars. Soon business was humming. In the period of a year, Elvis and the Blue Moon Boys played close to two hundred dates.

Once Elvis got busy on the road, he had to buy a car. Naturally, nothing but a Cadillac would do. Though he could only afford a second-hand machine (financed through Bob Neal), the day he got his first "Cad" Elvis felt that he had attained one of the great goals of his life. He sat up half the night gazing at the car from his hotel window.

Sad to say, on a run down to Texarkana not long afterward the rear of the car caught fire and the treasured vehicle had to be abandoned. With the insurance, Elvis went out and got another Cadillac. He had it painted pink and black, which now became his personal colors. Next, he bought his parents a pink and white Ford. By this point, the boy was launched on a career of car buying that probably has no equal in the annals of our car-crazy country.

What sort of show did Elvis put on in these early days? It was a country show, of course. It was also a corny show because both Elvis and Bill Black regarded themselves as comedians. Black, a big burly man with a big bull fiddle, did all the bits that were standard for entertainers who played "dog-house" bass. He twirled and slapped the instrument with all his might. He straddled and rode it around the stage as he played. He mugged and clowned, fighting hard some nights to break down the audience's resistance to Elvis's strange garb and no less strange style of performing. As the boys had to do forty-five minutes onstage, they couldn't confine themselves to their records. They ran the charts, doing all the current hits. The only thing that remained constant from one show to another was Elvis's determination to get to the audience and drive it wild.

In the country districts, deep in the Bible Belt, Elvis would work himself to the point of exhaustion, trying to get a rise from the house. When he had completed his frenzied performance, the staid farm folk would applaud politely and then come up to the stage to chat with the man whom they heard on the radio every morning between milking and breakfast, Bob Neal. They would talk to the DJ as if he were a preacher and ask him about his family as if he were a friend. They had no eyes for that wild spark, Elvis Presley. When the shows hit the bigger towns, however, the reaction would be entirely different. It was one night at Little Rock that Bob Neal saw an audience react so extravagantly to Elvis that it set his mind running on the stories he had read years before about the bobby-soxers swooning over Frank Sinatra.

Many nights on the way home, Elvis would sit beside Helen Neal and ask her earnestly: "Do you think I'll make it?" He wasn't talking about his singing career. From the jump, Elvis wanted to be a movie star. Mrs. Neal remembers Elvis's ideal as being someone like Clark Gable. Sonny Neal, three years Elvis's junior but a lot closer to him than his mother, recollects Elvis's hero accurately. Elvis aspired to be the second Rudolph Valentino. He fancied himself as a Latin lover. That was the real meaning of the famous sideburns. That was also the reason why at this time Elvis posed for beefcake shots, stripped to the waist with his hair tousled and his face set in a sullen, sultry leer. He even began to tell people that he had an Italian ancestor on his mother's side of the family.

This surprising identification with the film idol of the silent era, a man who was dead before Elvis was born, is the first unmistakable sign that Elvis had discovered the essence of his appeal and was starting to cultivate a corresponding image. It is also a sign of prescience, for nothing better defines Elvis's future role than the formula: teen Valentino. If you add to the basic image of the sultry Latin lover the further garnishings of an erotic style of music and dance, the tango for the twenties, rock 'n' roll for the fifties, the parallel is perfect. Soon Elvis would even have crow-black hair.

Elvis's sexual appeal brought a lot of girls around to the parking lot. Mrs. Neal used to pull her son and Elvis into the car right after the shows. Actually, she had no cause for alarm. Elvis behaved in a very puritanical manner. Sonny recalls: "Elvis was really a prude. Girls lost their appeal for him when they were easy to get. He always said that he wanted to marry a virgin." Though Elvis was uptight about girls, he was often threatened by tough teenagers who resented the way he excited their girls. It was largely to counter these threats that Elvis began taking along Red West, who would drive the car and act as bodyguard, just for the fun of getting out of town.

Once Elvis began to make some money, he bought the two things he most desired: a new pink Cadillac and a little house for the family. A big new car and a private home were every American's birthright in the fifties, like forty acres and a mule in an earlier era. The pink Cadillac was Elvis's personal symbol of success. He sang a song titled "Pink Cadillac" on his show, and when he recorded "Baby, Let's Play House," he put a pink Cadillac into the lyrics. (No one, incidentally, has asked why he made this change. The reason is that in the original version by Arthur Gunter, the lyrics ran: "You may go to college, You may go to school, You may get religion." References to religion were out of the question at Sun Records, whose proprietor regarded himself as something of a preacher. Phillips must have told Elvis to invent something new to replace the offensive line; Elvis inserted what he took to be the supreme symbol of hipness: a pink Cad.)

Most young boys fresh out of the slums would have behaved exactly as did Elvis Presley in buying a flashy car. How many, one wonders, would have taken their first real money and put it into a house? Here we see the other side of Elvis, the side that always contrasted so strongly with the flamboyant clothes and the punk attitude: the profound attachment to the notion of home and the longing to have a home of which he could be proud. This first house was a little brick bungalow stuck out on the pavement running along Lamar Avenue near the Airways Theater.

The house still stands, somewhat disguised by an addition
to its front, serving now as a day nursery. Walking through
the four rooms of the original building, you feel like you're
in a doll's house. The Presleys had no more space here
than in their apartment at the Courts, but the house symbolized a great change in the family's fortunes and status.
Now the one-time indigents were tax-paying property
holders. They had fulfilled the ideal of the Memphis Housing Authority: "From slums to public housing to private
ownership."

No sooner did the fortunes of the family improve than
Vernon Presley quit his job at the paint factory. Ostensibly, he was going to look for another job that wouldn't
put such a strain on his bad back, but he never found that
new job. The Neals were very friendly with the Presley
family at this point; they tried constantly to find work for
Vernon. Soon, however, they realized that no matter what
the job, Vernon was sure to quit after just a day or two.
One day when Bob Neal was talking to Elvis, he was
astonished to hear the youngster say that he was eager
to succeed because his folks were getting too old to work.
At the time, Vernon was not yet forty! The point of the
remark is not that Elvis exaggerated his parents' age, but
that Vernon exaggerated his disabilities so that he would
not be expected to work any longer. As matters turned out,
Vernon Presley never did have to go back to work. He
retired, in effect, at thirty-eight.

In February 1955, Bob Neal booked Elvis and the Blue
Moon Boys on a ten-day tour of the Southwest with a
number of well-established country acts, all traveling under the supervision of the show's headliner, Hank Snow.
The association which commenced at this time with Hank
Snow Enterprises was destined to continue until Elvis
broke away to headline his own show. Far more important
is the fact that through his work on the Hank Snow tours
Elvis first came into close contact with the booker of these
tours: Colonel Thomas Andrew Parker.

Chapter 10

The Flying Dutchman

COLONEL TOM PARKER is not a man about whom the world has ever harbored any doubts. Brash, flamboyant, out-front, the Colonel has always declared himself for just what he is: an old-time carny. The ideal portrait of the Colonel would pose him on the bally platform of a freak show, thrusting his elephant-head cane aggressively against a lurid, grotesque poster of Elvis, the Two-Headed Boy (a papier-mâché dummy), while bellowing through a mouth stopped intermittently with an enormous cigar: "This monstrous mistake of Mother Nature was born just as live as you and I. That's right, folks, born *alive!*"

The last great embodiment of that classic style of American show business epitomized by P. T. Barnum and his famous motto—"There's a sucker born every minute"—Colonel Parker is a figure that not only lives but looms inside the imagination. *Bigger than life!*—as he might ballyhoo himself—he seems to have stepped out of the gaslit, tanbark past or sprung from the rich, spermy soil of American folklore. Nothing could be more American than Tom Parker, unless it were the man with whom the Colonel is invariably identified, W. C. Fields.

Perhaps it is this mythic aura that makes so many people regard the Colonel as a lovable old rogue. Or perhaps his charm lies in the fact that he has always been so blatant about his tricks and impostures. Instead of trying to cover up his origins in the flimflam world of the carnival, the Colonel has always gloried in his past, boasting, like Barnum, of his chicanery. Writers have filled up whole chapters with tales of the Colonel's cunning. Millions of people have chuckled over such stories as how he sold foot-long hotdogs with no meat in the middle; how he painted sparrows yellow and sold them for canaries; how he put an electric hot plate under his dancing chickens, making them high step to "Turkey in the Straw"; or how he strewed manure over the exits from his tent show so that he could rent ponies to suckers who were afraid to step in the shit.

Reading over these endless accounts of shams and shucks, shifts and slights, shticks and scams, you recognize in the Colonel at last a primitive and elemental character, the hero of many folk cultures from the ancient Greeks to the nineteenth-century Yankees—the *trickster*. As for his literary archetype: How about something coarse and Germanic, like *Till Eulenspiegel and His Merry Pranks?* To really grasp the essence of the Colonel, however, you must descend even below the level of the mythic and folkloric to the primordial plane of the animal kingdom. Beneath his identity as the flashy carny, the merry prankster or the dissembling trickster, the Colonel possesses a totemic identity as the elephant man. The elephant is his personal symbol and fetish.

When you enter his office, for example, you discover before his desk two stools positioned to receive visitors. Each stool is supported on upholstered elephant legs terminating in big round feet with enormous toenails. As you gaze around the room, you see many statues and figurines of elephants carved in ivory, alabaster, marble and hardwoods. The Colonel's cane, never far from his side, is topped with an elephant's head. The elephant is, of course, a symbol of fortune. With his trunk down, he represents bad luck; with the trunk raised, good luck. All the Colonel's elephants hold their trunks arched aloft in triumph.

The elephant also figures largely in the Colonel's history. There is the story, for instance, about the time the Colonel was stranded in a town without enough money to pay his hotel bill. What does he do? What do characters in folktales do? They go out and find their totem animal, who soon rescues them from their predicament. This is precisely what the Colonel did. He found an elephant— such heroes always know how to summon their magic beasts—and strapped upon its massive back an old-fashioned icebox. Then he solicited ads and samples from local food merchants and paraded the beast through town bedecked with the stores' names and displaying their wares in the big wooden box. When the promotion was complete, Colonel had the money to pay his bill and enough food to sustain him for days to come.

Using the elephant as an attention-getting device has always been standard operating procedure for Colonel Parker. Back in the days when he was managing Eddy Arnold, the Colonel would arrive at the annual convention of the country music DJs at the Andrew Jackson Hotel in Nashville leading an elephant. Hobbling the beast outside the hotel entrance, the Colonel would drape its sides with an immense cloth reading "Never Forget Eddy Arnold." Even when the days of such promotions were far behind him, Colonel never lost his attachment to that legendary creature, the pachyderm. During the filming of *Follow That Dream* at Crystal River, Florida, in the sixties, Colonel insisted on visiting an ancient elephant he had known in his carnival days. The old elephant man could not rest content until he had fed the animal, which gave signs of remembering him: wagging its huge head and shuffling its ponderous feet in their shackles.

Yes, the Colonel and the elephant have a great deal in common. The elephant's vast bulk symbolizes the Colonel's gross corporeality. The elephant's thick hide represents the Colonel's imperviousness to pain or shame. The elephant's reputation for wisdom and mnemonic power correlates with the Colonel's sagacity and nostalgia. Even the elephant's longevity, its air of eld, is highly appropriate to the Colonel, who, even when he was a relatively young man, referred to himself always as the

"ole Colonel." Nor should it ever be forgotten that when
enraged the elephant is a very dangerous animal, especially the rogue elephant, the elephant that has left
the herd to roam abroad, terrorizing the countryside. Yet,
it's also highly characteristic of Colonel Parker, a classic
wise guy, that he should poke fun at his own cherished
totem. Once somebody asked the Colonel, "What's all this
stuff about elephants never forgetting?" Glancing keenly
over his cigar, the Colonel snapped: "What do they have
to remember?"

Just about everything that constitutes Colonel Parker's identity and modus operandi can be associated with
the carnival. The particular carnival for which the Colonel worked was, appropriately enough, the greatest in
the world. The Royal American Shows was the brain
spawn of the King of the Carnies, the late Carl Sedlmayr. Orphaned as a child in Nebraska, Sedlmayr struck
out on his own as a teenager and wound up with a job in
a touring carnival. Graduating from freak show operator
to carnival boss in 1921, Sedlmayr went to work to make
his show the best and most up-to-date on the road, voicing
his goal in one gruff phrase: "I want everything *massive*—
bigger'n everybody!"

Sedlmayr revolutionized the carnival business by
carting out to the most remote rural districts the fabulous
new thrill rides that were found hitherto only in the
innovative amusement parks of the metropolitan East.
Touring with huge roller coasters, airplane spins, loop-
the-loops, and Dodge-em cars, the Carny King pitched
Luna Park every night in the hinterlands of western
Canada or the American Midwest. Perceiving that "lights
draw people like bugs to a window," he decreed that
every ride must be outlined in garish neon. His competitors snickered at the thought of all that fragile glass
tubing being shattered in the rough and tumble of travel
by rail. Sedlmayr solved the problem by adding to his
train a wagon that housed a self-contained neon tube
factory.

The atmosphere in which the Colonel grew to maturity
was not, therefore, the stale air of some sleazy little tent
show. Colonel Parker started in the big time. Rallying

every spring at Tampa (where Parker had his home for sixteen years), over a thousand people would board the bright red-and-white pullmans of the Royal American's private train. Seventy cars, including many double-length flatcars, were required to haul this steel and canvas city, with its knocked-down rides, tractors, trucks, cranes, shops and motor-generators, with enough juice to light up a city of fifty thousand.

The Shows' itinerary was designed to carry it from coast to coast in concert with the annual fairs held in Canada and the United States. (Sedlmayr contrived the title of his carnival so that it would have one word, "Royal," that appealed to Canadians and another word, "American," that would draw his own countrymen.) The opening date was always the Memphis Cotton Carnival in May. (Elvis Presley, a typical carnival sucker, never missed an appearance of the Royal American. Colonel Parker had left the carnival, however, by the time the teenage Elvis began to throw baseballs at wooden bottles.) From Memphis the mighty train would roll north and west to St. Louis and then further north to Davenport, Iowa, for the Shriners Jubilee. Crossing the Canadian border, it would play the Red River Exhibition at Winnipeg and the regional fairs at Brandon, Calgary, Edmonton, Saskatoon, Regina and Port Arthur—Fort William. At the height of summer, the red-and-white cars would be rolling through the Midwest, heading for the Wisconsin State Fair at Milwaukee, the Minnesota State Fair at Minneapolis—St. Paul, the Mid-America Fair at Topeka and all the other state fairs in Kansas, Oklahoma, Arkansas and Louisiana. By the time the carnival had reached the Gulf Coast, it would be November and time to head back to Tampa for a quiet winter of repairing the equipment and repainting the rig.

Picture now the Royal American Shows as it looked in the thirties when Tom Parker was a young man. Arriving in town at a railroad siding, the carnival would form up in a parade and march through the city with its band blaring and all its performers in full costume. Arriving at the fairgrounds, the first job would be laying out the midway to the length of a mile and a half. Lining it would be countless booths and stands, wagons and tents manned by pitchmen, "sticks" (shills), barkers, showgirls, ticket sellers and chow slingers. Though the major attraction was the rides, the carnival offered all the traditional tent shows.

There was the Hawaiian Revue tent, with its grass-skirted, bra-topped dancers, ukelele plinking, aloha-shirted musicians and spectacular, near-naked fire-eaters. The White Revue tent offered a typical vaudeville show, full of hoofers, singers, novelty acts and a pit band. The Colored Revue tent was Negro vaudeville, which meant you could find everything from an old-time blues star down on her luck or a couple of clownish comics like Butter 'n' Beans to a brilliant jazz performer. The Illusion Show tent focused on spooky apparitions and truncated ladies. The Freak Show tent featured a dude who swallowed a glowing neon tube. The Midget Show was a big doll house, with all the midgets seated in their little chairs waiting to be introduced by the "head of the house," a testy, mean-faced little fellow with slicked-down hair, bow tie and Buster Brown shoes, who gave his spiel in a high-pitched voice without ever once losing the look of a chronic headache victim. The last and most exciting of these side shows was the Motordome: a nightmarish wooden funnel around which motorcycles roared until their riders were spinning at an angle of ninety degrees to the perpendicular.

Where was the young Tom Parker in this vast and complicated entertainment, which, as we know, is also a very tight, exclusive and hierarchical society? Accounts differ: Some place Parker in a "grab joint," dishing out cotton candy and red caramel apples; others put him in charge of the "pie car" or company commissary, a rather responsible job for a young man. All we know for sure is that after his marriage the Colonel and his wife were a fixture in the carnival for many years. Chances are that having joined the show when he was in his early twenties and having remained with it for nearly a decade, Tom Parker worked at a number of jobs that took him through the whole labyrinthine operation and gave him a marvelous grass-roots education in show business.

More important than what the Colonel did in the carnival is what the carnival did for the Colonel. Some of its lessons are obvious. The Colonel's whole notion of publicity, for one thing, comes straight out of the circus-carnival tradition of ballyhoo and bunkum. When the Colonel first started managing Elvis, he gave the new star of rock 'n' roll the whole carny treatment: elephants and midgets, banners and posters. Parker would get into the ticket booth to hustle like a pitchman or stand out in the lobby holding a fistful of programs on high like a hawker. Even in later years, after Elvis had earned hundreds of millions of dollars and become a household word the world over, every time he opened at Las Vegas, the Colonel would set to work like some hard-pressed front man papering the town before the arrival of the show. He would expend prodigious amounts of time, energy and money lining the highways with billboards, covering the placard sites with quarter sheets, transforming the hotel lobby into a forest of banners and posters. The radio would blare spot announcements every half hour and the newspapers were full of ads for the show. All this ballyhoo for a performer who had sold out the entire engagement weeks before he arrived in the city.

Ballyhoo, however, was the least of the lessons the Colonel learned in the carnival. Far more important was the education he received in manipulating the public. Most people don't realize that when Barnum made his famous remark, he was using the word "sucker" in its professional sense, as the term employed in the circus-carnival world for "customer." So basic is the notion of deception—of hokum, bunko, and bamboozle—to this world that no other concept of the customer exists but that of the *mark*. All the classic yarns of the carnival turn on acts of deception that enable the carny to fleece the sucker by exciting his desires and imposing on his credulity, while offering him nothing truly commensurate with either his expectations or the price he pays for the show. This is the philosophy that Colonel Parker imbibed in his youth and subsequently applied to his management of Elvis Presley.

The most important gift the Colonel developed in his carny days was his remarkable capacity for not only outwitting and getting over the sucker but for reading his mind. An interesting recollection by one of the Colonel's oldest associates has Tom Parker in his early years operating a "mit camp" or palm-reading booth. This sort of activity was forbidden in the Royal American, but it might have been something the Colonel did out of season. Even if the story is false in fact, it is true poetically, for Colonel Parker is a man of extraordinary psychic gifts. He is, for example, an accomplished hypnotist. Often during the years when the Presley organization was condemned to the tedious routine of making movies, Colonel would combine his love of practical jokes with his powers of mind control to produce scenes of irresistible humor.

During the shooting of *Kid Galahad,* for instance, the Colonel hypnotized Elvis's bodyguard, Sonny West, and instructed him to walk up to the film's director, Phil Karlson, and tell him that the movie stank, the acting was horrible, the direction disgusting and the whole production a terrible waste of time and money. As soon as the next break came, big, burly Sonny walked up to the director and launched into this outrageously insulting speech. The director's jaw dropped open in shock and remained hanging there while the Colonel drank in the scene, chuckling deep inside his mountainous belly without betraying his feelings on his face. Finally, Karlson screamed: "Who is this man? Get him off the set!" When the joke was explained to him, the director expressed astonishment that Sonny could have performed the prank at such length without ever once cracking a smile. "He was under hypnosis," explained the Colonel; "he couldn't have done it any other way." Turning to Sonny, the director demanded: "Is this true?" "Yes, sir, it is," avowed Sonny, who could never imagine how he performed all the strange and embarrassing feats he accomplished under the Colonel's direction.

The Colonel's powers as a psychic were not limited to hypnosis. He has suffered for years from a ruptured disc in his spine, which is why he always uses a cane. Yet he would never submit to an operation, preferring to control the sometimes excruciating pain by means of his special mental powers. The Colonel also claims to possess the evil eye. He would often recount to the Guys the story of the boardinghouse lady who hounded him so fiercely that he was compelled finally to do something to which he was profoundly averse. He put a hex on the woman and soon she came to disaster. When the old Colonel, sitting backstage like Tecumseh, leaning on his cane, would tell that tale, Lamar Fike recalls feeling chills running up and down his spine.

Depending on whether you view such capacities as evidence of possession of occult powers or simply as psychological acuity coupled with prodigious willpower, the fact is that the Colonel is a man with an enormous capacity for controlling other men or for hoodwinking them in ways that make them play into his hands. Like any great con man, the Colonel sees everyone as a mark and instinctively prepares to rip him off. Sometimes he gets his way by bluffing; sometimes by playing on the sucker's hopes and fears; sometimes by bullying. Whatever the means, the goal is invariably the same: The Colonel must always get the better of the other man.

Though Colonel has made as much of his chicanery as Jack Benny did of his miserliness or W. C. Fields of his detestation of children, nobody apparently has ever regarded the Colonel with distrust. Quite the contrary: When you talk to the Colonel's business associates, they invariably assure you that the Colonel is the soul of honor, a man whose word is his bond. Indeed, in some instances the Colonel's word has been his bond. The William Morris Agency, for example, represented Elvis throughout his entire career, and its president, Abe Lastfogel, is one of the Colonel's closest associates; yet the agency never had a formal representation agreement with Elvis Presley. In fact, if you believe the story that has been circulated in show business for the past quarter century and is credited even by Elvis's agents at William Morris, Colonel Parker never had a contract with Elvis Presley. All their multimillion-dollar deals were made supposedly on the strength of a handshake. What greater faith could a manager inspire?

Trading on his word, while developing relationships
of total trust, has enabled the Colonel to dispense with
a great many of the accustomed appurtenances of business. Though for the past quarter of a century the ole
Colonel has swum like a sea lion through an ocean of
money, he has contrived to do so without leaving many
more traces than a swimmer in the sea. Though his
signature appears on certain contracts, and he has owned
a couple of companies, he never incorporated officially
until 1974. He rarely writes a check, has never owned
a credit card and insists on paying for everything in cash.
Though he is a big man in a business that is thoroughly
internationalized, the Colonel has never owned a passport. Why doesn't he have a passport? According to the
Colonel, he could not provide the necessary proof of birth
because he was a foundling.

Avoidance of overseas travel—or is it just avoidance
of Immigration and Naturalization?—is paralleled in the
Colonel's life-style with avoidance of legal proceedings.
Though the Colonel is a highly combative man who has
spent many years in a business that generates a lot of
litigation, he has contrived never to be in the position
of suing or being sued in person. In this manner, he has
gone through a long life without ever once appearing in
court.

One other peculiarity of the Colonel's is worth noting
in this connection. He enjoys a reputation as one of the
Internal Revenue Service's very best customers. Where
other men go to great lengths to avoid paying taxes, the
Colonel is so eager to pay his tax bill and so careless of
opportunities to dodge behind shelters that it is said he
overpays the tax man.

When you add up all these eccentricities, they compose
themselves into a pattern that is not altogether unfamiliar. They constitute the low profile of a man who is
eager to have the minimum possible contact with the
authorities. By always making nice with IRS, avoiding
the courts, authorizing no credit investigations and not
subjecting oneself to the scrutiny of the immigration officials, a man may pass a long life in this country without
ever being required to divulge exactly who he is. Yet,

why should any man of Colonel Parker's wealth, power, probity and fame wish to pursue such a strange course?

As far as the Colonel's personal reputation is concerned, it is no less excellent than his reputation as a businessman. He appears to be a faithful husband, married to the same woman now for fifty years: the former Mrs. Marie Ross, née Mott. The Colonel has no children of his own but was always helpful to his wife's son, Bobby Ross, a Tampa public relations man who died of multiple sclerosis in 1977. Though extremely demanding of his employees, Parker has always been exceedingly generous toward them in money matters and retained the loyalty of his key men for as long as twenty-five years. Virtually unique in his profession for having limited himself to a single client, Colonel Parker has always been willing to offer advice and professional counsel to acts and fellow managers from whom he has no expectation of gain. Tommy Sands, for one, profited greatly for many years from the Colonel's discreet advice, as did Ricky Nelson. Though the Colonel is far from being a religious man, he has always made liberal donations to the Roman Catholic church near his official residence at Madison, Tennessee, and acted as a friend to the local priest and nuns.

Neither a drinker nor a doper, Colonel Parker appears to have, apart from work, only two passions. One is eating, which he has done on such a scale that he now tips the scales at three hundred pounds. Over the years, his oval face has melted like a lump of butter into a waffle stack of double chins. His protuberant belly and breasts give him the profile of Buddha in a loud Aloha shirt. His other passion is gambling.

Colonel Parker is a prodigious gambler at roulette and craps. In Las Vegas, where he maintains an apartment year round, he is considered one of the highest rollers in the history of the resort. He averages about ten months a year in the city and an hour a day in the casinos. He does all his gambling in public, though Vegas has opulent private accommodations for high rollers. At roulette, the Colonel likes to make the maximum wager: ten thousand dollars. As a good croupier will make the wheel spin every two minutes, it is possible to lose three hundred thousand dollars an hour. The Colonel's losses are reported to have sometimes exceeded a million dollars in a single month.

Gambling on this scale can be interpreted in many ways. Professional gamblers describe the Colonel as a "dumper"; that is, a man who plays without system or restraint, thus, in effect, throwing his money away. As earning this money has been the whole purpose and pride of the Colonel's life, we are faced here with the familiar paradox of the man whose pleasures invert his normal personality, presenting him in a totally unsuspected character. What could be more perverse than the spectacle of the Colonel, so shrewd, so manipulative, so masterful, submitting himself haplessly to games of chance that entail the minimum amount of skill and maximum amount of luck? No wonder he surrounds himself with so many trunk-up elephants! He has need of them. Actually, these talismans appear to do him no good. No one can ever recall his making a great score. Testing his luck every day, he finds it as uniformly bad at the gaming table as it is good at the bargaining table. The choice of the roulette wheel as his principal diversion is particularly ironic because it summons up the image of a perpendicular wheel of chance that you always find at carnivals. By playing at roulette, the old carny transforms himself into his opposite, the sucker.

Doubtless there is an element of addiction in the Colonel's dedication to gambling. One hears that he cannot keep the wheel out of his mind even when he is far from the casino. Sometimes, he will call from his home in Palm Springs and lay bets by phone. Also, he employs his great power in Las Vegas to increase the hazards of his play. On at least one occasion, he has insisted that the wheel be charged with *two* balls. There is an image to ponder: the man who plays with two balls!

No one doubts the Colonel's capacity to sustain his huge gambling losses, though some have questioned the propriety of incurring such losses in the same hotel with which he had to negotiate on behalf of his client. On the other hand, you don't hear those stories about Colonel Parker and Elvis Presley being owned by the Mob that you hear about so many entertainers in Vegas. Whatever the Colonel's problem, assuming that he has one, it would not appear to be the result of any criminal activity. More than one investigator has checked out the Colonel's record with the law. The finding has invariably been the same: "The man is clean."

Having considered other possible reasons why the Colonel would want to maintain a very low profile vis à vis the government, one comes at last to the possibility that there could be something buried in his past that he does not want to come to light. The Colonel was forty-seven years old when he first became famous through his association with Elvis Presley. It could well be that when the Colonel realized the magnitude of his lucky strike, he made a decision to inter his past and cover his traces permanently.

This view of the matter gains a lot of support when you investigate the Colonel at firsthand. The first name that a knowledgeable journalist crosses off his list of prospective sources is that of the subject himself. The Colonel's routine with would-be interviewers is notorious. He never turns down a request for an interview. What would be the fun in that? Rather, he grins like the shark eyeing the mark and replies graciously, "I'd be delighted to give you an interview. Do you want the short or the long version? The price of the short is twenty-five thousand dollars; the long is one hundred thousand dollars." That takes care of the inquiring reporter.

How about the Colonel's men, those long-term colleagues who have spent as many as twenty-five years by the Colonel's side? The answer is obvious. They are not going to tell you anything that the Colonel hasn't authorized. So a good many more names are scratched off the list. Now, we turn to the ex-employees, generally men who occupied minor positions as glorified go-fers. There are a number of them working still in Hollywood, New York or Las Vegas. When you tell them that you're interested in their experiences with Colonel Parker, they turn to stone. If they're frank, they'll tell you that it might be worth their current job if they talked freely about their former boss. The Man has big ears and long

arms. He's regarded as vindictive. He inspires fear and
rules by fear.

Or, perhaps, you do find some ex-errand boy or old
carnival grifter who doesn't feel vulnerable. What can
you learn from such a man? Just the usual little comic
anecdotes that have been rehearsed countless times. How
the Colonel bluffed this dude or conned that sucker or
how he likes his eggs and sausages in the morning. So
you give up on the go-fers and go to the couple of major
clients that the Colonel represented before his long stint
with Elvis. There's Hank Snow, for one, still wearing his
fancy western duds and sporting the kind of phony-look-
ing toupee that suggested the word "rug." When you
pronounce the name "Tom Parker" in Hank Snow's hearing, he sputters with rage: "I won't say anything for the
man or against the man!" Wham! That ends that interview. So you turn to the other surviving star with whom
Parker enjoyed a long relationship: Eddy Arnold.

Arnold receives you in a little off-the-highway office
on the outskirts of Nashville. The sign on the door reads
Logan County Utility Company. Ruggedly handsome still
at sixty-two, smiling genially as he parks his feet on his
desk as if it were the pot-bellied stove in the country
store, the Tennessee Plowboy appears quite willing to
kick back and run the story of his years with the man
he calls Tom Parker because when Arnold met the Colonel in 1945, he hadn't yet assumed his famous title.

Arnold reaches down into the inexhaustible bag of
stories about how the Colonel wheeled and dealed so that
his client got paid up front or how he cut into the concession operations: all the usual small-time hustles and
tricks that are the Colonel's stock in trade. Finally, growing impatient with this palaver, you pop the key question:
"If the relationship was so happy, why did you fire Parker?" Arnold smiles and waves his hand in dismissal of
the issue. "It was simply a matter of temperament. Tom
is a very flamboyant man. I'm a very conservative man."
With that fatuous remark, the interview concludes.

Once you've had enough of the freeze-out, the clam-
up, the what-he-eats-for-breakfast and how-he-chisels-
his-buck routines, you are free to draw certain conclu-

sions about Colonel Tom Parker. The first and most important finding is that though Parker has spent many years disporting himself inside one of the world's most intently ogled fishbowls, he has managed to deflect any serious attention aimed at himself. Now you see me, now you don't! That's his style. Clearly, he had been very careful to confine his activities to the smallest possible circle of colleagues and coworkers, maintaining these relationships unaltered for a lifetime. Most significantly, he has made it clear to everyone who ever worked for him that the price of talking about him would be a lot higher than anything they might be paid. In a word: The Colonel is impervious to investigation.

Once you abandon the effort to investigate the Colonel directly, there is nothing left to do but review once again the old press reports that are every writer's point of departure. The Parker file, you soon discover, consists for the most part of the same old stories and bits of information (or misinformation) endlessly hashed and rehashed. Much of this material has an apocryphal air and some of the stories—like the familiar yarns about the Colonel and the patent medicine Hadacol—are demonstrably false. What is most remarkable is not the hearsay character of the accounts but the sheer paucity of personal information. One would think he were reading about some legendary showman in the early nineteenth century rather than a living man with offices in Los Angeles and Las Vegas. How Elvis Presley's life was kept secret for so many years is no mystery at all: Elvis was the Howard Hughes of show business, living always behind thick walls of stone and flesh, a virtual recluse from the age of twenty-three. Colonel Parker, on the other hand, is a man who has been constantly visible for thirty-five years and whose work throughout that entire period has entailed continual contacts with the press. How he remained so undisclosed for all this time is quite another story. The ole Colonel turns out to be the best illusionist in the history of the stage. The man without a shadow. The man without a past.

As the Colonel grew a lot more visible after the time he met Elvis, in 1955, the best way to review his history

is to trace it backward from that point, observing where
the solid road of fact becomes the stumbling path of
legend and pure speculation. For the nine years from
1953 back to 1944, Parker managed Eddy Arnold. This
was a relationship that anticipated in several respects
the Colonel's career with Elvis. As with Elvis, so with
Arnold—it was a case of taking a young, virtually unknown singer and developing his career until he reached
stardom. Arnold had appeared on *Grand Ole Opry* and
had cut a few records for RCA when Parker took him
in hand, just as Elvis had performed on the *Louisiana
Hayride* and cut his handful of sides for Sun when the
Colonel hooked him. With Arnold, a far less original and
exciting talent, the climb was slower than with Elvis but
the results were eventually quite impressive. The Tennessee Plowboy recorded many hits, starred on his own
radio show, led his own touring company and eventually
obtained a two-picture contract in Hollywood. Parker's
attitude toward these pictures was prophetic of how he
would manage Elvis's movie career. He told his client:
"The pictures will be lean on artistic quality, but they
will be acceptable as movies." Those words could stand
as the motto of Elvis's entire film oeuvre.

Though Eddy Arnold was not a star of the first magnitude, he prospered greatly under the management of
Tom Parker. What's more, just as he did later with Elvis,
Tom Parker devoted himself body and soul, night and
day, to his only client. As Arnold himself has said: "When
Tom's your manager, he's all you. He lives and breathes
his artist. I once said to him when he was managing me,
'Tom, why don't you get yourself a hobby?' He looked me
straight in the eye and said, 'You're my hobby.'" Why,
then, did Arnold dismiss Parker?

Various stories are told at Nashville. According to one
account, Arnold had developed deep suspicions concerning
Parker. One day in 1953, while they were working at
Las Vegas, Arnold walked into Parker's room and saw
his manager snatch a piece of paper off the table and
conceal it guiltily. Arnold demanded to see the paper.
Parker refused to disclose what he was holding. The men
got into a violent argument, virtually coming to blows.

Not much later, Parker, resting in the garden of his home in Madison, Tennessee, received a telegram from Eddy Arnold. It read: "Your services no longer required. From receipt of this wire consider yourself dismissed."

Prior to his stint as Arnold's manager, the Colonel represented an old-fashioned pop singer in his declining years: Gene Austin, once universally familiar for his recording of "My Blue Heaven." Austin was one of the first generation of twentieth-century American pop singers, along with Henry Burr and Vernon Dalhart, voices known to the current generation only through the time-machine evocations of Tiny Tim. By the time Parker tied in with Austin, only old-timers would pay to hear such a hopelessly dated entertainer. When the war came along, imposing severe restrictions on travel and heavy taxes on entertainment, Austin and Parker gave up the ship.

The title "Colonel," which so well befits Tom Parker, is honorary, of course, having been bestowed on him first in 1948 by the governor of Louisiana, Jimmy Davis, himself a former country singer. The Colonel did have some actual experience of military life when he served in 1930 and 1931 in America's tiny peacetime army. He was stationed at Fort Barrancas, in the mouth of Pensacola Harbor, and at the legendary Schofield Barracks in Hawaii (which explains, most likely, why Elvis Presley, who so rarely gave benefit performances, did two free shows in Honolulu, both for the benefit of the military). Nothing is more characteristic of the Colonel's personal manner than his identification with the style of an old-time regular army officer. He speaks habitually in military jargon, orders his men about with a commander's brusqueness, signs his field orders "The Colonel," and even enjoys using his title to solicit salutes from unsuspecting servicemen. Indeed, if you didn't know better, you would swear that Tom Parker was in fact Colonel Thomas Andrew Parker, U. S. Army, Retired.

When the United States entered World War II, Tom Parker filled out the obligatory questionnaire from the Selective Service Bureau. When the draft board in Tampa received the form, it learned that the registrant was born

at Huntington, West Virginia, on June 26, 1909;[1] that he
was married with one child; and that his employer was
Gene Austin of Hollywood, California. A couple of weeks
later, Tom Parker was classified 3A: "registrant deferred
by reason of extreme hardship to dependents." In January
1944, with the war in its most critical phase and the
reserves of military manpower nearly exhausted, Tom
Parker was reclassified 1A. Two months later, after a
preinduction physical, his classification was altered to
4F. The Colonel was out of the war.

Prior to the war, Tom Parker was the dogcatcher of
Tampa. It is said that he took the job in 1940, after
failing to make a go of a pony ride at the Florida State
Fairgrounds. Parker was motivated to become the "field
agent" for the Hillsborough Humane Society, according
to a Tampa newspaper article, by two considerations: 1)
his fondness for animals; 2) a rent-free apartment located
above the animal shelter. As we shall see, this job, so
odd-looking at first glance, was actually an echo of the
Colonel's childhood. Perhaps that is why he threw himself
into it with such zeal. Not long after he set to work, he
got his picture in the paper performing a canine rescue
mission. At thirty-two, he's already very hefty; he's going
bald and covering the blemish with a natty hat, one of
those shiny-visored garrison caps worn in the old days by
bus drivers and filling station attendants. The picture
shows the back of the Colonel's old coupe which he has
adapted to his new work by lettering the trunk with the
word "Ambulance." The action of the carefully posed shot
consists of Parker raising the trunk door on an animal
cage, while his wife Marie, smartly dressed and coiffed,
looking a little like a magician's assistant, prepares to
stash inside the cage the cute little puppy in her arms.

Not content just to notify the papers of his latest
exploits removing stranded cats from trees or rounding
up vicious strays, Tom Parker dressed himself at Christ-

_____

[1]No record of this birth exists in the files at Huntington nor
was a recent investigation of Parker's origins by the local paper,
the *Herald-Despatch*, able to turn up a trace of the Parker family.

mas as Santa Claus and gave away puppies as presents to children. As if all this were not enough, he also renovated the dilapidated animal shelter and established the city's first pet cemetery.

It is when one tries to follow the Colonel's history back before the year 1940 that the trail begins to disappear. We know that he worked in the Royal American Shows in this period, but though the founder's son, Carl Sedlmayr, Jr., is still living, he is very reluctant to talk about Tom Parker. Another source who proved singularly unhelpful for this period was the Colonel's brother-in-law, Bitsy Mott, a one-time shortstop for the Brooklyn Dodgers and the Philadelphia Phillies. After one of those intolerably long and vague conversations that are the favorite pastime of good ole boys, Mott summarized his impressions of a lifetime acquaintanceship with the Colonel in a phrase that could serve as a motto for the whole enquiry: "That man's a mystery."

When you trace back everything that has ever appeared in print about the Colonel's early years, you find that it all originates in a unique interview with the Colonel conducted by an Associated Press reporter in 1956 and published in January 1957, on the first anniversary of the Colonel's takeover of Elvis's career. As this is the one and only time when Colonel Parker has ever pronounced publicly on his birth and upbringing, it's worth reading the original lines:

Parker was born 47 years ago in West Virginia, where his parents happened to be touring with a carnival. Mom and Dad died before Tom reached the fifth grade, so he wound up with his uncle's traveling show, the Great Parker Pony Circus.

At 17, young Tom struck out on his own with a pony and monkey act. Most of his stands were on the cherry soda circuit, an affectionate title given a business arrangement where a soft drink company pays the act about $3 a day to accept its bottle tops as the price of admission.

Parker soon traded in his pony for a typewriter and became press agent for a series of carnivals,

circuses, and showboats. He developed first name
friendships with Tom Mix and Wallace Beery, both
carnival men before the movies found them.

In 1932, while wintering with a carnival in
Tampa, he met, wooed and wed his wife, Marie,
who now helps with the bookkeeping.[2]

It seems astonishing that at this late date nothing
more is known of Colonel Parker's origins than these few
statements; yet they constitute the entire substance of
what passes as biographical accounts of the Colonel's
early years, the paucity of the information being disguised by padding and recasting and the enlargements
produced by speculation, association and sheer fantasy.
Actually, when you examine these skimpy little para-
graphs in a skeptical frame of mind, what they resemble
most are those potted "bios" that were cooked up in the
good old days by Hollywood publicity departments to
invest with glamour or pathos the otherwise drab or
disreputable life of some newly discovered star. I'm sure
it has occurred to more than one showbiz professional
that this bio is no less fictional than those produced by
the Hollywood flacks.

Having traced Colonel Parker's history back to its
beginnings, we have wound up in the dark; and that is
where we would remain, if Tom Parker had his way.
However, in the late sixties, a new clue to the Parker
mystery appeared in a very eccentric booklet titled *The
Hillbilly Cat*. Written by a Dutch fan, Hans Langbroek,
this book belongs to a genre of writing that focuses on
such esoterica as recordings rumored to have been made
but never released and bits of film that may once have
existed but can no longer be found. Written hippie-style—
"you know, yesterday, when i got home i did not feel like
much at all"—and suffering from a very inadequate com-

---

[2]The wedding must have taken place in another state or in
another year because the Florida Office of Vital Statistics has no
record of this marriage in its files for 1932.

mand of English, the book would not normally inspire much interest except as a curiosity. However, when the author comes to the subject of Colonel Parker, he makes a number of statements that are so bizarre that they stop the reader in his tracks. A quick check reveals that some of these remarks are simply false: for example, the assertion that Parker managed Tom Mix and brought him to London in 1947, where he rode his horse through the lobby of the Savoy Plaza. This amusing anecdote is undermined by the fact that Tom Mix died in the year 1940. What is one to make, however, of the statement that Tom Parker was born not in the United States but in Holland, at Breda, and that his real name is "Andre van Kuyk"?

"Preposterous!" you say. I would say so, too, but for the fact that the author is Dutch, which suggests, in turn, that he might have access to sources of information unknown to Americans. With that thought in mind, I made inquiries in Holland and—lo and behold!—a couple of really astonishing articles arrived by mail from a newspaper in Breda, *De Stem (The Voice)*. These articles, by a reporter named Dirk Vellenga, assert that Tom Parker is actually the long-lost son of a local family whose name is van Kuijk and whose surviving members include a sister and two brothers, to say nothing of the Colonel's boyhood friends. (Longevity appears to be a common trait amongst these folk.) The family has a lot of evidence with which to back up its claims. One of the prime proofs is the astounding resemblance between the surviving van Kuijks and Tom Parker. They also have some pictures of Parker as he appeared when he left home, pictures that are very hard to associate with the Colonel's current image. The best way to test the family's claim is to consider carefully the story the Dutch reporter collected from their lips.

Thomas Andrew Parker, according to this account, was born on the date he always cites, June 26, 1909; but his place of birth was not Huntington, West Virginia: It was the old Catholic city of Breda in the Brabant region of southern Holland. The Colonel's father, Adam van Kuijk, was originally a country man, born and bred

in the village of Raamsdonksveer, on the River Maas.
A soldier for many years, he was renowned for his ability
to manage horses. At the age of thirty-four, the elder
van Kuijk married Maria Ponsie, a woman of French
ancestry, whose family peddled at a small carnival that
moved from town to town on a barge in the Low Country.
The pair had nine children, of whom Tom Parker—whose
full name is Andreas Cornelis van Kuijk—is the fifth.
The father is remembered as a harsh and tyrannical man;
the mother as a very pious Catholic. One of her daughters
became a nun.

Van Kuijk the elder operated a livery stable in an
ancient quarter of the city, now demolished, called the
Vlaszak. The father's principal customer or employer was
a well-known warehousing and freight forwarding company, Van Gend en Loos. The social position of the family
was by no means a lowly one. The father enjoyed the
privilege of voting, and his relations included shipping
men and small merchants. The upper crust of Breda
society consisted then of military officers, whose position
was paramount because the city had been for centuries
a fortress town under the aegis of the Dutch royal family.
As the van Kuijks lived very close to a military barracks,
one of Andreas's earliest and most abiding impressions
must have been of the handsomely uniformed army officers to whom the townsfolk deferred, as to superior
beings. It is interesting to note that the van Kuijks lived
above their stable, just as the Colonel lived years later
above the animal shelter at Tampa. One is also struck
by the fact that the Colonel's mother bore the same name
as the Colonel's wife, Marie, who is the Colonel's senior
by eight to ten years.

Tom Parker's nickname as a boy was "Dries." A number of his childhood friends remember Dries quite well.
The picture composed by their recollections is that of a
very gay, audacious and headstrong lad, given to jokes
and stunts, fond of animals of every kind and wild about
circuses and fairs. Indeed, the whole personality of the
mature Tom Parker is quite apparent in these tales of
his childhood. One of his favorite games was to play
circus with the horses entrusted to his care and even

allow the animals to run free. The elder Parker was
enraged by this behavior, which threatened his job, and
punished the boy severely. Dries was not the sort of lad
that discipline could check. Soon he was back performing
some other prank, equally outrageous.

Even as a boy, Parker showed himself highly resourceful at getting what he wanted. He showed a playmate how to get into the soccer games for free by picking
up some bit of lumber and carrying it through the gates,
as if they were employees of the groundskeeper. Once,
when they were caught and barred from the stadium,
Dries went home, got the shovel from the coal scuttle
and then dug a hole under the fence for himself and his
buddy.

The young Dries van Kuijk was also very clever at
making money to buy sweets and other treats. It is recollected that he never ran an errand without being paid.
He even got into the ballyhoo business as a boy, driving
a wagon decorated with billboards around town to advertise a circus. The circus was an obsession with the
boy; he used every device conceivable to get tickets not
only for himself but for his little sisters. Once, hearing
that a circus was playing at a nearby town, he ran away
from school so that he could see the show.

As even repeated whippings would not make a scholar
out of Dries van Kuijk, he was apprenticed early to a
barber. When a customer wanted a shave, Dries was
supposed to apply the soap; then, after the shave, remove
the residues of lather. He didn't last long on the job
because every time he heard music in the street, he would
run out of the shop, leaving the customer in his chair
with soap still on his face.

As Dries grew older, his escapades became more daring. Once he stole a bike from a delivery boy and rode
to the inland port of Oosterhout, where his Uncle Willem
was a barge captain. When Dries was sixteen, his father
died. His uncle, Johannes Ponsie, a ship captain of Rot-
terdam, was appointed guardian of the children. Dries
went to live with him, but on his sister Adriane's birthday, September 15, 1927, came back to Breda. That night
he seemed in especially high spirits, rushing about serv-

ing the company and singing songs which he had composed himself. Shortly after his departure, his trunk was
delivered to the family's house. Inside were found his
clothes, his birthday presents and even his official papers.
Dries had slipped away from Holland.

He arrived in America at the age of eighteen and
found lodging with a Dutch family, who corresponded
with his family in Holland. No sooner had he learned
enough English to get about than he slipped away again
and traveled all over the United States riding the rods
of freight trains. After a year's adventuring, he returned
to Holland on the evening of his mother's birthday, bringing gifts for the whole family. How he must have relished
their astonishment at his startling and triumphant reappearance!

Once Dries van Kuijk got a taste of life in America,
it was just a matter of time till he took off again. Uncle
Johannes saw clearly how matters stood and told the
family: "Nobody can hold that boy down. When he wants
to go, he'll go." In the summer of 1929, Dries van Kuijk
left Holland for his second trip to America. Apparently,
he attached himself to a rich family on the boat, claiming
that he was an orphan whose family lived in the States.
He had told the Dutch family with whom he stayed the
first time that he was eager to enlist in the American
army. Now he put this plan into effect. He arranged that
five dollars a month be deducted from his pay (which
was twenty-six dollars a month) and sent to his mother.
The first check arrived in January 1930, which estab-
lishes the date for the start of his military service; his
period of enlistment would have been two years.

During these two years, Dries corresponded extensively with his family and friends in Holland. He sent
home pictures of himself in uniform and in civilian
clothes. His life appeared to be moving smoothly and
satisfactorily in the new path he had chosen. It was noted
that instead of signing his letters "Andre," he was now
using the mysterious name, "Tom Parker." Otherwise,
nothing occurred that could explain what happened next.
All the family knows is that in January, 1932, the letters

and the money orders stopped arriving—and *nobody ever
again heard a word from Dries van Kuijk.*

For thirty years the van Kuijk family speculated on
what had become of its missing member. At the end of
World War II, the family began to fancy that Dries might
turn up among the millions of American soldiers in Europe.
Every week, Tom Parker's mother lit a candle for
him in the Catholic church at Eindhoven, where she had
moved to live with one of her daughters. When the mother
died in 1958, she had no idea that her long lost son was
a famous figure in America, the prosperous manager of
the world's most successful entertainer.

It was not until 1961 that the van Kuijk family discovered
what had happened to the boy who had left home
thirty-two years before. One of Dries's sisters saw a picture
of Elvis Presley and Colonel Tom Parker in a ladies'
magazine, *Rosita*. She recognized Dries immediately because
of the strong resemblance he bore to another of her
brothers. The family took its story to the magazine, which
published an article that became, in turn, the source for
the statements in the little book by Hans Langbroek.
One of Parker's brothers, Ad van Kuijk, actually went
to the United States and met the Colonel and Elvis in
Hollywood. When he returned to Holland, he refused to
discuss the meeting. Other members of the family wrote
to the Colonel but never received answers. Among their
speculations was the notion that their brother was concealing
his identity because he had something shady in
his past: Perhaps he had entered the United States illegally
or had deserted from the American army. After
Elvis's death, efforts to reach the Colonel were redoubled.
The only thing that anyone received by way of reply was
a small American flag.

This account is supported by a number of witnesses;
but when you settle down to ponder it, you begin to have
your doubts. Could it not be simply a case of that familiar
phenomenon: the obscure claiming kinship with the great,
the rich, the famous? What, after all, are the grounds
for the identification? An old photograph that looks nothing
like the man we know. A couple of old letters signed
"Tom Parker." A brother who goes to see his famous

relative and returns with nothing to say. It's hardly evidence that would stand up in a court of law—or in that equally strict court of judgment which should be run by anyone presuming to the title of biographer. The only man, one concludes, who could resolve the issue is Colonel Parker—and he ain't talkin'! Or so I thought until that morning in January 1980, when, suddenly, the oracle spoke.

I was sitting in my office going over the story for the hundredth time with Lamar Fike. As usual, we were getting nowhere. Lamar, who had traveled extensively with the Colonel in the old days, did not see the man as remote and unapproachable. He was accustomed to calling up the Colonel and getting straight answers. It was natural, therefore, that when the discussion reached its customary impasse, he should say, "Why don't I call the Colonel and pop the question?" I stared at him with, I'm sure, the deepest skepticism imprinted on my face. Then, I replied, "Why not?"

When Lamar got the Colonel on the wire, he set the old boy up nicely. Speaking in the tone of the young disciple, which is so gratifying to the old master, he commenced by saying, "Colonel, you always told me, 'If there's somethin' you want to know from me, don't sit around stewin'—just ask!'" From Hollywood the voice of the aged man was heard in New York saying, "That's right, Lamar. What is it?" "Well, Colonel," says Lamar, as if this were the damnedest thing he'd ever heard tell of, "there's a book come out that says that your real name is Dries van Kuijk and you were born in Breda, Holland." There was a slight pause at the other end of the line and a perceptible change of tone. "Oh, yeah," answered the voice, obviously caught off balance and struggling to regain its composure. "That's appeared in about fifteen different places. That's as old…that's been out since I came out of the army fifty years ago. Hell, that's no news!"

Lamar was so flabbergasted by this unexpected rejoinder that he protested: "But Colonel, I've known you for over twenty years—why didn't you tell me that you were a Dutchman?" The Colonel, always fast on the comeback, snapped: "You never asked me."

Chapter 11

Under
New Management

THE MAN who brought Tom Parker and Elvis
Presley together was Oscar Davis, one of the pioneers
of country show business. Davis's was a world of county
fairs, livestock shows, rodeos, firemen's carnivals, circuses, fiddling contests, jamborees, tent shows and pro-
motional tours on behalf of patent medicines, flours,
chows and tobacco products. In contrast to Tom Parker,
who talked out of the side of his mouth and looked like
a huckster, Oscar Davis aspired to the image of the
tycoon. Small, dapper, with wavy iron-grey hair, he wore
always a four-hundred-dollar suit with his shoes polished,
his nails buffed. His most famous promotion was the
public wedding of country music's greatest hero, Hank
Williams.

Seeking a way to mend the fortunes of the alcoholic
and morphine-addicted Williams, Davis hit on the idea
of making the famous entertainer's second marriage a
well-promoted spectacle. Twice in one day he filled to
capacity New Orleans's 14,000-seat Municipal Auditorium—once for the rehearsal and once for the ceremony—with people who paid from seventy-five cents to
$1.50 to see the emaciated, balding, skull-faced singer,

181

costumed in fancy western duds, take as his bride a
diminutive, pretty, fresh-faced girl caparisoned in lace
and tulle. The wedding grossed $30,000, plus a mountain
of gifts which Davis wheedled out of the local merchants.
The ceremony was, to be sure, an imposture because
Williams had married already in secret to avert inter-
ference by his enraged first wife. The promotion, however,
was a triumph.

Having earned and lost millions in the course of a
long and billowy career, Davis found himself in difficult
straits when Hank Williams was delivered to his last
concert, on New Year's Day, 1954, stone cold dead in the
back seat of his car. Davis had no choice but to hire out
to other promoters as a front man: one of those ballyhoo
artists who blow into a town a week before the show and
start bombarding the airwaves with cannon-voiced announcers thundering: "COMING TO TOWN! THE BIG SHOW!
DON'T MISS IT!" It was, in fact, while spending a day at
WMPS in Memphis in October 1954, preparing his "spots"
for an upcoming Red Foley show, that Davis discovered
Elvis Presley. Always on the lookout for fresh talent, the
keen little promoter asked Bob Neal if he would play
some records by this new kid about whom there was so
much talk. Neal not only spun the discs but offered to
take Davis out to the Eagle's Nest, where Elvis was
working with Scotty and Bill. Davis found Elvis "sensational." Next time he sat down to cut up touches with
his old crony, Tom Parker, he told him about this amazing
boy in Memphis, who was driving all the women crazy.

Next time Colonel Parker got to Memphis, he arranged
to meet Elvis, Bob Neal and Sam Phillips in a little restaurant across the street from the Auditorium. Nothing
notable happened at the meeting. The Colonel had never
seen nor heard Elvis perform. All he could say was: "Oscar
tells me you're sensational. I'm going to see if I can book
you on one of my shows." It was all over in a couple of
minutes. The earth did not tremble. Contact, however, had
been established.

Early in 1955, Colonel Parker decided to get a firsthand
report on Elvis Presley. He summoned to his home at
Madison, Tennessee, just north of Nashville, Hank Snow's

son, Jimmy Rodgers Snow. The young Snow had grown up in the country music business and was himself a competent performer who was beginning to appear on his father's tours. The Colonel told Snow that he was sending him to Lubbock, Texas, where he would work a one-nighter at the Cotton Club with a young singer who was getting very hot. What the Colonel wanted was a complete rundown on Elvis on and off the stage.

Jimmy Snow had seen everyone in the country music business, but he had never seen anyone like Elvis Presley. "'Elvis the Pelvis,'" he writes in *I Cannot Go Back,* "as he was already being called, sauntered on stage in black pants with pink stripes down the legs, topped off by a black jacket and pink shirt with collar turned up to catch the ends of his hair. Guitar hanging from his neck, curls dangling over his forehead, eyebrows arching over lidded eyes, he grinned seductively at the girls in the front rows. Leaning forward with feet apart and clutching the mike, he warmed up with a slow ballad, then jumped into what the crowd came to see. Hips grinding and shaking, legs jerking and snapping, arms flailing the guitar to a fast drum beat, he drove the females into hysterics." These "females," it should be borne in mind, were not kids. Country music appealed to an adult public. It was mature women, not little girls that Elvis was turning on in the early days.

When Snow came back to Madison with an enthusiastic report on the new singer, the Colonel lost no time in booking him on a ten-day tour of the Southwest in February. Meantime, Parker went to Shreveport for three weeks to make a study of the possibility of establishing an artist management bureau for the *Louisiana Hayride.* It was during this period that he got his first eyeful of Elvis onstage. The Colonel was recovering from a heart attack at this time; the sight of Elvis must have given him a charge of vitality. The next time Parker booked Presley, it was for a big two-week tour in May.

The sexual excitement of Elvis's female listeners had already at this very early point in his career shaped his act into its distinctive form. Whatever his original intentions may have been when he first became an entertainer,

he had learned by now that his strongest drawing card
was his raw sex appeal. Consequently, instead of carrying
on like a wild young boy who doesn't know his own at-
tractiveness, Elvis had begun to study how to increase his
seductiveness. Bob Luman, a seasoned country singer, recollects the shocking effect of Elvis's opening, which by
now was as deliberately provocative as that of an old-time
jungle show.

"This cat came out in red pants and a green coat and
a pink shirt and socks, and he had this sneer on his face.
He stood behind the mike for five minutes, I'll bet, before
he made a move. Then he hit his guitar a lick, and he
broke two strings. I'd been playing ten years, and I hadn't
broken a *total* of two strings. So there he was, these two
strings dangling, and he hadn't done anything yet, and
these high school girls were screaming and fainting and
running to the stage. Then he started to move his hips,
like he had this thing for his guitar. That was Elvis Presley
playing Kilgore, Texas. He made chills run up my back,
man!"

This good description conveys the essence of Elvis's
act at the moment before his great breakthrough. The
note he strikes is one of erotic challenge. You can see
him standing there with his legs spraddled, his lip curled
in the famous snarl, green eye shadow giving his pale,
poached face a ghoulish hue, as he stares menacingly at
the girls with his broken-stringed guitar lying in his
hands like the child murdered unwittingly by Frankenstein's monster. By this point Elvis has joined the rogues
gallery of violent, crazy, sadistic teen heroes of the fifties,
alongside Marlon Brando in his black leather jacket and
visored military cap, leading his motorcycle gang into
Our Town; or the psychopathic Vic Morrow, switchblade
in hand, stalking Glenn Ford in the high-school classroom; or, closest of all, Michael Landon, watching the
girl gymnast flex her body sensuously on the parallel
bars, then, at the sound of a clangorous schoolbell, ex-
ploding before your eyes into the hideously hairy shape
of a teenage werewolf.

Elvis's genius lay in combining the movie myth of the
menacing teenager with rock 'n' roll music so as to create

a whole new performance idiom appropriate to that wild new form of entertainment, the rock concert. Out of his threatening poses, frenzied gyrations and spontaneous psychodrama sprang the whole tradition of hard rock. Overnight, the basic image for a hot young singer became a crazy-looking boy with a guitar in his hand cutting up all over a stage. So profound and pervasive is this image today that we can't imagine a rock singer under any other aspect. Consequently, you could say that Elvis's influence as a stage performer far surpassed his effect as a recording star because even though his musical idiom soon went out of style, every real rock act that followed him for the next twenty-five years derived directly from his stage rhetoric.

It's amusing to observe how quaint or even archaic are the resources which Elvis rediscovered for his highly innovative stage style. Those broken, hanging (carefully filed!) strings that awed Bob Luman, for example, were invented a century before Elvis Presley by Niccolò Paganini. The demonic violin virtuoso of the Romantic Age, also famous for his long hair, pale masklike face and aura of diabolic evil, would play madly on his fiddle until suddenly, twang!, a string would break and hang haplessly from his instrument. A signal to stop, to cool it, to get things back under control, the broken string worked on Paganini only as a challenge driving him on to even greater and more awesome feats of virtuosity. No sooner had he demonstrated that he could outplay the greatest violinist with only three strings to his instrument than twang!, he had suddenly broken another string! Now the challenge is even greater, the transpositions and fingerings more fantastic, as he fights to do with only two strings what other men can barely achieve with four. Then, twang!, my God!—he's broken yet another string! Now he's down to the G string, the thickest string, the string upon which he can perform like the devil himself, because, according to the legend, all his other strings rotted away during the years when he was confined to a damp dungeon for unspeakable crimes. Ah, the classics!

Once again we see that it was Elvis Presley's function

to recapture the past every time he took a step into the future, his talent lying precisely in his capacity to revive in the arid atmosphere of the Age of Ike the flamboyance and extravagance of the long-submerged romantic spirit. Nor should it be thought that Elvis's tricks were confined to matters of song or stage technique. He was also very crafty about his sex appeal.

Though it is holy writ that Elvis was the natural man instinctively vying with and defeating the uptight Goliaths of fifties philistinism, and though many a long rap has been laid down about how this simple—but heavily hormoned!—country boy overthrew with one mighty shot from his pelvic sling the enemies of a free, open, untrammeled sexuality, when you talk to those behind the scenes, you get a very different picture of the Simon Bolívar of the crotch. Consider the testimony of another young country singer of that day, David Houston, a friend of Elvis's from Shreveport, who traveled with him extensively in this period. According to Houston, here is how the natural man would prepare himself to go onstage: "He would take the cardboard cylinder out of a roll of toilet paper and put a string in one end of it. Then, he'd tie that string around his waist. The other end, with the cardboard roller, would hang down outside his drawers, so as when he got onstage and reared back with that guitar in his hand, it would look to the girls up front like he had one helluva thing there inside his pants."

Having discovered that he could drive the girls wild with his onstage performance, the shy, reticent, easily embarrassed Elvis began now to extend his stage image into his private life. If he drove the girls crazy, he was no less crazy about the girls. Everyone who knew him at the time recalls how obsessive was Elvis's pursuit of women. Every week when he came down to Shreveport, he would put up at the Al-Ida Motel, which was on the rough side of town in Bossier (Cajun = Boshur) City. One of the hottest tonk strips in the South, Bossier City was the "service center" for nearby Barksdale Air Force Base. "After dark," wrote Erskine Caldwell, "when the rainbow-colored, plastic-encased, rocket-shaped neon lights burst into all their crazy-crystal glory, Bossier City is a dazzling three-mile strip of booze, girls and ear-jarring nightlife." Though Elvis still didn't smoke or drink, he had become a night-prowling cat, who must have been thrilled down to the bottom of his penny-loafers by the antics he saw in this little sin city.

Elvis chased every girl he met. He never stopped cruising. He arranged his dates in shifts so that as one girl was leaving his room another one would be arriving. Sometimes he would have three or four girls in his room at once. If a girl proved coy, Elvis might resort to force to overcome her resistance. One girl threatened to sue him for rape, David Houston recalls. When her mother showed up at the hotel, Elvis had a long talk with her alone in the room. Afterwards, Elvis confided to Houston: "I think I could make the mother, too."

Persistent rumors in Shreveport suggest that Elvis may have gotten a girl pregnant during this reckless time. There's no way of verifying or disproving this tale. The woman is supposed to have had the baby, a girl, and subsequently married a man who had money and doesn't want any unpleasant memories being stirred up after all these years.

Elvis's first big tour with Hank Snow commenced on May 1, 1955, at New Orleans and then zigzagged through Louisiana, Alabama and northern Florida—classic redneck country—in a series of one-night stands. Elvis hit hard in every town along the route. He appeared on the first half of the program along with acts like Jimmy Rodgers Snow, the Davis Sisters and the Wilburn Brothers, all lightweight performers. The second half of the show offered the bigger names, commencing with the Carter Family and building up through Slim Whitman to the boss himself, Hank Snow. All through the tour, the performers on the first half of the bill kept complaining to Snow that they couldn't follow Elvis's act; so Snow put Elvis in the next-to-intermission spot.

It was in this slot that Elvis appeared on May 13 at the Gator Bowl at Jacksonville, Florida, before an audience of 14,000 people. Few of these folk had ever heard of Elvis Presley because they lived outside the range of the *Hayride* broadcasts. Elvis appeared onstage that night wearing a

pink suit with a lacy pink see-through shirt that resembled
a woman's blouse. In the course of his brief turn, he used
every trick he knew to turn on the girls. As he bowed off,
he shouted, "Thank you, ladies and gentlemen!" Then, lowering his voice and breathing heavily into the mike, he
leered, "Girls—I'll see you backstage!" It was meant to be
a gag. Some gag! In a flash, about half the audience leaped
to its feet and started running toward the dugout that led
down into the locker room where the performers dressed.

Elvis stayed one step ahead of the mob, receiving some
good downfield blocking from the police. Gladys and Vernon, seated in the stands, watched the flight and pursuit
in horror. When Elvis ducked into the dugout, he appeared
to be safe in his hole; but someone failed to close the door
and about a hundred girls came screaming into the locker
room. They attacked Elvis head-on and started tearing off
his clothes. He climbed out of reach atop a shower stall.
The police finally cleared the room, save for one scraggly
little girl who was found hiding behind a partition. As she
slunk out, one of the boys noticed an odd-looking hump in
her dress. Kicking at it, the dude dislodged what proved
to be one of Elvis's shoes. When it was finally judged safe
for Elvis to leave that night, he walked out in the parking
area and found his pink Cadillac had been scarified from
end to end with girls' names either scrawled on the finish
with lipstick or scratched into the paint with pins and
rings.

This startling outburst of violence, which terrified Elvis's parents, shocked his fellow troupers and brought
down denunciations on his head from the local authorities,
thrilled Colonel Parker to the core of his old carny man's
heart. What appalled and disgusted straight people made
the hustler's palm itch with greed. Elvis, the Colonel saw
in a flash, was sucker bait. He could be jounced and dangled
in front of millions of girls across the country who would
pay anything for a chance to get close enough to ogle him
and scream at him and reach out their hands in hysterical
fits trying to touch him. Elvis had to be handled right, of
course, like any freak attraction, or the whole thing could
get out of hand and result in some terrible disaster. He
would also have to be paced properly or his fad would burn

out quickly. It would take a lot of shrewdness to exploit this kid to the limits he suggested. The Colonel knew that he was the man for the job. From the moment of the first Presley riot, Elvis was, in the Colonel's mind, already his "boy."

Staking out Elvis Presley as his next mark and getting the boy safely into the net were, however, two very different things. Though none of the obstructions in the Colonel's path were formidable in themselves, in their aggregate they constituted a veritable obstacle course. The first and most fundamental job was to con Elvis and his family into believing that they would be much better off under the direction of Colonel Parker than they were with Bob Neal. This problem was made all the more difficult by the close familial ties which had developed between the Presleys and the Neals. Mrs. Presley often spent the evenings when Elvis was on the road visiting with Helen Neal, the two mothers sharing their concerns over their young sons, who were often out at work or play together. Then, assuming the Colonel could put away the Presleys, there were the problems presented by the professional people who had contracts with Elvis. Neal was the most obvious but not necessarily the most important of these businessmen. Sam Phillips was really a bigger problem because he controlled Elvis's future in both the recording and music publishing businesses. The Colonel was convinced that nothing could be done for Elvis's career in these areas until he was sprung from the grasp of Phillips and put into the hands of one of the major companies, which had the publicity and distribution apparatus to make Elvis's records big hits. Finally, there was the contract with the *Louisiana Hayride,* which the Colonel regarded as a sin and an outrage. Not only did the program pay virtually nothing for Elvis's services; it kept him running in and out of Shreveport all year long, when he should have been free to travel for weeks on end in any direction his career took him. Here was another hold that would have to be broken at the earliest opportunity.

Of all the problems facing the Colonel at this moment, none was more basic than the job of ingratiating himself with Elvis and convincing the boy that his future lay in allowing the Colonel to manage all his affairs. The first order of business, therefore, was gulling Elvis. Needless to say, this was not hard to accomplish. Elvis was just a naive young kid infatuated with his first taste of fame and indifferent to everything that did not feed his hungry ego. The first trick was to flatter the kid outrageously, tell him that he was much too good for these dumb little country shows. That he should have his own show. That he should be on TV. That he should record for RCA. Then, tell him what they all want to hear: "You should be in pictures." At the same time the Colonel was basting Elvis with butter and bullshit, he did not neglect to stuff his mouth with bread. Elvis's price was $250 a night for himself and the band. The Colonel would negotiate with Bob Neal to keep the price low and prove to Elvis that his manager wasn't very successful at earning him money. Then, when the Colonel got Elvis out on the road, the old boy would start slipping brand new hundred dollar bills in the kid's pocket or taking him shopping in the pimp clothing stores he loved. Soon Elvis was making more in "bonuses" than he was in fees. He was also calling Colonel Parker by a new nickname: "the Admiral."

Vernon Presley, who was both stupid and greedy, was no problem at all. The Colonel made a swift conquest of this spineless creature. The real problem was Gladys. The Colonel, with his shrewd eye for people, knew only too well how vital it was to his success that he get the mother's approval for his takeover. So concerned was the Colonel about making the proper impression on Gladys that he adopted an elaborate stratagem to put her away.

One of the Colonel's old cronies was the rube comic Whitey Ford, well known as "the Duke of Paducah." In the summer of 1955, Ford received a call from the Colonel that commenced, as did all the Colonel's scams, as an innocent bit of business. As a sideline to his showbiz career, Ford ran a sausage and egg farm; the Colonel asked Ford that day to bring over "a mess of sausage and a couple dozen eggs." When Ford made the delivery, he found his friend in a ruminative mood. Taking out a couple of records with yellow labels, the Colonel said: "I want you to hear a young singer I'm thinkin' o' managin'. I want your opinion of him." Ford was impressed by the freshness and vitality of the voice. He gave the records his enthusiastic endorsement. Then, the Colonel broke out his pictures of Elvis. Ford took one look at the boy and exclaimed, "If I had me a lad like that, I'd hop on the first plane to Hollywood." That was just what the Colonel wanted to hear. Now he leveled with Ford.

He told him that he was arranging a tour that would feature Elvis and Hank Snow's son, Jimmy Rodgers Snow, and the Carter Family. He wanted to place the Duke of Paducah on the bill. In exchange he wanted a favor. Actually, two favors. First, he wanted the Duke to keep an eye on these young boys and make sure they didn't do anything disgraceful. More important was another matter. When the tour hit Little Rock, its last date, Elvis's mother and father would be on hand. The Colonel wanted to meet the mother, but he was afraid that she might not react to him and his proposition in the right way. So what the Colonel wanted Ford to do was to go in first and soften up the mother. Ford was a nice, gentle, well-spoken man, a man with a reputation for God-fearing behavior. He would make a good impression on Mrs. Presley. When he had gotten into conversation with her, he could tell her all the good things about Colonel Parker—like how much money he would make for Elvis. Then, when the Duke had gotten the mother in the right mood, the Colonel would step in and take over.

When the tour reached its next-to-last stop, Monroe, Louisiana, the Colonel appeared. He had a meeting with Elvis; then, after the show he told the Duke of Paducah: "You're riding with me." As they rolled up the highway toward Little Rock, the Colonel gave the Duke his final instructions. "Here's the plan," he said, employing his customary military lingo. "When we get to Little Rock, I'm gonna stay outta sight. You will have a dressing room with Elvis. Elvis is gonna bring his mother and father in there. Then, Elvis is gonna say, 'Now, Mama, the Duke here has been with Parker for a long time. He knows him from A to Z. He'll tell you anything you

wanna know about him.' That's your cue to soft soap the
old lady."

That night everything went like clockwork. Gladys
and Vernon appeared in the dressing room after the show.
Elvis introduced them to the Duke and then beat it out
the door. He didn't go far, however; he laid his ear to
the keyhole and listened carefully to the ensuing conversation. The Duke took his time and brought the conversation around to the point slowly. He was a real country man, like the Presleys, a man who inspired confidence
and friendship. More than once during the conversation,
he described himself as a Christian. Once he had established the proper rapport, he came quietly but firmly to
the point. "Mizz Presley," he said in his thickest rural
accent, "ah've known Colonel a long time. Ah seen what
he done for Eddy Arnol'. Ah know his methods and how
he works. There's nobody else like him aroun'. He'll definitely make Elvis a star. He'll make Elvis so much
money, he'll never be able to spend it. That may sound
to you like an exaggerated statement, but you'll find out
that ah'm right."

Gladys was skeptical. Also a little distrustful. She
asked embarrassing questions, like: "What church does
Colonel Parker belong to?" That was a pisser! Colonel
Parker had never been in a church in his life, unless it
were to set up a bingo game. Somehow the issue was
skirted. Finally, Gladys fell back on her last line of resistance. She acknowledged that the Colonel might be
good for Elvis, but she didn't see any way that the arrangement could be made because Elvis "done already
signed with Mr. Neal and Mr. Phillips an' the radio
station down there in Shreveport." The old Duke chuckled
richly when he heard these fears. "Mizz Presley," he said,
"let me tell you sumthin'. Time the Colonel get through
with all these people not only will Elvis be free, but them
folk will be braggin' 'cause they onct worked with Elvis
Presley." At that moment, Elvis opened the door and
walked in, saying: "Mama, I want you to meet the Admiral—Mr. Parker!"

That night as the Colonel and the Duke drove toward
Nashville, the old carny was feeling both relieved and

concerned. He told Ford that though this was an important obstacle out of the way, there were still a lot of other problems before him. The biggest of these was Elvis's manager, Bob Neal. Neal, as the Colonel knew, was a man who had spread himself too thin. He had made so many commitments that he couldn't commit himself heart and soul to any one thing. That was his great weakness. Colonel Parker, on the other hand, was a manager who made it a point never to have more than one client, to whom he dedicated himself night and day. In the long run, therefore, the Colonel had more to offer Elvis than did Bob Neal. Still, what would happen if Neal refused to give Elvis up?

The solution proved to be simple. The Colonel went to Neal and told him that there was a good chance that RCA and Hill and Range would put up a big sum of money to purchase Elvis's recording and publishing contracts. This was a matter over which Neal had no authority whatsoever; yet, in exchange for his goodwill, the Colonel was willing to give Neal a percentage of the commission the Colonel would earn if he closed the deal. That put Neal in the Colonel's pocket. Neal informed the Colonel that offers for the contract were constantly coming through the office and the price was constantly rising. Sam Phillips had offered the contract originally to Owen Bradley at Decca for $5,000; Bradley had turned it down. Randy Wood of Dot Records was offered the contract subsequently for $7,500; he, too, turned it down. Then, the great Mitch Miller, the A & R genius of Columbia, called to ask the price; Neal relayed a demand from Phillips for $20,000. Miller rang off in a huff. The Colonel snorted when he heard these prices. He told the astonished Neal that the proper price for the contract was $50,000. That's what they should be shooting for. Fifty big ones!

Though every account of the translation of Elvis from small-time to big-time assigns all the credit for the advancement to Tom Parker, this is not just. It was Hank Snow, RCA's top country artist, who first brought Elvis Presley to the attention of Victor's man in Nashville, Steve Sholes. Snow also alerted his publishers, Hill and Range, to Elvis (as did Ernest Tubb), thereby initiating a relationship that was far more influential in the development of Elvis's singing and recording career than was his association with RCA. Though Hill and Range is not a household word, like Victor, this young company was then the most resourceful and innovative organization in the business. Its proprietors, Julian and Joachim (Jean) Aberbach, were highly sophisticated Viennese Jews who got into music publishing in Berlin back in the days of cabaret and "Goodnight Sweetheart." Though the most unlikely men in the world to become hillbilly music magnates, they saw the opportunity presented by the hitherto largely ignored field of country (Hill) and western (Range) and made a fortune.

Hank Snow was not being altruistic in promoting Elvis. He hoped to profit. He and Parker were equal partners in a tour-packaging agency called Hank Snow Attractions. They had taken under contract already a number of performers and were looking for fresh talent. Snow assumed that eventually he and Parker would manage Elvis jointly. This intention is reflected clearly in the very first contract Parker signed with Elvis on August 15, 1955.

According to the Presley Myth, Elvis and the Colonel never had anything more binding between them than a handshake. A relationship of twenty-two years that grossed over a hundred million dollars—all on a handshake! It is astonishing how universally this preposterous story is believed. What a great tribute to the Colonel that he could con the toughest suckers in the world into believing this audacious lie! In truth, the handshake story is not only false but repeatedly false; for on top of his first contract, Colonel Parker piled one after another, until, eventually, the articulation of his business relationship with Elvis Presley came to resemble a nest of jackstraws. All of these personally authored and sometimes legally ambiguous instruments betray the practiced hand of the hustler. Let us consider for a moment the initial contract. First, the document:

AGREEMENT

SPECIAL AGREEMENT between ELVIS PRES-
LEY, known as artist, his guardians, Mr. and/or Mrs.
Presley, and his manager, MR. BOB NEAL, of Mem-
phis, Tennessee, hereinafter referred to as the Party
of the First Part, and COL. THOMAS A. PARKER
and/or HANK SNOW ATTRACTIONS of Madison,
Tennessee, hereinafter known as the Party of the
Second Part, this date, August 15, 1955.

COL. PARKER is to act as special adviser to EL-
VIS PRESLEY and BOB NEAL for the period of one
year and two one-year options for the sum of two
thousand, five hundred dollars ($2,500.00) per year,
payable in five payments of five hundred dollars
($500.00) each, to negotiate and assist in any way
possible the build-up of ELVIS PRESLEY as an artist. Col. Parker will be reimbursed for any out-of-
pocket expenses for travelling, promotion, advertising as approved by ELVIS PRESLEY and his manager.

As a special concession to Col. Parker, ELVIS
PRESLEY is to play 100 personal appearances
within one year for the special sum of $200.00 (Two
hundred dollars) including his musicians.

In the event that negotiations come to a complete
standstill and ELVIS PRESLEY and his manager
and associates decide to free-lance, it is understood
that Col. Parker will be reimbursed for the time and
expenses involved in trying to negotiate the association of these parties and that he will have first
call on a number of cities, as follows, at the special
rate of one hundred, seventy-five dollars ($175.00)
per day for the first appearance and two hundred
fifty dollars ($250.00) for the second appearance and
three hundred fifty dollars ($350.00). San Antonio,
El Paso, Phoenix, Tucson, Albuquerque, Oklahoma
City, Denver, Wichita Falls, Wichita, New Orleans,
Mobile, Jacksonville, Pensacola, Tampa, Miami,
Orlando, Charleston, Greenville, Spartanburg,

Asheville, Knoxville, Roanoke, Richmond, Norfolk, Washington, D.C., Philadelphia, Newark, New York, Pittsburgh, Chicago, Omaha, Milwaukee, Minneapolis, St. Paul, Des Moines, Los Angeles, Amarillo, Lubbock, Houston, Galveston, Corpus Christi, Las Vegas, Reno, Cleveland, Dayton, Akron, and Columbus.

Col. Parker is to negotiate all renewals on existing contracts.

This agreement is fraught with conflicts of interest. Though Parker is now, in effect, one of Elvis's agents, he stipulates also for an enormous number of concert dates played in distant cities at reduced rates. He is, therefore, both the artist's agent and employer. What's more, we observe that Parker signs on behalf of Hank Snow Attractions, clearly committing himself to a joint arrangement with Hank Snow to promote and employ Elvis. Precisely how Parker aced Snow out his share of Elvis Presley has never been revealed. We do know that Snow threatened to take the Colonel to court, and, as we've seen, the mere mention of Parker's name even today makes the choleric Snow boil with rage. Clearly, the first person who got a screwing from Colonel Parker once he had cut into Elvis Presley was Hank Snow.

How did the Colonel propose to "build up" Elvis? A rare and revealing close-up of the Colonel's hustling is provided in *The Rockin' 50s* by Arnold Shaw, then the general manager of a New York publishing house, who paid a visit to Parker at Madison in August 1955, just at the moment when the Colonel was starting his new campaign. Devious, sly, always playing with an ace up his sleeve, the Colonel broached the subject of Presley with Shaw by playing a couple of the Sun recordings. Shaw was not impressed especially by the singing, but he was struck by the "animal sex appeal" exuded by the eight-by-ten glossies that the Colonel produced next. "In Georgia and Florida the girls are tearing off his clothes," the Colonel told Shaw, "but he's unknown north of the Mason-Dixon Line." Then, giving his mark an appraising stare, the Colonel came to the point. "You're a big man up North," he smiled, employing his half-flattering, half-mocking put-on style. "Let me see you get his records played in the Big City." "What's your interest, Colonel?" asked Shaw. The Colonel's answer was astonishingly frank. "This kid is now managed by Bob Neal of Memphis," he replied. "But I'll have him when Neal's contract finishes in less than a year."

When Shaw returned to New York, he was carrying two copies of each of Elvis's Sun releases. The first person to whom he gave the records was one of the most influential DJs of that day: Bill Randle, the successor to Alan Freed in Cleveland and a weekend jock in New York. Randle decided the records were too crude for his New York show, but when he played the two sides in Cleveland, one of the great strongholds of the new rock music, he got precisely the same reaction that Dewey Phillips had triggered a year before at Memphis. The Colonel's ploy had worked. Elvis was breaking now above the Mason-Dixon Line. Meantime, Colonel Parker was busy working on the project that he had neglected to mention to Shaw: negotiating the sale of Elvis's record contract to RCA. Getting the records on the air in the North had been vital to the success of this campaign.

Why did Sam Phillips want to sell the Presley contract? Phillips himself has said many times that he was strapped for cash and that he had no idea how successful Elvis would become. Why was he so lacking in vision? The answer is simple. Elvis was not selling great numbers of records for Sun. Though he was sensational on a stage, he was not a big item in the record stores. "That's All Right Mama" backed by "Blue Moon Over Kentucky" sold twenty thousand copies; the next record sold about five thousand. At that rate, it's no wonder that Phillips decided to cash in his chips and put his money into his next star, Carl Perkins. The exchange worked brilliantly at first; by the time Elvis got his first record out on RCA, Perkins's "Blue Suede Shoes" was the Number Two side in the United States. After that, the balance tipped dramatically toward Elvis, and Phillips must have been deeply chagrined.

Elvis's feeble sales record also explains why the nego-

tiations with RCA took so many months to gel. Steve
Sholes was eager to buy, but he had to persuade the corporate executives that this virtually unknown singer was
worth more money than anybody had ever paid for a new
performer in the history of the record business. All through
the summer of 1955 Sholes kept telling Parker, "Give me
some ammunition so that I can make headway in New
York." Finally, the Colonel got the break he was seeking.
In July, "Baby, Let's Play House" became the first Elvis
Presley record to appear on a national chart; it rose to
Number Ten on the country and western list and remained
a chart record during the entire period of the final negotiations.

A full step beyond the earlier Sun records and the
bridge to "Heartbreak Hotel," "Baby, Let's Play House"
exemplifies Elvis at the peak of his early style. The original recording by "Hardrock" Gunter is a grimy little blues
sung in an ambling back-beat style that goes nowhere.
Elvis's version is electrifying. His voice bursts out of the
loudspeaker with a searing cry; his fast staccato passages
crepitate eerily, thanks to the echo effect; and when he
settles into the final ride-out, riffing on the syllables of
"bababababy [hiccup] bababababy [hiccup]," he sounds
like a Hawaiian war chant. The fantasia on the blues
which had produced such witty and amusing effects on the
early Sun sides is now beginning to generate a bizarre
honky-tonk atmosphere that will soon permeate American
popular music and form the exciting but grotesque backdrop for the Rock Age.

November 21, 1955, was the date on which the prolonged negotiations for the purchase of Elvis Presley's recording and publishing contracts were finally concluded.
On that date a whole sheaf of legal agreements was signed,
sworn and filed away in New York, Memphis and Madison,
Tennessee. Colonel Parker updated his original agreement
with Elvis in a new instrument which designated him as
"sole and exclusive Advisor and Personal representative."
Parker also signed an agreement with Bob Neal that committed both of Elvis's agents to pool their percentages (fifteen percent for Neal, twenty-five for Parker) and divide
the sums equally, until Neal's contract elapsed on March

15, 1956. The other agreements were those which the Colonel had negotiated between Elvis and the various recording and publishing interests who were now to become such vital factors in the young star's career. These agreements have never been accurately reported.

RCA paid $35,000 to purchase the contract from Sun, all of which was charged against Elvis's future royalties. Elvis received a bonus of $5,000, which indemnified him for the money he was owed by Phillips in unpaid royalties. The term of the contract was three years with two one-year options.

The value of the recording contract purchased by RCA needs no comment. Not only did the firm obtain the right to make new records, but it acquired all the old records on Sun, as well as all the unissued material that was in Phillips's archives, including a number of songs that had never been issued but which would now be used to pad out Elvis's first album. The value of the publishing rights to Elvis's songs, for which Hill and Range paid $15,000, is another matter entirely. To grasp what was entailed in this deal and the profound effect it had upon the future career of Elvis Presley, it is necessary to have a clear conception of the modus operandi of the music publishing business at that time.

Unlike publishers in the past, who had made most of their money from the sale of sheet music, publishers in the fifties derived their principal income from the rights associated with the sale and commercial usage of phonograph records. One great source of income was the so-called mechanical rights in a song, which meant then the flat fee of one cent per side for each record sold by the manufacturer. The other principal source of revenue was the broadcast rights, a fee computed by an elaborate actuarial formula that reflects the amount of play the song receives over the air.

As there is an intimate connection between the commercial success of a song and the fame of the singer who records it, Hill and Range had adopted the stratagem of establishing for famous singers independent publishing companies that would obtain the rights to all the songs recorded by the singers so that they received not just the

royalties paid performers by record companies but a large
portion of the publishing royalties. The arrangement was
one of reciprocal benefit to all involved: The songwriters
would be eager to have their songs published by Presley
Music (BMI) or Gladys Music (ASCAP) because in this
manner they would be assured of having their songs recorded by Elvis. They would be so glad, in fact, that they
would voluntarily surrender one-third of their own royalties and even allow Elvis Presley to affix his name to
the song as one of its cowriters. On the other hand, Elvis
could be counted on, once the system was operating properly, to confine himself exclusively to recording songs to
which he held the publishing rights because on these songs
he earned far more money than he would if he recorded
a rival publisher's material. Finally, Hill and Range would
profit handsomely because they would receive as compensation for operating these new companies fifty percent of
all their income. This large sum was rationalized as being
fair compensation for the task of securing the songs, doing
the paperwork and running the enterprise on sound business principles. It's worth noting that in the years ahead,
Hill and Range, which had been founded only eleven years
before it acquired Elvis Presley, grew to become the largest
independent music publishing house in the world.

Bringing all this down to the level not of dollars but of
cents—music publishing counts its multimillion-dollar
revenues in pennies—we can imagine ourselves receiving,
as Elvis must have received, the primer explanation of
why it pays the performer to play the publishing game.
In the midfifties the standard royalty paid by the record
companies to performers was five percent of ninety percent
of the retail price of a record (with step clauses that increase the rate for sales above a quarter, a half, three-
quarters of a million records sold). As a 45-RPM record
sold then for eighty-nine cents, the per-record royalty was
approximately four cents. If the performer had a fifty-fifty
copublishing deal, he received in addition to this four cents
half of the two-cent mechanical fee (one cent for each side)
and half of the broadcast fee, perhaps another penny. Now,
instead of four cents, he has six cents. Putting it all together, the performer increases by half again his income.

That's what Professor Parker must have hammered into his young pupil's head, using a cigar for a ferrule.

With the money starting to come in on a greater scale than ever before and his credit reaching the sky, Elvis sold his little bungalow on Lamar and bought a new, more comfortable house on Getwell Street, in the vicinity of the Kennedy Veteran's Hospital. Instead of being set right out on the edge of the road, like the old house, this new dwelling had a large yard and was situated in a better neighborhood. It was at this time, too, that Elvis fulfilled a long-standing wish by purchasing for Gladys a pink and white Crown Victoria Cadillac that would match his own pink Cad. Gladys no longer drove a car, but the sentiment is what counts.

Elvis himself received a very valuable gift at this time: nothing less than his first great hit—"Heartbreak Hotel." It's ironic in view of the elaborate arrangements that had just been concluded to secure for Elvis precisely such valuable new songs that this now-legendary composition should have been offered to him by a couple of obscure writers who had never set foot inside the Brill Building and were far beyond the purview of the talent scouts at Hill and Range. Indeed, the story of the song's composition is interesting both for the light it throws on the mental processes of songwriters and for the way it anticipates instinctively, as it were, the method by which Elvis was to acquire not only new songs but the styles in which to perform these songs.

The tale begins in Gainesville, Florida, where Tommy Durden, an obscure band musician and songwriter, is conning the front page of the *Miami Herald*, before turning to the racing page. Splashed across the front page is the picture of a corpse with a headline that shouts: "Do you know this man?" The accompanying story explains that the man committed suicide after destroying every identifying mark on his clothing. A note he left contained only one scrawled line: "I walk a lonely street."

Durden was strangely excited by this incident, especially by the phrase, "I walk a lonely street." The line associated in his mind with his favorite kind of music, the blues. Getting in his car, he drove to the house of Mae

Axton, a publicist who had befriended Elvis on his appearances in Jacksonville, near Gainesville. This busy lady was, in addition to being a schoolteacher, publicity writer and "personality" on local radio and TV, a songwriter. One of her ambitions was to write Elvis Presley's first big hit. When her friend and writing partner, Tommy Durden, walked in that day with the paper and showed her the story, she agreed at once that they should try to turn it into a song—for Elvis.

Sitting down at the piano and starting to improvise blues licks, Durden concentrated on the phrase that had suggested the song. Mae Axton, who was struck more by the thought of the man's family seeing the picture and recognizing him with broken hearts, suggested that they arrange the lyric so that at the end of the "lonely street" there be a "heartbreak hotel." With those two themes to guide them, the partners plunged into the composition, only to be interrupted by the arrival of yet another of Mae Axton's writing partners, Glen Reeves, a local singer and entertainer in Jacksonville. When Axton explained to Reeves that she and Durden were writing a song for Elvis Presley titled "Heartbreak Hotel" and would welcome his help, Reeves said that the title was "the silliest thing I've ever heard." He refused to have anything to do with the project. Leaving to run some errands in the neighborhood, Reeves returned an hour later to find the song completed and recorded by Durden on Axton's tape recorder.

Now Axton went after Reeves again because she knew that her friend could do a perfect imitation of Elvis Presley's "shaky" style, and she anticipated that if she could demonstrate the song in Elvis's own style, he would be more likely to accept it. Reeves agreed to the request and in a few minutes, working from the chord symbols and the handwritten word sheet, he had shouted and shuddered the blues into the little mike of the home recording machine. To show her appreciation, Axton asked Reeves if he would like to have his name on the song and a share of the writers' earnings. For the second time that afternoon, Reeves refused to have anything to do with this "silly" song.

At this point, Mae Axton took off for Nashville, where

the annual DJ convention was in progress, to sell her new song. The moment Elvis heard the tape, his eyes lit up and he exclaimed, "Hot dog, Mae! Play it again!" Once Mae Axton saw that Elvis was taken by the song, she made him a proposition he couldn't refuse. Having heard at the hotel that RCA was about to buy Elvis's contract, Axton told Elvis that if he would agree to make "Heartbreak Hotel" his first record for Victor, she would make him the third writer and let him have a third of the song's royalties. The rest we know.

What isn't known but is really far more important and interesting is the fact that Elvis copied closely the style on the demo record of Glen Reeves. So close was the resemblance that, as Tommy Durden remarked: "I was convinced when I heard the record that Elvis was even breathing in the same places that Glen did on the dub." This curious circular relationship between the demo singer, who is struggling to copy the style of Elvis Presley, and Elvis Presley, who is copying the style of the demo singer, is one that will occupy us soon, when we come to consider Elvis's system of recording, a method that sprang up spontaneously the moment even such naive, semipro songwriters as Tommy Durden and Mae Axton began to pitch songs at Elvis Presley. For even at this early moment in his career, Elvis was more than a singer: he was—with that "shaky" voice that Sam Phillips had given him—an *image*.

Chapter 12

The Nation's Only Atomic-Powered Singer

JITTERY" is the word for Elvis at his first recording RCA session, held at Nashville on January 11, 1956, three days after he turned twenty-one. First, he paced all over the studio while the musicians were setting up.[1] Then, to break the tension, he did something that was to become the preparatory ritual for all his subsequent sessions: He sat down at the piano and, summoning the backup singers around him, launched into "I'm Bound for the Kingdom," followed by "I'll Tell It Wherever I Go." There is an amusing yet deeply revealing quality to this spontaneous outburst. At first glance, it must have seemed so incongruous. Here's this freaky-looking sex-teaser cranking up to record a jivey, salty black ghetto ditty in which he impersonates

---

[1]Steve Sholes decided to beef up Elvis's skimpy accompaniment with a vocal trio and a couple of additional rhythm players. Ben and Brock Speer of the Speer Family were hired to sing lead tenor and baritone; Gordon Stoker of the Jordanaires was engaged to sing first tenor. The band was enlarged to include Floyd Cramer on piano and Chet Atkins, Sholes's right-hand man, on rhythm guitar.

a cat whose only use for women is "Money, honey!"—and
how does he get in the groove? He sings hymns! Yet, at
the same time, in this schizzy behavior one recognizes the
essential Elvis Presley, the boy who wanted to be a gospel
singer and who has finally fulfilled this ambition in the
most bizarre manner by getting together at a Methodist
radio station with some of the same gospel singers he once
admired at the all-night sings to record rhythm and blues
songs derived from gospel music but fitted now with lyrics
that most people regard as "common," "low-down," or just
plain "dirty."

The first tune cut that morning was the Ray Charles
hit, "I Got a Woman." No sooner did Elvis go into the song
than producer and engineer were startled to see their new
star start bouncing around in the studio as if he were
onstage. Elvis was off mike more often than he was on.
Sholes stopped the session and told Elvis that he would
have to stand in one spot or they would never get an acceptable take. Elvis, always eager to please, replied
meekly, "Yes, Mr. Sholes." When they got the next take,
however, it was obvious that a lot of the rhythmic verve
had drained out of the performance. "Please, Mr. Sholes,"
Elvis begged, "don't make me stand still. If I can't move,
I can't sing!" Sholes told the engineer's assistant to rig two
more mikes on either side of the one Elvis was using. Now,
he would be picked up whether he bopped to the east or
bopped to the west. No sooner was this problem solved
than another surfaced. Elvis held his guitar so high and
hit it so hard that the sound interfered with the voice
recording. How were they to solve this problem? Someone
came up with the idea of giving Elvis a soft, felt ukelele
pick. With this feathery instrument, he could play hard
and not make a din.

As soon as the session got cooking, Elvis removed his
white buck shoes. Instantly, the small studio was filled
with a funky odor. "Ah'm sorry about the stink, guys,"
Elvis apologized, "but ah been out on the road and ah ain't
taken a bath in three days." This was typical of Elvis both
early and late. His doting mother hadn't given him any
guilts about dirt and body odor. Though he was constantly

grooming his gleaming hair, he was always, as Gordon Stoker puts it, "semi-dirty."

The harder Elvis worked, the more he reminded the musicians of an athlete playing a big game. At one point the pick flew out of his hand, but Elvis kept whacking the strings with his bare fingers until his hand began to bleed. "Why didn't you stop?" asked the astonished Steve Sholes. "Ah didn't wanna break it up, it was goin' so good," smiled Elvis, like an injured halfback reporting to his coach on the bench. Later in the session, Elvis hit the floor in a kneedrop that split the seat of his pants. He was always destroying his clothes. In fact, the reason he wore the oversized jackets that are now the hallmark of the punk style is not because he thought they looked better that way but because they gave him more elbow room.

The second tune recorded was one destined to make history: "Heartbreak Hotel." Long familiarity has made this song as unremarkable as the Empire State Building; yet, it is actually a very peculiar composition. A caricature of the blues, a sequence of melodramatic vocal gesticulations, it isn't so much a song as a psychodrama. This is precisely why it was of such immense value in establishing Elvis Presley as the startling new hero of pop music. More than any song Elvis ever recorded, this Method acting exercise set to music matched Elvis's image and projected it out over the airways that were the paths to fame.

The clamorous blues shout with which the song opens summons up the new hero in the act of raising his fist in a gesture of insurrection and triumph. But a moment later a tumbling scale passage carries the voice down, down, down until it is in the cellar mumbling and moaning in self-abasing despair, "I'm so lonely I could die!" Rebellion and submission, exultation and despair, pride and humiliation—you can paraphrase the song in countless parallel patterns; the important thing is the paradigmatic compression with which it delivers to the world that fascinating new character with whom everyone instantly identified Elvis: the down-in-the-gutter, ill-fated, nightmare-haunted Punk Hero.

"Heartbreak Hotel's" grotesquely exaggerated and histrionic quality matched perfectly the hysterically self-

pitying mood of millions of teenagers, who responded by
making the record an instant and immense success. The
record jumped on the charts in February; by the first week
in April, it was the Number One song on all three charts—
country and western, rhythm and blues, pops—the first
record in history to make such a grand slam. When Hill
and Range received the first royalty check, for a quarter
of a million dollars, the publishers decided against banking the sum because they thought it must be a mistake.

Two weeks after his first RCA session, on January 28,
Elvis made his first appearance on national television. The
program on which he appeared was one that would have
been totally forgotten but for the fact that it provided the
setting for Elvis's TV debut. *Stage Show* was the rickety
hobbyhorse of Jackie Gleason, whose enthusiasm for jazz
and the big band sound had inspired him to make the
aging Tommy and Jimmy Dorsey (reduced by this time to
being co-leaders of the same band) the hosts of a half-hour
variety show on CBS that was the warm-up for Gleason's
own program, *The Honeymooners.* Unfortunately for the
old band leaders, they found themselves confronting on
NBC the very popular *Perry Como Show,* which outclassed
the Dorseys so completely that CBS began urging the
Nestlé Company, which sponsored *Stage Show,* to put its
money into a more competitive offering. If the program
had not been in such desperate straits, chances are it would
never have tried such a long shot as Elvis Presley. As it
was, what sold Elvis to the show's producer, Jack Philbin,
was not his music but his physical appearance. Looking
at a photo of Elvis provided by William Morris, Philbin
exclaimed: "He's a guitar-playing Marlon Brando!" That
was good enough for one cheap shot ($1,250) and an option
on the following week.

The format of the program called for a lively opening
number by the June Taylor Dancers, a klutzy knockoff of
the Rockettes; then, the first and least important guest
would appear to do his turn. When Elvis marched out
onstage to receive the Dorseys' welcome, the contrast between the young rock singer and the old swing musicians
was shocking. "The Sentimental Gentleman of Swing" at
age fifty was white-haired, haggard and obviously bored

to death. He would die within the year, strangling on his vomit while so stoned on booze and pills that he couldn't rise from his bed. Beside him stood his "kid" brother, Jimmy, paunchy, baggy-eyed, smiling mechanically. He, too, would die shortly, of cancer. Looking at these two famous musicians, you could hardly believe they were the same men who had been the idols of American youth just fifteen years earlier. Elvis, plump, juicy, bursting with youthful hormones, appeared to have dropped from another planet.

Elvis made a good choice for his first number: "Blue Suede Shoes," which was not only the Number Two song in the nation but a rockabilly classic that he could sing better than anyone. He gave it a good performance and tried to whip up the band, yelling at Scotty during his solo, "Rock it...go, man, go!" On his second chorus, Elvis cut a fast step that got some applause. When the song ended, the audience reacted warmly, but there were no signs of unusual excitement. The next tune, the unknown "Heartbreak Hotel," could have put Elvis over the top; but the program's directors, following their usual procedure, had prepared a special arrangement for full band. What an arrangement! After a couple of screeching chords punctuating the opening shout, the drummer settled down to play straight stripper time until the band hit the instrumental break. Then, some hi-schrei trumpet player, left over from the days of Ziggy Elman, started screaming in his shaky topmost register. By the time he took his horn from his lips, nobody could remember the singer or even the song. Elvis came back and tried to recover the audience's attention, but it was too late. The second round had to be scored to the band. Elvis's first TV appearance had ended as a standoff.

Though the New York studio audience must have been asking itself, "What the hell was that all about?" the reaction in other parts of the country was swift and clear. CBS, a national network, nay, a national institution!, had just committed the unpardonable sin of filling the American living room with the obscene antics and barbaric yawps of a leering, sneering juvenile delinquent. It was like the opening shot of the Civil War. Suddenly, *Stage*

Show was the second Sumter. Next morning, the program's producers were flooded with wires, calls and letters denouncing the show and threatening reprisals.

When the Nielsen ratings came in, they showed that Como had taken 34.6% of the viewers compared with a lousy 18.4% for *Stage Show.* These initial ratings were prophetic of what happened on all of Elvis's subsequent appearances on this faltering program. Though "Heartbreak Hotel" soon reached the Number One position on the pop charts, Como beat Presley, hands down.

The most important result of the Dorsey shows was an offer from Hal Wallis, the famous movie producer, to give Elvis a screen test. Both Elvis and the Colonel were agreed that the goal of all their efforts should be a career in films. "Singers come and go," said Elvis, "but if you're a good actor, you can last a long time." The fact is that Elvis lacked any real commitment to rock music. He didn't even want to remain a singer indefinitely. In Elvis's eyes nothing was greater than being a movie star. That was what he had always wanted and if he could get it through singing—great! But, if you had to sustain your star status by continuing to sing, then you hadn't really made it into the big time: the class of the Rudolph Valentinos and James Deans. That was the sort of star Elvis had always aspired to be. So the opportunity to have a career in movies was for Elvis the beginning of a dream come true.

The screen test was set for April 1 at Paramount Studios. A veteran character actor, Frank Faylen, who had a few days free from Wallis's current production, *Gunfight at the O.K. Corral,* was asked to play opposite Elvis in a scene from Wallis's next picture, *The Rainmaker.* Stills of the session show Elvis dressed in rough-out clothes acting in a broadly macho style, chomping on a cigar, poking his finger in Faylen's belly and carrying on like a rough young stud. Faylen remembers that Elvis acted much too nice at first; the old actor had to urge the kid to get tough. Wallis, who had been impressed by Elvis in the first place because of his obvious sex appeal, was delighted by the test. "I felt the same thrill," he remembers, "I experienced when I first saw Errol Flynn on the screen. Elvis, in a very different, modern way, had exactly the same power, virility, and sexual drive. The camera caressed him."

The deal, which was the realization of Elvis's wildest hopes, was for seven years and three pictures, at a starting salary of $100,000 and increasing by increments of $50,000 in the two succeeding films. Wallis's most recent discovery before Elvis had been the comedy team of Dean Martin and Jerry Lewis; they had started at $50,000 a picture and worked up to $75,000. Clearly, Colonel Parker had done a good job of bargaining for the first picture. But by committing Elvis to a long-term agreement at fixed prices the Colonel made a big mistake. It wouldn't be long until everyone in the Presley circle was saying, "We don't make any real money on the pictures we do for Mr. Wallis."

Having no suitable picture in which to cast Elvis, Wallis decided to create for his new star a skillfully customized vehicle. He commissioned an original screenplay from Hal Kanter, who had fashioned for Wallis the adaptation of Tennessee Williams's *The Rose Tattoo,* which had won two Academy Awards the preceding year. While this project was in preparation, Wallis received an offer from Twentieth Century-Fox to stick Elvis into a picture it was preparing to shoot, titled *The Reno Brothers.* What Wallis received for the loan of his new acquisition, whose value was rising every week, is not known; but chances are the fee went a long way toward defraying the $100,000 promised Elvis for his first picture.

While the wheels were beginning to turn in Hollywood, they were spinning off their axles on the rock 'n' roll road. The summer of 1956 marks the dizzy apogee of Elvis Presley's career as a rock star. During these hot months, his life became a blur of one-night stands, broken only by quick dashes to radio, TV, film and recording studios. Typical of the fast pace was the thirteen-day stretch from June 22 to July 4. Elvis gave sixteen regular performances in half a dozen cities, flew up to New York to rehearse for a network TV show, came back again two days later to do the show, remained for another day to record two of his greatest hits, then wound up on the night of the Fourth headlining a big charity benefit at Memphis.

The run began with a three-day weekend at the Par-

amount Theater at Atlanta, where Elvis did four shows
a day between screenings of *Fury at Gunsight Pass*. The
bill was an all-country package (in Tom Parker's mind
Elvis was still a C & W act, not a rock 'n' roller), featuring
the Carter Family and two baggy-pants rube comics from
Grand Ole Opry: Rod Brasfield and Papa Sype. The great
moment of every show occurred toward the end, when Elvis
made a spectacular entrance riding up from the bottom of
the orchestra pit in an old-fashioned band car.

Stepping off the elevator into the lurid glare of a colored
follow spot, he would shout the first phrases of "Heartbreak Hotel"—and bring down the house! Then, he'd drive
straight into the current Little Richard hit, "Long, Tall
Sally," doing some of his fast jive moves. For a change of
pace, he would next sing "I Was the One," giving it that
under-the-echoing-overpass plangency that was so popular
at the time. Having cooled the mood with this exercise in
acne-spotted self-pity, he would reach back now to his Sun
days for "Baby, Let's Play House." Finally, the set would
reach its emotional peak with Elvis's first great R & B
ballad: "Hi want yew, Hi need you, Hi luh-huh-huh-huv
yew-hew!" Working in a blue spot and giving the song the
full gospel treatment, he would fall on his knees begging
and pleading and sometimes wind up lying face down with
his head in the footlight trough.

After this outburst, it was time to drive the kids out of
their kugels with three solid rockers in a row: "I Got a
Woman," "Blue Suede Shoes" and the song that would
become soon Elvis's trademark, "Hound Dog." Bowing and
waving and saluting the crowd, he would stand in sweaty
exultation for a moment. Then, the stage lights would dim,
the curtains would part and the screen would flash forth
the coming attractions.

The next stop was Savannah. Elvis traveled whenever
possible by road, using two of his fleet of four Cadillacs
(each a different color) to carry himself, his band and his
two cousins, Gene and Junior Smith. The Smith boys were
referred to by the other performers as "the hillbilly creeps."
Junior, the older of the two, looked exactly like what he
was: a psychopathic killer. A skinny, craggily handsome
young man, he resembled closely the actor Jack Elam.

Always grimacing, glaring and flashing forth from his disturbingly expressive face signs of his essential craziness, Junior disquieted a lot of people. They would have been terrified if they had known his real story.

Drafted during the Korean war, Junior had been sent to the front. The pressures of battle coupled with the tactics of the Koreans, which included the use of civilians as human booby traps, snapped his mind. One day, when a Korean family approached him with hands outstretched, he lowered his BAR and blew them all away. For this act of madness, he received a medical discharge. Now, the killer had been assigned a lifesaving mission.

Elvis's lifelong disposition toward nightmares and sleepwalking had been violently aggravated by the enormous emotional pressures of his big breakthrough. Gladys had become highly alarmed at the thought that some night in a strange city, all alone in a hotel room, Elvis would rise from bed to nip out a window or walk blindly, as he did once as a kid, into the middle of a highway. To guard her son from inadvertent self-destruction, she attached the Smith brothers to Elvis's side, with their most important duty being to sleep every night in the same room, or, preferably, in the same bed, with the somnambulist.

The *Elvis Presley Show* was preceded always by Oscar Davis, who launched the spot announcements over the airwaves and inserted the standard little ad in the paper, showing the picture of Elvis that appears on his first album, singing ecstatically with eyes shut and mouth wide open, slugged with the line Colonel had coined for his boy—"The Nation's First Atomic-Powered Singer." Colonel Parker himself was often away from the tour during this busy summer, negotiating new deals all over the country and getting signatures on his two-foot long contract, bordered with snapshots of the star and spelling out in the most minute detail how many inches of newsprint the concert promoter must provide, how many cops he must hire and how many yards before the gate must be cleared so that Colonel's souvenir hawkers would not have to compete with the local hucksters.

Elvis and his boys reached Savannah after driving all night from Atlanta. That night Elvis did two shows, one

at seven and the other at nine-thirty, each time packing
the 3,500-seat auditorium, mostly with screaming girls.
The behavior of the girls was described the following day
in the *Savannah Evening Press:* "They hung over rails
with glassy eyes and pawed wildly at the air. Those near
the stage held out their hands and screamed for Presley
to kiss them. One held up a baby to be kissed. One swooned
a genuine swoon. Cpl. C. C. Dickerson of the city police
said he took a 13-year-old girl to St. Joseph's Hospital in
a state of hysteria. It was frightening. Women have discovered burlesque—and they love it! He used the guitar
the way Sally Rand used to use a bubble." There were
some men in the audience. The reporter characterized
them as "strangely silent. They had a subdued, even
frightened look about them—sort of green around the
gills." After the show the reporter found Elvis in his dressing room with a towel wrapped around his neck, looking
like "a boxer who had gone fifteen rounds." Asked how he
felt after his ordeal, Elvis replied: "A show really wears
me out, but if I get to 'em, that's what counts."

The next night the show played in Charlotte, North
Carolina, in the big, domed Coliseum. The day before Elvis's appearance, the *Charlotte Observer* reprinted a piece
by TV critic John Crosby of the *New York Herald Tribune*
that denounced Elvis as obscene. Such attacks were commonplace at the time. Elvis was assailed all through his
first big year by a chorus of newspaper writers, pulpit
preachers, high-school teachers, police officials and local
politicians. These folk were not only genuinely shocked by
Elvis's antics but quick to identify him as a symptom of
the dread problem of juvenile delinquency. Not content
just to attack Elvis verbally, some of his assailants demanded that action be taken either to curb Elvis's performances or to run him out of town. It was not just the sting
of a damning article that Elvis was feeling the day he gave
an interview to a reporter from the local paper: It was the
fear that his newly won success might suddenly go up in
smoke.

The reporter met Elvis and Junior Smith in a lun-
cheonette near the hotel where they were staying. As the
boys ate up a mess of barbecue, the reporter jotted down

his impressions of Elvis. His "knees bounced while he sat," noted the writer. "His hand drummed a tattoo on the table top. His eyes, under his long lashes, darted from booth to booth, firing rapid winks at the girls who stared at him. 'Hi ya, Baby!' he breathed at one girl. She flopped back in her booth, looking like she'd been poleaxed." When the waitress brought Elvis coffee, he "reached down and fingered the lace on her slip. 'Aren't you the one?' she asked. He replied, 'I'm the one, Baby!'"

Once Elvis had filled his belly, he replied at length to the TV critic of the *Tribune.* "This John Crosby guy," he began, "who does he think he is? He says I'm obscene. Nasty. What does he know? Did you see the show [the second *Milton Berle Show,* June 5]? This Debra Paget was on it. She wore a tight thing with feathers on the behind where they wiggle most. Sex! Man, she bumped and pooshed out all over the place. I'm like Little Boy Blue. Yet, who do they say is obscene? Me! It's because I made more money than Debra. Forty thousand dollars a week! Them critics don't like to see nobody win doing any kind of music they don't know nuthin' about. The colored folk been singing it and playing it just the way I'm doin' now, man, for more years than I know. Nobody paid it no mind till I goosed it up."

The reporter asked the inevitable question about how long Elvis figured rock would last. Elvis replied that he didn't know but it didn't matter. "When it's gone, I'll switch to something else," he remarked confidently. "I like to sing ballads the way Eddie Fisher does and the way Perry Como does, but the way I'm singing now is what makes the money. Would you change if you was me?" With that parting shot, Elvis got up, paid his check and sauntered down the block with Junior until they reached a poolroom. The reporter left the star chalking his cue.

That night, he continued, "Presley burst onstage staggering and flailing like a moth caught in a beam of light." It took the efforts of twenty cops to keep the crowd from hurtling onto the stage. When the reporter cornered a fan and asked her what she thought of Elvis, she had the answer at the tip of her tongue. "He's a doll," she teased, "and I love to play with dolls."

Most of the young fans were content to dream about
playing with Elvis. The mature women who came to the
concerts were not content with dreams. They wanted action. On this night, for example, when Elvis got back to
his hotel room he heard a knock. Without thinking, one
of the Smith boys opened the door. In charged a highly-
wrought woman, who seized Elvis and hurled him onto
the bed. In the ensuing scuffle it took all three boys to
subdue the woman and push her out of the room. Elvis
loved football, but these female tackles! Hey, son, they wuz
somethin' else.

Wednesday night Elvis was in Augusta, Georgia, facing
a sellout crowd of six thousand at the Bell Auditorium.
When the local press caught him backstage after the show
and started quizzing him earnestly about his musical ac-
complishments, Elvis told them that he didn't know a
sharp from a flat. "In my kind of music," he joked, "you
just get out there and go crazy." The interview had to be
broken off abruptly because Elvis was heading out that
same night for Charleston, South Carolina.

His Charleston show was held in a dilapidated ballpark,
the stage a flatbed truck parked on the pitcher's mound.
The performance went off without incident. What happened afterward made the wire services. Elvis was sitting
in his Cad, preparing to leave for the railroad station.
Suddenly, a lady reporter came rushing up to him and
seized him by the sleeve. "I've got to make a deadline!"
she cried. Looking down at the woman's brightly painted
fingernails, Elvis leaned over and bit her on the finger.
She screamed and shouted, "What's the big idea?" "I was
only trying to be friendly, like a little puppy dog," Elvis
replied teasingly. "Well," said the woman, "that's the
first time anybody ever bit me out of friendship." Elvis
had the answer to that one, too. "Lady," he drawled, "if
you wanna get ahead in this business, you gotta be different."

Friday morning Elvis arrived in New York for a script
rehearsal of the *Tonight Show,* with Steve Allen, Imogene
Coca and Andy Griffith. Allen had launched his new Sun-
day-night program the preceding week. His competition
was *Talk of the Town,* the long-established Ed Sullivan

show on CBS. Obviously, Allen could not afford to have the kind of stink on his program that had occurred after the *Milton Berle Show*. On the other hand, Elvis was a hot new attraction, not the sort of act you'd want to cancel. The solution was to defuse the bombshell with humor. Elvis would be presented in a comic skit and do his solo in a funny setting. The audience would be invited to laugh its indignation away.

Elvis's appearance on the Steve Allen show was the most ridiculous performance of his life. It symbolized just as clearly as the famous from-the-waist-up appearance six months later on the rival Ed Sullivan hour the incapacity of television to either accept Elvis Presley or leave him alone. Allen and his gag writers had come up with two shticks for Elvis. He was to play in a skit that was a parody of hillbilly radio shows, like the *Louisiana Hayride;* and he was to sing, dressed like a concert violinist in tie and tails, his new song, "Hound Dog," to a real basset hound. Neither device produced any real laughs and both gimmicks prevented Elvis from giving the public what it wanted. The fans were furious at the way their hero had been treated. Next day they picketed the studio with signs reading, "We Want the Real Elvis."

The Steve Allen show played Sunday night. Monday morning, Elvis was back at work, this time at the RCA studios on East 24th Street. In the course of one long day's work, he produced two of his biggest hits: "Hound Dog"[2] and "Don't Be Cruel." Unlike "Heartbreak Hotel," which was composed with Elvis exclusively in mind, "Don't Be Cruel" was written by a man who had never heard of Presley. Otis Blackwell—once described by Jerry Lee Lewis (for whom the writer composed "Great Balls of Fire") as "a little colored fellow in a derby hat"—was out on the

---

[2]Elvis picked up "Hound Dog" from Freddy Bell and the Bell-boys during an engagement in April at Las Vegas. In July, Elvis recorded the song, copying Bell's version exactly, including the interpolated line, "You ain't never caught a rabbit." Hence the difference between Elvis's vocal and the original (superior) recording by Willie Mae "Big Mama" Thornton.

street scuffling to survive when he got his big break with this song.

Blackwell had started out in the music business as a singer who worked the round robins (going from one joint to another in the same night) in Brooklyn. By 1953, he was writing the jivey, jumpy R & B tunes typical of the day. On Christmas Eve, 1955, he was hanging out in front of the Brill Building, rock 'n' roll's Tin Pan Alley, on Broadway at Forty-ninth Street, when a hustler happened along and asked the down-in-the-mouth composer if he had any songs for sale. Blackwell pulled out a sheaf of compositions and was promptly ushered into the office of Moe Gale, one of the great wheeler-dealers of the game. Gale bought six songs for twenty-five dollars a shot. One of the six was "Don't Be Cruel."

Six months elapsed between the time the song was sold and Elvis Presley's recording session. During that time two important developments occurred: 1) Blackwell was conned into giving up half his royalties to Presley and allowing the singer to put his byline on the song; 2) Blackwell made up a demonstration record in which he sang his song in his own highly distinctive style, accompanying himself on the piano while beating a cardboard box in place of a drum.

"Don't Be Cruel" was Elvis's favorite among his early songs. It was also vitally important to his career because it established a new pattern for a Presley song. Hitherto, Elvis had been identified primarily with either C & W or R & B material. Now, he got a taste of the contemporary pop rock idiom. The song was a flirty, teasy, put-on of a lover's complaint. It had a catchy jinglelike simplicity that made it as contagious as a new slang word. In a word, it was slick.

The combination of Presley and pop proved sensational. The song not only became the Number One tune in the country but remained in that spot for nine weeks, not disappearing from the charts until clocking a total run of twenty-seven weeks—both incredible records. Significantly, the only Presley record to do better was another Blackwell tune, "I'm All Shook Up," which also stayed on top of the heap for nine weeks but remained on the charts for *thirty weeks*. Guided by these stupendous hits, Elvis quickly found his real groove. Henceforth, he and his publishers were always looking for tunes that conformed with the Blackwell formula.

"Don't Be Cruel" was released—in one of the greatest all-time marketing mistakes—as the B side of "Hound Dog." "Hound Dog," profiting from the heavy play automatically accorded the A side, rose swiftly to the top of the charts and remained there for a month. Then, the record flipped over and "Don't Be Cruel" followed "Hound Dog" as the Number One side. As in the parallel case of the Beatles' "Penny Lane" (A) and "Strawberry Fields Forever" (B), the decision to put both potential hits on the same disc resulted in a great bargain for the fans and a great loss of money for the singer and the record company. Elvis raised hell about this decision, but the simple fact was that RCA was just pumping out the product as it came to hand without any thoughts of stretching it. Nobody at Victor knew anything about the new world of rock. As far as they were concerned, Elvis was just a flash in the pan. The idea was to exploit him to the limit now that he was hot.

On the evening of July 4, Elvis played a charity benefit at Memphis. The place was Russwood Stadium, a now-demolished baseball field in the downtown area, once the home of the Memphis Chicks. The crowd was the biggest Elvis had ever faced: fourteen thousand people, stretching back from the red-white-and-blue bedecked bandstand on the third base line through the infield, the outfield and up into the bleachers. The program, which began at eight, was one of those interminable affairs, crowded with amateurs and semipros, which provincial cities generate out of their own resources. The MC was Dewey Phillips, juiced to the gills. For nearly three hours before Elvis appeared, ole Dewey kept bringing them on with a big hand: the orchestras of Bob Morris and Aaron Bluestein, the Admiral's Band of Navy Memphis, a barbershop quartet called the Confederates, Charlotte Morgan's dancing Dixie Dolls and one Helen Putnam, founder of Fat Girls Anonymous, who dedicated a song to Elvis—"A Good Man Is Hard to Find." Finally, just before eleven, when the hot,

restless, uncomfortably seated crowd—which had been
teased into squealing twenty-nine times by the mention
of Elvis's name—had had its patience stretched even further than Colonel Parker would have dared to try it,
Dewey bawled into the mike, "Here he is!"

Nobody needed to be told who "he" was. Instantly, the
vast crowd erupted in shrieks, shouts and tumultuous applause. Elvis bopped out onstage under the glaring arc
lights wearing a shiny black double-breasted raw silk suit
and a red tie. Pacing back and forth along the stage apron,
waving to the crowd and then bending down to shout greetings to his family in the first row, he finally came to rest
long enough for Dewey to make the presentation of a scroll
commemorating Elvis's contribution to the program. Then,
mindful of the fans who had complained about his disguised and muted appearance on the Steve Allen show,
Elvis collared the mike and barked: "I'm gonna show you
what the *real* Elvis is like tonight!" With that he went
into his usual act, ranging from "Heartbreak Hotel" to
"Blue Suede Shoes" and including a couple of his early
Sun numbers, such as "That's All Right Mama" and "Mystery Train." After he had worked himself into a sweat and
the audience into a fenzy, he grabbed the mike one more
time. With his blond hair falling in his face and his voice
like a mush-mouthed Jimmy Stewart, he made a vow that
was a prophecy of his whole future life. "Ah just wanta
tell y'awl not to worry," he drawled. "Them people in New
Yahk an' Hollywood are not gone change me *none!*" As
rebel yells split the night skies like skyrockets, Elvis was
into "Hound Dog" shouting: "They said you was high-
classed—but that wuz just a lie!" Then, he threw his hand
up in a farewell salute and left the stage, disappearing in
a phalanx of police who hustled him out of the stadium.

Chapter 13

The Early Days of Sexually Inspired Mass Hysteria

SUPPOSE you're a shrewd operator like Colonel Tom Parker, and you've lucked into the hottest new attraction in show business. Now, how do you go about making your star look like a star? Do you go out and find a bunch of other young dudes who are nearly as talented and put them all together in a great big flying circus with your man in the lead plane? Hell, no! Are you kidding? That's thinking like a chump. The trick is to go the other way entirely. That's right! Don't let another of those crazy rock 'n' rollers come within a mile of your boy. Don't let anybody who has a scrap of talent step on the same stage. Go out and shark up a lot of lames and lops, clowns and clods, who'll screw up so bad they'll make your kid look like Caruso. That's how you showcase a star!

So when Colonel Parker took Elvis under his exclusive management in March 1956, he called up a booker named Al Dvorin in Chicago, a guy from whom he used to buy midgets back in the days of Eddy Arnold, and he started ordering up every half-assed, two-bit, washed-up or wet-

nosed vaudeville act still shuffling around the old circuits.
Soon the Colonel had Elvis surrounded with a bizarre carnival of tap dancers, acrobats, magicians, comedy jugglers,
Irish tenors, xylophone players, nightclub comics, chan-
teuses and DJ MCs. The most amusing touch was the band.
Now, here's Elvis Presley, the hottest boy in the music
business. Shouldn't he have a great fifteen-piece show
band recruited out of the studios of Memphis and Nashville: guys who can really cut the mustard? Forget it! The
Colonel hires a club date sextet called the Flaim Brothers,
who are an economy version of the Lawrence Welk band—
accordion and all. They like to play tunes like "Every Little
Breeze Seems to Whisper Louise." Nice straw-hat, skating-
rink, Polish Falcon music. Also, the band is a little small
at six pieces. You can get away with that stuff in the
South. Up North, especially in the larger houses, the union
demands much bigger bands. In Chicago, for example,
where Elvis played a sports arena, the Colonel discovered
that the house contract called for twenty-two musicians,
including violins!

Well, Colonel paid them their scale; only he wouldn't
come up with a nickel for extra parts. So all night long
the extra musicians had to sit there faking! The horn players put their instruments to their lips, the fiddle players
ran their bows across the strings—but no music sounded
forth because the players were staring at empty music
racks. Colonel told Al Dvorin, who looks like the Great
Gildersleeve (and was once a band leader), to get up in
front of the orchestra and conduct with the tip of his lighted
cigar. Ha! That showed 'em! Colonel even did a little conducting himself. Gathering all his men backstage, he
shouted, "Now, what do we say?" Then, waving his arms
in time, he joined the swelling chorus of voices chanting:
"One, two, three—*fuck 'em!*"

The Elvis Presley Show may have been funnier than
the *Gong Show,* but only the Colonel was laughing. Here's
what happens on one of these occasions. In the afternoon,
the audience is like that for *Captain Kangaroo:* vast numbers of eight- and nine-year-old girls popping bubble gum.
In the evening, the average age is thirteen and the proportion of females may run as high as ninety percent. Now,

in those days, nice little girls, especially in the South, did not go to public performances dressed like the cast of *Grease*. It would have been unthinkable for any properly brought up child to appear at a theater or auditorium wearing pedal pushers or short shorts or jeans and a T-shirt. All that *Schlumperei* had to wait for the slovenly sixties. These junior misses wear long billowing skirts over crinolines or tight sheaths and chemises (cocktail dresses) over even tighter girdles and nylons. They curl and spray their short hair. They apply pancake, lipstick, liner and nail polish. They bedeck themselves with earrings, bangles, and charm bracelets (including always the gold calendar leaf with their birthstone). They jiggle on heels. Some of them are even wearing white gloves. If they are going steady, they wear their boyfriends' rings on chains around their necks. The other appurtenance with which they come equipped is a Brownie camera with a flash attachment. Elvis never walked onstage during those years without being irradiated by a barrage of flashbulbs.

So we have two or three or five thousand steamy, screechy, jittery, jabbery little girls jammed into some decaying movie palace or Masonic temple in Augusta, Richmond, or Savannah. For weeks, they've been waiting to see their god, Elvis Presley. Now, they've nestled down with a vast rustling of petticoats and a vast exhalation of baby powder, deodorant, and cologne in this crummy old theater. The house lights dim, the band strikes up and out in front of the brightly lit curtain steps a local DJ, some flattop nitwit with a bow tie, who's shouting "If anybody leaves their seats the show will be stopped!" Finally, the curtains part, but instead of the long-sought Elvis, here's this little girl, not much older than themselves, banging away on this xylophone and trying to sing. Well, girls: What are we gonna do about it? That's right! Everybody scream and boo and hiss! Or, better, start chanting rhythmically: "WE WANT ELVIS!...WE WANT ELVIS!"

Finally, the poor little girl with the mallets in her hands runs off into the wings crying. As the next act goes out to take her place, Colonel Parker—the old hypocrite!—comes to comfort the child. "They wouldn't listen to me!...They wouldn't give me a chance!" The poor child is crying her eyes out. Colonel is very kind and understanding. He comforts her. He dries her tears. He tells her, "That's show business. You have to learn to take it. You're gettin' paid." Meantime, the old Irish tenor is getting clobbered by the same hysterical screaming mob. Only this old dude is a veteran of many years on the stage. The moment he sees the game is up with "Mother Macree," he signals for "Donegal." He starts clapping his hands and yelling at the girls to join him. Pretty soon he's got them working as his rhythm section. He survives for a couple of tunes and runs for his life.

Wave after wave they come, the showbiz kamikazes, doomed to die in the face of an audience that has now been driven half mad by sheer frustration. The comic can't tell a single joke. He can't even make himself heard! Finally, he starts to work in dumb show and do pantomime. The acrobatic dancers have trouble hearing the pit band, there is such a roar and shriek of protest when they hit the stage. Finally, when the massacre is complete, the house lights go up and the audience scrambles out of its seats for what proves to be a very long intermission.

This is the Colonel's big moment, his star turn. Standing out in the lobby with a stingy brim hat on his head, a big cigar jammed into the corner of his mouth, holding aloft with one hand a sheaf of glossy photos while with the other he makes a constant jingle in the pockets of his change apron, Colonel is back on the midway hawking worthless trinkets for outrageous prices. He gets a buck for these "autographed" eight-by-tens of Elvis. It's a moody, bluesy, low-down Elvis in the picture, with his fist buried in one chubby cheek and his Novocain lip turned down in a sullen—or is it a sulky?—pout. You can also buy an Elvis Presley songbook, with a lot of songs he never sang, and a souvenir program, which proves you actually saw him. It's the Presley paraphernalia industry in its infancy.

When the girls get back in their seats after intermission, they're a giant mass of fidgets. The reappearance of the MC, wearing a sports jacket and white bucks, is greeted with hysterical screams. The girls feel that finally they are about to have their wish fulfilled. Their long wait

is over. Elvis is about to appear. Imagine what they do
when the MC shouts: "America's foremost gospel quartet—the Jordanaires!" Gospel quartet! Jordanaires!
Screeeeeeeeeeam! What a blast of baffled rage, what a
temper tantrum, greets the four neat young men dressed
in plaid blazers as they come bouncing out onstage to go
into "Let the Good Times Roll." Thank God, they have a
hit record at this moment, "Sugaree," which finally grabs
the audience. Then, they do a fast-stepping "Down by the
Riverside"—and run for their lives!

By now the Colonel's scheme has produced its intended
effect. The show has teased and tortured its highly vulnerable audience until just the name, *Elvis Presley,* will
bring down the house. That is what happens when the MC
bawls: "Ladies and Gentlemen: the man for whom you've
all been waiting—ELVIS PRESLEY!!!" At that instant
five thousand shrill female voices come in on cue. The
screeching reaches the intensity of a jet engine. When
Elvis comes striding out onstage with his butchy walk, the
screams suddenly escalate. They switch to hyperspace.
Now, you may as well be stone deaf for all the music you'll
hear. From this point on, you're gazing through a dense
wall of acoustic steam.

The Elvis of '56 wore traffic signal colors—a bright
green or a bright red sports jacket over navy blue slacks,
with red socks, white bucks (with blue soles) and sometimes a *cummerbund!* He dressed his guitar in a tan, hand-
tooled leather case with his full name carved conspicuously
on a diagonal across the skin. Elvis loved to tease his
audience. The moment he reached center stage, he would
collar the mike, bend it down like a tango dancer's partner,
spread his legs as if for a shootout and then shout,
"Welll..." Just as every girl in the audience leaned forward in anticipation of ecstasy, Elvis would stop suddenly,
laugh at the kids for having been taken in, then rear back
to start again with another "Welll..." This childish game
would continue until he released the band to go into
"Heartbreak Hotel."

The moment Elvis appeared, dozens of girls would bolt
from their seats and run down the aisles to the orchestra
pit, where they would snap their hero's picture. There must

be a million fading snapshots of Elvis Presley taken in
1956 alone. What did the girls see that drove them out of
their minds? It sure as hell wasn't the All-American Boy.
Elvis looked nothing like the stock young movie star of
the day: all those crisp-cut, white-buck, dumb schmucks
with names like Tab and Rock and Bob, names that rhyme
today with faggot. Elvis was the flip side of this clean-cut
conventional male image. His fish-belly white complexion,
so different from the "healthy tan" of the beach boys; his
brooding Latin eyes, heavily shaded with mascara; the
broad fleshly contours of his face, with the Greek nose and
the thick, twisted lips; the long greasy hair, thrown forward into his face by his jerking motions—God! what a
freak the boy must have looked to those little girls peering
at him through their camera finders. And what a turn-on!
Typical comments were: "I like him because he looks so
mean"; "He's fascinating—like a snake"; "I hear he ped-
dles dope"; "He's been in and out of jail"; "He's gonna die
of cancer in six months." Oh, those teenyboppers wailing
for their demon lover!

Like the gospel acts from whom he learned his trade,
Elvis's style onstage was busy, busy, busy! From the moment he hit the boards until he ducked off twenty minutes
later, he never stopped moving. Elvis's famous "gyrations"
came from the same source as his vocal tricks plus a few
things he picked up at local dances. Though Elvis was not
a dancer and had to lash his body to make it move, he
understood instinctively that his kind of music demanded
action. This recognition set him apart from all the other
white performers of his day and the character of his moves
distinguished him just as strongly from all the contemporary black acts.

John Lennon once remarked that every rock act he had
ever seen fell far short of the mental image of the performer he had formed listening to his records. Even the
great Little Richard, for example, presented an awkward
and constrained image onstage, half standing, half crouch-
ing at the keyboard of a piano, looking as though he had
caught his hands in the instrument's teeth or was receiving some Coppelia-like charge from the keyboard, without
which he might collapse like a rag doll. As for the famous

do-wop groups of the day, some of them moved skillfully, but they were all choreographed by the same man, Honi Coles (formerly of Coles and Atkins), which made them blur together in a slick, jivey idiom that did not convey the raunchy quality of rock music. In Elvis's moves, as in his original recordings, he exhibited a kind of genius: a capacity to project the substance of the music through the attitudes of the body that reinforced his singing and made him a total performer, his own best medium.

Lacking any training or natural flair for dancing, Elvis was forced like John Travolta in *Saturday Night Fever* to confine himself to the few steps he could cut. He would stand with his spraddled legs squarely before the mike shaking both limbs at once, as his band used to say, "wearing out his britches from inside." Suddenly, he would throw down his left hand, which would start fluttering like a hummingbird's wing. As a pained, ecstatic expression of possession crossed his face, his legs would start flailing like rubber hoses. Then, one-two! one-two!, he would snap his legs like scissors, the knees knocking, as in the Camel Walk, one foot coming to rest on toepoint. Next day the newspapers would report that Elvis did "bumps and grinds."

The suggestion of the burlesque dancer was especially strong when he would get down to the slow ball-and-sock-it conclusion of "I Got a Woman." Turning in profile, while grabbing his mike stand for support, he would shoot out his legs in a series of hot shots that were the pimp-walkin' daddy's equivalent of a bump. The difference was that where the stripper or the black jive dancer, like James Brown, works to make such moves sensuous or flashy, Elvis projected an idea of sex that was animalistic and violent, like a stamping stallion. His erotic pantomime suggested not so much the coitus of the burlesque dancer or the masturbation of the go-go girl as the aggressive and brutal motions of rape.

Though Elvis wasn't a stripper, he was a terrible tease. He played with his little-girl audience the way a little girl plays with her dolly. "I love you...I hate you...I kiss you...I kill you!"—this was the subliminal monologue he conducted through his onstage movements and gestures.

The great externalizing device for his erotic charade was
the standing microphone. Elvis was your classic mike
mauler. The moment he came on, he would seize the mike
by the neck and bend it down like the female partner in
an apache dance. He would haul it all over the stage.
Shake it violently. Straddle it. Force it down, down, down,
until it was parallel with the ground. Finally, he would
abandon it to throw himself down, taking care to fall just
short of those frantic fingers reaching out desperately to
touch him, just inches from those contorted, tear-stained
faces crying, "Please!...Please!"

No matter how much they begged and pleaded, it did
them no good. Oh, he might run one finger deliberately
across his forehead and then flick it in the audience's face,
sending the colored drops of sweat flying over the foot-
lights. That was the origin of the sweat-stained scarves
he flung into the house in his last years. Or, perhaps, he
did impulsively extend himself and kiss one girl on the
forehead. As she screamed and fell over backwards, he was
up on his feet again, whirling away from the stage apron,
dancing out of reach of all the thousands of other girls who
suddenly realized—"He kissed her!" Screeeeeeeeam!!!

In the gospel tradition, the goal of the performer is not
only to work the audience up to a feverish pitch of excitement but to keep pushing until they have been driven over
the edge of self-control and out of their minds. At this
point, the higher powers are supposed to intervene. What
about Elvis and his little girls? Did they experience states
of transcendental ecstasy and illumination? Or were they
possessed by the infernal powers and driven to commit
sins of the flesh?

Neither reaction was ever reported. The weaker sort
screamed and cried and finally were reduced by their tan-
trums to the hapless state of infants who have wet their
pants. The bolder sort were transformed into raging mae-
nads bent on violence and destruction. They didn't just
want to tear off their Orpheus's clothes. They wanted to
tear him to pieces. The Greeks had a word for it: *"Sparaga-
mos"*—the rending to bits of the sacrificial victim. That
sounds extravagant, but the fact is that on several occa-

sions Elvis Presley came very close to being killed by his adoring fans.

As early as 1956, Elvis had developed his famous escape technique for getting out of the theater alive. As he got into his last number, "Hound Dog," he would drag the mike further and further to the side of the stage. Finally, on the last note of the song, he would dive into the wings and race for the car standing beside the stage door.

As the audience threw its last fit, the MC would intone: "Elvis has left the building." Denied even a single encore, the fans were always left clamoring for more.

Chapter 14

Going Commercial

THE EPOCH-MAKING success of "Heartbreak Hotel" should have inspired a series of sequels that would have enabled Elvis to project his private psychodrama in a number of extravagantly emotional songs, precisely as his black counterpart, Little Richard, was doing at this moment with his even wilder and more frenzied persona. Sad to say, nothing of the sort happened. Elvis could never get the material that matched his act. Neither a songwriter, like Little Richard, nor a singer who was permitted to work with songwriters to produce the special vehicles his unique image demanded, Elvis was condemned from the start to fit himself to whatever material he was given.[1] So while Little Richard went on during the next two years

---

[1]Colonel Parker, who started isolating Elvis the moment he became his manager, made it a strict rule that no writer ever be allowed to get near the singer. For this reason many of Elvis's most important writers, such as Otis Blackwell and Doc Pomus, never met their famous client. What Colonel feared was that Elvis would say he liked a song to a writer who had not agreed to surrender the coveted one-third of his royalties. Then it would be impossible to make the writer kick back because he had his hook in Elvis's mouth.

etching the most powerful and indelible profile in the history of hard rock, Elvis went on patching together a crazy quilt of musical odds and ends—old songs, new songs, black songs, white songs, good songs, bad songs—that failed to add up artistically just as surely as it added up commercially to the greatest score in the history of the music business.

One of the reasons for this haphazard eclecticism was the long delay on the part of Elvis's new masters in the Brill Building in plotting his future course and in securing for him a steady supply of original songs. During most of Elvis's greatest year, 1956, he was obliged to adopt the same recording strategy as that employed by all the established white pop stars: the notorious practice of "covering" current R & B hits. Covering a record (*i.e.* recording the song anew) may produce a highly original recording with a distinctly new interpretation and sound, or it may entail little more than an act of licensed plagiarism. This latter practice was common at the beginning of the rock fad because the good records were coming out on the independent labels with relatively unknown performers; they were thus highly inviting to famous singers recording for major companies because the big names could displace the unknowns and the big labels could advertise and distribute their product much more successfully. Though Elvis didn't as a rule indulge in the worst form of this practice, which was to jump on a new record the moment it surfaced and steal the whole arrangement, which was not then protected by copyright law, he did copy virtually note for note a great many songs introduced by major black performers.

Setting aside the moral issues involved in such a blatant rip-off, one comes to the real issue: Why was the most original and creative white singer in America suddenly reduced to the practices of the outdated white pop singers? No satisfactory explanation of this behavior has ever been offered; but it's likely that Elvis suffered at this time from both the temptations presented by effortless success and by the difficulty of imposing a new vision onto material that was itself so new and powerful that he could not imagine any way of improving it. At Sun Elvis had recast originals by mediocre R & B men like Arthur Crudup, Junior Parker and Roy

Brown. Now he was up against all the greatest performers
in the style, commencing with Ray Charles and Little Richard and going on to Joe Turner, Fats Domino, Lloyd Price,
Willie Mae Thornton and Clyde McPhatter. Though it is
often said that Elvis sang black music better than any of his
white contemporaries, does anyone really believe that he
sang it better than the greatest black artists? Without the
enabling charge of contempt Elvis felt for the old-timers or
mediocrities he sent up at Sun, he could not work his magic.
You can't one-up something that is hipper than you are. So
instead of inflecting his mimicry into parody, he now settled
for just the mimicry, taking as his basic model Little Richard, whom he despised as a "screamer" but whose style he
appropriated for use not only on his covers of Little Richard's tunes but on those of other singers as well. It is at
this moment, therefore, that Elvis Presley first becomes
what it is usually assumed he was from the start: "a white
boy who could sing like a nigger."

The decisive moment in Elvis's recording career came
in September 1956, when Hill and Range finally got its
new Presley assembly line running. At this point two very
important things happened: 1) Elvis began to receive a
steady stream of music custom-crafted to his image; 2) his
image was modulated so that he became less the hard
rocker and more the masticator of black-flavored bubble
gum. For the old shlockmeisters in the Brill Building had
finally figured out how to deal with the rock 'n' roll fad.
After years of diluting and cleaning up R & B for the white
teen market, they finally recognized that real R & B wasn't
the most appropriate source for white rock because it reflected the raunchy life of the ghetto instead of the cars,
Cokes and pajama parties of white kiddieland. At this
point there commences the movement from rock to schlock
that would lead in a few years to the era of Fabian and
Frankie Avalon. Though Elvis Presley was vastly superior
to these travesties, he is the pivotal figure in the movement away from R & B and toward the cutesey, teensy
tunes epitomized by "Teddy Bear."

The manager of the new Presley tune and toy factory
was a genial Swiss named Freddy Bienstock, a nephew of
the publishers, Jean and Julian Aberbach. Bienstock's

principal responsibility was collecting material for Elvis
to record. If Elvis were making a picture with six scenes
in which he sang a song, Bienstock would circulate among
his six "contract writers" (typically words-and-music teams
whose royalty earnings were credited against a weekly
stipend paid by Hill and Range), a description of each of
the scenes, with the understanding that the writers were
free to submit material for every spot. Soon Swiss Freddy
would be winging his way toward Hollywood with thirty-
six musical chocolate bars.

RCA had no recording facilities on the West Coast at
this time, and Elvis could not tolerate the atmosphere of
the huge studio sound stages: so the sessions were held at
the best independent studio in town, Radio Recorders, on
Santa Monica Boulevard near Hollywood High. The engineer for all the Presley sessions down through the years
was a big, affable man named Thorn Nogar. His assistant
was Bones Howe, known today as an independent record
producer. Nogar and Howe were astonished at the way
Elvis Presley made records.

In those days studio time was doled out to musicians
like nights at Mt. Palomar are allotted to astronomers.
Recording sessions rarely exceeded three hours, and the
goal was to cut four sides an hour. When Elvis came to
town, RCA threw the rule book out the window. The studio
might be booked solid for as much as a month. The musical
instruments, mikes, baffles and other gear would be put
in place and there they would remain until the work was
completed. When Elvis was in the mood, he was a fast
worker: Once he cut *fifteen sides* in a single mammoth
session. If he were not in the mood, however, he might
abort the session in an hour. "It's not happening," he'd
say—and split!

Another source of astonishment was the way Elvis
turned a session into a party. He liked to stay "loose as
a goose"; so he would arrive with not just his band but his
boys. They would rib each other and clown around in the
studio. Then Elvis would seat himself at the piano, which
he played by chording in one of two keys, and spend an
hour singing hymns. As the all-night sessions wore on, the
young men would get hungry. Immense quantities of junk

food would be brought in and consumed: fifty or sixty hamburgers, mountains of greasy French fries, gallons of Pepsi Cola. When Elvis left a studio, it looked like it had been the scene of a sixth-grade picnic.

Elvis short-circuited all the customary preparations for recording. Instead of spending weeks closeted with writers, arrangers and producers, selecting songs, preparing scorings and rehearsing the new material, he would walk in cold and record everything at first sight. No performer since Fats Waller had ever displayed such a breezy attitude in the face of phonographic immortality. Elvis had absolute confidence in his powers. He could spot a hit at a glance. Memorize a song after hearing it only twice. After forty takes, he would tell the engineer to go back to number seventeen because that one had worked the best.

Though Elvis was a highly spontaneous performer onstage, who led his band a merry chase (Bill Black used to quip: "We're the only band in the business that takes its cues off the singer's ass!"), once he settled down to hone a hit, he became as compulsively repetitive as the most meticulous diamond polisher on 47th Street. He would lavish as many as *sixty* takes on a single song. His exhausting efforts to attain precisely the effect he was seeking were not determined, as might be supposed, by the struggle to achieve technical perfection. Far from it! Elvis would never hesitate to release a flawed performance if it had the right feel. He was seeking not to gratify the musician's ear but to tickle the teen fan's fancy. Commercial to the core, Elvis was the kind of singer dear to the heart of the music business. For him to sing a song was to sell a song. His G clef was a dollar sign.

Steve Sholes, a middle-aged man who had spent his entire life in the record business, soon realized that Elvis knew more about teen taste than any producer in the game. He confined himself to acting at these sessions as a benign and acquiescent father figure. Eventually, he was to spend the long nights sound asleep on a sofa in the lounge. Hal Wallis, on the other hand, would spend entire nights observing the sessions with fascination. He pronounced Elvis a "genius."

The real secret of Elvis's method lay not so much in his

genius as in that interesting professional device, the demonstration record. When Freddy Bienstock collected his songs in New York, he would hear them first in the time-honored manner: played on the piano and sung by one of the writers. After he had selected the most promising pieces, he would arrange to have them recorded as demos. Ostensibly, the demo was just a device for conveying the music to performers, like Elvis, who couldn't read notation. Actually, these recordings were selling devices, designed carefully to make the song appealing to the singer at whom they were aimed.

Making demos for Elvis Presley swiftly became a highly developed art. The canny writers who got a shot at the greatest hit-maker in the business did not neglect to study their target. They analyzed his style, his tastes, his favorite keys and rhythms and even his preference in titles—nineteen Presley records have the word *blue* in their titles. If one member of the writing team were a singer of professional caliber, he would do the singing. Otis Blackwell, for example, had a highly distinctive way of voicing and phrasing his songs. Elvis copied this delivery note for note on "Don't Be Cruel." As Blackwell recalls: "After he came out with 'Don't Be Cruel,' and I heard how close it was to the demo record I had done, I made sure I did all the demos for my songs. I didn't mind that he copied the demos so closely: I figured making good demos was a surer way of getting him to record my stuff." If neither of the writers were a man who could put a song across, one of several singers would be employed who were especially adept at mimicking Elvis (precisely the approach adopted by Mae Axton when she got Glen Reeves to demonstrate "Heartbreak Hotel" in Elvis's "shaky" voice).[2] Elvis's stan-

---

[2]In addition to Otis Blackwell, who demonstrated other writers' songs as well as his own, the singers on the Presley demos included such subsequently familiar performers as Brian Hyland ("Itsy Bitsy Teenie Weenie Yellow Polka Dot Bikini"), David Hill ("Two Brothers"), P. J. Proby ("Niki Hoeky"), Mort Shuman (later a big star in France), Dorsey Burnette (another Memphis rockabilly) and Ivory Joe Hunter.

dard instrumentation would be employed to give the records the Presley sound. Eventually, the demos became so important that they were recorded under the supervision of the young Phil Spector, who was brought to New York by one of Elvis's writing teams, Leiber and Stoller. When the demo was finished, it resembled a costly custom-tailored suit. All the song required to exhibit its perfect fit was to be tried on.

The fact that Elvis copied unknown singers who were endeavoring to copy him should not be dismissed as merely an amusing bit of irony. This practice offers a revealing insight into the character of all performers whose fame is based on projecting an enthralling image. An image is not simply an individual style: It is much closer to a Jungian archetype or a Platonic Idea. Because it transcends the individual and his limited consciousness, it can be enlarged and developed by the labors of many men, as one sees most clearly in the history of Elvis's only superior in popular appeal, Mickey Mouse.

Elvis Presley's genius consisted ultimately not so much in creating his style as in recognizing its constituents in the work of other men, commencing with Tony Curtis's haircut and leading through Jake Hess's vocal mannerisms to Otis Blackwell's campy black phrasings to the score or more of other sources and influences that comprised Elvis's substance throughout the course of his long and evolutionary career. Like so many artists, great and small, high and low, of the twentieth century, Elvis operated on the principle that a man has a right to take what belongs to him by nature.

The first step on a Presley recording session was invariably the audition of the demos. Like every feature of Elvis's life, this procedure quickly hardened into a ritual. First, Freddy Bienstock would go into the control booth with his stack of discs. Removing from its tan sleeve a shiny, oddly smelling, ten-inch seventy-eight RPM acetate, he would lay the record on the turntable, lower the tone arm and send the music blaring into the studio. There Elvis would stand, surrounded by his musicians, poised to make the decision on which the fate of the teen world might turn for the next six months.

Elvis's responses to the auditions were as curt and decisive as the gesticulations of a Roman emperor judging
a gladiatorial combat. If the song did not appeal to him,
he would make a slashing sign across his throat, signaling,
"Cut!" If the song attracted him, he would rotate the palm
of his hand above his head, signifying, "Take it from the
top!" Once Elvis had made a selection, the audition would
stop and the recording process would begin.

If Elvis liked the arrangement on the demo, he would
order his men to copy it note for note. If he objected to the
arrangement, he and his players would concoct a "head"
(unwritten) arrangement. The only parts lacking on the
demo were the vocal echoes: These colorless vocables, like
the styrofoam chips employed in packing a valuable object,
were manufactured swiftly by the Jordanaires, who were
typically facile studio musicians.

As nothing matters on Elvis's RCA records but the star,
most listeners instinctively tune out the mediocre playing
and singing of Elvis's accompanists. Elvis should have
tuned them out himself and replaced them with players
at least as good as those on the demos. Making any change,
however, even the slightest, in his customary dispositions
was something that was unthinkable for Elvis at any time
in his life. So his original backing remained on his records
until, ironically, it was the accompanists who quit Elvis.
(The first defections occurred in the summer of 1957 when
Scotty and Bill quit in protest against the fact that they
were still being paid $150 a week [$250 on the road] while
Elvis was making millions.)

Though Elvis constantly improved as a singer in his
early years, developing a voice as "phonogenic" as Caruso's, he just as consistently declined as a creative force
in music. Clearly, he was the victim of his own success.
Instead of struggling as he had to do at Sun to come up
with an original version of each tune he recorded, he could
now turn out dozens of records by simply copying his best
demos, giving the songs the little idiosyncratic touches
that teased the teenyboppers to ecstasy. As his music deteriorated into a series of simple-minded formulas, as his
demos got consistently better, as his fans became habit-

uated to acclaiming every new record as if it were a revelation, Elvis found himself rolling toward the pinnacle
of success in a rocking chair. Never has anyone ever been
so richly rewarded for doing so little.

The only thing that could have saved Elvis's soul at
this point would have been to refuse, as did the Beatles,
to take the easy, obvious way to success. Such thoughts
never crossed the mind of the young Elvis Presley. He
assumed his success was only momentary so why shouldn't
he cash in on it in every way he could? He had no higher
values than those represented by chart positions, gold records and gross sales. Elvis was, in short, the classic commercial artist.

Among the first songs he cut on the West Coast were
the pieces intended for *The Reno Brothers* (later retitled
Love Me Tender). This stock western, set at the end of the
Civil War, was planned originally as a straight drama.
When Elvis was added to the cast, Fox decided to capitalize
on the great commercial opportunity presented by his first
appearance by interpolating four tunes. Just the year before, Mitch Miller had scored an enormous hit with an
authentic Civil War song, "The Yellow Rose of Texas."
Now, music researchers everywhere were feverishly turning over old songbooks looking for more of the same kind
of material. One of the most popular songs of the Civil
War was "Aura Lea," a sentimental salute to a golden
girl couched in that idiom preserved still in fraternity
house drinking songs and high school anthems. Simple
and mellifluous, wistful and haunting, this period piece
was perfect for the picture. The only problem was the
verses—"Aura Lea! Aura Lea! Maid of golden hair!"—
which were too quaint and literary for all those gum-chew-
ing pubes in tight toreador pants. So for the limpid English
of the original was substituted "Love me tender," which
sounds like a TV commercial with a talking steak.

Listening to Elvis's recording of the song today, one is
astonished at how badly he sings it. His voice is husky
and lacking in resonance; his delivery at the slow, demanding tempo is uncertain in pitch. He still has great

difficulty in a ballad making himself sound sincere. One imagines with what wistful beauty Bing Crosby would have voiced this pretty period piece. Needless to say, Elvis's vocal inadequacies made not the slightest difference to his doting fans. Before the record could be shipped to the stores, RCA booked 856,327 orders. In those days when you "shipped gold," it wasn't fool's gold.

The primary reason for this tidal wave of demand was the extraordinary preview that the song received in the course of Elvis's first appearance on the *Ed Sullivan Show*. This performance is one of the great pseudoevents of entertainment history. Not only has its importance been grossly exaggerated, but the facts have been remodeled by the fantasies that shaped the Presley Myth. According to the widely publicized legend, Sullivan was so scandalized by Elvis when he first appeared on the tube that he was moved to say, "I wouldn't touch him with a ten-foot pole!" Then, when Elvis appeared on the rival Steve Allen show, raising its ratings, Sullivan was compelled to eat some very expensive crow. Even in the act of surrendering to Elvis, however, Sullivan is said to have expressed his distaste for "The Boy Who Dared to Rock" by ordering his cameramen to shoot Elvis only from the waist up. As Elvis performed in this truncated manner, Sullivan stood in the wings fuming and murmuring audibly, "Sonovabitch! Sonovabitch!"

This famous tale is about ninety percent fiction. Sullivan knew nothing and cared nothing about Elvis Presley when he was first approached by William Morris to put the young rock star on his program. What made Sullivan explode with rage at the suggestion was an infuriating experience he had had the year before with Bo Diddley. When Sullivan heard Diddley's big hit, "Bo Diddley," at rehearsal, he had reacted in much the same spirit as those people who were outraged by Andy Warhol's Brillo boxes. To the impresario's ears, the song was a bad joke: just the same stupid phrase repeated over and over again with the singer's name comprising the bulk of the lyrics, like a soap jingle. Determined to have Diddley sing some "real" music, Sullivan told Diddley to do Tennessee Ernie Ford's new hit, "Sixteen Tons." Diddley could not believe that he had been forbidden to plug his hit record—the whole purpose of his appearance on the show. He assumed instead that he was being given the coveted opportunity to perform *two* songs.

That night he led off with "Bo Diddley" and then went into "Sixteen Tons." Sullivan exploded with rage. He cut Diddley off in the middle of the tune. Then, cornering the singer backstage, he ranted: "You're the first colored boy who ever crossed me up on a song!" When Diddley received his check for seven hundred dollars, he was ordered to endorse it and hand it back. After such a fiasco, it's easy to imagine how Sullivan felt about having another of these rock 'n' roll weirdos on his program.

Eventually, of course, Sullivan did have to come to terms with Elvis. Instead of paying the $5,000 that had been asked originally, he was forced to ante up $50,000. Fearful that next time the price might go even higher, he made a deal to have Elvis on the show three times in the next six months. The first show was a remote from Hollywood on September 9. Elvis was not shot from the waist up on this program: That famous incident—which has come to symbolize more than anything else the moral tone of the fifties—occurred on the last show. And it had nothing to do with morality. It was, in fact, the very opposite of censorship, being a deliberate tease intended to suggest that there was a lot more going on "down there" than in truth there was. Likewise, it is ridiculous to imagine Sullivan standing in the wings during the first show fuming with moral indignation because actually he was recuperating from a car crash and the show's host was Charles Laughton.

So much for the fictions—what of the facts? The most important fact is that the program provided an occasion for the whole nation to tune in on the phenomenon about which it had been hearing for the past nine months. Elvis's fame and his position as the greatest showbiz sensation of the day had now been firmly established. It was Elvis who made this program famous, not the program Elvis. As a show, it was nothing that anyone would want to see

again. Elvis was never comfortable on TV—what rock act
has ever been shown to good effect on this medium, saving
the Monkees? Rock and TV are the ideal illustration of
Marshall McLuhan's dictums about the incompatibility of
hot performers and cool media. What's more, Elvis had
gotten so much flak about his TV performances in the past
that he must have felt morally obliged to ride this rocket
to fame with a very tight rein.

Whatever the reasons for his poor showing, he talked,
looked and performed like an amateur on a local talent
show. He developed such a case of fidgets during "Love Me
Tender" that he appeared like a little boy desperate to go
to the bathroom but too embarrassed to ask the way.

This amateurish performance was witnessed by 82.6
percent of the viewing audience or an incredible fifty-four
million souls, one-third of a nation. (The record stood on
the Sullivan show until 1964, when it was broken by the
Beatles.) On the strength of the appearance and the subsequent flood of orders for the new song, RCA tossed out
seven new 45s on the market and Fox changed the title
of *The Reno Brothers* to *Love Me Tender,* increasing its
customary order for three hundred prints to five hundred
and fifty.

If TV was not the secret of Elvis's overnight fame, what
was? Clearly the number of people he reached in live performances was relatively small. The amount of attention
he received in the national press was far less than a comparable phenomenon would receive today. What's more,
the tone of all the articles was either ambivalent or antagonistic. Elvis's phonograph records were crucial to his
success, but the public had first discovered these records.
Almost invariably this crucial discovery was made through
radio.

Radio, the medium that Marshall McLuhan likened to
the "tribal drum," was the great evangelizing voice not
only for Elvis Presley but for rock in general. Significantly,
the first rock hero—the man who named the music, established the rock concert, made the first rock movies and
reached the widest audience with the sound he dubbed
"The Big Beat"—was a disc jockey: Alan Freed. The Pied

Piper of Rock and the 1,700 DJs of the fifties dictated the
cultural climate for seventeen million teenagers. As these
kids got up in the morning or came home from school, as
they rode in cars or lay on the beach with their portables,
as they did their homework in the evening or snuggled in
their beds at night with the lights out and their minds
open in the most suggestible condition, the DJs enjoyed
an incomparable opportunity to mold the imagination of
an entire generation. Some of these men achieved a tremendous hold on their young audiences and were transformed in the kids' fancies into surrogate fathers: a point
well made in the otherwise over-idealized but beguiling
film about Alan Freed, *American Hot Wax*. Television, by
contrast, meant very little to the teens because until the
advent of shows like *American Bandstand* (not broadcast
nationally until the summer of 1957), television programming was aimed exclusively at adults and children.

By the end of 1956, Elvis Presley was being universally
acclaimed as the King of Rock 'n' Roll. The boy who began
the year as an obscure country singer broadcasting from
a hillbilly station at Shreveport, the regional entertainer
who spent his life out on the highway rushing from one
schoolhouse or community center to another in the Deep
South, the Sun recording artist whose greatest achieve-
ment was landing a side on the country and western charts
was now, less than twelve months later, an American hero.
Nobody in the history of show business had ever made it
so big so fast.

Even the Beatles, who broke all of Elvis's early records
eventually, seem like shleppers when you compare their
hard, steady pull to the top with Elvis's breathtaking as-
cent. Instead of characterizing Elvis's triumph in conventional metaphors—the long, billowy road, the steep ladder, the tightly closed door—you are obliged to seek
images that suggest speed, violence and, above all, the
sheer inadvertence of the man who walks into a room filled
with volatile gases, lights a match—and is blown through
the ceiling! Clearly, if you want to understand the phenomenon of Elvis Presley or how he "did it," you have to
start with the powerfully explosive vapors and not with

the puny little match.

The vapors are, of course, the frenzied atmosphere of youth culture in the fifties. From the start of the decade down to the advent of Elvis, history's first generation of culturally autonomous teenagers had been working itself up to a climactic outburst. As the endlessly incited energies of this rebellious generation charged the national atmosphere, they furnished a classic demonstration of William Blake's great vision in *The Marriage of Heaven and Hell* of the schizophrenic character of any true revolution, which will appear to those whose authority is threatened like a monstrous fire-breathing dragon risen from the deeps, whereas to those who welcome the new order, it will seem as sweet as a harpist by a pastoral stream. As the new generation seethed and heaved like the proverbial sea before the storm, the adult world struggled to anticipate the shape of things to come.

All the famous youth movies of the fifties can be interpreted as images of terrified anticipation. First, the teenagers appear in *The Wild One* (1953) as Nazi Huns, riding across the steppes of Sonoma on their snarling mechanical ponies led by that grim-visaged Attila, Marlon Brando. Then, they are seen as vicious, sneering slum bums, mugging an idealistic young teacher in *Blackboard Jungle* (1955), whose theme song is "Rock Around the Clock." Finally, the ultimate image of the teenager—as a weird and hideous monster, a Grendel assailing the split-level mead hall—is snapped in focus in *I Was a Teenage Werewolf* (1958). Thus was youth viewed by adults in that day. More importantly, thus did youth regard itself: as a new, perhaps monstrous race.

When youth culture swung into the traditional path of a great song and dance mania—instead of a mass outbreak of juvenile delinquency—the guardians of the fifties should have breathed a sigh of relief. Rock, though of an unprecedented coarseness, vulgarity and violence, conformed fundamentally with historically sanctioned patterns of adolescent behavior. That's what men like Alan Freed—the type of older man who identifies with the kids, the Timothy Leary of his time—kept telling the country.

The fifties, obsessed with its "menaces"—the Commie menace, the Pachuco menace, the Black menace, the Beat menace, the Hipster menace, the Teenage menace, the menace presented by everything that did not conform to the constricting canons of "normalcy" in that most abnormal age—had no ears to hear. Rock, a relatively harmless and innocent enthusiasm, was condemned as obscene, insurrectionary, criminal and "racious." This relentless opposition assured its success.

Rock swiftly became what anthropologists call a "peripheral cult": a rite of the excluded and powerless, who exhibit symptoms of possession by alien demons (whose presence is manifested by the appearance of foreign words in their mouths, words like "man," "cat," "baby," "rock"). To exorcise the demons and restore the "sick" to their normal selves, the cult contrives through the use of inciting music and dance to arouse its members to a state of ecstasy. In this open condition, they can be freed of their demons through the ministrations of a charismatic shaman, who possesses the remarkable gift of taking the evil spirits into his own body and soul, where he either defeats them in combat or placates them by sweet offerings.

If this analogy appears farfetched, reflect again on the paramount image of the whole era—the spectacle of thousands of young girls screaming out their lungs while they exhibit first one, then another stereotyped posture of frenzy, like the illustrative plates in Charcot's books on hysteria. How do these hapless agonies differ from the frenzies of black charwomen hurling themselves into the cathartic service of some ghetto storefront church? The truth is that rock ministered to its young devotees and relieved them of distresses that were no less real than those of oppressed minorities for being the products of prosperity.

All cults develop eventually a profound yearning for a great leader or hero or messiah who will embody the ethos of the group in a totally fulfilling and redemptory image. So great was the craving for such a hero in the rock cult that its frantic devotees acclaimed some of the most preposterously amateurish or mawkish performers ever seen

on the American stage. Though today it seems hard to
believe, when Bill Haley landed in England for the first
time in 1956, there were riots at the docks. Riots for a
moon-faced, spit-curled clod like Bill Haley! Critics and
showbiz professionals of that day were driven to the limits
of exasperation by the spectacle of such crude and inept
performers attaining unprecedented popularity. What the
old pros were slow to recognize was that the kids cared
nothing for professional skills and talents; what they demanded were projections of themselves. The identification
between the rock public and the rock star was the most
blatant event witnessed. The moment a performer opened
his mouth at a rock concert, he found himself drowned out
by an enormous echo, as every kid in the house sang the
same song in the same voice. As Mel Brooks makes his
archetypal rock star, Fabiola, explain: "They're doin' the
singin'—I jes' got the mouth!"

The obvious mediocrity of the first white rock stars
could not be tolerated for long, however. Inevitably, the
kids, brought up on slick professional showbiz and Hollywood movies, began to yearn for a rock star who was
handsome, talented and dynamic. The ideal rock star had
to meet a very elaborate set of specifications that had been
established by the complex course of youth culture during
the preceding years. Obviously, he had to be very young,
unlike the Benny Goodmans or even the Frank Sinatras
of the previous generation; for rock was not, like swing,
a style that aspired to sophisticated adulthood, but a
frankly regressive music fixated on the moods of early
adolescence. Instead of looking clean and wholesome, like
the Hollywood youth idols, the rock star had to exhibit a
totally different ideal of beauty—hoody and dangerous,
mysterious and demonic—because one of his basic functions was to scare the hell out of the parents and teachers
who were persecuting his "people." At the same time that
he presented the image of a motorcycle hoodlum or a
Brooklyn hitter, he had to appear to the gaze of the initiated as a sensitive and vulnerable soul, like the first
great teen saint and martyr, Jimmy Dean. Finally, it was
vital—because the music was steeped to the lips in the
sounds and lingo of the black ghetto and best performed

with the corresponding black body English—that the new hero be a cultural mulatto: a "white nigger." In fine, what rock 'n' roll demanded was a handsome young stud who looked dangerous but was really a pussycat who could sing and swing his ass like a jiveass black bluesman.

Chapter 15

The New Jimmy Dean

THE GIFT of perfect timing that accounts so largely for Elvis's success in the nascent world of rock 'n' roll did not desert him when he arrived in Hollywood to make his film debut. Far from it! In the film capital, he found an opportunity awaiting him just as great as anything he had encountered in the music business. Only the year before, Hollywood's most brilliant young star, the fascinating Jimmy Dean, had died on the highway in his white 550 Porsche Spyder. His demise opened up a gap in the Hollywood pantheon that could easily have become a niche for Elvis Presley.

Indeed, from the beginning of the decade down to the moment of Elvis's advent, there had been a clear line of development in pictures that made the youth star and the film about modern youth one of Hollywood's most promising new genres. Marlon Brando had established this idiom with *The Wild One,* a cinematic treatment of a real incident in which a gang of bikers took control of a small town and terrorized the citizenry until the arrival of the state police. That film had projected a mutely intense, almost enigmatic image of the youth hero as a young man of feeling, a sort of Byron of the motorbike, posing, musing and communing with his counter-wiping beloved, while his good-natured but potentially dangerous gang parties

it up in a whirl of hipster slang, street-gang high jinks
and progressive jazz. Morally, the picture said that the
failure of the parental generation to act with firmness and
authority was responsible for the damage the delinquent
kids were inflicting on society. Dramatically, the film projected the incapacitating anguish that is the most characteristic response of American parents when confronted
with their children's misdeeds and defiant nonconformity.

The next film to take up the theme was *Blackboard
Jungle,* which substituted for the jivey, inadvertently destructive but basically good-natured kids of Brando's motorcycle gang a really threatening and ugly group of slum
school punks who are prepared to use criminal tactics in
their assault on the social authority represented by the
school's teachers. Again the anguish of the parental generation—coupled this time with its idealistic belief in the
goodness of youth and its eagerness to educate young people—is projected vividly by Glenn Ford, who finally suc-
ceeds in detaching the good kids from the leadership of
the bad kids, thus resolving the dilemma of juvenile delinquency by removing the rotten apples from the barrel.

By 1956, when the best film in this tradition, *Rebel
Without a Cause,* appeared, the debate over rebellious and
delinquent youth had gone beyond the old beliefs in discipline or the segregation of good and evil. This film was
the classic statement of enlightened popular opinion in
that day, which held that the disturbed behavior of kids
was the product of the psychological and moral flaws of
their parents. In this picture, the implicit ideal is a strong
father, a mother who is supportive instead of domineering,
and a set of moral principles that is not canceled the
moment some danger impends that can be averted by lying
or covering up the truth. Without such parents and principles, the film argues, youth is condemned to the role that
James Dean so brilliantly realized: the kid who would be
good if only he were given the chance to be good by an
ugly world that comprises, on the one hand, his cowardly
and role-reversed parents, and, on the other, the violent
and self-destructive kids who kill each other playing
chicken with their hot rods. Never before or since in
American movies has any actor so resourcefully and so

beautifully portrayed the type of modern middle-class
youth, with all his charm and sensitivity and moral confusion, his pain and rage and bafflement, his curiously
sexless yearning for love and his highly romantic capacity
for friendship, all leading up to one of those remarkably
lyrical and dreamlike catastrophes that were the great
ideal of a theater and cinema inspired by the poetic mel-
odrama of Tennessee Williams.

Whatever value one assigns to these films and actors,
the point is that when Elvis Presley arrived in Hollywood
he had a marvelous opportunity to step into a vigorously
welling stream of cinematic energy, a genre and a tradition
already well established, which could have offered him
opportunities to play parts that were suitable to his age,
appearance and public and that would have satisfied his
ambition to become a good actor and to count for something
more than a box office attraction. He was intensely aware
of the opportunity created by the death of Jimmy Dean—
at this time Elvis's favorite actor—and was nearly frantic
with the desire to jump into Dean's shoes. The very first
article on Elvis in *Photoplay*, written by a reporter who
interviewed Elvis on the first day of shooting for *Love Me
Tender*, represents the rock star discussing earnestly with
his producer, the young and much-admired David Weisbart (who had produced *Rebel*), the possibility of starring
in a projected *Jimmy Dean Story*. Elvis is quoted as saying,
"I could do it easy. I want to play that more than anything
else."

In another interview, Weisbart made an extended comparison between Elvis and Jimmy Dean. Pointing out the
differences in the two young stars' temperaments—Elvis
he found gregarious, Dean a loner; Elvis an enthusiast,
Dean a calculating professional—Weisbart concluded by
explaining just where he thought Elvis's strength lay and
how he could be expected to succeed without either the
training or the experience in acting that Jimmy Dean had
gained from Lee Strasberg and the New York theater
world. "Elvis's great charm," argued the producer, "lies in
his immaturity; but he is still a shrewd kid, with all of
Jimmy's knowledge and ability to use charm.... Acting
skill will probably ruin him because his greatest asset is

his natural ability. That is what Jimmy appeared to have, and that is what made him a great actor." If ever prophecy were perfectly phrased and absolutely fulfilled, it was this astounding prediction by the late David Weisbart, which sums up Elvis's entire film career, twenty-nine feature-length pictures in twelve years, in a couple of astute sentences.

Elvis, as Weisbart saw clearly after working with him in *Love Me Tender,* was a natural. This one word says it all. He produced instinctually effects of "charm" that real actors attained through art. If his career were managed so as to preserve this innocent and natural appeal, he might score the same kind of success as Jimmy Dean. Tamper with the magic, however, try to make the kid an "actor," and you would reduce him to a condition that was valueless. Many people will scoff at this notion, but how much does it differ from the facts of Elvis's singing career? Everyone who has examined Elvis's recording history has come to the same conclusion: that his first records were his best, though, paradoxically, he became infinitely more artful as he gained experience. As Elvis was just a boy with virtually no professional experience when he first stepped into the recording studio, what is one to conclude but that the subtle amalgam of common styles and individual talent that he had brought to focus instinctively was worth more than all he learned and developed in a lifetime of prodigious musical activity and success.

The condition of being a natural is a highly precarious one that is not likely to survive long unless it is carefully guarded. Had David Weisbart gone on to make the *Jimmy Dean Story* with Elvis Presley, it's quite possible that Elvis's career might have been given an entirely different direction in Hollywood. As it turned out, however, Elvis went from *Love Me Tender,* in which, as we shall see, he offers what is far and away his most appealing film performance, to film after film in which he became a stock figure until, step by step, he was reduced to one of the ugliest and most repulsive presences on the American screen. It was a long and deadly fall, a decline so drastic that no performer less mindlessly adored by his public could possibly have survived it.

Once Colonel Parker had tossed Elvis into the first picture that came along, heedless of whether or not the part suited him or whether he would receive the proper direction or whether he should he fortified with acting lessons, all the rest was up to Elvis. It was a simple case of sink or swim. Elvis turned on his charm at the first cast party and started wooing his fellow actors, appealing to their sympathy for the greenhorn, while they marveled that anyone so successful could act so humble. In adopting this sucking up to the stars approach, Elvis revealed how totally dissimilar he was from his idol, Jimmy Dean. When Elia Kazan called Dean out of his dressing room on the set of *East of Eden* to introduce the other, well-established players, Dean had gone from one actor to another, sticking his mid-finger up and snarling, "Fuck you!...Fuck you!...Fuck you!" Jimmy Dean had no intention of being coopted by a Hollywood he despised. Elvis Presley just wanted to be accepted.

Elvis took a lot of crap from the other actors on his first film: jokes about his blue suede shoes—which he gave away to the crew; jokes about the neck-brace posture he adopted to avoid spoiling the erectness of his collar when he turned his head; jokes about his mascara and his accent and his eagerness to please, which extended to putting on a show for the visitors to the set during breaks in the shooting or after lunch in the commissary.

Lunch was the one moment of the day to which the other actors on this dumb picture looked forward because they had a standing invitation to join Elvis and the Colonel in a special dining room. The ole Colonel liked playing host to the young players. He was like that kind of mother who seeks to make friends for her shy darling (while keeping a sharp eye on him) by inviting his classmates every day to lunch in a tearoom near the school. Elvis's classmates were repulsed by the Colonel. Richard Egan was grossed out by the old man's habit of wearing his undershirt as his only shirt. Bill Campbell got angry when the Colonel tried to pin a big pink button on his jacket reading "I Love Elvis." "Parker," he snapped, "what in hell do you think you're doing? I'm trying to make a name for myself in this business and you want me walking around like a

guy wearing a sandwich board!" "We don't generally give
away these big buttons," jived the Colonel. "You'll be sorry
you didn't take it some day."

Still, lunch with Colonel meant that you could eat steak
every day—while Elvis ate mashed potatoes, gravy and
burnt bacon. One afternoon, when they had all settled in
their places and were eagerly awaiting the sirloins, they
noticed the Colonel was missing. "Oh," says Elvis, "he
went over to the office to do something. He'll be back."
Finally, at the end of the meal, the Colonel appears. He's
red-faced and angry. "What's up?" everybody choruses.
The Colonel isn't loath to say. "Those goddamned people!"
he bursts out, glad to have a chance to blow off steam.
"They called me up there and asked how much they'd have
to pay to get Elvis for this picture they're planning. They
said it was for one of those extravaganzas where they use
a lot of people from the musical end of the business. All
Elvis had to do was sing two songs which they had all
orchestrated and set to go. 'He doesn't have to do much
work: Just fly in, make the session and go home.' 'Well,
sir,' I said, 'that'll cost you seventy-five thousand dollars.'
Jesus! They went crazy! So after they huddled and whispered and argued over the money, I got fed up with their
game. I said: 'I'll tell you what I'll do. You got a pair o'
dice?' They said, 'What do ya wan' 'em for?' I said, 'Well,
I'll roll you for him. Double or nothing!' An' ya know something? They wouldn't do it! So I walked out on them. To
hell with 'em!"

While the Colonel was recounting this bizarre business
meeting, which, after all, concerned Elvis closely—even
presenting him with the startling image of being diced
over in just the way the old southern planters used to
gamble for prize slaves—Elvis went right on eating his
meal, as if nothing of consequence were transpiring in his
presence. Bill Campbell marveled over this indifference,
especially to the constant wheeling and dealing for great
sums of money that went on continually around Elvis. As
Campbell saw it, Elvis had simply resigned himself to
being a "property." "He was absolutely aware of the fact
that he was not his own individual, that he belonged to

a bunch of people—not just Colonel Parker. It went far beyond that!" Indeed, it did!

After the day's shooting, Elvis would go to the screening room and watch the rushes until perhaps seven. Then, he would duck into Bill Campbell's Thunderbird, shoot out the back gate onto Olympic Street—to avoid the crowds of fans hanging around the main gate—and dash back to his hotel, the Knickerbocker, off Hollywood on Ivar. Here, on the eleventh floor, he shared a suite with his country bumpkin cousins, Gene and Junior Smith. Though Elvis was now living smack in the heart of that wonderland which he had been reading about for years in the pages of *Photoplay* and *Silver Screen,* he never had any time to explore Hollywood. After he had eaten his supper in his room, talked to his mother on the phone and studied his lines for the next day's shooting, it would be time to turn out the light and fall into a troubled sleep. On the weekends, the best fun he could find was an amusement strip in Long Beach, where he could limber up his arm throwing baseballs at wooden bottles or go flying on the thrill rides. That would have been the extent of Elvis's amusements in Hollywood, if at this moment he had not run into the only man whom he would ever befriend in the movie colony: Nick Adams.

Actually, you didn't run into Nick Adams; he ran into you like a fast-talking, brightly smiling, exhaustingly aggressive door-to-door salesman for baby pictures or white leatherette Bibles. Though Adams was only a couple years older than Elvis and a relative newcomer to Hollywood himself, he had already carned a well-deserved reputation as the biggest pain-in-the-ass in town—the sort of guy who, when you saw him coming, dictated an immediate change of course and acceleration in the opposite direction. What Adams was forever selling was himself: a property which, to hear him tell it, was nothing less than sensational—"the greatest little actor to hit this town in years." In fact, he had very little going for him either in terms of looks or talent or professional experience. He was just another poor kid from the sticks who had grown up dreaming of the silver screen.

Born Nicholas Adamshock, son of a Lithuanian coal

miner in Nanticoke, Pennsylvania, Adams had come out
of the same grinding poverty in which Elvis had grown
up. After serving a hitch in the Coast Guard, he took off
for the Heavenly City with two hundred dollars in his
pockets and an extraordinary determination to make
something of himself. Scuffling to survive, he worked as
a filling station attendant, a short-order cook and once
obtained a free room by offering to care for an old lady's
cats. Not having money to buy food, Adams ate the good
liver which the lady provided for the animals and fed the
beasts on scraps from garbage cans. The story of how Adams got his first part in the movies sums up his character
perfectly. Slipping onto the set of *Mister Roberts,* he
jumped in front of the famous director, John Ford, and
went into a lousy impersonation of Jimmy Cagney. "Throw
him out!" bawled Ford; but then, when the kid kept popping up again and again on the set, Ford finally surrendered and gave Adams a three-line part to shut him up.
Adams made those three lines stand out like a major
speech. But it's doubtful he would have gotten much further at this time if it hadn't been for his knack of cutting
into difficult, withdrawn stars, the first of whom was
Jimmy Dean.

Adams ingratiated himself with Dean precisely as he
was to do a year later with Elvis Presley. He offered himself to the shy, emotionally contorted and rebellious Dean
as a friend, a guide, a boon companion, a homosexual
lover—whatever role or service Dean required. Dean ridiculed Adams publicly, but he did get him a bit part in
Rebel Without a Cause. Getting tight with Jimmy Dean
meant also becoming friendly with the whole circle of
young actors and actresses who hung out with Dean at the
Villa Capri and Googie's, the all-night hash joint next door
to Schwabb's. Adams was soon on close terms with Jack
Simmons, Dean's mousy, bespectacled roommate; Natalie
Wood and Sal Mineo, teenagers who were still attending
school three hours a day on the studio lot; Rafael Campos,
the Dominican actor familiar from his role as the Puerto
Rican kid in *Blackboard Jungle;* Russ Tamblyn, another
screen hoodlum, married at the time to Venetia Stevenson;
and Dennis Hopper, with whom Adams was sharing a

house when he met Elvis. All of these friends of Jimmy
Dean were introduced to Elvis by Adams, who saw Elvis,
whom he contrived to meet almost the day he stepped off
the train in Los Angeles, as a substitute for the late Jimmy
Dean.

Meeting all these famous young actors must have convinced Elvis he had really arrived in the movie business.
What would have pleased him a lot more was making some
progress in his hapless efforts to woo his leading lady, the
sizzling Debra Paget. Elvis—later so canny about revealing his romantic attachments—wore his heart on his
sleeve unashamedly at this time. He even violated his
strict rule of addressing everyone as "Miss" or "Mister" by
referring to Debra as "Debbie." When a reporter asked
Elvis if he had any favorite female stars, he replied: "I
love 'em all, but I've got one special gal—and she's the
only gal for me. But she keeps me 64,000 miles away."
"Who could that be?" blurted the reporter, hot for the big
scoop. With a boyish grin, Elvis sighed—"Debbie!" An
hour later, the reporter caught up with Debra Paget, who
was having lunch. "What's this about cold-shouldering
Elvis?" he asked. "Oh, that!" she exclaimed, going into the
nervous laugh with which she follows every statement.
"I'll admit," she continued, "that my impression of Elvis,
before I met him, was the same as many others who don't
know him. I figured he must be some kind of moron. Now,
I think the best way to describe his work is to say it's
inspired." Still, she didn't deny that there were a lot of
miles still separating them, even though they played man
and wife in the film.

Elvis, for his part, could never understand why he
wasn't making more ground with Debbie. Every night, he
would pour out his heart to his only trusted confidante,
his mother, seeking some solution to his problem in her
wisdom. Gladys told her friends in Memphis that never
had she heard Elvis go on so before about any girl. Between
the pressures of appearing before the camera every day
and the frustration of pining for the distant and inaccessible Debbie every night, Elvis's wire-strung soul began
to jangle. Gene Smith recalls that Elvis walked in his sleep

every night. One night Gene caught Elvis going out the window of their suite on the eleventh floor.

Awakening the somnambulist was a risky business. If you shook him, or even touched him lightly, he was likely to gather you into his dream and punch you out as his nearest assailant. Gene Smith solved this problem by employing a special hands-off technique. The trick was to switch on the lights and then, in a low soothing voice, call out—"Elvis?" At that moment, the dreamer would suddenly snap out of his trance and demand earnestly, "What was I doin' this time?" As soon as he heard his latest caper, he would burst out laughing. Though everyone around him was deeply concerned by his obvious propensity toward self-destruction, Elvis took the matter very lightly. He always said that he would live forever. The truth is that if he hadn't been so carefully guarded, he might have followed his hero, Jimmy Dean, to an early grave.

Why was Debra Paget so resistant to Elvis—a handsome, famous, prosperous, well-mannered and universally adored young star? True, she was a couple of years older than he at an age when every year counts. Also, having been reared in show business and having appeared in pictures since her fourteenth year, she was more sophisticated than the young rock star. Then, there was the fact that Debra was Jewish. For a young man as devoutly Christian as Elvis, this might pose a problem; yet, as we shall see, Elvis was always drawn to Jewish people and even, on occasion, expressed the wish that he might himself be one of the "chosen people." So even the barrier of religion would not have posed an insuperable obstacle to a serious relationship, and it was precisely such a relationship that Elvis had in mind when he began courting "Debbie."

As for Debra Paget, everyone in Hollywood agreed that she was a very nice girl. She lived with her mother, father and sisters in a very theatrical house in Beverly Hills that was celebrated for its menagerie, which included a chimpanzee (Elvis acquired one himself eventually), an orange gibbon, a macaw and numerous other tropical birds and fishes. Elvis became familiar with the house and family when he asked Debra Paget for a date, and she astounded him by replying that she had never gone out on a date, but that he was welcome to come and visit her at her home. Virtually any man would have been titillated by this reply; but for Elvis Presley, it was an incredible turn-on. It was nothing less than the sudden, unexpected realization of his most fervid longing: to find a perfectly beautiful, lusciously erotic girl, who was, at the same time, a very proper and well-bred virgin.

Once Elvis began visiting his beloved's home, he realized that the dominant personality in the family was Debra's mother, who had been in the theater and still used her stage name, Marguerite Gibson, or as she was known to everyone, Maggie. In finding the family firmly under the rule of mother, Elvis was once again discovering a condition that fulfilled his natural inclinations. How startled he must have been when soon it became apparent that this mother was nothing like the kind of mother he had always known. Maggie was brassy. She drove around town in a jewel-studded Cadillac. She used very salty language. Some people said her stage experience had been primarily in burlesque. In fact, she was your classic Jewish stage mother: the female equivalent of Colonel Parker. Not only did she control Debra, like a puppet at her fingertips, but she managed her in the formal business sense. Like the Colonel, she lived and breathed her "artist."

Maggie had groomed Debra very carefully for her career. She had brought her up to be a movie star in the classic forties mold: a second Jane Russell, one of those smolderingly erotic beauties whose slightly flawed facial lines were eclipsed by their bustlines, which were always dramatized for the movie viewer by their plunging necklines. Having done a certain amount of, shall we say, "exotic dancing," Maggie had taught her shy, soft-spoken giggling daughter the same arts. In fact, once, at Las Vegas, where some bigwig like Bob Hope was putting on a benefit, Debra performed a routine that was so vulgar that even the hardened showbiz types who were running the show were outraged. Nobody blamed Debra, of course; everybody recognized her for what she was: a puppet in her mother's hands, the kind of girl who could exist all day on a single glass of water because her mother had forbidden her to

drink and gain the few ounces the water would add to her
body weight. What pissed the show people off was the way
the old girl made sweet, innocent Debra camp it up like
some cheap hooker.

It would be wrong to suppose, however, that Maggie
crushed a blossoming romance between Elvis and Debra.
True, the old lady didn't dig this pimple-faced kid worth
a damn. She had very different ideas about the sort of man
who should get her carefully treasured daughter. It was
Debra herself who turned thumbs down on Elvis. Even
today—now the wife of a wealthy Texas oilman and the
mistress of five homes—Debra Paget retains a slightly
patronizing air when she talks about Elvis. "He was a very
sweet, very simple kind of person," she recalls. "He just
liked to get on his motorcycle and go off into the night."
Then, she laughs in a low throaty voice. Reflecting on the
experience, she confides: "I never told anyone before, but
Elvis asked me to marry him after the film. He called long
distance from Texas. My family didn't go for the idea."
Elvis, as we shall see, proposed to several women in this
period of his life. That he made the offer to Debra after
the film is interesting in view of an incident that occurred
before the picture was completed.

One night while he was visiting Debra at her home,
Elvis raised again the issue of their having a proper date.
She told him that she never dated because she devoted
herself entirely to her career. Then, she said that he would
have to excuse her this night because she had a pressing
business appointment. Elvis got aboard his bike and rode
off into the night. Only he didn't go far. In fact, he doubled
back quietly and kept watch on the house, suspicious of
what a business appointment late in the evening might
signify. Sure enough, not long after he took up his post,
he saw a Chevrolet sedan pull up with a couple of very
straight-looking dudes inside it, dressed in conservative
business suits. One of them went to the door, rang the bell,
passed inside; then, shortly afterwards, he came out escorting Debra, who was beautifully dressed. They all got
into the car and drove away. Elvis memorized the license
number and the next day made some inquiries. He was

astonished when he learned that the car and its crew were
the possessions of no less a person than Howard Hughes.

At the same time that Elvis was courting Debra Paget,
he was introduced by Nick Adams to Natalie Wood. The
actress was at this time an eighteen-year-old girl living
with her working-class parents in Sherman Oaks. In taking up with Natalie Wood, Elvis was swinging to the opposite extreme from Debra Paget. If Debra Paget was the
sizzling Jane Russell type, Natalie Wood was everyone's
cute little pansy-eyed daughter, now a pixieish teenager
in pedal pushers and babushka, riding around Beverly
Hills perched on the back of a motorbike. Actually, Natalie
Wood was just as dedicated to her career as Debra Paget;
both girls had studied in different grades at the same studio school. (In the Mother's Room, Maggie Gibson always
managed to say something so shocking that Natalie's
mother had to fight to keep herself from fainting dead
away.) At eighteen, Natalie Wood was a veteran of fourteen years in pictures. She was an instinctively independent and mature young woman who resented being treated
as a carefully chaperoned child. When she got involved
with the Jimmy Dean crowd, she found just the world she
had been unconsciously seeking. "They were the gods,"
she recalls. "I just wanted to be exactly like them. What
we used to talk about was how unhappy we were. Whoever
was the unhappiest, whoever came closest to suicide the
night before, he was the winner."

Now this young woman, full of the heady lore of Stan-
islavski, bongo drums, Porsches and existentialism, eager
to be free and independent, identified with Hollywood's
handful of New Wave actors, comes face to face with Elvis
Presley—her antithesis. Naturally, she's fascinated. Elvis
is "wonderful looking—such a sensuous mouth"; he's "tre-
mendously sweet"; but the most intriguing, almost startling, thing about him is that he's "terribly conventional"!
"He was the first person of my age group I had ever met
who said to me: 'How come you're wearing makeup? Why
do you want to go to New York? Why do you want to be
on your own? Why don't you want to stay home and be a
sweet little girl? It's nice to stay home.'" Elvis was so
square, he was fascinating. "We'd go to P. C. Brown's and

have a hot fudge sundae. We'd go to Hamburger Hamlet
and have a burger and a Coke. He didn't drink. He didn't
swear. He didn't even smoke! It was like having the date
that I never ever had in high school. I thought it was really
wild!"

The other thing that was remarkable about Elvis was
the fact that he was genuinely religious. "I hadn't been
around anyone who was religious," explains Natalie. "He
felt he had been given this gift, this talent, by God. He
didn't take it for granted. He thought it was something
that he had to protect. He had to be nice to people, otherwise, God would take it all away."

Before Elvis went back to Memphis, he and Natalie
discussed the possibility that she might come and visit
him in his new home on Audubon Avenue. "His parents
called my parents and asked if I could be their house guest.
I would be very fully chaperoned and Nick Adams would
be there. My parents were quite strict. Normally, they
would have said, 'No.' But they liked him so much . . . they
thought he was such a religious boy and his parents
sounded so nice over the phone that they decided they
would let me go." So it came about that on October 31,
three days after Elvis's second appearance on the Sullivan
show, Natalie Wood, dressed in a black sweater and black
pedal pushers and toting three stuffed tigers, arrived at
Memphis, where she was greeted by Nick Adams and Elvis
and escorted through a crowd of fans and autograph hunt-
ers to a $12,000 custom-fitted white Lincoln Continental,
which Elvis piloted home.

When Natalie saw the hundreds of fans besieging the
little spruce-green tract house, served by souvenir ped-
dlers, hot dog and popcorn vendors, she was shocked and
horrified. She came from a world where all the biggest
celebrities lived, but she had never witnessed anything
like this carnival atmosphere around a film star's home.
When Elvis tried to pull into the driveway, the fans
blocked his path. Nonchalantly, he leaned out the window
and said: "As soon as I pull the car into the garage, we'll
all come back out here and talk to you all." "Don't forget
now, you promised!" chorused the fans. If Natalie figured
this was just a line to get into the house she soon learned

differently. No sooner had they parked the car than Elvis marched them out to the low iron fence, embellished with metal musical notes, where they chatted with the fans for half an hour and Natalie had to field endless questions about whether she was having a romance with Nick or planning to marry Elvis.

A few hours later, having had supper and met Mr. and Mrs. Presley (Natalie found Gladys "very laid back"), the three young stars took off into the glamorous Memphis night—after first signing more autographs at the gate. Elvis drove around town, stopping a couple of times so that Nick could hop out of the car and buy ice cream cones. At 11:30, the big white car pulled up in front of the Chisca Hotel on Main Street; Elvis ushered his guests up to the mezzanine, where Dewey Phillips was laying his crazy rap on the city. An off-the-wall interview followed, with much playing of Elvis records and goofy laughter. When the show went off the air at midnight, Elvis and his party descended to the street, where they found a crowd of one thousand people assembled outside the hotel. In front of the crowd were numerous flashbulb-popping photographers and newspaper reporters, asking questions not much brighter than those the fans popped.

Five or six hours having passed since supper, Elvis was now hungry. Regaining his car with considerable effort, he started driving out Union Street followed by a motorcade of about fifteen automobiles. Arriving at one of his favorite joints, the Gridiron, he ushered his party inside the cheap interior, fired up the juke box and settled down for a solid breakfast of tough-fried eggs and burnt bacon. By 1:30 in the morning, the party was back at Audubon Avenue, where the crowd still numbered two hundred souls. Once again Elvis had to negotiate to get inside his driveway. Once again, all three young celebs had to oblige with answers and autographs till two in the morning.

Throughout the following week, the same routine was followed day in, day out, with the only variations being movies in place of Dewey Phillips and spins on Elvis's Harley-Davidson bike in the afternoon instead of tours in the big white car. Natalie was accustomed to riding on the back of a bike from her days with Jimmy Dean. What she

could never accept was the long tail of cars that followed
Elvis everywhere he rode. The drivers of the foremost cars
sometimes pulled abreast of the bike and conducted neigh-
borly conversations with the local hero.

Just as bizarre was the fishbowl atmosphere of the
house. One afternoon, while Elvis was playing Ski Pool
with Nick Adams in the den, five teenage girls, standing
on tiptoe, witnessed the whole game from an open window.
The rule was that any fan was welcome to wander around
on the property so long as he was not disruptive. If he
made too much noise, he was asked to leave. When Natalie
asked Elvis why he put up with this outrageous violation
of privacy, he said that he owed his success to the fans and
that it was his duty to tolerate their behavior and fulfill
their requests for appearances and autographs every day.

On that responsible note the visit ended, and Natalie
Wood, accompanied by Nick Adams, emplaned for L.A.,
that peaceful place.

Love Me Tender opened on November 15, 1956, at that
ancient citadel of youth culture, the New York Paramount.
Long before daybreak, hundreds of kids from the five bor-
oughs came bubbling up out of the subway entrances of
Times Square to form a queue around the theater, which
had erected on its marquee a thirty-foot colored cutout of
Elvis playing his guitar. When the first kids to see the
show were quizzed about their reactions, they objected
vehemently to the fact that the movie was not a rock 'n'
roll picture, did not deliver the real Elvis and made the
horrible mistake of killing off their new hero in the last
reel—an error that the Hollywood hacks tried to rectify
by summoning up the ghost of the dead Elvis in the last
frames to sing a spooky reprise of the theme in Wraithe-
Vision.

Though all of these criticisms were valid, they don't
alter the fact that in his first film Elvis makes his most
appealing screen appearance. This movie is a monument
to Elvis the Good: a young, innocent, healthy, clean-look-
ing blond, with an irresistible smile and cuddly teddy-bear
quality that makes him the ideal playmate for every thirteen-year-old girl who ever lived. David Weisbart said:
"Elvis was the character, even to the sideburns, the minute

he stepped off the plane." It's true: This accidentally adopted role suited Elvis better than any part he was ever to play in his subsequent career of twenty-eight starring roles.

His first appearance sets the tone for everything that is to follow. By this point in the picture a lot of stock action has gone by—a train robbery, a chase, a big welcome-home scene. Then, finally, the camera catches its first sight ever of Elvis Presley. He's dressed in shirt-sleeves, rough trousers and peasant boots and he's plowing behind a team of mules: the archetypal southern farm image. You glimpse him first from a distance, as he's being called to the house to welcome home his brothers. As the camera zooms in for the close-up, Elvis breaks into a big smile, a lovely, sweet, unself-conscious smile that radiates its warmth across the screen. At this moment, teenage audiences all over America burst into uncontrollable screams. If anything in the history of pop culture could be called an epiphany, this moment is it—Elvis Presley dawning upon the movie consciousness of America.

To review the picture properly, you would need an instrument not yet developed but likely to come some day soon, as our culture evolves ever more in the direction of the tactile, the gustatory, the olfactory, the universe of the infant. This instrument, something like the infrared camera, will respond not to the visual outline of the object but to its *vibes*. Point the instrument at *Love Me Tender*, and you observe in scene after scene a characteristic pattern. There will be Debra Paget, seething with repressed sexuality like a severely contained but unmistakable nymphomaniac: her finely shaped breasts always protruding, her voice low but hot, her face that of an elegant cat in heat. Richard Egan produces a contrasting signal: He is a man of steel with a face carved of the same cold, unyielding material. Everyone else is dead, inert, a prop brought in and set up for the shooting. The only fluently live creature in this curious cast is Elvis, who at every moment is giving off waves of sentient feeling: one moment tender and affectionate; the next, troubled and hurt; the next, furious and violent, a being composed entirely of feelings that surface as naturally as notes from a singer's mouth.

The only false notes he strikes are in his livelier songs, where he slips into the body rhetoric that made him famous but which is utterly anachronistic in this archaic and rustic time frame. When he sings "Love Me Tender," addressing it to Mildred Dunnock, playing his mother seated in a rocking chair, the love and tenderness that beams from him is delicious. How apt that in his first picture, he sings a love song to his mother! It reminds one of the only real anecdote still told in Hollywood about this film. Elvis was supposed to pull a gun and brandish it, while his mother said, "Put down that gun!" In the first take, the moment the mother gave the command, Elvis instinctively complied, saying, "Yes, ma'am."

It is revealing of the mental set of the more sophisticated reviewers of this charming performance that not one of them had a good word to say for the picture. In fact, *Love Me Tender* inspired the most famous put-down that Elvis Presley ever received. It appeared in *Time* as a neat little column of print resting on a picture of Elvis standing beside his mule's hindquarters. It read:

Is it a sausage? It is certainly smooth and damp-looking, but who ever heard of a 172-lb. sausage 6 ft. tall? Is it a Walt Disney goldfish? It has the same sort of big, soft, beautiful eyes and long, curly lashes, but who ever heard of a goldfish with sideburns? Is it a corpse? The face just hangs there, limp and white with its little drop-seat mouth, rather like Lord Byron in the wax museum.

But suddenly the figure comes to life. The lips part, the eyes half close, the clutched guitar begins to undulate back and forth in an uncomfortably suggestive manner. And wham! The midsection of the body jolts forward to bump and grind and beat out a low-down rhythm that takes pace from boogie and hillbilly, rock 'n' roll and something known only to Elvis and his pelvis. As the belly dance gets wilder, a peculiar sound emerges. A rusty foghorn? A voice? Or merely a noise produced, like the voice of

a cricket, but the violent stridulation of the legs?
Words occasionally can be made out, like raisins in
cornmeal mush. "Goan...git...luhhv..." And then
all at once everything stops, and a big, trembly
tender half smile, half sneer smears slowly across
the Cinemascope screen. The message that millions
of U.S. teenage girls love to receive had just been
delivered.

Thus spake *Time*.[1]

[1]This squib was the first in a long series of sneering send-ups
of Elvis composed by *Time*'s anonymous but unmistakable movie
reviewer, Brad Darrach.

Chapter 16

Starring Vehicles

Putting rock 'n' roll on the big screen of the Hollywood exploitation movie proved almost as difficult a task as putting it on the little screen of the network variety show. The moviemakers' problem was not one of the incompatibility of art and medium: their difficulty was entirely one of talent and tradition. No major director ever addressed himself to the task of translating the rock world to the screen; on the other hand, those hacks who did undertake this job were pre-programmed to an extraordinary degree by the long history of movies about jitterbugs and swing bands compiled in the late thirties and early forties.

From the first rock movie (Sam Katzman's quickie, *Rock Around the Clock,* starring Bill Haley and Alan Freed) to the last, the basic effect was simply déjà vu. Rock came across as swing in crinolines. Not only had you seen the story a hundred times before, with its preposterous dialogue peppered with archaic jazz slang and vintage handclasps, but you had witnessed, if not performed, all the supposedly original dance steps, been startled by the purportedly "barbaric" sounds and enjoyed countless times the ritual triumph of youth over age, hot over cool and inspiration over constipation.

Part of this time-loop effect can be blamed on rock itself, which in its early years was often little more than a gag

reflex regurgitating the high-school enthusiasms of the
Swing Age, commencing with the Lindy and the Boogie-
Woogie and going on to the cult of the jalopy, the jukebox,
the screaming, swooning bobby-soxer, the anguished young
singing star, et cetera, et cetera. The real problem with
these pictures, however, was not simply the repetitiveness
of pop culture: It was the fact that the filmmakers were
middle-aged men who were so confident they knew what
was happening in the youth culture that they never both-
ered to give their subject a thought or even a look.

The one exception to this repetition compulsion was
Hal Wallis, whom we have seen sitting in on Elvis's recording sessions, getting a firsthand impression of the real
thing. Now that it was time to launch Elvis in his first
starring vehicle, Wallis ordered the writer and director of
the film to go down to Memphis to meet the star on his
home turf and see the new hero do his stuff. Elvis was
about to take leave of the *Louisiana Hayride* in a grand
farewell performance that would bring his whole phenomenon into vivid focus.[1] Unfortunately, by this time the
writer had completed his screenplay. The suggestion
proved valuable all the same, for something of Elvis's inspiration did penetrate Hal Kanter, which is the reason
why his film, *Loving You,* is the most full-blooded rendering we possess of the early Elvis.

No damned Yankee, Kanter had grown up in Savannah
and retained his capacity to speak in flawless dialect
of "crocus sacks" and "flying Jennys." He trained a
shrewdly appreciative eye on Elvis Presley and his milieu.
Picked up by Elvis himself, driving an orchid-colored
Fleetwood, Kanter was carried out to the house on Audubon. Giving it a fast once-over, he was particularly
amused by Elvis's bedroom, which was papered in a yellow
sheet covered with blue and orange flowers, and embel-

[1]In April 1956, after eighty-four appearances, Elvis ceased
broadcasting on the *Hayride.* As his contract did not terminate
until September of that year, Colonel Parker bought him out for
ten thousand dollars in cash and a commitment to play a farewell
concert at some future date.

lished with ceramic minstrels on plaques. The twin beds were cozied up with fancy quilted coverlets and adorned with blue stuffed poodles.

No sooner had the menfolk settled down in the den than Elvis raised a question about the script. Wallis had expressly forbidden Kanter to bring with him a copy of his screenplay for fear that Colonel Parker or Elvis himself might raise objections to the story before the shooting had commenced. As it turned out, Elvis was interested in just one rather obscure point. "Mr. Kanter," he said thoughtfully, "is it the kind of part where I have to smile into the camera or smile at people?" "Well," replied Kanter, taken aback by the oddity of the inquiry, "I don't recall offhand.... I don't think there is anyplace where I wrote, 'He smiles.' That will all be in the playing. Why do you ask a question like that?" "Well," said Elvis deliberately, "I've been studying the people in the movies that have made some kind of impression on me: Humphrey Bogart, Jimmy Dean, Marlon Brando. There's one very interesting thing about them— *they never smile!*" "Son of a bitch!" exclaimed Kanter, "I never thought of that!" "That's why people remember 'em," persisted Elvis, rounding out his point, "'cause they don't smile. Everybody smiles—except the people you remember." After that observation, Hal Kanter concluded that "Elvis was going to be around for a while because he was not quite the simple, charming country boy that some people tried to make him out to be."

Kanter got his next surprise when, after considerable prompting by Gene Smith, who kept saying to Elvis, "Show him! Go ahead and show him!" the rock star stood up at one end of the room and recited, with all seriousness, from beginning to end, General Douglas MacArthur's farewell speech to Congress. This was supposed to demonstrate to the director that Elvis was not just a boy who sang foolish songs but a young man who could really *act*. Kanter took due note of his star's audition, concluding that "If you were a real General MacArthur kind of fellow, you would have jumped up, saluted and even cried a bit." Hal Kanter was not this sort of fellow. "I didn't give a shit whether he could act or not," he explains today, "because we had already signed to do the picture."

Yet, as Kanter spent more time with Elvis and began
to observe the Rock King's world from close up, he started
making mental notes for revisions of his work. What most
impressed him was the nighttime drive from Memphis to
Shreveport on the eve of the concert. It was necessary to
travel under cover of darkness because by this time, Elvis
could barely get through the streets of Memphis once his
car was recognized. So, after dark, the band boarded a big
yellow Cadillac stretch-limousine with a one-wheel trailer
for some of the instruments and for the others a canvas-
covered roof rack (Kanter got a big kick out of Bill Black,
who would look thoughtfully at a voluptuous girl passing
by and remark with a dead pan: "When I see something
like that, it makes my asshole pucker up like a yellow
caution light.") Elvis took the wheel of the lead car in the
caravan, a white Lincoln Continental, installing "Mr.
Kanter" in the place of honor in the front seat, while the
rear seat filled with Gene and Junior Smith and the Colonel's brother-in-law, the ex-baseball player Bitsy Mott,
who was now a regular member of the entourage.

Riding through the back country, they pulled up at a
roadhouse to get a cold Coke. Elvis was ushered deferen-
tially to the back room, but Kanter could see that the star
wanted to be recognized. He got his wish. Not more than ten
miles out of town, they were overtaken by a cop with his
siren screaming. Elvis leaned out the window and demanded, "What the hell's goin' on?" The cop shouts: "Wait
a minute! The radio station is sending its mobile unit after
you." At that moment, a van appears and out of it pops a
local DJ with a mike on a wire. At one in the morning, way
out in the country with the crickets sounding in the background, Elvis Presley did an interview leaning out the window of his white Lincoln. That was broadcast journalism
circa 1956.

Late that night, the boys in the back fell to sleep and
Hal Kanter got as close to Elvis Presley as he was ever
destined to come. At one point, they drove by a shack and
saw a hound dog on the front porch. Elvis was inspired to
soliloquize: "That little dog lies on that porch all day.
Nighttime comes, and he has a whole life of his own. He
does all kinds of things in the night. When day comes, he

goes back and lies on that porch. The old man that owns him ain't got no idea what that dog been up to all night. Man, that's great! It's just like us. We're drivin' through the night in this big sonovabitch. Nobody knows what we're doin'. Not even the ole boys in the back seat!" It's entirely possible that the young Elvis Presley, that guarded and evasive being whom no one ever knew, came as close in that speech as he ever did to articulating his real slant on life. Life, as Elvis saw it, was a matter, as they say down South, of "slippin' away."

When the party arrived at the Captain Shreve Hotel at five in the morning, all hell broke loose. Kanter heard chanting outside in the street. Looking out the window, he saw a crowd of kids yelling for Elvis. They would not stop until, finally, Elvis stuck his head out of his room and shouted: "Hey, you all! Let me get some sleep. Now, go 'way! I'll see ya later!" That did it. They left.

The farewell concert, staged at the Louisiana Fair Grounds on December 15, 1956, was a typical Elvis Presley rave-up. Nine thousand kids going out of their minds, Elvis entering the hall behind a flying wedge of burly cops, a preshow press conference that consisted of fifteen DJs, each with his portable tape recorder and mike, lined up in a row, as Elvis went from one to the other giving them three- or four-minute interviews. Then, the warm-up acts, all exact replicas of Elvis Presley, doing his songs with his gestures and dressed in his clothes. Finally, the apocalyptic moment when the star appeared in a hall that was crepitating with the heat lightning of thousands of popping flashbulbs. At that instant an immense scream was heard, which rose and fell without ceasing throughout the entire time that Elvis was onstage, so loud a noise that you couldn't hear enough of the music even to know for a certainty what song Elvis was singing. Hal Kanter, an old pro, was highly impressed. He determined to put this milieu on the screen. "If I came to scoff," he reflects today, "I went away a prophet."

After the Christmas holidays, when it came time to start work on the new picture, Elvis invited his family to join him in Hollywood. For Vernon and Gladys, this was a startling suggestion. In all their lives, they had never

gone further than the 104 miles from Tupelo to Memphis.
Now, they were expected to cross the entire continent. Like
their son, they sought company for the journey. During
the alterations to their house, they had made friends with
the building contractor who had built their swimming
pool. He was named Carl Nichols. His wife, Willy, became
a special favorite of Gladys, who rarely made friends. Willy
Nichols recollects Gladys as being a very different person
from the mater dolorosa that one sees in all the family
photographs. "Everybody played up the sadness," says
Mrs. Nichols, "photographing her when she was real sick
or when Elvis was drafted. She was happy. She liked to
eat and cut up. She loved to ride around and see everything."

The happiest moment in Gladys's life, Willy Nichols
believes, was the night they all agreed to go out together
to Hollywood. "She called us up one night," Mrs. Nichols
remembers, "and she was in the best mood you've ever
seen. She was laughing and she said, 'Willy, we're goin'
to California!'" When the Nichols arrived at the Presley
house, Gladys was beside herself with joy. She told Willy,
"You're the truest person I ever met." Then she presented
her friend with a little brass bracelet that had a locket
containing Elvis's picture, a piece of jewelry that Elvis had
originally given to his mother. As the evening wore on,
Gladys's hilarity became so extreme that Vernon was
moved finally to tell her she had better quiet down. She
was becoming hysterical.

No sooner did the preparations for the trip commence
than Gladys began to display a side to her personality that
no one had ever before divined. The simple soul who always wore "dusters" and spent her life preparing crowder
peas and thickenin' gravy suddenly became the well-
groomed mother of a movie star. She went to Lowenstein's
Department Store and with the aid of a "costume coordi-
nator" bought an entire wardrobe of very attractive
clothes. She paid a great deal of attention to her hair,
having it styled every day. She began to anticipate all the
things they would do when they reached movieland. She
told Willy that as soon as they got there, they would buy
French poodles, the old-fashioned movie stars' favorite

pets. They bought them, too, Willy naming hers Pierre and Gladys dubbing her dog Duke, after her favorite movie star, John Wayne. Gladys also lectured Vernon on how to behave during the trip, telling her husband, who was very tight with a buck: "We have to tip big. We're expected to do it and we're in a position to afford it." Gladys showed so much savoir faire about this Hollywood trip that Willy began to wonder whether her friend had not once been screenstruck, just like her son.

The two middle-aged couples spent four days riding across the country on America's dying railroads. They would sit in their compartments, laughing and telling stories. Gladys had been feeling quite ill after Christmas; in fact, in January, she had entered the hospital for two weeks to receive a thorough checkup. Now on the train she had trouble sleeping, but she was determined to enjoy herself. When Gladys was in a good mood, she would sing in a deep vibrant voice that reminded Willy of Elvis's voice, especially after it deepened and darkened in later years. One day Gladys said, "I can't understand all this fuss over Elvis. I think I have a better voice than he does." Then, she broke into "Heartbreak Hotel." Mrs. Nichols was astonished at how well Gladys brought off the song with its difficult leaps. Indeed she could never stop marveling over how similar were mother and son. Their faces showed a marked resemblance. They both mumbled when they talked. They were both brooders and loners. What's more, they were both destined to early deaths, a fact of which Gladys appeared to have foreknowledge.

One day she told Willy Nichols that she did not expect Elvis to live beyond the age of thirty-five. She was fearful he would be killed by a lunatic or by a jealous lover. She was appalled at the crazy ideas and emotions that were revealed in the fan mail that came pouring into the house, so much fan mail that even at this early date the Presleys had to hire a professional secretary to answer it. Most of all, though, Gladys feared that Elvis would be killed by his own life-style: his lack of sleep and headlong rushing from one activity to another. She always saw the boy burning himself out. As for herself, she was convinced that she would soon be dead. She was resigned to dying. She warned

Willy to say nothing of the matter to Elvis. This trip to Hollywood was Gladys's last—and only—fling.

Willy also obtained some insight into the relationship of Gladys and Vernon. She observed that Gladys was the master in the house and a very jealous master at that. Vernon was a handsome man at forty: tall, well-proportioned with a great head of wavy hair, just beginning to turn grey. He liked to wear flashy clothes, just like his son, and drive around in luxurious automobiles. Gladys noticed that Vernon often spent a great deal of time out at the fence in front of the house talking to the pretty young women who hung around waiting to see Elvis. On more than one occasion, she cautioned her husband. If Gladys got upset, Elvis would always assume that his father had done something wrong. He'd get Vernon out in the car and demand: "What have you done to her now?" Poor Vernon. He was always on the defensive with these two allied against him.

When the Presleys and the Nicholses arrived in Hollywood, they received a royal welcome. Elvis quartered them in the Knickerbocker Hotel, where he was staying, and brought them out to the lot every day to watch the shooting. Willy Nichols found the routine of moviemaking boring. Gladys appeared very pleased to meet the actors and especially Mr. Wallis. Hal Kanter could appreciate the pride of a southern mother in her little boy. He arranged to give the Presleys a marvelous souvenir. In the scene at the end of the picture in which Elvis performs in a theater, Kanter seated the Presleys and the Nicholses among the film extras and flashed their pictures on the screen. After Gladys died, Elvis refused ever again to see *Loving You*.

On the weekends, when Elvis wasn't working, he would take his family and their friends sightseeing. He would show them the homes of the stars. Two places excited him particularly: Red Skelton's house, which he admired for its ostentatious decor, and Debra Paget's house, which he now contemplated with nostalgia. The Presleys and the Nicholses also met Elvis's latest actress friend, the beautiful Joan Blackman, who at eighteen had just begun working in pictures.

She had met Elvis on the Paramount lot, while walking

in the company of some other girls, distinguished not just by her looks but by the fact that she was wearing red pants. Elvis came cruising along in the hot rod which he drives in *Loving You*. Taking one good look at the shapely brunette in the red pants, he shouted—"Hey, you, c'mere!" That started what turned out to be a typical Presley affair. He introduced his new girlfriend at once to his mother. Then, they all went to the movies. It was the premier of *The Ten Commandments*, a picture after Elvis's own heart. He became so excited during the showing that he started narrating every scene for his guests, as if the film were in a foreign language. As he went over the biblical scenes, he would throw in a lot of technical details about filming he had picked up recently. Gladys kept trying to hush him to avoid being embarrassed, but Elvis continued to lecture heedlessly throughout the entire movie, as was always his wont when a picture turned him on.

Joan Blackman concluded that Elvis was not naive about women, just scared. She was a virgin and Elvis was quite content to leave her that way. She interpreted his timidity as anxiety that something nasty would get back to Gladys. Actually, Elvis was always loath to have sex with any woman he respected. What's more, at this particular moment, he was probably still upset by the first paternity suit ever to be brought against him, by a girl who had filed an affidavit in Ohio. In any event, the hot but adolescent affair with Joan Blackman was soon over. Eventually, the pair were reunited in a couple of movies, but there was no further romance. Years later, the actress ran into Elvis backstage at Las Vegas. He looked at her, obviously stoned, and said: "You had your chance." That became a standard line with Elvis.

The Presleys and the Nicholses left Hollywood after a one-month stay. Elvis followed hard on their heels, returning to Memphis in mid-March. When he got back, he learned from his family that they had just found a beautiful new house. Elvis had been insisting for months that they leave their home on Audubon because it afforded so little privacy and produced so much tension with the neighbors, who resented bitterly the carnivallike atmosphere created by the fans. In fact, at one point the neigh-

bors had banded together and brought a public nuisance
suit against Elvis. The magistrate did not find in their
favor. He said the behavior of the fans was not Elvis's
responsibility and that otherwise he was a good house-
holder. In fact, the judge remarked, with some asperity,
Elvis Presley's house was the only one on the street that
had been paid for in full. Nonetheless, it was time to move,
if for no other reason than the fact that Elvis was now a
wealthy man and a movie star, who should have the sort
of home that befitted his impressive status. It was with
the intention of fulfilling Elvis's dreams that the former
tenants of the Lauderdale Courts set out on their house-
hunting expedition. It was typical of their hapless approach to any sort of business that they entrusted this
serious and costly undertaking to the first person who
came along.

Virginia Grant was a young and inexperienced real
estate agent in 1957, one of those gushy southern ladies
whose mouths go a mile a minute but never manage to
keep up with the frothing volatility of their exuberant
temperaments. One day in February, Mrs. Grant was waiting for a client at Lowenstein's East, a suburban branch
of Memphis's leading department store, when she spied
standing at the curb a "gorgeous pink Cadillac." Naturally, she had to see who was sitting inside the Cad. When
she recognized Gladys Presley, the young woman summoned up her courage and knocked on the window of the
car. "Hello," she said, "aren't you Elvis Presley's mother?"
"Why, yes," the lady said, "how did you recognize me?"
"From pictures in newspapers and magazines," came the
flattering reply. That was all it took to get the conversation
going. The real estate agent was too wise to identify herself
as such at first; but, when Gladys asked her if she worked,
her profession emerged naturally. Once the ice was broken, Gladys informed the keen young agent that the Presleys were in the market for a big house with some land
not far from town. One month later, Virginia Grant was
driving the Presleys around Memphis, looking at houses.
It was after they had rejected a property because it was
too small that suddenly the young woman thought of
Graceland.

A typical southern suburban mansion, built about 1910 of pink Tennessee fieldstone and adorned with an imposing white-columned portico, the house was owned by Mrs. Ruth Brown Moore, whose deceased husband had named it after his wife's aunt. Long unoccupied, it was badly in need of repairs, having become over the years a white elephant. The only use that anyone had found for the place was to house the Sunday school of the Graceland Christian Church. On the other hand, the fabric was sound, the grounds extensive and the district, Whitehaven, was at this point the fastest growing upper-middle-class neighborhood in Memphis.

On the morning of March 19, Virginia Grant meets the Presleys again at the house. This time, Elvis is present. Mrs. Grant is so stunned by his appearance that she almost blacks out. Elvis, for his part, acts as if nothing of consequence is taking place. He walks through the rooms, giving them a very casual once-over. Then, discovering a piano in the drawing room, he sits down and starts to chord out a tune. Having gotten this bit out of his system, he gets up and continues his breezy survey of the house, remarking that the place "sure needs a lot of work." As he proceeds, he starts coming up with ideas for decorating: colors, contrasts, types of furniture. Finally, he voices his goal: "It will be a lot nicer than Red Skelton's house when I get it like I want it." With that bit of heavy name-dropping to indicate the league in which Elvis Presley bats, he reaches for the tentative agreement and without deigning to even glance at its stipulations, he scrawls his signature across the bottom. Hell! Didn't he sign all his contracts that way? Never did him any harm, did it?

No sooner does the word of Elvis's purchase appear in the papers than Mrs. Grant is faced with her next challenge: The Presleys had offered their house on Audubon as part payment on Graceland. Mrs. Moore's representatives had allowed Elvis $55,000 for the property, which he had bought for $40,000, but which he had improved considerably with the den and the pool. Elvis had agreed to add ten thousand dollars in cash and take a note for $37,000 at three or four percent interest with Equitable Life to make up the balance of the total price of $102,500.

At the last minute, however, a bubble gum company came up with a much heavier offer for the house on Audubon, which it wanted to demolish, chop up in pieces the size of matchbooks and give away as a premium: for every five packs of bubble gum a free piece of Elvis Presley's house. The idea delighted Elvis, who pronounced it a "cute little gimmick." It made Vernon rigid with greed. Nothing could be done until the deal had been cleared with the Colonel, who had extensive dealings with franchise and souvenir companies. Imagine everyone's disappointment when it turned out that they couldn't close with the offer because Elvis already had a deal with another bubble gum company!

The truth was that by this point in his career, Elvis had a deal with every sort of company that could profit by his endorsement. In August 1956, Colonel Parker had signed an elaborate contract that was aimed at spinning off from the basic product—Elvis—a half-hundred satellite products, ranging from lipsticks to phonographs, from jeans to fountain pens. He had assigned the rights to merchandise the name and image of Elvis Presley to Special Projects, Inc., the corporate label of a very sharp merchandiser named Hank Saperstein, who also held the rights to the Lone Ranger, Wyatt Earp, Lassie, and Ding Dong School. This deal put the Colonel in hawker's heaven. Now, instead of having just a souvenir program, a songbook and a couple of glossy pictures to sell, the Colonel could preside over a whole store filled with Presley paraphernalia.

In the clothing department of the store, a young girl could purchase an entire Elvis Presley outfit: jeans (black twill with emerald green stitching) with Elvis's signature stamped on a leather pocket patch; an Elvis Presley Ivy League button-down shirt; canvas shoes with tops and linings stamped with a drawing of Elvis and his guitar, and Elvis Presley rock 'n' roll bobby-sox to wear with the shoes—or without shoes at the next sock hop ball. In the novelty department, the young lady could buy an Elvis Presley wallet or a statuette of Elvis or a charm bracelet, selling for just one dollar, whose charms included a tiny framed picture of Elvis, a guitar, a hound dog and a cracked heart, symbolizing "Heartbreak Hotel." At the cosmetic counter, she had her choice of a variety of lipsticks in shades like "Tutti Frutti Red" or "Hound Dog Orange." In the music department, she would discover in addition to Elvis's records two new portable RCA phonographs covered in blue denim (to suggest "Blue Suede Shoes") and embossed on the lid with Elvis's signature in gold. On a special stand at the door, she would find the most inspired product of all: a portrait of Elvis in phosphorescent ink that would glow in the dark. Just the thing for the Elvis idolator who lies abed at night listening to his records and dreaming of one day meeting and even kissing him.

Saperstein knew his business. In just six months from the starting date of his franchise operations, he reported gross sales of twenty-six million dollars. Elvis's cut ranged between four and eleven percent of the wholesale price: say, three-quarters of a million dollars. Colonel Parker, who coveted above all else Elvis's merchandising income, took a fifty percent commission.

Elvis's third film, *Jailhouse Rock,* is far and away the most interesting picture he ever made and the most penetrating treatment ever accorded the murky world of rock 'n' roll. Unlike *Loving You,* which weaves a sophisticated comedy, sustained by professional players, around an Elvis who is not required to do much more than what he always did on stage, *Jailhouse Rock* focuses exclusively on Elvis, taking him step by step through the archetypal life of a rock 'n' roll star. Instead of offering a conventional plot, with intrigues, discoveries, reversals and bold dramatic climaxes, this taut, acerbic black-and-white picture *(Loving You* is in candy color) has the air of an exposé or an anatomy of a world concealed from the public. Though the picture never makes any big splashes, it absorbs the viewers and offers something interesting at every carefully scripted moment. It also has the gall to present Elvis Presley as an obnoxious young punk and a shallow, egotistical Hollywood show-off. Elvis detested the picture and never had a good word for it. It was too close to the truth.

The success of *Jailhouse Rock* owed nothing to the

circumstances under which it was conceived, produced, played or timed. The film was the product of the same Hollywood B-movie machine that ground out all those horrible pictures that soon made Elvis Presley the biggest putz in the history of filmmaking. In fact, this picture was less carefully nurtured than many other Elvis movies because it was conceived strictly as a one-shot, low-budget gamble aimed at cashing in on a passing fad. The producer, Pandro Berman, stood at the time at the mid-point of a thirty-year career that comprised no less than eighty films, including all the Fred Astaire classics. He regarded Elvis then, as he does today, with scant respect. "Let's say, he had a lot of personality; he was not an actor," remarks the brusque, businesslike Berman, who is totally devoid of cant. "The important thing is: We got a break. Instead of going out and hiring a guy like Irving Berlin or Jerry Kern and paying a fortune for music, these punks from hillbilly Tennessee wrote the music, and we paid twenty cents for it." (The "punks" in question were, of course, the "legendary" Leiber and Stoller.)

Money was the only consideration in the making of this picture, as it was in all of Elvis's movies. As they say in the business, the money was "duplexed": There was all the money you *saved* by making the whole film depend on the star's appeal; then, there was all the money you might *earn* if the picture caught on with the rock-hungry youth audience. Even so, Pandro Berman, if left to his own devices, would never have thought of making a movie with Elvis Presley. He was engrossed at the time with more important things, like his production of *The Brothers Karamazov*. It was Berman's wife (and sometime assistant producer), Katherine Hereford, who came up with the idea of building a movie around Elvis. She had seen him in *Love Me Tender*, and, like millions of others, she had observed: "When you saw his face come up on the screen, it said something."

The deal for the picture was made by MGM's boss, Benny Thau, negotiating with Abe Lastfogel, the president of William Morris, who was the mouthpiece for Colonel Parker. At first glance, the terms appeared to be a triumph for the Presley interests: a quarter of a million dollars in salary against fifty percent of net profits plus all the publishing rights to the songs—all this for a young star who had only one picture in circulation. The other end of the deal was not something you would read about in press releases or movie chitchat columns; yet, it was no less, perhaps much more, important. MGM, which had no proprietary interest in Presley, was determined to make this movie on a shoestring. The entire budget, apart from Elvis's salary, was $400,000: probably the smallest sum of money ever allocated to a Presley picture. Such a budget normally guaranteed that the product would be Grade Z schlock.

Colonel Parker couldn't have cared less about the quality of the movie. When Berman asked the Colonel if he should send the script to Elvis, the Colonel said no. "Do you want to read it?" persisted the surprised producer. Again, the Colonel said no. Suspecting a trap, Berman insisted; "What *do* you want?" The Colonel, no less surprised, replied: "I don't want nothin', except to get all the music I want in the picture and have it done by my boys." Even if the movie profits were small, the Colonel would reap his profits from the record sales and publishing royalties. No wonder he was so indifferent to the picture's quality. As for Elvis, he could always console himself with a fleet of new Cadillacs.

Holding down the budget meant in practical terms that none but the most mediocre supporting players would be employed, that the sets would be the cheapest back-lot interiors, that there would be no production numbers and that the shooting schedule would be the tightest humanly possible. Here the key man was the director. Berman knew from the first whom he would use on this film; in fact, this director was to work with Elvis again so it's good we get his professional profile from his boss. As Pandro Berman saw him: "Richard Thorpe was the fastest director on earth. He never looked at a script. He never tried to butt into the story. He never interfered with casting. He was just the most efficient shooter you could buy. Any time you wanted a picture shot on a budget and a schedule that was very tight, you got Richard."

Born under so many bad signs, *Jailhouse Rock* was

saved from its natural fate by one man and one man only: its writer, Guy Trosper. Already a respected scenarist and later a writer who was nominated a number of times for awards in connection with such successful films as *Birdman of Alcatraz* and *The Spy Who Came in from the Cold,* Trosper was not the sort of man who would normally be called on to crank out this kind of film. Both Berman and Hereford were apprehensive that he would decline the job; but they played their hand right, promising Trosper that if he helped the studio with this little project, he could expect something much better the next time around.

Virtually every screenwriter who ever did a Presley picture made some use of the Presley Myth: What sets Trosper and his screenplay apart from the others is his debunker's attitude toward the Myth. Instead of treating it sympathetically in the Hollywood tradition of glamourizing the star as an innocent kid with an unwitting genius for turning people on, Trosper inverts the convention and makes the Myth into a rock 'n' roll version of *What Makes Sammy Run?* His rock star is a once-innocent but always hot-tempered and violent kid who has been embittered and wised up by a stretch in prison. A cruel, ego-tripping punk, he's interested less in fame than he is in money and power. Being basically a prick—or sometimes a bitch—he is a character with some dramatic definition instead of being the juvenile jellyfish that Elvis was normally condemned to play.

Looking at the film today, it reads almost like a deadpan but caustic documentary on the early days of the rock and record business. Instead of showing the hero as a charismatic figure flailing around in front of madly enthusiastic audiences, the whole picture takes place behind the scenes, in the then unfamiliar world of the recording studio, the TV studio, the offices of larcenous record producers and shyster attorneys. The heroine, a good-natured, attractive but essentially maternal girl, is introduced as being an "exploitation girl" for a record company. How's that for an "inside" characterization? Instead of the characters talking about the thrills of performing or how much they love the fans, the conversations are normally confined to commercial strategies and money: Elvis is even made to pronounce the phrase "capital gains" (which in his mushmouthed accent is irresistibly funny). In short, this pioneering account of the Big Rock Candy Mountain is much closer to the truth than any picture about rock ever made subsequently, the scammy, squalid and often tragic history of the music having never once made a dent in the simpleminded adolescent infatuation on which the whole Rock Age rests.

The picture, which is informed throughout by a very sarcastic sense of humor, opens up with a shot that is a parody of Elvis's first appearance on the screen in *Love Me Tender*. Instead of showing this son of the soil plowing behind a mule team with reins around his neck, you see Elvis, sporting his famous smile, riding a grotesque-looking excavating machine like a mechanical camel. He's a working stiff, as always; and, as soon became the convention in all his films, he's pretty quick with his fists. On payday, he's drinking it up with the boys in a bar when one dude makes some very ungentlemanly remarks about an aging slattern. The honorable young Elvis punches him in the mouth. In the ensuing brawl, Elvis inadvertently kills his adversary. Like the hero of any old blues, he goes straight to prison. Here he is caged with a marvelous character: a barrel-shaped good ole boy named Hunk Houghton, who is an ex-country music singer and the boss of all the prison rackets. Elvis is dumb and slow; Hunk is hip and fast. He works earnestly at giving the kid the game. He also demonstrates his singing prowess, offering to teach Elvis a few guitar chords. Elvis responds by outsinging Hunk, which earns him a spot on a corny little TV show which is broadcast from the prison to prove how jolly life is in the joint.

When a load of fan mail arrives at the prison for Elvis, Hunk suddenly snaps to the fact that the kid might be a property. Concealing the mail from Elvis, he cons him into signing a fifty-fifty partnership deal. Naturally, there would be those in the audience who would associate this scene with the way they imagined the fat ole Colonel got Elvis's name on the dotted line.

Even in prison Elvis's temper is not dampened; he gets

into a free-for-all in the mess hall that leads up to one of the kinkiest scenes in any rock movie: a stripped-to-the-waist, wrists-tied-to-the-rail flogging that must have brought some very troubled memories back to haunt Vernon Presley. Eventually, however, the kid is cut loose to make his way in the world doing the corny country songs and licks that he has learned from his music teacher, Hunk. Big-hearted Hunk even gives the kid the name of a cabaret and its owner in some distant city, implying that all Elvis has to do is walk in the door, say, "Hunk sent me," and he'll be given a job.

Now we get some of that classic guitar-man imagery that springs right out of the soul of rock, but which quickly fades from the genre, Presley picture. Elvis is shown a room in a SLEAZY HOTEL; he goes to a cheap JOINT (which has neon champagne glasses on its façade); he meets the classic bald-headed, cigar-smoking, geriatric NIGHTCLUB OWNER; he discovers that the only job he can get is as BUSBOY! Ah, it's a good, solid shaming he takes here; and, with his temper, you know he ain't gonna take it but *so* long! There's one worse thing that can happen to him, however: He can jump onstage without permission, crank up his guitar, sing his song, and then BOMB! In fact, he can do even worse: All the while he's singing in a very soulful voice, some middle-aged jackass sitting at ringside with a cute young chick can be telling stories (traveling salesmen jokes, doubtless) and braying with LAUGHTER right through Elvis's song. Well, sir, that leads to the kicker: the moment when the kid comes leaping off the stage like a cougar and SMASHES HIS GUITAR to smithereens right on the jackass's table. Now, that's what you call good early punk and it's a pity that Elvis, the proto-Punk, never got to do it again.

No sooner does Elvis go charging out of the club than this girl he met at the bar, this "exploitation girl" for Geneva Records, which has a big star named Mickey Alba (read Frank Sinatra, Perry Como, Vic Damone), comes running out after him. As they go driving off in her convertible, she tells him that he wasn't very good. When he won't listen to her, she urges him to make a custom recording and hear how he actually sounds to the public.

Here, of course, we're tracking right into the famous Sun studio; and in the sequence that follows, one wonders whether Elvis, who was in charge of the music in this picture, might not have reproduced pretty accurately what happened at the famous first session in 1954. His new girl brings him a backup band that consists of Scotty Moore, Bill Black and D. J. Fontana plus Mike Stoller on piano.

The first time he sings his song, "Don't Leave Me Now," it's very similar to those sentimental things he did first at Sun. Then, after he hears the playback, he decides to jump up the tune just as he jumped up "That's All Right Mama." Like many features of this highly realistic movie, this sequence hovers on the border between a fiction that is based on reality and a reality that is like something out of fiction. In any case, the session ends with a new style being born. Now it's just a question, so Elvis thinks, of getting the record produced.

Elvis has yet to learn the truth about the record business. When he plays his demo for a coolly indifferent producer at Geneva, he's told that they aren't interested. As he's leaving, though, the producer suggests that the demo be left with him overnight so that he can play it "over the wire for J. R. in New York." Inevitably, the whole concept is pirated. Elvis discovers in the booth of a record store that the tune he was on the verge of bringing out on another label is already Mickey Alba's latest hit on Geneva. "He stole my style, my—everything!" cries Elvis, the boy who in real life stole so much from so many singers.

The movie Elvis rallies quickly and decides to take the game into his own hands. Forming a partnership with his record lady, he goes into business for himself. Next time you see him in the studio, he's Elvis Presley for sure: doing a typical Leiber and Stoller tune and making with the motions, just as Elvis always did while cutting his records.

At this point in the story, the relations between Elvis and his partner have become rather sticky. She's in love with him, of course. But he's so self-absorbed, he hardly knows she exists. He insists, when asked, that their relationship is based strictly on money. What confuses her is the inconsistency of his behavior. One night she takes him out to suburbia to see her folks. They're typical of

college-town eggheads. When they learn that Elvis is in
the music business, they start to gabble about progressive
jazz. This drives the movie Elvis just as crazy as it would
the real-life Elvis, who hated jazz because he couldn't understand it.

When Elvis and the girl hit the street, she scolds him
for his attitude. He silences her with a very brutal kiss.
When she angrily demands: "How dare you think such
cheap tactics would work with me?" he replies, "That ain't
tactics, Honey. It's jes' (smirk) the beast in me." Again,
proto-Punk, but, alas, as so often happened when Elvis
tried to act tough and "hoody" on the screen, he muffs the
line, which has to be delivered with a rather complex
amalgam of scoffing, sneering and swaggering.

Success follows now that Elvis has taken everything
into his own hands. He ties in with a creepy lawyer, who
manages the business. He talks percentages and volume
sales. He's just about to make his first big appearance on
TV, when out of nowhere comes old Hunk, fresh out of the
can after doing an eighteen-year stretch. Hunk demands
a shot at the tube; the kid warns him that he's hopelessly
out of date. Hunk's number is cut by the producer, but
Elvis stars in the most brilliant song and dance routine
to be found in any Presley picture: the "Jailhouse Rock"
number.

This famous bit of footage was just an afterthought by
the producers of the film. It wasn't part of the original
scenario or budget but when Alex Romero, the dance director, came up with the idea of choreographing the title
song, another $25,000 was found for the sequence. Presley
purists put down this number as too slick and chorus-
boysy. Actually, it was the one time in Elvis's entire career
when somebody with a bit of skill and authority got the
kid to move as if he knew where he was going. The jivey
strutting style he adopts is perfectly in keeping with his
natural body language; the only difference is that instead
of faking all his moves with the force of a football lineman
hurling himself down a row of staggered car tires, Elvis
makes his moves with definition and style.

The worst feature of the picture is its melodramatic
ending. Hunk, a schlub but still a man, grows enraged at

the way Elvis abuses his long-suffering exploitation girl. He socks the kid in the jaw and then—God forbid!—in the throat. Elvis loses his voice and there is much pother about whether he will ever sing again. When he strikes up "Young and Beautiful" you're supposed to be overwhelmed with joy, but if you're a music buff, you note with disgust that Leiber and Stoller have failed, as usual, to write a good ballad.

The other criticism of the film is that Elvis walks through it like a storeroom dummy instead of an actor. The sweetness he projects in his first picture and the sullen self-involved anger he exudes in his second picture are followed here by what became his standard screen role: the smug, stupid, embarrassingly self-conscious screen rooster. It's too bad the bait didn't take because Elvis never again got to appear in any picture that offered him such marvelous opportunities to confront himself.

Chapter 17

Boy-Man

WHEN ELVIS got back to Memphis in the summer of 1957, he found Graceland completely renovated. The walls were pure white with cornices of gold-leafed dentilation. The floors were covered with thick white shag carpeting. The windows were hung with floor-to-ceiling drapes, red for the winter, blue for the summer, opened and closed by concealed motors. The furniture was oversized and custom built: huge slabs of foam rubber upholstered in nubby fabrics. Smoked-glass mirrors covered whole walls and glass-topped tables added to the feeling of lightness and glitter in the once dark and decrepit rooms of the old mansion.

Elvis exulted in the appearance of his rock palace. He was also amused by the homey country touches that his parents had added to the grand design. The original Beverly Hillbillies, Gladys and Vernon had installed behind the neoclassic, Victorian eclectic house such humble rural structures as a chicken coop and a hog pen. Vernon, who had claimed that he was no longer able to work, labored for hours stuffing sausages in his big garden, where he grew purple hull and crowder peas, cabbages and tomatoes, pole beans and peppers, "Eyetalian" squash and eggplant. Around the grounds strutted a couple of screaming peacocks that would enrage everyone when they jumped up on the hood of a gleaming Cadillac or Lincoln to scratch at their reflections in the windshield. In the afternoon, the folks would go out for a drive. Gladys would take her tin of Garret snuff, her snuff-dipping stick and a Maxwell House coffee can for a spittoon. Vernon would take a chaw of good tobacco, Bull of the Woods or Day's Work. Then, they'd get into a brilliantly hued Fleetwood and take off for a little run over to the Nicholses' place or out the road, where they could buy ripe watermelons.

Elvis, for his part, threw himself into all those pleasures that appealed most to his adolescent heart. Indeed, you could say that his primary goal once he became famous was to turn back the clock to that time when he was a wretched little cipher at Humes and relive those bad old days so as to experience them the second time around in precisely the opposite manner. Instead of being a pariah, he was now the richest, handsomest, most popular kid in the school.

Instead of appearing at the Rainbow Rollerdome teetering self-consciously on a pair of skates he couldn't manage, praying for some young girl from church to recognize him, Elvis would rent the whole damn place after midnight, when normally it shut down, and throw a wild skating party for at least forty kids that would last till dawn. Everything would be laid on in a style that would thrill any teenager's heart. The electric organ would play Elvis's favorite skating tunes. The chili dogs and Hoagies would be on the house. When you went to the skate-renting counter and gave the man your size, he would offer the skates for free. Presiding over the entire entertainment would be your gracious and charming host, the boy with the most, Elvis! Yeah!

The appearance of this palace of pleasure? On the outside, it rather resembled a rambling one-story brick church, with high arched windows and gothic parapets. Inside, it was a typical high-school gym: a Quonset-arched ceiling supported by exposed steel trusses; suspended from the ceiling, a couple of big gas heaters with whirling fans and shiny, galvanized tin exhaust pipes; a vast wooden floor marked off in circles and quadrangles; a pipe railing protecting the spectator seats; bare walls adorned with a

number of large reproductions of religious paintings, such
as a Crucifixion; some swags of red-white-and-blue bunting hanging from the rafters; and there, in the middle,
suspended from a crossbeam, a big electric sign, ribbed
with neon, flashing imperatively: "Couples."

Not content with just throwing the party, Elvis would
dictate every move on the floor. Inspired to fulfill his most
cherished fantasies, he invented a novel game called War.
Oh, it was hell on wheels! Just the preparations for the
event would scare off many of the guests. First, a large
supply of pads and protective bandages would be handed
about, as if in preparation for a nice lethal game of ice
hockey. Then, the first-aid team would take up its position
at the side of the arena, busying itself with opening boxes
of Band-Aids and uncorking various flasks and bottles of
antiseptics, anesthetics and restoratives. Next, sides would
be chosen, with perhaps eight men to a team. Girls were
not allowed to play as a rule, though an exception was
made for one extraordinarily tough tomboy named Linda
Mulinex. Linda was Miss Hell on Wheels.

The object of the game was to floor the members of the
opposite team by any means possible. Basically, it was a
free-for-all on skates. The two teams would line up at
opposite ends of the rink, with Junior Smith, who acted
as referee, standing in the middle of the floor. Junior would
glare right and left—making psychotic grimaces—to assure himself that everybody was ready. Then, he would
blow a shrill blast on a whistle, straining so hard that he
would double over from the waist. Instantly, the two ranks
of players would come charging down on each other,
wooden wheels slamming against the wooden deck, bodies
going into bends and crouches, with elbows thrust out in
postures of attack or defense.

Sonny West recalls vividly the first time he played War.
He was introduced to Elvis by Red West, Sonny's cousin,
who identified the big boy in the flattop as "fresh meat."
The next thing he remembers is skating full tilt at this
Linda Mulinex. "Hell!" thinks Sonny, a 190-pound football
player, "I don't wanna hit no girl!" Veering off to one side,
he tries to skate past her. Linda comes right at Sonny,
spinning in a dizzying cartwheel. Instinctively, Sonny

throws out a muscular arm and knocks her to the floor.
Next thing he knows, Linda has recovered and is hard on
his tail. Before he can make his clumsy feet execute a turn,
she comes up behind him and gives him a sharp chop with
her forearm right behind his knee. Sonny drops as if shot.

Scrambling to his feet gamely, he's about to get under
way again, when he feels another hatchetlike chop behind
his knee. Again, he takes a header. After he's been cut
down a few more times, Sonny scrambles for the safety of
the sidelines. There, he hangs to the wall, panting hard
and looking ruefully at the busted-out knees of his new
Levis. Instantly, Elvis is beside him, demanding, "What
are ya doin'?" Sonny waves toward Linda and gasps, "I'm
stayin' away from *her!*" "Then you're not playin'?!" raps
Elvis. "I *can't* play!" cries Sonny. "Every time I get ready
to hit someone, I find myself on my butt! You keep that
damn girl away from me, an' I'll git out there." Elvis gave
the necessary orders and got Linda off Sonny's ass. That
did not end the big boy's problems, however. Before the
night was over, he had had his cheek split open and been
knocked cold by a shot to the head from a pair of skates.
Each time he was laid out, the first-aid team rushed to his
rescue. Sonny was impressed at how efficient they were:
They even had sophisticated "butterfly" bandages to close
the cut on his cheek instead of using a needle and thread.

Though War was violent and dangerous, the game that
frightened Sonny the most was the Whip. Once he was so
unlucky as to wind up at the tail end of a giant whip that
numbered thirty skaters. As they raced around the rink,
the speed of their motions went up and up. On a fast turn
at the end of a line of thirty people, a skater could be doing
thirty miles an hour! It was on one of these racecourse
turns that Sonny suddenly lost his grip and went flying
off at a tangent like a man shot from a cannon. He hit the
guard rails at the side of the floor and went flying over
them to land in the wooden seats. He was lucky that night
to get out with his life.

Did Elvis expose himself to similar risks on the floor?
His participation in these violent skating games, as in the
equally dangerous games of football he loved to play, appears to have been something less than absolute. Though

he threw himself into the game for all he was worth, there was an understanding among the players that Elvis was not to be damaged. If someone got into the game who didn't understand the unspoken rule or who had the temerity to go after Elvis deliberately, Red and Sonny would soon improve this fool's knowledge of the sport. Once one of the skating instructors got the dumb idea of impressing his girlfriend by dumping Elvis. Red and Sonny soon settled his hash. While Red skated into the hapless pro from one side, Sonny struck the showoff such a blow that he flew clean through a hole in the guardrail and smashed himself to bits against the seat barricade. When a player's injuries were too grave for the first-aid team, it was customary to summon an ambulance and cart him off to the hospital.

When the roller rink no longer appealed to him, there were always other and even more dangerous recreations. One of these was motorcycle racing. Elvis would have the Shelby County police shut down a stretch of Highway 51 late at night. Then, he and one of the other boys would crank up their big Harley-Davidsons to enjoy some sport. As everyone knows who's ever ridden with one of these massive hogs between his legs, there's something deeply thrilling about the experience of being astraddle a really mighty bike. If you run the monster up to those speeds, in excess of 100 m.p.h., which it's capable of attaining, the thrill becomes even keener. What Elvis most enjoyed was putting the final cherry on top of this elaborate sundae of nocturnal speed and danger. As he and Lamar Fike would roar down the empty highway, they would pull up beside each other, adjust their positions and then reach out—to touch hands at 120 m.p.h. A Michelangelesque moment!

Was all this just good clean fun? No, of course not. It was the kind of crazy, compulsive behavior that characterized everything Elvis Presley did. Not only was Elvis intent on rewinding the dreary spools of his dismal high-school career to relive the past in triumph: He was just as determined to live down the reputation of being a sissy, which he had incurred when he was under his mother's thumb. Elvis was bent on demonstrating to his little world—and later, to the whole world!—that he was a macho man. He would take all the risks, including the

risks nobody has to take. He would play with the big bad
boys and beat them at their own games. He would experience what southerners have always been best at experiencing: the ecstasy of self-destruction. They call it "Going
to Jesus."

Elvis's other amusements in Memphis were of a more
pacific, if not of a more conventional character. He had
always enjoyed the movies. Now that he was a movie star,
he enjoyed them even more. Only, he felt that he should
enjoy movies in the manner that best suited him. Why
should he experience the inconveniences of viewing films
in public theaters? Why should he have to incur the cost
of building a movie theater on his property at Graceland?
There was another solution readily available to him. He
could lease a neighborhood movie house for the hours when
he most wanted to see the latest pictures. This sensible
decision soon gave rise to a remarkable practice: nothing
less than the King's first full-blown courtly ritual.

Like everything Elvis did for fun, the movies would
invariably begin after midnight. Their venue would change,
depending on circumstances, but the typical site was the
Memphian: a small, 1940-ish Art Deco house located in
the area of Overton Square, about a fifteen-minute drive
from Graceland. During the day, one of Elvis's boys would
have called the man who booked the first-run pictures for
the big downtown houses. Elvis had his pick of all the
pictures scheduled for release in Memphis within the next
six weeks. His tastes could be summed up in one word—
action. He had no use for love stories, musicals or straight
dramas. He wasn't keen on westerns either. His real joy
was who-done-its, terror movies and certain kinds of comedy. To make sure that he would not be disappointed by
the selection, at least three or four feature films would be
on hand when he arrived at the theater.

Elvis displayed an attitude compounded of magna-
nimity and exhibitionism at his private screenings. He
didn't mind if as many as a hundred fans or other members
of the hoi polloi shared the picture with him, provided they
knew their place and showed him the proper respect. This
crowd of commoners would gather at the front of the theater long before Elvis's arrival, tipped off by the members

of the young King's entourage. Elvis would enter invariably through the stage door and take his favorite seat in the empty theater, about twelve rows back in the center. No one was permitted to sit in front of or beside him except his date, who was always seated to his left. On his right, a small table was placed on which were arranged his little Hav-a-Tampa cigars, his Pepsi, his chewing gum and, later in the evening, his food, which was brought in from all-night hamburger stands and pizza parlors. Once the King had been enthroned, the front doors of the theater would be thrown open and his guests would enter, taking their seats at the back of the house.

During the hours from midnight to dawn, the regular staff of the theater would be on duty. You could go back to the snack stand and get your fill of hot buttered popcorn. You could give an order to a go-fer who would run out to bring back pizzas and cheeseburgers. If you wanted to go to the men's room while Elvis was inside, you had to wait until the King had completed his toilet. Elvis never went to the john without his henchmen, who stood guard at the door until he was ready to return to his seat. In this as in every other feature of the evening, he enjoyed absolute control.

If the film did not interest him, he would shout at the projectionist to turn it off and go on to the next offering. If, on the other hand, the movie interested him greatly, he might order it rerun. Once he saw *Dr. Strangelove* three times running, from about 1:00 in the morning till 5:30; then he had the last reel repeated about three times more, explaining that Peter Sellers was such a subtle actor you could not understand exactly what he was doing in just a few viewings. If the movie were interesting but it slowed down for a love scene, Elvis would do a little spontaneous editing, demanding that the unexciting scene be omitted and the projectionist get on to the next good part. Sometimes, so much footage was omitted that the party had to break up early because the supply of film on hand had been exhausted.

Elvis enjoyed the acting of heavies: his favorites numbered Marlon Brando, George C. Scott, Clint Eastwood and even Frank Sinatra in a serious role. He wasn't im-

pressed by women on the screen, and he virtually never
looked at one of his own films. On the very rare occasions
when he would screen one of his own pictures, everyone
would be barred from the theater but Elvis and his closest
associates. Generally speaking, he found his own pictures
very hard to take. "Who's that fast-talkin' southern sonovabitch up there?" he would challenge, looking at himself.
In later years, he would examine his image with horror,
exclaiming, "Too fat! Too fat!"

The only quiet, private pleasure that Elvis enjoyed was
the poignant experience of nostalgia. Though revisiting
the scenes of one's childhood is a satisfaction sought generally by the middle-aged or elderly, from the age of
twenty-one on Elvis Presley was often engrossed in con-
templating his humble origins. Taking along a trusted
confidant, he would drive slowly and thoughtfully around
the Lauderdale Courts, past Humes High, through Overton Park, recalling aloud the experiences and emotions he
associated with these places. Sometimes, he would drive
down to Tupelo and show his friends where he had grown
up, stressing the extreme poverty of his childhood and
brooding deeply over the most dilapidated sections of the
town. To avoid attracting attention, especially in Memphis
where the appearance of one of his cars was certain to
summon up a spontaneous escort, he would put a disguis-
ing cap on his head and go out for his reminiscent cruise
in a panel truck that was used to haul garbage off the
property at Graceland. Driving along in low gear, sometimes late at night, once again a truck driver with a little
cap on his head, Elvis would get deep and bluesy contem-
plating his awesome translation from a slum project to a
palace.

Elvis always stressed the vital fact that he had made
his money while he was still young and able to enjoy it.
The attainment of wealth in middle age was a goal he
scorned. Happiness, in his view, was a condition possible
only in youth. No matter what you had when you were
older, it would be vitiated by the very fact that you were
older. Age was the enemy of joy. The real goal of life was
never to succumb to age. One of the reasons Elvis would
spend so much time examining his face in mirrors was to

see if he could discern the first faint traces of the aging process.

If he discovered a line forming in his skin, he would quickly apply facial creams or lotions designed to restore the skin to its babylike natural smoothness. If he detected some slight loss of hair from his comb, he would shout in anguish. Sometimes he made minuscule marks on his scalp with his eyebrow pencil, taking care each day not to wash these little dots away. They marked his hairline and their purpose was to enable him to measure any recession of this vital line, this lifeline. As for grey hair, he knew that would come early because premature greying was characteristic of the Presleys. Fortunately, it posed no problems once he had begun to dye his hair. In his thirties, Elvis's hair was thickly streaked with grey. To paraphrase the ad, "Only his hairdresser knew." He also began to dye his eyebrows and even his eyelashes. No hair was too small or inconspicuous to escape his careful scrutiny. If the enemy of life were age, a man had to confront his foe with the vigilance of a soldier posted on a dangerous frontier.

The only other danger that Elvis faced were the cranks whom Gladys dreaded so much. The first serious threat from one of these crazies surfaced one morning in August, when word came up from the gate that an FBI man had arrived who wanted to speak with Elvis. Elvis and the boys met the agent in the living room. He showed his identification and then popped open an attaché case. Reaching inside, he confronted them with a letter which he held between the second knuckles of each index finger. "I want you to look at this carefully," he said. "This is a death threat from somebody upstate. We already know the town where it was postmarked. What I want you to tell me is do you recognize anything about this letter?" Elvis looked at the letter closely and read it slowly aloud. "No matter how you try to get away from us, we will kill you by gun or by bomb. Either from another car or a person or an airplane." Elvis was shocked. "Is this for real?" he asked the agent. "You have to treat it as if it were," the man replied. "Do you carry a weapon?" Elvis replied, "No, but

I think I'll start." That marked the beginning of a practice
that eventually developed into a mania.

After the FBI man left, Elvis and the boys sat down to
breakfast. "I don't understand this," said Elvis. "Why
would someone want to kill me?" Lamar replied: "Hey,
man, maybe somebody's so pissed off at what you've become that he just wants to cut you down out of envy."
"Well," said Elvis, "they're not gonna get me without a
battle." The boys looked at each other mutely. Then Elvis
exclaimed: "This is ridiculous! Let's go see some movies
or something!"

Lamar was all for seeing movies that afternoon. "All
right," the big fat boy said, "let's go!" Elvis hesitated for
a moment; then he said with studied casualness, "Go outside and crank the car—I'll be with you in a minute."
Lamar made a face: half smirking, half quaking. "This is
like one of those Al Capone movies," he complained. "You
want me to go out and crank the car. If it blows up, I'm
the one that goes!"

By the time they got out of the last movie, it must have
been nearly eleven o'clock in the evening. Elvis had his
whole gang with him that night: George Klein, Gene
Smith, Cliff Gleaves and Lamar. As always, they had
parked the car in an alley behind the theater. "Lamar, go
crank it up," says Elvis. Lamar went through the ritual,
opening the hood, getting under the car, doing the whole
checkout, while Elvis explained to the other guys what he
feared. Finally, Lamar jumped in the driver's seat, hit the
ignition and jumped out like a madman. The car hummed
smoothly. At that point, all the boys piled aboard and took
off for Graceland, with Elvis at the wheel.

As they drove home through the night, a rainstorm
came down on the car, dampening the mood of hilarity.
Approaching the gate at Graceland, they were just about
to start up the driveway when suddenly, out of the darkness, stepped a strange man. He signaled to Elvis to open
his window. Lamar was frantic. "Elvis, go on through,
don't stop, don't open no window, this may be it!" Elvis
said, "I gotta find out what this guy wants." With that he
rolled down the window and the man stuck his head in the
car. His approach was so sudden and direct that Elvis

whipped out his gun and Lamar backed him up instantly
with another gun which they had stashed in the car. Holding two pistols just inches from the man's face, they demanded virtually in the same breath: "What do you want?"
The man stared at them in astonishment for a moment.
Then, he gasped: "I want an autograph for my daughter."[1]

The most curious feature of Elvis's life-style in this
early period is his pattern of relations with women. Almost
any other boy, given the opportunities that Elvis was
granted, would have behaved more wickedly. Nothing
wipes out moral restraints and psychological inhibitions
faster than enormous wealth, popularity and power.
Though everyone who derives his success from public endorsement, from rock stars to ministers of the gospel, recognizes the necessity to be wary of public disgrace, the
greater the powers a man achieves, the greater the possibilities for dissembling his sins. Elvis Presley at the
height of his glory could have indulged himself in the most
outrageous manner if he had so desired. The curious thing
is that once he became famous, Elvis behaved as if he
didn't dare to step over the line of conventional morality.

In this connection, it is illuminating to see what Elvis
made of his sexual opportunities once he had become a
movie star. Hollywood and Las Vegas offered him endless
possibilities for gratification. In a couple of years he might
have compiled a record of conquests that would have put
Casanova in the shade. Instead, what did he do? First, he
dedicated himself to a couple of self-involved stars, who
regarded him as either a foolish bumpkin or the ideal Coke
date. Then, having extended the field of his conquests to
Las Vegas, where *everybody* gets laid, Elvis fell into the
pattern of inviting the more appealing girls to Memphis
and Mama—not precisely the behavior of a rake. Finally,
having had his first little fling with the starlets and the

[1]The FBI apprehended the writer of the threatening letter,
who turned out to be an emotionally disturbed young woman. In
striking anticipation of John Lennon's murderer, she had threatened first to commit suicide. Instead, she committed herself to a
mental institution.

show girls, he gave up the whole enterprise as a bad show
and retreated to the pleasures of his home town.

Most of these pleasures had nothing to do with sex. If
Freud hadn't destroyed the notion that there is some time
in life when we have not yet discovered sexual pleasure,
one might be tempted to describe Elvis's adventures in
Memphis as "presexual." They were certainly highly immature. His most gratifying relationship with the members of the opposite sex was a very cozy foursome he established between himself and three fourteen-year-old
girls who were ardent fans. These girls accompanied him
to the movies, the amusement park and roller rink. They
joined him in warm weather for evenings around the swimming pool. They would grieve when he left for a tour or
a film production. They would rejoice when he returned
and their accustomed life with him resumed. They spent
the last days with him before he entered the service and
visited him in Texas before he left for Germany. Not until
Elvis had returned from the service and invited Priscilla
Beaulieu to live with him at Graceland did the trio Elvis
called "the old gang" break up. Because they spent so much
time with Elvis and because their relationship was of a
sort that was clearly an ideal fulfillment for Elvis, it is
important to see how the first rock star related to the first
circle of groupies.

Gloria Mowel was the first of the three girls to meet
Elvis and the one who introduced to Elvis the other two:
Heidi Heissen and Frances Forbes. Gloria's father worked
for an Oldsmobile agency that operated a garage the Presleys patronized. One day when this kind father saw Elvis's
car in the garage, he got the idea of trying to wangle an
invitation for his daughter to meet the hero of Memphis.
When Vernon Presley came in to pick up the car, Mr.
Mowel told the star's father about his teenage girl, who
was such a dedicated Elvis fan. Vernon agreed to arrange
a visit.

On that great day, whose date Gloria can never forget—
October 11, 1956—she rang the bell at 1034 Audubon
Avenue. Instead of being ushered into the presence by a
maid, Gloria was suddenly confronted by Elvis himself.
Entering the house, she recognized "Ruby Baby," a recent

hit by Johnny Moore and the Drifters (whom Elvis loved), playing loudly on the phonograph in the den. Elvis offered her a Pepsi and they started a conversation—which continued on and off for the next five years. Elvis, Gloria soon perceived, was both very emotional and very lonely. He was drawn to girls, but he didn't trust them because he couldn't be sure whether they were crazy about him or just his public image. Though Elvis was always the center of attention wherever there was a crowd, a position he demanded and sometimes connived to obtain, when he was alone with Gloria or the other girls, he seemed better pleased. In such intimate meetings, he was very lowkeyed, quiet, playful and apt to chatter endlessly about the most trivial things.

Once Elvis found a person or a thing he liked, it became an obsession with him. As soon as Gloria had won Elvis's confidence, she was always invited to the house. She would accompany Elvis on his usual round of amusements, but she also spent a lot of time with him at the house, either out in the back, where he would shoot his BB gun, or in his bedroom, where they would sometimes engage in furious pillow fights with feathers flying everywhere. Elvis loved to roughhouse with his teenage girls. They loved it, too—until he went "too far." As Gloria recalls: "We'd tickle, fight, laugh, mess around; but all you'd have to say is, 'Stop!', and he'd roll over and quit. It would never be mentioned again that night. But next time, it would be the same thing exactly. You'd fight with him, kid around and scuffle. The next thing, he'd get serious and you'd just push him away. I think that if he really pushed, I would have done it. But he had a saying he told me once: 'I'll never break a virgin. There's too many prostitutes walking around.'"

Though all three of these girls were going to junior high, their nights with Elvis generally ran till three or four in the morning, his usual hours. Making the rounds with Elvis, they might drop in on Dewey Phillips's show and then drive out Poplar Avenue to Joe Cuoghi's record store, Popular Tunes, where they'd sit around after closing, playing all the new sides. Then, Elvis would want to go home and eat a big meal, or, if it were warm, find some

place that had cold watermelons and bring them back so
that they could cut out their sweet red hearts and enjoy
the southern farmer's late-night treat.

The best times were those nights when after tumbling
in and out of the pool for a couple of hours, they would go
upstairs with Elvis to have a real teenage pajama party.
Elvis had a dressing room at the top of the stairs with a
long mirror. The girls would bustle around Elvis, blowing
his hair dry. He would say to Gloria and Heidi: "Frances
was jealous tonight because I was throwing you in the
pool." The girls would giggle and continue grooming their
mutual "lover." When they had finished restoring Elvis
to perfect condition, he might turn the tables and start
lecturing them on how to apply their makeup. Elvis
wanted them to wear heavy eye shadow and sophisticated,
sexy makeup. He might even take the eyeliner and apply
it himself. When everyone was looking pretty, they would
troupe down the hall to Elvis's bedroom.

Elvis's favorite color at the time was dark blue, a drastic
change from the pink and black he had favored a couple
of years earlier. His bedroom had white walls, but the
drapes and the spread over the enormous bed were blue
with white leather piping. Behind the bed was a big
smoked-glass mirror. Elvis and the three girls would all
sit on the bed, yoga style, with him in the middle. He'd
tickle one of the girls and make her toss and giggle. Then,
he'd kiss her. Turning to another one, he'd say, "Gloria is
jealous 'cause I kissed Frances" or "Frances is jealous
'cause I kissed Heidi." After they had tired of this play,
Elvis would turn out the light. Then, he would lie down
on the bed with an arm around a girl on each side and the
third girl lying across his feet.

Nothing would be said during this blissful teenage *Lie-
bestod*. The ecstasy was of that intensely quiet and motionless character that suggests the bliss of the fetus floating in the amniotic fluid. "You never wanted it to end,"
murmurs Gloria, when she thinks back on that experience
today. "When you were in that room, you wanted to shut
out the whole world for the rest of your life."

When the hour got very late, Elvis would sit up and
kiss each of the girls in turn, saying: "I love you and I'll

see you tomorrow. Now, get Lamar to take you home." The girls would come marching down the stairs to find Lamar dozing upright on the sofa. The fat boy's job was to sit up and wait for them. When he'd look at his watch and discover it was four A.M., he often panicked. What would the girls' parents say? Would he have to take the tongue-lashing that was directed at Elvis? Actually, nothing ever happened. Elvis had a great gift for disarming parents and persuading them that though their fourteen-year-old daughters spent a lot of time in his bedroom, nothing improper was going on. Perhaps he drew strength and conviction from the fact that these pajama parties were so innocent.

What Elvis found in the company of his three fourteen-year-old groupies was an ideal relationship: a system of relations, in fact, that both through what it offered and what it forbade fulfilled him deeply. The girls' age—precisely the same as that of Priscilla Beaulieu when Elvis fell in love with her—was that of his fans, the age group to whom he made the strongest appeal because it was the most appealing to him. With such girls Elvis could feel himself most a man, which, in turn, made him much more pleasant and charming and even, paradoxically, less assertive and arrogant. On the other hand, the effect of being surrounded by three adoring girls was roughly the equivalent of being bathed as a child in the love of an adoring young mother. Yet there was none of the discomfort Elvis would have felt with a mother figure because the plurality of this relationship coupled with the puerility of the girls constituted an absolute denial of anything like the idea of mothering. This denial was symbolized most absolutely by the fact that the girls were virgins. (It's significant in this regard that Elvis could never tolerate the idea of having sexual relations with a woman who had borne a child. Such a woman was undeniably, to him, a mother.) As for his rationalization that he was too ethical to deflower a virgin, this, as we shall see, he soon abandoned. In any case, it's perfectly apparent that, sexually, Elvis was fixated at precisely the age of his typical fan: thirteen or fourteen.

Though Elvis was most fulfilled by plural relationships,

in one aspect of his ambivalent identity as a boy-man, he
did crave a single woman who would play the role of the
steady girlfriend with the promise of becoming his wife.
Dixie Locke was the first of a number of women who sustained this part in Elvis's life. Not long after he became
involved with Gloria, Heidi and Frances, he developed
another such relationship with a young woman of nineteen
who combined the character of the simple, ordinary, small-
town southern girl, which was the type of Dixie, with the
character of the ambitious performer, which was the type
of the Hollywood actresses and the Las Vegas showgirls
whom he had dated in the past year. Commencing in June
1957, and continuing until the arrival of Priscilla in 1962,
Elvis's steady girl was Anita Wood.

"Pert" was the word they used for Anita Wood back in
the late fifties, when the story of her romance with Elvis
was being detailed in the movie mags under titles like,
"'You Are My No. 1 Girl...' Or Is She Just the Girl Who
Waits and Waits?" "Pert" meant that although Anita was
stacked to kill (35-23-35), she was just five foot three,
weighed a mere 110 pounds, wore her blonde hair bobbed
short and smiled her dimply, pimply smiles like the perfect
little southern miss. Like a lot of pert misses, Anita's compact form was compacted of ambition, pride, energy and
a measure of talent for show business, especially singing
pop tunes. Though she had grown up far from the centers
of the entertainment industry, in Jackson, Tennessee, she
had been in contention for a professional career since she
was eight. "Contestant" was another word that fitted her
very well. From the age of twelve, she had been appearing
in talent contests with great success. At sixteen, for example, she won the Youth Talent Show at the Mid-South
Fair in Memphis, singing "Oh, What a Dream!" At seventeen she had her own radio show in Jackson, *Antics of
Anita,* which was soon carried on local TV. At eighteen,
she won a Sammy Kaye *So You Want to Lead a Band*
contest. At nineteen, she moved to Memphis to become the
hostess on the *Top 10 Dance Party,* a local version of
American Bandstand. It was shortly after she began appearing on this program that she met Elvis.

George Klein, the dark, Semitic-looking local DJ who

had been the president of Elvis's graduating class at
Humes and a long-time friend of the Presley family, was
the intermediary between Elvis and Anita, as he was to
be many times in the years ahead between Elvis and a
whole series of local girls down to the last important relationship of Elvis's life, with Ginger Alden. Elvis was
always very reticent about approaching new women and
George, a popular figure in town, was ideally situated to
find and introduce to the King all sorts of appealing young
ladies. In this case, however, it was Anita who made the
initial suggestion, remarking in a joking style when she
first met George: "I think you ought to introduce me to
Elvis some time. After all, he's a Memphian and I'm a
Memphian now, too." Just two days after planting that
suggestion, Anita received her first offer of a date with
Elvis.

It wasn't Elvis who called: Lamar Fike was entrusted
with the job. When Lamar, who liked nothing better than
playing Elvis's stand-in, made the suggestion that Anita
go out with Elvis that very night, she was dismayed to
have to say that it was impossible because she had a date
already. Lamar could see no obstacle in a prior engagement: All Anita had to do was break the date with the
insignificant little nobody with whom she was planning
to spend the evening and prepare herself to meet the King!
Anita was a girl of strict principles; she would hear nothing of breaking a date with one man just in order to see
another one who was more important. When she declined,
Lamar became highly indignant and began to chew her
out on the phone, just as he used to chew out those maitre
d's who did not pass Elvis into the restaurant immediately
when he arrived unannounced and found himself preceded
by a line of people waiting for a table. "Oh, lord! This is
unbelievable!" the fat boy burst out. "How often do you
get a chance to go out with someone like Elvis Presley?"
The more Lamar tried to beat Anita down, the more stubborn she became. Finally, she said, "Tell him to call me
again," and hung up the phone. Now, there was nothing
for Lamar to do but acknowledge that the invitation of
which every young woman in America dreamed had just
been rejected.

Actually, Anita started crying the moment she got off the phone. She was convinced that Elvis would never call her again. She had lost her great opportunity. It was true, of course, that she was not an Elvis Presley fan. She had never bought one of his records nor gone to see him in person or on the screen. The only time she had seen him, in fact, was once when her mother called her into the living room and pointed at the TV set, saying, "Look at this boy from Memphis. Isn't he cute?" Still, you didn't have to be an Elvis Presley fan to know who Elvis was or what it meant to be asked out by him, especially if you were a girl trying to make a career of singing. Anita's principled behavior paid off, however; it made an impression on Elvis, who was always measuring people by the way they reacted to him, tempting them to grab and then despising them when they took. Two weeks later, he told Lamar to call Anita again. Meantime, George Klein had spoken with the young woman and made it clear that Elvis watched her show and was very taken with her appearance.

Her first date was a perfect introduction to the glamorous world of Elvis Presley. A huge black Cadillac limousine pulled up at Anita's door. The hulking Lamar, wearing a dark suit like a chauffeur, bustled out and escorted Anita to the car. When she sat down at some distance from Elvis, she got an instant flash of annoyance from the handsome star. The principal object of the evening was to cruise by the Strand Theater on Main Street, where the staff was erecting a cutout of Elvis above the marquee in preparation for the opening of *Loving You*. Back and forth the limousine crawled, as Elvis and his boys appraised the display. Then came the most impressive move of the night. As Anita recalls: "After a while we headed back out toward Whitehaven. Elvis called Chenault's, his favorite restaurant, on the car phone and asked them to have the private dining room ready in fifteen minutes." Sounds pretty heavy, doesn't it? The luxurious limousine, the car phone—whoever heard of such a thing in Memphis? Hey, this was the big time! The results of all this pomp and circumstance were not what might be anticipated. "When we got to Chenault's," continues Anita, "my hamburger and Elvis's special—a cheeseburger with bacon instead of hamburger meat and all the trimmings—were already fixed and waiting for us." At least they got what they ordered.

Once Elvis began to court Anita, he pressed his suit very hard. Just two nights later, she was picked up again and taken to a special midnight showing of *Loving You* that was restricted to Elvis, his family and friends. Anita made a good impression on everyone. Three nights later, Elvis picked her up again, this time in his white Lincoln, to "carry" her to Graceland for supper.

The meal, which had been cooked by Mrs. Presley, was served by a black maid. The menu? It was that traditional southern home cooking that Elvis prized above any food in the world: sauerkraut and wieners, blackeyed peas, tomatoes, potatoes and a huge coconut cake that Mrs. Presley had baked herself. The only uncomfortable part of the evening occurred when Elvis invited Anita upstairs to see his quarters. She was very impressed by the smoked-glass mirror covering an entire wall behind the enormous bed and the way the thick navy blue carpet ran into the bathroom. No sooner had he shown her the bathroom, though, than he started to get fresh with her. "I think he was fixin' to test me out," is the way Anita sees it now. "Boy! He got testy real quick! I was nervous. I didn't know what to expect. I had heard so much back then about him. I stood my ground and said, 'I think it's time for me to go home.' That was about it."

Though Elvis had picked up his date, it was Lamar's job to take her home. Lamar was not happy about the way the evening was ending. He identified totally with Elvis: A rejection for his boss was a rejection for Lamar. "Look," he stalled, "is there any way you can keep yourself around here?" "No," insisted Anita, "I'll be going." Poor Lamar. He was struck dumb. Always so loquacious when it didn't matter, now the best he could offer was a hapless, "My God!" As Anita marched out the front door, clutching the pink and black stuffed poodle that Elvis had given her, the big fat boy with the gleaming D.A. opened the door of the car and then slid behind the wheel to make his delivery.

Once again, standing her ground did Anita Wood no

harm with Elvis Presley. Elvis was accustomed to dividing women into good girls and the other kind. Eventually, he would get to the point where, when he first met a girl, he would say: "Are you a good girl?" If the answer were, "Yes," that would be the end of his play. With Anita, Elvis felt that he knew where he stood. There would be no crossing the line. They could kiss and pet and carry on all they pleased, but the thing itself would never happen. Not unless he married her. So, in all essential respects, Elvis's relationship with Anita was no different from his relationship with the Three Mousketeers, Gloria, Heidi and Frances. In both cases there was a lot of playing around, but there was no boogeyin'. As Anita says, "I'd been taught that there were some things that you just save for marriage. I don't care what the situation is. Still, he knew that I loved him. He didn't have to worry about me. I think there were plenty that were always available. I saw evidences of it everywhere. I think he respected me."

Though Anita was not pressured to submit to Elvis sexually, she was forbidden on pain of instant banishment ever to reveal to anyone, even her closest friends, the character of her relationship with Elvis. No matter how much time they spent together or how long they were involved or how seriously they discussed marriage and having children, Anita was not permitted even to say that she was Elvis's steady girl. "Colonel Parker was the one he blamed for everything," says Anita. "Colonel Parker, he said, would not let us get married. For the sake of his career, we could not publicly admit that we liked one another or were going together. I always had to say that we were just friends because otherwise the publicity would hurt his image. He had to be free so that all the girls, the fans, could love him."

Though Anita could not assert that she was Elvis's steady girl, the relationship was common knowledge. When Elvis left in late August to tour the Pacific Northwest, he gave his "Little Beadie Eyes" a diamond ring garnished with sapphires. He kissed her publicly at the train station at Memphis, and the press published pictures both of the kiss and the ring on Anita's finger. Matters appeared to be taking their course.

At this moment Anita won yet another contest: *The Hollywood Star Hunt*. The semifinals took place at a movie house in New Orleans. Anita took along her entire family. As she stood in the backstage gloom behind a giant screen hearing the muffled voices of Jayne Mansfield and Tony Randall in *Will Success Spoil Rock Hunter?*, she offered up a little prayer. It was the same prayer that she always uttered before she stepped onstage: "Dear God, let me do my best and let me make the best of whatever happens." Then she strutted out under the glaring lights in a gleaming white bathing suit. After a quick change, she was back onstage in an evening gown singing in a husky, bluesy voice, "Walkin' After Midnight." She was declared the winner. What was even better, one of the judges offered to fly Anita to Hollywood immediately for a screen test. When Elvis called her that night from Spokane, he seemed as delighted as she was about the victory. "I told you all along you'd win, honey," he said. "It's wonderful. I'm so glad. My little girl's gonna be a movie star." A week later, they were reunited in Hollywood.

Elvis put Anita up at the Knickerbocker and showed her around town, just as he had done his parents. When the night of his big concert at the Pan-Pacific Auditorium arrived, however, he did not invite Anita to the concert or the party afterwards in his hotel suite, a celebration to which all his friends in Hollywood had been invited. The absence of Anita Wood was noticed the next day by the gossip columnists. Undoubtedly, it was another instance of the policy Elvis had adopted—at the Colonel's behest— of holding himself apart from Anita on public occasions.

In any case, Anita had her own career to think about. Her screen test had been successful, and she had been signed to appear in two pictures, the first of which was titled *Girl in the Woods*. At this point, however, a sudden cloud appeared, which cast a pall over Anita's rosy prospects. The production company began to have financial troubles. Anita found herself unsure of what would happen next. It was a critical moment for her, a moment at which she needed support and counsel. Elvis could have provided the support and the Colonel the counsel; instead, matters took a very different and disappointing course.

Though Elvis had at first greeted Anita's success with
enthusiasm, he now appeared to have cooled to the idea.
Instead of sustaining her through this crisis in her career,
he pleaded with her to give up the fight and come back to
Memphis, where he was idle and wanting her. "Come
home, Little," he would urge. "Just come home right now!"
Anita, alone, confused, anxious, out of her depth, finally
decided to give up and take comfort in her lover.

When she got back to Memphis, however, she found
Elvis no more ready for marriage than he had ever been.
Soon, Anita was back at work, picking up the pieces of her
shattered career.

Chapter 18

The Last Days of Elvis the Pelvis

LATE in August 1957, Elvis and his entourage took off on what proved to be his last concert tour until the seventies. A three-week sweep of the Pacific Northwest, reaching up into Canada, this tour corresponded to a similar string of one-nighters that Elvis had played in the spring, commencing at Chicago and working up through the Northeastern states and over the border to Toronto, Montreal and Ottawa. The territory in each case was familiar to the Colonel from his days with the Royal American. The style of the tour was also reminiscent of the carnival. Elvis played nothing but football and soccer stadiums, using a flatbed trailer as a stage. His entrance was classic. Gotten up in a ten-thousand-dollar thread-of-gold and rhinestone tuxedo, which Colonel Parker had ordered from Nudie of Hollywood, Elvis would make the complete circle of the arena seated on the back of a white Cadillac convertible, waving at the crowd as if he were a circus star.

The ole Colonel was back in his element, traveling from town to town, in a private pullman, just as he had in his carnival days. He indulged himself in a frenzy of ballyhoo and contemplated the crowds with satisfaction. They were

not impressive by modern standards. Ten thousand people
was the largest audience Elvis drew; the gross receipts for
twenty shows were a mere $375,000. Alan Freed had taken
in $300,000 the year before during twelve days at the New
York Paramount without a superstar like Elvis. Freed,
however, enjoyed the advantage of drawing on the greatest
concentration of rock 'n' roll fans in the country; whereas
Elvis Presley was never allowed to play New York at the
height of his fame, being condemned instead to tour most
of the time out in the sticks.

This observation raises the vital issue of the Colonel's
basic ability as a manager. It is quite likely, for example,
that even in 1957 Elvis had the same capacity to draw
gigantic crowds that the Beatles evinced just eight years
later. Nothing happened between 1957 and 1965 to make
it easier to go from the little stadium to the big stadium;
in fact, during those years rock 'n' roll lost its original
power and lay dormant awaiting the revival produced by
the "British Invasion." If the Colonel had been the genius
of management that he appears in the Presley Myth, he
would have seen and seized the fantastic opportunity that
presented itself at this supreme moment. Instead of hustling Elvis through the provinces, Colonel should have
steered his great attraction through all the major population centers of America and Europe, just as Barnum did
with General Tom Thumb and later Jenny Lind. Instead
of earning $25,000 for a show, Parker might have antic-
ipated Sid Bernstein's mighty score at Shea Stadium in
1965, when 55,000 fans paid $385,000 to see a single per-
formance by the Fab Four. Colonel Tom Parker was no
Barnum. He was not even a Bernstein. He was just a
canny, cautious, tight-assed old tent-show man who was
so busy thinking of all the nickels and dimes he could
collect with his corny pictures and programs that he never
had the time or the mind (or did he just lack the *nerve?*)
to go for the big score. It was not until other, more audacious men had blazed the way that Colonel Parker finally got into the biggest time and toured the aging Elvis
through the super-bowl circuit in the seventies.

The Pacific Northwest tour ran smoothly until it
reached Vancouver; then, all hell broke loose. The ar-

rangement that night was the standard setup: the flatbed parked down near the goalposts and protected by a portable iron fence, which was guarded by a detachment of Canadian Mounties. The first half of the program passed without incident. The MC, an ex-vaudeville juggler named Howard Hardin, an old friend of the Colonel, told a couple of corny jokes, tossed a few objects in the air and then brought on the acts, which included: the Burns Twins and Evelyn, a tap trio; Joe Termini, a comedy violinist; Wells and the Four Fays, a fast acrobatic team; Paul Desmond, an impressionist; and the Jordanaires, working the closing slot before intermission.

When Scotty, Bill and J. D. came out on the trailer to set up their instruments after the intermission, there was a noticeable swelling and heaving in the crowd on both sides of the field. When Elvis appeared, the crowd screamed so violently that it seemed they could not contain themselves. They couldn't. After the second number, both sides of the stadium were suddenly transformed into human waterfalls. Thousands of kids leaped out of their seats and came pouring onto the field so that they could get a close-up view of Elvis.

Now the Mounties were driven back to the iron fence, where they formed a thin red line. Elvis was getting a kick out of the fans' reactions. He began to tease and taunt the kids, sitting on the very edge of the stage with the mike bent down nearly parallel with the ground, making all sorts of inciting signs. For half a dozen numbers, he kept up his childish game, while the Mounties struggled ever more valiantly to hold back the surging mob. Finally, as Elvis leaped into a wild fast rocker, the crowd could take no more. Giving a tremendous shout, they came vaulting over the barricade.

Some kids were impaled on the iron and began to scream in agony. Others locked in hand-to-hand combat with the cops. Elvis yanked the mike off the stand and began to retreat, singing all the while. Suddenly, the Colonel screamed: "Get your ass off the stage!" Two guys reached out and grabbed Elvis, one under each armpit. They picked him up bodily and threw him into a car. Scotty Moore remembers running for his life with his guitar clutched in his hand. The crowd mounted the stage and began seizing everything in sight: music, equipment, chairs, stands. It was a good old-fashioned ass-kicking rock 'n' roll riot.

Next day the local press complained loudly, adding ruefully that not only had Elvis provoked the riot but he had also outdrawn the Canadian Exposition and was now somewhere south of the border, running like a bandit with all those Canadian dollars. The Colonel read the newspaper accounts aloud for the boys with great relish. Yes, sir! They had left town just like a scammy little carnival on the run.

When Elvis hit Hollywood in the last week in October for a pair of concerts at the Pan-Pacific Auditorium, he was all charged up and dying to show the movie people what he could do on a stage. He had played their game through three pictures; now they would play his! This moment was actually the pinnacle of his entire career. His album of songs from *Loving You* was Number One on the album chart. "Teddy Bear" was still among the top ten on the singles chart. The *Peace in the Valley* EP (extended play) was the top record in that genre. The title song from *Jailhouse Rock* had just been released and would be by November 1 the Number One record in the country. On top of all that, the premier of *Jailhouse Rock* was scheduled for the week before Elvis's two concerts. No performer in the history of the business had ever had a greater concentration of hits and scores at a single moment in his career. Nor had anyone ever remotely approached this kind of success at the age of twenty-two. Elvis was on top of the world.

The old Colonel knew that this was a golden opportunity to demonstrate to the Hollywood brass just what his famous boy could produce in terms of both performance and box office. The Pan-Pacific was a big old exposition building with an interior shaped like an enormous Quonset hut. The seating consisted of temporary bleachers; the stage was built on nine-foot risers draped with blue velour. The capacity of the house was 9,200 admissions. The Colonel decided to sell 9,200 tickets. He gave strict orders that there was to be no "paper": not one free ticket, even for

the most important members of the press. By exacting
every last dime from the dates, he contrived to gross
$56,000 for two nights' work.

Elvis's first concert at the Pan-Pacific was the most
notorious performance of his career. He had provoked scandal and complaints of obscenity many times before. He had
had police cameras focused on him and outraged parents,
teachers, clergymen and journalists denounce him aplenty.
These things had always occurred, however, in provincial
areas, where, presumably, the people were very square.
L.A. was another story. Los Angeles, while not enjoying
the reputation for tolerance that San Francisco has earned,
was nonetheless one of the most sophisticated towns in
America when it came to entertainment. When the Colonel
stood in Elvis's dressing room on opening night and urged
his boy to give "one helluva show," Elvis had no fears of
censorship. Not in L.A. In fact, he probably wouldn't have
had any trouble if it were not for the very special audience
he had drawn.

Stacked up on the bleachers of the old hall that night
were not nine thousand adults but nine thousand kids.
Ninety percent of these kids were girls. The average age
of these girls was thirteen. They were the hard-core Elvis
fans: the ones who ran out and grabbed the first tickets
that went on sale, which was the reason they had tickets
when thousands of other people who wanted to see the
show were turned away at the box office. These junior high
girls had sat for nearly an hour in a state bordering on
desperation as they viewed the idiotic antics of Colonel
Parker's Time Loop Variety Circuit. Then, they had been
turned out for an intermission so that the Colonel's hawkers could cut into the kids with an endless variety of souvenirs and chatzkahs. Now, at last, they were back on
their hard board seats waiting with nearly hysterical tension for the appearance of their god.

When Elvis swaggered onstage that night, he got a
blast of screams that nearly knocked him flat. He was a
juicy piece of beefcake, all right, wearing the gold tux
jacket with its rhinestone lapels over black trousers. (He
had destroyed the gold trousers by leaping off the stage
onto a cinder track in Seattle.) He was wearing one of his

George Raft gangster black shirts with a gold four-in-hand
tie. By now he had eschewed his trademark guitar so as
not to spoil his new Hollywood look. When he slashed into
his first number, "Heartbreak Hotel," the deafening wave
of screams commenced again. It never stopped for the next
forty minutes. As the girls screamed and cried and tore
their hair and beat on each other in a frenzy; as they
shouted and hollered and moaned in ecstasy; as they spoke,
sang, cried aloud the words of each song in unison with
Elvis—or even, according to some reports, lost control of
their natural functions and reduced themselves to the condition of hapless infants who have to be "changed"—Elvis
met every fresh outburst of mania with ever more extravagant gestures and grimaces, leg movements and hip
swayings, knee-drops and flat-out falls on the stage.

After all these years in the "live," he had dredged up
out of his memory of all the movies he had imbibed in his
adolescence and all the gospel shows he had witnessed
back home in Memphis an extraordinary vocabulary of
stage antics and mannerisms. He loved above all else to
impersonate the jive-ass nigger pimp, who snaps his elbows into his waist as he flings his long fingers out from
bent wrists and then with a head tilted provocatively awry
and a killing look in his eye, runs those tight elbows up
his sides in a pants-hitching gesture that says, "Ah'm ready
for *anything,* bitch!"

To the naive young girls, highly charged but highly
repressed, these gestures were experienced as heavy turn-
ons. They also were noted grimly by a number of local
reporters. Yet, what really provoked the scandal that
erupted the next day was none of this behavior but a purely
spontaneous outburst of high spirits with which Elvis concluded the show.

Colonel Parker insisted always that when Elvis performed onstage, he should have parked conspicuously beside him the symbol of the company that sold his records.
So on this, as on countless other nights, sharing the spot-
light with Elvis was Nipper: the familiar RCA Boston Bull,
with his head cocked cutely listening to "His Master's
Voice." It had become Elvis's custom to reach out from
time to time and give Nipper a friendly pat on the head.

After all, the poor thing sat there so patiently all night.
How could you ignore him completely? Especially during
his last number, "Hound Dog," Elvis was likely to make
play with Nipper. On this night in Hollywood, however,
carried away by the audience's frenzy and by his own desire to give the greatest and most uninhibited performance
of his career, Elvis suddenly abandoned all restraint.
Throwing his arms around the huge dog, he flung himself
with it on the floor and rolled over and over toward the
stage apron. The girls went out of their minds at the sight
of Elvis embracing this big, cute, lovable dog, almost as
yummy as a teddy bear. They screamed their approval, as
Elvis leaped to his feet and rushed offstage and into the
waiting limousine. Some evil-minded adults, however, left
the theater with the idea that Elvis had capped an obscene
performance by pretending to bugger the dog!

When word was received at the headquarters of the Los
Angeles Police Department that Elvis Presley was bug-
gering a huge dog onstage as part of his show at the Pan-
Pacific Auditorium, you can imagine the officers' reactions. They determined to do their duty. They called up
Colonel Parker and warned him that Presley had better
clean up his act and tone it down or face possible charges.
Then, borrowing a leaf from the well-publicized procedures
of the Jacksonville, Florida, authorities, the police arranged to have three sixteen-millimeter motion picture
cameras set up in the auditorium for the second show to
provide ocular evidence of the "act," in case it was deemed
advisable to press obscenity charges.

When Elvis sat down to breakfast the afternoon following the first concert, he found the Colonel at the table,
immersed, as always, in the morning papers. He made a
point of reading aloud to Elvis a column in the *Mirror-
News*, written by the entertainment editor, which read the
riot act to Elvis. Commencing with its first word, "Sex-
hibitionist," and running on for more than a dozen para-
graphs, the article assailed Elvis bitterly for giving an
obscene performance aimed at exciting the "libidos" of
"little girls." The writer was not content to castigate Elvis
for doing "bumps and grinds" or "contrived sensual gestures" or producing music that was "a lascivious steaming

brew": He went on to compare him with an "ancient Caesar" and the concert to "one of those screeching uninhibited
party rallies which the Nazis used to hold for Hitler." It
was a pretty startling review for a boy who prided himself
on being so religious and so pious toward his mama.

When the Colonel concluded his reading, Elvis burst
out in that rage that was always smoldering beneath the
surface of his carefully contrived cool: "Those muthafuck-
ahs! Ah never been obscene in mah life! Ah'm 'bout sick
o' this shit! Ah tell ya one damn thing—ah'm gonna do
one helluva show tonight! Ah'm not gonna let 'em put me
up agin a wall!"

When Elvis stepped out onstage that night, he found
sitting at his feet a galaxy of young stars: Carol Channing,
Rick Nelson, Russ Tamblyn, Venetia Stevenson, Sammy
Davis, Jr., Nick Adams, Vince Edwards, Tony Franciosa,
Rita Moreno, Debbie Minardos, Tommy Sands, and a number of others whose names mean nothing today. This was
Raphael Campos's party. He had collected money from
everyone who wanted to see the show and secured from
Colonel Parker the entire first two rows of seats. In other
parts of the hall were many other movie bigshots, including Hall Wallis and Abe Lastfogel. Colonel Parker, who
had cornered the (battered secondhand Japanese) binoc-
ular concession, got his big thrill of the evening when he
rented a pair of glasses to the famous producer and closed
his hand around the big man's cash.

After Elvis had sung his first tune, he pointed to the
cameras aimed at him and quipped: "I wonder if they're
gonna release this in theaters?" Then, he continued in a
more earnest vein: "I'm sorry this came up, but we're not
gonna let it stop us from puttin' on the best show we can
for you people. If they think it's obscene, that's their problem, not mine!" With that, he winked at the camera and
put his hands around his head to form a halo. "I'm gonna
be an angel tonight!" he cried. Then, as the house roared
its approval, he went into his next song. Despite his defiant
rhetoric, he did tone down his show, which met, nonetheless, with hysterical applause.

When Elvis got back to his dressing room, he found
awaiting him a reporter from the British music journal,

Melody Maker. "I made over a million dollars this year,"
Elvis crowed, "but I'm no musician at all. I can't play the
guitar, and I never wrote a song in my life. Yet I get my
name on songs, and I collect a third interest of *all* the
songs I sing." Flashing a wry grin, he added: "There doesn't
seem any point in my studying music." Having delivered
these lines, which could have come from the script of *Jailhouse Rock,* he went off to the party that was awaiting
him at the Beverly Wilshire.

Though Elvis was now a big man in American show
business, he still partied like an adolescent kid. No drinking was permitted in his presence, no drugs—God forbid!—
and, as far as eating was concerned, sandwiches and chocolate cake furnished forth the victory banquet. With a
room full of movie stars, what would you suppose the entertainment to be? Believe it or not, those who were disposed to be entertaining took turns imitating famous
movie stars. Sammy Davis, Jr., got behind a desk at one
end of the room and arose as the good Dr. Jekyll. Then,
he ducked back down, and came up as the evil Mr. Hyde.
Nick Adams did his amateurish takes on Cary Grant, Bogart and Brando. Vince Edwards offered Clark Gable. Billy
Murphy, of *G.I. Joe* and *Sands of Iwo Jima,* also did Gable.
Chump-change movie stars doing real movie stars. The
mediocrity is the message.

Actually, the only real excitement felt on the occasion
was that which thrilled through the fifteen-and-a-half-
year-old Ricky Nelson. Ricky had recently done an Elvis
Presley imitation on the *Ozzie and Harriet Show.* Instantly, he had received a mountain of fan mail and a
contract from Imperial Records. Now, he was about to go
out on the road and play his first big dates. Having
achieved overnight fame by imitating Elvis, Ricky was a
little self-conscious about showing up at Elvis's party.
Marcia Borie, the maternalistic editor of *Photoplay,* had
to sit with Ricky for about half an hour at the pharmacy
in the lobby of the hotel while he soothed his nerves by
slurping down a thick chocolate malted. Finally, he said:
"You know Elvis—you go first!" With that they proceeded
to the Presidential Suite, the disciple quaking at the
thought of encountering the master face to face.

When they stepped into the foyer, Elvis spotted them immediately. "He rushed through the crowd like Andrew Jackson at the Battle of New Orleans," recalls Borie, "pushing everyone aside. He took Ricky in his arms and lifted him. Ricky was about five feet ten—not a little boy! 'You're Ricky Nelson,' Elvis cried. 'I've seen you. Did David come, too? Mom and Daddy here?' Ricky was so nervous, he jumped up to get a Coke." Borie said to Elvis, "'Ricky's in awe of you and now he's starting off on his first tour. If you could give him a few tips, it might make a world of difference to him.' Elvis took Ricky by the shoulder and led him into another room and shut the door." When Borie talked to Ricky later, he said that Elvis had filled him up with dos and don'ts. "He was enormously helpful. The funny thing was that Elvis was in awe of Ricky because he had watched him so many times on his dinky little TV at home. All that night, the two of them never took their eyes off each other." What's more, when Marcia Borie went out on the road shortly thereafter with Ricky, she saw him get virtually the same response from thousands of screaming fans as Elvis had produced at the Pan-Pacific.

Ricky Nelson was, of course, just the first of a legion of Elvis imitators, many of whom would enjoy highly successful careers for a few years. Nothing demonstrates more clearly than this phenomenon how much the success of such simple performers as rock stars depends on the tastes of their audiences rather than upon the performers' own skills. Once some innovative entertainer has cut the die, any number of copies can be stamped out, as long as the public's tastes remain fixed. Let the tastes change even a little, however, and virtually all the imitators blow away. This, in brief, is the history of rock in the fifties.

King Creole, Elvis's last movie before entering the army, is generally regarded as his most successful performance as an actor. Based on Harold Robbins's *A Stone for Danny Fisher,* the film was transposed from Chicago to New Orleans to allow Elvis to get down closer to his roots and do his songs in the honky-tonks of the French Quarter. Actually, the picture brings Elvis around very close to the point where he entered the movie world with his viewing of Tony Curtis in *City Across the River*. Allowing for the difference between tough neighborhoods in the North and South, the type of character, the basic milieu, the conflict of whether to fall in with the J.D.s and gangsters or stand free as a good guy, all these things make the picture a kind of confirmation of Elvis's first intuitive divination of his role as a movie star. His performance is quite believable, for once, but not especially exciting. As always he moves through his role with a curious sort of preoccupied and self-obsessed defensiveness that flares up easily into rage. Elvis the movie star is rather like Elvis the sleep-walker.

The gain in histrionic credibility is, unfortunately, offset by a loss of conviction in the musical numbers. They are all staged in backlot cabarets that don't ring true and with onstage performances by Elvis that offer nothing that anybody else couldn't do. Instead of the innocent charm of *Love Me Tender* or the punk violence of *Loving You* or the slick, arch choreography of *Jailhouse Rock,* we get for the first time in a Presley picture that dumb, head-on treatment of the guy with the guitar in his hand that became forever after the albatross hung by Hollywood around the neck of the once-charismatic Pelvis. Instead of grieving over the fact that Elvis was never given a great dramatic part, what should trouble Presley fans is the fact that Hollywood, by this time in its history, had lost its effortless knack of knocking out brilliant and inexpensive musicals. The notion that Elvis was an unfulfilled actor is a pipe dream. Elvis was an entertainer, a type of performer who is basically the opposite of an actor. Instead of having the gift of impersonating or at least suggesting a personality other than his own, the entertainer's gift is for making everything he does a vehicle for the exhibition and exaltation of his own personality.

On December 20, 1957, Elvis Presley received his army induction notice. This ended a period of more than a year during which both Elvis and his public had lived in constant dread of his being drafted. No period in Elvis's early life was more painful or injurious to him than the two years he spent in the service; yet, when you read the pub-

lished accounts of this ordeal, you get the impression that
he spent his time in uniform experiencing no more discomfort than the ordinary soldier. In fact, if you're a believer in the Elvis Myth, you will argue that the army
experience was highly beneficial to Elvis because it
quashed once and for all the criticism of him as a menace
to American youth and earned him the respect and admiration of every real red-blooded American male.

The absurdity of this view becomes apparent the instant
you stop seeing Elvis Presley as a pawn in a public relations game and start empathizing with him as a human
being. For from Elvis's viewpoint, he had nothing to gain
from the army and everything to lose. At the time he
entered the service, he was at the very peak of his fame.
With fads and fashions in pop music changing constantly,
with a host of imitators and rivals springing up to steal
his stuff, with fame itself such a freaky and chancy thing,
what likelihood was there that he could come back two
years hence and pick up exactly where he left off? There
was none; and, in fact, Elvis never did regain the momentum he lost when he entered the army. So, from Elvis's
point of view, his conscription was the worst sort of disaster
that could have befallen him as an entertainer and a new
star.

As for his personal emotions, apart from considerations
of career, anyone who appreciates the extreme sensitivity
and vulnerability of the young Elvis will realize with what
feelings of anxiety and despair he must have regarded the
prospect of giving up his friends and family to live in a
barracks among total strangers, many of them men who
might regard him with envy and hostility. Instead of being
the master of his fate, he would now be transformed overnight into the passive victim of circumstances. Instead of
protecting himself by building up layer upon layer of in-
sulation against the world, he would be suddenly alone
and naked. Instead of being able to use his talent to put
a magic circle around himself, he would now have to rely
entirely on his capacity for physical endurance and blind
obedience. Any way he looked at the army, it had to strike
him as a nightmare.

All this anyone could see by simply viewing Elvis's

predicament from his perspective. What no one could have seen, if Elvis had not revealed the truth to a trusted confidant, was the ultimate horror of this nightmare: Elvis's conviction that he did not have to go into the service but had been persuaded to volunteer by the arguments or trickery of Colonel Parker. To get this story straight, we have to skip ahead six months to a time in the summer of 1958, when Elvis was undergoing his basic training at Fort Hood. True to his nature, he found on the base a man in whom he could confide as he would a parent: Master Sergeant William Norwood, now retired and living at Killeen, Texas.

As the company sergeant of Elvis's unit, Norwood was the man immediately in charge of Private Presley. An unsentimental but kindly man, married, a father, he responded instinctively to Elvis's need for sympathy and understanding. When Elvis wanted to see Anita Wood during the recruit training period, a time when no recruit is allowed off limits, Sergeant Norwood arranged for the young couple to meet in his house, which was on the base. When Gladys became gravely ill and Elvis was having trouble gaining an emergency leave, Sergeant Norwood exerted himself to solve the problem. This was the sort of man whom Elvis adopted as his protector and counselor during his months at Hood. It makes sense, therefore, that Elvis would confide in the sergeant and reveal to him what Elvis believed to be the true story of how he got into the army.

In October 1956, more than a year before Elvis received his draft notice, *Billboard* published an article datelined Fort Dix, New Jersey. Purporting to be the inside dope from the army brass, the article prophesied that Elvis Presley would be drafted the following December and would go into Special Services. He would receive only six weeks of basic training; then, he would be released to resume his career on behalf of the army. His hair would not be cut. He would be given a lot of dental and orthodontic work. He would be given leave to do another picture for Paramount. He would be free to continue recording and appearing on television. In short, Private Presley would

get the softest deal that any man had ever received from
the U.S. Army.

But at this time Elvis Presley had not even taken his
preinduction physical examination and been classified 1A.
Consequently, as far as the army was concerned there was
no reason to assume that Elvis would ever serve in the
military, much less to concern itself with what sort of deal
he should be offered. What's more, even if the army had
been anticipating this special case, it is unbelievable that
it would have considered making him such an offer because
it would be sure to provoke a storm of criticism. The true
source of the report, therefore, could not have been the
army. What was it?

When Elvis heard the story, he was profoundly shocked.
He had approached his draft board long before and requested that they notify him confidentially and in advance
when his number was about to be called. Now, he felt
betrayed. Rushing to the office of the draft board in Memphis, he said, "Hey, I thought we had a deal!" The chairman
of the board, Milton Bowers, assured Elvis that they did
have an understanding, which the board had honored to
the letter. Elvis was not in danger of being drafted and
the board had just released a denial of the whole report,
which certainly had not come from Memphis. When Elvis
persisted in demanding an explanation, the only suggestion Bowers could offer was that some evil reporter held
a grudge against the star or was just seeking to create a
stir with some sensational copy.

Neither explanation is very likely. Reporters have to
clear their copy through editors, and editors are prone to
ask where sensational stories come from when they have
no clearly attributed sources. In this case, a clue to the
true source is provided in the article, where it is said that
the only people who would know the date of Elvis's induction were army officials and some of his "closest business associates." Elvis Presley had only one close business
associate in his entire lifetime: Colonel Thomas Andrew
Parker. Could the Colonel have leaked this damaging
story? Why would he do such a thing?

No sooner had Elvis received assurances from his draft
board that he was not about to be called up than Colonel

Chapter 19

A Deadly Induction

WHEN ELVIS drove up before the office of the draft board on Main Street on the morning of March 24, 1958, he saw a crowd of fifty or sixty reporters and photographers gathered to witness his induction. Colonel Parker was clearly visible in their midst, holding a big cluster of red balloons stamped, "See Elvis in *King Creole*." This was the Colonel's big day. He and the army, after close consultation, had worked out a deal. The colonel would give the newsmen a free hand so that he could benefit from their stories in launching his campaign for the New Elvis, the boy who gave up everything—fame, fortune, the glamour of stardom—to do his bit for Uncle Sam. The army would employ the same publicity to get off its back all those congressmen, columnists and veteran's organizations that had been beefing about Elvis getting a soft deal in Special Services. Both the Colonel and the army would come out winners. The only loser would be Elvis.

The result of this strategy was the greatest carnival ever staged at the induction of an American draftee. By the time Elvis and the dozen other boys who were entering the service with him had been brought to Kennedy Veterans Hospital for their medical examinations, the crowd of media representatives had swelled to two hundred, enlarged further by numerous fans and bystanders who were

329

attracted by the rare opportunity to see the star at close range. At every step of the normally confidential examination procedure, Elvis was dogged by photographers determined to give their public the most candid view possible of the event. Elvis was photographed clothed, half-clothed and virtually naked, standing against a measuring scale stripped to his Jockey briefs. As the beam of the ophthalmoscope went into his eye and the probe of the ornascope into his ear, the ubiquitous news camera followed the medical instruments. Everything was recorded save the moment when the doctor slipped the vinyl glove on his hand and shoved his finger up Elvis's ass. What a pity that this, the most eloquent and emblematic moment of the entire ritual, could not have been recorded for posterity!

In the late afternoon, Colonel Parker dragged Elvis before the movie and TV cameras to read some of the congratulatory messages that had come pouring in on this occasion. Governor Frank Clement wired: "YOU HAVE SHOWN THAT YOU ARE AN AMERICAN CITIZEN FIRST, A TENNESSEE VOLUNTEER, AND A YOUNG MAN WILLING TO SERVE HIS COUNTRY WHEN CALLED UPON TO DO SO." The Colonel urged Elvis to read some more of this malarkey into the camera. Elvis demurred. When the Colonel spurred his colt harder, he reared. Suddenly, Elvis's true feelings flashed forth: "It's me that's goin' in and what happens will be to me—not you!" Virtually no one reported the remark. When the day's work was done, there was nothing left but the time-honored act of raising the right hand, swearing the oath of allegiance and taking one step forward. At that moment—as the press never tired of repeating—Elvis Presley became US53310761.

When the Greyhound bus bearing the recruits to Fort Chaffee, Arkansas, left the hospital, the fans took off in hot pursuit. Cutting in and out of its path, like a flock of speedboats racing around a steadily advancing tug, the "Elfans," as they had started calling themselves, tracked their man all the way to his barracks on the base. When, finally, long after dark, a couple of white-helmeted M.P.s finally put a stop to the pursuit, admonishing the girls, "These barracks are for men only," one fourteen-year-old teenybopper glared at the military cops and spat out the single word—"Balls!"

If Elvis thought his media ordeal was over, he soon learned differently. His first chow hall breakfast was reported more exhaustively than any meal in history. Two dozen photographers gathered around the table to capture the star in the act of spooning up his cereal or forking in his sausage and eggs. Colonel Parker directed the shooting himself, as he did the afternoon clothing issue. The Colonel was in such high spirits that he even tried to slip a string tie, such as he was wont to wear, into Elvis's stack of uniforms. Elvis didn't enjoy the joke. "No, sir," he said, tossing the tie aside, "if I wore a string tie in here, I'd have to take the punishment, not you!" The Colonel comported himself more discreetly at the crowning event of the whole procedure. Elvis's G.I. haircut.

As the floodlights blazed and the cameras ground, a smiling civilian barber in a white smock welcomed Elvis to the chair. Switching on his electric clippers and brandishing them in the air, he ran them up the mythic sideburns. As the hair came off, he tossed it playfully in the air, letting it drift to the ground. Elvis had prepared himself for this event. Rather sheepishly he joked: "Hair today, gone tomorrow!" Now, the humming clippers were plowing up the back of the celebrated coif, shearing the hair off in disfiguring lanes. The photographers, whipped to a frenzy by this primitive rite, begged the barber to go slower. *LIFE* alone filed 1,200 pictures from Chaffee.

The instant the clipping was complete, a specially coached porter rushed forward with a broom and swept all the hair into a pile, which he then dumped into a bin to be taken out for immediate destruction. As the sweep-up proceeded, Colonel Parker lectured the newsmen on the enormous value of the hairs thus wantonly destroyed. Elvis was upset despite himself. He forgot to pay for the haircut with his sixty-five-cent chit. The barber called his famous customer back, thus redoubling his embarrassment. Elvis ran out of the shop and ducked into a phone booth. When the photographers sought to press their lenses against the glass, the Colonel interposed, intoning with the solemnity of a jailer, "The boy's entitled to speak to his mother without being disturbed." When Elvis got through to Graceland, he discovered that his mother had taken to her bed and was "grieving."

That word became now the motto of Gladys's declining life. The shock of having her baby snatched from her was more than she could bear. Elvis was gone and there was no saying when he would be back. When people sought to console her, she would burst out weeping, "They're not going to take care of my boy...he has a quick temper...he'll get confused!" There was no comforting her. All day, she would go about the house wringing her hands and saying, "I feel that something's happened to him."

After a few days at Chaffee, Elvis was dispatched to Fort Hood in Texas for training as a tanker. When the Colonel turned up at the head of his press corps, he was met by a very determined WAC colonel, who told him, "You will have carte blanche, as promised—but just this one day. After today, nothing!" By the end of his first week in the army, Elvis was able to call home and report, "They finally got the reporters off my back. These cocksuckers! They really got me locked up here." Private Presley had been assigned to A Company, First Medium Tank Battalion, 32nd Regiment, of the famed Hell on Wheels Division, formerly commanded by General Patton. Now his future was clear for the next few months. He would receive eight weeks of "basic"; a fourteen-day leave; another eight weeks of special training in tank warfare; two weeks of unit training; then, his unit would he shipped to Germany as replacements in the Third Armored Division, the cutting edge of the NATO armies.

Fort Hood was an open base, which meant that Elvis could receive visitors any time he was off duty. One of his first and most welcome callers was a former disc jockey, then a motion picture theater operator in Waco, Eddie Fadal. As soon as Elvis could get away on weekends, he made the Fadal home his retreat from the base. Often he would arrive with Anita Wood, who spent almost every weekend with him in Texas. Elvis would always inspect every room in the house before he settled down, explaining that he had a great fear of hidden photographers. Then he and Anita would vocalize in the den until supper, which was prepared by Fadal's wife La Nelle to conform exactly to Elvis's tastes. Elvis never ate beef, preferring the meat of the hog. His especial delight was a rich dessert, like banana cream pie or Bavarian chocolate cake. He would start with one big slice and then consume the entire pie or cake. Eddie Fadal made it a practice to drive down to Hood early every week with a freshly baked pie or cake plus the latest 45s and copies of *Box Office* and *Motion Picture*. He quickly became the second most important person in Elvis's private support system. The first was Master Sergeant Bill Norwood.

A wiry little dude with a country voice that must have reminded Elvis of his Uncle Vester, the sergeant had been a recruit instructor since before World War II. Once he had allowed Elvis to use his private phone, the sergeant found himself the recipient of many more visits, which gradually developed into a routine that included coffee in the morning and supper at night. Elvis complained constantly of homesickness and depression. One night he broke down and cried bitterly. When the tears had stopped flowing, the sergeant spoke: "When you come in my house," he advised in his dry Texas drawl, "you can let it all out. Do whatever you want to and don't worry about anything. But when you walk out of my front door, you are now Elvis Presley. You're an actor. You're a soldier. So, by God, I want you to act! Don't let nobody know how you feel on the inside." Elvis mumbled, "Yes, sir."

The final exercise of the first eight weeks was the toughest moment of basic: a week in the field entailing fourteen-mile marches under the broiling Texas sun with seventy-pound packs. About half the men in Elvis's outfit collapsed under the strain, but Elvis made it through, even though he had the extra burden of being the assistant squad leader. Sergeant Norwood, no mean judge, was delighted with his famous pupil's performance. He told him: "Presley, you're a natural-born soldier!"

When Elvis got back to Memphis on his first furlough, he looked fitter than at any other time in his life. He had dropped twelve pounds and lost a lot of the baby fat in his cheeks. His jaw was long and lean; his chin as squared off as any army corner. Many people were surprised to see

him again a sun-bleached blonde. The only question about
his physical condition that couldn't be answered by looking
at him was, "How's your voice?" That issue was soon resolved when he took off on June 10 for Nashville for the
only recording session of his army years.

The Colonel had been receiving a lot of requests from
both the army and RCA to allow Elvis to perform publicly
and to record. There was nothing in army regulations to
prevent Elvis from making dozens of records, providing he
cut them on his own time. As Elvis was the fastest hit-
maker in the history of the industry, even a handful of
sessions would have provided Victor with enough product
to carry it comfortably through the next two years. Colonel
Parker was dead set against these proposals. He told Elvis,
"I want the can empty!"

Colonel's strategy was aimed both at RCA and at Elvis.
Emptying the can was always the Colonel's first move
before any contract negotiations. Already the Colonel was
preparing to renegotiate Elvis's contract when he re-
emerged in 1960. On the other hand, emptying the can
would mean that when Elvis got out of the service, he
would be forced to resume his recording career from ground
zero: a point of psychological disadvantage which, along
with all the other problems he would face at that time,
would make Elvis more dependent than ever on his manager. The Colonel also knew that having an empty can
would compel RCA to reissue a lot of Elvis's old records.
To a hustler like the Colonel, it was far more gratifying
to sell the same record twice (in different wrappings) than
it would be to come up with a new record. The former
course could be represented as a triumph of merchandising
skill—almost as good as a hot dog with no meat in the
middle. Any damn fool could sell a new Elvis record. So
Elvis got his orders: "You will go in there and do one
night's recording. After that—nothing for the duration."

No sooner did Elvis get back to Fort Hood than the rest
of the family began arriving. Lamar turned up first, driving a white Mark II Continental that made a sensation in
little Killeen. The next day Vernon, Gladys and Grandma
arrived in a white Fleetwood towing a trailer full of household goods. Elvis had worked a fast deal with a man who

sold house trailers to obtain the use of a three-bedroom
model for a couple of months. When the family checked
out the trailer, they realized that it was hopelessly inadequate. A quick house hunt turned up a three-bedroom
ranch house that belonged to a local politician. The politician scalped the Presleys, charging them $1,400 a month.
Elvis shrugged off the cost. What did it matter as long as
they were all together and comfortable? Why, the house
was virtually a carbon copy of their old home on Audubon
Avenue.

Despite the perfection of his living arrangements, Elvis
could never persuade his mother that they were well off
in Killeen. Gladys missed her home. She dreaded the day
when Elvis would be shipped overseas. When Elvis would
tell her that they would live overseas just as they lived
here in Texas, Gladys would shake her head and say, "I
jes' can't see mahself over theah in a fereign country. Ah've
left nuthin' over theah, and ah'm not tryin' to find anythin'. It grieves me." Everything grieved Gladys at this
time. She complained of pains in her abdomen and would
get so nauseous in the morning that she couldn't stand the
odor of eggs frying. She would pick quarrels with Vernon,
hollering insults at him, especially her favorite epithet for
her husband, steercottled (i.e. castrated). If Elvis were
present during the fight, he would get very upset and seek
to intervene. Sometimes, in the evenings, it was obvious
that Gladys was drunk. Her voice would glide up into a
foolish falsetto; her speech would be badly slurred. Elvis
hated to see his mother drunk. He would cry out at such
moments, "Momma! momma! what are you doin' to yourself!" Then he would embrace her and lead her off to bed.

Though Elvis never looked so healthy in all his life,
Gladys kept harping on the dangers of military service.
She was not entirely wrong. One day, after Elvis had been
out firing .50 caliber machine guns, he came home complaining about the ringing in his ears. Gladys warned:
"Elvis, you better be careful with your ears. You know you
play by ear and you can't read music. You should be careful
with your ears." She may have reminded him also that
when he was a child he had chronic ear trouble for which

he was treated in the good old southern way by having
urine poured in his ears.

Next morning, when Elvis turned up at Sergeant Norwood's quarters to have his customary cup of coffee, he
repeated his mother's warnings. Norwood told him to take
sick call and have his ears checked. When Elvis got back
from the dispensary, he was carrying a note from the doctor. It said that Elvis had a perforated left eardrum. He
was not to be exposed to any loud noises, especially gunfire.

Norwood puzzled over this news. He told Elvis that it
posed problems. If they obeyed the doctor's orders to the
letter, Elvis's training would suffer. He would attract attention. It might be said that he was goldbricking. Elvis,
for his part, did not want to withdraw from any part of his
training. So they decided that henceforth when they went
to the firing range, Elvis would stuff his ears with cotton.
When he wasn't firing the guns, he would stay far away
from their concussions by going to the rear of the unit to
handle ammunition. Meantime, Sergeant Norwood would
work to get Elvis's classification changed from a tanker
to a reconnaissance scout, a job that would keep him with
the division but well away from gunfire. Despite the sergeant's efforts, Elvis remained with the tanks and their
.90-mm. guns for another two months, until his unit
shipped out for Europe. (In later years Elvis's hearing
deteriorated markedly. When he returned to the stage in
the early seventies, he complained constantly that he could
not hear himself through the stage monitors. No matter
how high the monitors were set, Elvis demanded that they
be turned up higher. Soon he had the "hottest" stage in
the business.)

During the first week in August, Gladys called her doctor in Memphis. She asked him to come down to Killeen
to examine her. He replied that he had no license to practice medicine in the state of Texas. Vernon took her to a
local practitioner in nearby Temple. He could not diagnose
her condition. She began to turn sallow and finally yellow.
Lamar grew alarmed at her appearance. He told Elvis that
his mother should go back to Memphis and get proper
medical attention. Elvis would not allow her to leave.

Finally, Gladys's condition grew so alarming that Elvis

was forced to relinquish his mother. Reluctantly, he drove
her and Vernon to Temple and put them aboard the Sante
Fe. When she turned up a couple of days later at the
doctor's office in Memphis, he insisted she enter Baptist
Memorial Hospital for tests. He was not alarmed, but he
was puzzled at this sudden jaundice in a normally healthy
woman.

The most obvious cause of her condition was hepatitis,
but the diagnostic specimens did not indicate the presence
of infectious disease. The liver was inflamed, but it was
difficult to determine why. Specialists were brought in for
consultation. They argued over whether the cause might
be cirrhosis of the liver or perhaps a clot that was blocking
the portal vein. Meantime, the condition of their patient
worsened.

Gladys's doctor was not entirely familiar with his patient nor was she entirely honest with him. Gladys Presley
was a woman of very unhealthy habits and temperament.
She was grossly overweight from improper diet. She never
got any exercise. She drank to the point of drunkenness but
never confessed this to her doctor. The most sinister ingredient in her self-destructive way of life was the consumption of diet pills. Gladys had started using these amphetamine compounds years before and increased their
usage as she became increasingly dependent on them. It
was said in her family that she was ashamed of her obesity
and wanted to improve her appearance, especially when
Elvis became famous and photographers were constantly
taking her picture and printing it in magazines and newspapers. Eventually, the amphetamines were bound to have
a deleterious effect: if not on her body, then on her mind.
Extreme irritability of the sort which Gladys displayed in
the final months of her life is a typical effect of amphetamine abuse. Being of a secretive nature, Gladys confided
nothing of this history of drug use to her doctor.

As Gladys's condition worsened, Elvis tried to obtain
an emergency leave from Fort Hood. Significantly, Gladys
had broken down on the eve of Elvis's departure for Germany. His whole unit was on point of embarkation status.
As the request was processed through the chain of command, Gladys's life began to slip away. Elvis was on the

phone with the doctor every day and the reports were increasingly alarming. Finally, Elvis could no longer tolerate delay. He announced that if he didn't get his leave that day, he was going to take off for Memphis without leave. Some wires were pulled in Washington and Elvis was released.

Elvis reached his mother's side late Thursday night. She rallied when she saw him, but the doctors warned that her condition was still grave. For the next thirty-six hours Elvis and Vernon kept a vigil at the hospital, where they were joined by the family and Elvis's friends. Finally, on the second evening, Elvis was persuaded that his mother was feeling better. He left the hospital, picked up Frances, Gloria and Heidi and went to the Crosstown Theater to see Paul Newman, one of his favorite actors, in *The Long Hot Summer*. After the show they all went back to Graceland and sat talking to a late hour. Then Elvis told Lamar to take the girls home.

At three in the morning, the phone rang. It was Vernon. "Elvis, your momma just died." Then he went on to explain how she had been "suffering for breath" and had suddenly been killed by a heart attack. Elvis was so stunned, he didn't know what to do. He had to talk to someone who could help him. Instinctively, he picked up the phone and dialed Sergeant Norwood.

The sergeant describes Elvis's tone as "livid." He was talking and crying at the same time. He told Norwood the story of the deathbed vigil, the sense of relief he had experienced when he went to the movies, then the shock of being awakened by his father telling him that his mother was dead. His long rambling monologue went on until four in the morning. At that point, Sergeant Norwood told Elvis that he should hang up so that Norwood could get in touch with Elvis's superiors and arrange for an extension of his leave.

Lamar, returning a few minutes later, saw the front door of the house standing wide open. A night wind was blowing through the trees. An eerie feeling was in the air. Without switching off the motor, he started to get out of the car, when he saw Grandma come bustling out the door. "Lamar," she snapped, "you gotta take me down to the

hospital, Gladys just died." When they stepped off the elevator on Gladys's floor, Lamar was startled by a fearful
sound. It was Elvis and Vernon keening, sending up the
heartrending cries of hillbilly folk afflicted with grief.

"I heard this horrible wailing," Lamar recalls. "It just
made my skin crawl. I had never heard anything like that
in my life. I came around the corner and Elvis saw me.
'Oh, Lamar, my baby's gone!' He was hugging me and
crying on my shoulder. Then, he grabbed hold of Grandma.
Finally, he said, 'Come on, Lamar. Mama really wanted
to see you. She's always askin' about you. She was always
worried about you.' Then he grabbed hold of me and we
went in her room. The body was all covered up. He started
patting her stomach. 'Look here, Satnin',' he said, 'here's
Lamar.' I couldn't handle it. I had to get out."

Elvis remained beside the body rocking back and forth
in grief, until the hospital attendants asked him to leave.
He and Lamar made their way downstairs and went out
the back of the hospital into a loading area. Dawn was
just breaking. At that moment a hearse drove up. Elvis
seized Lamar by the arm to detain him. Lamar saw a look
of hate come into Elvis's face, the jaw flexing spasmodi-
cally. They stood there waiting until the body was wheeled
out with a red velvet pall over it. When Elvis saw the
body, he burst out again. "Oh, Lamar, what am I gonna
do without Satnin'? Oh, Lord, they're taking her away
from me!"

The doctors, puzzled by Gladys's death, requested an
autopsy. Elvis didn't want to know why his mother had
died; he was intent on keeping her alive in his mind. No
autopsy was permitted. As in the case of Elvis's death
years later, no one was ever to know precisely what killed
Gladys. Instead, all the energy inspired by the occasion
was lavished on preparations for a great funeral. Vernon
wanted to have loudspeakers put out on the grounds of
Graceland and the ceremonies turned into a huge public
event. He got in touch with James Blackwood and requested that the famous gospel group sing at the funeral.
Next, the casket had to be ordered. Elvis wanted the finest
available. Then, arrangements had to be made at the house
to lay out the body in the music room.

Later that same morning, the hearse came up the driveway bearing Gladys's body. Elvis was on the lookout. The moment he saw the big black coach driving up the hill, he shouted to Vernon: "Daddy! Momma's comin' home! Look, Momma's here!" When the huge casket, silver finish on copper, had been mounted on the catafalque in the music room and the lid raised, Elvis threw himself on the body. Then, he stepped back to admire his mother. "Look at my Mommy!" he exclaimed. "She's fixed up so pretty!"

Gladys had been beautified by the undertakers. Her hair had been styled, her eyelashes brushed out. She was dressed in a costly outfit which Elvis had bought for her. "My Momma loved beautiful things—but she wouldn't wear them!" cried Elvis, who had always been exasperated by Gladys's refusal to allow him to lavish on her furs and jewels. As he stood there, consuming Gladys with his eyes, he demanded to see her feet—"her itty-bitty sooties!" The undertakers exchanged perplexed looks. Reluctantly, they obliged, raising the satin coverlet and exposing the slipper-clad feet. Instantly, Elvis clasped Gladys's feet and fondled them, pouring out a stream of unintelligible baby talk.

When Anita Wood arrived, she found Elvis sitting in front of the house wearing his favorite outfit: a frilly white tuxedo shirt, open at the neck, with tight white pants and white buck shoes with high backs and big square tongues. "Come here, Little," he commanded, "I want you to see Momma. Come on...she loved you." The moment they arrived beside the coffin, Elvis fell again into the baby-talk blandishments, pointing to each part of Gladys's body and exclaiming over her "itty-bitty lips" and her "itty-bitty hands" and working down finally to her "itty-bitty sooties," which he insisted that Anita examine carefully. Anita was disturbed by Elvis's bizarrely infantile behavior, but what really shook her was the moment when he whipped out his comb and began to run it carefully through Gladys's hair.

Eddie Fadal arrived at Graceland that afternoon. He was greeted by Elvis, who threw his arms around Fadal's neck and then led him straight to the casket. "Look at those hands!" Elvis exclaimed. "How those hands toiled and worked for me...all the things that Momma did for me.... Oh, those beautiful hands!... How they toiled, emptying bedpans in a hospital!" Elvis was clearly becoming hysterical at this point, and Fadal began to long for the presence of a doctor who might prescribe some soothing drug. No sedative was administered; instead, everything conspired to make Elvis frantic.

Word had gotten around Memphis that there was to be a great wake at Graceland and that everyone should come bringing gifts of food and drink. As dozens of women— many of them with designs on Vernon—came bustling up the driveway and into the house with shopping bags, cardboard cartons and dishes covered with silver foil, cellophane and Saran Wrap, the house began to look like the site of a church social. Half-eaten sandwiches, wet paper cups, soiled plates, crumpled paper napkins and other garbage littered the once immaculate rooms with their elegant gold cornices. Heaven knows what might have happened if at that moment the ole Colonel had not appeared, like Lee before Richmond, instantly taking command of the situation and driving back the hordes of milling women.

The Colonel saw at a glance that the fans would demolish the house if they were allowed another day of freedom on the property. He told Vernon that the funeral must be held at the funeral home. Vernon, usually so humble before the Colonel, insisted that the funeral be at Graceland. That was how country people always did their burying—from home. The Colonel was not to be dissuaded. When the director of the Memphis Funeral Home arrived that evening, he found the two men at each other's throats. Finally, the Colonel prevailed. Arrangements were made for the services to be conducted the following afternoon at the funeral parlor.

That night Elvis was completely distraught. He could not be persuaded to leave his station beside the casket. The more people who arrived at the house, the more extravagant Elvis's behavior became. Finally, he turned in exasperation to Lamar and cried: "I can't stand to see anybody else! These people are driving me crazy!" Lamar went to work at once clearing the house of guests. Vernon was furious, but he had his hands full with the Colonel.

When it got late, a doctor was summoned who gave Elvis
a shot to put him to sleep. He suffered violent nightmares.

Early the next morning, the body was conveyed to the
Memphis Funeral Home, a massive old Spanish colonial
mansion with white brick walls and a heavy tile roof that
spreads its bulk under the lofty shade trees on a corner
of Union and Pasadena. For four hours that morning, an
endless stream of people entered the front door of the funeral parlor, filed past the silver casket in the state room
and then departed through the back door of the building.
When they got out into the street, they remained waiting
to catch a glimpse of Elvis and his family. By the time of
the funeral, about one in the afternoon, three thousand
bystanders had gathered in the normally quiet and empty
neighborhood.

That morning at Graceland, Elvis had come staggering
downstairs, appearing at the point of collapse. He was
wearing a very handsome new suit. "My Momma would
have loved this suit," he exclaimed to Willy Nichols. Willy
understood: It was a new suit that Gladys had never seen.
At that point, Elvis went rubber-legged and a couple of
people rushed up to support him. All the rest of the day,
he staggered and stumbled, as if drunk with grief.

Now that Gladys was out of reach, Elvis began to fondle
Vernon just as he had always done with his mother. "Oh,.
Daddy...it's a grey haired Daddy...he's a Satnin' Daddy...
he don't know how to do any better," Elvis would drool,
as he patted his father fondly on his head.

As the time for the funeral approached, Elvis demanded
that Gladys's doctor leave his patients and come to Graceland. He wanted the doctor to sit at his side during the
ordeal ahead. When the doctor arrived, he found Elvis and
Vernon taking turns rubbing salt in each other's wounds.
Elvis would say to Vernon: "Well, Dad, she's not gonna be
feedin' those chickens no more." Vernon would echo: "No,
son, she won't be feedin' those chickens any more." The
Colonel, meantime, was busy barking orders into the
phone. He had arranged in just one night the route of the
funeral cortege, the extensive security measures to be
taken by the Memphis police and the notifications to be
given to the press. Always averse to even the slightest

passing reference to death, the Colonel snuffed out his sense of mortality on this occasion by indulging himself in an orgy of work.

By the time the limousine with the Presley family pulled up at the funeral home, the body had been moved to the West Chapel, a life-sized version of those cardboard churches with celluloid windows that are placed beneath Christmas trees. Decorated in mock-Tudor style, the room boasts golden yellow walls pierced with fake stained-glass windows lit from behind with garish green floodlights. Massive brown pews flank a crimson-carpeted center aisle which leads up to an area that is called the "stage." With its flat proscenium arch, draw curtain and backdrop of a Palladian window filled with opaque panels, the "stage" resembles closely a college drama club setting for *Gammer Gurton's Needle* or *Ralph Roister Doister*.

While the nearly four hundred guests who could squeeze into the chapel were taking their seats, the funeral directors were busy behind the curtain carrying in the flowers from the state room and banking them around the massive silver casket raised on a low plush prie-dieu. Just before the ceremony commenced, Elvis and Vernon were ushered behind the curtain to pay their last respects before the casket lid was closed.

Elvis, his face swollen, his eyes red and heavy-lidded, could hardly draw himself away from the body long enough to embrace tearfully James Blackwood and J. D. Sumner, who had arrived just in time. Reminding the Blackwoods that he had come to the funeral of their brother, Elvis choked out, "I know you understand what I'm going through." Then Elvis, Vernon, Grandma and some relations were ushered into the family room, which is contrived so that the family of the deceased may have a full view of the stage without being visible to guests in the pews. At that point, the Blackwoods and the organist disappeared behind the fake windows, the Reverend James Hamil took his stand at the lectern and the curtain was opened.

The prayers and the eulogy were not long in duration, but the singing was extended far beyond what had been planned. Elvis dashed behind the window screen repeatedly, demanding every hymn that came to mind. The Blackwoods obliged with "I'm Redeemed," "Precious Lord Take My Hand" and "In the Garden." The hymn that had the greatest effect, however, was Gladys's favorite: "Precious Memories."

Singing like a solemn barbershop quartet, the Blackwoods intoned the sentimental verses:

> *Precious memories, unseen angels*
> *Sent from nowhere to my soul.*
> *How they linger, ever near me,*
> *And the scared past unfolds.*

Then the ringing tenor of James Blackwood blared:

> *As I tread down life's pathways,*
> *No matter what the years may hold,*
> *While I ponder, hope grows fonder.*

Finally, after a swelling statement of the refrain, J.D. Summer reached down into his deepest, most sepulchral range to sing with flesh-creeping effect:

> *In the stillness of the midnight,*
> *Precious sacred scenes unfold.*

Vernon Presley faltered at this point and Eddie Fadal had to brace him. By the time the service had concluded, Elvis was wracked with grief.

No sooner had the curtain been drawn and the funeral workers begun to remove the casket to the hearse than Elvis commanded them to stop. He insisted that they open the lid again so that he could have one last moment with Gladys alone. The men obliged. As they stood in embarrassed silence, Elvis threw himself over the casket and mumbled incoherent words of baby talk.

A hundred and fifty uniformed policemen comprised the funeral detail. Officers were stationed at every block along the route to the cemetery and patrol cars were positioned at every major intersection. The cortege was led by the commanding officer, Inspector Legg, in a patrol car with a flashing dome light. Following next came the long black Cadillac limousines of the funeral director, the preacher and then the funeral coach, bearing the casket and flowers. The train of family cars followed, led by Elvis's limousine. Eight motorcycle patrolmen rode up and down the line as flankers. As the cortege rolled down the tree-lined blocks of old Memphis, making for the highway, thousands of people stood along the sidewalks watching silently, the men covering their hearts with their hats.

Forest Hill Cemetery is off Highway 51, just three miles distant from Graceland. When the procession reached the cemetery gate, a sizable crowd had already assembled. Reverend Hamil got out of his car and led the way up the hill to the gravesite, followed by the pallbearers carrying the coffin. When the casket had been put upon the lowering mechanism and dropped part way into the grave, Elvis and Vernon were brought to the graveside.

The ceremony at the grave was brief. After the last prayer had been said, Elvis half leaped, half fell on the casket, crying aloud: "Oh, Satnin', I wanna go with you! I don't want to stay here! I can't be without you!" The extravagance of his grief shocked the bystanders. Lamar reached down and seized Elvis, trying to drag him to his feet. "Get up, people are watching you," he hissed. "Get away, man, get away!" Elvis snarled. He was holding fast now to the lid of the casket as if he would never allow it to be buried. It took the combined efforts of several men to get him to relinquish his grip. At last he was led stumbling down the hill to the waiting car.

Chapter 20

A Lonely Little Boy,
5,000 Miles Away

A GREAT CHEER broke from the throats of five
hundred kids the moment Elvis set foot on German soil.
All that morning, October 1, 1958, they had watched the
S.S. *General Randall* come creeping spectrally through the
fog into its berth in Bremen. Then, as the ship was made
fast and the gangplank was lowered, the kids had begun
to jostle the American military police and duck through
their lines. When Elvis appeared, wearing his dress uniform and toting his bulky duffel bag on his right shoulder,
the kids went berserk. Elvis must have felt he was back
in the States, as he smiled and waved and then boarded
the troop train surrounded by an escort of shiny-helmeted
M.P.s and marines in dress blues.

The train with Elvis's eight hundred-man battalion
rolled south all that day and late into the night bound for
Friedberg, in Hesse, about an hour's drive northeast of
Frankfurt. When the men finally stepped off the coaches,
around one in the morning, they registered instant disappointment. Not allowed even a glimpse of the quaint
little town, with its picturesque castle, they had been de-
posited directly upon U.S. government property.

The weather was cold and damp. The fog was so thick

you could not see ten feet in front of your face. After a
night's sleep in receiving quarters, they rose early next
morning to take a look at their new home. Ray Barracks
consisted of nothing but long lines of austere grey-brick
buildings. Back in the thirties, it had housed Hitler's S.S.
troops. Now it was garrisoned by the 32nd Battalion of the
American Third Armored Division. Still it looked like
what it had always been: Friedberg Kaserne, the next step
up from a military prison.

After a couple of days of reclaiming baggage and being
issued winter clothing and combat gear, the men could see
how they had fared in the military lottery. Elvis had been
assigned to Headquarters Company as a jeep driver in a
reconnaissance platoon. All his noncoms and officers were
new. It was a case of starting all over again from scratch.
Elvis, who hated change and dreaded Germany, could not
have been happy. The only cheering development he could
anticipate was the imminent arrival of his family.

Vernon, Grandma, Lamar and Red (who had joined the
family during its last weeks at Fort Hood) were still at
Graceland when Elvis left for Europe. His departure from
the Army Marine Terminal in Brooklyn had been another
of those pseudoevents staged by the brass with the "aid
and advice" of Colonel Tom Parker. While 2500 relatives
of the departing troops stood about on the heavily fenced
and guarded dock, Elvis conducted a lengthy press conference. Every moment of it was recorded by movie cameras and tape machines so that it could be rebroadcast
around the country in the evening and eventually released
as an EP, titled *Elvis Sails*.

The Presley family had seen bits of the conference that
night on TV. They had laughed heartily when Elvis explained to the American people how delighted he was to
be giving up his career and leaving the country for a year
and a half. "I'm glad to be going," he assured the press.
"Before I was drafted, I'd been trying to arrange a European tour. Now I'll get to see Europe anyway. I'm looking
forward to my first furlough in Paris. I'd like to meet
Brigitte Bardot." Then, he marched bravely up the gangplank with his duffel bag on his shoulder while an army
band played a ponderous medley of "You Ain't Nothin' But

a Hound Dog," "I'm All Shook Up" and "Teddy Bear." If
the family could have seen how that finale was produced,
they would have laughed a lot harder. Elvis had walked
the plank no less than eight times carrying that borrowed
duffel bag.

Bad Nauheim, the town in which the Presleys settled,
is an old spa that had a population, in that period, of
14,000. Its narrow cobblestoned streets wind around blocks
of five-story Victorian buildings whose steeply pitched
roofs are crowned with quaint towers, ornamental spires
and lacy weathervanes. During the afternoons, all the cure
guests engage in the great central-European pastime of
the *Spaziergang*, the reflective or convivial walk, with
hands clasped behind back or linked arm-in-arm, under
the elms, oaks and poplars of the allées that lead to the
band shell, where an orchestra of frail violins and reeds
plays light-opera airs.

Though the population of this staid old place was elderly
and valetudinarian, the arrival of *Der Elvis* brought an
immediate influx of young people. On his very first weekend off the post, Elvis was walking in the park with Lamar
when they were accosted by a German photographer. He
was accompanied by a cute little blonde of high school age
with a provocative ass. The photographer suggested that
Elvis pose with the girl. Elvis put his arm around her and
faced the camera. When she looked up into his face, he
stared down at her. Suddenly his sullen pout dissolved into
a charming smile. She smiled back mutely. That smile
opened up a whole new life for Margrit Buergin.

Up to this moment, she was one of millions of kids in
dreary postwar Germany, growing up in homes with no
man, a hard-pressed mother and the whole emphasis of
life on learning some skill that would get the girl out of
school and into the business world. At the age of sixteen,
Margrit was already working a double shift: as a typist
for a Frankfurt electrical goods company during the day
and at night as a student at a secretarial school. Once
Margrit smiled back at Elvis Presley, she was no longer
a little typist: She was Cinderella.

Elvis got her number from the photographer and called
her apartment. Margrit's mother could not speak English,

but she ran out and got a neighbor, who delivered the
stunning news that their caller was *Der Elvis!* When Margrit got home from school she was dumbstruck. She sat by
the phone all that night wringing her hands, as if the next
day she had to face a firing squad. Sure enough, at 10:30,
the phone rang again. Like every German teenager of her
generation, she had a few words of English. Through the
dense emotional fog of the moment, she managed to comprehend that *Der Elvis* was asking her to go the following
weekend to the movies. *Shrecklich!*

Elvis, for his part, was thinking just like any young lad
eager to make a good impression. Instead of dispatching
one of his minions to fetch Margrit, as he would have done
in Memphis or even Hollywood, he got in a Mercedes cab
driven by his new chauffeur, Joseph, and had himself
driven to Frankfurt. Arriving at the tiny flat occupied by
the Buergins, he endeavored to charm Frau Buergin, who
was beside herself with excitement.

Frau Buergin dispatched her daughter with the notorious rock star, without a moment's compunction. She had
no illusions about life. Actually, she had nothing to fear.
Elvis was into his little southern gentleman bag. Instead
of taking the virtually paralyzed girl to the nearest hotel
and getting down, he brought her back to Bad Nauheim
and introduced her to his father, his grandmother and his
closest friends. Then, he began taking her out two or three
times a week, giving her money for cabs and clothes and
escorting her to every entertainment he could discover,
from the Frankfurt zoo to a nightclub in town, called La
Parisienne. Naturally, it was Margrit's first *Nachtlokal.*

Needless to say, this steady dating did not go unre-
marked by the local press, the national press or the international press. Overnight, Margrit Buergin, sixteen-
year-old typist and after-work secretarial student, became
an international figure. She was soon receiving forty letters a day. The letters came principally from other women
in America and Germany. American women hysterically
called Margrit a "whore" and a "tramp." The Germans used
a more complicated expression that translates "plaything
of the occupying American prick." For Christmas Elvis gave
his "little Puppy" a gold watch studded with diamonds.

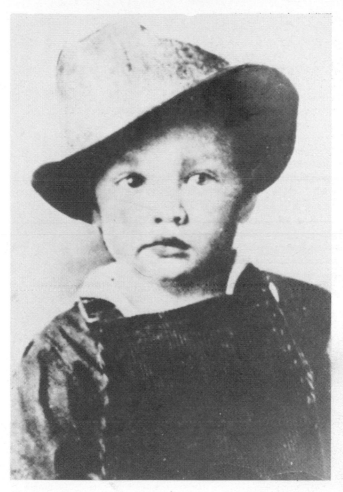

BIB OVERALLS: The first shot of the most photographed man in history. *(United Press International Photo)*

THE LITTLE FAMILY: Vernon was fresh out of prison when this shot of the family in its Sunday best was snapped in East Tupelo, about 1941. Elvis favored his father strongly as a child, but in adolescence he began increasingly to resemble his mother, a likeness that showed most strongly at his death. *(Globe Photos)*

DIONYSIUS AT 19: Elvis just after the release of his first record on Sun. The King label, one of whose records Elvis is holding, was a pioneer in recording R & B records with country singers and C & W records with R & B voices, precisely the two things that Elvis did on his first record. *(United Press International Photo)*

TEDDY BEAR: When word got around that Elvis liked to win stuffed animals at carnivals, he was inundated with padded beasts. Shown here in his girlish boudoir in 1956, he can almost be heard saying, "I don't collect 'em, but if people send 'em to me, I keep 'em." *(Globe Photos)*

THAT'S MY BOY: A classic shot used to illustrate the 1957 AP story that marked the first anniversary of the Colonel's takeover as Elvis's exclusive manager. Elvis offers his practiced lip curl while Colonel plays PR man, employing his hunt 'n' hit typing technique. The original caption offered this penetrating analysis of Elvis's character: "He's like most other twenty-one-year-old fellows," says Colonel Tom. "He has a few dates, takes care of his folks, and tries hard to live right." *(AP Newsfeatures Photo)*

THE HILLBILLY CAT: This famous shot embellished all of Elvis's contracts in the early days; another, nearly identical photo, snapped a second before or after, appears on the cover of Elvis's first album. He never again looked so skinny. *(Wide World Photos)*

THE MUSIC GATE: For twenty years the rallying point of Elvis's fans, the gate had just been installed in April 1957 when this picture was taken. *(United Press International Photo)*

MIKE MAULER: Elvis's real instrument was not the guitar, which he never really learned to play, but the microphone. The erotic pantomime that made him famous demanded a passive partner he could seize, bend over and ultimately get down with. The small size of the theater, the ecstatic, almost exclusively female audience and the flashbulb-popping fans are typical. The guitarist behind Elvis in this top picture is Scotty Moore. *(Black Star)*

G.I. BLUES: Shorn of his sideburns and dressed for the German winter, Private Presley stares glumly at the star he used to be. *(United Press International Photo)*

DEATH BLOW: The family on the eve of Elvis's induction into the army. Elvis is registering the deadly blow which was to change him permanently. Gladys appears dazed; she would be dead within five months. Vernon is bearing up very well. *(Wide World Photos)*

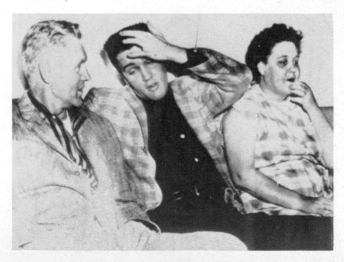

AT LAST: After six years of living together, Elvis and Priscilla were married in 1967. Marty Lacker designed Elvis's tuxedo; Priscilla embellished her own gown. The hairstyles were pure Elvis. *(United Press International Photo)*

PATERNITY: Nine months to the day after they were married, Elvis and Priscilla became parents. Elvis described himself as "happy but shaky." *(Wide World Photos)*

HOT SHOT: Elvis in his most spectacular and uncomfortable costume, starved to perfection and knocking them dead at the taping of the Singer special in 1968. *(United Press International Photo)*

DON ELVIS: At the marriage of his bodyguard Sonny West to Judy Jordan, Elvis officiated as best man. He wore a bell-bottomed suit of crushed black velvet and his diamond-studded sheriff's badge belt and carried his scepter, a Kel police flashlight. *(Wide World Photos)*

BLACK BELT: Elvis became obsessed with karate in his later years and bought his way up from a second- to a seventh-degree black belt. Here he is putting on a demonstration with a supremely cool Red West. *(Globe Photos)*

MARTIAL ARTISTS: Elvis with his Memphis karate master, Kang Rhee, in July 1970. Though generally too stoned to do much on the mat, Elvis sought in every way to achieve recognition as the "king of the bad-asses." *(Karate Action Photo)*

THE MEMPHIS MAFIA: Elvis was on a law-and-order kick when he had his Mafia deputized en masse by Sheriff Roy Nixon of Shelby County just before Christmas, 1970. Back row: Billy Smith, Bill Morris, Lamar Fike, Jerry Schilling, Roy Nixon, Vernon Presley, Charlie Hodge, Sonny West, George Klein, Marty Lacker. Front row: Dr. George Nichopolous, Elvis (wearing pearl-handled pistol in shoulder holster), Red West. *(Collection of Lamar Fike)*

HEROES OF THE SILENT MAJORITY: The Oval Office, December 21, 1970. On the eve of his speech proclaiming drugs "America's Number One Problem," President Nixon appoints the drug-saturated Elvis Presley (just look at his eyes!) a special agent of the Bureau of Narcotics and Dangerous Drugs. *(Courtesy of National Archives and Records Service)*

THE CARY GRANT PICTURE: The twenty-year-old Dries van Kuijk as he looked on the eve of his departure for America.

THE FLYING DUTCHMAN: Andreas Cornelius van Kuijk, AKA Colonel Tom Parker, was born and reared above a livery stable in Breda, Holland. In this archive shot of the now demolished Vlaszak district, the van Kuijk house is the second from the left; the ground-floor doors of the stable are partially visible.

HOW MUCH DOES IT COST IF IT'S FREE?: Colonel Parker in the rare act of giving something away. *(Globe Photos)*

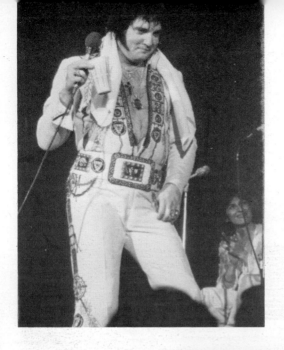

DEAD WEIGHT: The most obvious sign that something was terribly wrong with Elvis Presley during his last years was the obesity which overwhelmed him after a lifetime of starving himself down to his normal weight before making a public appearance. *(Globe Photos)*

THE ROYAL TOMBS: The little family united in death in the meditation garden adjacent to the swimming pool at Graceland. The eternal light beneath the symbol of the Memphis Mafia appears to have blown out. *(James Hamilton)*

Though Elvis had found himself a German girlfriend, he didn't for a moment consider this relationship any betrayal of his long-standing love affair with Anita Wood. In fact, he thought that his only problem with Anita was the temptation his absence offered her to date other men. To affirm his good intentions and warn her against the dangers of her situation, he did something one day that was unprecedented in his life: He wrote Anita a letter.

"I haven't dated a single girl," he assured his "Little Beadie," adding, "when I marry it will be Miss Little Wood Presley." Above all, he implored her to trust him and to "keep yourself clean and wholesome." Then, with many anxious warnings about revealing the contents of the letter to anyone, he signed himself "Yours alone and forever"—and went back to playing with his "Little Puppy."

One month after Elvis's arrival in Germany, his unit received orders to proceed to Grafenwöhr for special training. Loading their tanks aboard flatcars and boarding coaches themselves, the men of the 32nd Armored Battalion journeyed about a hundred miles southeast to a point just short of the Czech border. "Graf," as the G.I.s called it, had a well-deserved reputation as the Hellhole of Europe. It was the Nazi Fort Hood: a vast tract of hilly, wooded country that had been cleared of people twenty years before and fitted out with gunnery ranges, antitank traps and every other device necessary to train tank crews. During the winter the weather was bitterly cold and the ground covered with snow. Most American tanks had no heaters and a jeep, such as Private Presley was driving, was about as comfortable as sitting in a big ice-cube tray.

Visiting troops at Graf were restricted to the base during their stay. The only pastimes open to enlisted men at Graf were drinking beer, shooting pool or going to the movies. Naturally, Elvis chose the last. It was one night at the post movie house that he met the second German girl to become part of his life-support system overseas: Elisabeth Stefaniak.

Elisabeth was also a product of the war and the wrenching effects it had on German society. Born in 1940, she was too young to remember her father when he went off to the Russian front to fight for his Führer. When the war

ended, Elisabeth and her mother were safe, having lived
always in western Germany: The problem was what had
happened to her father. He was reported simply "missing."
Then, one day in the early fifties, he returned from Rus-
sia—with a Russian wife. An acrimonious divorce followed, and Elisabeth's mother ended by marrying an
American sergeant named Raymond McCormick. The sergeant did one tour of duty in the States; then he was
returned to Germany, winding up at Graf, where he was
an instructor in ammunition loading and handling.

After living in the States for several years, coming back
to this dreadful outpost on the front lines of the Cold War
was no joke for a young girl. Sergeant McCormick was an
Archie Bunker type. He took a low view of the morals of
most G.I.s. Though there were thousands of men on the
base, Elisabeth, who was now eighteen years old, was not
allowed to date a soldier. Nor could she get a job because,
technically, she was an American citizen; the Germans
preferred to hire cheaper-paid Germans. Putting it all together, you could say that Elisabeth Stefaniak's prospects
were dim.

Like every other teenager in the world, Elisabeth was
very curious about Elvis Presley. When she learned that
he was on the post and went to the movies every night,
she quizzed the manager of the movie theater about his
famous guest. The manager confirmed that Elvis would
slip into the movie house every night about ten minutes
after the picture began; then, he would slip out again a
few minutes before it ended. The trick was to get to him
before he made his getaway.

A few nights later, Elisabeth, having been presented
to Elvis by another G.I. at the movie house, is walking
with him through the wooded area that leads to the seg-
regated zone where the married noncoms live in apartment
buildings. When they reach Elisabeth's apartment house,
she invites him to come up and meet her mother and her
stepfather, the sergeant. Elvis declines instantly. Still, he
lingers. He prolongs the feeble conversation. Finally, he
bends down and kisses her. Then he strides off alone into
the woods, calling out as he disappears: "Come on back to
the movie and I'll be seein' ya!"

Elisabeth stumbled up the stairs to her apartment and lay awake all night thinking of the extraordinary thing that had befallen her. The next morning, she told the story to her mother and stepfather. Sergeant Bunker made a face and shrugged, "Who cares?" Elisabeth's mother was enormously excited. She, too, was an Elvis fan.

That night Elisabeth was back at the movies—and so was Elvis. They met every night for a week. Every evening he would walk her home, but always he refused to go upstairs and meet the family. Then, without any invitation or announcement, Elvis came to the McCormicks' house on Thanksgiving Day.

Once Elvis had gotten his foot not only through the door but under the table, he started showing up at odd times of the day. He might pop over at ten in the morning, driving his jeep, and come up for coffee in the kitchen. Or he might come around in the evening for supper.

Once a good ole boy has filled his belly, what's he gonna do next? You got it. He takes himself a nice long snooze. Once Elvis had made himself at home at the McCormicks', he would stretch out on the couch after breakfast and cop some Zs. He also took to borrowing the sergeant's old Buick, hauled over from the States. Pretty soon Elvis was driving Elisabeth to the movies every night.

Now, the boy has taken his girl to the movies. The night is still young. They have the car. What are they going to do? There's only one thing Elvis wants to do. Drive slowly around Grafenwöhr and talk to Elisabeth. Not talk about the scout problem they were given that day or how all their tanks have parts missing or how he got a new heater for his jeep. No, Elvis wants to have that deep communion, that solacing confessional hour, that he enjoyed for so many years with Gladys. A man has problems and there's no better way to get them off his chest than to tell them to a woman, a sweet, sympathetic woman, who will just soak them up like a sponge.

One night Elvis got so deep into his musings and his confessions that he violated one of his deepest taboos: He talked about his father. As Elisabeth listened, hardly daring to breathe, much less speak, Elvis told her that when his mother was hardly cold in her grave, his father had

started running after other women. As he described the
scenes he had witnessed just before they left Killeen, and
even more recently at Bad Nauheim, he grew more and
more upset. Finally, he pulled the car over and burst into
loud racking sobs.

Elvis left Grafenwöhr just before Christmas. On the
day of his departure, he came to say good-bye. He explained
that he had need of a secretary back at Bad Nauheim who
would lend a hand with the mail and act as interpreter in
the daily business with the Germans. Elvis was offering
this job to Elisabeth.

A couple of days later, Elisabeth, wearing a red coat for
identification, was standing on the train platform at Bad
Nauheim waiting for Elvis to pick her up in his spanking
new white BMW sports car, which the press had dubbed
"Der Elviswagen." Soon she had met Vernon, Grandma
and the Guys. Everything was delightful until she realized
what lay in store for her.

Elvis, as usual, was looking for unlimited service at a
rock-bottom price. Elisabeth was informed that her duties
would not be confined to answering letters and translating
the chatter of the local merchants. She was also expected
to help out Grandma with the cooking and the dishes, to
aid Vernon with the shopping and to do any other odd
chores that seemed inappropriate for the menfolk who sat
around idle all day long. Her remuneration was the grand
sum of thirty-five dollars a week. (Elvis always paid his
salaried employees thirty-five dollars a week in the early
years because that was the amount he received while
working for Crown Electric.)

What was worse than the pay was the discipline imposed on her. Having just escaped from a man who
wouldn't allow her to date the only men available, Elisabeth was startled to hear from Elvis's own lips that she
must not think of dating anyone while she lived in his
home. He insisted in fact, that she not even *look* at the
boys who lived in the house or came there on visits. If he
discovered her in this forbidden act, he would growl,
"*Caught!*"

It was a blue Christmas for everyone in the Presley
family that year. Red and Lamar had to squeeze Vernon

to get a few dollars to buy gifts for their families at home. Elisabeth was distressed about her situation. Elvis moped around the house brooding on his dead mother. Even Grandma, normally so cheerful, couldn't get herself together to make a real Christmas dinner. Vernon and the boys went to the dining room at the post in Friedberg and had G.I. turkey.

The more depressed Elvis became, the more he complained about being in the army. He would sit on the edge of his bed and let it all out to Lamar: "It's like starting all over again," he would lament. "It's like when I was working for the Loew's State and Crown Electric. Seventy-eight dollars a month—shit! I make that in a minute!" Lamar would pour his soothing platitudes over the irate Elvis, but the monologue of complaints would only grow keener. "Here I am a singing star and a movie star and I gotta act like one o' the guys! It ain't easy bein' one o' the guys. I ain't never been one o' the guys, and I never will be one o' the guys!"

Adding to Elvis's gloom was the steady stream of letters from Anita, who was now getting upset over all the stories in papers about his relationship with Margrit. Elvis decided to write Anita and deny everything. This time he concedes that he had "seen" the German girl about whom Anita was reading; but, he insists, it had been only once when she was in the company of a photographer. As the girl didn't speak a word of English, how could they possibly have been dating? The real truth, Elvis protests, is that never in his whole life has he been so "lonesome and miserable." His only consolation is to lie in bed at nights thinking about his "Wittle Beadie," about her little eyes and little nose and little hair, which some nights he imagines brushing his cheek and getting him so hot that he starts swearing! No matter. Like General MacArthur, he vows: "I shall return." Meantime, he urges her to get Tommy Edwards's (actually The Four Fellows) record of "Soldier Boy." From now on, he says, that will be their song. Then, he signs off with a tremulous P.S.: "No one ever reads this, OK?"

If the characters in *Grease* wrote letters, they would be exactly like these soliloquies Elvis mailed from Germany.

He sees himself as a character in a wailing R & B ballad, a "lonely little boy 5,000 miles away," accused falsely of loving another girl when all he really wants is Little Wittle Beadie. Oh, it all begs to be poured into a microphone and stamped on shiny vinyl and blasted out over the airways, with a fast-talking DJ jumping in at the end to blither, "'Lonely Little Boy' by Elvis Presley—for Anita and the gang out there in Whitehaven!" Yes, it's a very teeny Elvis that you find in these sad-assed letters from Germany: that lonely melancholy boy who spent his life dreaming of things he wanted, only to discover when he got them that they didn't make him happy.

Chapter 21

Teen Angel

Goethestrasse 14, the blocky, three-story, white stucco house into which Elvis settled after he and his boys had been kicked out of a couple of hotels for disturbing the elderly guests with water battles and playful acts of arson, was full of heavy, overstuffed furniture and that fusty, dreary, old-world atmosphere that Elvis loathed. An even bigger problem than the house's depressing atmosphere was its owner, a widow named Frau Pieper. One of those big, hard, busty jobs straight out of *The Katzenjammer Kids,* Frau Pieper was the human equivalent of a German tank. She was loud, aggressive and ugly, all of which would not have mattered a damn if she had been willing simply to rent her house for ten times its proper value and clear out. The difficulty was that she made it a condition of the rental that she remain living in the house in a room next to the kitchen. She argued that she had no other place to live and that her services were essential as housekeeper. Like a fool, Vernon acceded to this outrageous demand and the family was saddled for the next fifteen months with a universally detested house mother.

Once Elvis settled into the house, his life locked into a routine that never varied. Reveille at Goethestrasse 14 would sound raucously at four-thirty in the morning, when

357

Lamar would wake up the whole neighborhood by gunning
the mighty engine of the *Elviswagen*. If it had snowed the
night before, as it often did, Lamar would have to lay his
ponderous bulk behind the haft of a broad shovel to get
the car clear of the house. When Elvis got up, everyone
got up: That was an unspoken rule. Grandma and Elisabeth would go into the kitchen and prepare a breakfast
designed to please only one person—but served to everyone. There were always lots of big, fat, round "cat's head"
biscuits, thick gravy made from bacon drippings, hard-
fried eggs and burnt bacon, jam, syrup, butter, coffee and
ice-cold cling peaches out of cans. Elvis would mix the
butter, syrup and jam together, spread the mixture on the
split biscuits, then convert them into "soaks" by dipping
them deep in his coffee. The bacon he would eat with his
fingers, holding it by the fat end and nibbling on the lean.
The peaches were his dessert, icing the fat in his belly and
leaving a sweet taste in his mouth as he set out bitterly
to drive the seventeen kilometers to the base.

As soon as the boss was out of the house, everyone
would go back to bed. They would get up again at a normal
hour and set to their tasks. Elisabeth and the boys would
go into a glassed-in back porch that served as an office
and start reading and answering the vast amounts of mail
that were delivered daily by the APO. The volume of the
mail, even over here in Germany, was so staggering that
it would take the three of them many hours each day to
reply to the most likely correspondents. Virtually everyone in the household had become adept at forging Elvis's
signature so it was possible to make thousands of teenagers in Europe and America happy in the possession of
an authentic letter written and signed by Elvis himself.

Vernon loved to play the hard taskmaster. Orville Bean
at last! Though he paid the boys nothing, giving them at
most fifty cents or a dollar a week for beer money, he didn't
hesitate to chastise them if they were remiss in their duties. Even Elisabeth, who was such a sweet and obliging
girl, always busy about the house from early morning to
late at night, was chewed out fiercely for the slightest
infractions of discipline. Once Elvis came home for lunch
and found Elisabeth writing in the office. "What are you

doing?" he asked. "Writing my mother a letter," she replied innocently. That afternoon, as soon as Elvis had cleared the house, Vernon came down on her like an angry Egyptian overseer. He reprimanded her severely for engaging in personal business on Presley time. Elisabeth protested that all her time was Presley time, that she had no set hours or duties and was expected to toil from before dawn to long after dark. Vernon bore down even harder at this sign of insubordination, giving her that hard, mean, nasty redneck tongue.

Apart from bossing the hands, Vernon's other duties took him often to the commissary, where he would lay in supplies of Hormel chili, Pepsi, canned Vienna sausage (Elvis pronounced it "Vaih-ennah"), peanut butter, canned crowder peas and dairy supplies. By this point, Vernon had bought himself a good burgherlike black Mercedes that would lend him dignity. His trips abroad often lasted much longer and produced much less yield than a time and motion analyst would allow reasonable. Like most southern men, Vernon had a knack for slippin' away that baffled the curious.

Supper was served at six. Sauerkraut and weenies were the standard fare. Sometimes there'd be steak and gravy— but only when Elvis was away on field exercises. Elvis's absences tended to encourage a very different life-style: trips to the movies and meals in German restaurants where, like renegade Jews, the boys and Elisabeth would stuff themselves with forbidden foods like Hassenpfeffer, Wienerschnitzel, Sauerbraten and red cabbage, even Wildschwein (wild boar), marinated for nine days in strong spices. Living as prisoners of a juvenile egomaniac, Elisabeth, Lamar and Red didn't often get a chance to go out and play.

In the evening, the townsfolk would gather before the house to watch the ceremony of the autograph signing. Elvis had established this ritual as a device for relieving his family of day-long disruptions by concentrating the unavoidable requests into a half hour in the early evening. All day the house would stand there blank, apparently deserted, almost spooky, with its black-green rolling shutters repelling the gazes and the lenses of the inevitable

priers and gawkers. On the wooden blind that covered the
French windows at the front of the house, there would be
displayed a placard that gave directions to visitors. Hand-
printed in defective German, it read:

Wegen vorgeschriebener   To preserve the
Ruhe Der Kurgäste is   prescribed rest of the
das Betreten des   medical patients
Grundstucks untersagt.   traffic in this area is
                                forbidden.

AUTOGRAMME VON 19:30   20:00
Autographs between 7:30–8:00 P.M.
    Only Please

When the magic hour arrived, Elvis would appear before the house, dressed in his army fatigues and cap, to
sign the postcards, pictures and album sleeves handed to
him by fans. There was never any violence or disorder
during these sessions, but after a while they began to bore
him. At that point, the routine was altered. Lamar or Red
would come out of the house and explain that Elvis was
indisposed but eager to sign their souvenirs. Then the boys
would collect the stuff, bring it indoors, forge Elvis's
signature upon it and return it to the patiently waiting
fans.

Once this chore was out of the way, the family would
gather for the balance of the evening in the parlor, which
boasted a piano as well as a radio and a phonograph. Elvis
might seat himself at the piano to play and sing or they
might tune in a disc jockey show on the Armed Forces
Network, the only station they ever listened to in Germany. Elvis's favorite record was "The Bells," Billy Ward's
weird and lurid evocation of the funeral of a sweetheart.

By nine, Elvis would be hungry again. He would give
Elisabeth the high sign and she would go into the kitchen
to prepare his bedtime snack. Peeling several bananas,
she would slice the fruit and mash it in a bowl with lots
of peanut butter. Then she would spread this mulch on
slices of bread, cap the sandwiches with more bread and

toast them under the grill. Elvis would eat four or five of
these rich concoctions. His other nighttime favorite was
even more leaden. This was a fried potato sandwich. The
potatoes were sliced a quarter inch thick and browned in
the fat of bacon that had just been removed from the frying
pan. The sandwich would consist of fried potato, burnt
bacon and onions, plastered with mustard. This mess, too,
would be seared under the grill.

By ten o'clock, Elvis would be climbing the stairs to his
bedroom on the second floor. He would lie abed for a while,
reading the latest issue of *Mad* or *Cracked,* laughing aloud
at the gags. When he fell to sleep, Red and Lamar might
go out to the Beck's beer bar, where they would nurse two
steins for the balance of the night.

The weekends would see some lifting of the gloom that
clouded the week. Elvis, freed of his duties at the post,
would invite some of his army buddies to the house. One
of his favorites was a clean-cut, well-bred young man
named Rex Mansfield, who had been by Elvis's side since
they were inducted together at Memphis. "Rextus" earned
Elvis's respect in the first weeks at Hood by refusing to
accept payment for taking Elvis's duty as corporal of the
guard during a visit by Anita. Rex had said, "I'll expect
you to do as much for me." That was always the best way
to talk to Elvis, who automatically divided everyone he
met into those he could take for granted and those whom
he would have to take seriously.

A very different sort of man was Joe Esposito, a dark,
stocky, second-generation Italian from Chicago, who was
a company clerk. Joe was a hustler who had studied accounting by day and hung out with Mob guys by night; he
even boasted of having dated the daughter of Tony "Big
Tuna" Accardo, the alleged boss of the Chicago Family.
Perhaps it was from these wise guys that Joe picked up
his skills as a shylock, which he used to good effect in
Germany. Lending money to G.I.s at a hundred percent
premium, Joe made an extra seven or eight thousand dollars a year. It was in this manner that he first met Lamar,
who borrowed money from Joe and then repaid him by
introducing him to Elvis.

The most entertaining of Elvis's new army cronies was

a little dude from Decatur, Alabama, named Charlie
Hodge. This lad grew so close to Elvis in the years to come
that he became Elvis's shadow. He was a shrunken
shadow, only five feet three. He had a big, man-sized face
on him, but his body was like a suit draped on a hanger:
good fit at the shoulders and the rest hanging over nothing.
Charlie was an accomplished gospel singer and country
musician, who had gone to the Stamps Gospel School and
worked for years as one of Red Foley's Smokey Mountain
Boys. Of all the men who got tight with Elvis, he was the
only one who was a professional musician and entertainer.

Evenings on the weekends would start out much as
they did during the week; but around midnight on Friday,
Elvis would always get the itch to go out and run around
in the cars. He would go upstairs and comb his hair and
prepare himself carefully to leave. Then, he would come
down and give the command to move without allowing
anybody else as much as a moment to take a leak. If someone complained he were tired or seemed reluctant to go,
Elvis would whip out his quart jar of Dexies, obtained from
a pharmacist on the post, and shake out four or five. "Take
a cup of coffee with this," he would urge: "it'll get into
your bloodstream faster." Then the boys would jump pell-
mell into the cars and take off for Frankfurt.

Elvis's favorite entertainer in this big modern city was
a female contortionist who worked in a club that was
rigged for gymnastic performances. After watching her
twist her body into astonishing knots, Elvis finally obtained an introduction to the lady and even dated her. All
the boys chuckled in lubricious delight at the thought of
what this chick could do in the sack. The Pelvis never
divulged what sort of relationship he enjoyed with the
Pretzel.

During this winter, Vernon met Dee Stanley, the wife
of Master Sergeant Bill Stanley, a much-decorated veteran
who had been General Patton's personal bodyguard during
the invasion of Europe. The Stanleys lived with their three
little boys in nearby Wiesbaden. The relationship commenced when Dee Stanley, a vivacious, high-strung little
woman from Tennessee, called Elvis and invited him to
supper. Elvis countered by inviting her to his hotel for

coffee and then substituting his father as host. Vernon took a shine to Dee at once; soon he and the Stanleys had become a threesome. One afternoon, he got Dee into bed and the threesome became a triangle. The romance was cross-hatched by guilt, conflict and anxiety. Bill Stanley, a heavy but contrite drinker, sought to enlist Vernon's help in averting a divorce. Dee, who rendezvoused with Vernon at Graceland after flying back to the States to put her children into a home, was concerned that Elvis would block her marriage to his father. It was while matters were at their most precarious that Vernon went out shopping with Elisabeth one day and nearly killed them both.

Vernon accelerated to pass a car in front of him on the Autobahn. Just at that moment, the car he was trying to skirt moved into the passing lane to get ahead of another car. Vernon hit his brakes so hard that his machine went into a skid and struck the median. Flipping over and rolling three times, the car flew across the oncoming lanes and crashed into a tree on the far side of the highway, coming to rest upside down.

When Vernon extricated himself from the car, he stuck his head back inside and yelled: "Honey, are you all right?" Elisabeth had been struggling to get free, but she had discovered that she was paralyzed. "My back hurts—I can't move!" she cried. At that moment, some motorists stopped and pulled her free of the car. She told them to call Frau Pieper. Shortly afterward, an ambulance arrived and took Elisabeth off to a nearby hospital. Vernon chose to remain with his car, which is where Elvis found him when he came roaring up in the *Elviswagen* with Lamar.

The call to Frau Pieper had found Elvis at home. Terrified at the thought that his father might be injured, Elvis pushed his BMW up to 150 miles an hour getting to the wreck. Once he saw that his worst fears were unfounded, he grabbed Vernon and took off for home. He never suggested that they go to the hospital to learn how Elisabeth was faring. She was very lucky. X-rays disclosed that her back was not broken and that her paralysis was only a temporary condition owing to shock. She would have to remain in bed for days, but she would suffer no permanent disability.

When the ambulance arrived at Goethestrasse, Frau
Pieper was horrified at the girl's appearance: white from
shock, her hair still full of bits of glass and broken egg-
shells. The landlady would not hear of the stretcher bear-
ers carrying Elisabeth upstairs; she insisted they put the
girl to bed in Frau Pieper's apartment on the ground floor.
Immediately, Red and Lamar were at Elisabeth's side,
hugging her and telling her how happy they were that she
was not badly hurt. Vernon and Grandma appeared also,
giving thanks for Elisabeth's miraculous escape from
death. Only Elvis was absent.

Finally, when all the others had left, Elvis came into
the room and closed the door. His face bore that ugly,
distrustful expression so characteristic of him. Without
pausing for a moment to inquire how Elisabeth felt, he
came to the point of his furtive visit. Bending down close
to the pain-racked girl, he hissed: "What were you and my
daddy doin' that caused that wreck?" For a second, Elisabeth could not believe her ears. Here she was, lucky to
be alive after nearly being killed by Vernon's bad driving,
and Elvis was accusing *her* of causing the wreck! When
she tried to assure him that she was innocent, he refused
to believe her. Nothing would persuade him until she had
gone over the entire story in great detail, point by point,
the sheer weight of the facts finally dispelling his suspicions. At that point, he relented and made some perfunctory inquiries about her condition, adding that he was glad
she was not seriously hurt. The truth was, however, that
the only thing that gladdened him was the relief of learning that his father had not been playing around with a
girl whom Elvis regarded as his own property. That was
the thing which at this moment he feared above everything
else.[1]

In June, Vernon and Dee went to visit Elvis at the
Frankfurt Military Hospital, where he was confined with
tonsilitis, to get his permission to marry. Elvis received

[1]Just before Elvis sent his people back to the States, Elisabeth
began dating Rex Mansfield on the sly. They were married a few
months later in the U.S. Elvis was deeply chagrined.

them propped up in bed. He was smiling and cheerful. He had made his decision already. When Dee brought the conversation around to the inevitable topic, Elvis made a little speech. "Mrs. Stanley," he began, "I want my daddy to be happy. He was a wonderful husband and father, and I've always wanted a brother. Now, I guess I'll have three. We can just add another room onto Graceland." As always, he contrived to make an event he dreaded seem welcome. Dee took him at his word. "From that moment on," she recalled later, "I knew that I would marry Vernon Presley."

No sooner had Vernon found a wife than Elvis found one, too. It was in August 1959 that Elvis first met Priscilla Ann Beaulieu. He was sitting in his parlor one weekend night, preparing for another of his dull little at-homes, when he looked up and saw one of the prettiest teenage girls he had ever beheld. "She looks like an angel!" exclaimed Elvis when he recovered from his shock. She was dressed in a blue middy outfit with her rich auburn hair wound in a single massive curl. Though she had just turned fourteen, she looked considerably older, being quite fully developed and heavily made up.

Priscilla would have made an impression on Elvis at any time. Appearing at this desperate moment, she must have seemed the answer to all his lonely and fretful prayers. She excited him so much that instead of coming on like the charismatic King of Rock 'n' Roll, he regressed to the awkward, embarrassed manner of the boy next door. When Priscilla entered the room, Elvis sprang out of his chair and stuck out his hand, exclaiming, "Hi! I'm Elvis Presley." Having introduced himself about as suavely as Howdie Doodie, he blurted out next some teasing remark about Priscilla's little turned-up nose. Instantly, like any sensitive teenager, she flushed with anger.

Elvis was quick to detect his gaffe and just as quick to cover it up. Dashing to the piano, he started putting on a show. He sang in his richest, most succulent tones. He flashed his most engagingly boyish smiles. He worked his ass off to recapture his audience. After about ten minutes of showtime, he ducked into the kitchen to get a glass of cooling water. Elisabeth was sitting at the table with

Grandma. Elvis, his mind filled with Priscilla, exlaimed
in wonder at this visitor's beauty. Then, he darted back
to the parlor.

The evening passed swiftly after its rough start. When
Currie Grant—a noncom in Special Services who had
brought Priscilla to meet Elvis—saw the hands on the
clock approaching eleven, he started his disengagement
maneuvers. He had promised Priscilla's parents to have
their daughter home by midnight. Elvis, not the type to
relinquish any pleasure till he had drunk his fill, would
not hear of such an early departure. Hell, he was just
hitting his stride, getting into his rap, starting to get something going with this little honey. Finally, after getting
Grant so uptight that he was practically dancing a jig on
the living room floor, Elvis released his guests. They piled
into Grant's car and took off up the Autobahn.

When they arrived home, they found Captain and Mrs.
Beaulieu sitting up and waiting for them with grim
expressions on their faces. The Captain dressed down the
enlisted man. The mother scolded her daughter. There
were to be no more visits with this Elvis Presley. That
much was fixed, settled, beyond discussion. Priscilla was
not brokenhearted. From the start she had seen the whole
idea as a fantasy. What's more, she couldn't believe that
Elvis would ever want to see her again. Why should he,
when every girl in the world was dying to meet him?
Imagine her surprise when she learned through Grant
that Elvis was pressing for another meeting the following
weekend. Now she would have to persuade her parents.

Captain Beaulieu was actually Priscilla's stepfather.
An enlisted man in the marines in World War II, he had
worked his way up from the ranks, qualifying after the
war for an air force training program that had landed him
a navigator's berth at the big air base at Wiesbaden. He
had married Priscilla's mother several years after she was
widowed. Her first husband, Priscilla's father, was a handsome naval pilot named James Wagner. While flying home
in 1945 to visit his wife and five-month-old infant daughter, Lieutenant Wagner had crashed and died. Priscilla
still carried a yellowed picture of him in her wallet. One
of the reasons for her apparent maturity was the fact that

she was the oldest child in a family that now numbered four younger brothers and her little sister, Michelle.

Currie Grant did a splendid job of reassuring the Beaulieus about Elvis's character and intentions. He explained that far from being one of those crazy showbiz types, Elvis was an exemplary young man who lived with his father and grandmother in the most respectable manner; that his little weekend parties were chaste entertainments, where the boys and girls sat around the piano singing songs or snacking on pizza and Pepsi. As for the problem of conforming with Priscilla's curfew, Elvis was so keen on avoiding any future difficulty that he had offered to provide a car and a driver expressly for this purpose. That weekend, Priscilla returned to Bad Nauheim.

Gradually, the rhythm of her visits changed from weekends only to twice a week, three times a week, eventually four times a week. It must be borne in mind that these visits were not just little runs across town. Lamar would collect her in Wiesbaden very early in the evening and drive for nearly an hour until they got to the house on Goethestrasse. Then, when the evening was over, they would have another long drive, this time at night in winter with the road often blanketed by heavy fog. Visibility was so poor sometimes that Priscilla would have to get out of the car and lead Lamar through the thick vapors. Many a night they got home long past the appointed hour.

As the frequency of Priscilla's visits increased, the venue of these little trysts also changed. Now, instead of a party around the ole pie-ano, with lots of other boys and girls present, as well as Daddy and Grandma—those watchful chaperones!—in the kitchen, the famous sex hero and his teen angel were spending the whole evening alone together in his bedroom. In a word, Elvis had contrived to transform Bad Nauheim into Memphis, Goethestrasse 14 into Graceland, and his empty, lonely evenings into deeply absorbing pajama parties.

Still, there was one important difference. Instead of cavorting or communing with a collective identity comprised of three fourteen-year-old girls, Elvis was now focusing all his attentions on just one fourteen-year-old girl. This was an unprecedented event in his life. In the past, whenever Elvis had sought to establish an intimate relationship with a girl of the age on which he was fixated, he had found it impossible to achieve any real rapport. Junior high girls were always so overwhelmed with Elvis's fame and mystique that they could never relax and accept him as their teenage boyfriend. They always kept harping on the fact that he was a star, a hero, a king! This was the ironic and exasperating price that Elvis paid for success. He had priced himself right out of the fourteen-year-old market.

Priscilla, however, was different. Even years later, Elvis was still marveling over this child's self-confidence. As he told an interviewer: "Priscilla was just a kid—more than ten years younger than me. But she wasn't like so many of the other girls. I guess most of 'em were a little overawed by me, by what I'm supposed to be. Dunno why, because I'm shy myself and do my best to make other people feel at ease. But with this chick, it was different. She didn't give the impression that in any way she was tongue-tied." In fact, as Elisabeth Stefaniak recalls: "It's like she could get away with more smart talk than the other girls. He would put them in their place real quick but not her." Priscilla's appeal was not confined to youth, beauty, innocence—important as those things were to Elvis. What made her unique was the fact that she could hold her own with the famous star, sitting up there in the bedroom talking about cars, movies and eye makeup, and even evincing at times a certain pertness, even sassiness, suggesting that she held herself nearly equal to Elvis. What a wonderful thing that must have been to him; for if she treated him as an equal, he was equal: He was free at last to regress to that age where he was most comfortable: sweet sixteen.

What did the Beaulieus make of the fact that their daughter was constantly being carried off by a fat man in an expensive Mercedes to spend the evening with a notorious sex symbol? Clearly, they were given something more reassuring than Currie Grant's Norman Rockwell portrait. As soon as Priscilla told Elvis that the lies she was forced to invent every night to explain her late arrivals at home were creating a threat to the continuation of the visits, Elvis decided to go straight to the heart of the problem. He and Vernon paid a call on the Beaulieus. What precisely they told the Captain and Mrs. Beaulieu is not known, but it must have turned on the fact that some day—once he had gotten out of the service and had reestablished his career—Elvis would want to settle down and marry and live just like any other successful young man. Though no promise of marriage was made at this early date, the thought of marriage was clearly in everyone's mind. Nor is this surprising in view of Elvis's lifelong penchant for proposing marriage at the earliest possible moment. Whatever the substance of this conversation, the facts speak for themselves. Having started off by telling her daughter, "I wouldn't send you across the street to meet Elvis Presley," Mrs. Beaulieu was now telling Priscilla that her relationship with Elvis represented a "once in a lifetime opportunity."

After a long summer at the post in Friedberg, Elvis's unit received a red alert. Captain Betts, the company commander, told the men: "Don't leave anything behind that you want to keep." Elvis took alarm immediately. "This is it!" he shouted as he entered the house that day: "They're going to ship all civilian personnel home." Lamar, fearing an immediate invasion by the Russians, cried: "I hope they send us soon! I don't wanna be here when a war starts!"

The alert turned out to be merely a test of the unit's readiness, but the 32nd Armored did ship out immediately for Wildflicken, a mountainous region near the Swiss border that was already deep under snow and ice. During the ten days the exercise lasted, the battalion lost about half its equipment. One slip on the narrow mountain roads and a tank would plunge down a two- or three-hundred-foot declivity. Elvis had put a tank heater in his jeep in anticipation of the cold. One bitter night, he turned on the heater, pulled a poncho over his head and went to sleep. In the middle of the night, he awoke gasping and choking, feeling that he was about to die. Carbon monoxide from the engine had filled the tent made by his poncho and would have killed him, if a chance breeze hadn't blown the covering off his head and revived him. Elvis staggered out of the jeep and collapsed on the ground. Lying there, he looked up at the stars and thanked God for sparing him.

When Elvis returned from the field in the fall of 1959, he found the first unmistakable signs of his reviving career. Hal Wallis had come over from Hollywood to supervise the work of a second-unit production crew, which was going to film backgrounds for Elvis's first movie when he got out of the service. Predictably, it would exploit his past two years in the army and dramatize the lighter-than-life adventures of a G.I. tanker in Germany. Elvis was not happy with the idea. Naturally, he kept his disappointment to himself and his most trusted confidants. He craved roles that were not simply thinly disguised and fantasized versions of Elvis Presley. Being a professional good guy, always eager to please, however, he couldn't level with Hal Wallis or with anyone in a position of authority. He would spend the rest of his long career in Hollywood lamenting the fact that he never got any good parts. What he never learned was that actors don't just *get* good parts: They *demand* them.

The other news at Goethestrasse was downright unpleasant: Vernon informed his son that Dee would be coming soon to live with them. Why Vernon and Dee did not marry at this time is a mystery. She had her separation agreement and was, presumably, well along in her divorce. A few more months of separate domiciles and the pair could have married and cleared the air of any questions of impropriety. By moving in with Vernon before the divorce, Dee created fresh threats of scandal. Elvis could not have approved of such an arrangement; but he was in a compromising position himself, carrying on with Priscilla up in his bedroom four nights a week. (Vernon and Dee were married at Huntsville, Alabama, on July 3, 1960. Elvis was conspicuously absent.)

The last months in Germany went by so rapidly that they are just a blur in the minds of those who lived with Elvis. When the date for departure had been set, three weeks short of the two-year term of the draft, Elvis sent the family home. On the final day, when Elvis climbed aboard the DC-7 at Frankfurt Airport, the crowd around the plane was so dense that Priscilla could not get beyond

the outer fringes. Elvis had promised to wave to her when
he entered the cabin—and he did wave. The crowd took
the wave as intended for it and roared back a farewell that
would have drowned the voice of a dozen fourteen-year-old
girls. One photographer who knew the truth did contrive
to capture Priscilla at the final poignant moment. The
photo he snapped is one of the most touching in that immense album stamped ELVIS.

The picture is of a very young but very pretty girl, one
of those young girls who bear already on their faces the
unmistakable signs of a woman's beauty. The finely cut
lips are parted. The hand is held up in an arrested salute.
The feature that rivets the viewer's gaze is the eyes. They
are beautiful eyes, nearly innocent of makeup. What is so
extraordinary about them is their clouded ecstatic focus,
as if they were the eyes of a seer gazing raptly into the
future.

the other fingers. Elsie had continued to watch others busy
at auction, the casino... and began to see that she had took
... saw being used for illustration and these... drawer, that
would have the machine... just a dozen... chair... ful
with. One photographer who knew the... subjects
to confine Priscilla to the final... record. To
... note in casual... of his most touching in that immense album stamped as...

The pictures... of a very young but very pretty girl, one
of those young girls who bear a smile... on their face that
immediate... still more that women's beauty. The... lip
their...hand in hand to hold... an unrelieved subtle
... The feature that struck the young... pure... She was. They
are beautiful eyes, meant... another of... What is so
extraordinary about them is their shielded external focus.
It is as if they were the pupil of a... gazing deeply into the
future.

Chapter 22

About Face!

A BLIZZARD was driving over McGuire Field, near Fort Dix, New Jersey, when the DC-7 carrying Elvis and his detail began its landing approach. Terrified of flying, Elvis had anesthetized himself by swallowing a handful of sleeping pills before he took off at Frankfurt. After the refueling stop at Prestwick, Scotland, he had dropped into a deep sleep. Now, after fourteen hours in the air, he was wide awake and staring grimly out the window into a wall of glimmering white.

Down and down the plane glided, an interminable descent, punctuated by hysterical sick jokes about crashing. Elvis, tense with fear, his left leg jiggling frantically, dug his fingers into the armrests and braced his body. Suddenly, it seemed his worst fears had come true. The plane struck the ground with a violent impact and hooked sharply to the left. Just as the soldiers started shouting in terror, the ship straightened out and rolled down the tarmac. Coming in on instruments with the ceiling zero, the pilot had missed the runway.

Though Elvis's landing was bumpy, the rest of the road was as smooth as love and money could make it. The Colonel had engaged a railroad magnate's luxurious private car to spare Elvis the stress of any further flying. The forty-eight-hour journey quickly became a royal progress.

Everywhere the train paused, even if it were just a whistle stop in the middle of the night, jubilant crowds appeared to salute their King's return from exile. Elvis would appear on the coach's "back porch," attired in his stunning dress blues, three stripes and a rocker on his sleeve, smiling and waving like a war hero. When the train pulled out of the station, the Colonel would start tossing photos and flyers at the crowd.

Elvis's arrival at Memphis's Union Station was tumultuous. Under heavy police escort he was conveyed to Graceland. When he stepped through the door and embraced Dodger, his happiness was complete. Nothing had changed. Everything would be as it had been before. He was still the King. If any doubts remained about his status with the public, they were wiped out in the first week.

One million orders were received for Elvis's first new record—even before he could set foot in the studio. On top of this million-dollar blank check, Elvis received the unheard-of fee of $125,000 from Frank Sinatra for a guest shot on the Timex special. Imagine receiving $125,000 (worth three times that amount today) for singing two songs! *LIFE*, which had pilloried Elvis in 1956, offered now to plaster his picture across its glossy cover. Colonel Parker had the gall to ask for $25,000—offering to refund the money if *LIFE*'s newsstand sale that week did not increase thirty-five percent. *LIFE* was so outraged that it canceled Elvis's picture for the cover. Meantime, Hal Wallis was urging Elvis to leave at once for Hollywood to start work on his new picture, which was already in production. RCA was equally insistent that its greatest star do nothing before he filled up the "can."

The overwhelming demand for Elvis was not simply a product of his long absence from the scene. It was also an expression of the desperately imperiled state of his kingdom. During the years when he was in the army, rock 'n' roll had fallen on evil days. The original power of the music, derived from the great tradition of R & B, had been frittered away in the adaptation of black adult experience to white teenage innocence. In the mouths of Elvis travesties, like Frankie Avalon and Fabian, the stars of

American Bandstand, rock had swiftly been reduced to rubbish.

At the same time that the teen twerps were taking over, the real rockers, the young men of talent, were being wiped out in an extraordinary plague of disgraces and disasters. Rock had established all-time records for unwarranted success; now it set comparable standards for undeserved misfortune. Buddy Holly, Richie Valens and the Big Bopper perished in a plane crash. Little Richard ran up such an enormous bill with the IRS that he was forced to take refuge, first in the ministry and then in Europe. Chuck Berry was indicted (later convicted and imprisoned) for a violation of the Mann Act. Jerry Lee Lewis's burgeoning career was blighted by scandal. Carl Perkins never recovered his momentum after cracking up with his band on the road to the *Ed Sullivan Show.* Eddie Cochran was killed in a cab crash in London that permanently crippled Gene Vincent.

As if all this weren't enough, in November 1959 commenced the climactic disaster—the payola scandal. The first shock was felt one afternoon that month, when Alan Freed came on the air sobbing, right in the middle of "Shimmy Shimmy Ko-Ko-Bop" by Little Anthony and the Imperials. In the voice of a dying man, he announced that as of that moment he was resigning from WABC. Swiftly, it was revealed that he had refused to sign a statement declaring that he had never taken money to plug records. Two days later, on his *Big Beat* TV show, he took his final farewell of the New York public, leaving the kids in tears and inspiring one girl to cry at the camera—"Now, they've taken away our father!"

Overnight, the atmosphere of the music business changed from the cheerful uproar of Tin Pan Alley to the eerie silence of an abandoned boom town. "No longer are the lobbies of the Brill Building thronged with businessmen, wildly ecstatic over a newly recorded song or newly released disc," wrote a trade reporter. "The crowd that used to stand in front of the Turf and Dempsey's or Hanson's Drugstore has faded away. Disc jockeys cannot be reached by phone, distributors are out of town, A & R men are suddenly vacationing, and many record company officials

answer their phones in soft, whispering voices." Suddenly,
the Big Beat had become the Big Stink.

At the very moment of Elvis's return, a congressional
investigative committee, fresh from hearing how Charles
Lincoln Van Doren had repeatedly deceived the public on
the *$64,000 Question*, was now learning that RCA dis-
tributors wrote checks to DJs with the name of the record
to be plugged on the check, that Morris Levy of Roulette
Records held two unpaid mortgages in the name of Alan
Freed and that Dick Clark, a twenty-nine-year-old DJ
from Philadelphia, held an interest in thirty-three record
and publishing firms which provided him with an income
of $500,000 a year. Under orders from Mr. Clean over at
the White House (whose closest aide, Sherman Adams,
had received a vicuna coat, electric appliances and a very
expensive business trip from Bernard Goldfine, a Boston
businessman) to "clean up the mess," the committee had
jolted the whole country with its revelations of corruption
in the music and broadcasting industries. (The industries
defended themselves with more honesty than brains by
asserting that one of their oldest traditions was "pay for
play.") Rock 'n' roll, long the target of parental rage, the
fury of the old pops establishment and the public press,
was now hanging on the ropes, waiting for the knockout.

The final defeat of the old rock was produced not by its
political opponents but by a hard-punching young black
contender called the Twist. With the advent of Hank Bal-
lard, Chubby Checker, the Peppermint Lounge and the
Philadelphia Sound, American popular music, that part
of it at least that was alive and happening, suddenly
jumped into a new groove called soul. As the disillusioned
white teenagers mourned the demise of their heroes, the
rest of the country put an invisible hula hoop around its
hips and merrily shook its ass.

Elvis Presley, that cat's whisker on the crystal of popular consciousness, was quick to pick up the S.O.S. from
the sinking ship. He was just as quick to make off in the
opposite direction from the wreck. His first recording session, thrown together on the spur of the moment to capitalize on the enormous excitement produced by his return,
does look backward at the days of do-wop. Its only hit, a

scratch single, "Stuck on You," sticks a hook reminiscent of "I'm All Shook Up" into the mouth of a black gospel drone, a contrivance just good enough to ring the Pavlovian bell and send the schlocky tune to the top of the charts. With his second session, however, at the new Studio B at Nashville, a landmark event, running all night long from the evening of April 4 to the following afternoon, Elvis revealed his new course bearings.

The two great hits that came out this session, "It's Now or Never," which sold nine million copies, and "Are You Lonesome Tonight?," which sold a mere five million, were both unabashed, middle-of-the-road, lily-white pops. Elvis vocalized these tunes, as he did almost everything in this extraordinarily eclectic session, as a crooner. His voice has a honeyed mellowness and even in some of the songs an effeminate softness and sensitivity. He caresses the phrases of the romantic tunes with a tremulous-lipped intimacy that is the vocal equivalent of bedroom eyes. These famous hits prophesied the Presley movies of the sixties. "It's Now or Never," a Caribbean version of "O Solo Mio," embellished with exotic castanets, mandolin twitters and a rhumba rhythm, summons up perfectly the atmosphere of all those tropical resort milieus in which Elvis was destined to star in the succeeding decade. Not only a symbol of the abrupt volte-face which Elvis executes at this time in his career, the song declares the direction in which he is soon to head.

The ringing high A with which this Neapolitan classic ended demonstrated another important feature of the new Elvis: His voice had finally matured. Always a singer of unusual vocal endowments for the pop market, Elvis now revealed himself in possession of an instrument with an enormous range of two and a third octaves, extending from the baritone's low G to the tenor's high B. Though he never mastered completely the knack of moving smoothly through the "channel" from the low chest tones to the high head tones, he demonstrated a great improvement upon his early records, which, as in a song like, "I Want You, I Need You, I Love You," sound sometimes like the product of two distinctly different voices: one a strong dark baritone, the other a high nasal country tenor. From this time

forth, the vocal inadequacies that marred the early ballads
will vanish, and Elvis Presley will take his position in the
long tradition of romantic crooners, commencing with
Russ Colombo and Rudy Vallee and leading down through
Bing Crosby and Frank Sinatra to, on one side, the white
epigones of the "Groaner" and the "Voice," Dean Martin,
Perry Como *et al.*, and on the other, the "sepia" side, Billy
Eckstine, Roy Hamilton, Arthur Prysock and Brook Benton—the latter four Elvis's very special favorites.

Having now aligned himself with traditional pops, an
identification that was enforced further when he appeared
on television with Frank Sinatra looking, in his Miami
Beach tuxedo, like a candidate for the Rat Pack, Elvis
retired from the stage and exchanged his identity as the
King of Rock 'n' Roll for that of an old-fashioned Hollywood
juvenile. One would think, reading most accounts of this
astonishing about-face, that nothing was more common in
show business than for enormously successful superstars
to abandon at the height of their popularity the image,
the medium and the act which made them rich and famous
to go off in search of a fresh career. Elvis's commitment
to the movies was nothing new, of course; the question is:
Why, having found a way to combine a successful career
in film with an even more successful career as a stage
performer, TV attraction and recording artist, did he sacrifice all these mutually reinforcing activities to the one
for which he was least gifted?

Clearly, he grossly overestimated the importance of
being a movie star and grossly underestimated the power
of rock 'n' roll to endure and revive. (Or was it a case of
scorning that at which one excels and envying what is
beyond one?) Whatever Elvis's motives in making this
false step, they could not have carried him far if they had
not been reinforced by Colonel Parker, who dictated that
Elvis concentrate entirely on films to the exclusion of every
other sort of activity.

The Colonel appears to have arrived at this decision
after prolonged discussions, during the years when Elvis
was out of the country, with his Hollywood cronies, Hal
Wallis and Abe Lastfogel, president of William Morris.
These three showbiz veterans worked out between them

a comprehensive strategy for exploiting Elvis when he got out of the service. Their basic goal was to widen his appeal by making him over into the image of a latter-day Bing Crosby, a good-looking, charming crooner with a flair for comedy. They were inspired partly by the fear that Elvis's public was too narrow and his stance too controversial; partly by the opportunity, which was offered by his military service, to make a fresh start with a clean, wholesome image.

Colonel Parker was attracted to the plan not only because it promised to make Elvis a major movie star but because it offered a means for rigidly controlling his star's public exposure. The plan was as mechanical as clockwork. Three times a year, at Christmas, Easter and during summer vacation, Elvis would be made available to his fans. Each motion picture would spin off a soundtrack album and each album would yield a hit title song. The title song would become a vital part of the ballyhoo for the picture and inspire DJs to play other cuts from the album. All three components of the package would reinforce each other. Then, when the product had been exploited to the limit, there would be a total blackout of Elvis in all media. The fans, deprived of their hero, would start to build up fresh expectations, which would be gratified when the whole process was repeated four months later.

Everybody stood to make a lot of money from this system. Abe Lastfogel's agency would take a flat ten percent off the top for negotiating on Elvis's behalf and drumming up new customers. The Colonel would take his customary twenty-five percent of Elvis's gross income plus whatever he could hustle for himself as technical director, publicity consultant or supervisor of security. Hal Wallis, the principal but by no means the only moviemaker, would obtain an easily marketable and relatively inexpensive supply of pictures.

Elvis Presley films were budgeted generally so that fifty percent of the budget was allotted to Elvis's salary. If Elvis received seven hundred fifty thousand dollars, the total cost would be one and a half million dollars. Assuming that profitability commences when the producer has recouped twice the cost of the negative, everything over three million dollars would be gravy. A successful Presley picture earned about five million dollars, a not-so-successful film about four million dollars. As everything moved swiftly, the filmmaker could earn one to two million dollars in the space of a year. What's more, a really clever producer like Wallis could use a Presley picture in a cross-collateralization deal, a financing device that Wallis may not have invented but which he certainly pioneered.

Elvis was "bankable," which meant that you could take his commitment to make your cheap-shot, teeny-weenie-bikini beach-party movie to the bank and use it as collateral to raise the enormous sum required to make a major motion picture that could win you an Academy Award. Cross-collateralization enabled Wallis in 1964, for example, to bank the shlocky *Roustabout* into his last great picture, *Becket.* As the famous (and enormously wealthy) producer remarked in 1969, when the game was up: "The Presley pictures were made, of course, for strictly commercial reasons." Hal Wallis never had any delusions about Elvis Presley's value in motion pictures. He looked at the meat and stamped it "commercial."

There was, unfortunately, one slight drawback to this otherwise perfect scheme. It assumed that Elvis Presley was like Kickapoo Joy Juice, one of those alcohol-laced tonics that could be bottled and peddled in any manner that was most convenient. All the medicine man had to worry about was doling out the product so that each bottle had its full effect but not so great a kick as to diminish the demand for the next bottle. What those mighty minds, Tom Parker, Hal Wallis and Abe Lastfogel, lost sight of was the obvious fact that Elvis drew his extraordinary power as a star (and his immense draw at the box office) from the fact that he was the King of Rock 'n' Roll, the emotional focus of seventeen million teen minds in America alone and as many more in the rest of the world. Take him off his throne, deprive him of his essential image, remove him from living contact with his people and their world and reduce him to the level of a traditional Hollywood musical comedy star—and what did you have? Just another version of those Tads and Tabs, Rocks and Rickys, who were the dying Hollywood's notion of where kids were at in the sixties.

It can be argued that the picture pundits proved their point by grinding out twenty-five Presley films in one decade, all of which made money. But the challenge was how to make the money without destroying the property. When the picture people got through with Elvis Presley in the late sixties, he was the laughingstock of the entertainment industry. What's more, the rockers who did not desert the sinking ship soon found that the vessel had been transformed into an immense transatlantic steamer that plied back and forth from England to America with a whole new crew of musicians to replace those who had been lost in the fifties. Soon the new "rock" was a vastly bigger and more profitable business than anything ever dreamed of in the days of rock 'n' roll. The opportunity that Elvis would not abide was seized by other performers, who eventually broke all of Elvis's records and made him seem like some old father figure lost in the mists of the past.

Elvis's first postarmy picture, *G.I. Blues,* launched the campaign on behalf of the new, "mature" Elvis Presley by producing the greatest anticlimax of his entire career. Millions of kids had waited for many months to witness the first full-length performance by Elvis since *King Creole.* Finally, the moment had come. They poured into six thousand theaters across America and what did they see? A creaky old service musical of the sort that was ground out while the movie industry marked time during World War II. The story was trivial, the characters cardboard, the music corny military call-and-response routines. The most terrible disappointment was Elvis. The famous sideburns had been shaved off. The classic D.A. shorn to regulation length and covered with a garrison cap. The bop clothes, the hoody windbreaker, the blue suede shoes—all gone! With them went Elvis's face. Instead of the Novocaine lip, the pale, poached skin, the heavy-lidded, kohl-eyed look, the Presley phiz was now as straight and square as that of Ken, the Barbie Doll.

So keen was Hal Wallis on domesticating the Hillbilly Cat and making him "family" that he undercut the movie's wheezy old plot, about a bet made by two G.I.s to see who

can score first with a sexy nightclub dancer, by presenting
Elvis—whom the story requires to be a lady-killer—in a
Dagwood Bumsted routine with a bawling baby and, in
another bit, singing with wide-eyed innocence a cutesy
Bavarian folk song behind a puppet show. No mere soft-
ening of the Presley image, *G.I. Blues* turned Elvis inside-
out and upside-down. It also turned him off.

Elvis didn't go down without a fight. He disliked *G.I.
Blues* and put the heat on Colonel Parker, who was dick-
ering again with Twentieth Century-Fox, to get him better
parts, a serious role. Elvis's keenest wish in Hollywood
was always to be given a chance to prove himself in a
dramatic film in which he sang no songs and strummed
no guitars and demonstrated that through sheer force of
his soul and talent he could thrill a movie audience the
way he thrilled a concert audience. In *Flaming Star*, his
second film after his return from the service, he got the
chance he had been seeking.

Cast as the half-breed son of a white rancher and an
Indian woman, Elvis returned to that legendary world of
nineteenth-century America in which he had made his
movie debut. He got to play tense confrontational scenes,
shoot guns, suffer wounds, ride horses and explore the
whole western macho movie ethos. He certainly looked
the part. He even brought off some of the early scenes,
especially where he is seen guarding his Indian mother
from the marauding local ranchers. As the action gets
heavier and more violent, however, the artificiality of his
performance becomes increasingly obvious (just as it does
in *Love Me Tender*) until, eventually, Elvis and the picture
collapse in a jumble of silly clichés.

This largely unconvincing and tediously plotted western was followed by *Wild in the Country*—a picture that
seems to have been compounded (by the washed-up Clif-
ford Odets) of reminiscences of Tennessee Williams and
Peyton Place. Elvis's part, that of a sullen, sexy, southern
youth being driven to violence—though destined for final
salvation—derives very clearly from *King Creole*. What
makes the film interesting at moments is the appearance
in it of the young Tuesday Weld, who plays a sluttish
unwed mother living with her conniving father and con-

stantly inviting the brutal advances of that smoldering young stud, Elvis. Menacing sullenness, overbearing arrogance—these are notes that Elvis could strike convincingly on the screen because they were characteristic of his true personality. The subtle balance, however, by which a good actor could sound these repellent notes and at the same time retain the audience's sympathy was something that Elvis never mastered. Either he looks and acts ugly, producing a feeling of disgust; or else he is not convincing as a heavy and you don't take him seriously.

These two pictures mark the end, for all practical purposes, of Elvis's career as a serious film actor. Neither film received the sort of notices that would have encouraged Elvis in his acting ambitions; more importantly, neither picture made much money. At this point, Colonel Parker, Hal Wallis and Abe Lastfogel could say to Elvis: "I told you so." Henceforth, Elvis was confined to lighthearted musical comedies, commencing with his most commercially successful film: *Blue Hawaii.*

Concocted by the same team of Hal Wallis and Hal Kanter that had produced Elvis's best movie, *Loving You, Blue Hawaii* demonstrates the complete lack of respect for Elvis that had now become characteristic of his Hollywood manipulators. The picture completes the job, well begun by *G.I. Blues,* of metamorphosing Elvis the Pelvis into Elvis the Putz.

Taking up the story of Elvis after he gets out of the army, the picture offers us a characterless young man with two very vivid parents: a Mai Tai-drinking pineapple planter and his kooky southern-belle wife, played with a caricatured accent by Angela Lansbury. The rebellion of that once dangerous insurrectionary, Elvis Presley, has been muted now to cranky reluctance to follow in his father's footsteps. Instead of planting pineapples, Elvis (who never learned to swim) plays at being a beach boy, displaying a disappointing physique—flat chest, skinny legs, weak arms—and no apparent familiarity with water sports. His girlfriend is the handsome but maternal Joan Blackman, to whom he relates like a college boy to his older, married sister.

The picture's only complication is provided by a sulky

and sassy teenage girl, one of a party of four which Elvis is guiding about the islands. When this naughty creature throws herself at Elvis in her nighty, he turns her firmly across his knee and gives her a good parental spanking. Having proven his maturity by punishing a girl similar to his former fans, he now completes the rites of conformity by getting married. The wedding is represented in an almost hieratic ceremony in which Elvis and his bride, mounted like human effigies on a barge, are conveyed with preternatural smoothness across a lagoon to a quaint old missionary chapel. The symbolism of the once wild, exotic and rebellious Pelvis frozen into the immobility of a figure atop a wedding cake and conveyed like a glazed-eye somnambulist toward the altar was one that profoundly gratified the drive-in crowd. The picture grossed many millions.

Marco Millions would have been the most appropriate property for Elvis in the sixties. Once Elizabeth Taylor had established the benchmark of the million-dollar salary with *Cleopatra,* the Colonel could not rest until he had found a way to raise his boy's price to this mystic number. Eventually, he succeeded. In Elvis's palmiest years, his price was one million dollars against a sizable percentage of the producer's profit. By the midsixties, Elvis Presley was the highest-paid actor in Hollywood.

What wasn't revealed was the fact that Elvis had to surrender half of this money to the government in taxes. The Colonel never permitted his boy to employ any sort of tax shelter. In fact, the only advice on taxation which the Colonel offered took the form of holding up before Elvis's anxious gaze all those poor devils, like Joe Louis, who had once been big stars but, who through failure to pay their taxes, had come to grief. Elvis was glad to pay when he heard what happened to you when you tried to beat Uncle Sam.

After the great success of *Blue Hawaii,* the Hollywood moviemakers demanded that Elvis appear henceforth in pictures concocted to a fixed formula. The Presley picture soon became one of Hollywood's most stereotyped products: the entertainment world's equivalent of a franchise hamburger. Like the burger, the picture looked big and ap-

petizing—until you got into it. Then, you realized that it
was totally synthetic, devoid of any genuine satisfaction.
Compounded with mechanical precision out of the same
invariable ingredients, prepared with astonishing rapid-
ity, sold for a good price but actually scrimped in the making and aimed at a totally indiscriminate public, the product got steadily worse over the years until its grand and
total effect was sheer nausea.

The prime ingredients of this beefcake formula were
Elvis, a famous vacation resort and a bevy of good-looking
girls led by some young "sex kitten" whose career was just
beginning and whose price was rock bottom. The story
lines, some of which were old, like *Kid Galahad,* some
new, were stupefyingly similar. Elvis was always cast as
a handsome young stranger of working-class status who
has just blown into town and stumbled over the most incredible looking collection of girls. His identity as a racing
driver, a sailing captain, a helicopter pilot, a deep-sea diver,
a boxer, an acrobat, a photographer, a roustabout, a ranch
hand, gambler, etc. was simply a matter of the costume
he wore. His silicone-cheeked face, his tooth-capped smile,
his helmet of shiny jet-black hair ("five inches of hot-but-
tered yak wool": *Time*) varied no more than does the head
on a display window dummy. Though Elvis spoke lines,
threw punches, and did a lot of driving in these pictures,
his basic identity was that of a dummy.

In the movies, Elvis always displays an "attitude." He's
aloof or annoyed, impudent or sarcastic; he walks around
with a chip on his shoulder. These adolescent postures are
reflected by the girl, who is bitchy and standoffish, ostentatiously indifferent to his appeal. The whole first part of
the picture is always devoted to their huffs and sneers, as
they trade put-downs or toss curtain lines over their shoulders. What brings her around eventually is simply the fact
that she is the weaker of the two: not the weaker person
but the weaker sex. The attitude toward women in Presley
pictures is extremely condescending. The assumption is
that the only thing women have on their minds is men.
If they reject a man, he need not take the rejection seriously because it is simply a sign that the woman is playing

hard to get. Elvis is a cool customer who jives along, confident that he'll come up a winner in the last reel.

As the new morality of the Swinging Sixties began to soak down to the grass-roots level, the moviemakers began to insinuate first a little and then a lot of dirt into these pictures. The girls now wear bathing suits that reveal their nipples and creases; they talk in double entendres and pose provocatively. Eventually, the movies became soft-core pornography played, like an old burlesque routine, with a very dead pan. Elvis's entrance in *Tickle Me* is a classic of the genre. Carrying his saddle to the bunkhouse of a dude ranch, he stumbles (literally, with a big pratfall) over a group of yummy young things exercising in short shorts. The camera ogles their leader so that both Elvis and the audience view her from behind and between her legs.

Perhaps the most preposterous feature of all these pictures is the way their hero constantly bursts into song in the most unlikely places. The flat, banal tone, the travel brochure settings, the obvious effort to create an illusion of verisimilitude subverted completely the conventions of musical comedy. As for the quality of the music, it matched perfectly the level of the movies, both combining to plumb below the level of pop culture to what might be called pap culture.

Blue Hawaii is the best of the postarmy Presley film scores; of the worst, one is not obliged to speak, if only out of respect for the dead. Elvis's Brill Building writers, it should be borne in mind, were not accustomed to composing for dramatic situations, as were the famous songwriters of the thirties and forties, who had grown up in the New York theater. The only man who could consistently contrive something that would work in the absurd situations offered by the scripts was an obscure tune tailor named Ben Weisman. Ever hear of Ben? No? Well, you're not alone. Nobody outside the business has ever heard of Ben Weisman. Yet this dude composed no less than *fifty-seven* songs for Elvis Presley. Imagine: Elvis Presley, the King of Rock 'n' Roll, at the peak of his life and career— and what does he do for ten years? He devotes himself to realizing with every nuance of style and soul the immortal songs of Ben Weisman!

In 1964 Colonel decreed that henceforth Elvis should record nothing but movie soundtrack albums. After all, there's no sense in competing with yourself! Elvis despised these songs and would often explode in the studio, crying: "What am I gonna do with this piece o' shit?" Eventually, he grew so dejected that he relinquished the last bit of control he held over his career, the supervision of his recording sessions, and bowed his neck to the same yoke borne by the paid-by-the-hour jingle-makers. He would allow the musicians to record the entire soundtrack; then, he'd go into the studio alone, put on the earphones and pour his voice like molasses over the trash that came pouring out of the "cans." Colonel Parker would take it from there.

Colonel's power increased in direct proportion to the decline in Elvis's power. Power was, in fact, the Colonel's ruling passion, not greed. Having obtained total control over Elvis Presley, it was no great trick for the Colonel to obtain extraordinary influence in all the big entertainment companies that were dependent on Elvis's enormous popularity. RCA Victor, for example, was an ailing and ill-managed company when it hired Elvis Presley. After failing to shove the "45" down the throat of the record-buying public, the company started losing ground rapidly to its competitors. Elvis stopped this retreat single-handedly and revived the company's fortunes. From 1956 to 1962, Elvis produced thirty-one of Victor's thirty-nine million selling singles. For ten years straight, he accounted for about twenty-five percent of the company's total business. Imagine what a man like Colonel Parker could do with this sort of leverage! He not only exploited his position to obtain extraordinary benefits for himself and his client, but he made damn sure that he would never have to share his power with any new rival.

Many students of rock music have puzzled over the fact that, having scored such an enormous success with Elvis Presley, RCA did not follow up this great coup by hiring many other rock acts. The usual explanation is that RCA, identified primarily with classical music, was just too

snooty to mess around with the likes of Buddy Holly or
Frankie Avalon. This is like saying that General Motors,
the manufacturer of the Cadillac, resented the success of
Chevrolet. The truth is that every time RCA would start
to show interest in another potentially competitive act,
Colonel Parker would threaten to deprive the company of
Elvis Presley. As no new star could possibly compensate
Victor for the loss of its greatest asset, the once-powerful
record maker had to limp through not only the fifties but
the *sixties* with only one other major rock act on its roster,
the Jefferson Airplane.

Colonel's success in bamboozling the record executives
was matched for a number of years by equal success in
bulldozing the movie companies. In the midsixties the
Colonel cut into the faltering MGM, negotiating a series
of deals that culminated with Elvis being put on salary
at the beginning of 1966 at the staggering sum of $75,000
a week. Needless to say, the more Colonel got for his boy,
the more he also got for himself.

One of the most frequently repeated of all Colonel Parker stories has a fifties TV executive offering Parker the
once awesome sum of $50,000 for a single appearance. The
Colonel's famous comeback is: "That'll do just fine for me,
but how much are you gonna give the boy?" It's a good bet
that none of the millions of people who have chuckled at
this bit of con-man repartee has ever grasped its true
meaning. What it confesses is that Colonel Parker always
expected to receive something for himself over and above
what he got as Elvis's representative. The Colonel's favorite action was "side action."

The most obvious thing he got at both Paramount and
MGM was a large suite of offices, which he decorated in
his inimitable manner and outfitted so that every day he
could enjoy lunch in an atmosphere reminiscent of the
carnival cookhouses of his youth. One large room of the
office was always equipped with a big table covered in
authentic old-timey oilcloth, a huge freezer-refrigerator
combination, an electric range (courtesy of RCA) and an
immense and continually restocked supply of the Colonel's
favorite foods donated by some well-wisher. As there was
never anything for the Colonel and his large staff (whose

salaries were paid by MGM, RCA, and William Morris) to do in the office, the Colonel drilled his "army," as he came to call them, in the arts of looking busy.

The moment the security officer announced the approach of a visitor, Colonel would sound the alarm. Instantly, the feet would come down off the desk tops, the letters to absent friends would be thrust in drawers, the phones would be raised for imaginary conversations and the men would start shuffling big stacks of quite meaningless papers. Colonel would press a button under his desk and activate a ticker-tape, which he would appear to examine with great concern, muttering like Billy Rose on a bad day, "Not good . . . not good!" When the visitor entered the office suite, he would be impressed by the extraordinary bustle of business.

The Colonel's favorite guest at lunch was Abe Lastfogel, the "Little Square Man," as he was once known, in allusion to his doll-like stature and his impeccable reputation for honesty in business dealings. One of the most powerful figures in the history of entertainment management, Lastfogel became the Colonel's most valuable ally in Hollywood. Lastfogel knew infinitely more about the picture business than did Parker, who had come to Hollywood knowing virtually nothing. Equally important was the fact that Lastfogel possessed that image of rabbinical respectability so precious to a man like the Colonel, who exuded from every pore the bad odor of the carny. With the well-connected Lastfogel initiating the deals and astutely conducting the negotiations, the Colonel was free to kibitz and direct the game from behind the scenes. The "Little Square Man," for his part, gained a lucrative account plus the pleasure of indulging his humor, which delighted in clever rogues. The price he paid was eating a lot of ham and pork.

As the years wore on and public tastes changed, Colonel didn't have to put on an act when he murmured, "Not good . . . not good!" The first sign of Elvis's diminishing popularity was the drop in his record sales. Colonel's solution was to rig the market. He got RCA to apply pressure to its distributors and dealers to preorder each new Presley record in huge quantities. When a million orders had been booked, the Colonel would signal the company to release the disc. RCA would announce that it was "shipping gold." A certificate would be granted. When the record failed to sell, the merchants would quietly exercise their right to unlimited returns. Then it would be the stores' turn to ship gold, fool's gold, back to the fools who mined it.

When the movie business began to decline, Colonel had no such simple device for maintaining the illusion upon which Elvis's fame depended. At best he was able to counter arguments that the general public had lost interest in Elvis by pointing out that Elvis had a hardcore following of two hundred fifty thousand fans who saw every Presley picture three times, thus assuring a minimum paid attendance of seven hundred fifty thousand persons.

Elvis had, as everyone knows, the most devoted fans in the history of show business. Once he cleaned up his act, he lost a lot of the kids, but he gained in their stead great numbers of middle-aged matrons and even old grannies, who murmured reflexively at every mention of his name: "He was so good to his mother." Mother's Day became, in fact, one of the major festivals of the Presley cult, marked generally by a radio promotion featuring Elvis singing hymns.

The most interesting aspect of the fans' behavior was the instinctive manner in which they indemnified themselves for the loss of the King's living—as opposed to his "canned"—presence. Like the loyal followers of an exiled ruler or holy man, the fans built in their homes shrines to the King that were remarkably similar to the shrines to the emperor once found in every Japanese house. One wall or sometimes one whole room would be converted into a domestic chapel, more or less elaborately decorated with devotional pictures, books, relics, mementoes and symbols of the cult. By playing Elvis's records and concentrating on his familiar image, a really devout fan could achieve an effect of communion with his King that was no different essentially from that of a religious person meditating on his god.

Such passive contemplation, however, was never enough for the Elvis zealots. They demanded a more vigorous and

physical form of worship, which was first brought to perfection by the greatest of all the Presley organizations:
Britain's Official Elvis Presley Fan Club. Once a year, this
group, virtually none of whose members had ever seen
Elvis in the flesh, would have a big jamboree at which
many of the members would appear onstage to give their
impressions of Elvis (thereby anticipating by many years
the race of Elvis impersonators who sprang up when the
hero died). Clearly, when the King is away, the cats will
play—at being the King.

To maintain the profitability of the Presley movies in
the face of declining box office receipts, ever more drastic
cost cutting became necessary. The Colonel worked tire-
lessly to get the resort hotels and the local tourist bureaus
to pick up the tab for the location shooting. Film directors
were superseded by TV directors because the latter could
work faster. When Hal Wallis indicated he had had enough
of Elvis, the Colonel took up with Sam Katzman, "The
King of the Quickies": a man with a genius for low-budget,
low-mentality movies. Eventually, the shooting time for
an Elvis Presley feature was reduced to seventeen days.

As Elvis saw his dream of becoming a great movie star
turn into the nightmare of grinding out three horrible
pictures a year, he became bitter, cynical and estranged.
The aura of acrimony that envelops him in these films,
which comes off him like body odor, was really the leakage
of rage and self-hatred produced by the ordeal of appearing
in what he called "my latest travelogue."

Chapter 23

The Fun Years

WHEN ELVIS PRESLEY returned to America after his years in the army, he was a changed man. His mother's death, his father's remarriage, his own sufferings in the service, as well as the prolonged interruption of his career and his anxiety about its revival, had eroded the great self-confidence he displayed in his early years. His first TV appearances, particularly his queer showing on *Frank Sinatra's Welcome Home Party for Elvis Presley,* testify to the change in the man that underlay the change in the image.

The first signal that something important had happened to Elvis was sexual. The Elvis who had appeared on the Dorsey, Berle and Sullivan shows, who had starred in *Loving You* and *Jailhouse Rock,* was butch. He had a chunky, clunky aura as he stood four-square before the camera and blasted out his soul with total indifference to public opinion. Even his legendary shyness, cunningly exploited in those scenes in *Loving You* in which he plays opposite the sophisticatedly sexy Lizabeth Scott (who has a wonderful time toying with this *enfant terrible,* alternately seducing and mocking him), comes across as a kind of strength, the coiled-up power of a boy whose manner warns: "Don't get me started or you'll be sorry!"

After the army, Elvis appears very delicate and vulnerable, as if he were recovering from major surgery. He wrings his hands as he talks. He has become extremely wary. With his preposterous Little Richard conk, his limp wrist, girlish grin and wobbly knees, which now turn out instead of in, he looks outrageously gay. When he confronts the much smaller but more masculine Sinatra, Elvis's body language flashes, "I surrender, dear."

Nor is this sudden loss of his former virility merely a deceiving appearance: It is paralleled by many more significant changes in Elvis's manner of conducting his life and career. Instead of partying with his peers, the young actors and actresses of the Jimmy Dean clique, Elvis locks himself up now in a house with six stooges and never goes out to play. Instead of falling in love with a beautiful film star, he herds hundreds of anonymous groupies through his bedroom. Instead of being basically a sympathetic character with some ugly traits, he becomes an arrogant punk who closely resembles the character he portrayed in *Jailhouse Rock*. As for his career, he abandons all control over it and submits himself completely to the machinations of Colonel Parker and his cronies in Hollywood. All these changes attest to a profound metamorphosis in the character of Elvis Presley. Though they first become manifest when he is discharged from the service, we must search for their source in that deadly wound Elvis suffered when his mother died.

Gladys was as much the source of Elvis's self-confidence as she was the cause of his extreme dependency. She was also his only confidante and his moral governor. Once Gladys died, Elvis found himself desperately alone and naked. His first instinct was to retreat from the world and wall himself round with people who were devoted to him, body and soul. His second impulse was to drown his sorrows in an endless round of parties and games that would keep him perpetually distracted from his real state of mind. His ultimate resolution was the most fateful: It was to sever the link between his past and present by totally inverting the relations between his life and his image. Instead of being an innocent and naive kid who impersonated publicly a wild and orgiastic figure, Elvis would now play in public the All-American Boy, while off camera he indulged himself in an endless debauch of sex and drugs.

The inception of Elvis's new life-style was a two-week furlough that he took in the summer of 1959 in Paris with several of his boys. Settling down at the posh Hotel Prince de Galles, he swiftly discovered an old-time nightclub on the Champs Elysées called the Lido, which had a chorus line bearing the lengendary title, The Bluebelle Girls; in other words, the descendants of those turn-of-the-century chorus girls who had swarmed over the original Prince de Galles or Prince of Wales, the future Edward VII. Elvis, wearing for the first time his elegant dress blues and looking like a latter-day version of the Student Prince, instinctively fell into the pattern of his renowned and royal predecessor. Every night he ate dinner at the club; then, after the first show, he swept up the entire chorus line and carried it back to his hotel, where they partied extravagantly, until the phone would ring and the manager of the club would beg Elvis to return the girls so that the supper show could commence. Elvis would witness that show as well and afterward return to his suite with the girls, with whom he toyed till dawn.

When Elvis returned to Hollywood, he showed no sign at first of adopting this orgiastic pattern so close to home. He was still a little inhibited, still exhibiting traces of his mother's morality. Then, one night, a random occurrence initiated a chain of events that concluded with Elvis finding himself once again in a position to indulge his appetite for orgiastic parties. The decisive event was being asked to leave the Beverly Wilshire Hotel for precisely the same reasons that had led to Elvis's expulsions from hotels in Germany: extreme rowdiness.

On this particular night Elvis and the Guys were involved in one of those childish games in which he spent so much of his spare time in the early years: a water battle with squirt guns. What made the battle characteristic of Elvis was the violence with which he drove it, that innate violence that always made him take everything to the limits and beyond, never feeling that he had had enough of any game until limbs broke and blood flowed and screams of pain accompanied the pleasure.

First, one of the boys had slipped on the wet kitchen
floor and gashed himself deeply on a broken bottle. Then,
Red, Joe and Sonny grabbed Elvis and threw him on the
floor. As Sonny held Elvis's legs and Joe his midriff, Red
rubbed his palm back and forth over Elvis's nose, driving
him completely crazy. When he had brought Elvis to the
ultimate peak of rage, Red shouted, "Let go!" At that moment, Red and Sonny leaped up and ran for their lives.
Joe, seeking to do the same, slipped and fell on the floor.
Instantly, Elvis was on top of him, kicking him like a log
as he rolled across the floor. Then, Elvis seized a guitar
and, swinging it like an axe, hit Joe a stunning blow on
the elbow. Joe screamed in pain and lay there watching
his arm inflate like a balloon. Red and Sonny, who had
circled back, realized now that the fight had gotten out of
hand. They made a dash through a fire escape door and
took off down the hall with Elvis in hot pursuit. When
Elvis saw he couldn't catch up, he threw the guitar with
all his might after the fleeing figures.

At that moment, an elderly lady who lived on the floor
opened her door. Just as she was about to step out into the
hall—whoosh!—a guitar flew by her nose, almost hitting
her. Jumping back, she slammed the door and picked up
the phone to call the manager. A few minutes later this
worthy was upstairs demanding to know what was going
on and inspecting with a horror-struck countenance the
damage to the rooms. Next day, Elvis and his boys were
asked to leave.

The Colonel decided at this point that it didn't make
sense to confine these rambunctious boys to a hotel. They
needed more space to stretch out—and they needed to be
kept away from the little old ladies of this world. The
solution to the problem was obviously a good-sized private
house in some secluded spot. A short search turned up a
unique residence in Bel Air that had formerly belonged
to Ali Khan. It was a doughnut-shaped structure, ringed
around a fifty-foot patio edged with shrubbery. Situated
on the side of a winding hillside road called Perugia Way,
the house overlooks the greens of the Bel Air Country
Club. Carpeted with thick white shag, filled with expensive California-style furnishings and staffed by a black

cook and houseman, this flying saucer was the perfect playpen for a wealthy young playboy. Soon it became legendary as the headquarters of the Memphis Mafia, the most intently partying group of bachelors in the history of Hollywood.

The Presley parties are invariably depicted as tedious get-togethers whose only singularity lay in the disproportion of men to women. Though literally thousands of young women were guests at these parties over the years, those who got beyond the formalities would not have been eager to recount their adventures for the benefit of the press. Nor would any reporter or editor who valued his job in Hollywood have been willing to publish such scandalous tales. Though one hears a great deal about the outrageous violations of privacy suffered by the stars, if we are to judge by the example of Elvis Presley, in his day one of Hollywood's greatest stars—and one about whose private life curiosity reached unprecedented proportions—there are few limits to what a celebrity can do and escape exposure in the film colony.

The parties, which swiftly became the focal point of Elvis's life, would commence every night after supper, at about ten. The basic idea was to fill the house with attractive young women who had been especially selected to conform to Elvis's exacting criteria. Elvis's tastes in women were just as fixed and unvarying as his tastes in food. It was only natural that a man who could subsist for six months at a time on a steady diet of burnt bacon, mashed potatoes, sauerkraut and sliced tomatoes would want one and only one kind of girl. The interesting question is: What is the female equivalent of the aforesaid diet?

Elvis liked small, kittenish girls who were built to his ideal proportions. They were to be no higher than five feet two and weigh no more than one hundred ten pounds. The prime areas of erotic interest were the ass and legs. Hair coloring, complexion, facial features were not important, though beauty was, naturally, desirable. What was critical was that the girls be as young as possible, certainly no older than eighteen, and that they be not too far removed from the condition of virginity. Married women were out of the question and a woman who had borne a child was

a complete turn-off for Elvis Presley. As for clothing, Elvis
liked to see a pretty girl dressed all in white. When she
undressed, he was hoping to see that she wore white un-
derpants. White panties were Elvis's erotic fetish.

All the Guys became at Elvis's urging quite accomplished procurers. Their readiest source of supply was the
studios where Elvis worked. Most Presley pictures had
party scenes that called for as many as a score of pretty
young girls. The moment the first call for such extras went
out, the Guys were busy among the applicants, like cooks
in the morning market, making their selections for the
Boss. After the studios, there were many other sources for
Presley chicks: talent agencies, nightclubs, theaters,
stores—Hollywood is full of pretty young girls, many of
whom will do anything to advance their careers. All one
of the boys had to do was mention that Elvis Presley was
having a party that night at his home in Bel Air and the
prey was winging toward the net.

Once the parties became an institution in Hollywood,
a lot of girls started trying to crash the gate. On a typical
evening, the whole street and the parking area before the
house would be swarming with scores of young women
who behaved very much like the crowd seeking admission
to a popular discotheque. Like the patrons of a disco, they
came in all sorts of costumes from simple cotton dresses
to sweater and pants outfits to stylish frocks topped with
fur jackets. Parking their cars along this once-quiet street,
they would stand, lean or sit all over the property, chattering and gossiping and looking each other over carefully.
The focus of everyone's attention was the heavy brown
door to the house, which was opened from time to time by
one of the boys, who would admit the girls he knew and
tell the others to "try later." As at Studio 54, the decision
as to how many and which girls to admit depended entirely
on the demands of the party going on inside the house.
Some of the more determined girls would remain standing
in front of the door until two in the morning.

Once a girl was admitted to the house, she would be
ushered about with great politeness by one of Elvis's man
mountains. Her first impression was invariably one of
great luxury and style. As you entered the house, for ex-

ample, you could look straight through the foyer to the
patio, which was romantically illuminated at night and
filled with the plashing of a fountain at its center, where
a statue emptied endless jugs from its shoulder. Sinking
into the deep-pile carpet and following her guide as he
turned to the left, she would enter first the living room,
which was dominated by a fireplace above which hung a
painting, actually a painted photograph, of Elvis, Gladys
and Vernon in front of Graceland. The next room around
the circle was the den; here the parties were always held.
Loud rock music would be playing from an illuminated
jukebox filled with Elvis's favorite records; a wet bar at
the far side of the room would be piled high with refresh-
ments suitable for a Sweet Sixteen party—soft drinks,
potato chips, pretzels, cookies—and in the middle of the
room a TV set, whose back was concealed by a folding
mirrored-glass screen, would be playing with its sound
turned off.

Facing the television, on a huge built-in sofa, the King
would be enthroned with his feet up on a cocktail table.
Flanked by a couple of his men and surrounded by a bevy
of young women, he would be watching TV. No matter
who arrived, even if she were the most famous or beautiful
star in Hollywood, Elvis would not rise to greet her. "Get
her coat...find out what she wants to drink." With such
bossman orders, Elvis would beckon Tuesday Weld, Joan
Blackman or Connie Stevens into the circle around him.

Elvis had a very sarcastic and vulgar sense of humor
that would emerge when he settled down at ease and removed the phony mask of southern gentlemanliness that
he wore in public. From years of listening to the local wits
in his hometown—that type of southern joker who responds to every situation with a proverbial line and a snap
of his extended fore- and midfinger—Elvis had developed
quite a patter of Memphis jive. As the aspiring young
extras and starlets sitting at his feet constantly looked
back and forth from the silent video screen to the immaculately groomed and carefully dressed star, they would be
treated to an endless stream of witticisms.

Watching Jerry Lewis caper on the screen, Elvis would
sneer and drawl: "That's about as funny as a turd in a

punch bowl." Or perhaps he'd say "as funny as a Smitty
on a hearse." (A Smitty was the Memphis name for a device
designed to make a teenager's motor roar.) Every time
Elvis got off one of these gags, the Guys would roar with
laughter. Their response would encourage Elvis to continue his bizarre commentary, which soon blurred into
what must have sounded to the girls like a code:

"He's stronger than Tarzan's armpits.... He's been
there since Hitler was a corporal.... He's wilder than a
peach orchard boar.... Tell 'em where the cow et the cabbage!... That cat's lower than a whale.... Cute as a bug's
ear.... So uptight you couldn't drive a straw up his ass
with a ten-pound sledge!" Watching two guys back off from
each other in a western, Elvis might crack: "He's scared
and the other's *glad* of it!" Or if someone said, "If only so
and so were to happen, then..." Elvis might retort scorn-
fully, "If my aunt had nuts, she'd be my uncle!" The moment the laugh died, the whole party would fall silent and
return to the basic activity, which was watching Elvis
watch TV.

As there were perhaps forty or fifty girls in the house
and only eight men, it would have been natural for the
Guys to start hitting on some of these chicks. This was a
practice that was sternly forbidden. Elvis considered any
such advances highly improper, an act of *lèse majesté,* until
he had exercised his prerogative to make the first choice.
Allowing Elvis what was called "the pick of the litter" was
an obligatory act of deference. To behave differently would
be to invite some terrible explosion.

Elvis's temper and his overbearing manner had gotten
much worse during his years in the army. The boys who
had known Elvis for long said that the army had made
him "mean." His ugly traits were greatly exaggerated by
the presence of women. When girls were around, Elvis felt
obliged to play the big shot, the boss. He would put one
of his little cigars in his mouth, his Hav-a-Tampa Jewels
or Rum Crooks, and hold it there a moment. If one of the
boys didn't jump up and give him a light, Elvis would
explode. "Goddamn it to hell! Am I gonna sit here all night
like this, or is one of you lardasses gonna gimme a light?"
That sort of behavior was supposed to impress the girls.

Elvis didn't stop at just being overbearing. Sometimes he would humiliate his men so grossly that even these faithful flunkies were compelled to rebel.

Sonny West recalls a night when Tuesday Weld came to visit Elvis, bringing along a very attractive friend named Kay. As Elvis and Tuesday got deep into conversation, Sonny started promoting Kay, while preparing a drink at the bar. In the middle of Sonny's pitch, Elvis pops up suddenly between them, stares provocatively at the girl and says admiringly, "You're really pretty!" Then, he flits off to continue talking to Tuesday. Sonny resumes his efforts to woo the young woman and is starting to make progress when Elvis appears again, gives the girl one of his patented heavy-lidded stares and murmurs, "My man!" Just as Sonny is recovering from this fresh intrusion, Elvis swings back for a third pass at the target. This time, he gives the girl a little peck. When she doesn't object, he kisses her firmly on the mouth. She kisses him back. Sonny gives up in disgust and retreats to the other side of the room, where Alan Fortas and Gene Smith are watching the scene.

"He's smooth as silk," rumbles the admiring Fortas. "Yeah, he shot me right outta the saddle," concedes Sonny. Gene leans in confidingly at this point and, nodding his head toward the two women, he says: "Sonny, if you had your pick, which would you take?" Sonny replies without hesitating, "Tuesday—she's got some body on her!"

Elvis, who is always scanning the room, spots Gene and Sonny with their heads together. Instantly, he assumes that they're bad-mouthing him. Jumping up and walking over to the boys, he says, "What the hell are you two whispering about?" Sonny is dumbfounded. He's too embarrassed to repeat the conversation. His confusion confirms Elvis in his conviction that he was the topic of conversation. "If you don't tell me," he warns Sonny, "you're in big trouble." Sonny, exasperated, hurt, angry, looks at Elvis and exclaims: "Man, you have *changed!* I *quit!*"

In a flash, Elvis grabs a Coke bottle. Sonny barks, "You're not gonna hit me with no goddamn bottle!" Elvis backs down and relinquishes the bottle, but he can't control his anger. The moment Sonny starts walking out of the room, Elvis plants himself in the big boy's path. "You're not quittin'," snarls Elvis, "'cause you're *fired!*" "Call it anything you want!" shouts Sonny. "I'm gettin' outta here!" Nobody could talk back to Elvis and get away with it. Flashing red, Elvis swings from the floor and hits Sonny squarely on the jaw.

If Elvis had been on a movie set, where he was always punching guys out, Sonny would have flown halfway across the room, smashed into a wall and come sliding down onto the floor like a stiff. Instead, he simply twisted his head with the blow and then turned back to stare at Elvis in shock and pain. As the tears started coming to his eyes, Sonny gasped: "I never thought you would hit me, Elvis!" Then, he turned and left the room.

It was the only time in Sonny's life that he didn't return a punch. If he had struck back, he would have knocked Elvis into the middle of next week. It never crossed Sonny's mind, though, to defend himself. Nobody ever hit Elvis. Though he abused them, humiliated them, hit them with his hands or kicked them with his feet or even drew weapons and threatened their lives, *nobody ever struck back at Elvis Presley.*

Sonny went to his room and packed. He called his girl and told her that he had quit his job. When he came to the front door, he found Elvis standing there alone. "You got any money, Sonny?" he asked. Sonny said he was okay. Elvis handed him a check, which he had had one of the boys draw. "Can one of the Guys take you someplace?" asked Elvis. "No, I called a cab," replied Sonny. When he pulled away from the house in the cab, Sonny saw Elvis standing in the doorway.

The other disaster that could ruin a party was a girl who dared to talk back or challenge the "Boss." Elvis had strict rules for feminine behavior. As long as women deferred to him, he was gallant to them. If, though, they "got down on his level," as the Guys put it, then Elvis was freed of the obligation to play the gentleman's role and was allowed to teach the girl her "lesson." One night, for example, the sophisticated daughter of a famous movie star came up to the house. Appalled, most likely, by the court of the Hillbilly King, she made the mistake of getting into

an argument with Elvis. Galvanized by a terrible flash of
rage, he leaped to his feet, seized the young woman by the
hair, dragged her stumbling head over heels across a marble coffee table and into the next room, where he planted
a very vigorous kick in her ass and ordered one of the boys
to throw her out in the street.

Another night, while he was entertaining a young actress, Elvis got so enraged at something she said that he
picked up a watermelon and threw it at her, hitting her
a mighty thump on the ass. Throwing things like a hysterical woman was one of Elvis's more dangerous habits.
One night, many years later, when he was having supper,
Joanie Esposito, Joe Esposito's wife, said something that
infuriated Elvis. Instinctively, he hurled the knife that
was in his hand straight at her face. If Sonny West hadn't
flung up his hand to block the knife, Elvis might have
knocked out one of Joanie's eyes.

In 1963, Elvis did inflict a disfiguring injury on a young
woman in this manner. She had demanded that one of the
boys playing pool with Elvis move his car so that she could
leave the party. Elvis was so enraged by the woman's
insistence that he hurled his pool cue at her, striking her
on the breast. The cue paralyzed a nerve in the breast,
causing it to sag permanently. The most interesting fact
about the story is that no compensation was offered the
woman and none was sought. As always, Elvis walked
away from his misdeed without any apology or desire to
make amends. As far as he was concerned, the fault was
all the woman's who had provoked him.

Assuming the party was not spoiled by some "fool" or
some "bitch," the final phase, about 2:00 A.M., after the
late movie, would consist of the "slipaway." Elvis would
finally rise and make his way past the bar to the adjoining
room, which was the master bedroom. This was the signal
for all the Guys to take off the wraps. Like beggars at a
royal feast, they were free now to enjoy the scraps. All the
girls who had been passed over by the boss were fair game.
If the boys could score, they carried their girls off to the
other bedrooms. If they were failures, as was poor Lamar
so often, they were delegated "night duty," which meant
they lay down fully clothed in the living room to snatch

some sleep before they were roused before dawn to carry home Elvis's girls.

"Girls" is the word because Elvis almost invariably retreated to his bedroom with two or three young women in tow. His preference for groups rather than for one-to-one encounters had hardened now into a habit. Most young men with such tastes are assumed to be prodigiously virile studs whose sexual appetites are so enormous that they cannot be satisfied by a single woman. This was certainly not the case with Elvis Presley. Generally speaking, he never had normal sexual relations with these girls. The reason? Elvis was a pervert, a voyeur.

What he sought as his erotic goal was a group of girls who would agree to strip down to their panties and wrestle with each other while Elvis stared out his eyes with a rocklike hard-on pressing up against his underwear. He accounted for this obsession by recalling an incident from his childhood: a moment when he had seen two little girls tumbling together on the ground with their dresses rising to show their crotches. In fact, with the fine focus characteristic of his kind, what Elvis described as his ultimate fulfillment was not the sight of the girls or even the crotch but the vision of black pubic hairs protruding around the edges of white panties. Out of all the sexual excitements in the world, this one teasing image represented the ultimate in arousal to Elvis Presley.

The panties were not just a tease, like the fan dancer's fan or the bubble-dancer's bubble. They were also a protective shield. Elvis could not tolerate the sight of a completely naked woman. If one of the gorgeous showgirls or actresses who filled his bed night after night were to disrobe completely in his presence, he would protest: "You have a beautiful body but I would feel better if you put something on." Elvis was just as loath to show his own body. As a rule no woman ever saw him undressed. His shyness focused on his penis, which he called "Little Elvis" and went to great lengths to hide. Instead of pissing in a urinal, for example, he would always go inside a stall, like a woman. He was not modest but ashamed. Like most country boys of his time, he was uncircumcised. A sensitive adolescent at heart, he saw his beauty disfigured by an ugly hillbilly pecker.

He complained also that when he engaged in intercourse, the foreskin, pulled back and forth in the grip of the vulva, would fray and tear, sometimes emerging bloody. There was an obvious solution to this vexing problem, but Elvis could not bear the thought of a knife cutting into Little Elvis. (Vernon was much braver. In his last years, when he became involved with a young woman, he submitted to the dread operation in the hopes of reviving his deadened dick. Perhaps that was what he meant when he once told Elvis: "You'll never be half the man your father was.")

In addition to being an orgiast and a voyeur, Elvis was also a lifelong masturbator. Every month one of the boys would be dispatched to those extended newsstands off Hollywood Boulevard to buy the boss all the latest "fuck books." The man might spend as much as forty dollars obtaining enough material to satisfy his master's appetites. Elvis would take a different magazine to bed with him every night and jerk off looking at the pictures.

If Elvis became sufficiently aroused by the spectacle of the girls wrestling, he might go down on a girl or dry hump her. Gene Smith recalls Elvis changing clothes after a date and looking like he sprayed his Jockey briefs full of whipped cream. If Elvis were feeling particularly daring, he might allow a girl to jack him off. One of the familiar tales of the Presley circle concerns the night Elvis went to bed with a famous Hollywood sex kitten. When this aggressive young woman—who had slept with half the men in the movie industry in the effort to advance her career and who had learned through that ordeal as much about men as any old hooker—divined where Elvis was at, she not only jerked him off with great skill but, when he ejaculated, she caught the semen in her hand and rubbed it all over her face like cold cream. Those two moves put Elvis completely in her hands.

If Elvis did have intercourse with an unfamiliar woman, he would never allow himself to ejaculate inside her. He was terrified of an unwanted pregnancy or a paternity suit—or so he averred. The Guys interpreted his anxiety

as the product of some episode in his early years, when
Elvis had gotten a girl pregnant. An exaggerated fear of
knocking a girl up, however, is also characteristic of young
men, especially adolescents, who suffer from sexual anxiety and are afflicted with other sexual problems, like premature ejaculation. Though Elvis Presley was always girl-
crazy, this obsession can sort very well in a young man
with a deep underlying fear of women, of marriage and of
begetting children: all signs of masculine maturity.

These sexual predilections explain also how it was possible to go through so many women without ever once
contracting venereal disease, the universal fate of the
swinger. That Elvis escaped all the dangers of the game
was owing not to good luck but to the most extraordinary
self-control: a lock-hold on his sexual behavior that must
have been powered by uncontrollable sexual phobias.

Looking at half-naked girls grappling with each other
or jerking off while ogling the centerfold of *Playboy* were
by no means the full extent of Elvis's voyeurism. As soon
as he moved into the house on Perugia Way, he made
provision for indulging his letch on the sly. He observed
that the closet of his bedroom had a common wall with
an adjacent bedroom. In the neighboring room, the wall
was lined with floor-to-ceiling bookcases. Elvis and the
boys removed a portion of the wall between the shelves
and installed in the space a two way mirror. Now, they
were in a position to view everything that happened in
the bedroom from a secure location in the closet. The
only problem was that normally nothing was happening
in this room. Elvis quickly solved this problem by ordering a couple of the boys to get girls into the room and
have intercourse with them while he watched with the
other Guys.

This sport had only one danger: With so many guys
crowded in the closet chortling and whispering about the
"action" they were watching, there was the distinct possibility that the sound would carry through the wall and
alarm one of the girls who was being exploited. Again,
Elvis came up with the answer: Whenever one of the boys
was about to get down with a girl, he must make a point
of turning on the radio in the room. He could say that it

was more romantic that way or there was such beautiful music on such and such a station. Girls would go for crap like that and the sound of music would mask the mumbling behind the wall. Eventually, however, it was agreed by all hands that the little window they had opened was not adequate for the proper enjoyment of the show. In the next house the boys occupied, they installed a mirror that was as big as a suburban picture window.

Elvis's second house in Bel Air offered a total change in atmosphere from his first. Instead of an architectural whimsy, redolent of a sheik's tent, the new mansion on Bellagio Road was a classic 1920s movie star's mansion. Modeled upon an Italian villa of the Renaissance, the exterior boasted statues in niches, a steeply landscaped terrace and an old-fashioned swimming pool off to one side. The decor was baronial: a grand entrance foyer paved with marble and adorned with a sculptured fountain, an imposing open staircase to the second floor, an ornamented fireplace rivaling that at Pickfair.

People who have special appetites are very quick to spot novel ways of fulfilling them. No sooner had Elvis moved into this old mansion than he noticed a peculiarity in the dressing room that adjoined the swimming pool. Rather than waste time describing the vision that inspired this latest and grandest peephole, let's examine the finished product.

First, you have to imagine the King and his lusty men bidding a momentary good-bye to a covey of beautiful young women whom they have urged to change into bathing suits so they can all enjoy a dip in the pool. The moment the girls go clattering down the steps beside the pool to the dressing room cut into the sloping hillside, Elvis and the Guys dash around to the side of the pool where there is a little louvered door at ground level that looks like a utility hatch. Opening this door, they crawl into a dark low space which they have laboriously excavated by hand from the foundation of the building. The dirt floor is covered with blankets because there is no room to stand. One wall of the room is a huge plate-glass window that looks directly into the women's side of the locker room. To the women, of course, this huge window appears as a mirror.

Lying on their sides and trying to breathe as shallowly as possible—heavy breathing fogs up the glass and spoils the view—Elvis and the Guys fall to studying the girls as they undress. Though it is often said that voyeurism is a scaredy-cat perversion, this new four-by-eight-foot window was, as the boys discovered, a great test of nerve. As long as the girls removed their clothes or made their toilettes from a distance, the peek effect was perfect. When a girl walked up close to the mirror and stared directly into it— while holding up, perhaps, one breast and then the other for examination—the more timid guys, like Lamar, would be terrified. It was hard to believe that this girl, just inches from your face, couldn't see you lurking there in the darkness.

Eventually, Elvis got anxious about this king-sized window and ordered it removed for transport to Graceland. There the boys sought high and low for a suitable place to install it, but the old house was very ill-suited to such contrivances. Finally, the mirror was stored in the attic, along with many other abandoned toys and devices for recreation. Meantime, the house on Bellagio Road received a new inhabitant who was destined to compensate Elvis for the loss of his old toy by sending the girls screaming around the house every night in a manner that was positively provoking.

Scatter was the ideal frat house mascot. A forty-pound, three-foot-tall chimpanzee, he had been trained by his first owner, a Memphis cartoonist who used him on his local TV show, to wear clothes, drink whiskey and raise hell with women. When Elvis first brought the beast out to Hollywood, he was enthralled with his antics. Elvis would treat him like a baby, carrying him around on his shoulders, showing him off for company and even changing his diapers. What tickled the Guys most about Scatter was the fact that he was so damn horny. Just let a girl step in the house and old Scatter would be hot on her tail. He would lift up her skirt and stick his head up toward her crotch. He would follow women to the bathroom or try to get inside while they were on the toilet. He would also chug-a-lug a few drinks at the bar, and then turn around on his stool and start whacking off in some girl's face.

Elvis was always thinking of fresh ways to use Scatter as a device for driving people crazy. He would have the chimp dressed up in his cute little middy suit and tennis sneakers. Then Scatter would be enthroned in the back seat of the Rolls-Royce Silver Cloud and driven about by one of the Guys wearing a chauffeur's cap. That night Elvis would scream with laughter as the chauffeur, generally Alan Fortas (who has a somewhat simian build), would recount the stories of how this motorist almost ran off the road staring at the chimp or how that old lady looked shocked or a cop on a corner did a triple-take as the car went by. What really bugged Elvis was that they could never find one of those trick cars, like they have in the circus, that can be driven from the rear by a hidden operator, while the ape sits up front turning the driving wheel. To roll down Hollywood Boulevard of an afternoon with Scatter at the wheel of a big costly Cad, casting Ubangi-lipped looks to right and left with a driver's cap on his head and his long funky fingers wrapped around the wheel—oh, God! Wouldn't that be heaven!

Short of the ultimate thrill, however, there were lots of other tricks you could play with the chimp. One of his most celebrated exploits was the time he got loose at the Goldwyn Studio and climbed up the drainpipe to the second-floor office of the boss, Sam Goldwyn. When Scatter came swinging through the window, Goldwyn's secretary screamed in horror and fled from the room. Scatter kept on going until he was in the Big Man's private office. Before the astonished movie mogul could utter a word, the ape had leaped on his desk and was cavorting among his contracts, pub shots and pictures of his grandchildren. Fortunately, the animal was well diapered so he couldn't do anything totally outrageous.

The best fun Elvis had with Scatter was always some stunt involving sex. It was as if Elvis were using the beast as his proxy, as the perpetrator of all those crazy sex pranks that he would have liked to have played but didn't dare. There was a little stripper, for example, who was a regular at the Presley parties. Elvis would entice this girl to come up to the house; then he would persuade her to get down on the floor and wrestle with Scatter. She wasn't

much bigger than the chimp. If you didn't look too carefully, you would swear that the horny ape and the hot
little chick were getting it on. That killed Elvis.

Another time when one of the Guys went upstairs with
a young woman who was an aspiring songwriter, Elvis got
Alan and Sonny to slip Scatter into the bedroom after the
couple had started balling. Scatter outdid himself on this
occasion, eliciting from the girl some of the loudest and
most piercing screams of his entire career. Sad to say, the
Guy was so outraged that he picked up the beast and
hurled it about ten feet down the hall.

Poor Scatter! He soon suffered the fate of all Master
Elvis's other toys. He lost his charm and was shipped back
to Graceland, where he was installed at the back of the
house in an air-conditioned cage. Neglected after all the
attention he had received for years, he pined and drooped
and turned vicious. Late in the sixties, he bit a maid who
was feeding him. Two days later, he was found dead in his
cage.

About the time Scatter died, the steady advance of electronic technology provided Elvis at last with the perfect
toy for a man who was an orgiast, a voyeur and a masturbator. It was the first Sony videotape machine for
"home use." Once Elvis got this machine, he was enabled
to seek relief from the monotonous routine of acting in
films by getting behind the camera and functioning as a
director. He soon found some cooperative young women
and set to work turning out an endless series of bedroom
follies. What he was after in these films was what he had
been after all his life in sexual encounters: a chance to
watch while beautiful young women grappled with each
other and simulated lesbian sex. Naturally, no one but
Elvis was permitted to view these hot reels. Once, however,
one of the Guys found the opportunity while Elvis was
away from home to view some of the forbidden footage.
What he saw shocked him profoundly. The two girls, naked
save for white panties, who flashed on the screen were
intimates of the Presley circle. They were giggling and
wrestling and taking turns diving into each other's crotches.
At the end of the film, Elvis suddenly popped up before

the camera with a full erection and a very smooth jack-off motion.

Eventually, Elvis made a great auto-da-fé of his private videotapes. Yet some of the tapes escaped destruction. They are allegedly being peddled in Los Angeles at high but not exorbitant prices: five hundred dollars for a five-minute quickie and fifteen hundred dollars for a long-playing orgy. In that great black market that consists of bootleg Elvis records, TV out-takes and other scraps from the cutting room floor, these home movies must be the most sought-after items. As biographical documents, their value is also enormous. What could be more basic to the study of a great sex hero than a filmed record of his sex life? Perhaps that is what Elvis meant when he said that some day he wanted to write an autobiography entitled *Through My Eyes*.

Eventually, Elvis discovered a curious genre of soft-core pornography that appealed to him even more than his private videotapes or the hardcore Danish stuff that came on the American market in the late sixties. As this type of pornography pleased him more than any other, we are justified in regarding it as the clue to his basic sexual fantasies. Interestingly, these were of a highly hostile yet not conventionally sadistic variety. The films Elvis relished are called in the trade "cat films." Their subject is women fighting. The typical film opens up on a shot of a couple of tough, coarse-looking broads sitting on a sofa and having a violent quarrel about a man. Suddenly, one of the women reaches over and slaps the other's face. The second woman retaliates by grabbing her opponent's hair. Then, they really get into it like a couple of cats, screaming and clawing. Inevitably, their legs go up and the viewer gets a flash of their panties, which was the part that most excited Elvis. By the end of the film, the women have reduced each other to wrecks.

As it's impossible to watch two people fighting without identifying with one or the other, these films offered Elvis Presley the opportunity to experience vicariously the pleasure of beating up a woman while at the same time protecting himself psychologically from the shame or guilt that would have been entailed if it were a man with whom he was identifying, a man who would obviously be a stand-in for himself. That Elvis's basic relations with women took the form of push and shove is clear from his behavior during his teenage pajama parties. That there was an angry hard-on behind these little games we should not have known but for the cat films. His excitement in viewing these films suggests not just his fundamental hostility toward women, which is pretty clear from his stage act, but also the source of that hostility.

The typical woman in a cat film is a hefty, older woman of a type that Elvis could easily have associated unconsciously with Gladys. If this sounds improbable, bear in mind that nothing is more basic to a mama's boy than deeply buried hatred for the woman who has enslaved him and frustrated him and imprisoned him psychologically for a lifetime, including all the years after her death. To take a celebrated example of this phenomenon, the literary world's most famous mama's boy is Marcel Proust. After his beloved mother's death, Proust donated the furniture of her house to a male brothel he patronized, and he arranged to have rats, animals that he associated with his mother, trapped, caged and then impaled on long needles while the illustrious author watched their death agonies with fascination. It would be a very naive observer of the relations between Elvis and his mother who did not suspect that beneath the surface of obsessive love there did not lurk, as a kind of psychic counterpoise, an opposite and no less powerful emotion, which finding no outlet in relation to its proper object had necessarily to be worked off on some substitute target.

One cannot relinquish the subject of Elvis Presley's sex life without considering the widespread suspicion that he was latently or actively homosexual. Perhaps the most perceptive way of viewing this issue is to stress the fact that Elvis was above all an adolescent sex hero. Adolescence is a period of imperfect sexual differentiation, a fact that was once proclaimed by our very language: the word "girl," meaning in the vocabulary of Chaucer a young person of either sex. What Elvis projected through his epoch-making act was not just the enormous sexual excitement of puberty but its androgynous quality. Much of Elvis's out of his stupor. If Gene Smith had been allowed to lie in his bunk a couple of hours more, Elvis and the Guys would have brought him home dead.

This was by no means the only time when Elvis's reckless dispensing of drugs nearly caused a death among his friends and lovers. Like all heavy drug users, Elvis was keen on having everyone around him doing what he was doing. This pattern of imposing his addictions on his entourage is readily explainable by two of his basic character traits. On the one hand, he loved to wield authority, to be the boss and force others to do his bidding. On the other hand, like most drug abusers, he suffered from a vague sense of guilt that he sought to dissipate by telling himself that everyone was doing just what he was doing. Polypharmacy loves company.

It needs no saying that in forcing all this junk down other people's throats, Elvis was imposing on their trust and naivete. Ultimately, what he was doing was exploiting their attachment to him to gather them into the embrace of his own profoundly self-destructive life-style. Though Elvis figures in the Myth as a refulgent Lifegiver, a priestly figure dressed in white and dispensing love and vitality to the world gathered at his feet, in his private aspect he was precisely the opposite figure to that projected by the Myth. No less glamorous, possibly even more beautiful and seductive than the Lifegiver, in his private world he was that ancient figure of Hebrew legend, the *Maloch HaMovet*—the Angel of Death.

It is worth remarking in this connection that though Elvis turned square in his public image after the army years, he never altered in the direction of his private development, which carried him swiftly down the well-worn grooves of the drug underworld. Though he made his peace with the establishment and danced to the Colonel's tune on the day shift, at night he was still the same old cat, perpetually on the prowl, sniffing his way along the trail that led to ever more bizarre sexual perversions, drug addictions and spiritual and mental delusions and hallucinations.

Elvis Presley is therefore that classic American figure: the totally bifurcated personality. Always professing his

power over young girls came not just from the fact that he embodied their erotic fantasies but that he likewise projected frankly feminine traits with which they could identify. This AC/DC quality became in time characteristic of rock stars in general, commencing with Mick Jagger and the Beatles (who had such ravishingly girlish falsettos) and going on to include Jim Morrison, David Bowie, Elton John and many figures of the punk pantheon. It's also worth noting that "punk" in its original meaning, as prison jargon, signifies the passive homosexual lover of a tough, typically older convict. (The subliminal meaning of Elvis's role in *Jailhouse Rock* is that he is Hunk Houghton's punk.) Indeed, it has always been a tradition of the rock world that the young studs who are the stars should have managers who are homosexuals and who "style" their boys in accordance with their own ideas of what is cute and kissy. Such was Brian Epstein with his punk, John Lennon. Though Elvis was not homosexual, his image was "rough trade."

When you dig down to the sexual roots of an Elvis Presley, you detect a profound sexual ambivalence. Elvis plays the strutting, overbearing macho in public; but in private he loves nothing better than to rough-house with teenage girls with whom he exchanges beauty secrets. His basic erotic image is a crotch covered with white panties and showing a bit of pubic hair—an image no different essentially from male to female. Eventually, as we shall see, he staged orgies in which the star was an aggressive lesbian who not only wrestled with other girls but dominated them sexually, just as an aggressive man might dominate a submissive woman—while Elvis got his kicks by watching. The inference is irresistible, therefore, that at bottom Elvis identified with a strong, aggressive woman rather than a strong, aggressive man. As his mother was precisely such a woman, threatening to bash in his father's head with a heavy skillet while calling him "steercottled," it makes sense to conclude that Elvis was his mother's son in sex as in everything else.

The flourishing of Elvis's perverse sex appetites in the sixties is paralleled by the sudden escalation in his consumption of drugs during this period. Prior to 1960, there is no evidence that Elvis was habituated to any sort of drug but benzedrine or amphetamine compounds. These pep pills had been part of his life since his first days on the road, and his use of them had continued straight through the period of his service in the army. Once he got back to Hollywood, however, he suddenly began consuming a whole range of drugs that produce narcotic and hypnotic as well as stimulant effects. How he first discovered and familiarized himself with these drugs is unknown; but, considering his later practices, it is very likely that he owed his introduction to these dangerous pills to the doctors to whom he complained of his inability to sleep.

Elvis was always an insomniac; now, under the stress of making movies and overstimulated by the constant use of Dexies to get him going after nights with little or no sleep, he must have quickly approached that manic, round-the-clock sleeplessness that is typical of the speed freak. To one who believed that the solution to any problem of mind or body was a drug, nothing would appear more logical as an antidote to uppers than the use of downers. So, it is not surprising to learn that as soon as he became established at the Beverly Wilshire, he came to an understanding with a druggist at the Milton F. Kveis Pharmacy in the lobby. This man began to supply Elvis with unlimited quantities of drugs without prescriptions at the price of one dollar a pill.

Soon Elvis was buying seven or eight thousand dollars' worth of pills at a time and paying for them by check. No less great than the volume was the variety of drugs that Elvis and the Guys began to experiment with at this time. They were into Dexamyl, Quāalude, Percodan, Demerol, Seconal, Tuinal, Valium, Nembutal and Placidyl. One of the reasons there were so many different drugs is that Elvis discovered in this period what was to be, along with the Bible, his favorite book for the rest of his life: *The Physician's Desk Reference*. This bulky volume, with its exhaustive enumeration of every pill in the pharmacopoeia, accompanied by a full clinical description and a very tantalizing picture, became Elvis's favorite study. With his prodigious appetite for pleasure and his quick, retentive memory, he had both the motive and the means to

explore all the resources of the legal drug world. So obsessed did he become with this theme that he even made a sly public confession. In an interview in *Parade* in November 1962, he is quoted as saying, "I've got very simple pleasures. I like to read medical books. One time in high school I thought I'd become a doctor."

Elvis's way of playing doctor soon produced near-fatal results. Gene Smith recalls driving back to Memphis at this time in a Dodge mobile home that Elvis used instead of taking the train. Smith was so overstimulated from being awake for three days and two nights on speed that he could not fall asleep. He complained to Elvis, who quickly upped with the cure: a 100-milligram dose of Demerol, a synthetic opiate. Smith popped the tiny white pill and waited for the anticipated relief. For another forty-five minutes he stared at the highway with his mind still racing the van. Finally, good ole Doc Presley gave the insomniac another 100-milligram pill. Smith retired to the back of the van and lay down on one of the beds.

An hour later, Billy Smith, who was riding up front with Elvis, who was driving, went to the rear to check on his cousin. He found Gene laid out cold, barely breathing and with a heartbeat so slow and faint that it seemed he must be near death. Billy had only recently been the one who discovered Junior Smith dead in his bed, probably the victim of an overdose. Now he realized that he was witnessing the same thing happening all over again. He rushed into the front of the van and warned Elvis. "Pull off!" he shouted, "I think there's something the matter with Gene!" "What do you mean?" demanded Elvis, steering the bulky vehicle off the road. "I shouted as loud as I could in his ear, and he didn't move a muscle," cried Billy. "I think he's dead!"

Bringing the van to a lumbering, lunging halt, Elvis scrambled into the back compartment, followed by Billy and Joe Esposito. After trying everything they knew to rouse the comatose drug victim, they hauled him out onto the highway. It was a freezing cold night. The unconscious man was clad only in jeans and a T-shirt. For three hours, the boys took turns dragging the limp body back and forth along the road. Finally, the drugged boy began to come

undying love and loyalty to Ma, Country, and Corn Pone, always an unregenerate southern redneck who stopped just short of the Klan and the John Birch Society, he was also the first great figure in that devolution of American society that has led to the narcissistic, anarchistic, junked-up heroes of the world of rock and punk. A Faustian figure, like most of our American mythmen, he registers both poles of the American schiz with perfect clarity. What makes him so appalling and alarming—but, again, so *echt Amerikan*—is his incredible innocence and self-righteousness, his stunning incapacity to recognize or even sense subliminally the total contradiction that informs his being. Accustomed to living in two worlds simultaneously, the day world of the squares and the night world of the cats, he embraces disjunction as the natural and inevitable condition of human existence. It is this Janus-like existential stance that makes him appear so often an enigma. Yet, though he lacks a middle term that could unite the opposite and opposing halves of his soul, he makes perfect sense as a totally responsive being who found himself alive at a time when the national values pointed in divergent directions and who reacted by rushing off in both directions at once.

Chapter 24

Three Sisters

ELVIS prolonged his unconsummated relationship with Anita Wood until late in the year 1961. Then, one day, Anita came downstairs at Graceland and walked into the dining room, where Elvis and Vernon were engrossed in conversation. Out of the blue, she announced: "I've just decided that I'm going to leave." Before either man could respond, she looked intently at Elvis and delivered her curtain speech.

"We've been together for four and a half years," she said firmly, "and we just aren't going anywhere. I understand that Colonel Parker doesn't want you to get married, that it would be detrimental to your career and all that— but I'm getting older. I want a family and children. So I've made my decision."

No sooner were the words out of her mouth than Vernon started pouring soothing oil on the seething waters. "Anita," he said, "maybe you all will get back together. People...a lot of times, they'll go through bad passages and a few years later they'll be together and it'll be great!" Anita was not to be deflected by this nonsense from the main issue. "I've got to make a life for myself," she persisted. "I don't want to live this way for the rest of my years." Elvis had been sitting at the table during this

419

unexpected outburst, saying nothing. Now, at last, he spoke.

"Little," he said solemnly, "are you sure? Are you *sure,* Little?" "Yes," affirmed Anita, without a moment's hesitation. "I've got to go." "Well," intoned Elvis, getting very churchy, "I pray to God that I'm not making the wrong decision by letting you go." That remark almost knocked Anita off her feet. Fuming, she thought to herself, "Well, you can't do anything about it—I'm going!"

She would have been even angrier if she could have heard Elvis discussing her with Sonny about this same time; in fact she would have been furious. For while Elvis was pretending that Anita's departure was a grave matter that demanded prayers for guidance, he had long since set his heart on another girl and was just waiting for Anita to blow away. When Sonny asked Elvis if he thought he might marry Anita, Elvis replied with the air of a man who has considered a matter carefully and come to a settled decision: "She's sweet, she's cute as hell," he smiled; then, with a significant look, he concluded, "but, I can do better!"

Undoubtedly, he was thinking of Priscilla. He had talked to Priscilla on the overseas phone many times since his return to America. He had shown her picture proudly to all the Guys, who marveled at how mature she looked for her age. He had even received some letters from her, which Anita had discovered in the house in Bel Air, stuck in the pages of a book. Though Priscilla might look mature, her letters proved that she was still a child. That was, of course, a great part of her charm for Elvis. Indeed, he had begun to think that if he could get her into his hands while she was still so young and pliable, he could mold and shape her into the woman of his dreams. This Pygmalion fantasy was not just an idle whim. It sprang from the depths of his egocentric character. What's more, having experienced love first and most strongly as the child of a totally controlling parent, it was only natural that he should express his own love in precisely the same manner.

So, the moment Anita was safely out of the house, Elvis called Wiesbaden and begged Captain Beaulieu to allow Priscilla to fly to Memphis for a Christmas visit. After giving lengthy assurances that she would not be living under the same roof with him but would stay with his father and stepmother in their home, Elvis got his way. Priscilla was dispatched to him as a marvelous Christmas gift.

The visit proved a great success. It confirmed Elvis in his determination to gain possession of Priscilla. Persuading her to come live with him was no problem. The real difficulty lay in persuading the Beaulieus to agree to such a highly unconventional arrangement. To anyone but Elvis Presley, it would have appeared an utter impossibility. What respectable middle-class American family would send its beautiful fifteen-year-old daughter to live with the world's most notorious sex symbol? How could a man who was a professional officer even entertain such a shocking proposal? How could any mother stomach it? Even if the parents could be prevailed upon to agree, how would they answer to their friends, to the press, to the world at large, so insatiably curious about every little detail of the famous star's life?

Elvis had always enjoyed great success in conning the parents of his local groupies; yet, what he had wanted in the past was nothing in comparison with this outrageous fantasy. We know most of the things he promised Priscilla's parents: That he would see to it Priscilla was well educated in a Catholic school. (As her education was virtually complete by this time, this promise wasn't worth much.) That she would be treated like a young woman of means, given her own car, fine clothes, etc. (Buying the girl outright, like the bride of some Arab sheik, was not, one presumes, a proposal that either party could entertain.) Finally, that he would marry Priscilla at some unspecified future date.

Priscilla's arrival at Graceland, in May of 1962, was kept as quiet as possible. Though everyone was told that Priscilla was living with her "guardians," Vernon and Dee, the staff at Graceland knew different because they saw the girl running around in the morning, wearing shorty pajamas. Though this story would have made a juicy item for the scandal sheets, virtually nothing appeared in print. It was yet another striking instance of how successful Elvis was at keeping his private life concealed from the press and the public. Indeed, it was a matter of critical importance that the truth about his relations with Priscilla be kept secret, for only recently two of the greatest heroes of rock 'n' roll had been crucified publicly—and one of them locked up in prison—for doing precisely what Elvis was doing now: cohabiting with a teenage girl.

Elvis's closest rival in the rockabilly world, Jerry Lee Lewis, had been the first to suffer. The irrepressible Jerry Lee had arrived in England in 1958, riding high on a tremendous wave of popularity generated by such legendary hits as "Whole Lotta Shakin' Goin' On" and "Great Balls of Fire." Received with tremendous enthusiasm by the British public, Jerry Lee was making a triumphal tour of the country when the news broke that he had married his fourteen-year-old cousin, Myra Brown. Instead of evading the issue, Jerry Lee brought his child bride onstage to greet the fans. The resulting explosion of public outrage blew Jerry Lee out of show business for the next ten years. After his English tour was canceled, his latest record blacklisted and his concert dates wiped out, he found himself right back where he started from down in Loosiana. The fact that he had *married* his teen queen did not mitigate the crime one bit in the eyes of the public. Imagine what the reaction would have been if this same public had discovered the rock star and his little girl were living together in sin!

An even worse fate befell Chuck Berry, who at this time was also at the peak of his career both as rock's greatest songwriter and one of its most popular performers. In 1961 Berry was convicted in St. Louis of transporting a fourteen-year-old girl across a state line, a violation of the Mann Act, and sentenced to three years imprisonment and a $5000 fine. On February 15, 1962, he was incarcerated in the United States Medical Center for Federal Prisoners at Springfield, Missouri. He was released on parole on October 18, 1963.

In cohabiting with a minor, even in arranging to transport her across state lines, Elvis was playing with dynamite. What's more, Elvis hardly knew Priscilla at this time and had no way of assessing what his success would be in his mad scheme to shape her into the perfect woman. Clearly, in this, his first major decision since his mother's death, he had run completely off the rails. The whole undertaking was crazy from the start. In time, it produced the disaster that finally broke Elvis Presley.

Though virtually every feature of Elvis's relationship with Priscilla was dubious, the public transformed this foredoomed affair into a fairytale romance. Priscilla was seen as Cinderella and Elvis as Prince Charming. Though Elvis's homes resembled Hugh Hefner's playboy pad a lot more than they did the enchanted castle, the infatuated fans insisted on viewing the pair as ideal lovers. Priscilla was perceived as a delicately budding flower which Elvis was guarding jealously for his very own. Not since Edward left the throne for "the woman he loved" has any such relationship been more totally misconstrued.

Once Priscilla had settled down at Graceland, she began to receive her training from Master Elvis. The first lessons were in makeup and hairstyling. Elvis liked his women to wear the heaviest kind of theatrical makeup: black mascara, batwing eyelashes, lots of color laid on in pancake appliers. Always obsessed with hairstyles, he insisted that Priscilla tease her hair up about twelve inches in a towering, heavily lacquered beehive. Marty Lacker recalls that the first time he met Priscilla, "she looked like she had about eight people living in her hair." Though Priscilla had an exquisite, doll-like kind of beauty, when Elvis got through with her, she looked like a tart.

Another feature of her appearance that changed immediately was the color of her hair. She dyed her towering, teased-up coif the same jet-black color that was Elvis's trademark. In fact, some people began to insist that Elvis and Priscilla were coming to look alike, that they were becoming twins. An extreme narcissist like Elvis might well have wanted his mate to be a female copy of himself. She was certainly his shadow or reflection at first: studying his tastes, conforming to his wishes, copying his style and personality. In making such a profound identification with Elvis, Priscilla might well have been motivated by a very deep desire to *be* Elvis. Envy so often passes for love.

In October, after Elvis left for Hollywood to start work on *Kid Galahad*, Vernon Presley enrolled Priscilla at Immaculate Conception Cathedral High School. The school is located in midtown Memphis on Central Avenue at Belvedere Boulevard. Considered one of the better Roman Catholic schools in the city, it was an obvious choice because of its convenient location. School had already begun when Vernon had his meeting with Sister Adrienne, the principal. She recalls that the enrollment was preceded by an extensive correspondence between her and the Presley attorney. Transcripts of Priscilla's academic records arrived, indicating that she should be placed in the senior class. In fact, Priscilla had so many credits already that it was decided that she should attend only half a day, leaving at lunchtime. At first, Sister Adrienne assumed that Priscilla was a member of the Presley family; but when the nun saw the transcripts from schools in Germany, she put two and two together and concluded that this was the girl Elvis had been dating in Germany.

Once Sister Adrienne realized that she was being asked to enroll in a Catholic girls' school a young woman who might be living with Elvis Presley in questionable circumstances, she sought the advice of her close friend on the faculty, Sister Loyola, who recollects the conversation clearly.

We were working on the school paper that day— I taught journalism—and the girls said to me, all excited: "Sister, Elvis's father is in the office talking to Sister Adrienne." Then they confessed that they had all been down on the floor looking through the keyhole to see Mr. Presley. I said, "Get back to work, girls; we're not concerned with Elvis's father; We're working on the paper." I was curious myself, but I didn't let them know it. When everyone left, I went into the office and Sister Adrienne said: "You'll never believe this, but Elvis has a protégée who wants to go here to school." I said: "Do you think he's in love with this girl? Do you think it's a girlfriend? It seems very strange." We discussed it at length and Sister Adrienne said, "This girl is supposed to be

Catholic and her parents have agreed to let her come
to Memphis from Germany and she will live in Mr.
Presley's home—not at Graceland—and she will be
properly chaperoned." Then she said, because we
were very close, "Sister, do you think it's all right
for me to take this girl?" I said, "If he assured you
that she will be properly chaperoned and if she's
living with Mr. Presley and not with Elvis, it seems
to me that it will be all right."

The next day Priscilla arrived and was assigned
to my class. I tried to prepare the girls because in
a girls' school, they're much more given to emotional
outbursts about boys than they are in a coed school.
I explained the circumstances and said, "She's probably Elvis's girlfriend." They were very excited.
Then this lovely little girl arrived. I remember she
was very shy. She had very little to say. She came
in and I assigned her a place and gave her the book
list. Her face was packed with makeup and her hair
was in a beehive. She had on so much makeup that
you could not really tell what kind of girl was underneath all that stuff. Sister Adrienne told her,
"Now, we don't say the girls can't wear makeup,
Priscilla, but we like for it to be inobvious. Also we
wear uniforms, and we will see that you have one.
When you get the uniform, take all that makeup off.
I think you will fit in better with the girls." It took
a couple of days to get the uniforms and I noticed
that she was coming to school overly dressed. Then
one day she walked in wearing her uniform. It was
a lovely uniform the girls wore: white blouse, plaid
skirt and a little waistcoat. She looked darling. Her
real beauty was showing.

The only thing I taught her was religion. I've often
wondered since if she was really Catholic because
when she was married to Elvis, they were not married by a priest and their little girl was not baptized
as a Catholic. Sister Adrienne and I have discussed
whether Elvis's father just wanted her to have the
cloak of security that a Catholic school would pro-

vide. Maybe she wasn't Catholic at all. She didn't
know the most basic things about our religion.

I had the top students in English. She was not a
top student. Her grades were average or below. She
rarely committed herself a whole lot to anything. We
have a lot of activities in sports, drama, school paper
and yearbook. She didn't participate in any of the
activities. The minute school was over, she was
whisked away or she drove off in her Corvair. She
told me that she was exhausted every day because
she would stay up at night for parties and movies.

I asked her about her parents in Germany: if she
missed them very much, if she wrote to them, if she
heard from them. She would respond but not as most
girls do, telling you all about their parents. She gave
very short answers. She was never very close to her
teachers, but she was very friendly and nice to the
other girls. The girls would say to me: "Sister, Priscilla is a cute girl. She's neat." They used that word
when they liked someone. "She doesn't brag, she
doesn't put on, she doesn't mention Elvis." The girls
were impressed at first by the fact that Elvis's father
brought her to school in a big car. "Sister, she rides
in that Cadillac with the television in it!" they said.
But after about ten days, she came to school in a
little red Corvair, and the girls were delighted with
that. We had a custom here that once a week the
girls could go out to lunch. She'd fill her Corvair full
of girls and they'd go out to lunch. They were all
excited to get a ride with Priscilla. They learned soon
that she was the sort of girl who never did say a
whole lot.

When graduation time came, we wondered whether
Elvis would come and disrupt the ceremony. Graduation was held in the cathedral. That night I passed
through the yard and I saw that Cadillac and I said
to myself: "Oh, there he is!" I went over to get the
girls lined up, to see that their robes were on right
and everything. Two or three other young sisters
went over to the car and spoke to Elvis and got his
autograph. They asked him if he were coming in. He

said: "No, Sister, I'm not going in. This is Priscilla's
night. If I went in, it would disturb the graduation.
I'll wait out here in the car until it's all over."

As soon as Priscilla was graduated from high school,
she enrolled in a school that taught modeling and dancing.
Her basic inclination was toward the world of style and
fashion. Though Memphis was the worst place imaginable
for a girl with such interests, she made the best of the
situation, anticipating the time when she would spend
more time in the much trendier milieu of Los Angeles. The
West Coast was doubly certain to figure in her future
because not only did Elvis spend a great part of every year
in the area making movies but Priscilla's family was living
now near Sacramento as a result of Captain Beaulieu's
transfer to Travis Air Force Base.

It was while she was visiting her family in the summer
of 1963 that Priscilla first became a target for the news
media as a result of Elvis's love affair with Ann-Margret.
The actress, who was now being called "the female Elvis
Presley," had been thrown together with Elvis that August
in Las Vegas, where most of the shooting was being done
for *Viva Las Vegas*. At first relations between the stars
were strained because Elvis swore that the picture's director, George Sidney, was sweet on Ann-Margret and was
lavishing on her the best camera angles, the greatest number of close-ups and the other advantages that Elvis was
accustomed to claiming. Naturally, he raised hell about
this favoritism to Colonel Parker, who swooped down on
the picture's producer, Jack Cummings. The Colonel was
already very annoyed with Cummings because he had refused to allow Colonel his customary "side action."

Colonel had suggested, for example, that all the resort
shots be done at the Sahara, which was owned by the
Colonel's friend, Milton Prell. Cummings had pointed out
that the Sahara was highly unsuitable and had cut a deal
with the Flamingo. Colonel had offered next to contract
a security force for the entire company. Cummings had
told Colonel to worry about his own boy, while Cummings
took care of his workers. Now the two men were ready to
square off for the final round.

Cummings was a tough, acid-tongued veteran of twenty years in Hollywood. He also had the enormous advantage of being the son-in-law of Louis B. Mayer. The Colonel's attack took a typically childish form. He waited until a major sequence had been completed, entailing the title song of the picture. Then, he demanded that the whole costly take be shot again because the camera had not caught Elvis's feet. Cummings said that Elvis wasn't a dancer and his feet could be safely omitted. Colonel insisted on taking the matter to the top studio executives. Normally, in such a situation, the executives would have given in to the Colonel's demands just to placate the old man. This time, however, they were caught between the Colonel and the boss's son-in-law. The sequence was not reshot. Colonel was so enraged that when the movie was completed, he tried to sell Elvis's fifty-percent interest just so they could disassociate themselves with the project. *Viva Las Vegas* grossed $5.5 million, which is considerably better than most of the Presley pictures.

The principal reason for the success of the film was the remarkable Ann-Margret, who proved to be just what Elvis should have been in the movies: a talented, vivacious and erotically enticing performer who balanced nimbly on the line between the sexy and the lewd—the lifeline of every Presley formula movie. Even without the assistance of the director she was dating, she would have upstaged Elvis and outperformed him consistently. It is to Elvis's credit that he recognized her ability and did not allow their professional problems to stop him from paying his customary court to his costar. By the time the shooting on the picture had ended, Elvis and Ann-Margret were clearly involved in what was the only authentic romance in Elvis's long career of dating Hollywood actresses.

A sign of how infatuated Elvis became with Ann-Margret is the fact that for the first time in his life he began to disappear from his house for a day or two at a time, spending the stolen hours at Ann-Margret's place up in the Hollywood Hills. This violation of the rule that women had to come to him was just one of several signs that the Guys interpreted as indications of real passion. For her part, Ann-Margret announced that she and Elvis were going steady and she told one reporter that her huge round pink bed was a gift from Elvis. (Elvis gave fancy beds to more than one woman.) Some people interpreted the actress's remarks as just another publicity ploy. The truth would appear to be that there was a brief but intense affair, conducted right under Priscilla's nose.

Ann-Margret later became completely mute on the subject of her romance with Elvis. Evidently, the affair was broken off abruptly on Elvis's initiative and without any clarifying explanations. Not long after the two had ceased seeing each other, a couple of the Guys spotted Ann-Margret riding through Hollywood. Pulling up beside her, they struck up a fast conversation. "I thought you were in love," said one of them. "I thought we were, too," replied the actress. "Well, what happened?" said her questioner. "Ask your boss," the lady replied. "I haven't the faintest idea."

The explanation is probably quite simple. Ann-Margret was dedicated to her career; therefore, she was not a suitable mate for Elvis. His record of noninvolvement was virtually unblemished; it probably cost him no great effort to keep it perfect. Elvis's life was designed to allow him an endless series of one-night stands and short affairs, his commitment to marry Priscilla providing a perfect rationalization for his reluctance to become emotionally involved with any women.

By late 1963, however, Priscilla was out of school and beginning to show signs of restlessness. Life in Bluebeard's Castle was pretty dull. It was about this time that Priscilla began to display an interest in other men. At a gospel concert at the Auditorium (one of the very few public events that Elvis ever attended), she had seen a good-looking, blond, nineteen-year-old singer with the Stamps Quartet named Milan Lefevre. Though it was taking a great chance to reach out to another man in Elvis's hometown, filled with gossips and spies, Priscilla managed to get in touch with this young man and meet him several times either at the Auditorium or at the Whitehaven Shopping Center. Lefevre thought Priscilla was a real "fox." He felt she was pursuing him. Yet, nothing came of their meetings. The fox was not yet ready to pounce.

While Priscilla was flirting in Memphis, Elvis was

grinding through three movies a year and thirty parties
a month in Los Angeles. This schedule had gotten him so
depressed that he was becoming quietly desperate. His
consumption of downers was escalating steadily. His irritability was growing more marked every month. He was
also starting to buck under the Colonel's yoke.

According to the Presley Myth, Elvis and the Colonel
were deeply devoted to each other. Their stock exchange
consisted of Elvis saying, "I love you, Colonel," and the old
man replying, "You're all I live for, Elvis." The truth is
that from the earliest years of the relationship there was
a deep and ever-widening conflict between this famous
pair. Elvis disliked the Colonel instinctively and dreaded
those occasions when he had to confront his master. It's
generally assumed that the total control that Parker exercised over Elvis's business was entirely owing to Elvis's
distaste for business. It might have been Elvis's distaste
for the Colonel that made him willing to do anything or
sign anything just to get the old man out of his life again.

Once Elvis had concluded that the Colonel had conned
him into going into the army, a development that led
shortly to Gladys's death, Elvis's sufferings and Vernon's
remarriage, Elvis must have viewed the Colonel with feelings of hatred. Yet he couldn't break with the old man
because he was totally dependent upon him to revive his
career. Once Elvis felt confident again, however, he started
to give the Colonel the freeze. It was noted that the two
would walk past each other on a movie lot without even
saying hello. Colonel Parker soon demanded that every
day he receive a report on Elvis from his foreman, Joe
Esposito. Elvis resented this so much that he found a pre-
text for firing Joe in the fall of 1963. At that point he gave
the job to Marty Lacker.

Fat, balding, Jewish, married with two children, Lacker,
who had joined Elvis in 1961, was a one-time local announcer and DJ. Under his veneer of good ole boy conformity he was a rather different type from the rest of the
Guys. (Elvis's predilection for Jews—George Klein, Alan
Fortas, Marty Lacker, Larry Geller—is remarkable considering his background. Vernon was outspokenly anti-
Semitic, always complaining that "Elvis is bein' screwed

blind by them Jews out in Hollywood." The Colonel used
to warn the Guys: "Watch what you say about Jews and
homosexuals out here in Hollywood because you never
know when you're talkin' to one of 'em." By entrusting
Jews with important positions in his organization, Elvis
was rebelling against the prejudices of his little world and
especially against his father.) Lacker was completely devoted to Elvis and unresponsive to pressure from Colonel
Parker. He could have performed a very valuable service
for Elvis by jealously guarding his employer's privacy.
Instead, he evinced a passive and acquiescent temperament, which led him eventually to second Joe Esposito's
efforts to get back into Elvis's good graces. During the
year 1964, however, Elvis was in the unique position of
not having as his foreman a man who reported every day
to Colonel Parker.

The rebellious attitude that Elvis evinced during this
period toward the Colonel soon embraced every feature of
his life. The rebellion was fueled by all the pressures,
frustrations and disappointments of the postarmy years.
Above all, it was incited by the disgust with which Elvis
viewed his once enthralling life and career. Elvis had always interpreted his success as a sign that he had been
singled out by providence to accomplish some great mission here on earth. The problem was that as the years
wore on, instead of the goal becoming clearer, it became
ever more difficult to perceive. When he was younger,
Elvis had enjoyed the reassuring effects of progress: He
had seen one landmark after another race past him as he
pursued his giddy career. With everything happening so
swiftly, he could tell himself that if he just kept going, he
was bound to reach his destination. Now, he had lost that
simple faith. He had begun to suffer from the thought that
he wasn't going anywhere. What *was* he doing? Just standing still, grinding out one crappy movie, one mediocre
soundtrack album after another. Then, as reward for all
his labors, he was always throwing foolish parties with
foolish girls, parties that pleased the guests a lot more
than they did the host. In fact, in his more depressed moments, Elvis began to think that he was actually worse
off than he used to be because now, instead of exalting

him, his life was beginning to degrade him. Elvis the Bad had been glutted, while Elvis the Good had been starved.

The self-hate of a narcissist is one of the most deadly of all emotions. It is the sadism of the self toward the self. Carried far enough, it can lead to a nervous breakdown or to suicide. During the spring of 1964, Elvis began to experience a crisis of self-loathing. He abandoned his customary life-style and instead of rushing maniacally from one sport or prank to another—denying his innate depression by the mindless pursuit of fun—he locked himself up in his bedroom at Graceland for days at a time, refusing to speak with anyone. The gloom that closed over Elvis alarmed all the Guys. Some of them said that if Elvis didn't find something fresh to live for, some new inspiration, he might crack up. Such was the situation on April 30, 1964, when word was received at the house on Perugia Way that Elvis's hairdresser, Sal Orifice, would not be able to pay his accustomed call. He suggested that a barber be summoned from Jay Sebring's fashionable salon. The appointment was booked and that afternoon, when the doorbell rang, one of the boys answered—and in walked the Swami.

Chapter 25

The Swami

LARRY GELLER was a young man slightly ahead of his time. A tall, slender, good-looking New York Jew, he was an early example of a type that swiftly became common: the low-pressure, low-profile West-Coast hippie spiritualist and health food faddist, who, as he labors every day at his manual craft, babbles endlessly about meditation, vitamin E and the Third Eye. Elvis sometimes referred jokingly to Geller as his "guru"; but you wouldn't get far imagining their relationship in the terms suggested by that appellation because Geller was no master and Elvis could never maintain for more than a few moments the posture of the disciple. The truth is that far from being Elvis's mentor, Geller was just the match that touched off the emotional tinder that was Elvis Presley.

Imagine in the first place how exotic Larry Geller must have appeared in the dumb jocko-schloko Memphis-in-Bel-Air milieu in which Elvis was imprisoned. In contrast to the beefy, blowsy look of the Guys, Geller is thin, dark, *spirituelle;* his thoughtful face with its dark soulful eyes is crowned by a great turban of black hair. Everything about him proclaims the swami. Then, as the skinny scissors snip and the spray nozzle hisses and the precious jet-black dyed locks fall to the floor, words are spoken and looks exchanged and heavy etheric vibrations registered

that soon have Elvis hanging on every word, oscillating
moment by moment from surliness to sincerity, from suspicion to faith, from despair to joy. One of the most telling
exchanges occurred when the breezy, arrogant, spoiled-
rotten Elvis said, "Don't worry about the hair on the
floor—the maid will clean it up!" Instead of responding
like any ordinary mortal and saying, "Okay," Swami
Geller, the servant of servants, the beggar's bowl of bar-
bers, the humble picker-up of learning's crumbs, murmured in his spooky spiritual voice: "I like to do my own
cleaning."

Once Geller had hooked Elvis, his task became that
of a spiritualist "connection." Every few days he was
expected to deliver a new load of occult literature and
engage in prolonged discussions of the books Elvis had
already consumed. Elvis fell on these strange books with
an appetite equal to that of the keenest Ph.D. candidate
sitting buried in the stacks of some great library. In fact,
you'd have to have the stomach of a bookworm to read
the stuff that Elvis gobbled up in this period. He said
his favorite subject in high school was English? You can
believe it! Suppose you enrolled for a course in spiritualism and the professor handed you this list of required
readings:

Vera Stanley Adler: *The Initiation of the World*
David Anrias: *Through the Eyes of the Masters*
Alice A. Bailey: *Esoteric Healing*
McDonald McBain: *Beyond the Himalayas*
Anne Besant: *The Masters*
H. P. Blavatsky: *The Secret Doctrine;*
                 The Voice of Silence
Paul Brunton: *The Wisdom of the Overself*
Richard Maurice Bucke: *Cosmic Consciousness*
Cheiro's Book of Numbers
Joel Goldsmith: *The Infinite Way*
Manley Palmer Hall: *The Mystical Christ;*
                    The Secret Teachings of All Ages
Corrine Heline: *Sacred Science of Numbers*
Max Heindel: *The Rosicrucian Cosmo-Conception*

Krishnamurti: *The First and Last Freedom*
C. W. Leadbetter: *The Inner Life*
The Leaves of Morya's Garden
Nicholas Roerich: *Flame in Chalice*
Dane Rudhyar: *New Mansions for New Men*
Baird Spaulding: *The Life and Teachings of the
Masters of the Far East*
Tibetan Book of the Dead
Paramahansa Yogananda: *Autobiography of a
Yogi*
The Urantia Book.

Heavy! Right? The real hard-core, mystogogical, table-rapping, apparition-looming, spirit-voices mumbo jumbo. The stuff you find in those dim little bookshops down at the bottom of Fourth Avenue or along Hollywood Boulevard with "OCCULT" lettered across their windows. Old these books are, many of them dating back to the days just before and after World War I, when this kind of rubbish enjoyed such a tremendous vogue that T. S. Eliot used it in *The Wasteland* as a symbol of the degradation of myth and ritual in the modern world.

Actually, it never makes any difference when these books are written because they are always composed of the same banal or preposterous ideas in the same familiar code phrases. Each successive author or age gives this stuff another stir in the pot and then pours out the familiar stew. Sometimes these authors go on pouring through a score of volumes. Getting the spirits to speak is as nothing compared with the difficulty in making them shut up. Or make sense. The reader is always being hailed, or better, *haled,* by pseudo-biblical prophet voices that cry out with the urgency of a great revelation. Then, as they maunder on for page after page of empty prose or kooky verse or abandon language in favor of diagrams, paradigms and arrangements of lotus blossoms, you realize that you've been had again by the spiritual hucksters, the heavenly con men, the charlatans of the soul.

What would make a young man like Elvis Presley spend

years and years in the perusal of these queasy writings?
What sort of compulsion could propel him through all this
bad prose and quack verse? Just reading two or three of
these books is a test of one's powers of self-discipline.
Imagine what it takes to read hundreds of such volumes
and then reread many of them and ponder their unreal
substance! That he did read these books with great care
is evident even from the appearance of his copies, dog-
eared, travel-stained, heavily underscored on almost every
page. Elvis committed many of the key passages to memory and would recite them aloud while Larry Geller held
the book like a stage prompter.

The customary explanation of this mania is that Elvis
was "profoundly religious." The difficulty with that answer is that none of these books deal with religion either
in the strict theological or the common everyday meaning
of the word. Spiritualism is not religion. It may be a substitute for religion or it may mask itself as an ancillary
to religion in order to lull the fears of the pious and win
for its dubious doctrines a wider following. At bottom,
however, spiritualism is antagonistic to orthodox religion
because so much of its substance is derived from heresies,
superstitions and magical beliefs and practices that the
great Western religions long since proscribed.

The particular tradition of spiritualism from which
stem most of the writings to which Elvis Presley devoted
himself for the balance of his life was established in the
1870s in New York City by the notorious and fascinating
Madame Blavatsky. Elvis always had on hand copies of
Madame Blavatsky's writings and those of her disciples,
like Anne Besant and C. W. Leadbetter. In fact, one little
volume purporting to be translations by Blavatsky of the
most ancient runes of Tibet, *The Voice of Silence,* was such
a favorite of Elvis's that he sometimes read from it onstage
and was inspired by it to name his own gospel group, Voice.
Though Elvis was so well acquainted with the Blavatsky
school, who called themselves "Theosophists," he does not
appear ever to have understood who Madame Blavatsky
was or even what was the true purport of her writings.

Like Immanuel Velikovsky in our day, Madame Blavatsky argued that the world was once occupied by a mas-

ter race, the Aryans, who possessed a special language and
a vast store of knowledge that was so superior to anything
the human race has created since that everything that is
really profound in our modern philosophies and religions
is just a broken and often miscomprehended fragment of
the "Ancient Wisdom." The goal of Madame Blavatsky's
labors in her two immense books, *Isis Unveiled* (1877) and
The Secret Doctrine (1889), is to restore the Ancient Wisdom to something resembling its original character by a
gigantic labor of synthesis, collecting bits and pieces of the
shattered system of the Aryans in every civilization and
culture on earth, ranging from the Indians and Tibetans,
to the ancient Greeks and Egyptians, to the early Mexican
and American Indian civilizations. All of this sounds
pretty impressive until you start reading one of these
books; then, you recognize that you are in the presence of
a mind that is either very disordered or completely untutored or fundamentally fraudulent. For instead of a synthesis, these books produce about the same impression as
would the pages of *The Golden Bough* if they were torn
out in fascicles of two, three or four pages and then rear-
ranged by being blown in a heap by a powerful fan. Mes-
merism, vampires, mediums, the Vedas, spirit materialization, charming serpents by music, witchcraft, the
resuscitation of buried fakirs, levitation, Atlantis—the
whole range of the occult is crammed into these volumes
without the slightest semblance of order or reason.

The explanation of the books' mad methodlessness and
total want of synoptic intelligence is simple: They are pas-
tiches of plagiarisms: passages filched from other authors
and copied so crudely that even the spellings of the more
difficult words are wrong.[1] The ancient documents that
Madame Blavatsky claimed to have discovered in her ex-

[1]Madame Blavatsky was not the only plagiarizing prophetess
of her period: The principal theologian of the Seventh Day Ad-
ventists, Ellen Gould White, who wrote forty-six volumes total-
ing twenty-five million words, has been convicted by modern
scholarship of plagiarizing eighty percent of her writings—which
are still accepted by the faithful as the voice of God.

tensive travels in the Orient, including Elvis's favorite
Tibetan runes, are forgeries in the style of Macpherson's
The Works of Ossian. Madame Blavatsky was simply a
charlatan, an imposter who was exposed many times in
her own day, being driven from country to country, as in
each place the truth about her was discovered. She died
in the midst of a last great scandal precipitated by the
confessions of her accomplices, who revealed that their
mistress had practiced on the credulity of her financial
patrons by employing cabinets with secret doors, disguised
handwriting in metallic inks (for messages from the "Masters") and even life-sized puppets for apparitions. Apart
from being one of history's great phonies, Madame Blavatsky was also vehemently anti-Christian. Her books
contain chapters with titles like "The Church: Where Is
It?" and "Christian Crimes and Heathen Virtues." Putting
it all together, therefore, one is impelled to ask: Is this
something that a nice Christian boy should be reading and
laying to heart?

Elvis did soon begin to display unmistakable signs of,
shall we say, heterodoxy. Instead of viewing Jesus as the
son of God and his appearance on earth as an act of special
creation, Elvis took the view that Jesus was just one of a
number of great Masters and that he had gone through
numerous incarnations in the course of his cosmic development. Such a heretical notion would not make a ripple
in a company of spaced-out hippies; in the strict little world
of Memphis Fundamentalism, Elvis's discourse over the
afternoon breakfast table shocked his employees and set
his father to wondering what had become of his son. As
for Elvis, his absorption in the notion of the Masters, the
"White Brotherhood" that lives out there beyond the Himalayas and constantly sends down messages through the
"ether" to certain select "Adepts" on earth, was gradually
building up to the notion that he just might be a Master
himself!

He took at this time as his primary guide a little book
that soon became as much a symbol of the new spiritual
Elvis as the guitar had been of the old worldly Elvis. *The
Impersonal Life* must be visualized first as an object, a
personal prop, because from this time forth you could never

come into the presence of Elvis Presley, whether at one
of his homes or in a hotel room or an airplane cabin, without finding a copy of this book either in his hand or near
his person. Over the course of the next thirteen years he
must have given away hundreds of copies of this book, like
an eager evangelist distributing a favorite tract. A little,
blockish-looking volume, measuring about four by five
inches, covered in paper coated to look like black leather
and stamped in gilt with gothic letters, the book resembles
a Bible or missal. Though no author's name appears on
the title page, a couple of letters (addressed "Dear God"
and "Dear Father") attached in place of a preface make
it appear that the author was Joseph S. Benner and that
he completed this book in the year 1917.

The reason for the absence of the author's name in the
accustomed place is explained by the startling assertion
that the Voice which speaks throughout this book in such
an authoritative tone—and with such quaint locutions as
"mayhap" and "perchance"—is not the voice of a man but
the voice of God. Joseph S. Benner holds himself forth as
nothing less than the amanuensis of the Divine Being. At
one point, for example, the Voice remarks, "In one of my
other Revelations, called the Bible...." You get the idea.

To Elvis Presley, the notion that God was not some
bearded old patriarch riding on a thunderhead but the
Voice within must have been a startling revelation and
one that was fraught with enormous significance. For if
God is inside us and we are, in a manner of speaking, God,
then it follows that we need not concern ourselves over-
much with external authorities, neither ministers, churches
nor even that "other Revelation." The source of all true
spiritual inspiration is within ourselves.

This idea of divine immanence soon became the master
principle of Elvis's life. By inflecting it this way and that,
he found that it explained everything he wanted to know
and validated everything he wanted to do. Elvis had always disliked and distrusted ministers, whom he saw as
basically greedy, self-serving imposters holding their con-
gregations in line by frightening them out of their wits
with phony hellfire sermons. Now that Elvis realized the
voice of God was within him, he arrogated to himself the

functions of a minister, preaching at the boys (and girls)
endlessly, off-loading on them every night what he had
read in his books the preceding day. Elvis had always been
the Great Explainer, holding forth on every subject under
the sun; now, he began to wonder whether his true vo-
cation might be that of spiritual leader, a kind of super-
evangelist preaching a great crusade of spiritual enlight-
enment and moral regeneration. Who, after all, had
greater power over people than Elvis Presley? Whose presence had more charisma? Who could work those ballparks
and football stadiums with greater authority and skill? It
was a vision that tantalized Elvis till the last days of his
life.

The notion of the "divine I" also furnished a perfect
rationalization for Elvis's untutored and unsystematic
study of all the world's most baffling mysteries. Most men
embarking on some prolonged and difficult investigation
would want to solicit the aid of experts, wise men, rabbins.
Not Elvis Presley. A born autodidact, he felt himself capable of sounding the greatest depths and scaling the most
sublime heights all through the efforts of his own intellect,
guided, of course, by the inner light. What's more, Elvis
must have found such unguided study a natural extension
of the Fundamentalism in which he had been reared. To
this day, the principal activity of the little churches in the
country around Tupelo is a kind of discussion class in
which the members of the congregation are invited one
after the other to offer their personal interpretations of a
particular passage of scripture. As for the credulity that
Elvis evinced in swallowing uncritically the fantasies of
the spiritualists, it corresponds to the atmosphere of ancient superstition and belief in the weird which was the
real religion of Gladys Presley. In becoming a total believer in occult doctrines, Elvis was merely substituting
one set of superstitions for another: the hip new fashions
of the yogurt yogis for the corny old saws of the hillbilly
faith healers and snake handlers.

Or, perhaps, as Elvis was always such a naif, such a
child at heart, we should view his mental excursions in
the light of imaginative experience, like a kid reading
fairy tales. Certainly there is no way that a rational crea-

ture could entertain many of the notions in these books.
It may also be significant that after this period, Elvis
turned to the reading of science fiction and became a firm
believer in UFOs.

So between the years 1964 and 1967, we must imagine
him as a young but crackbrained Don Quixote sitting in
his bathroom-study with a plastic mantle over his shoulders and a whining hairdryer parching his skull while he
discusses with his svelte Sancho Panza the entire range
of mystical, occult and spiritualistic doctrine and practice.
During this time, they pondered the evidence of materialization and dematerialization, karma and reincarna-
tion. They examined each other's palms for telltale signs.
Elvis discovered a tiny cross on his mound of Venus. The
problem was that there were so many rival ways of interpreting this doubtless significant sign. The same difficulty
arose when Elvis computed his number, employing the
formulas in Cheiro, one of his favorite books. Elvis's number was eight; but this displeased him for some reason and
he found ways of calculating his name so that he arrived
at both five and six. Even so he was not pleased; what he
really wanted was to be like his father, a ten.

Elvis also made many efforts to communicate by mental
telepathy, though invariably he wound up using the telephone. Nonetheless, he always assured the Guys that if
he died, he would find a way to communicate with them
from the beyond. Elvis was especially curious about the
mysteries of death and the afterlife. He not only studied
the ancient Buddhist manual for the dying, *The Tibetan
Book of the Dead,* but he visited mortuaries and observed
the methods employed in preparing bodies for burial. Birth
also intrigued Elvis, particularly the subject of his own
birth, about which he built up gradually an elaborate legend. The most spectacular products of this obsession with
transcendental phenomena were the voices and visions
that Elvis apprehended and the miracles he claimed to
have worked.

On one occasion, while driving across the desert toward
Los Angeles, Elvis and the Guys were peering up into a
brilliant blue sky stretched behind the mountains south
of Flagstaff, Arizona, when suddenly Elvis cried out: "Do

you see what I see? That's Stalin's face up there!" As everyone craned their necks to see the cloud, they agreed, one
by one, that the resemblance to Uncle Joe was remarkable.
At that point, Elvis got so excited that he drove the vehicle
off the road and braked to a sharp stop. Calling for Larry
Geller to follow him, Elvis dashed off into the desert. With
tears streaming down his face, he babbled: "My prayers
have been answered. I have seen Christ and Antichrist
and I know what I have to do!" Nobody but he had seen
Christ. Yet Elvis felt that this was the moment in his life
when, like Paul on the road to Damascus, he was vouch-
safed the vision and shown the way.

Elvis reported many other, less dramatic, visions and
voices. He told Marty Lacker that once while listening to
the song of a bird, the meaningless warbling had suddenly
turned into the voice of Jesus. On another occasion, Elvis
sought to direct the movement of a sky full of clouds, claiming success for his efforts. Other times, he showed how the
power of his "vibes" made the leaves in the garden tremble.
The calling he experienced most keenly, however, was not
that of visionary or cloud shifter but that of healer of the
sick. He had always wanted to be a doctor, and he had
been reared in a culture that believed in faith healing. It's
even possible that he may have witnessed ministers laying
hands on sick people and literally tearing the illness out
of their diseased bodies. Now he undertook to do the same
thing himself, explaining to his friends that these efforts
cost him a great deal because he had to take the pain of
the afflicted one up into his own body. Like all healers, he
experienced both failure and success. Consider a case that
occurred in 1973, when Elvis sought to heal Sonny and
Judy West's little boy, Brian, who was suffering from a
burning fever.

By this time Elvis had had quite a bit of experience in
his role as spiritual doctor; consequently, when he arrived
at the Wests' home he had with him the tools of the trade.
He produced a large green scarf, explaining that green
was the healing color. He set upon his head a massive
turban with a big glittering stone in its center. Laying the
child on the green cloth, Elvis assumed the lotus position
and went into deep meditation. Then he began to address

the child, exhorting him to relinquish the fever and let it pass into Elvis. As Elvis bent lower to place his hands on the critical points of the child's body, little Brian became fascinated with the big stone flashing from Elvis's turban. The child reached up and tried to snatch the bauble. "Don't do that, Brian!" Elvis warned. Sonny and Judy sought to suppress their laughter. The kid was screwing up Elvis's act! Finally, having laid his hands on both sides of the child's head and on his solar plexus, Elvis turned to the parents and said: "I think the fever's breaking." Sonny touched his son but he discerned no difference. He humored Elvis by saying, "Yeah, I think it is." Meantime he made a mental note to give Brian two more aspirins. Next day, however, Brian's fever broke. When Elvis called and got the report, he said: "Good, that pleases me. If you notice any change, let me know."

By the summer of 1966, when Elvis started filming *Spinout,* he had gotten so far into his role as Master that the performance he gave off the set surpassed by far his work before the cameras. No sooner did he arrive on location at Nagoura, just outside Los Angeles, than he began what the film magazines would have called a "whirlwind romance" with his costar, Deborah Walley. Every moment the pair were not before the camera, they shared together, from breakfast in Elvis's trailer to lunch in the same luxuriously appointed vehicle to the hours-long phone calls that filled the evening after the rushes. It looked like one of those hot and heavy affairs that are supposed to boil up spontaneously on film locations. Actually, it was something much crazier and fraught with more serious consequences. Elvis had decided to blow Miss Walley's mind as only a great Master can affect a hungry and adoring disciple.

What made Deborah Walley so hungry was precisely what had made Elvis so frustrated before he discovered spiritualism. This young actress, who was always playing silly little ingenues like Gidget or, in this picture, the kookie-pookie girl drummer in an all-guy rock band, this perennial teenie-weeny jumping bean with the bangs and the pop eyes was in fact a highly skilled and highly professional actress who had been born into show business and

had been working in the theater since she was twelve. She
had been on the verge of becoming a star of the Off-Broad-
way theater of her day (appearing in Chekhov's *Three
Sisters* at the age of sixteen), when she got sucked into the
movie business and became an overnight sensation. Picked
up like a toy train and put down again on a new set of
tracks leading in precisely the opposite direction to that
on which she had set her heart, she had allowed herself
to be conned into playing the whole Hollywood game to
the hilt. She had done the dumb beach-party pictures,
appeared on the covers of the movie mags and the women's
mags, and, finally, she had even made the ultimate commitment by marrying a very handsome and successful
young actor with whom she had a child. Oh, she was a
fabulous success! Didn't everyone around her on the location address her as "Miss Walley"? The only hang-up
was that she missed the life she should have had and the
people she should have known.

Comes now the Master. She had no big thing about
Elvis Presley. She was never a fan. She didn't even regard
Elvis as an actor. At the most, she observed that his physical appearance reminded her a little of her husband, John
Ashley, who was then in the Philippines making a picture.
Suddenly, Elvis was coming on to her: not in a sexual
manner but in some strange new way that she had never
before experienced. He was very intense, very earnest. At
the same time, he was very warm and physical, always
putting his arms around her and even kissing her. Yet he
wasn't being seductive in any ordinary sense. It was more
as though he was trying to communicate with her in a
language she didn't yet understand.

No sooner do they commence their conversations than
he lays on her a copy of *The Impersonal Life*. She's very
bright, eager, the perfect pupil. That very night she goes
through the whole book. Next morning in the trailer, he
starts to give her a quiz. She makes an A+. Elvis is encouraged to go much further. He takes her home in his big
Rolls-Royce. He takes her into his bedroom. There, he lifts
up the lid on a trunk and starts going through all the
books it contains. He's like some little kid showing off his
toys. Deborah starts to get the bug. After all, Elvis Presley

is one helluva salesman. A great "communicator," as they say on Madison Avenue. She's a born enthusiast. Mental touchwood. Poof! Up in smoke she goes as she burns through the books, the long swami raps, the silent sessions of unvoiced rapture as they hold each other tight in the trailer and strain for the still, small voice of Him!

Soon they're on that exhilaratingly naked plane of interaction where two people confront each other with a clearly declared purpose and nothing else to distract them. He tells her: "Look, we've only got this moment together: so let's have it completely. No holding back. No wasting time on trivialities. I've got the word. I want to give it to you. I'm not a man. I'm not a woman. I'm a soul, a spirit, a force. I have no interest in anything of this world. I want to live in another dimension entirely." Deborah, a lapsed Roman Catholic, was thrilled. "I ate it right up," she says today, "like it was chicken soup. He treated me like an angel. I couldn't have had any more with him because I hated that macho lifestyle of his. In that world, I wouldn't have lasted ten minutes." Deborah Walley's marriage didn't last any longer than it took to have one final session with her husband after he got back to Los Angeles.

In the movie with Elvis she played a rock drummer. Now she began an affair with a real rock drummer. She became a "cosmic flower child." She started dropping acid. She became the guru to her drummer, persuading him to get high with her. By the time of the Monterey Pop Festival the following summer, Deborah is the perfect freak. She's sitting in the front row gonged to the gills, her hair out like Struwelpeter, bells around her neck and the world's biggest grin. Next, she's into photography, painting, songwriting. Finally, she gets so far out on acid that she has this final trip that takes her from being atop a mountain way down into a narrow corridor, where she meets a guy who says to her (like Elvis): "You're about to receive the word; but, when you get it, you won't be able to remain any longer on earth." At that point, she becomes alarmed. She realizes that not only has she thrown her career away but she is risking her sanity. A nervous breakdown follows and a period of hospitalization. Eventually, she pulls herself up and out of the breakdown and resumes her life,

forming fresh relationships, having another child and
eventually winding up today as a writer. It's quite a trip
on which Elvis launched her, rather more dramatic than
that which he took himself, but probably expressing the
same urgencies only in a far more confident and liberated
spirit.

The world into which Deborah Walley went spinning
after her mindblowing encounter with Elvis Presley was
the brave new world of Rock. Commencing in 1963, when
the first Beatles records made their way to America (on
an obscure Chicago label named Vee-Jay that specialized
in black R & B) and mounting to a sensational crescendo
in 1964 with the arrival of the Fab Four in America, where
they played to no less than seventy million people on the
Ed Sullivan Show, the new rock—so called to distinguish
it from the corny old rock 'n' roll of the fifties—had by the
year 1967 reached a level of messianic fervor that impelled
many observers to compare it to the Great Awakening or
even the Crusades. Never before in the history of the world
had any mass cultural phenomenon developed such power,
authority and pervasiveness. One moment, there was this
new fad among the teenagers for British boys in pipe-stem
suits and soup-bowl haircuts; the next, there was this awesome human tide, this *Völkerwanderung*, that gathered
up tens of thousands of young men and women, as in *The
Invasion of the Body Snatchers*, and transformed them
overnight into blissed-out Flower Children traipsing around
like whacked-out Ophelias speaking in riddles and dancing like Isadora Duncan and gathering at immense en-
campments in unlikely places like Monterey or Woodstock,
from which they had to be extricated by prodigious feats
of paramedical ingenuity.

To anyone who was even semiconscious in this period,
it was obvious that something big was happening. You
couldn't switch on a radio or TV, pick up a newspaper or
news magazine, without getting Rock right up the kazoo.
Yet to that original Magical Minstrel, Elvis Presley,
locked up in his luxurious bath-study in Bel Air like a
Jacuzzi Faustus, there was nothing to Rock save a few
cute tunes by the Beatles and the dread spectre of Commie
drug-inspired youth revolt and youth degeneracy. On

those rare occasions when Elvis came down from the
mountain and surveyed the Cities of the Plain, the modern
Sodom and Gommorah, strung out on Sunset Strip; or,
when he listened with dark, angry brows to the obscenities
of Mick Jagger and the horrible caterwauling of acid-rock
bands—imagine! naming a kind of music after a *drug!*—
Elvis would hurl down thunderous bolts of Jehovahan rage
and righteous indignation.

No wonder, then, that when the Beatles first came to
America—welcomed on the *Ed Sullivan Show* by a telegram wishing them every success and signed by Elvis
Presley (though dispatched without his knowledge by
Colonel Parker)—Elvis refused point-blank to meet these
dubious young men who aspired to the hand of his daughter, the American youth audience. "Hell, I don't wanna
meet them sons o' bitches!" exploded Elvis when the Colonel ran the proposition by him for the first time during
the Beatles' initial tour in 1964. Even if Elvis hadn't entertained deep doubts about where these dudes were coming from, he wouldn't have been eager to meet them. Had
he ever been keen to meet the stars?

The Colonel was not a man to take no for an answer,
especially when the refusal came from his puppet, Elvis.
Continuing his campaign to create the illusion of good
feelings between his famous client and the Beatles, the
Colonel sent next to the English boys a gift he knew would
blow their minds: four fabulous suits of cowboy clothes,
with ten-gallon hats and fancy boots and real six-shooters
in leather holsters. It was the national equivalent of the
key to the city. When the Beatles returned in 1965, they
wore the outfits for one of their prodigiously successful
dates. That was the signal to the Colonel to bear down
hard on Elvis and make him receive his natural foes the
next time they came around, as they were scheduled to do
in the third week of August when Elvis was in Los Angeles
working on one of his schmuckiest travelogues, *Paradise,
Hawaiian Style.* "Okay, okay," sighed Elvis, conceding,
once again, that he had been defeated. "But," he warned,
"they're going to have to come up here to the house!" That
was good enough for the Colonel. Now, he would be able

to sit down face to face with Brian Epstein and tell him:
"Elvis is dying to meet the Beatles."

At this time, Elvis was back in the circular house on
Perugia Way, after living for a couple of years on Bellagio
Road. During his absence, the circular patio in the center
of the house had been roofed with glass and the space
turned into a large game room with a pool table and various other adult toys. Elvis was still holding court, however, in the den, the scene of all those parties in the early
sixties.

On the great night, Elvis took his accustomed seat on
the long sofa against the wall, flanked by all his men:
Marty Lacker, foreman at the time; Joe Esposito; Billy
Smith, Elvis's little cousin; Jerry Schilling, a good-looking
young man from Memphis; Alan Fortas; Sonny West; and
a couple of new men: Mike Keaton and Ray Sitton, a 280-
pound hanger-on from the Music Gate, whom everybody
called "Chief." Soon this group was joined by the Colonel
and Tom Diskin. The wives and children were sequestered
in another room until the men should have finished their
business.

Around nine in the evening, the Beatles arrived in a
black limousine with a couple of bodyguards, a British pop
journalist and Brian Epstein. Virtually the entire Bel Air
security force was on hand plus a contingent from the
LAPD to prevent the fans from mobbing the stars or breaking through the gate into the parking area. On the way
to the house, the Beatles had speculated on how they would
find Elvis. "I expect we'll find he's just like one of us,"
remarked John Lennon. George Harrison was less confident. "I hope so," he said doubtfully, "some people are a
let-down." Now as the new princes of rock were ushered
across the thick white carpet and into the den, they could
hear their records blasting from the jukebox.

When the Beatles entered, Elvis rose to greet them.
Tanned by the Hawaiian sun, dressed casually in a red
shirt, black windbreaker and skin-tight grey trousers, he
looked healthy and relaxed. As Elvis smiled in recognition,
John, affecting comical nonchalance, quipped, "Oh, there
you are!" Formal introductions were made all round. Then,
Elvis resumed his seat, with John and Paul on his right

hand, Ringo and George on his left. As the jukebox continued to blare, alternating hits by the Beatles with hits by Elvis, nobody said a word.

The Beatles stared at Elvis. Elvis stared at the Beatles. None of the Guys felt it was his place to speak. Even the Colonel was oddly silent. Finally, when something like five minutes had elapsed, Elvis could bear the silence no longer. "Well, look," he protested, "if you damn guys are gonna sit here and stare at me all night, I'm gonna go to bed! Let's call it a night! I didn't mean for this to be like a thing—the subjects call on the king—or something like that! I just thought we'd sit and talk. We can talk about some music and maybe play a little, jam a little." The instant he said, "jam," all the Beatles cried, "What! God, we'd love to play with you!" The ice had been broken.

Soon the group had broken into separate circles. Elvis, John and Paul drifted into a quiet spot. "How many hits have you written now," asked Elvis, preoccupied as always by numbers and the sheer weight of the Beatles' triumph. John and Paul began earnestly reckoning, as if the figure had some special importance. When it was John's turn to ask a question, however, he wanted to know something crucial. "Why don't you go back to your old style of record," he asked. Elvis, who hadn't cut a rock single in years, offered his usual cop-out. "It's my film schedule," he explained. "It's so tight...but," he smiled, "I might do just one more for kicks." Lennon's comeback, "Then we'll buy it," was intended as a joke, but it signified clearly what the Beatles thought of Elvis's current work.

As Elvis chatted with John and Paul, Ringo started shooting pool on the table in the patio, surrounded by all the children of the entourage. Meantime, Colonel Parker and Joe Esposito laid hands on a cocktail table that opened up to become a roulette table. Appointing Joe croupier and himself pit boss, the Colonel called out in a formal tone: "The casino is open!" Immediately, he was joined by Brian Epstein, who had been as eager to meet the Colonel as the Beatles had been to meet Elvis.

After shooting some pool, Elvis broke out a bass guitar, which he was just learning to play. Ordering that the Beatles be equipped with guitars, he started to lead the jam session. The high point of the rave-up was Elvis picking out the bass bit on "I Feel Fine." "Coming along quite promising on bass, Elvis," said Paul encouragingly.

Then, it was time for one final chat on the long sofa about the fans and how it feels to face such immense and intimidating crowds as the Beatles had recently confronted at Shea Stadium. The once unimaginable range of experience that Elvis had been the first to traverse had now been scaled at an even higher altitude by the Beatles. The evening ended with the five young men comparing notes like astronauts discussing their trips to the moon.

The meeting was adjudged by all a success, except for George Harrison, who withheld himself from the conversation and behaved all night as if he were suffering from a fit of the pip. When it was time to leave, the Beatles said, "We'd like for all of you to come up to the place where we're staying tomorrow night." Elvis replied, "Well, I'll see. I don't know whether I can make it or not." Then, the Beatles turned to the Guys and said, "You're welcome with or without him." Several of the Guys said, "Fine!" The cagey ones, like Joe, held back because they didn't want Elvis to think they were too eager to hang out with his principal rivals. That sort of thing could make Elvis rage with jealousy.

The next night Marty Lacker, Jerry Schilling, Richard Davis and Sonny West went to see the Beatles in the house on Mulholland Drive which they were occupying for their week in Los Angeles. It was a big house with a spectacular and commanding view of the city. Once the Guys had settled into conversation with their hosts, John Lennon spoke up and in that marvelously candid style of his clarified the Beatles' intentions with regard to American celebrities. "Let me tell you guys something," he said: "There's only one person in the United States of America that we have ever wanted to meet—*not that he wanted to meet us!* And we met him last night. We can't tell you how we felt. We just idolized him so much. When we first came to town, these guys like Dean Martin and Frank Sinatra and all these people wanted to come over and hang around with us at night simply because we had all the women, all the chicks. We don't want to meet those people. They don't

really like us. We don't really admire or like them. The
only person that we wanted to meet in the United States
of America was Elvis Presley. We can't tell you what a
thrill that was last night!" There is John Lennon for you,
telling it, as always, just like it is.

At this point, Paul offered to show the Guys around the
house. As they are proceeding through the wing with the
bedrooms, Paul opens a door, proclaiming, "This is George's
room." As the Guys troop inside dutifully, they're startled
to see that the room is not empty. George Harrison is in
the room with Joan Baez. When the Guys appear at the
door, she says "Hi!" Jerry Schilling is a great fan of Joan
Baez; bumping into her in this manner renders him
speechless. Paul continues on the tour breezily, as if nothing had happened. The moment Schilling can recover his
breath, however, he's at Paul begging him to use his influence so that Schilling can get Joan Baez's autograph.

By this time, the tour has led outside the house to the
pool, which sits atop a cliff that falls away from the house
on the side overlooking the city. As the Beatles and the
Guys emerge from the house earnestly discussing how they
are going to obtain Joan Baez's autograph, a great racket
reaches their ears. It turns out that two desperately determined teenage girls have risked their lives by climbing
straight up the cliff face to reach the Beatles' house—and
get their autographs!

The Guys had left Elvis sound asleep at the house on
Perugia Way. Now they were eager to get back before the
master arose and found them missing. The Beatles urged
them to stick around and go out that night to the Hollywood Bowl and see the show. There was nothing in this
world that the Guys would sooner have done—but the
very thought of Elvis waking up and asking for them and
then learning that they were off with the Beatles sent
tremors of terror through their hearts. They declined the
invitation and when they saw the Beatles again the following year on their third tour of America, the Guys had
to decline again. A man may not serve, or even visit over-
long, two masters.

In the spring of 1966, Elvis resolved, after an absence
of two years from the recording studio, on making a major

effort at reviving his moribund recording career. The Colonel's insistence on producing nothing but movie soundtrack albums had by this time made Elvis the laughingstock of the record business. For years his records had been mediocre, but at least they sold. Now they were so dreadful that even the fanatical Presley fans wouldn't buy them. Clearly, if Elvis were going to continue making records, he would have to take a new tack. Such a change was facilitated by the fact that Elvis's long-time producer, Steve Sholes, had retired for reasons of health and been replaced by a new man, Felton Jarvis, who was very eager to refurbish Elvis's reputation. RCA, prohibited from cashing in on the new rock, must have been desperate to get something out of its once great pop star. Vast sums were being made again by rock stars: far more money even than had been made by Elvis in his greatest years. Bob Dylan, the Beatles, the Rolling Stones were not only piling up hit singles but selling albums in unprecedented numbers. The age of the "45" was over; now when people talked about a record they meant an album.

Having spent the past two years intensely involved with spiritualism, it was only natural that Elvis should have been inspired at this moment to record a great gospel album. Gospel had always been his favorite form of music; gospel was a music he had never stopped performing for his own pleasure; gospel would give him a chance to unite his deepest personal preoccupations with his musical talent to create for once a work that expressed his total being. It seemed like a very promising idea, and everything Elvis did by way of preparation increased the likelihood that he would produce a uniquely expressive album.

He decided, for example, to hire Jake Hess and his new quartet, the Imperials. Not just Hess but the old arrangements of the Statesmen were to be used in the album. A group of four female singers was also added so that the sound would have the fullness of a mixed choir. The band was recruited from among the best studio musicians in Nashville. The session was prolonged for three whole days so that every song could be brought to perfection. If ever in his career Elvis went all the way to achieve a work of art, this was the occasion.

How Great Thou Art was certified for a gold record. It also won a Grammy as the best gospel album of the year. (Colonel Parker got quite active in the Grammy organization and for the first time in years RCA began to receive some awards.) Commercially, therefore, the album bore at least the appearance of success. Artistically, however, it is one of the most disappointing performances in the Presley canon. Ever since "Crying in the Chapel," recorded in 1960 (though not released until 1965), Elvis had been singing gospel songs with a sugary and artificial voice that harkened back to the days of the first crooners. Now he orchestrated this phony religioso tone to create a new idiom that could best be described as religious easy-listening or Nashville Soul.

The essential ingredient in this musical pap is Elvis himself, whose holy crooning suggests the mock piety of a spooky funeral director. Swelling the concoction and giving it a specious fullness is the vocal chorus, which harmonizes everything in the tritest barbershop chords embellished with a high, other-worldly soprano. Through the entire first side of the album, every song is extruded from these vocal nozzles at the same slow puling tempo and with the same frozen attitude of spurious devoutness. The image that best fits this sacred snow job is of one of those gaseous, gelatinous, synthetic confections called Smoothies.

If spiritualism couldn't revive Elvis's talents, it was of no greater avail in the even more difficult struggle in which Elvis engaged in this period to change his head. One of the great principles of yogic literature, Elvis discovered, was the notion that to hear and feel the "high vibrations" through which the Masters communicate with the Adepts on earth, you have to be very quiet, very still, a human ssssh! Now this was an ideal diametrically opposed to the temperament of the world's greatest rock star. Elvis was as tightly strung as a violin, as manic as speed, as quick-tempered as a wildcat and perpetually onstage. How are you going to make a guy like this into a cigarstore Indian? One of his principal propaedeutics was a book titled *Autobiography of a Yogi* by Paramahansa Yogananda.

This book reads like a fairy tale. The young Adept is forever meeting great gurus who perform the most astonishing feats of mental telepathy, levitation, materialization and dematerialization. One of them even enables the future yogi to pass his college exams by putting all the right answers in his brain with a telepathic crib book. As for Yogananda himself, he's the original flower child. Nothing in his entire life ever sours for an instant the essential sweetness of his disposition. He's Yogi Bear.

Nor did anything become the Yogi in this life so much as the leaving of it. According to the report of the morticians at Forest Lawn (reprinted as a testimonial in all the brochures of Yogananda's Self-Realization Fellowship), "No physical disintegration was visible in his body even twenty days after death.... No indication of mold was visible on his skin.... No odor of decay emanated from his body.... This state of perfect preservation of the body is, so far as we know from mortuary annals, an unparalleled one." When Elvis was confronted by Doubting Thomases and men of little faith, he would throw this testimony in their teeth. How could you argue against incorruptibility?

Though this great guru died in 1952, long before Elvis discovered the Way, he left behind him a fully developed spiritualist academy with its main campus atop a mountain overlooking Pasadena. To this Laputan ashram Elvis loved to go because it fulfilled so perfectly all his ideas of how the higher life should appear. First, there was the winding journey up to the top of the mountain, commencing in the wicked valley and ending after countless hairpin turns on the heights. Your arrival in Shangri-La was signaled by two golden lotus buds atop the gate posts. The retreat was a perfect Raymond Chandler setting: a turn-of-the-century vacation hotel, with verdurous lawns constantly crossed and recrossed by mysterious women swathed in pale green, orange, blue and champagne-colored saris. There was a meditation garden, which Elvis duplicated immediately at Graceland. Down where the hill sloped toward the sinful city, the paths were barricaded because this portion of the grounds contained the quarters of the brothers and sisters who lived in celibate serenity, spending their lives in spiritual exercises, good works and meditation. When Elvis was told that this area was closed to him, it was all he could do to restrain the impulse to declare himself a celibate and plunge into the mysteries beyond.

The resident djin was a sweet, cooing pouter pigeon of a woman who called herself Daya Mata. Years before she had been Fay Wright of Salt Lake City. Then she had been drawn into the ineffable presence of the yogi, who, like most of his kind, had a great fondness for female disciples. (Remember the scandal when the Beatles, meditating on the banks of the Ganges, discovered the Maharishi making a pass at Mia Farrow!) Elvis was very taken by the soothing aura that emanated from Daya Mata. He called her fondly, "Ma."

When Elvis first met Ma, he asked her to authorize him to learn the secrets of Kriya Yoga, which is the ultimate notch on the scale of self-realization: the power to materialize and dematerialize at will, like a Homeric god. Ma laughed at this brash and naive proposal. She counseled patience, humility, perseverance—all the virtues in which Elvis was most lacking. He, in turn, offered money, which she gratefully accepted on behalf of the Foundation. (Giving money to these heathen so infuriated Vernon that he ordered the office staff at Graceland not to forward any letters from the SRF to Elvis.)

No matter how spiritual Elvis became, he could never attain the slightest degree of control over his terrible temper. Even when he was fresh from a soothing session with Ma, conducted in her top-floor retreat atop the mountain, the moment he got back on the level, he was prone to acts of irrational violence. Once as he was heading home from his Shangri-La, he drove past a Gulf station at the foot of the hill where a couple of attendants were shadowboxing. Elvis ordered his big limousine to pull into the station. Rolling down the window, he made some sort of remark to the boxers, admonishing them to embrace love, not hostility. As his car pulled away, one of the dudes thrust up his finger in a fuck-you sign. That did it!

Instantly the car screeched to a stop and Elvis came charging out of the rear door. Advancing on the foremost attendant, Elvis threw a high karate kick that missed the man's body but sent his tire pressure gauge flying up in the air. Then Elvis whipped out a .38 from his shoulder holster and was just about to lower it when Hamburger James came rushing up from behind and shouted, "Gimme the gun!" Automatically, Elvis turned around and handed the astonished valet the weapon. In a second, they were back in the car and running for their lives, terrified that the evening paper would arrive with the headline: ELVIS PRESLEY THREATENS TO SHOOT GAS STATION ATTENDANT.

Whenever Elvis sinned against the great god Cool, whenever he tore up his living room with a barrage of karate kicks or drove through the closed gates of Graceland because they weren't opened swiftly enough or whipped out a gun and shot up some offending car (that wouldn't start) or some enraging TV set (that wouldn't hold the picture), he would experience pangs of guilt. If the pangs were keen enough, he would make amends. Interestingly, this atonement took the form of the penalty for murder in ancient civilizations: what the Anglo-Saxons called *wergild,* or man-money. Each time Elvis went crazy with rage, he would buy all the Guys extravagant and undeserved gifts. They might all receive Harley-Davidson motorcycles or Cadillac convertibles or even more expensive Mercedeses. Elvis didn't care whether the men kept the cars or sold them the next day. The important thing was that he bought his freedom from guilt.

Once this practice became common, it alarmed both Vernon Presley and the Colonel. Vernon was unable to do anything but beg his son to desist. His powers of moral suasion were limited by the fact that he was on the payroll for $72,800 a year and owed everything he had to Elvis. The Colonel was in a different position. When he saw that Elvis was likely in the future to literally throw his money away, the Colonel may have decided it was much better that he get the money instead of a lot of yes-men and girlfriends.

On January 2, 1967—on the eve of his negotiations with RCA for a new seven-year contract—Colonel Parker dictated a letter of agreement addressed to Elvis Presley that commenced: "As per our understanding on the telephone a few weeks ago, here is the amended agreement to our existing management agreement. As of this date all

existing contracts change. The renewals will be 50% to
Elvis Presley and 50% to All Star Shows [Colonel Par-
ker]. All overages and profits, all expense payments will
be 50% to Elvis Presley and 50% to All Star Shows." The
letter goes on to stipulate that a like fifty-fifty split would
be made of all income deriving from merchandising agreements and that the term of this new agreement would be
January 22, 1976.

Fifty-fifty splits are rare in the modern entertainment
business; but in the bad old days when unscrupulous white
managers exploited black artists to the limits of rapacity,
such outrageous spoliations were quite common. Duke
Ellington surrendered fifty percent of everything he
earned throughout most of his career to Irving Mills, as
did Louis Armstrong to Joe Glaser. In defense of the old
agents, it could be said that they were unique in even
deigning to represent black artists and that the sums involved were never great. Colonel Parker, on the other
hand, was representing the most famous entertainer in
the world in deals that entailed millions of dollars. His
only excuse for taking an exorbitant commission was that
Elvis Presley was his only client.

Subsequently, Colonel Parker would argue that his relationship with Elvis Presley was unique and beyond comparison with normal manager-artist arrangements. He
would assert that he was not Elvis's manager so much as
he was the star's partner. Unlike other manager-artist
partnerships, however, the Parker-Presley partnership
worked only one way. Colonel was entitled to half of everything that Elvis earned, but Elvis was not entitled to any
share in Parker's other business. Colonel's reasoning appears to be that whatever Elvis got he owed to the Colonel's
skill as a bargainer; whereas what Colonel got for himself
he owed only to the same cause. The real earner, therefore,
was Colonel Parker. Elvis was just a passive property in
the Colonel's eyes, who, in another man's hands, might
not have been worth anywhere near what the Colonel got.
Such reasoning earned the Colonel another 25%.

Chapter 26

Love and Marriage

IN OCTOBER or November of 1966, Elvis received a very distressing call from Major Beaulieu. It was a reminder, in no uncertain terms, of Elvis's promise to marry Priscilla. The Beaulieus, the major told Elvis, had taken him at his word. They had been very patient. They understood the problems that marriage might pose for his career. Nonetheless, over four years had elapsed since Priscilla had arrived at Graceland and still no date had been set for the wedding. As far as the Beaulieus were concerned, there could be no further excuse for delay.

How did Elvis feel about Priscilla after all these years together? Probably, he felt much the same as he did after his divorce, when he confided his final view of the relationship to Linda Thompson: "I tried to mold her into what I thought I wanted. I realized too late that you just can't do that. You can't teach a person to be affectionate. By nature, she's a cold person. She's reserved. She's very disciplined. She was brought up in a military environment. Very disciplined. Very reserved. Very cold. So I tried to teach her to be warm and funny and loving and affectionate. She tried to do it, but you really can't teach someone to be what they aren't." What's more, as Priscilla grew to maturity, Elvis was outraged to discover that she had a will of her own. He characterized her as suffering from a

459

"Napoleon complex." The reason, he explained, was her size: "She's just mad 'cause she never grew." Then, he'd admit ruefully, "When I first met her, she had a cute face. I thought, 'She's short but she'll grow.' Then, the years went by and she never did!"

Elvis reluctantly set a date "during the holidays or right after." When the holidays came, Elvis managed one more delay of four months. During that time, he threw himself into the greatest spending binge of his life. Before we consider this astonishing spree and its consequences, we should understand Elvis's basic stance toward the whole question of marriage: not just marriage to Priscilla but marriage in general.

It's obvious in the first place that Elvis had far less to gain and much more to lose through marriage than most men. He certainly didn't need a woman to provide him with the comforts of home. He had a huge domestic staff that was carefully trained to anticipate and fulfill his slightest whim. As for finding companionship in marriage, the truth is that one of his greatest fears was that marriage might cost him those companions with whom he had spent many years in comradely pleasures. Even at this early date, Elvis was regarding with dismay the defections from the ranks of the Guys caused by their marriages and new families. If he himself were to marry, the whole life-style that he had spent a lifetime developing might be destroyed. As for marriage as a means of holding a woman, Elvis was capable of maintaining a relationship with a woman he liked for years without marriage: That was precisely what he had done with Priscilla and before with Anita Wood and Dixie Locke. When you got right down to it, therefore, the only thing that Elvis could gain through marriage would be children. He was fond of children. He was sure that some day he would have children. Still, what was the hurry? A man could have children at any age.

Even though Elvis had little to gain through marriage, the most decisive factor was not the calculation of gaining or losing but rather Elvis's emotional response to the idea of marriage. Whenever Elvis got on this topic, he would always make the same speech: "Man, I wasn't made to be married. I don't like it. Look at the typical American fam-

ily scene: Man walkin' around fartin'. Woman walkin'
around scratchin'. Kids goin' around hollerin'. Hey, man,
fuck that! I never did fit in that scene and I never will.
I'm not your average American male and I don't aim to
be that sucker."

If Elvis loathed marriage, why did he marry? The basic
reason—paradoxical as it must sound—is because Elvis
associated love with marriage. As we have seen already,
he had the sort of temperament that was highly susceptible
to intense, love-at-first-sight affairs. All he needed to fall
madly in love was just a glimpse of the right face. The
very first time he laid eyes on Priscilla Beaulieu, for example, he experienced such an infatuation. He saw her as
a teen angel, and no sooner did he feel the rush of romantic
love than he associated it with the thought of marriage.
This is precisely what he had done some years before with
Debra Paget. Though the actress regarded him at first
with scorn, he was willing after just a few weeks to make
her his wife. Prior to Debra Paget, Elvis had sought to
marry Dixie Locke, packing his bag and making as if to
leave his parents' house. Marriage to Elvis was like orgasm to sex: It was the climax of his most passionate encounters. Yet, like orgasm, the urge to marry was not an
enduring condition: It was just a feverish spasm of desire.
If the offer was not soon consummated by the act, the
impulse to make it soon subsided.

Once Elvis was past his first romantic infatuation with
a woman, the character of his relationship with the woman
began to change radically. The erotically charged emotion
of the initial phase would vanish, and in its place would
arise a totally different kind of connection. Instead of passion, the theme would now become play. Instead of heavy
macho wooing, the roles would reverse and the woman
would be expected to take the initiative. Soon, even this
playful kind of love would evaporate, and Elvis would slip
into his basic role, which was that of the child being babied
by his adoring mother. It used to astonish the Guys, how
swiftly this transformation could occur: how a girl whom
Elvis had dated just a few times would suddenly start
mothering him and pampering him and speaking to him

in baby talk. He struck a chord in women, all right: the umbilical cord.

Once Elvis had brought a relationship around to this baby-mommy level, the promise of marriage was totally forgotten. After all, one doesn't marry one's mother. Quite the contrary: He enjoys the warmth of the maternal embrace while looking about for some nice little girl with whom, once again, to fall in love. This pattern explains every relationship Elvis ever had with a woman—except one: Priscilla. Elvis got himself in so deep with Priscilla he couldn't get out. Though Elvis prolonged his relationships with other women—Anita Wood before his marriage and Linda Thompson after the marriage—for just as long as he kept Priscilla dangling (five years seems to have been his proper limit), he did not make the mistake of committing himself in advance to these women as he did to Priscilla. By demanding and obtaining a mere child, by pledging his honor to a stern military figure like Major Beaulieu, Elvis created conditions of compulsion that would have made many men buckle under. Elvis was not, after all, a strong or rebellious personality. Elvis the Obedient was always stronger than Elvis the Rebel. Elvis the Angry was quickly smothered by Elvis the Guilty. Though Elvis was capable of cruel and ruthless behavior when he was operating behind a blind, he was extremely sensitive to any threat of public dishonor.

Having conceded this much to his character and his predicament, one must add that Elvis was perfectly capable of reneging on a promise or breaking a contract or backing out of any deal that he felt posed a deep threat to his own best interests. If the only pressures that had been brought to bear upon him in this case were the pangs of conscience or the distant rumbles of Major Beaulieu, it is very doubtful that Elvis would have married Priscilla and thereby placed in jeopardy both his career and his future happiness. No, the process by which Elvis was brought to marriage is far more bizarre than anything that would have befallen a more rational person.

The reason for the last-minute postponement of the marriage, after everyone had agreed that the ceremony should take place during or immediately after the Christmas holidays, is unknown and probably insignificant. What is important is Elvis's behavior during this time. Unlike the traditional bachelor who enjoys one last fling before he settles down to become a husband, Elvis, absorbed in spiritual pursuits, was not in the least disposed to his customary dissipations. Nothing is more characteristic of the man who cannot face some grave problem than the development of a saving distraction. This is precisely what happened to Elvis Presley on the eve of his marriage.

Late one afternoon in February, while out riding in the country south of Memphis in Mississippi, Elvis steered his big Harley-Davidson motorcycle down a narrow blacktop road in the vicinity of the little town of Walls. Snow was on the ground and the light was already failing, when suddenly out the gloaming appeared to him the signal he had been so desperately seeking. There in a lonely pasture not far ahead arose before his astonished gaze an immense cross, standing over fifty feet high, illuminated eerily against the dun sky. What could such a portent mean? Elvis pulled of the road and scrutinized the scene carefully.

The cross was a massive object made of cast concrete and weighing many tons. At its foot was a small lake over which arched a distinctively oriental bridge. Nothing else was visible on the property except a charming little house set beside a gate in the chain-link fence that surrounded the acreage. Off in the distance there were some cattle barns and behind them, barely visible, a stand of trees. These physical properties were of no account. What mattered was the atmosphere of the place, which was fraught with strong religious overtones.

When Elvis got back to Graceland, he immediately put in motion an inquiry that soon revealed the property belonged to a man whom Elvis knew: Jack Adams, an airplane salesman. Back in the fifties, Adams had tried to sell the star a plane for his tours. Nothing had come of the effort because Gladys had told Adams that she was very alarmed at the thought of Elvis flying. Since that time, the men had never met again. Adams was still in the same business; he had an office not far from the farm Elvis had seen at a little local flying field called Twinkletown Airport. Just two days after Elvis first saw the great white cross looming from the pasture of Adams's farm, he and his boys pulled up outside the salesman's office in two big black Cadillac limousines.

Adams, an extremely polite and diffident sort of man who could easily compete with Elvis for the number of times he says "Yes, sir" or "No, sir" in an ordinary conversation, was startled when he looked out his window and saw the big cars disgorge their loads of heavyset men wearing western clothes. (The Guys had been doing a lot of horseback riding recently at Graceland and, at Elvis's urging, they had all adopted the western look.) The first men to confront Adams were Marty Lacker and Alan Fortas. They demanded to know whether his farm was for sale. Learning that it could be purchased for $530,000, they said that it was vastly overpriced. Just as the haggling began, Elvis walked into the room, having paused in the foyer to provide himself with a Coke from the machine. He asked if they could inspect the property. Adams immediately arranged for a guided tour. The visit wound up at the little house at the corner of the property. There Elvis and Vernon went into the sitting room alone and discussed the deal for fifteen minutes. When they were finished, Vernon asked Adams if Elvis could spend a night in the house. Adams pulled the key off his ring and told his prospective customer: "Delighted to have you."

A couple days later Elvis and Vernon turned up at Adams's office again. They told him that they liked the place and wanted to buy it just as it stood: with the cattle, the equipment, the furnishings in the house, everything on the property right down to the last roll of toilet paper. The moment the property was securely in Elvis's grasp, he started improvising what turned out to be a whole new design for his future life at home.

Dubbing his new place the Circle G Ranch, Elvis declared that it was time he and the Guys exchanged their old life-style at Graceland for a new way of life at the new Graceland, which would be constructed on the ranch. When they were just a bunch of young bachelors, nothing more was needed than a big house with a few servants to do the cooking and cleaning. For a group of solidly married mature men, the accommodations would have to take another form. Instead of one house, they would all require houses. Elvis would have the big house and each Guy would have a small house. It would be like a castle surrounded by cottages. Or, as a couple of the boys pointed out, it would be like that new phenomenon they were hearing so much about out on the West Coast—the commune!

Yes, that was the idea. Elvis Presley was going to establish the first commune in Mississippi. What's more, he was going to do it quickly. In fact, he wanted it done overnight. So whipping out the magic wand inscribed all over with dollar signs, Elvis began summoning up on this quiet and remote tract of land, not far from the crossroads called Bull Frog Corner, a whole new plantation.

The first thing was to get all the Guys properly mounted. Elvis had bought some horses for Graceland—a beautiful golden Palomino for himself called Rising Sun, a little horse for Priscilla called Domino, and some other animals for the Guys. Now everyone had to get in the saddle and play cowboy. That meant even the enormously obese Lamar, whose horse reared up one day and threw him violently to the ground—to everyone's vast delight. Mounting the commune on horseback, however, wouldn't help them get around the rough back-country roads or trails on the ranch. So Elvis decreed that everyone must now be equipped with a pickup truck.

In no time a score of Rancheros and El Caminos had been delivered to the ranch. Buying trucks, though, tickled some nerve in the one-time truck driver that responded so delightfully that he couldn't stop with just outfitting the family and the Guys—he had to go right on with his truck buying until he had equipped everyone in sight. Eventually, plumbers, carpenters, surveyors, anybody who showed up on the property were subject to an off-the-wall offer of a shiny new truck. Elvis got so carried away in the course of this binge that he started offering trucks to people to whom he had already given a truck. When they balked, he ordered them to find somebody else to whom to give the truck. In this manner, in a couple of weeks, Elvis bought enough trucks to outfit a company of motorized infantry. Marty Lacker recalls standing in front of the ranch office one night at two in

the morning, watching Elvis operate a tractor, and suddenly finding Vernon Presley beside him looking distraught and holding out in the cold night air an enormously long strip of adding machine ribbon. "Marty, what
am I gonna do?" cried out Vernon. "He done bought ninety-
seven thousand dollars' worth o' trucks!"

Once the rancheros had been equipped with Rancheros,
the next problem was how to house them. By this time
word of Elvis's spending binge had spread like wildfire
over the whole area. Salesmen for every conceivable item
made a beeline to the ranch and laid siege to the gate.
Every time Elvis went in or out of the place, these hustlers
would jump the Big Spender and start describing or demonstrating their wares. One dude was a salesman for mobile homes. He provided Elvis with the solution to his
housing problem. If Elvis were in such a big hurry, why
should he bother constructing buildings? All he had to do
was buy a flock of mobile homes and park them on concrete
pads. Elvis agreed and gave the necessary orders, but then
a hitch developed because it turned out there were zoning
rules even out here in the country. You couldn't just slap
down a colony of mobile homes. This demanded an all-out
effort to obtain variances from the zoning regulations.
When the variances were obtained, the wand waved again
and in a few days no less than six huge mobile homes were
trucked onto the property and lined up in a row on their
concrete pads.

Naturally, once the fans got wind of their hero's change
of venue, they came flocking down to the ranch in great
numbers and made a nuisance of themselves by standing
around the gate or even climbing over the five-foot fence
to check out the action at close quarters. Elvis had hoped
to have more, not less privacy on his commune. Instantly,
he waved the wand again and overnight fifteen-foot walls
of cypress were erected along the borders of the property
to shut off the view of the goings-on inside the ranch. These
wooden walls didn't stop the curious. People who owned
houses overlooking the ranch began to construct observation platforms on their rooftops, which would enable
them and their guests to enjoy the forbidden spectacle.
Soon Elvis was dismayed to discover that every move he

made was subject to scrutiny from observers with field glasses, telescopes and photographers with telescopic lenses.

When Elvis bought the ranch, it was stocked with 150 head of prize cattle: Santa Gertrudises developed by Winthrop Rockefeller on the King Ranch in Texas. That was a good start, but it wasn't much fun simply owning the cattle: The real thrill was in adding to the herd or even in finding some new kind of livestock that would be more distinctively Elfan. Not far away, at Colliersville, Tennessee, Elvis learned there was a ranch that bred prize Tennessee walking horses. Elvis went immediately to the GLL Farms and met the owner, George L. Lenox, Jr. Though there were three hundred horses at the ranch, the only one that interested Elvis was the prize of the lot: a famous stud named Carbon Copy. The asking price for this one animal was $100,000. What restrained Elvis from buying it is unknown; but after repeated visits and discussions, he finally relinquished his plan to purchase the horse and establish the Presley stud.

Perhaps Elvis was dissuaded by the need to spend a lot of money on other things at the ranch. After all, he wanted to build a fine house there for himself and Priscilla. He had decided also that he needed a cattle barn with a capacity of a hundred animals. Meantime, his infatuation with every conceivable kind of vehicle had him now into buying three-stall horse trailers and tractors and all sorts of odd-looking farm machinery. There is no knowing how far Elvis might have carried this crazy binge, if the Colonel had not succeeded in heading him off by negotiating a fast movie deal that demanded Elvis's presence in Hollywood by late March. Vernon was on the phone constantly at this time begging the Colonel to find some way to avert the financial ruin looming in the wake of Elvis's mad prodigality. Vernon's own efforts to put the brakes on by presenting Elvis with itemized lists of his expenses had met with no results at all. Elvis wouldn't even stop to look at the tabulations. The only hope was to employ the tactics used to curb bulls or tantrum-throwing infants—distraction.

By the time Elvis left to make *Clambake*, he had blown

more than a million dollars in cash. He had also increased his already heavy payroll by engaging new men to run the ranch, and he was about to blow another large sum of money by purchasing and decorating a new $425,000 house in the Trousdale Estates, adjacent to Beverly Hills. Though the finances of the Presley organization have always been guarded like the gold at Fort Knox, there are a couple of very clear signs that indicate how close this binge came to breaking the Elvis bank. One is the fact that for the first and only time in his life, Elvis had to make some of his purchases on credit. The other is that later in the same year, he was forced to sell portions of his two publishing firms—Elvis Music and Gladys Music—to Hill and Range. Putting it all together, it is clear that this spending spree was not just a prank or eccentric fling. It was a statement, inspired by extreme psychological stress.

Apart from his effort to hold the Guys together by providing them with new homes and new toys in his immediate vicinity, one can see the spree as a desperate and reckless effort to indemnify himself for the enormous sacrifice he was about to make by getting married, as an effort to assert once again his complete control over his life, as an act of defiance against all the old fogeys who worshipped money—like the Colonel and Vernon—and simply as an exhibition of power and a manic outburst of that curious kind of euphoria that some people experience from throwing their money around.

Once the binge was over, however, Elvis woke up back in Hollywood, set to begin another of those horrible pictures that he had now come to loathe from the bottom of his heart. He was also suffering from the worst burden of excess weight he had ever acquired. For this is another and highly significant feature of his behavior at this time: He had indulged himself not just in a shopping spree but in an eating binge. Bringing one of his black cooks down to the house on the property, he gave her orders to bake him every day pan after pan of corn pone. Then, at mealtimes, he would take a glass that held a pint of buttermilk and soak inside it great chunks of the rich, heavy pone. Stuffing himself with this soggy, infantile food, he started putting on weight. As if this were not bad enough, he also indulged himself at this time with huge bowls of mashed potatoes and gravy as well as platters of sausage and home-baked biscuits. One month on this diet and Elvis weighed 210 pounds. When he stepped off the plane at L.A., the Guys who had remained on the Coast couldn't believe their eyes. Elvis was big as a hog.

Before Elvis could rid himself of the weight by his usual combination of powerful drugs and crash dieting, the director of the picture or one of the studio officials got sight of him. He communicated his alarm to Colonel Parker, who was quick to pass the message along to Elvis. Guilty as hell about having bloated up like a ballon, galled by the necessity of having to make another "travelogue" and disturbed most of all by the irrevocability of his commitment to marry Priscilla, Elvis fell into a profound state of depression.

On the night before the first day of shooting, he rose from bed—drugged, doubtless, with sleeping pills—and made his way to the bathroom of his latest Bel Air house, on Rocca Place. A TV set had been placed next to the tub, with its wire running across the floor. Elvis tripped over the cord and went head foremost into the tub. He lost consciousness and lay there for an indeterminate period of time. Then, gradually recovering consciousness, he hauled himself out of the tub and went back to the bedroom, where he fell sound asleep. The next morning, when he emerged from his room, he complained of a severe headache. Describing vaguely the fall he had taken during the night, he showed the Guys a large bump on his head. When Joe Esposito examined the swelling, as large as a golf ball, he notified Colonel Parker and summoned Elvis's doctor.

The doctor and a medical team arrived at the house almost at the same moment as the Colonel appeared with several film company officials in tow. The Colonel went into Elvis's bedroom alone and conferred there with the doctor. When the old man came out, he explained to all present that Elvis had suffered a severe brain concussion. He would be laid up in bed for some time and would require round-the-clock nursing. Work on the film would have to be postponed for at least several weeks. Then the Colonel turned on Larry Geller and told him to clean out all the books he had brought to the house. Geller was shocked, but he would have been far more shocked if he had known what Colonel Parker had in store for him.

The Colonel had been watching his chance to get rid of the Swami for a long time. He had smiled at Geller and complimented Geller, telling him that he would have made a marvelous magician because he knew so well how to control people and promote illusions. These little jokes were deadly signs, if Geller had known how to read them right. They signaled the Colonel's real view of Geller and portended an all-out effort to discredit the Swami in Elvis's eyes and then banish him forever. The moment Elvis took his fall, the Colonel saw the long-awaited opportunity. He represented to Elvis that all his problems were produced by the Swami and his books. If Elvis would just give up this spiritualist nonsense and go back to being the good boy that he had been in the old days, insisted the Colonel, everything would be fine again. The Guys would be happier, the Colonel would be happier, Elvis himself would be happier. They would be one big happy family again.

Though Elvis knew very well what the Colonel was about, he was in no condition to resist. He always shrank from any sort of confrontation with the Colonel and now was hardly the moment to make a stand. Elvis was weak, frightened, confused. He was like a sick little boy. The Colonel got everything he wanted. Elvis agreed that the books had damaged his mind. He did not object when the Colonel insisted that one of the Guys be present when Geller cut Elvis's hair so that there would be no temptation to go back to discussing the books. (This rule assured that Geller would soon throw up his job and quit, which is exactly what he did.) Finally, Elvis agreed to allow all his books to be taken out and burned.

After a couple of weeks of close confinement to bed and severe restriction of visitors, the patient was finally allowed to get up and dress. On that day the Colonel called an important meeting of the entire group. The meeting commenced with the Colonel and Joe Esposito going into Elvis's bedroom for a private conference. Then, all three came down to the living room where the Guys had assembled. Elvis looked pale, listless, out of it. Colonel sat four-square, cigar fuming in the side of his mouth, hands criss-crossed on the head of his cane. As Larry Geller recalls the scene in the book he wrote with Jess Stearn, *The Truth About Elvis,* the Colonel minced no words.

"Things are going to change around here," he said. "First of all, the payroll is going to be cut back. Elvis has been spending too much money lately, and has gone beyond what he can afford."

Larry looked at Elvis, half expecting a protest. But Elvis's eyes were on the floor. At no time did he look any of the group in the eye.

"And don't," continued the Colonel, "bring your financial burdens and other problems to Elvis. If you have any problems, mention them to Joe Esposito. He will get in touch with me.

"Leave Elvis alone. Don't expect him to be your counselor." His eyes fell on Larry for a moment. "What do you think he should do, walk down the street in robes like Jesus Christ, and save people? No, this boy has had a bad fall. He's not well. He's not in a position to help anybody. He's going back to the studio to start a picture. There's a lot of people depending on him to fulfill his obligations." His eyes moved around the group. "And I'm depending on you to help us."

As he took in the attentive faces, his head nodded in satisfaction.

"Elvis is an entertainer," he stressed. "He shouldn't fill his head with anything distracting him from what he is supposed to do." Again, his gaze fell on Larry. "You're all lucky to be here. If any of you don't like the way things are, you can leave. The door is open."

Everybody nodded. Nobody was leaving.

The Colonel leaned on his cane, and said, more amiably, "When things get back to normal, the pay cuts will be restored." He turned to the silent Elvis. "We're more than fair. Aren't we, Elvis?"

Elvis nodded, his face devoid of expression.

Finally, the Colonel announced: "From now on,

there is going to be a new foreman—Mr. Esposito." Then, turning to Marty Lacker, who was taken completely by surprise by this announcement, the Colonel added: "Mr. Lacker, you will be in charge of special projects. The first project is preparing for the *wedding*."

The Colonel had decided that Elvis should marry.

Chapter 27

The Colonel's Wedding

THOUGH Marty Lacker was ostensibly in charge of Project Wedding, it was all the Colonel's show. The Colonel contrived the event not to please Elvis or Priscilla, but to fulfill his own notions of what was appropriate. Indeed, it would be no exaggeration to say that Elvis's wedding was really the Colonel's wedding. The Colonel ordered the wedding, arranged the wedding, determined who should or should not be invited to the wedding and probably found a way to pay for the wedding by sticking someone else with the bill. The sucker was the Colonel's close friend in Las Vegas, Milton Prell, who had just purchased the Aladdin Hotel.[1]

[1]Milton Prell was the front man for Moe Dalitz, well-known gambling figure who, along with Meyer Lansky, wielded such enormous influence over the development of Las Vegas into the gameing capital of the Western Hemisphere. Prell's first job in Vegas was running the Sahara Hotel, which both Colonel and Elvis made their headquarters when they visited the city. When the hotel was sold to the Del Webb interests, Colonel and Elvis obtained shares in the business, a unique transaction. Prell, a man like Parker, who rarely made friends, was also the Colonel's neighbor in Palm Springs, the two men being constantly in and out of each other's houses.

Sin City was a very unnatural place for a man to marry who lived in Memphis and had spent years defining himself not as a flashy showbiz type but as the All-American Boy. Vegas was the perfect place, however, for Colonel Parker. Not only could he freeload the wedding, but he could play hide and seek with the press much more easily here than in Memphis and he could use the distance of the event from Elvis's home as a convenient excuse for failing to invite all those people he was intent on humiliating.

Rewarding and punishing the Guys according to their desserts was one of the Colonel's major obsessions at this time. He had always detested the Guys as wasteful parasites and feared that the brighter ones like Red and Marty might find some way of gathering power into their own hands. He had put them in their place after Elvis's accident; now he decided to give them another dose of the same medicine just to make doubly sure that they didn't repeat their former indiscretions, like advising Elvis what songs he should sing. The Colonel's plan was to keep the wedding a deep dark secret from everyone but the principals until the very last minute. Then he would clap his hands and make all his puppets dance.

On April 29, 1967, the Colonel gave the signal. Elvis, Priscilla, the favored Guys and some of the other important guests were gathered together in a house in Palm Springs. Despite the Colonel's precautions, word of the impending marriage had leaked out and the press was all over the little town. On the night of April 30, Elvis and Priscilla flew into Vegas and went to the city clerk's office at four in the morning to obtain the wedding license. The following morning, May 1, was the time that had been appointed for the ceremony. The Colonel made it appear, however, that the wedding was to be held that afternoon. He told reporters that if they gathered at the Aladdin Hotel at 1:00 P.M., he would have an important announcement to give them. They assumed the announcement would be that Elvis was about to get married, not that the event had already occurred.

That morning Marty Lacker—who had been asked at the last moment to share the honor of being best man with Joe Esposito—learned for the first time that none of the

Guys save Joe and he would be allowed to witness the ceremony. This shocked him profoundly. He knew what such a slight would mean to the men who had shared Elvis's life for years. When he entered the suite where Elvis was to be married, he recognized that the excuse he had been given—that there wouldn't be space for the Guys—was just a lie. Red West, puzzled at not getting any word about the ceremony, went to Joe Esposito's room to find out what was happening. When he saw Joe dressed in a tuxedo and learned from his lips that the Guys were not to be present at the ceremony, Red went wild with rage. He charged down the hall and banged on the Colonel's door. When the old man opened up, Red denounced him and threatened to seize his cane and beat him up. Then, having vented his spleen, Red went back to his room, where his wife was in tears, and announced that they were not going to attend the reception. They were going to boycott the whole event.

With these sweet vibes filling the air, Elvis prepared himself for the great moment. He was extremely agitated and told Marty that this was the "showdown." His appearance and Priscilla's that day have been preserved in a lot of photographs. Both of them look comically vulgar. Elvis had his hair piled up in a huge conk like that worn by such black singers as Bobby "Blue" Bland. His tuxedo was so short in the jacket and so jivey in the cut that it might have graced some salesman getting married in the Bronx. Priscilla wore the traditional white gown, veil and train. She ruined the effect of bridal beauty and virginity by giving her face the full Cleopatra treatment with the heaviest kind of kohl-black eye makeup and a mane of dyed black hair that would better have suited a witch than a bride.

Despite Elvis's lifelong involvement in Christianity, his marriage was no different from that of any free-thinking, atheistic entertainer from Broadway or Hollywood. The service was not performed by a minister but by a Jewish judge, David Zenoff, who was—naturally!— an old friend of the Colonel. Priscilla had tinkered with the then traditional vows so that "love, honor and obey" now read

"love, honor and comfort." Elvis completely missed the
implications of this modification.

Present at the ceremony in Milton Prell's private suite
were Vernon and Dee; Major and Mrs. Beaulieu with their
two oldest remaining children, Donny (seventeen) and
Michelle (thirteen); Colonel and Marie; Billy and Jo Smith;
Patsy and Gee Gee Gambill; George Klein; and the two
best men, Joe Esposito and Marty Lacker, with their wives,
Joanie and Patsy. Grandma Presley could not attend because she was not up to the journey.

Once the ceremony had been completed, the Colonel
ushered the newlyweds into a press conference. Answering
a lot of stupid and embarrassing questions about his private life must have been the last thing in the world that
Elvis Presley wanted to do at this moment; but the Colonel,
operating according to his customary policy, was intent on
getting some mileage out of the wedding now that it was
a fait accompli. When the old man felt the reporters had
had enough time, he signaled the end of the conference
and led the way to the reception.

The guests included the Colonel's staff and many of his
business colleagues. They did not include such Presley
stalwarts as Lamar Fike and Sonny West, both of whom
learned about the marriage through the media. The whole
affair was right out of the top drawer of a hotel caterer.
The food was rich and varied but it offered nothing that
would appeal to Elvis's palate. The music was that stroll-
ing violin and accordion stuff that would have set Elvis's
teeth on edge. Devoid of appropriateness, originality or
taste, it was a perfect expression of Colonel Thomas Andrew Parker.

The least that Elvis might have salvaged from his wedding was a nice restful honeymoon in some lovely setting.
Not even this was he allowed. Rushing back to Palm
Springs that night, he was installed with his bride in a
rented house. For the next couple of days, he was obliged
to return to Hollywood to put the finishing touches on
Clambake. One wonders why, after stalling so long, it was
necessary that he suddenly marry at such an inopportune
moment. When he was finally released from work, the best
he and Priscilla could do by way of having a honeymoon

was to go back to the ranch, where they holed up for a week or so with Lamar. Both of them were eager to go to Europe; but the Colonel told Elvis that Europe was off limits because his appearance there would produce complaints from fans that he never played in their countries. Instead of Europe, the Presleys wound up going to the Bahamas, which Elvis imagined would be similar to Hawaii. When he realized what a dull, stodgy place he'd chosen—and got a few days of rain—he made a quick retreat to Memphis.

On May 28 the couple held a reception for all the people in Memphis who should have been at the wedding reception. Events of this sort were always torture to Elvis. He wandered around that afternoon with a fixed smile on his face. His only consolation lay in the thought that this celebration marked the end of all the obligatory festivities attendant on the wedding. Not long afterward, he learned that Priscilla was pregnant. It's said that she was very unhappy about becoming pregnant so quickly. As she had lived on the most intimate terms with Elvis for five years, it's hard to believe that this sudden pregnancy was an accident.

During the winter following the marriage, Elvis made *Speedway* with Nancy Sinatra, who had always been an adoring fan and who, now that she was divorced from Tommy Sands, was feeling even more vulnerable to the attractions of her hero. Elvis, for his part, was inspired to indulge himself with Nancy in an orgy of the sort of pajama-party roughhouse that he always enjoyed with his teenage groupies in Memphis. Every day at lunchtime, Elvis and Nancy would go back to her dressing room trailer and play their games. Elvis would start by messing Nancy's hair or disarranging her clothes so that it would appear that they had been intimate. Or if he got really inspired, he might get her down on the floor of the trailer and dry hump her. As they tossed and turned, he would gasp in mock passion: "Did you come yet?" She would laugh hysterically, but at the same time she could feel his penis getting hard. He could feel it, too. He'd lean down close to her ear and whisper: "Do you feel Little Elvis?" When they walked out of the trailer to begin the afternoon's shooting, they'd get off on the fact that people were staring at them or whispering behind their backs.

One day Priscilla turned up on the set to have lunch. She told Nancy that she was pregnant and was expecting the baby around the first of February, which was just a couple of months distant. Nancy Sinatra could not believe that Priscilla was at such an advanced state of pregnancy because it was virtually impossible to see any signs of the baby. "How do you keep looking so slim?" she demanded. "When I get hungry," Priscilla replied, "I eat an apple." "Good for you," said Nancy, thinking: "She's got her hands full trying to hold onto this man."

As the filming drew to a close, Elvis's pranks in the dressing room got more and more out of hand. One afternoon, Nancy's maid helped her undress and then left for the day. Nancy, clad only in jeans and brassiere, went over to her closet to remove the brassiere and put on a shirt. Just as she reaches in for the shirt, out of the closet pops Elvis! Feeling very vulnerable in her half-naked condition, she gives Elvis a startled look. Then she laughs and he grabs her and holds her close. "He just got very quiet," she recalls. "He just held me. He held me very quietly, very closely to him, and he lifted up my face and he kissed me and I started to melt. I really thought I was going to die. Then he pulled away and looked at me and said: 'I'm sorry. . . . I'm sorry.' And he went out."

Nancy Sinatra was determined not to have an affair with Elvis now that he was married. At the same time, it was impossible not to be tempted. On the last day of shooting, they were having lunch in the trailer out on location and the time came to do the final shots. "Well, Silly," sighed Nancy, "see you around." Then she rose to leave. "Wait a minute," he said, "come back." Then he pulled her down on a sofa at the back of the trailer. Putting her head on his shoulder, he held her for a while. Finally she said: "I really have to leave. I don't want to. I really have to." He responded by kissing her. "I kissed him back," she remembers. "I really kissed him back. With all my heart. Not sensually. No French kissing. It was a warm, sincere, I-love-you kiss. He looked at me and said, 'That's the first time you've ever kissed me, isn't it?' 'That's right,'

I said. 'Why?' he wanted to know. I said, 'Cause I'm saying good-bye.' He gave me a big, brotherly hug and off I went. That was the last romantic moment. I treasure it dearly."

When Elvis got back to Graceland around Christmas time, everybody's mind was on the impending birth of his first child. Priscilla had gotten a book of names; from it, she and Elvis chose two pairs of names, one suitable for a boy, the other for a girl. Priscilla was convinced that she was going to give birth to a boy. She and Elvis determined his name should be John Baron. To Priscilla these names denoted "great strength and masculinity." If the child were a girl, they decided to call her Lisa Marie (after Colonel's wife).

Elaborate preparations were made for the birth of the baby. Elvis summoned all the Guys to stand by him during this critical period. Though they didn't count for enough to be present at his marriage, they were expected to support him during the birth of his child. Actually, of course, there was nothing for these big dudes to do except drive Elvis and Priscilla to the hospital and sit around there waiting for the child to be born. Even so they managed to invest this simple action with a great deal of cloak and dagger persiflage.

Two cars were to be used: A blue Cadillac, which Charlie Hodge would drive, would carry Elvis and Priscilla to Baptist Memorial Hospital, not twenty minutes from Graceland. Another car, a big black Cadillac gangster-mobile, would carry the Guys, who would act as decoys, drawing off the fans who were apt to give chase once they saw one of Elvis's cars leaving Graceland. Arrangements had also been made to alert Vernon and Dee the moment everyone else headed for the hospital; and, of course, the other relatives who lived at Graceland would be expected to come along. To accommodate this mob an extra room adjacent to Priscilla's room had been engaged just as a lounge for the family. A couple of off-duty Memphis cops had also been hired to guard the mother and baby.

Shortly after eight on the morning of February 1, 1968, Priscilla felt herself going into labor and warned Elvis that it was time to leave. Elvis alerted the boys and the long-perfected plan was put into operation. The moment the two cars got outside the gates of Graceland, however, there was a mix-up and the decoy car went off to the wrong hospital, while Elvis's car was chased all the way to the hospital driveway. Having gotten Priscilla to the hospital, there was nothing for Elvis and the boys to do the rest of the day but sit around in the doctors' lounge on the second floor and make idle conversation. Elvis finally decided that he didn't look well enough for such an important event and went home to change his clothes. When he got back in the early afternoon, he was wearing a powder blue suit with a dark blue turtleneck. Now he was prepared to face the cameras.

As an only child who had been for his entire life the center of his world's attention, Elvis could not but have felt highly ambivalent about the birth of a child. As a man who had lived always in the midst of adoring women, he must have preferred instinctively the idea of a daughter. Yet as a highly conventional male, he would have been pleased with the notion of a son who would bear his name. As a perpetual adolescent, the idea of becoming a father, that is an adult, must have also produced very mixed emotions. As we shall see, Elvis never allowed parenthood to alter his behavior in the slightest or to cause him to add even one millimeter to his growth or maturation as a human being. Even so, no matter how keenly a person clings to his youth, no matter how resolutely he blocks out all signs of age, certain events signal the passage of years and the inevitable change of roles. The extreme nervousness and the signs of intense withdrawal which the Guys observed in Elvis that afternoon were not simply evidence of the customary and comical anxiety of the expectant father. They were the signs of a very rare crisis in the life of Elvis Presley: a moment of mortality that could not be ignored.

At 5:10 in the afternoon, Priscilla's obstetrician, Dr. Turman, walked into the lounge smiling. Addressing Elvis, he said: "It's a girl! Born nine minutes ago. A perfect, beautiful little girl. Priscilla is fine. It was a perfectly normal birth." "Thank God!" gasped Elvis. Then as the congratulations of the Guys rose around him, he exclaimed: "A telephone!" Rushing out into the hall accompanied by Vernon, Elvis called Minnie Mae while Vernon tried to reach the Beaulieus in California. A few minutes later, he's back in the lounge smiling. "You know what Grandma said?" he asks with a big grin on his face. "She said, 'I know she's a beautiful baby—always take care of her.'" Vernon returned at that moment to announce that he couldn't get through to the Beaulieus because their phone was continually busy. By this point the news of the birth has spread outside the hospital and the reporters and photographers and TV crews who have been standing by all day are clamoring for an announcement.

"You go, Dad," Elvis begged his father. "Tell them I'm a happy but shaky man." Vernon and Dee promptly left for the lobby of the hospital, where they confronted the press. Looking at some notes in his hand, Vernon announced: "It's a baby girl. She was born 5:01, February 1, 1968. She weighs six pounds, fifteen ounces and is twenty inches long. Her name is Lisa Marie. No special reason for that. They picked it out of a baby book. Both mother and baby are doing fine. The father is still shaky but very happy."

"How are you doing?" shouted a reporter. "How does it feel to be a grandfather?" Vernon smiled and drawled: "I can't tell yet. I haven't had time. It's been a long time since I've been a father. But my hair's turning gray.... I guess it should now that I'm a grandfather."

By this point Elvis was on his way behind a nurse to the fifth-floor nursery to see Lisa Marie. Gazing through the glass window, he sees the raw little infant held aloft by another nurse. The baby has dark hair and blue eyes. Her hair has been brushed back, tied in a knot and bound with a pink ribbon. The nurse offers to allow Elvis to hold the baby, explaining that usually this privilege is reserved for the mother but that Priscilla is still too groggy to take the baby. (She had been given Demerol and gas and awoke later with no recollection of having given birth.) Elvis stammered and said: "No, ma'am, Priscilla—Mrs. Presley—should be the first."

That night Elvis was wired for speed. No matter how many sleeping pills he took, he couldn't knock himself out. Finally, he called up Nancy Sinatra, who took his call in her kitchen. After it had gone on for an hour she slowly

sank down onto the floor for the balance of the conversation. Elvis was in a highly characteristic frame of mind
that night: brooding on how fortunate he had been and
how fortunate his child would be. "I just don't know how
I got to be so lucky," he exclaimed at one point. Still, such
good fortune always put him in mind of those who weren't
so fortunate. "I am so lucky and my little girl is so lucky.
But what about all the babies born who don't have anything? Who don't have food!" As he explored this line of
thought, he gradually drifted into his spiritual mood. Finally, he confessed to his unseen listener: "I should have
been a preacher. I should have stayed with the church."
This thought was always at the back of his mind now, and
it would remain fixed there to the very end of his life. Like
so many should-have-beens, it was just a sentimental
fancy that was not supposed to bear any real weight. Na-
ively, Nancy Sinatra remarked: "You probably wouldn't
have this awareness now if you hadn't done what you did.
You could go back into the church—Little Richard did it.
You can do it." At that point, Elvis changed the subject.

Four days later, Priscilla was released from the hospital. She appeared before a throng of admiring spectators
on the pavement before the main entrance riding in a
wheelchair pushed by Elvis. She had teased her hair up
into a towering Cleopatra mane and put on her batwing
eyelashes and heavy makeup. She wore a suit with a mini-
skirt that rode up her thighs. Holding the baby in a big
blanket like pharaoh's daughter with the infant Moses,
she made a bizarre madonna.

The day after Priscilla was brought home from the hospital, the news media blared forth the story of Nick Adams's sudden and mysterious death. Though the public
never got all the facts, Elvis was immediately informed
of the truth. Adams, who had just gone through an acrimonious and painful divorce, had become profoundly depressed over the failure of his career. Deciding to take his
life, he had written a long suicide note and then swallowed
a bottle of pills. His body was discovered by a friend, who,
failing to reach the actor by phone, had entered his house
surreptitiously. This fast-thinking friend realized the moment he read the note that such unambiguous evidence

of suicide might cost Adams's children their father's life insurance benefits. Acting with courage and canniness, the man pocketed the note, crept back out the window through which he had come and notified Adams's lawyer, who alerted the police.

What Elvis made of this startling death, coming as it did hard on the heels of the birth of his daughter, is unknown. Along with so much else that concerns the inner life of Elvis Presley, his thoughts and emotions about the death of his only close friend in Hollywood appear to have been swallowed up by his steadily increasing introversion.

Chapter 28

The Singer Special

AS 1967 drew to a close, the fortunes of the Presley organization continued their long decline. The British Invasion of 1965 had now been echoed by a tremendous upsurge of pop music right under Elvis's nose on the West Coast. Jim Morrison and the Doors, Grace Slick and the Jefferson Airplane, Janis Joplin with Big Brother and the Holding Company, the Byrds, the Beach Boys, the Grateful Dead, the first concerts and light shows at the Fillmore West—all signaled the onset of the most feverishly creative period in American pop music since the midfifties. As the music industry rushed forward to exploit this frothing new wave of trend and talent, Elvis Presley, that fifties figure all alone in the sixties, was washed away by the tide and beached like a shipwrecked sailor marooned on a desert island. His record sales sank to an all-time low. No major studio would ante up the million dollars to make another of his silly beach-party, racing-car exploitation movies. Even the loyal Presley fans began to go whoring after strange gods. Judged by all the relevant standards, Elvis Presley was now just another famous has-been. His theme song could have been "I'm All Washed Up!"

At this moment of tight money, Elvis was still in the midst of his greatest spending spree. He blew $425,000 on

a trashy new house atop a Beverly hill. It looked as though
it had been designed by an architect from Hallmark Cards.
A cardboard villa bedecked with a couple of ornamental
features intended to suggest the French Riviera, the house
was not even functionally adequate for Elvis's needs. It
wasn't big enough to house his new family and his old
entourage. It was also much too exposed to the incursions
of the fans, to say nothing of the new race of crazy killers
and kidnappers and assassins, about whom Elvis had been
obsessed ever since the murder of Jack Kennedy. Soon,
the new house would have to be abandoned. As for the
ranch into which Elvis had poured so much money—without even counting the hundred thousand dollars worth of
trailers and trucks he had bought for the use of his boys
in the country—that dinky home on the range had lost
its charm just as rapidly as any other toy. Meantime, it
continued to eat up more money. As if all this weren't bad
enough, Vernon, who didn't have enough business sense
to run a corner grocery, had decided at this moment to do
some speculating in the Texas cattle market. He soon lost
his shirt: only it wasn't his shirt he lost—it was Elvis's.

As the ole Colonel sat in his carnival cookhouse office
at the front of the MGM lot, the atmosphere was thick
with foreboding. Was it possible that the game was up?
Could the master player be running out of tricks? Though
the endless round of busywork continued as always, there
was a feeling in the air that if the Colonel didn't soon pull
a rabbit out of the hat, they might all be looking for jobs
elsewhere. It was at this crucial moment that the Colonel
began to send out signals to NBC through his connections
at RCA that he might be willing to do something he had
always said was out of the question: star Elvis Presley in
a TV special.

When this surprising news was passed along to NBC's
vice-president in charge of operations on the West Coast,
Tom Sarnoff, youngest son of the other famous showbiz
commander, General David Sarnoff, a meeting was arranged to explore the idea. The Colonel, like any hustler
eying a fresh mark, at first affected indifference to the
proposal, treating it as if it were entirely NBC's idea and
nothing in which he was eager to get involved. What he

appeared most interested in talking about was his very
own "special." Pulling out a radio press release headed
"Elvis Presley Christmas Program," the Colonel proceeded
to lecture Sarnoff on the beauty of this radio syndication
that was being gobbled up by local stations all over the
country. The Colonel had spliced together out of Elvis's
old Christmas records a little program into which he had
stuck, like the raisins in a plum pudding, several inane
"greetings" from his boy. Especially in the South and
Southwest, the sale of this piece of trash was going pretty
well. As the show cost nothing to produce, it was turning
a profit. In fact, the Colonel urged, training his canniest
look on Sarnoff, if NBC wanted to do an Elvis special on
TV, they might just want to follow the Colonel's lead and
make it a Christmas show. Call it *Elvis and the Wonderful
World of Christmas*.

Sarnoff expressed his appreciation of the Colonel's "creative input." Then, he reverted to the business that had
brought him here to the kitchen: the terms on which the
Colonel would allow Elvis to appear as the star of a one-
hour special on NBC. He suggested that the Colonel bear
in mind that one successful appearance by Elvis on the
tube would lead naturally to further appearances in subsequent specials, perhaps three or four in as many years.

The Colonel replied that more was involved in a show
like this than just a simple appearance on the air. For one
thing, there would be reruns. What's more, the show was
certain—like Elvis's movies—to generate a very valuable
soundtrack album. RCA would appreciate that feature of
the deal. As RCA and NBC were members of the same
family, they could have a nice little thing going there.
Then, of course, there was the matter of *prestige*. This
would be the first time that Elvis had appeared on television since 1960—that was a long time ago! They couldn't
complain that Elvis Presley had been overexposed. No, sir!
Even more important was the fact that Elvis had never
done a special. This would be a *first* for NBC. That, too,
was a consideration. Oh, the more you looked into a deal
like this, the more you saw in it.

The deal the Colonel cut didn't show any shakiness in
his hand. From the demands he made, you'd never know

his client was flat on the balls of his ass. Colonel Parker sold Elvis Presley to NBC as if he were offering them the first appearance in America of the Beatles. What was he asking? Here, basically, were his terms:

1. Elvis is to receive $250,000 for the first showing; $125,000 for the second showing the following Christmas. This is predicated on a fixed schedule of work: so many weeks at so many hours per day. If they go five minutes over the schedule, they will have to pay for the overtime on a pro-rata basis calculated on the boy's per diem salary.

2. NBC will have the option to replay the program on the third and fourth successive Christmases. After that, the Presley organization has the right to buy the show. There will be the usual 50/50 split of the profits Elvis receives in his movie contracts.

3. The soundtrack album: This will be owned outright by the Presley organization, which will market it through RCA, according to the usual arrangement. This is a customary clause in all Elvis Presley contracts. Music is the Colonel's game. He has never given anyone a piece of an Elvis record.

4. Movie tie-in: NBC will produce a motion picture starring Elvis. He will receive $850,000 in salary plus 100% of the first $150,000 of net profits, subsequent profits to be split fifty-fifty. (This was the origin of *Charro,* produced through Universal.)

Once the terms of the deal had been set, Sarnoff receded from the picture and a new man came to the fore: Bob Finkel. The son of a pioneer motion picture exhibitor in Pittsburgh, Finkel had grown up in show business. He operated a so-called "in-house" TV production company called Teram, which put together programs for NBC-TV. Finkel had never worked with the Colonel or Elvis, but he knew them very well by reputation. He realized that he was stepping into a potentially explosive situation as the middleman in this first collaboration between the star

with the world's most demanding manager and the giant
network that was his boss. It was vitally important to the
success of the project that a creative producer be found
who had the special talents necessary to make this show
an unqualified success. If Elvis Presley was going to make
his first TV appearance since 1960 and do his first special
ever, the eyes of the entire entertainment world were going
to be keenly focused on the show—and on Bob Finkel.

Finkel made a decision at this point that was to have
far-reaching consequences. Instead of calling in one of the
make-no-waves hacks who were abundantly available to
him, he got in touch with the most imaginative—but also
the most independent, incorruptible and controversial—
variety producer in the history of TV, the young Steve
Binder. Even today, after twenty years in the business,
Binder impresses one on firsthand acquaintance as being
the type of earnest and idealistic young college instructor
who is forever embarrassing the administration by his
demands that students sit on the faculty council or that
avowed enemies of the state be permitted to speak in
chapel.

In 1967 he was still enveloped in the scandal produced
by his latest show, which had violated one of the business's
oldest taboos. In the finale of this program Binder had
ordered his black male star, Harry Belafonte, to touch—
yes, physically touch with his big copper-palmed hand!—
his white female star, Petula Clark. Imagine! Here are
these millions of conventional-minded Americans sitting
comfortably in their living rooms being given this wonderful opportunity by Plymouth to relax and forget about
the problems of their crazy country, when all of a sudden
they're looking at the thing that disgusts them the most:
a big buck nigger putting his hands on a pretty little white
girl!

The hullabaloo raised by that idealistically inspired
little embrace nearly blew Binder right out of the business.
When the network's southern affiliates refused to air the
show, Plymouth began to raise hell with the network.
Soon, even the show's stars, who had reacted enthusiastically to the suggestion that they get "close" on camera,
were recoiling in horror from their terrible sin. Petula

Clark fled back to England and Harry Belafonte got so
indignant that it looked like he might go on the *Tonight
Show* and tell the public *not* to buy Plymouth. Now, in
view of this subversive history, what would induce a showbiz veteran, a born survivor like Bob Finkel, to start in
with a troublemaker like Steve Binder?

The answer lay in another Binder production, this one
dating from 1965: *The T.A.M.I. Show.* As everyone in
television knew, this documentary was not only the first
but the finest full-scale treatment of rock and soul music
ever put on the tube.[1] From its opening shots—Jan and
Dean skate-boarding across L.A. jump-cut to Diana Ross
applying lip gloss at a distance of about six inches—*The
T.A.M.I. Show* had squeezed into one dazzling synopticon
nearly everything important that was happening in the
music world at that glorious moment. From Diana Ross
and the Supremes to Gerry and the Pacemakers, from
Chuck Berry to Marvin Gaye, from the Rolling Stones to
the Barbarians (a Boston group that featured a drummer
with a hook for a hand),—the program had blown the
viewer's mind as no live music show has done before or
since in the entire history of TV.

The climax of the show was provided by the most dramatic demonstration ever witnessed of the superiority of
the traditional black R & B style over the newfangled
English-oriented white rock 'n' roll. Like a professor il-
lustrating a course in popular culture, Steve Binder had
put on the screen back-to-back James Brown and Mick
Jagger, each at the peak of his performing career. For ten
electrifying minutes, Brown had jigged on one leg like an
African witch doctor, while his fellow celebrants in this
strange black rite had struggled to draw him off the dancing ground and lay him to rest under a series of ever more
gaudy cloaks. Each time they appeared to have captured
this madly possessed creature straight out of a voodoo
hongan, he had erupted again in even more violent par-

[1]The *T.A.M.I. Show* (Teenage Music International) was produced originally as a movie but it got its greatest play as a Dick
Clark TV program.

oxysms of song and corybantic ecstasy. When Brown finished his act and jivey Jagger came sashaying out to do his London School of Economics version of the "real" Negro rhythm and blues, you could practically see the flop sweat streaking his pale fleering face. Not even the sight of Meredith Hunter being knifed to death under his nose at Altamont made Mick so sick as the thought of having to follow Soul Brother Number One. If Steve Binder had set out deliberately to illustrate Elvis's dictum—"Black musicians have more talent in their little finger than whites in their whole body"—he couldn't have found a more convincing illustration. One thing star and producer would share from the outset would be a common enthusiasm for the power of black culture.

What troubled Binder initially was simply the thought that Elvis Presley might have reached a point in his career where he was so locked into the pattern established by his movies that all he would want to do on a TV show was just standard stuff that every long-established entertainer runs through every time he is wound up and set ticking. Binder was an ambitious young Turk in his medium: He wasn't interested in "showcasing" once-exciting stars who had become showbiz automatons. What he had to know before he took even the first step toward producing an Elvis Presley special was whether Elvis Presley was willing to do something *special* or whether it was too late for him to make a fresh departure.

The first meeting commenced with the usual platoon arrival of Elvis, the Colonel and the Memphis Mafia. Binder had spent many years watching stars play games with their entourages. Elvis's Al Capone entrance struck him as par for the course. He suggested that the supernumeraries be allowed to rest their feet in the outer office while the principals withdrew to the conference table. Once Binder and his producing partner, Bones Howe (the same man who had once been a gaffer at Radio Recorders), had settled into their seats and confronted Elvis and the Colonel, the game of chess commenced. The Colonel made the opening move. It was a carefully considered gambit.

Colonel Parker told Binder/Howe that the historic show they were about to produce should be conceived in the first

place as a costly "gift" to the American public from Elvis
and the Colonel. The image summoned up by the Colonel
was that of a mink stole or a gold watch, beautifully
wrapped and lovingly placed beneath every American family's Christmas tree. As the card that accompanied the gift
would bear also the signature of that eminently respectable American institution, the Singer Sewing Machine
Company, it was essential that the producers maintain
the proper moral tone for such an occasion.

They were fortunate, the Colonel continued, in being
able to showcase a star who was synonymous with everything that was fine and wholesome in American life. Elvis
was the dream of every little old lady in every Singer
sewing machine center in the country. These women knew
how good Elvis had always been to his mother. They also
knew how deeply religious he was. As the success of Colonel Parker's recent radio syndication proved, everybody
loved to hear Elvis sing Christmas songs. So, the obvious
way to produce the show was to have Elvis sing about
twenty Christmas tunes—carols, ballads, novelty numbers, nicely mixed, like a bouquet of pretty flowers (or a
bag of freshly roasted nuts). Then, at the end of the show,
he would give the little old ladies and their families one
of his famous smiles, say "Merry Christmas everyone!"—
and fade! Now, how's that for a prime-time winner?

When Steve Binder heard the Colonel's proposal, he
was so appalled at the idea that he was struck dumb. For
a long time, he could say nothing. Grimly, he realized that
he was now face-to-face with the principal cause of Elvis's
precipitate decline from the great fame he had once enjoyed. Here, sitting opposite him, was the real architect
of all those horrible movies that were Elvis's celluloid
tomb. Finally, Binder recovered his voice and began, like
a shrink feeling out a new patient, to ask a few questions
aimed at establishing where Elvis's head was at. Getting
into a rap about a recent experience he had had with a
group he was producing called the Association, Binder told
Elvis that these singers had been offered the first crack
at "McArthur Park" but had turned the tune down because
it didn't fit their image. Coming now to the kicker of the
story, Steve looked earnestly at Elvis and said: "What

would you do if someone had brought you that song? Would you have recorded it?" Elvis didn't hesitate for a moment: "Sure, I'd record it!" he snapped. "I love that piece of music." Steve said nothing in reply, but he was impressed. If Elvis Presley could picture himself stepping that far out of character, perhaps he might go even further.

"What is your feeling about facing the public again on TV?" continued Dr. Binder. "Sheer terror!" confessed Elvis, never one to bullshit when he spoke of his fears. As the discussion continued, Elvis made his real feelings perfectly clear to his new producer. "You know," he explained, "for nearly ten years I have been kept away from the public. And the one thing that I always loved doing was performing in front of the public. But I'm not sure they're gonna like me now. I may be past that point in time." That was the whole issue as far as Elvis was concerned: "Will they still like me?" It was just what he had wondered at the very start of his career. Now, after all these years, he was right back where he had started—thanks to the skillful management of Colonel Tom Parker.

The meeting ended with an agreement. Elvis would go off to Hawaii to lose weight and get into shape for the big comeback bout. Binder and Howe would huddle with their production people and rough out the program for the show. Binder would be given a free hand save for one job: that of musical arranger. The Colonel made it clear that his slot must be filled by Elvis's own arranger, Billy Strange. Who is Billy Strange? Binder knew him well. Everybody in the business knew him. He had a little tag that some producer once stuck on him. It read: "You wind him up and he shows up." That was his rep. He was just one of those nothings who attach themselves to names. The first name he had latched onto was Nancy Sinatra, at the moment when she made her recording debut.

Binder was not happy having to put the music, such a vital part of the show, in the hands of a guy who was always turning up at sessions and saying: "There must be a mixup—I didn't get a call!" "Yeah," the producers would say, "I guess we goofed, Billy. But sit down, there's your chair and you got your guitar, and, no sweat, man, you're on the date!" But what could Binder do? Elvis was one of

those stars who gave every twerp who shines their shoes
a lifetime annuity.

Now Binder began to address himself to the great problem faced by every creative TV producer: "How do I get
a good idea and, after I've got it, how do I get it past all
the people who want to shoot it down?" The most important
thing was to restore Elvis to the milieu in which he had
attained his true fame, as a hot-as-a-pistol rock star shooting his wad right down the throats of hundreds of screaming teenies ga-gaing over him from ringside. That was the
important thing: to put Elvis back in the ring.

The ring! Why, sure. Why not present him in the boxing
arena? The great thing about the ring is that it cuts off
the performer's retreat and compels him to work in every
direction at once like a modern dancer. What's more, by
surrounding the stage with cameras, including one directly overhead, Elvis could be literally gobbled up on the
screen. Just to make sure that not one morsel of man-meat
would be lost, Binder conned NBC sports into letting him
have a hand-held camera and a special operator who could
duck around the ring and catch Elvis at all the odd angles
that are inaccessible to the clumsy floor and crane cameras.

In a couple of weeks, Binder and his staff of unknown
but highly talented production people had hammered out
the basic formula for the show. They all agreed that this
rare occasion should be used as much as possible to illuminate the real Elvis. Though many people thought that
at the age of twenty-one Elvis had sprung full-blown out
of Colonel Parker's head, the truth was that he had his
roots, his sources, in the culture of his own world. So they
would do numbers on the gospel scene, on the rhythm and
blues world, even on karate, which translates so naturally
into choreography. At some point, Elvis would have to do
a medley of his old hits, but this needn't be a mere rehash
of old favorites or an exercise in nostalgia: they could make
the old music and style come back to life again.

The most important thing in Binder's mind was to get
Elvis out from behind his mask, to make him step forth
and declare himself as a man, not just a living legend.
Some way would have to be found to interview Elvis, to

draw forth his ideas. Then, when the show reached its conclusion, Elvis ought to offer something more than just the usual kiss-off to the audience. He ought to make a statement: come right out and say that he knew what was happening these days and that he cared which way the world was heading. It was a big demand to make of a performer who was so swallowed up in such a dumb image; but what were they here for if not to do something original? That was Binder's goal. Now, could he sell it to Elvis Presley?

When Elvis got back from Hawaii, the big meeting was held: the meeting at which the producer pitches his idea of the show to the star. Binder didn't stop with just outlining the show. He told Elvis that this program was his Rubicon. If he chose to do the conventional show, like Bing Crosby or Perry Como going through their mindless routines, Elvis would condemn himself to following those older singers into that twilight zone where once-vital but now exhausted talents always end: enthroned in a dozing court surrounded by their faithful followers dreaming of the past. If, on the other hand, he rose to the challenge and took the risk of doing something fresh and different, he could be reborn! Millions of people would see the show. They would sit there like a jury. Then, they would deliver an instant verdict. If it were favorable, Elvis could take off again with the excitement of a new discovery.

Binder saw immediately that he would have no problem selling this dream to Elvis Presley. Elvis was willing to take the dare. The problems lay with the network executives and with Colonel Parker. The network people were really scared at the idea of making the whole program an examination of Elvis. Though they were eager to exploit his fame, they didn't want to commit themselves to a one-man show. What they wanted was some "insurance": maybe a couple of guest stars to enlarge the attraction. Say... Milton Berle! Now, there was a good idea! Get a few laughs into the show. Or Sammy Davis, Jr.! Elvis dug Sammy. Sammy dug Elvis. Wouldn't hurt to have a black dude on the program: might do a lot for the ratings in cities like New York, Chicago, Detroit and Philadelphia. Binder had to do some fancy talking to get this idea out of the VPs' heads; he had to tell them how important Elvis really was as an American culture hero and how absurd it would be to dilute the impact of his first TV appearance since 1960 with the acts you could see on any other show. Finally, he won the argument. Then, he had to deal with the Colonel.

Colonel Parker had made it clear from the first day they met that if this show didn't meet with his approval, it would never go on the air. He wasn't telling them what to put on the air, but if they tried to do something that was bad for his "boy"—well, they wouldn't have a show. So, with this ominous guillotine hanging above his neck, Steve Binder began his pitch to the ole Colonel.

Binder soon perceived that the Colonel was not going to insist that Elvis do twenty Christmas songs and split. One thing the Colonel would not allow, however: that was any effort to make Elvis come out on the tube and deliver a statement that could be given a social or political interpretation. Elvis was an entertainer, pure and simple. He wasn't running for office or saving souls or doing an editorial for *The New York Times*. Binder could forget about social consciousness. The show would end just where it was supposed to end, with Elvis saying, "Good night and Merry Christmas."

Having prevailed on all the basic issues but one, Binder felt he had the green light to go into production. Bones Howe had told Binder how Elvis used to run his sessions at Radio Recorders: so it was decided that they should make every effort to get Elvis once again to produce himself. They established a pattern of daily meetings at three o'clock every afternoon in the Binder/Howe offices in the glass-tower building on the Strip, where Elvis could kick around ideas not only with his producers, but with the two clever young writers who had been hired for the show: Allan Blye and Chris Bearde. Soon these spark sessions began to produce interesting results.

Stimulated by the unique experience of being treated as a human being with his own ideas on how things should be done, Elvis relaxed and opened up his store of amusing recollections and anecdotes from his early years. He was also very funny on the subject of his famous image. He would suddenly stop in the middle of his rap and say, "Whoops! There goes my lip again!" Then twisting his lip into the celebrated crooked smile as if it were an uncontrollable facial tic, he would joke, "This is how I got through twenty-nine pictures." "Aha!" thought Binder, "that must definitely go in!" Bit by bit, they worked up the lines and the songs and the moves that would reveal the real Elvis. After a couple of weeks, Binder was telling Howe: "We don't have to worry about the interview: Elvis will interview himself."

One afternoon, Elvis got into his familiar complaint about how fame had made him a virtual prisoner. He could never do anything or go anywhere, he said, without being mobbed. Fame has forced him against his will into becoming a recluse. It was a curse. After listening to this rap for a while, Binder spoke up. "You know, Elvis," he said, "I'll bet you exaggerate this problem. Times have changed. You don't have to live this way any more. I'm sure that if we went downstairs right now and just hung out in front of the building, nobody would mob you." Soon they were all out in the street, leaning up against the building, watching the passing parade.

This was the summer of 1968. At that time the Strip had become a psychedelic midway. Hundreds of cars were passing by carrying thousands of kids dressed in all the bizarre costumes of that kooky day. It was probably the first time in his life that Elvis had ever stood on an American street corner and seen the new generation at close quarters. As the minutes ticked by and the crazies passed by, *nobody recognized Elvis Presley!*

There he was, standing right there, leaning against the building, looking just like he looked in all those movies. The hair, the features, the clothes, the image was unmistakable—but no one paid him a moment's attention. After a while it got boring, just standing there waiting for something to happen. Finally, Elvis said: "Okay, you win!" With that they went up the glass shaft to the office and resumed the conversation about how they were going to renew Elvis's career.

One of the people who stood on that corner was Joe Esposito. You can bet your bottom dollar that the minute

he got to a phone, he called the Colonel and reported this
latest development. You can also wager that the Colonel
didn't take this little bit of off-the-wall psychotherapy
lightly. Isolation was the principal device the Colonel had
always employed to maintain his hold on Elvis. By keeping
Elvis locked up always in a house or a movie lot or recording studio, by carefully watching his every move
through a network of domestic spies, by quickly identifying and dealing with any threatening influences that
showed up inside the prison, the Colonel had been able to
manage Elvis for years like a monkey in a cage. Okay,
there was this one time when this goddamned hair stylist
slipped behind the Colonel's back with his line of spiritualistic hokum. Otherwise the strategy had worked fine.
However, there was always the danger that another swami
would come along, another of these self-anointed ministers
running that classic pimp line that begins: "It's not me I
care about but *you*, baby, what's good for *you!*" Yeah, Elvis
was just like any little two-dollar hooker when it came to
that line. This Binder would bear watching. He might have
little wings on his back.

Once the production got rolling, the key people were
assigned offices at the Burbank Studios, where the filming
would be done. Colonel Parker insisted on being given a
small office and often went into a rap about how little he
required to satisfy his needs. One guy who knew how much
the Colonel needed was Bob Finkel. The executive producer of the show had a lot of heavy responsibilities, but
he soon realized that his heaviest job was keeping the
Colonel happy or at least occupied. The Colonel was bored
by the process of preparing the show. To entertain himself,
he would play practical jokes on everybody around him.
One day he dressed up the two William Morris flunkies
who were assigned to him as Coldstream Guards. Wearing
their towering beavers and fancy red uniforms and carrying rifles, they were posted in front of Bob Finkel's office.
When Finkel came to work that morning, he found himself
barred from his own office.

Finkel, getting in the spirit of the thing, rushed over
to wardrobe and had himself outfitted as an officer of the
Guards. Colonel Parker got a kick out of that one. A few

days later, he invited Finkel to lunch. As they sat in the
Colonel's office eating an excellent meal, the Colonel kept
filling Finkel's glass with superb champagne. Finkel complimented the Colonel on his taste in wine. The Colonel
beamed and said: "Tell you what, Mr. Finkel, you called
my bluff the other day with that uniform of yours. I'm
gonna show you how much I appreciate your sense of humor. Tonight, when you get home, you'll have a case of
this champagne waiting for you." That night Finkel found
the champagne and told his wife that next time they entertained, they should break out the good stuff the Colonel
had sent them. As it happened, they were giving a dinner
party that weekend. When the guests sat down to the table,
Finkel went around the table filling their glasses and telling them they had a treat in store. This was the best
champagne he had ever tasted, and it came straight from
the famous Colonel Tom Parker. Finally, seating himself
at the head of the table, he raised his glass on high, offered
the toast and took a long sip of the wine. As he looked
down the table in dismay, he saw everybody staring at
him, equally dismayed. The splendid champagne proved
to be mineral water.

Billy Strange was still working on the Nancy Sinatra
album when the time came to begin the music rehearsals.
Binder had been watching Billy's strange performance for
a long time, noting how time and again the arranger made
excuses that allowed him to delay doing the arrangements.
Now, at the eleventh hour, Binder called Strange and told
him: "If the lead sheets for the music are not on my desk
at ten A.M. the day after tomorrow, you're fired!" Strange
snapped back: "You can't fire me. I'm your line to Elvis."
Binder snapped back: "I'm running this show and if you
don't deliver, either you go or I go!" Two days later, the
lead sheets had still not been delivered. Getting in touch
with Finkel, Binder explained the situation. Finkel heard
him out; then, he said two words: "Fire him!" That was
good news for Binder; now, he could bring in a man whom
he considered the best arranger in the business, Billy
Goldenberg.

Goldenberg, who had been Frank Loesser's arranger on
Broadway, was remarkably gifted at working up music for

theatrical presentations. Unfortunately, he disliked Elvis Presley. When he heard what Binder wanted of him, he refused flat out, saying: "Look, I don't *like* Elvis Presley's music. I'm wrong for him. Get..." Binder wouldn't take no for an answer. He started appealing to their long and successful association, bringing up all the great times they had had working on *Hullabaloo* and the Leslie Uggams show and blah, blah, blah. He pressed so hard that he forced Goldenberg into an emotional outburst. "Steve!" he shouted. "You know I'd do anything for you. But I'm not doing Elvis Presley! There's a *limit!*" That night he started working on the arrangements.

The very next morning, Binder walks into the rehearsal hall. Word has spread that he fired Billy Strange. Suddenly, the Colonel appears. He demands an explanation of the firing. He gets it. The Colonel extracts the long cigar from his mouth and examines the soggy tip intently. Finally, he says, "Well, Binder, I just don't know whether Elvis is going to show up." When Binder doesn't flinch, the Colonel turns on his heel and disappears. Half an hour later, Elvis appears. He never said a word about the dismissal of his arranger.

As the show took hold on everyone and the morale of the staff soared, it began to look like Colonel Parker had booked himself a winner. The only problem was that the Colonel didn't think so. He kept raising hell about the fact that the program had nothing at all to do with Christmas. "Where's my Christmas music?" he would demand. Then he would direct his fire straight at "Bindel." (The name had started appearing regularly on the Colonel's lips after the Billy Strange incident. It could be regarded as a joke or as a slur or both.) Once the argument would get going hot and heavy, the Colonel would demand a meeting. Soon they were having one of these pointless meetings every other day.

The meetings were conducted along the classic lines the Colonel had drawn years before: the old Svengali-Trilby routine. Binder and Howe, Finkel and the network people, would be called into the Colonel's office. Elvis would be produced in his most passive and zombielike condition. Then the Colonel would proceed to lay down the law, making it appear always that he was merely the mouthpiece for his "boy"—who was sitting right there and should have been able to open his own mouth. "Now, Elvis" the routine would begin, Svengali carrying on a one-way conversation with the mesmerized Trilby, "you want to do so and so, is that right?" Elvis would look unhappy and stare at the ground and say, "Yes, sir." "Well, son," the Colonel would continue, "it's been brought to my attention that Mr. Bindel here has been telling people that we're going to do so and so. But you really want to do it the other way, don't you?" Elvis (very humbly): "Yes, sir." Then, as soon as the meeting broke up, Elvis would come up to Binder and say, "Don't worry, Steve, it's going to be all right."

Actually, the Colonel had gotten himself one helluva deal. Here were all these highly gifted, enormously ambitious, still unspoiled young creative people knocking themselves out day and night to revive a star that the Colonel and his cronies had reduced to the level of a storeroom dummy. Elvis was so irrelevant to the contemporary entertainment scene that some entertainment critics received the announcement of the program as a great howling joke. "Look who they're bringing back! Soon it will be time for the woolly mammoth!" That was the attitude among the hipper people in the entertainment business. What Binder and his boys were doing was not just resuscitating Elvis but putting him back in touch with the contemporary world. Instead of presenting a carefully embalmed mummy from the fifties, they were striving to present a living, breathing, and hitherto unrecognized human being. And all the Colonel could say was: "Where's my Christmas music?"

Another advantage of the deal, as it turned out, was the fact that NBC was heavily committed to making this show one of the best specials ever produced on the network. The money the network got from the Singer Corporation didn't begin to pay for the cost of producing the show. As the scuttlebutt about this production spread through the industry, all sorts of sponsors began to call up Binder, asking to be cut in on the show or even given the full sponsor's role, which they said Singer had gotten for a song. They were right: The show was a monument to deficit financing. Every day, some fresh demand came from the production staff that spelled heavy bucks. Like this thing about the hundred guitarists for the opening sequence.

Steve Binder had decided that the show should have a really socko logo. He had constructed for the purpose a set of enormous three-dimensional letters that spelled out in lights the magic word: ELVIS. Then, he got another flash. Instead of just lighting up the letters or having the dancers and singers cavort around them, why not reach deep into the old Busby Berkeley bag and do a whole production number right on top of the letters? The Elvis image—what was it? Young man with a guitar—right? Okay. They would make the logo and the image into one gigantic visual knockout punch. Animate the sign. Have it crawling with Elvises. That's it! Have a hundred black-clad, guitar-slingin', rock 'n' rollin' Elvises up there on those letters sockin' it to the people in stark silhouette. Normally, that kind of thinking is just a pipe dream. On this show, all it took was a phone call.

"Hello, Bob? This is Steve. Listen, for the opening number, I've just decided what we really need is a hundred guitar players. Yeah, I said a hundred." Oi! Imagine taking that one to the top! Still, Finkel did it. And he got Steve his hundred guitar players—for about one and a half minutes on camera! It made a pretty heavy one and a half minutes, though. Most important, it set the scale for the show as THE MOST.

As Binder got tighter with Elvis, he discovered that what his star needed to feel comfortable was to be surrounded at every moment by his special environmental bubble. Elvis always had to have his boys and his toys and his little world. That was the way to keep him happy and productive. Not one to mess around, Binder gave orders that the largest dressing rooms at the Burbank studios be converted at once into a hotel suite and furnished with every contrivance that could please Elvis Presley. As time neared for the actual filming of the show, Elvis moved into his dressing rooms and lived there just as he would at a hotel. Why, it was just like the good old days when he and the boys were at the Beverly Wilshire!

Once Elvis had been installed in his new quarters,

Binder noticed another interesting feature of his star's life-style. Instead of knocking off at the end of the day's work and going out or falling asleep, Elvis loved to get the boys around him and have spontaneous sings that would last all night. Sometimes, when the crew would arrive at the studio in the morning, they would find the Guys still sitting in their rooms playing guitars and singing and having a ball with their boss. This recreation gave Binder his final inspiration for the show.

If the challenge of the program was to bring Elvis Presley out of the closet and into the open world of the TV camera, what better way could they do it than by simply borrowing the techniques of cinema verité filmmakers and rolling the cameras straight into Elvis's dressing rooms while he was playing and singing and joking with his famous Memphis Mafia? This idea got to be such an obsession with Binder that he decided finally that all the elaborate and costly production numbers didn't mean a damn in comparison to these behind-the-scenes scenes. Now, he had to go to work all over again to persuade Elvis and the Colonel that the very best footage they could shoot would be a private party in a dressing room.

This latest brainstorm produced the greatest resistance to date. Even Elvis, who had gone along with everything up to now, began to shake his head and raise objections. Sure, he loved to sit around in the privacy of his rooms and have a ball—but putting it all on camera for a zillion people to watch! Hey! That was going pretty far, wasn't it? When the Colonel heard the idea, he not only balked: His mind went into paranoid overdrive. He didn't just want to know how the idea would work or even whether it would work. He wanted to know why Binder would want to do such a thing. What was he up to?

At the inevitable meeting, Steve Binder found himself obsessively conscious of the Colonel's steely blue eyes focused in a look that he still can't forget. Binder knew all about the Colonel's prowess as a hypnotist. How could he not? So many times when he came out of his office after a long sit-down with Elvis, Binder found his staff running around on all fours acting like cats and dogs while the old Colonel sat in his chair with a big grin wrapped around his cigar watching his victims disport themselves on the carpet.

Now, Binder found himself getting the same treatment. "The Colonel," he recalls, "used to sit at a meeting with those cold steel-blue eyes staring at me like he was trying to get a subliminal message into my brain. I'd stare back, knowing that there was nothing he could do. Yet, he did convince me that there is such a thing as *mind control*. That strange hypnotic way he had of exercising total control and power over Elvis. That kind of hold is totally unexplainable in terms either of deals or loyalties between people."

The highly suggestible mind that surrenders so swiftly and so completely to one master, however, is capable of surrendering just as swiftly and completely to another. What Steve Binder didn't know was that he was beginning to exercise a very considerable power of his own over Elvis Presley. He was coming into focus in Elvis's mind precisely as had Larry Geller just a few years before.

Larry had popped up in Elvis's life just at the moment when Elvis was feeling total dissatisfaction with both his career and his life-style. Without even intending to do so, Larry had presented Elvis with a sudden revelation: There was another way to live that would get him out of this horrible bind. In a flash, Elvis had been converted to spiritualism. In no time, he was up to his eyeballs in occult literature and self-abnegation and having visions and even threatening to give up his career and become a monk in a monastery. The Colonel had nearly lost Elvis that time. If it hadn't been for the opportunity presented by that brain concussion, that timely blow to the head that knocked the stuffing out of Elvis, God knows what might have happened! Now, here was the same pattern, the same danger, asserting itself all over again.

One thing the old Colonel knew: You never get anywhere trying to lead a high-kicking bronc by the nose. No, you have to be shrewd, canny. You watch and wait. You let the horse knock himself out. Then, when he gets tired, you walk in and lead him away. Colonel was smart enough to see that this damn Binder wasn't completely wrong. He would produce one helluva show, and it would earn the

Colonel a lot of money. After one more showing, they could
buy the show. What's more, the success of the show would
make Elvis's price go way up for the next show. To cap it
all off, they would start shooting *Charro* in March, 1969.
The Colonel's strategy, therefore, was not to block the show
or cause it to fail in any way. The trick was to make Binder
work his tail off handing the Colonel a winner; then, when
they had gotten their mileage out of Binder, toss him into
the junk pile. Meantime, though, the best policy was to
fight this dude every inch of the way and psych him out
fore and aft just to make sure that he wasn't getting his
hooks any deeper into Elvis than was absolutely necessary.

As for this crazy scheme of filming Elvis fooling around
in his dressing room—why stop it? Let them do it; *but,*
demand a veto on showing it if it did even the slightest
damage to Elvis's image, that lovingly fondled and carefully gilded image that the Colonel had spent his life shin-
ing and polishing and peddling to millions of suckers and
marks the world around.

After many sessions designed to suss out Steve Binder's
secret designs, Colonel Parker gave his conditional approval to the plan to shoot Elvis at play. Steve, meantime,
had decided to bring back Elvis's original band, Scotty
Moore and D. J. Fontana. (Bill Black had died in 1965.)
He was so keen on the impromptu jam-session atmosphere
that he wouldn't even let D.J. touch his drum kit. He was
going to sit in front of an empty guitar case or a newspaper
and whack out the time with a pair of soft brushes. Wasn't
that how they did it in those old thirties movies about jazz
bands out on the road and doing a little home cooking in
their berths on the Pullman trains?

Never in his entire career did Elvis ever look better
than he did for the Singer Special. At thirty-three, he was
at his peak. The years had taken the baby fat out of his
cheeks and given him a more masculine appearance. Maturity had also made him seem less like the callow youth
and more like the youthful man. Having paid some dues
to life, he had a much more soulful expression in his face
than he did when he was a smart-alecky punk teasing the
girls at ringside. As the cameras, poring over him from
every angle, would reveal, his classic features were even

more finely molded than before and less encumbered than
ever by the vulgarity of his youthful personality.

Another reason why Elvis looked so great that night
is that he was wearing the best costume he ever donned.
Bill Belew, who after this show became Elvis's clothes
designer for life, had decided that the most dramatic way
of snapping Elvis into focus for the reminiscent segments
of the show was to suit him up from head to toe in wickedly
glinting black leather. He designed a fabulous black
leather motorcycle jacket with a stand-up collar, heavy
welts along the seams and a broad, double-buckled strap
around each wrist. Leather likewise were the trousers,
whose crease was a long, mean-looking leather welt. No
shiny metal studs or ornaments of any kind were allowed
to trivialize the effect of the costume. Elvis was a human
truck tire.

(It has often been pointed out that this costume is in-
authentic. Elvis never wore leather in his mythic period:
that was Brando [or, later, Gene Vincent] whose crude
jacket and ugly farmer jeans would make any self-respect-
ing S/M freak gag because it was so baggy and gauche.
The real model for Elvis's costume was Jim Morrison, who
had just emerged as the surf-born Dionysius of West Coast
rock, clad from head to toe in shiny black vinyl. What
Belew did was bring Elvis back not as a waxworks replica
but as an echo of a past that existed only in the imagination
of the current generation, which was the best way to bring
him back with a bang.)

Just before Elvis stepped out on the stage, the Colonel
appeared for their final huddle. Everyone was ordered out
of the dressing room. Binder used to wonder what these
last-minute encounters comprised. Did the Colonel fix his
steely-cold gaze on Elvis and tell him he was the hottest
act in history? Or did he actually hypnotize him? It was
apparent that whatever happened, it made a startling difference in Elvis. One moment he would be his usual quiet,
diffident self: the bashful boy from Memphis town. The
moment the Colonel finished with his protégé, the boy was
another person. Now his theme was "I'm All Psyched Up!"

When Elvis climbed into the ring that night, he found
his old sidemen, Scotty and D.J., waiting for him, looking

remarkably the same as in the early days. Charlie Hodge
was also on hand with his guitar, which made three musicians and one clown: Alan Fortas, who had been given
a tambourine to bang and jiggle. Alan had been chosen for
the role of henchman because Steve thought he corresponded best to the image of the Memphis Mafia: those
big, gross, good-natured shlubs who were Elvis's abundant
human ectoplasm.

According to the Elvis Myth, what happened next was
one of the greatest moments in the history of rock, if not
of show business in general. Elvis Presley, barred from
the stage for years, cut off from his true love, the live
audience, a refugee from a celluloid nightmare, armed
with nothing but his trusty guitar and backed with nothing stronger than a couple of good ole boys, suddenly broke
the symbolic silence of eight long years by raising his voice
in the greatest shout since Achilles roared before the walls
of Troy. As always, the Myth is totally false. As it happens,
we can now go back and examine that moment in the most
minute detail, thanks to a remarkable bootleg album issued by an underground outfit in Glendale called audifön.
No microphone up the sleeve, tape recorder in the briefcase
job, this album was ripped off the original soundtrack by
someone at RCA. It offers not only the first show but the
second show as well, recorded before a fresh audience a
couple of hours later on the same evening.

The first thing it tells us is that Elvis was quite right
in describing his emotion on confronting a live audience
for the first time in eight years as "sheer terror." The only
way to excuse the performance he gave on this momentous
occasion is to say that he was just too uptight to give a
good account of himself. Though nothing was expected of
him but the same songs and the same patter that he had
been delivering all his life, he practically collapsed under
the impact of the occasion. He couldn't think. He couldn't
talk. He couldn't remember either the lines of his script
or the lines of his songs. Everytime he made a remark, he
turned on his last word with decimating self-conscious-
ness and started putting himself on.

At first, he hardly speaks at all: He thumbs his guitar
and jumps into a song, "That's All Right Mama." The script-

ers and producers had decided that his first recording was
the natural point from which he should take off. The only
problem with the plan was one that evidently never
crossed the minds of those who conceived it: the vocal
register, the tessitura, of the song was too high for the
Elvis Presley of 1968. Elvis's voice had dropped perceptibly
since he was a kid (he used to say that on his early records
he sounded like a "chicken"), but he still thought of the
song in the same key. The result is a very hoarse and
painful effort to vocally get it up. It sets the tone for what
follows.

Most great performers put into this same situation
would not have behaved as Elvis did. They might have
floundered, fumffered, fucked up; they might have found
themselves tongue-tied and hoarse and short of breath: all
classic symptoms of panic. As they felt themselves bomb-
ing, however, they would have rallied. They would have
jumped to their feet, taken command, thrown away the
script and, if necessary, dropped their pants. Not Elvis. He
sits there with the water running out of the bath and
makes feeble jokes about how much he'd like to get up and
leave. He reaches for the script and starts to read it out
loud—without really getting a laugh by doing the imper-
missible. Eventually, he does struggle to his feet; but he's
ready to sit down again when he finds that the mike doesn't
rise to meet him. Charlie Hodge, a natural-born performer,
who worked his ass off during this session to keep up the
infield chatter and cue Elvis into his lines and try to make
the debacle a success, picks up the mike and holds it up
to Elvis. Then Elvis starts complaining that there is no
strap for his guitar. So Charlie starts singing the words,
"no strap at all," to the tune of "One Night." Finally he
gets Elvis functioning well enough so that this little bit
could be cut out of the hour-long tape and exhibited in the
final show as an example of Elvis's marvelous "spontane-
ity."

If this home-cooking session fails as a performance, does
it succeed any better as a document, as a revelation of
Elvis, which, after all, was the primary intention? The
spectacle of a famous performer dissolving in self-con-
sciousness and stage fright does have, it's true, a clammy,

to be the most successful since 1960, yielding two gold albums, three singles that sold in the millions and several minor hits. Binder, Howe and Goldenberg had restored Elvis to himself just as successfully and in exactly the same way as Jerry Wexler did at this time with Aretha Franklin, who had also drifted far away from her roots in the gospel-toned world of soul. The only difference was that Wexler was acclaimed a genius but nobody outside the business recognized what had brought Elvis back to life musically.)

When Goldenberg pulled the wraps off his dazzling new translation of Elvis's favorite gospel, R & B and rock standards, the effect was startling. No Elvis Presley album either before or since has ever delivered so much musical energy, excitement or imaginative stimulation. Sure, the tempos are fast, the transitions abrupt, the atmosphere crepitating with heat lightning. This is show music, designed to propel dancing bodies and stand up to glaring scenery and reach out through that tiny, tinny, two-bit little speaker in the TV set and set the somnolent viewer's feet tapping and blood pressure rising. Sometimes the band blares like Saturday night on Beale Street; sometimes the sound hushes to the lonely soulful wail of a harmonica or the cat litter–matchbox scratch of pick on guitar frets. Sometimes the violins fill the atmosphere with a thick blue haze; then, the page turns and the trumpets screech like those big fat mamas shoutin' at the East Trigg Baptist.

The score was a feast for the ear and a revelation for Elvis. At four o'clock in the morning, he was up in the booth with Bones demanding to have the tapes spun again and again! Never again was he to walk out onstage without thirty pieces behind him. He had been weaned at last from the tuppenny sound of rock 'n' roll.

As the last numbers were put in the can, the filming and recording of the show was declared complete save for the finale. This was the last loose screw, the last unsettled issue. Steve Binder was still, after all these months, holding out for his original idea: Elvis should walk out on camera and say: "I care!" Colonel Parker was just as set as ever on having Elvis wind up the show in the customary

clinical kind of fascination. Though it makes one as uneasy as the sight of an open incision, you do get some startling glimpses of the patient's guts. What comes through is deeply ingrained self-doubt and self-derision: a great longing to have done with this terribly embarrassing subject of Me. Nobody who listens attentively to this recording is going to conclude that Elvis Presley was fond of himself. Quite the contrary: What one infers is that all of Elvis's fabulous success simply piled up on the surface of his being without ever seeping through to his resolutely self-hating and self-castigating core.

It's very interesting, in this connection, to observe what happens in the other "live" segment of the show, which was a stand-up solo performance of Elvis's early hits sung before an audience with the orchestral accompaniment prerecorded and piped onto the stage through shotgun speakers. Once Elvis gets up on his feet and frees himself of the encumbrance of his mind, his body starts to function, projecting forcefully and with growing conviction those deep erotic images that turned on audiences at every point in his career. It can't be said too often that the source of Elvis's onstage power was not his vocal performance but his erotic pantomime. The actual rebirth of Elvis on the Singer Special occurs at those moments, when holding the mike in his fist and sinking down on his knees, he bends back in the phallic posture of the Limbo dancer, with his pubis thrust toward the audience, and scrunching up his face like a man coming to orgasm, he hollers from the bottom of his soul. That is the essential Elvis.

The aspect of the Singer Special that was to have the greatest influence on Elvis's future career was, interestingly enough, not the self-revelatory breakthroughs for which Steve Binder fought so hard, but the new musical horizons that were revealed to Elvis through the work of Billy Goldenberg and Bones Howe. It is no exaggeration to say that Goldenberg and Howe reeducated Elvis in contemporary commercial music and set him down in the groove in which he was destined to ride until the day he died. The reason they were able to exercise this profound influence on such a willful and self-repetitive performer is because they caught Elvis at just the moment when he had opened himself for once to far-reaching changes in his professional outlook.

Prior to the Singer Special Elvis had been trying, with the aide of his new A & R man, Felton Jarvis, to climb back up out of the terrible hole into which he had fallen during the period of his mass-production moviemaking. Having allowed Colonel Parker to persuade him that there was no need to go into the studio and work with other musicians, Elvis had done no studio work at all during the years 1964–1966. Matters might have gone on like this even longer, if RCA had not started competing with the Colonel by releasing old Elvis recordings which invariably outsold the movie soundtracks. When the hapless Steve Sholes, a man whom Elvis despised, retired and Jarvis took over, the Colonel agreed that Elvis could go back into the studio at Nashville and resume his recording career. By this point, however, Elvis's career was so shot that it was very hard to say how it should be resumed. Elvis's position on the musical *mapa mundi* was Nowhere. Until he did the Singer Special.

This show put him into a tight working relationship with a brilliant arranger and a hotshot engineer who was hip to the revolution in recording methods that had occurred during the sixties. Ironically, the essence of the whole recording revolution lay in an idea that Elvis Presley had helped to pioneer: the use of electronic devices not only to record but *create* fresh sounds. It was an electronically produced echo that had given Elvis's first and best records on Sun their distinctive acoustic aura. It was another electronic echo device that had made Scotty Moore's guitar sound with such a weird and haunting plangency. The young and inspired Elvis Presley had been packaged with all sorts of primitive electronic gimmickry and had ridden to fame with those tricks up his sleeve. Instead of remaining alive and open to all the new sounds that were pouring in on listeners during the sixties, however, Elvis stopped his ears and fell asleep. Pretty soon the Hillbilly Cat was swooning to corny Hawaiian beach lullabies, singing back-beat versions of Neapolitan love songs, doing the Mambo, the Cha-cha-cha and coming on like the last of the middle-aged crooners. From being one of the most

sharply etched profiles in the history of pop music, Elvis had become a faceless hack who stood for nothing musically: or at least nothing that belonged to the modern world.

As far as learning to make full use of the modern recording studio, Elvis never caught up with his day. That challenge was beyond him. Though Bones Howe put him into the best studio on the West Coast, Western United, there was no way Elvis could work except to put on a show for the band with a hand-held mike in his fist. Still, he did get an idea of what modern recording techniques could do and began to look at sixteen-track boards as something more than engineers' toys. The really big breakthrough came, however, in the area of his instrumental sound, which, for the first time in his entire career, was produced by a full-scale studio orchestra. Here, he profited enormously from the vision of Billy Goldenberg.

The arranger's problem was essentially the same as the costumer's—only on a vastly greater scale. What Goldenberg was expected to do was to take the traditional Presley repertoire and whatever current music was used on the program and give it all a thrillingly contemporary treatment. Instead of the stale old sound of Sun or Nashville, these new arrangements had to pop, crack and sizzle with the extravagant new energies of the sixties. His solution to the problem was both brilliant and highly ironic; for, what he decided to do was to voice the music of Memphis's most famous singer in the marvelous new idiom of the Memphis Sound: the style created by Stax/Volt records, a black-oriented record company in Memphis that was now giving Motown a run for its money. You wouldn't think that you would need a Broadway showbiz arranger who didn't even dig the Presley idiom to show Elvis Presley how to renew his music by dipping it in the strong dark colors of his own hometown; but that is precisely what Goldenberg did—and what Elvis loved so much that he canceled his next recording session at Nashville and for the first time since his days at Sun employed a Memphis studio (Chip Moman's American Studios) and a backing comprised of many of the same musicians who are heard on the Stax/Volt records. (These Memphis sessions prov clinical kind of fascination. Though it makes one as uneasy as the sight of an open incision, you do get some startling glimpses of the patient's guts. What comes through is deeply ingrained self-doubt and self-derision: a great longing to have done with this terribly embarrassing subject of Me. Nobody who listens attentively to this recording is going to conclude that Elvis Presley was fond of himself. Quite the contrary: What one infers is that all of Elvis's fabulous success simply piled up on the surface of his being without ever seeping through to his resolutely self-hating and self-castigating core.

It's very interesting, in this connection, to observe what happens in the other "live" segment of the show, which was a stand-up solo performance of Elvis's early hits sung before an audience with the orchestral accompaniment prerecorded and piped onto the stage through shotgun speakers. Once Elvis gets up on his feet and frees himself of the encumbrance of his mind, his body starts to function, projecting forcefully and with growing conviction those deep erotic images that turned on audiences at every point in his career. It can't be said too often that the source of Elvis's onstage power was not his vocal performance but his erotic pantomime. The actual rebirth of Elvis on the Singer Special occurs at those moments, when holding the mike in his fist and sinking down on his knees, he bends back in the phallic posture of the Limbo dancer, with his pubis thrust toward the audience, and scrunching up his face like a man coming to orgasm, he hollers from the bottom of his soul. That is the essential Elvis.

The aspect of the Singer Special that was to have the greatest influence on Elvis's future career was, interestingly enough, not the self-revelatory breakthroughs for which Steve Binder fought so hard, but the new musical horizons that were revealed to Elvis through the work of Billy Goldenberg and Bones Howe. It is no exaggeration to say that Goldenberg and Howe reeducated Elvis in contemporary commercial music and set him down in the groove in which he was destined to ride until the day he died. The reason they were able to exercise this profound influence on such a willful and self-repetitive performer is because they caught Elvis at just the moment when he had opened himself for once to far-reaching changes in his professional outlook.

Prior to the Singer Special Elvis had been trying, with the aide of his new A & R man, Felton Jarvis, to climb back up out of the terrible hole into which he had fallen during the period of his mass-production moviemaking. Having allowed Colonel Parker to persuade him that there was no need to go into the studio and work with other musicians, Elvis had done no studio work at all during the years 1964–1966. Matters might have gone on like this even longer, if RCA had not started competing with the Colonel by releasing old Elvis recordings which invariably outsold the movie soundtracks. When the hapless Steve Sholes, a man whom Elvis despised, retired and Jarvis took over, the Colonel agreed that Elvis could go back into the studio at Nashville and resume his recording career. By this point, however, Elvis's career was so shot that it was very hard to say how it should be resumed. Elvis's position on the musical *mapa mundi* was Nowhere. Until he did the Singer Special.

This show put him into a tight working relationship with a brilliant arranger and a hotshot engineer who was hip to the revolution in recording methods that had occurred during the sixties. Ironically, the essence of the whole recording revolution lay in an idea that Elvis Presley had helped to pioneer: the use of electronic devices not only to record but *create* fresh sounds. It was an electronically produced echo that had given Elvis's first and best records on Sun their distinctive acoustic aura. It was another electronic echo device that had made Scotty Moore's guitar sound with such a weird and haunting plangency. The young and inspired Elvis Presley had been packaged with all sorts of primitive electronic gimmickry and had ridden to fame with those tricks up his sleeve. Instead of remaining alive and open to all the new sounds that were pouring in on listeners during the sixties, however, Elvis stopped his ears and fell asleep. Pretty soon the Hillbilly Cat was swooning to corny Hawaiian beach lullabies, singing back-beat versions of Neapolitan love songs, doing the Mambo, the Cha-cha-cha and coming on like the last of the middle-aged crooners. From being one of the most sharply etched profiles in the history of pop music, Elvis had become a faceless hack who stood for nothing musically: or at least nothing that belonged to the modern world.

As far as learning to make full use of the modern recording studio, Elvis never caught up with his day. That challenge was beyond him. Though Bones Howe put him into the best studio on the West Coast, Western United, there was no way Elvis could work except to put on a show for the band with a hand-held mike in his fist. Still, he did get an idea of what modern recording techniques could do and began to look at sixteen-track boards as something more than engineers' toys. The really big breakthrough came, however, in the area of his instrumental sound, which, for the first time in his entire career, was produced by a full-scale studio orchestra. Here, he profited enormously from the vision of Billy Goldenberg.

The arranger's problem was essentially the same as the costumer's—only on a vastly greater scale. What Goldenberg was expected to do was to take the traditional Presley repertoire and whatever current music was used on the program and give it all a thrillingly contemporary treatment. Instead of the stale old sound of Sun or Nashville, these new arrangements had to pop, crack and sizzle with the extravagant new energies of the sixties. His solution to the problem was both brilliant and highly ironic; for, what he decided to do was to voice the music of Memphis's most famous singer in the marvelous new idiom of the Memphis Sound: the style created by Stax/Volt records, a black-oriented record company in Memphis that was now giving Motown a run for its money. You wouldn't think that you would need a Broadway showbiz arranger who didn't even dig the Presley idiom to show Elvis Presley how to renew his music by dipping it in the strong dark colors of his own hometown; but that is precisely what Goldenberg did—and what Elvis loved so much that he canceled his next recording session at Nashville and for the first time since his days at Sun employed a Memphis studio (Chip Moman's American Studios) and a backing comprised of many of the same musicians who are heard on the Stax/Volt records. (These Memphis sessions proved to be the most successful since 1960, yielding two gold albums, three singles that sold in the millions and several minor hits. Binder, Howe and Goldenberg had restored Elvis to himself just as successfully and in exactly the same way as Jerry Wexler did at this time with Aretha Franklin, who had also drifted far away from her roots in the gospel-toned world of soul. The only difference was that Wexler was acclaimed a genius but nobody outside the business recognized what had brought Elvis back to life musically.)

When Goldenberg pulled the wraps off his dazzling new translation of Elvis's favorite gospel, R & B and rock standards, the effect was startling. No Elvis Presley album either before or since has ever delivered so much musical energy, excitement or imaginative stimulation. Sure, the tempos are fast, the transitions abrupt, the atmosphere crepitating with heat lightning. This is show music, designed to propel dancing bodies and stand up to glaring scenery and reach out through that tiny, tinny, two-bit little speaker in the TV set and set the somnolent viewer's feet tapping and blood pressure rising. Sometimes the band blares like Saturday night on Beale Street; sometimes the sound hushes to the lonely soulful wail of a harmonica or the cat litter–matchbox scratch of pick on guitar frets. Sometimes the violins fill the atmosphere with a thick blue haze; then, the page turns and the trumpets screech like those big fat mamas shoutin' at the East Trigg Baptist.

The score was a feast for the ear and a revelation for Elvis. At four o'clock in the morning, he was up in the booth with Bones demanding to have the tapes spun again and again! Never again was he to walk out onstage without thirty pieces behind him. He had been weaned at last from the tuppenny sound of rock 'n' roll.

As the last numbers were put in the can, the filming and recording of the show was declared complete save for the finale. This was the last loose screw, the last unsettled issue. Steve Binder was still, after all these months, holding out for his original idea: Elvis should walk out on camera and say: "I care!" Colonel Parker was just as set as ever on having Elvis wind up the show in the customary noncommittal manner of all the big entertainers. After having listened to so many arguments and pleas against the good-night-and-Merry-Christmas bit, the Colonel was willing to make a concession. He said that Elvis could end with a song like "I Believe." Binder and Howe were nauseated at the idea of their original vision of Elvis Presley gurgling down the drain with something as phony and fraudulent as "I Believe." Even in Las Vegas, the idea would have been offensive.

Finally, Steve Binder thought of a possible solution. What if they were to write a piece of special material for Elvis? A song with an affirmative tone, an air of social awareness—not anything that would make the Colonel say no automatically but something that caught the tone of the message without spelling it out in so many words? It was a pretty vague and abstract set of specs that he delivered to Billy Goldenberg and the songwriter, Earl Brown, but they agreed to go off that night and give it a try. That was how the real pros worked, wasn't it? After six weeks in rehearsal and an exhausting five-hour tryout at the Nixon Theater in Pittsburgh, the old dudes who wrote the Follies and the Scandals and all that jive would sit down on the stage apron at four in the morning with a bottle of bootleg booze and hack out the song that would be the big hit of the show when it reached Broadway.

Next morning, the pair showed up in Steve Binder's office. It was the tensest moment of the entire production. Now that they were almost finished with everything but the final edit, all the parties to the enterprise had closed in on Binder. In the very next office was Colonel Parker laying down the law to Bob Finkel and Tom Sarnoff and anybody else who would listen. He was explaining in no uncertain terms why Elvis could not, would not and should not go out and make some sort of incriminating lefto-pinko statement to millions of conservative-minded Americans just fresh from their Singer sewing machines. In Binder's office, Billy Goldenberg was seating himself at the piano while Earl Brown got set to plug the song he had written the night before: "If I Can Dream."

The song, which became Elvis's first big hit in years, was a typical piece of white soul concocted out of remi-

niscences of Ray Charles and lifts from the new Memphis
Sound. It was frankly stagy and even a little hokey. But
it struck the note of social aspiration without preaching,
and it gave Elvis a chance to wind up the long show with
a big powerful theatrical roundhouse punch. Elvis listened
to it carefully; then, he demanded to hear it again and
again. Finally, he turned to Binder and said: "I'll do it!"

Stepping into the adjacent office, where the Colonel was
still holding forth on the impossibility of doing anything
heavier than "I Believe," Steve announced: "We've got a
new finale. It's called 'If I Can Dream.'" The Colonel
turned white with rage. The people from NBC and RCA
rushed into his adjoining room to hear Elvis sing the song.
No sooner were the last notes out of his mouth than everybody was jumping on the bandwagon, congratulating Elvis, clamoring for the publishing rights and telling the
Colonel that it was already a smash hit. The Colonel said
nothing.

"If I Can Dream" was recorded by Elvis as a voice-over.
After the band had left the studio, Elvis asked that all the
lights be turned out. Taking the hand-held mike, he lay
down flat on the floor of the blacked-out studio with the
"cans" on his ears. Then, as the recorded orchestra finished
its Burt Bacharachish intro, Elvis started singing and
gradually worked his way up to the hoarse, shouting finale
so reminiscent of the blind Ray Charles crying out in anguish from his darkness.

The last scene in the long saga of the Singer Special
must be titled "The Colonel's Revenge." When RCA was
preparing to release the single of "If I Can Dream" and
the soundtrack album of the Special, Steve Binder and
Bones Howe demanded of the Colonel that they be cut into
the royalties of the records they had produced and recorded. This was the moment the ole Colonel had been
awaiting for a long, long time. He told the producers to
read their contracts—and weep! He not only refused to
give them more than a tiny token payment—which they
rejected—he even refused to put their names on the single.
(They finally did get credits—but no bread—on the album.) It was the old story of the music business all over
again, the same story that once featured Arthur Crudup

being screwed by Hill and Range, that once featured Elvis's name as author on songs of which he didn't write a word or a note, the story of crass commercial exploitation of creative talent that is the national anthem of American pop music.

The moment Elvis came charging offstage after his triumphant bout with the ghost of the past, he appeared a different person. "They still like me!" he blithered as he rushed into the dressing room. Then, confronting the Colonel, he swore: "I've got to get back in front of the public. We've got to go out on the road again!" Whatever Colonel Parker might have said or thought of this command, he realized soon that it had to be carried out. To the ole Colonel's credit be it said that no more than a year after Elvis came to his senses, he was opening in the greatest showroom in the world at the International Hotel in Las Vegas. Like a successful "analysis," the Singer Special had cured Elvis of his illness and pointed the way to his new happiness.

Chapter 29

Revival at Las Vegas

ONE of the greatest moments of the Presley Myth is Elvis's famous comeback at Las Vegas in 1969. If you read the story in the rock press or in one of the innumerable Presley fan books, it assumes the proportions of a showbiz legend. Elvis is portrayed as down and out, lost and rejected, the object of scorn to all but the faithful few. Then, through a combination of Colonel Parker's magical management skills and Elvis's wondrous talent, in one night the whole picture is reversed. Elvis is once again the darling of the American people, the greatest entertainer in the world and the king of rock 'n' roll. The refusal of even the best informed writers to present this episode in its correct colors is yet another example of the peculiar status of Elvis Presley as a figure of popular idolatry, a folk hero whose exploits must always conform to the pattern of a fairy tale.

Great comebacks are, of course, the stuff of showbiz legend. The miraculous resurgence of Al Jolson in *The Jolson Story*, Sinatra's triumphant comeback in *From Here to Eternity*, the poignant recoveries of Judy Garland in her later years, these are tales that attest to the capacity of the great performer to rise to the most difficult challenges and reimpose his mystique on even the most indifferent or unsympathetic audiences. Such stories do not

517

sort well, however, with the story of Elvis at Vegas. For
one thing, Elvis's professional history was radically different from that of just about any entertainer in the history
of the business. He was not a flash in the pan who suddenly
died, only to be reborn many years later. He was not, on
the other hand, like Jolson and Garland, a performer who
had enjoyed great success for many years and then either
through a change of public taste or a series of private
misfortunes been reduced to the status of the has-been.
Elvis was an entertainer who walked off the stage after
just two years of unexampled popularity to devote himself
to another medium, which made him rich but dimmed the
luster of his original fame. There is absolutely no poi-
gnance in this history, no sense of defeat or rejection. Elvis
wanted the money and the opportunity that Hollywood
offered, and he got both to an unprecedented degree.

Elvis was only twenty-two years old when he left the
stage; when he returned twelve years later, he was still
a young man at the height of his powers. He was better
looking than in youth; his voice was richer and stronger;
his command of performance technique was greater.
What's more, the timing of his return, though not deliberately chosen, was highly favorable. Nineteen sixty-nine
marked the first year of rock 'n' roll revival, the irresistible
longing to loop back, as in a time machine, to the magic
moment in 1956 when it all began and experience once
again—or for the first time ever!—the incomparable pleasure of being a screaming teeny submitting to that first
musical rape. Not only is this a phenomenon that far transcends what has been traditionally understood as nostalgia: It is a mania that has persisted ever since, giving rise
to wave after wave of rock 'n' roll revival, so that even
today there is nothing more trendy than turned-up collars
and gooey hair and the raucous sound of rockabilly. As
students of contemporary culture have been remarking
since the sixties, we are no longer a civilization that is
capable of creative innovation; instead, we have become
a civilization that survives through the incessant recycling
of cultural waste products: cast-off clothes, old comic strips,
rerun (or remade) movies, and, above all, that monoto-
nously revolving kaleidoscope loaded with bits of shrewdly

selected, skillfully cut and electronically enhanced gospel, blues, rock, jazz, pop, folk, pop, blues, rock, and so on, in endlessly shifting combinations of this week's, last season's, tomorrow's "sound."

Elvis Presley didn't launch rock 'n' roll revival nor even give it a distinctive image, as he did the original rock. The great downbeat for this regressive symphony, the first clear signal that it was time to play rock da capo, came from rock's greatest innovators and creative geniuses, the Beatles. It was in the winter of 1967–68, the fateful winter that blighted the brief spring and summer of the hippies, that the world's greatest trendsetters decided to do an about-face and retreat (with hip finesse) to their earlier manner or even to the styles of the old masters who had preceded them, like Buddy Holly, Chuck Berry, Little Richard and, of course, Elvis Presley. Their example was quickly copied by such enormously popular groups as Credence Clearwater, who demonstrated that even without the mystique of the Beatles, a band that could recover and concentrate the essence of the old rockabilly sound could achieve consistent top-of-the-chart success. At that point, the cells of memory burst open and out poured all those ancient rockers who had been Elvis's contemporaries. By the summer of 1969, you could see back on the boards every survivor of the fifties: Fats Domino, Little Richard, Bo Diddley, Chuck Berry, the Everly Brothers, Jerry Lee Lewis and the indomitable Bill Haley. Small wonder that by this time Elvis was beginning to drop hints that he would like to go back on the road.

Even so, his manager was very reluctant to make the move. Which brings us to the other part of this mythically distorted episode: the role of Colonel Parker. According to the Presley chroniclers, Elvis's reemergence at Las Vegas was a masterpiece of managerial manipulation. The Colonel, after shrewdly withdrawing Elvis from public performance at the height of his drawing power, now, no less astutely, decided to launch him again after nurturing the appetite for his reappearance by burying him for thirteen years in the unreal world of Hollywood exploitation flicks. Las Vegas was chosen as the launching site because it would offer Elvis the ideal audience—a couple thousand

middle-aged people sated with food and drink—and because it would offer vast amounts of money.

The truth is that when Elvis began to have thoughts
about returning to live performance, he gave no consideration to Las Vegas because he saw the resort as a most
unsuitable place for his style of entertainment. How else,
in fact, could he have seen it? Rock music had never attained any popularity in Las Vegas. All attempts to introduce the style had failed miserably. Las Vegas was, in
fact, the one totally secure bastion of the traditional entertainment idioms, deriving from the Broadway theater,
the New York nightclub and the Parisian follies. The heroes of Vegas were sophisticated old pros like Frank Sinatra, Dean Martin, Tony Bennett, Sammy Davis, Jr., Don
Rickles, Buddy Hackett and Shecky Greene: performers
with whom Elvis had no identification. Everything in Vegas was oriented to the "over thirties," a euphemism for
the middle-aged and the elderly. Putting it all together,
any sensible person would have said that Las Vegas was
the worst place in America for Elvis Presley to attempt
a comeback. As if all this were not bad enough, Las Vegas
also had the distinction in Elvis's mind of being the only
town in America where he had ever bombed.

Back in the spring of 1956, as he was making his spectacular take-off into national celebrity, Colonel had booked
him into the New Frontier for two weeks. He was the star
of a show that featured the silky string arrangements of
the Freddie Martin Orchestra and the booze and gambling
jokes of Shecky Greene. Elvis cut such an incongruous
figure in that company that *Newsweek* likened his appearance to "a jug of corn liquor at a champagne party."
The Las Vegas audience was described as sitting through
Elvis's act "as if he were a clinical experiment." After two
weeks of getting the cold shoulder from the old folks—as
well as suffering the humiliation of seeing his name go
from the top to the bottom of the marquee—Elvis exploded,
telling the press: "I don't want no more nightclubs." For
any other entertainer the recollection of this early mishap
would have become a joke after the passage of thirteen
years, especially if the performer had been as incredibly
successful as Elvis and had reoriented his image and his

career to middle-of-the-road comformity with popular taste. This was not, however, the way Elvis Presley's mind worked. He had forgotten nothing and forgiven nothing. At thirty-three he felt about Las Vegas precisely as he had felt at twenty-one; namely, that it was a good place to party but a bad place to play.

What Elvis thought, felt or wanted, was rarely a decisive factor in any decision concerning his career. The important consideration was what the Colonel thought. The joke is that even the Colonel, who spent half his life at Vegas gambling, had never considered booking his boy back into the resort until he received an offer that put the once unthinkable notion of Elvis in a showroom into a new and enticing perspective. To appreciate the significance of this offer, especially from the Colonel's standpoint, one has to recover for a moment a little of the curiosity and excitement that was aroused by the much-publicized announcement by Kirk Kerkorian in 1968 that he was going to lead America's most popular resort into the golden decade of the seventies by providing it with the world's largest and most lavishly equipped hotel.

As the news stories and prospectuses depicted the International Hotel, it sounded like one of those "world of the future" conceptions that used to tease the imaginations of Americans back in the thirties. Every feature of the hotel was colossal: a capacity of 1,500 rooms (two and a half times the size of the reigning favorite, Caesar's Palace); a height of thirty stories ("the tallest building in the State of Nevada"); the pool, a reservoir of 350,000 gallons ("the second largest man-made body of water in Nevada, second only to nearby Lake Mead"); the shopping concourse, with a score of boutiques, offering everything you could buy in a fair-sized town; the dining facilities, half a dozen American and ethnic restaurants—Mexican, German, Italian and Benihana Japanese; the casino, the largest in the world—natch!—with over a thousand slot machines. As for entertainment, the International would have not one but three major facilities—a lounge, a legitimate theater and a showroom—each offering a production that would rival or surpass anything that could be found in the entire resort. Clearly, therefore, the In-

ternational was the ultimate resort hotel. In fact, it was
not so much a resort hotel as it was a resort *in* a hotel: a
totally self-contained, round-the-clock pleasure dome, where
one could check in for a weekend or a week and never once
feel the need to step out the door.

The Barnumesque grandeur of this conception was certain to have impressed itself on Barnum's foremost living
descendant, Colonel Tom. The canny Colonel saw at once
the great advantage he could reap by launching the publicity for Elvis's return atop the enormous wave of ballyhoo
that would be generated by the hotel's first season. He
recognized that the scale of this undertaking corresponded
to his favorite billing of Elvis as "The World's Greatest
Entertainer." What's more, as a deeply addicted gambler,
the Colonel was attracted by the possibility of combining
profit with pleasure.

Booking Elvis into the International for two weeks,
however, wouldn't solve his career problems. If he were
going to match the millions he earned in the movies with
income from personal appearances, sooner or later he
would have to go where the real money was—out on the
road. What this gig would offer was a chance to break in
his new act and get back into the rhythm of regular performing. So just when Elvis was starting to kick against
the traces of his old routine, the Colonel was readying a
new harness and surveying a new track at Las Vegas.

The man with whom the Colonel was dealing was the
general manager of the hotel, Alex Shoofey. A tough little
Lebanese whose nickname is "The Cleaver," Shoofey had
a well-deserved reputation for being one of the shrewdest
operators on the Strip. He had come to the Keno Kingdom
back in 1948 in the same random manner that characterized the arrival of so many of the greatest figures of this
Topsy-grown town. Having become a CPA in New York
after the war, he had gone out to California to make his
fortune running a gas station. When the business failed,
he packed up his gear and started driving home. Going
through Vegas, his old car broke down in front of a joint
called the Club Bingo. Shoofey strolled inside and—
Bingo!—he had a job working for the owner, Milton Prell.
When Prell bought the Sahara, he made Shoofey its man-

ager. It was at this time that the astute CPA first met
Colonel Parker, the man who was fond of saying, "Fuck
capital gains!"

When Kirk Kerkorian decided to build the International, he wooed Shoofey and his whole staff away from
the Sahara and established them at the Flamingo, where
their job was to recruit and train the staff for the International. Shoofey made such a good thing of the Flamingo
that Kerkorian decided he would operate two Las Vegas
hotels. Now, Shoofey was looking for big names to lend
prestige to the International's first and most critical season.

Colonel and Shoofey couldn't agree on a price. Colonel
took the position that his man was vital to the showroom's
success; Shoofey argued that Elvis had been out of the
game for a long time and was an unknown quantity in Las
Vegas. When the Singer Special played, Shoofey was disappointed. "The show was not the big, big success they
expected," he recalls. "In fact, it didn't come off. Elvis came
on wearing his old leather jacket. It was a throw-back. It
was unacceptable for Las Vegas."

When Shoofey did not call the Colonel with the anticipated offer, the Colonel called Shoofey. Once more they
negotiated, and this time they made a deal. Shoofey had
several acts in mind to open the room. He asked the Colonel if Elvis would like to have the honor. "Absolutely not,"
snapped the old man. "We will not open under any conditions. It's much too risky. Let somebody else stick his
neck out." The Colonel was shrewd in making this stip-
ulation, as events were to prove.

The showroom of the International is comparable in
scale to every other feature of the building. Similar in plan
to a huge municipal auditorium, one of those dreadful
houses that are all spread and no height—the sort of stage
that is perfect for only one famous act, the Rockettes—the
Showroom Internationale is a solo performer's nightmare.
Don Rickles, whom Shoofey had been very eager to engage,
took one look at the looming balcony and said there was
no possibility that he could do his act in such a vast and
impersonal space. Finally, it was decided that the room

should be opened by the hottest entertainer of the day, Barbra Streisand.

Elvis was very unhappy about the Vegas booking. Once again, the Colonel had thrown him into the lion's den. Now, it was his job to find a way to lick the beast. The Colonel's decision to keep him off the stage all these years had destroyed Elvis's confidence. No longer a cocksure kid who had but to walk onstage to have the audience at his feet, he was now a young old pro, smart enough to recognize all the pitfalls that lay before him. One big problem was that he had no act. What was he supposed to do—go onstage with a five-piece rock band and start singing "Heartbreak Hotel"? That's what the Colonel wanted him to do. Now, how could Elvis do something as dumb as that? It would risk typing him as a relic of the past, a campy character out of a rock 'n' roll cartoon. What was even worse was the fact that he didn't dig the old rock any more; he had gone on to other things and so had the world. Why should he put himself in a rock strait jacket when he preferred so many other kinds of music?

What was the alternative? Put on a tux and play Dean Martin? That was just as ridiculous. Elvis had an image that was bigger than life. Whatever he thought about rock, people still loved it and he was its king. He couldn't disappoint the public and risk his neck by suddenly assuming a totally new identity. Then, there were all the problems that related to the Vegas audience. Elvis had spent his great years driving little girls to tears. Now he would be looking at bouffant hairdos and evening gowns and cleavage. He'd have men out there who were old enough to be his father and women old enough to be his mother. He sure as hell couldn't come on to these people the way he had to the teenyboppers.

He began to haunt the hotels. One night he walked into the lounge at the Flamingo and found the solution to his problem. The performer was a young, virtually unknown Welsh singer named Tom Jones. He was a good-looking, well-built stud dressed in a sharp tux with a vest and wearing a tight, groovy Afro. His voice was powerful, though his held notes sometimes wavered unpleasantly. His stance was commanding. As he would hit the long high notes, he would bend way back from the waist, giving the women at ringside a good long look at his crotch. His pants were so tight that they appeared to have been sprayed on. In the strong stage lights, you could see clearly the outline of his dick and his balls. In fact, the best word for his act was "ballsy."

The most astonishing thing about this young man was the effect he had on the women in his audience. As the show reached its peaks, stylishly dressed, carefully soignée young matrons, many of them seated beside their husbands, would scream and throw their room keys at the singer. (Afterward the poor husbands would have to go onstage and retrieve the keys.) Some of them even got so nutsy, they pulled off their panties and tossed them into the lights. As Elvis looked on in astonishment, he realized that these women were feeling just what the little girls had felt at his shows back in the fifties.

When Elvis checked out Jones, he discovered that he was hot as a murder weapon. His records were going gold, he had a great new TV show in the works, his price was shooting up. The Flamingo was so eager to push him that they had launched a whole promotion keyed to the theme of "Tom Jones Fever." When you sat down at the table, you found a little bottle filled with pink "fever pills." When you turned on your radio, you got the latest report from the "fever clinics." The whole hype. The amazing thing was that it worked! Night after night, Tom Jones packed the room. It was said that the pit bosses and stickmen were complaining because their wives were pestering them constantly for tickets to the show.

Elvis got very friendly with Tom Jones. He even told the Guys, "Tom is the only man who has ever come anywhere close to the way I sing. He has that ballsy feeling, that 'I'm gonna shove it up your ass attitude.'" The only fault Elvis found in Jones's act was its blatant sex appeal. "I think that's very lewd," Elvis would frown, "showing his cock and his balls." "Hell, Elvis," Lamar Fike would carol, "you did the same shit in your time!" "No," Elvis would demur, "I was never vulgar."

All the same, the two men soon became fast friends. Elvis would hang out in Jones's dressing room, even walk

out onstage while Jones was working. After the gig, they
would go out together and get drunk. Jones drank champagne, Elvis vodka with orange juice to disguise the taste.
Then, when they were mellow, Elvis would talk to the
young singer, only five years his junior, like a father to
a son. At the same time, this father was getting a lot of
good ideas from this son.

When Elvis opened in Vegas, the professional show
people who worked with both Elvis and with Tom Jones
were astonished at how much the famous star had taken
from the man he treated as his protégé. Nick Naff, director
of publicity at the Flamingo and then at the International,
sums up the borrowings neatly:

> What Elvis got from Tom was the trick of working
> the Vegas show stage. Tom showed him that you
> have to be dynamic and sensual in a way that gets
> through to the over-thirties. You gotta hit 'em right
> in the cunt. Tom gave Elvis those head shakes, the
> vocal accents on the bridges, the freeze poses at the
> end of the songs, the trick of wiping the sweat with
> a cloth and then throwing it out in the house—all
> those things. The big difference was that Tom did
> all this stuff instinctively. He just didn't know any
> other way to work. Elvis was much smarter. He
> wasn't so spontaneous, but he knew a good thing
> when he saw it. He took Tom's stuff, translated it
> into his own style, rehearsed his ass off and went
> over big with it. Elvis was much the brighter of the
> two.

Tom had given Elvis the key to the house. The rest, for
a performer of Elvis's talent and resources, was relatively
simple. The whole trick was the image, the attitude. Once
Elvis got that straight, he knew just what to do. He wasn't
going to stand there in a fancy tux flashing his pecker. He
had a better gimmick. For years he had been studying
karate. He was a second-degree black belt. Now what was
ballsier than karate? Those studs paced around on the
mats like big cats. When they attacked, they screamed
like jaguars. They had dozens of great moves that were as

beautiful as any choreography. They also had that great look in their eyes: that killer look, where the soul, the *ki*, comes flashing out of the eye. Finally, there was the karate uniform, the *gi*. If you were going to do karate moves, you couldn't have a better costume.

Calling up Bill Belew, the costume designer whom he had met on the Singer Special, Elvis ordered a number of specially designed *gis* in black mohair. Some were in the traditional two-piece pattern; some were all-in-ones to keep the jacket from flying up and exposing his midriff. For the sash, Belew suggested that he have a macrame belt made by a Hawaiian-Japanese who was into the martial arts and would weave into the belt all the appropriate karate symbols. This idea thrilled Elvis. It was as if he were receiving a magic talisman that would protect him on the stage.

Sartor resartus. When Elvis put on the new *gi*, he assumed instantly his new image. He didn't jiggle and jerk any more. He took his stand and held it, firm as a statue. He didn't walk in that old butchy style. He padded back and forth like a cat-footed karate killer. When he got into a hard-hitting tune, like "Suspicious Minds," instead of throwing his body into some awkward rendition of the Shimmy or the Camel Walk, he started throwing karate punches: kicks and chops that projected powerfully the force of the music. In no time, he had his new act together.

Now it was time to attend to the music. Elvis started rehearsing a full month before his opening. For the first time in his career, he assembled a band of first-rate Los Angeles studio musicians: no more Nashville cornballs or boyhood pals, like Scotty and D.J. Las Vegas was a big challenge and Elvis was determined to meet the challenge with all the power he could marshal.

Two weeks before opening, Elvis brought all his forces together at the International Hotel for a series of full-scale rehearsals. One of the things that had impressed him about Tom Jones's act, especially when he saw him work in Hawaii in May 1969, was the way the Welsh singer matched his powerful voice with the sonority of a full orchestra, producing those smashing showbiz climaxes that give you goose pimples. Though Elvis had only recently been carping at Steve Binder and Bones Howe about the dangers of "over-producing" his songs with a big studio orchestra, he now became passionately convinced of the importance of working with the largest possible backing. In addition to his five-piece virtuoso rock band, he engaged: the Imperials (a pop gospel quartet); the Sweet Inspirations (a black female soul trio); a harmonizing soprano with an extremely high "angelic" voice; and a thirty-five piece orchestra with a conductor. With Charlie Hodge standing at his side with his acoustic guitar, Elvis mustered onstage *fifty* musicians and singers.

Naturally, the Colonel was furious at this extravagance. In a flash, he saw that Elvis's anxiety would wipe out their joint profits. In fact, he may have suspected that this was Elvis's true intention: an act of revenge inspired by the Colonel's callousness toward Elvis's feelings about Las Vegas. Elvis was heard to say at the time: "I don't care if I don't make any money so long as I give a good show." This was the kind of speech calculated to give the Colonel another heart attack. Colonel, for his part, went about puffing his cigar to a hot glow and demanding of no one in particular: "What the hell does he want all these people for? He doesn't need them! He's just *insecure!*" Ah, a line like that was designed to ricochet back off the Guys to Elvis, where it would hit him square in the balls. Elvis would send back his answer through the same set of human bounce boards. "I've got to have my *power!* I've got to have *dynamics!*" he thundered to the Guys. "You saw that stage, you saw what I've got to cover! What the fuck does that old bald-headed bastard think this is all about!"

By the time Elvis arrived in Las Vegas, Barbra Streisand had been working the showroom for two weeks. At this moment, she was at the peak of her career. She had just won an Oscar for *Funny Girl*. Her talents as a singer, an actress, a comedienne and an analyst of public taste promised that her Las Vegas debut would be one of the greatest events in the history of the resort. It was confidently expected that her engagement would establish attendance records, set benchmarks for musical and theatrical excellence and push the whole level of local entertainment onto a higher plateau. Then, the unthinkable happened. Streisand, ignorant of Vegas, puffed up with success, not really at her best before a live audience, came to town with an audaciously simple show. It was essentially a rehash of a program which she had given the previous summer at New York in Central Park. There were no warm-up acts, no jokes, no choreography or sets: just Barbra standing there under the lights with a fantastic hairdo, a splendid gown and the longest fingernails since the Manchu dynasty, singing her heart out into a jeweled hand mike. It was a stunning exhibition of vocal and stylistic virtuosity by the Heifetz of pop song. In New York, it would have killed the audience. In Las Vegas, after the stellar opening night, it produced shrinking houses and even snores.

Elvis slipped into the back of the balcony one night to watch his rival work. He pointed mutely to all the empty seats around him. Then, he settled down to listen to the program. He gave no signs of pleasure. He made sour faces when Barbra got into her Jewish obsessions. When it was all over, he turned to Lamar Fike and said two words: "She sucks!" Then, he went downstairs to the dressing room to tell Barbra how much he had enjoyed the performance. When he was admitted to the dressing room, he was astonished to find the great star alone. Elvis had never been alone for one moment in his entire life. Two or three men always accompanied him even to the bathroom. Streisand made no bones about her disgust with the audience and the hotel. "This place isn't even built yet!" she fumed. "I wouldn't be surprised if some night while I'm out there working some schmuck doesn't walk by with a ladder on his shoulder!" Then, vowing that she would never play Las Vegas again and wishing Elvis well on his engagement (doubtless with the same degree of sincerity as he had evinced with his phony congratulations), the two parted company.

As Elvis was straining every fiber of his being during the final days of rehearsal, even going so far as to strap weights on his legs as he worked to build up the muscles, Colonel Parker was having a field day blitzing the town and the nation with his publicity. Setting up his headquarters in a three-room suite at the end of the hall on the fourth floor, the old boy and his henchmen—Tom Diskin and Jim O'Brien—swiftly seized control of the hotel's public relations apparatus and readjusted it for their style of pitch. The hotel, for example, had wanted the radio spot announcements to be low-keyed and tasteful, with Elvis's voice in the background as the announcer extended an invitation. Colonel Parker would not hear of such a thing.

Soon the airwaves were filled with raucously echoing pitches: "ELVIS!))) ELVIS!))) ELVIS!))) NOW!))) NOW!))) NOW!))) INTERNATIONAL HOTEL!)))" The roads were lined all the way in from Los Angeles with socko billboard sheets. Every store in town was offered a window placard or a poster. Every unguarded wall was plastered with a quarter sheet. The newspaper ads were not just ads: They were two- and three-page sections devoted entirely to Elvis. You couldn't watch TV for an hour without getting an urgent spiel. All this round-the-clock activity, however, was just the buildup to the circus-hits-town bit the Colonel did the moment Barbra Streisand's engagement ended.

That night, the Colonel was standing in the hotel lobby with a huge crew, equipped with ladders, staple guns, lumber and vast quantities of posters and placards printed up by his old buddy Clyde Rinaldi, in Tampa. Abiding by the rules of professional etiquette, the old man did not permit one banner to be hung announcing Elvis's appearance until the contractual time of the Streisand engagement had run out. Then, at the stroke of midnight, he shouted at his crew: "Hit it!" Instantly, the men went into action. In a matter of hours, they had papered every public room in the hotel with Elvis's name and picture. They had constructed a booth next to the hotel entrance that sold souvenir programs, styrofoam straw hats, teddy bears. They hung banners from the ceiling, they supplied the maids with stand-up announcements to be placed conspicuously in every room on top of the TV set or the dresser. Next morning, when the hotel executives came to work, they were appalled to discover their immaculate new lobby buried under this junk blizzard. What could they do? As the marquee announced, in the largest lettering available and with a silhouette figure of the star, Las Vegas was now under the rule of ELVIS!

Opening night, July 26, 1969, the hotel offered a free dinner show to a specially invited audience. Naturally, the Colonel got control of the guest list and invited all his cronies from Tampa, Nashville and Hollywood, his doctor from Palm Springs, his wife's relatives and other such important figures. Oh, it was a star-studded assembly. The Colonel knew George Hamilton quite well. Minnie Pearl and Earl Scruggs were invited. Fats Domino attracted quite a bit of attention because he was virtually the only man of color among the two thousand guests.

The decor of the Showroom Internationale was just as preposterous as everything else in Las Vegas. Grander than the "Fountainblue," grosser than Grossinger's, it was adorned with three-dimensional putti stringing yards of swagging chiffon between plastic classic columns. The maitre d' and the captains wore frilly blue shirts under their elaborate tuxedos, and seated each guest according to a vast, astrological-looking chart. The New York rock press had been flown in en masse on Kirk Kerkorian's private DC-9, a stunning two-bedroom aerial yacht. Accustomed to nothing better than a paper plate laden with "soul food" and a plastic cup filled with sour wine, they were overwhelmed by the largesse that characterized the Presley opening. Small wonder that their notices of the event were so rhapsodic.

The two warm-up acts, the Sweet Inspirations and the comic Sammy Shore, can be passed over without comment as they were observed without interest by the audience. Then, the giant gold curtain fell. When it rose again, it revealed the philharmonic-sized forces of Elvis's accompaniment belting out a hot show-time rhythm. Suddenly, without a word of announcement, a figure dressed in black emerged from the wings at stage left. There was a gasp of recognition, then a mounting roar of applause that instantly became a standing ovation. Elvis, meantime, had stridden to center stage, received his guitar from Charlie Hodge and assumed the classic spraddle-legged stance to kick off his first number. The uproar in the house was so great that he was stopped in his tracks. Smiling foolishly but unwilling to break the spell by saying anything, he held the band in check for a few moments. Then, he cried:

"One for the money!" The band shouted back, *"Ba-dum boom!"* "Two for the show!" *Ba-dum boom!* "Three to get ready and *go, cat, go!"* He was off and running on fast "Blue Suede Shoes."

What followed was a case of old Cokes served up in shiny new cans. Elvis's special arrangements, which could not match the rock poetry of Billy Goldenberg's, had the effect at fast tempos of seizing the singer, as if in one of those old vibrating belts, and shaking him violently on what sounded like one note until he was breathless. Then, panting, gasping, apologizing—at one point he said, "You all just look at me a couple minutes while I get my breath back!"—he would swig down a cup of Gatorade, like a spent athlete, and return to his musical exercise machine. On the first slow tune, "Love Me Tender," he strolled around the stage apron, kneeling down to kiss one woman after another. He was determined to make contact with the "over thirties." His first medley—"Jailhouse Rock," "Don't Be Cruel," "Heartbreak Hotel" and "All Shook Up"—betrayed a sarcastic and spoofing attitude, as if he were saying: "I'm not twenty-one any more and neither are you, so we won't take these old toys too seriously."[1] All the best material appeared in the latter part of the show, where he got into his recent hits, "In the Ghetto" and a six-minute take-out on "Suspicious Minds," which built up to a bacchanalian climax, the trumpets screaming, the drums roaring, the choral voices shouting out their lungs. All in all, it was a show that offered a lot more to the eye than to the ear and a lot more to the viscera than to the mind. Elvis was blowing it out, belting his songs, producing broad, coarse effects that were appropriate to all the broad, coarse sensibilities in his audience. When he walked off that night, the flacks, the fans, the rock critics and the music businessmen hailed the performance as a

---

[1]Elvis grew so disgusted with rock 'n' roll in his later years that every night at Vegas after his obligatory rock medley, he would turn to J. D. Sumner and say: "Thank God we're through with that shit! Now maybe we can sing some real music."

triumph. As such it was reported the following week from coast to coast.

Next day at noon, Colonel Parker met with Alex Shoofey in the deserted and eerily lit showroom. Originally, they had agreed to get together just to talk over the opening and make any little readjustments that might be necessary. Shoofey arrived, however, with something drastically different in mind. He had been enormously impressed by Elvis's new show. He hadn't attended the rehearsals and didn't know what to expect. After his experience with Barbra Streisand, he was very worried. Then he had seen something that he hadn't even dared to hope for: a real honest-to-god Las Vegas stage show. Instantly, his mind had started spinning like a computer. He saw the chance of a lifetime. Now, he was going to grab it.

Seating himself at a table about the size of a roulette wheel, the small but tough-looking CPA confronted the obese man with the long cigar drooping from his lips. The two of them looked exactly like what they were: the dealer and the dumper. Now, they were going to play a little game. The stakes? Elvis Presley's future. Shoofey knew exactly how to deal with the Colonel. The best approach was always to lay it on the line, which is just what Shoofey proceeded to do.

"Colonel," he said in his raspy New York voice, "I'd like to draw up a new agreement with you—for five years." "No!" snapped the Colonel, astonished at this development. "It's too big a risk. I know what you're thinking. You were impressed by the show last night: but, remember, that was only *one show!* You don't know what will happen next." Shoofey's mouth drew back in a sharklike grin. "Colonel," he said, "I'm a gambler. I'm willing to go right now, take a five-year contract. Two appearances a year, four weeks each appearance." Colonel was still shaking his head. This wasn't good business. "Alex," he said, getting personal, putting on his I'm-old-enough-to-be-your-father air: "I wouldn't do it this way. I would go on the basis of the right of first refusal." Shoofey was not dissuaded in the least. Leaning across the table and fixing the Colonel with a hard, unwavering look, he reached for his sinker. Speaking the language of the professional gambler, he croaked: "I'll take the cut!"

As Shoofey spoke, the Colonel started scribbling figures on the tablecloth. It was an old dodge of his, a device to give him more time to think—without looking the other man in the eye. The more he scribbled, the more the proposition appealed to him. What was it that appealed to him so much? Money? A giant figure that would eclipse any price ever paid in Las Vegas? That's what everybody thought at the time, and that's what most people believe to this day. Every article, every book says it. Elvis Presley made a million a month in Vegas. Or was it even more? With all the expenses and freeloading and stock options, the smartest operators in Vegas figured Elvis was good for $400,000 a week. The truth was far otherwise.

Elvis had come into Vegas with a four-week contract calling for a salary of $100,000 per week. Now, Shoofey upped the offer to $125,000 a week for two months per year, with the price to hold for the next *five years*. Believe it or not, the Colonel bought it. He gave Elvis away for a price that would soon be surpassed by attractions of far less drawing power. Shoofey himself was staggered by his own success. He calls it "the best deal ever made in this town." That is probably an understatement. Consider what he got that day.

The International's showroom was rated at a capacity of 1,500. By squeezing (and paying off the fire inspectors), the room could actually accommodate two thousand. With a fifteen-dollar minimum, that comes to a minimum of $30,000 a show for the house. Figure two shows a night for twenty-eight consecutive nights, and you get a bottom figure of $1,680,000. Naturally, the room took in much more because half of these shows were dinner shows with big tabs. The gross for the month, therefore, far exceeded two million dollars—and this happened twice a year for five years. The punch line to this golden yarn is that the showroom was budgeted, as are all Las Vegas hotel entertainment facilities, to operate at a *loss*, entertainment being in Vegas just one of the baits that are offered the suckers to get them to the gambling tables. You always hear about the records that Elvis established at Vegas.

The record that most impressed hotel men was that Elvis
Presley was the first act in the history of the resort to earn
a hotel a profit on its show.

When the Colonel and Shoofey finished negotiating the
big issues, they came around to the fringe benefits. Kirk
Kerkorian had lured men like Shoofey to his side by offering them options on the new hotel's stock. He had instructed his manager to offer options to all the big acts
that played the hotel. It was a way of binding the entertainers to the establishment, making them feel that they
were working for themselves. Shoofey offered the Colonel
options on twenty thousand shares of hotel stock at five
dollars a share. Barbra Streisand had snapped up the stock
without a moment's hesitation. Shoofey expected the Colonel to follow suit. Instead, the old man said: "Keep your
stock. I don't believe in stocks." The stock soon rose to
$70 a share.

The Colonel said that he would expect a bonus if they
continued to do good business. Shoofey was perfectly agree-
able. He was also very clever about the bonuses. Instead
of setting a limit on what he would offer, he used to ask
the Colonel at the end of each engagement what *he* wanted.
Shoofey was counting on a modest demand. If the demand
were too great, he could always try to cut it down; but if
it were an appropriate sum, it would make both him and
the Colonel look good if they played it like gentlemen.
Shoofey was not disappointed in his reckoning. The Colonel's demands were very modest. Though Elvis made millions for the International Hotel, he never got more than
$50,000 over his contract price. As for his personal ex-
penses, they amounted to very little. The same, however,
could not be said about Colonel Parker's expenses. Here,
we come to the other side of the Colonel's most peculiar
deal.

In selling Elvis short—and never obtaining more than
$150,000 after four years of fantastic success—Colonel
Parker appears to have made a colossal error of judgment.
What's more, he appears to have acted completely out of
character. After all, what is the Colonel's essence? Making
demands! Asking for unheard-of sums of money. Squeezing
the suckers for every last dime. In a word, getting *his!*

Now, here we see him suddenly going for a long-term deal
that he doesn't believe in on principle and which, in practice, turns out to be a bad deal, which he doesn't even seek
to renegotiate. How does one explain such a thing? If the
Colonel had been a ten-percenter or even a quarter-sharer,
it would have been bad for him. As a fifty-fifty partner in
every deal Elvis made, it looks as if he screwed himself
out of a pile of money. Appearances are deceiving, however, especially when you are considering the activities of
a man as devious as Tom Parker. Consider the deal from
his angle.

Colonel saw from the jump that Elvis was always going
to blow an enormous amount on these Las Vegas shows.
He knew that the nut would never get any smaller; in fact,
it was bound to get bigger and bigger as the supporting
acts and the musicians increased their demands. As the
Colonel's share was of the net, not of the gross earnings,
no matter how hard he bargained to raise Elvis's price, his
own income was never going to be anything extraordinary
in Las Vegas. What he needed, therefore, was some way
of getting *his*. Now, as an inveterate gambler, as, in fact,
one of the highest rollers in the history of Las Vegas, the
Colonel had an interest in the resort that had nothing to
do with the showroom. What he really needed was a break
at the casino.

Once Elvis was established at Vegas, the Colonel began
to gamble on a scale that astonished everyone. The old
man would drop every night between $50,000 and $75,000
on the roulette wheel and the crap table. One night Lamar
Fike saw the Colonel gamble steadily for five hours. Soon,
according to Alex Shoofey, the Colonel's losses amounted
to at least a million dollars a year. Elvis's gross annual
income never exceeded seven million dollars. Deducting
expenses and taxes from this sum, the Colonel's share
could never have exceeded by much what he dropped at
Vegas. The question arises, therefore, how did the old man
sustain this level of expenditure?

The answer is that the Colonel had mastered the art
of living on nothing a year. Just consider what he got out
of the International Hotel alone. The hotel provided the
Colonel with a year-round three-room suite, all of his food

and drink, much of his transportation costs, the food and dining paraphernalia for his Palm Springs home and— virtually unlimited credit at the casino. In turn, the Colonel kept Elvis working until the end of his life for a salary that never exceeded $150,000 per week, the figure he negotiated on the expiration of the first five-year contract. Though Elvis's contract was not an exclusive arrangement and every hotel in Las Vegas was bidding for his services after he finished his semiannual appearance at the International, Colonel never entertained such an offer for a moment. He offered his hotel a monopoly on the greatest attraction in the history of the resort in exchange for various arrangements by means of which he got *his*.

Elvis was destined to return to Las Vegas again and again in the next seven years, falling into one of those treadmill patterns that characterized his entire career. Every August and February, like clockwork, Colonel Parker would throw a switch and the machine would spring into action. At first Elvis got some pleasure from his new success. He tinkered with his image and his repertoire. When he opened for the second time, in February 1970, he had a totally new look.

Not since Marlene Dietrich stunned the ringsiders with the sight of her celebrated legs encased from hip to ankle in a transparent gown had any performer so electrified Las Vegas with his mere physical appearance. Bill Belew, who had been very cautious up to this point about designing any costume that would make Elvis look effeminate, decided finally to kick out the jams. Now Elvis faced the house encased in a smashing white jumpsuit, slashed to the sternum and lovingly fitted around his broad shoulders, flat belly, narrow hips and tightly packed crotch. And then there were his pearls—loads of lustrous pearls, not sewn on the costume but worn unabashedly as body ornaments. Pearls coiled in thick bunches around his neck, pearls girdled his tapered waist in a fabulous karate belt, rope of pearl alternating with rope of gold, the whole sash tied over one hip with the ends dangling down to brush one knee. With his massive diamonds flashing pinks and purples from his fingers and his boyish smile flashing sheepishly through his huge shag of shiny black hair, Elvis

looked like a heaping portion of male cheesecake ripe for
the eyeteeth of the hundreds of women ogling him through
opera glasses or lunging at the stage like gravid salmon
hurtling a cataract.

Elvis also relaxed and regained his old confidence. He
would kick off the show now James Brown style by collaring the mike and shaking it to the beat of "I'm All
Shook Up," the kettle-drumming orchestra shaking its
elephantine body behind him. Coming to the guitar break,
Elvis would strum the acoustic instrument slung on a
white band about his neck with the carelessness of a practiced faker. Then the number would end abruptly with the
martial artist snapping into profile and thrusting his guitar bayonet-wise at the chorus.

The rest of the evening would pass smoothly as he
glided through medleys of old tunes or lounged in elaborately upholstered versions of his new anthems. Every
number would end with a classically struck profile, the
white-clad figure with the Grecian features suggesting a
spaceage version of the Discus Hurler or the Laocoön. Between numbers he would offer glimpses of his wry humor:
"My mouth's so dry, feels like Bob Dylan slept in it all
night." Finally, the performance would come to its conclusion with the Vegas equivalent of one of those sunset-
in-the-Rockies numbers from the old *Ziegfeld Follies*.

Silhouetted against a cerulian blue cyclorama, the Las
Vegas Philharmonic, the front rank of black-clad, guitar-
slingin' Memphis Mafiosi and the integrated chorus of the
Imperials and the Sweet Inspirations would be transfigured by a flood of rich amber light pouring in from the
Valley of Loose Gold. As the massed players and singers
sustained a mighty cathedral chord, the Sun King would
fall on one knee in the classic Jolson-gladiator pose, flinging wide his arms in a grand salute to his assembled court,
over which he seemed destined to reign forever in eternal
youth and jollity and jamboree.

Chapter 30

The President Will See Mr. Presley

ELVIS was just winding up his first appearance at Las Vegas in August of 1969 when the Sharon Tate murders burst like a bomb in his brain. He saw in these murders a prophecy of his own doom. As he pored over the newspaper accounts and talked on the phone with law enforcement officials in Los Angeles, he became obsessed with the idea that he, Priscilla and little Lisa Marie might be the next victims of the crazy killers. Wasn't he an object of envy and hatred? Didn't he and his family live in a cul-de-sac up in the hills of Los Angeles, where it would be easy to enter in the middle of the night and kill, kill, kill?

Instantly, Elvis ordered the house on Hillcrest Drive guarded by uniformed security men night and day. He vowed to spend as little time as possible in Los Angeles, whose inhabitants he had said always were the biggest bunch of freaks in America. Still, the more he thought about his danger, the less these protective measures reassured him. Putting rent-a-cops around his Trousdale house was not sufficient. What Elvis required was absolute security, the kind of security that was enjoyed by the president of the United States. The president had his uniformed guards, alarm systems and all the mechanical protection that human ingenuity could devise. Ultimately, though, what really secured him from harm? The Secret Service. Those neat, efficient-looking dudes in dark suits, who were sworn to put their body between the president's body and the onslaught of any assassin. That was the sort of protection that Elvis craved: a wall of human flesh. A group of men who were tough, well-trained, well-armed, totally dedicated and willing to take the bullet that was meant for him. Now, where could he find such men? It must have been with a great sense of relief that he recognized that he had them already. Sure, they were the Guys!

Some of the Guys were worthless as bodyguards. Charlie was just a little mascot. Joe was strictly for business. Lamar, if he fell on you like a Secret Service man, would kill you with his weight. Still, Elvis had some boys who were real bad-asses, like Red and Sonny West. Ole Red had been working since leaving Elvis with Bob Conrad on the TV series *Wild, Wild West.* Now that the show had gone off the air, Red had returned to Memphis where he had gotten involved with Chips Moman at the American Recording Studio. Elvis was sure he could bring Red back into the fold. Meanwhile, he had already put Sonny on the payroll. With the proper training, Sonny could become a real gunslinger. He was huge, fearless, naturally loyal and aggressive. Elvis would soon have that big boy leading his security forces with a snub-nosed Colt Python stuck up his armpit, barrel foremost, in a quick-release holster. Still, he needed a lot more hired guns.

Guns, Elvis reasoned, were really the whole secret of security. If everybody had a gun and knew how to use it, who would dare to mess with them? Elvis himself always owned guns, carried guns, shot guns and believed in guns. Now, he decided to get everybody guns. In the course of the next four years, he must have bought at least 250 guns. All the Guys carried guns. There were guns in all of Elvis's homes, in Elvis's cars, on Elvis's own person at all times. He started putting a gun next to his bed when he slept and next to his plate when he ate. There were so many guns that after a while, they lost track of them all. (Becky Yancey, one of Elvis's secretaries, remembers her

husband sitting down on a sofa at Graceland one day and
feeling something hard under the cushion. It was a gun.)

Elvis purchased most of these weapons himself, his favorite store being Kerr's Sporting Goods, a couple of blocks
from the Beverly Wilshire Hotel, in the heart of Beverly
Hills's swank shopping district. Kerr's is one of those
fancy, snobbish, super-WASPy establishments, like Aber-
crombie & Fitch was in New York, whose clerks develop
as they get older a very icy and condescending manner
that virtually challenges each new customer to prove that
he's good enough to deserve the store's merchandise. As
these prim and alum-mouthed gentlemen of the counter
saw it, to buy costly, finely crafted guns, you ought to be
either an authentic sportsman, a marksman or a gun col-
lector. It's easy to imagine the disgust the salesmen felt
when Elvis would blow in, wearing his latest street costume: an all-black outfit with a high Napoleonic collar, a
white four-in-hand tie, numerous gold chains and perhaps
a cape and a gold-tipped ebony walking stick. Instead of
examining a few weapons carefully and asking a lot of
technical questions—or recalling the time when he was
out in the bush and this big rhino came charging through
the zanzenoobie bushes—Elvis would say, "Lemme see
that one and that one and that one..." until he had bought
every fancy engraved, inlaid, chased and gilt pistol in the
case at prices that went as high as $3,500 a pop. What's
more, instead of acquiring these weapons as esteemed ar-
tifacts with the intention of mounting them in special cases
under glass, Elvis would heft them, sight them, load them
with live ammunition and stick them under his belt. Then,
he'd walk out the door, jump behind the wheel of his yellow
De Tomaso Pantera 265 or his black Dino Ferrari and try
to beat the light!

Eventually, Elvis's collection of weapons constituted a
veritable reliquary of pop culture heroes. Just by fondling
these guns or strapping them on his body or, best of all,
firing them, Elvis could experience the thrill of identification with his favorite military, law-enforcement or gangster types. His gilded, pearl-handled nine-millimeter Beretta automatic, for example, was the same weapon that
James Bond carried, only the snobbish 007 would have

turned up his nose at Elvis's gaudy model, preferring the
hi-tech chic of a steel-blue barrel and a skeleton grip. Elvis's Walther PPK/S double-action automatic, so square,
compact and sinister looking, with its blue-black finish
and snub nose, is, like the Beretta, a favorite weapon of
undercover agents, particularly the CIA. The graceful
Mauser Luger, on the other hand, summons up the world
of the *Wehrmacht* in the Great War: a German officer in
a tight field-grey tunic with the Iron Cross dangling at his
neck and his machine-pistol strapped high above his hip
in an elegant enclosed holster, like a camera case. The
Colt .45, of which Elvis owned many copies, likewise
evokes World War I; in fact, the replicas that Elvis purchased were stamped with the dates 1917–1967, indicating that they had been manufactured to commemorate the
fiftieth anniversary of this classic and klutzy weapon.
Drastically different associations hallowed the nickel-
plated, long-barreled Colt .44 magnum revolver. This hand
cannon had been made famous by its use by Clint Eastwood in *Dirty Harry*. As soon as Elvis saw this movie,
which made an enormous impression on him, he went out
and bought this enormously powerful weapon, which can
penetrate an engine block or even shoot down an airplane.
Like Clint Eastwood, Elvis wore his .44 in a bulging shoulder holster.

Some of Elvis's weapons had very dubious associations.
His antique Carl Hauptmann-Ferlach double-barreled
hunting rifle was the prize weapon of Hermann Goering.
A magnificent specimen of the nineteenth-century gunsmith's art, the rifle has a stock of Circassian walnut,
hand-carved and inlaid in ivory carved with deer and elk;
the barrel is chased in gold. Goering was a prodigious
hunter who would butcher hundreds of animals in a single
day, shooting from blinds past which his beaters drove
whole herds of beasts. Elvis scorned hunting because it
was a sport that demanded quiet, patience and cunning.
The only hunting Elvis ever did was shooting snakes along
a mudbank. He owned enough shotguns and rifles, however, to have furnished the armament for an old-fashioned
African safari.

Most of Elvis's weapons possessed a distinctly lethal

character. They did not suggest sport, marksmanship or
gun collecting so much as they did an obsession with killing human beings. He owned, for example, a .300 magnum
assassination rifle that broke down to fit inside an attaché
case. Naturally, it was equipped with a telescopic sight.
Elvis owned also some very intimidating machine guns.
He possessed an early model of a .22 caliber machine gun
with a horizontal drum, the design of a famous gunsmith,
Dick Casule of Salt Lake City. With this weapon, now
widely used by the police, a lone man could lay down a
tremendous barrage, all of it quite deadly at short range.
Elvis's prize automatic weapon was his classic 1927
Thompson submachine gun, the original Tommy Gun,
with the perpendicular drum and the slotted muzzle brake
to reduce the bucking recoil from the big .45 caliber shells.
This gun was obtained for Elvis by his friends in the Chicago Mob.

In some periods of his life, Elvis was a pretty good shot
with a handgun. It all depended on how much he practiced.
Here he experienced a certain difficulty, for as the district
around Graceland became thickly settled, Elvis's middle-
class neighbors began to complain every time he and the
Guys would indulge in an orgy of shoot-'em-up target practice. The shooting was done, to be sure, under rather un-
safe conditions. Adjoining the low building in the backyard
of Graceland that was used for an office was an old smokehouse. Elvis had installed inside the door of this wooden
structure two rows of sawed-off telephone poles that sustained targets shaped like human silhouettes. The idea
was that all the spent or ricocheting bullets would be
caught inside the shed and not fly loose so that they could
cause injury. The problem was that the power of the weapons that Elvis was firing was so great that sometimes the
bullets would drill through the walls and carry many yards
before they fell to the ground. These red-hot slugs also had
incendiary properties. Once Elvis set the building afire
with a prolonged burst from an M-16.

When the neighbors' complaints about the constant
gunfire at Graceland had brought the police to his door a
score of times, Elvis reacted as he did always in such situations: He vowed that he would make himself proof

against complaint even if he took it into his head to fire
his guns all night long. A contractor was summoned and
plans were drawn for a four-stall firing range that would
be sunk nine feet below ground in the backyard. When it
came time to begin the excavation, Elvis lost interest in
the project. It joined the circular movie theater, the recording studio, the helicopter pad and all the other dream
projects that were designed at one time or another for this
same backyard.

Shooting at targets, no matter how you did it, could
never rival the pleasure of shooting at human beings: the
most dangerous game. So Elvis introduced a new sport at
Graceland that deserved the title War far more than his
old collision combats at the Rainbow Rollerdome. The new
version of War was fought by teams armed with explosive
fireworks. First, the Guys would drive over to West Memphis in Arkansas, where fireworks were legal, and buy
two or three thousand dollars' worth of Roman candles,
skyrockets, baby giants, firecrackers and "nigger chasers"—jet-propelled snakes that took fast, unpredictable
turns along the ground until they exploded. Then, they
would don air force jumpsuits, with gloves, helmets and
goggles. Dividing themselves into Red and Blue teams,
they would face off at point-blank range with as many as
twelve Roman candles in each hand and engage in two-
or three-hour shootouts.

Invariably, there were painful and sometimes serious
injuries. Richard Davis almost lost an eye once when a
ball of flaming phosphorus struck him in the face. Elvis
had a big scar on his neck from a hot shot that slipped
down his collar and burnt him fearfully. As with so many
of Elvis's games—the skate battles, the daredeviltry on
the roller coaster, the midnight racing in cars and on motorcycles—the fun was edged with terror. Elvis seems
never to have enjoyed himself fully unless he was tempting
fate to roll him a seven.

Once Elvis got on his gun kick, guns became, after cars,
his favorite gift item. He gave guns not only to the Guys
but to the men he most admired, like President Nixon, to
whom Elvis presented one of his commemorative Colt .45s,
and Spiro Agnew, for whom Elvis selected a Colt .357

snub-nosed magnum.[1] Though you might expect that a heavy macho type like Elvis Presley would think that guns were exclusively a man's prerogative, you would be completely wrong. Elvis gave many guns to women, insisting that they ran no risk from the law in carrying weapons concealed in their purses because any real he-man lawman would respect a lady's desire to protect herself from injury or dishonor. This passing out of guns to girls became so habitual with Elvis that every time he dismissed a young woman with whom he had spent the night, he would give her with his farewell kiss a sinister-looking .38 Python. As Elvis saw it, guns are a girl's best friend.

When Chemical Mace was made available for civilian use, Elvis bought dozens of canisters and distributed them among the women in the group, as well as to his female employees. Unfortunately, the little gold-finished canisters got mixed up sometimes with other items in the ladies' purses. When Elvis opened at the Sahara Tahoe in July 1971, he arranged to have Priscilla, Norah Fike, Joanie Esposito and Judy West flown up from Los Angeles aboard a Lear jet. As the plane was preparing to land, Priscilla asked Judy: "Do you have your breath spray?" Judy reached inside her bag and pulled out the dispenser. Opening her own mouth wide, she pushed down on the release — and gave herself a searing and asphyxiating blast of Chemical Mace! As she screamed and gasped for breath, the vapor from the dispenser spread through the cabin, causing all the other women to start coughing and crying. Drifting further, through the open door to the pilot's cabin, the irritating mist produced the same symptoms in the crew, which was now in the midst of its landing maneuvers. Taking the ship aloft again, the pilots circled the airport until the air cleared.

When Judy came staggering off the plane, everyone was shocked by her appearance. She looked like a purple-snouted mandrill. The Mace contained an indelible dye designed to mark fugitive "perpetrators" so they could be

---

[1]Agnew declined his gun, explaining that a public official could not accept gifts from a citizen.

easily identified and captured. The injury to her vanity was transitory; the painful chemical burn she suffered in her mouth produced permanent scarring. When Elvis heard the story, he laughed. What the hell! He didn't tell her to shoot herself in the mouth, did he? Nonetheless, he changed his policy with regard to issuing dispensers of Chemical Mace. Now he insisted that the canisters be finished in black.

Elvis's security mania soon stirred up one of his oldest and deepest fantasies: his longing to be a highway patrolman. After he got out of high school, his ambition was to qualify for the force when he reached his twenty-first birthday. Now that he was nearing his thirty-fifth birthday, he finally realized his long-deferred aspiration. First, he had himself appointed a special deputy to the sheriff of Shelby County, the politically ambitious William N. "Bill" Morris. When a new sheriff, Roy C. Nixon, took office in October 1970, Elvis had himself reappointed as chief special deputy. Subsequently, he persuaded Nixon, who was destined soon to become mayor of Shelby County, to deputize all the Guys, including Vernon and Dr. Nichopolous. These appointments entitled them to receive official identification cards, wear a badge and carry a concealed weapon. The presentation of badges didn't end there, however. At Christmas, Sheriff Nixon and Elvis's friends presented Shelby County's most famous deputy with a gold belt buckle that bore a replica of his star engraved with his number, six, and encrusted with diamonds. Elvis presented the sheriff, in turn, with a pistol.

Having made such a good start at becoming at last a shield-wearing peace officer, Elvis was inspired now to acquire comparable badges and credentials from all parts of the country. Soon he had obtained through Colonel Parker's influence the badge of the Palm Springs police department. With the aid of his powerful attorney, Ed Hookstratten, Elvis became a member of the Beverly Hills police department. Eventually, he would carry about with him a leather attaché case into whose lining had been fixed no less than thirty different badges, representing as many communities or law enforcement agencies, including even the Canadian Mounted Police. Elvis treated his badges exactly like a kid who collects bubble gum cards or postage stamps: He would give an expensive gift to a captain in Denver so that he could "trade up" from lieutenant to captain in that town, with the ultimate goal being to cop the chief's badge. Though the badges were treated like pop bottle caps, they were potent symbols of authority. They offered Elvis a marvelous opportunity to misrepresent himself as an authentic law enforcement official, an advantage he employed on numerous occasions, stopping airliners at the point of take-off, countermanding the orders of local police officers and threatening with arrest anybody who got in his way.

Once he had his deputy's star, Elvis began hankering after another important symbol of office: the blue identification lamp that is used in Tennessee by the police when they are working out of an unmarked car. After pulling a few strings, Elvis obtained Sheriff Nixon's very own blue flasher. Now, fully equipped at last, patrolman Presley embarked on his long-deferred career.

Picture the scene. You are driving along a road on the outskirts of Memphis and exceeding the speed limit by ten or fifteen miles an hour. You glance in the rearview mirror and are startled to see rapidly overtaking you a mysterious midnight-blue Mercedes sedan with a blue light flashing imperatively from its dashboard. Without a moment's hesitation, you apply the brakes and pull over on the shoulder of the road. The Mercedes pulls to a stop beside you. Out the window on the driver's side appears the head of Elvis Presley. "Sir," says the world-famous superstar, "do you realize how fast you were travelin'? We got a law in this town, and we aim to see that it's kept." Then, holding up his sheriff's badge to make the proper impression of authority, Elvis continues: "I'm putting you on warning now. If you are caught speeding again, you will be subject to arrest and fine. Blah, blah, blah." Then, having laid down the law to the astounded motorist, Elvis cranks up his powerful car and speeds off in search of more lawbreakers.

It's not likely that anyone stopped by Elvis in Memphis would fail to recognize the city's most famous native son; this same instant identifiability didn't always hold in other parts of the country. Elvis's stepbrother, Rick Stan-

ley, recalls driving along the freeway in Los Angeles with
Elvis in his Dino Ferrari and coming upon a wreck at the
side of the road. Elvis stopped his car immediately, got out
and approached the policeman who had taken charge of
the situation. Introducing himself and offering to be of
assistance, Elvis was anticipating a warm welcome. Instead, the cop rounded on him and snarled: "Man, I don't
care *who* you are—just get in your car and get out of here!"
Actually, you can't blame the cop. Here he is hard at work,
when out of the blue comes some fat freak in a Prince
Valiant costume claiming to be Elvis Presley! Now, what
the hell would anybody do but tell this Hollywood weirdo
to get back in his Batmobile and split? Elvis was so shocked
by the cop's command that he jumped back in the car and
roared off. As he drove away, though, he mumbled angrily,
"Tell *me* what to do! *Me*, a federal agent!"

Yes, Elvis's career in law enforcement had carried him
to the top of the profession in a rise almost as spectacular
as that of his early years in the music business. In just
one year, Elvis rose from the lowly position of deputy sheriff of a county in western Tennessee to that of agent in one
of the federal government's most exciting and glamorous
anticrime forces: the Bureau of Narcotics and Dangerous
Drugs. Even more impressive is the fact that having received his first appointment from a local sheriff, he received his last from the president of the United States:
Richard Milhous Nixon. As this story has never been told
before in all its bizarre detail, we have to begin early in
1970, when Elvis got very friendly with a former sergeant-
in-charge of the Los Angeles police department's narcotics
squad, John O'Grady.

O'Grady came into Elvis's life when Ed Hookstratten
recommended that Elvis hire the ex-cop, now a private
eye, to investigate a North Hollywood waitress named Pat
Parker who had brought a paternity suit against the star.
The suit was based on false and preposterous accusations,
but it entailed a lot of pretrial preparations: lie detector
and blood tests, background investigations, depositions,
etc. During this time Elvis got tight with his new private
investigator, a man with a very colorful background and

a talent for spinning tales, as his entertaining book, *O'Grady,* testifies.

During the fifties, when he was "The Big O," the terror of Sunset Strip, the most gung-ho narc on the West Coast, O'Grady racked up an incredible total of 2,500 busts of drug dealers and drug users. His specialty was busting jazz musicians, whom he detested especially because as youth heroes they set a bad example for the younger generation. O'Grady felt exactly the same way about drug-using rock stars, but he made an exception for Elvis Presley.

To the veteran narc, it was obvious from the first that Elvis was a "hype." In the course of their initial meeting at O'Grady's office on the Sunset Strip, Elvis rose to go to the men's room and walked straight into a wall. Yet, it was just as clear that Elvis was a passionate believer in law enforcement, especially the rigorous enforcement of the drug laws. O'Grady decided to resolve this ambivalence by involving Elvis at every opportunity in police work. He imagined that the more Elvis learned about drugs, the greater his fear or his shame would become, until eventually he would renounce the stuff. What O'Grady could not imagine was that Elvis was perfectly comfortable leading a double life in which at one moment he was going out to bust a bunch of dope-smoking hippies and the next he was using all his wiles to con some druggist or doctor into giving him an illegal prescription for some dangerous and strictly controlled drug.

O'Grady did succeed, even beyond his wildest dreams, in making Elvis a dedicated champion of drug-law enforcement. Night after night, he would sit with his client recounting an endless series of fascinating stories about raids and busts, undercover work out on the street and famous entertainers who were really hypes. Elvis, who reacted to this sudden opening of a new and mysterious world in much the same way that he did to the appearance of the Swami, would sit spellbound, urging O'Grady on to further revelations of secret police techniques. Soon, Elvis had become so infatuated with his new friend that after every story, he would sigh wistfully and say, "Man, I wish I could be an undercover narcotics detective!" O'Grady, giving his glass of Jack Daniels a swish, would reply with his customary deadpan sarcasm: "I wish I could be Elvis Presley."

Though the tough ex-cop made light of Elvis's dreams of joining the LAPD as an undercover man, Elvis's hankering for this new role, this new thrill, became obsessive. One night Elvis was seated in an upstairs room at the La Scala Restaurant on Santa Monica Boulevard with Priscilla, Joe, Charlie, Sonny and O'Grady. The maitre d' came to the table and told Elvis that Paul Newman's kids would like to meet him. "Fuck Paul Newman and his kids!" burst out Elvis, who had run into the actor recently at Kerr's and become convinced that Newman, preoccupied with his shopping, was snubbing him. With that sort of reaction fresh in his mind, you wouldn't expect that O'Grady would have reacted positively when, a little later, a waiter came to the table and whispered in the eye's ear that Paul Frees was downstairs and was eager to come up and meet Elvis.

Frees is a man both known and unknown to every TV watcher and radio listener in America. He is the voice of the Pillsbury Doughboy, the Pittsburgh Paint Peacock, Kellogg's Toucan Sam, Walt Disney's Ludwig Von Drake, Captain Crunch, Boris Badenov, Inspector Fenwick and so on through a thousand and one commericals, animations and narratives for the past thirty-five years. If this had been all that Frees had to recommend him, however, he would not have gained an audience that night with the King. What made O'Grady turn around and start talking up this old acquaintance to Elvis was the little known fact that Frees was America's foremost police buff.

For years the invisible man with the ubiquitous voice had been performing at police benefits, contributing to police charities and cutting into cops like O'Grady, who would reciprocate by taking Frees out on drug raids. As Frees earned a million dollars a year and the narcs were often reduced to scrounging for wheels, O'Grady would sometimes throw his surplus prisoners into Frees's Rolls-Royce for conveyance to the station house. O'Grady estimates that in drug-saturated Marin County, Frees must have participated in at least two hundred raids. In fact, it wasn't long before his meeting with Elvis that Frees had become the recipient of a remarkable honor bestowed upon him by the Bureau of Narcotics and Dangerous Drugs at the behest of its special counsel, John Dean. With all this background at his fingertips, O'Grady didn't have much trouble in getting Elvis to agree to meet this remarkably interesting but oddly mysterious character.

The man who appeared next was short, stocky, middle-aged and flashily dressed with a massive gold chain swagged across his vest. His head was leonine, the hair brushed forward across the bald brows, the eyes masked with big shades and the golden mouth covered by a thick, brushy RAF mustache. If you didn't know who he was, you might have mistaken him for a South American don. Elvis was intrigued by him immediately, and soon the two flamboyantly attired vocal virtuosos were engrossed in conversation.

They found common ground in their mutual hatred for rock groups like the Beatles, who sang about drugs and used drugs and by their example encouraged millions of kids to become heads. Elvis explained that this was all part of a Communist conspiracy to weaken America by undermining the morals and health of the youth. He then went on to attack stars like Jane Fonda, who in his opinion were "Communist sympathizers," or stars who exhibited a profound scorn for lawfully constituted authority, like the Smothers Brothers.

Once the similarity of their opinions had brought the men into an amiable intimacy, Elvis asked Frees if he could demonstrate some of his famous voices. Frees, a born performer and master of a hundred shticks, obliged instantly. As the table roared with delight, like children at a birthday party, the vocal magician segued effortlessly from his March of Time Stentor to his kooky Nutty Peanuts to his bemused ole Cap'n Crunch to his slyly humorous Inspector Fenwick to all the twerpy little villagers in the Green Giant commercials, until he got down finally to the voice of a disgruntled ant, who sounded exactly like the late Ned Sparks.

Once the show was over, O'Grady suggested that Frees do an encore. As everyone present was united in a common loathing for junkies, pushers and drug smugglers, what

would be the harm if Frees were to show Elvis and his
family his "credential"? At that point, Frees reached inside
his jacket and produced a flat leather case like a passport
wallet. Flipping it open, he laid under Elvis's nose a remarkable document. It was emblazoned with the official
seal of the Department of Justice and the insignia of the
Bureau of Narcotics and Dangerous Drugs. It displayed
an identification photo of Frees, along with his finger-
prints and vital statistics. It was signed by John E. Ingersoll, the director of the drug agency. The most impressive feature of this credential was the title it bestowed on
its bearer. It informed the reader that Paul Frees was an
"agent at large" of the Department of Justice. In other
words, this fifty-five-year-old radio-TV entertainer, this
million-dollar-a-year residuals tycoon, was a full-fledged
federal narc with ambassadorial privileges and immuni-
ties.

O'Grady, who practically drooled with envy every time
he ogled this "beautiful credential," explained its full purport to Elvis. At that moment, Elvis realized that instead
of having to sate his cop lust by collecting dinky shields,
like those of a deputy sheriff of Shelby County or a member
of the Palm Springs police department, he could have the
boss badge. He could go after the magic emblem of a federal
narc! Gazing raptly at the document, as if he were be-
holding the Holy Grail or the Shroud of Turin, Elvis murmured: "There isn't much that I've got that I wouldn't give
to have one of those!"

The Saturday before Christmas, 1970, Elvis gave the
folks at Graceland a stunning exhibition of how a narc
goes underground. On that day, Elvis got into a big fight
with Vernon and Priscilla over the issue of his Christmas
shopping. Vernon had just received some shocking bills
from Los Angeles. At Kerr's, Elvis had bought thirty-two
handguns, including a gold-inlaid .357 Colt Python
($1,950) and a gold-plated .44 Ruger Blackhawk ($1,850).
The other weapons had ranged in price from a thousand
dollars down to sixty-six dollars for a tiny, two-shot over-
and-under Derringer. The total bill for handguns was
$19,792. This was nothing, however, compared to the bills
from the car dealers. Elvis had purchased *ten* Mercedes

sedans, which he planned to give away like three-speed bikes. This tab added up to $85,000!

Elvis could never bear to be challenged about anything and especially could he not tolerate criticism of his spending sprees. Vernon and Priscilla, on the other hand, were both as tight with a buck as Elvis was prodigal. Elvis's spending alarmed and horrified them in precisely the same degree that it made him feel happy and fulfilled. They were always at war about money. This day would have been no different from many others if Elvis had not seized the opportunity to punish both his father and his wife while at the same time giving himself a rare thrill.

Rushing up to his room, he dressed himself in one of his most extravagant and swashbuckling costumes. He donned a purple crushed-velvet suit and cape, with the immense gold-buckled belt bestowed on him by the International Hotel for breaking all attendance records. Slipping a massive Colt .45 into his shoulder holster and a Derringer in his boot, he topped off the outfit with a jeweled white cane. Stalking out of the house, he jumped in a car and drove to the airport alone. Walking up to the American Airlines counter, he asked when the next plane was leaving. Informed that a Washington flight would soon depart, Elvis bought a ticket with his gold star American Express Card and allowed himself to be ushered into the VIP lounge.

At this point, Elvis must have felt like he was flying around in outer space. Never before had he left the city alone. Only the heady game of Undercover Narc could ever have inspired such derring-do. Merely being *alone* must nearly have given him the bends.

Once he settled into his room at the Washington Hotel, a drab old establishment near the White House, his mood began to change. Sure, it had been fun, riding in a cab. Fun when he ordered the driver to stop at the doughnut joint, where some dumb "nigger" recognized him and screamed about the diamonds on his hands. Elvis had told that black boy that he aimed to keep all his diamonds— then he gave him an eyeful of the .45 under his arm. The best fun was when he registered at the hotel desk. He had used the name Colonel Jon Burrows, which was a variation

of the name Colonel Parker always used when he didn't
want to reveal his identity.

When Elvis settled down in front of that hotel room TV,
the manic phase of the high began to wear off. Here he
was, the most popular man in the world, and he didn't
know a soul. Finally, he got an inspiration. Why not fly
out to L.A.? Picking up the phone, he put through a call
to London Towne Livery Service in Beverly Hills. This
was a limousine service that Elvis used often. It was operated by a British actor, Gerald Peters, who has appeared
in scores of movies and TV shows playing immaculately
groomed and utterly imperturbable English butlers. Elvis,
who had a nickname for everyone, called Peters "Sir Gerald." It was late Saturday night when Peters received a
call from a Mr. Jones in Washington, D.C. The first thing
that Mr. Jones wanted to know was whether Peters was
alone. When Peters confirmed that he was alone, the voice
on the other end of the line said, "Do you know who this
is?" "Why, you're Mr. Jones, sir," replied Peters instinctively. The voice, suddenly shrinking to a whisper, responded: "Sir Gerald, it's *me!* Are you sure you're alone?"
Recognizing his caller now as Elvis Presley, Peters assured
him that he was alone, though now he suddenly realized
why he had been receiving calls all evening from Elvis's
men in Memphis and Los Angeles pretending to be motivated entirely by sociability but asking a lot of pointed
questions about the whereabouts of the Mercedes limousine which Peters rented from Elvis when the star was out
of town.

"I'm flying into L.A. tonight, arriving at three in the
morning," continued Elvis. "Will you meet me?" Peters,
concerned by his client's strange manner, replied by asking him if anything were wrong. Elvis reassured him, but
he ordered Peters to say, if he received any inquiring calls,
that he had not heard from Elvis. "Very good, sir!" sang
out Sir Gerald to the King.

Elvis could not long survive without the supportive
presence of the Guys. He decided now to call Jerry Schilling, who was not currently on the payroll but working as
a film editor in Hollywood. Jerry agreed to meet Elvis at
the airport that morning. When Elvis disembarked from

the plane, he was accompanied by two TWA stewardesses, one on either arm. He was not feeling well: one eye was infected and his face seemed slightly swollen. As soon as they arrived at the house on Hillcrest Road, a doctor appeared and gave Elvis a shot that knocked him out till the next afternoon. That day when Gerald Peters reported for work, Elvis told him the story of his quarrel with Vernon and Priscilla. Peters recalls that Elvis sounded just like a bewildered little boy as he said: "I can't understand it, Sir Gerald. Why were they so mad at me? It was *my* money. I earned it."

Now that Elvis had recovered from his journey, he decided it was time to turn around and fly back to Washington. He wanted Jerry to accompany him. Jerry said that he was due to report for work on a new job Monday morning and that if he didn't show up, he might be fired. Elvis acted hurt. Jerry felt guilty. As always Elvis's selfish whim took precedence. At ten that night when he took off for Washington, Elvis had his baby-sitter in the next seat.

On the same Red-eye Special was Senator George Murphy. Soon the famous singer and the old hoofer were deep in conversation. Elvis explained that he was bound for the nation's capital to offer his services to the government in the war against drugs. He planned to pay a call at the Bureau of Narcotics and Dangerous Drugs and then seek a meeting with J. Edgar Hoover. Could Murphy give him a hand? The Senator replied that he would make an appointment for Elvis the following morning with the director of BNDD, John E. Ingersoll, and also call the offices of the FBI. Encouraged by this unlooked-for support, Elvis now got a real inspiration. He decided that while he was in Washington, he would make an effort to see President Nixon. As there was no time to arrange this meeting through intermediaries, Elvis would request an appointment himself.

He set to work at once and wrote a letter to Nixon. He explained the dangers the country faced from entertainers like the Beatles and Jane Fonda. He offered to throw his own weight onto the other side of the scale. Then he rounded off the note with a request for an immediate appointment, stating that he could be reached at the Wash-

ington Hotel, where he was registered as Colonel Jon Burrows. As soon as Elvis and Schilling got off the plane, they
drove to the gates of the White House where Elvis, dressed
still in his bizarre costume, got out of the car and introduced himself to the guard. Handing the smiling but perplexed sentry the letter, Elvis got back in his car and drove
on to the hotel.

At this point, Jerry Schilling demanded that Elvis allow
him to call Graceland to assure the people there that Elvis
was safe and also to summon Sonny West, Elvis's bodyguard, to Washington so that Schilling could fly back to
Los Angeles and salvage his job. While these arrangements were being made, Elvis went off to the Justice Building for his keenly anticipated meeting with the top narc.
As it turned out, he had to make do with the deputy director of the drug agency, John Finlator.

One can picture Elvis sitting beside Finlator's desk,
like a naive but idealistic pupil explaining to the school
principal why all the students should be organized at once
into companies, platoons and squads so that they could
drill every day and prepare to defend their country. When
Elvis wound up his pitch by requesting that he be given
a BNDD badge to facilitate the good work he intended to
do with the youth of America, the official replied that such
a request ran directly counter to government regulations.
Only bona fide agents of the Bureau could be issued the
Bureau's badges. Finlator was also obliged to decline the
offer of a cash donation from Elvis: $5,000—to an agency
whose annual budget was about fifty million dollars. When
the meeting ended, Elvis was just where he should have
been: standing in the office of the drug agency with egg
on his face.

When Elvis phoned Schilling at the hotel to report the
failure of his mission, he received electrifying news. Schilling had just put down the phone after receiving a call from
the White House. He had just been speaking with the
President's secretary. "The President will see Mr. Presley." That's what the woman had said! Can you dig it!
Nixon had cleared time on his schedule just so he could
see Elvis that day. The letter had turned the trick!

Why was Nixon so eager to see Elvis? Clearly, it is to

the advantage of any politician, even the president, to press the palm of a great celebrity. But to drop the business of state on the spur of the moment and give his undivided attention to a rock 'n' roll singer—that goes a bit beyond the usual behavior of even the most celebrity-conscious president. No, the reason Elvis got such a royal welcome that day at the White House was quite specific. As always, Elvis's unconscious timing was perfect.

Richard Nixon was poised to launch at that very moment a mighty new crusade against drugs. He planned to label drug abuse "America's Number One Problem." Not content with just denouncing drugs or beefing up the federal drug budget, Nixon was already planning to set up a drug superagency, modeled along the lines of the FBI and the CIA, called the Drug Enforcement Agency. The cost of this new secret police force would be staggering. By Fiscal Year 1974, Nixon would have raised the drug law enforcement budget 1,100 percent above what it was when he took office in 1968. From $69 million in FY 1969, the crusade against drugs would inflate this cost by FY 1974 to an astounding $719 million. Now, just as he is about to sound the clarion call to the nation—which kept insisting foolishly that there were bigger problems than drugs, like the war in Vietnam—along comes one of the greatest heroes of American youth, Elvis Presley, America's Number One Entertainer, proposing to talk to the Number One American about America's Number One Problem! No wonder Nixon cleared some time in his crowded schedule. This was an opportunity for a real summit!

Nixon's right-hand man in the new drug crusade was a young zealot with an oddly ornithological name: Egil Krogh. When Elvis, Jerry and Sonny (who arrived in the nick of time) were ushered into the Oval Office, they were met outside the door by Krogh. He told the Guys that they would have to wait in the adjoining Federal Building because if more than one visitor joined the President at a time, special security measures were required. The Guys were disappointed because Elvis had promised them that they would meet the President; but they marched off be-

hind an aide, Jeff Donfeld, to await the outcome of the
historic confrontation.

When Elvis walked into the Oval Office, he was high
as a kite. He had cranked up on speed for this great moment. He was also exhibiting the signs of another drug
problem in the red and itchy rash which had developed in
the past twenty-four hours over his face and neck. Eager
to look cool and in command, Elvis had topped off his cape
and cane outfit with a pair of amber-tinted shades. When
Nixon got a load of Elvis's fancy threads, he said, "You
dress pretty wild, don't you?" Without dropping a beat,
Elvis answered: "Mr. President, you got your show to run
and I got mine!" That took care of that issue. Actually, as
Elvis looked over Nixon, with his bent back, neck-brace
posture and long, jowly face, he must have felt he was back
on the Ed Sullivan show.[2]

Elvis's rap began with the advocacy of himself as "living
proof that America is the land of opportunity." Overnight,
he had gone from truck driver to superstar, proving the
reality of the American dream. Now, he explained, his
greatest concern was with the youth of America, who had
been seduced into drugs and immorality by the "filthy,
unkempt appearance and suggestive music of the Beatles."
Likewise, he inveighed against the Smothers Brothers,
Jane Fonda and others of their ilk, who had "poisoned
young minds by disparaging the United States in their
public statements and unsavory activities." Now, Elvis
claimed, he was devoting much of his free time to meeting
with small groups of young people, including "anti-estab-

[2]Richard Nixon did not wire the Oval Office until February,
1971; therefore, we have to make do with a rough reconstruction
of this historic event. Fortunately, just ten days after Elvis visited
the White House, on December 21, he paid a visit to FBI headquarters and a memorandum of his interview with the Bureau's
Assistant Director, Thomas E. Bishop, was prepared for the benefit of his chief, J. Edgar Hoover. As Elvis invariably made everything he did into a routine, we are justified in assuming that the
tone and substance of his remarks to the FBI director echoed his
line with the President.

lishment" college students, and using his authority to
change their ways and solve their problems. (He neglected
to say that these little groups were invariably composed
of good-looking girls and their greatest problem was that
they were not permitted to remove their white panties.)
Elvis, was, therefore, ideally suited to become the President's ambassador to troubled youth.

As Elvis delivered this inspiring speech, marred only
by his incessant scratching and rubbing of his drug-in-
flamed face and neck, Richard Nixon must have been profoundly gratified. He not only agreed that Elvis had the
power to work miracles with youth, he told Elvis that any
time he desired he could exchange his career in show business for an equally successful career in politics. Already
former entertainers like Senator George Murphy and Governor Ronald Reagan had demonstrated the power of showbiz in the political arena. What was their power in comparison to Elvis's power, the power of the "King"? There
was just one rule that he must never forget, warned Nixon,
raising a minatory finger: "Never lose your credibility."

Oh, it was a marvelous meeting, a great coming together of matching minds. Why, they were like two politicians with the same constituency—what Nixon had so
poetically characterized as "the Silent Majority." Now
Nixon realized that the Silent Majority had found its voice
in Elvis Presley.

Finally, the moment came when Elvis turned to the
President and told him that if he were to accomplish the
greatest amount of good in this new crusade to free the
nation's youth of the curse of drugs, he should be able to
carry the badge of a full-fledged narcotics agent. Nixon
smiled and said wistfully, "I don't have much power around
here, you know. I'm really just a figurehead. Getting you
a badge, though, is one thing I can do!" With that, he
switched on his intercom and gave the order to have a
BNDD badge and a complete set of credentials prepared
immediately for Elvis Presley.

Elvis thanked the President and then made one more
modest request. Would the nation's leader agree to take
another minute to meet Elvis's personal bodyguards, the
men who watched over him night and day? Nixon agreed

and his receptionist was ordered to summon Jerry Schilling and Sonny West. While the boys were on their way to the Oval Office, Nixon excused himself for a moment so that he might sign a stack of documents that had just been laid on his desk. As Elvis wandered around the Oval Office, taking in the chintz-covered furniture, the pictures of Nixon and Ike on the wall, the fire in the grate and the impressive stand of flags flanking the President's desk, he kept watching Nixon out of the corner of his eye. Imagine his astonishment when, after signing the papers on his desk, the President turned to the aide waiting to remove the documents and said: "What was this I just signed?" Elvis would repeat that story till the day he died.

Over in the Federal Building, meantime, the call from the Oval Office had been received by Jeff Donfeld. As Jerry and Sonny sat there watching, they saw their guide pick up the instrument and say: "Yes...yes...well, I'll be damned!" Then, he announced, "Fellas—you're goin' to see the President!"

See him is exactly what they did. When the doors of the Oval Office were opened, the President was standing at his desk reading a document, just as if this were a scene in a movie. Jerry and Sonny were so awestruck that they didn't dare to move. Elvis had to go to them and practically haul them into the room. As soon as the introductions were made, Nixon balled up his fist and gave Sonny a friendly shot in the shoulder, remarking to Elvis, "Boy, you've got a couple of big ones here! I'll bet they take good care of you." "Yes, sir!" echoed Elvis.

Pictures of everyone standing together were snapped now by the White House photographer. Then, Nixon presented the boys with pairs of cufflinks stamped with the presidential seal. The historic meeting was over—only Elvis wasn't quite satisfied. "Sir," he confided, leaning in toward the President—"they have wives, too." "Oh, of course!" bumbled Nixon, repairing to his desk, from which he extracted a pair of pins with the presidential seal. Now, all smiles, the King of Rock 'n' Roll concluded his audience by presenting the President of the United States of America with a deadly-looking Colt .45.

Ten days later, Elvis was back in Washington with his

entire entourage for another visit to the Justice Building, this time to the headquarters of the FBI. Elvis and the Memphis Mafia were scheduled to receive what the FBI described as a "very special" tour of the Bureau's facilities and Elvis was to have a private meeting with the Assistant Director, Thomas E. Bishop. Hours were consumed in visiting the various laboratories, record-keeping facilities, firing range, etc. Like visitors to a distillery, who are offered from time to time samples of the product, VIPs at the FBI get to examine a Manlicher Carcano of the type that was used to assassinate President Kennedy and, as a special treat, they are invited to don ear protectors and fire the G-man's trademark weapon, the Tommy Gun. Naturally, it is an iron-bound rule that visitors must surrender on entering the building any weapons they may be carrying. Elvis decided to see if he could get away with violating this rule. He had nearly completed the inspection tour when his concealed weapon was revealed in a most embarrassing manner. Leaning over a water cooler, his two-shot Derringer slipped out of his breast pocket and landed squarely in the wet basin. The escorting agents were blasé about the infraction. In fact, they claimed they knew all along that Elvis was "packin' heat" because of the way he carried his left shoulder.

All this rubbernecking was interesting, but the real payoff for the visit was Elvis's appointment with Hoover's assistant director. What Elvis had in mind for the FBI was something a little heavier than just his customary denunciations of Commies and junkies. As he got deep into his rap, he offered to help the Bureau in its work. Speaking of the people in show business "whose motives and goals he is convinced are not in the best interests of this country," Elvis volunteered, according to an FBI memo, "to make such information available to the Bureau on a confidential basis whenever it came to his attention." Slashing through the bureaucratic gobblydegook you could sum it all up in one line: Elvis offered to work as an *informer*.

The interview concluded with Elvis paying fervent tribute to J. Edgar Hoover. "Presley noted," according to the memo prepared after the occasion for the Director, "that in his opinion no one has ever done as much for his country

as has Mr. Hoover, and that he, Presley, considers the
Director the 'greatest living American.'" This paean led
up to an urgent request for a face-to-face interview with
the "greatest living American," Elvis giving as his contact
"Col. Jon Burrows, 3764 Highway 51 South [the address
of Graceland], Memphis, Tenn., telephone EX7-4427."

Elvis left FBI headquarters confident that he would
soon meet the legendary Director. If he had been able to
read what the Assistant Director reported to his boss, Elvis
would have been highly indignant. "Presley's sincerity and
good intentions notwithstanding," wrote Bishop, "he is
certainly not the type of individual whom the Director
would wish to meet. It is noted at present that he is wearing his hair down to his shoulders and indulges in the
wearing of all sorts of exotic dress." *Sartor resartus*.

Just one year after the Tate-LoBianca murders, Elvis
was suddenly faced with the deadly threat for which he
had so long been steeling himself. On August 26, 1970,
the chief of security at the International Hotel in Las Vegas (where Elvis had opened two weeks before) received
a call from a man who identified himself as "Jim Reeds."
He said that he had information that Elvis was to be kid-
napped that night by two men who had attended a party
with Elvis prior to his departure from Los Angeles. The
next afternoon, Colonel Parker received a call from a man
with a southern accent who said that Elvis would be kid-
napped that weekend. The following night, this series of
threats reached its climax with a call of a more disturbing
character. Joe Esposito's wife, Joanie, who was at home
in Los Angeles, received an anonymous call, actually two
calls, in the course of which a whole extortion scheme was
presented. The unknown voice said that a madman who
felt that Elvis had "done him wrong about a year ago" was
on his way at that moment to Las Vegas, armed with a
gun that had a silencer and bent on murdering Elvis. The
caller demanded $50,000 in small bills in exchange for the
killer's name and license number.

Nothing was said to Elvis about these threats for fear
that he would not be able to perform. Colonel Parker and
Joe Esposito got in touch with the local FBI agent, as

did Ed Hookstratten, who believed that the threats were associated with the paternity suit against Elvis that was still in progress. The FBI man was impressed by the fact that the anonymous caller had been able to learn Joe Esposito's unlisted number in Los Angeles; otherwise, he saw no cause for alarm.

A few days later, one of the Guys went down to the lobby to collect the group's mail, which was kept in a special box behind the registration desk. In the mail, he discovered a showroom menu bearing Elvis's picture on which had been drawn a gun pointing at Elvis's head. Some sort of message was printed beside the gun, but it could not be deciphered until it was recognized as mirror writing. Putting the menu up against a looking glass, the words became legible. They read: "Guess who, and where?" This time the FBI man said, "We have to take this one seriously."

Seriously is exactly how Elvis had been taking the possibility of assassination for a long time. So serious had he been that he had armed everyone in his entourage, drilled himself and them at the firing range, sent Sonny West to school at the sheriff's office in Memphis and worked out the most elaborate security arrangements with the International Hotel that human ingenuity could suggest or money could buy. Now that the threat that had inspired all these precautions had materialized, you might suppose that Elvis would derive some comfort from the fact that he was so well prepared. Nothing of the kind!

Elvis reacted as if he were standing naked before the killer's gun. He panicked. He broke down, sobbing uncontrollably and crying, "Why would anyone want to kill me?" He called to his aid every tough guy he could recruit. Karate coach Ed Parker was flown in from Los Angeles. Red West was brought in from Memphis. When Red walked into the Imperial Suite, Elvis threw himself into his old protector's arms. John O'Grady recommended that Elvis hire the former bodyguard of the mayor of Los Angeles, a steely-eyed human panther who walked on the balls of his feet and was a fast-draw expert and a dead shot with his nine-millimeter, fourteen-shot automatic. Six to eight FBI agents were rushed to Las Vegas and even a couple of Secret Service men. Elvis Presley was now guarded even better than the president of the United States.

The hotel, which looked on all these preparations with dismay, urged Elvis to cancel his engagement. Elvis, after prolonged consideration, decided that he must take the risk. If word got out that he could be intimidated so easily, blackmailers all over the country might try to shake him down. Even so, he was not going to step onstage until every conceivable precaution had been taken. Two doctors and a complete medical emergency team, with resuscitation equipment and a supply of the right type of blood, were stationed backstage. Two ambulances were parked at the stage door. Lamar Fike was put in charge of the showroom lights, with orders to keep the room half lit at all times, while being prepared to raise the lighting to the maximum at the first sign of trouble. Everyone was given orders that if he saw anything that looked suspicious, he was to shout the code word "Floor!" At that signal, Elvis would throw himself to the floor, while Sonny or Red, whoever was closest, would hurl himself across Elvis's body as a human shield.

By the next night Elvis's panic had turned into a snarling sadistic rage. He called a meeting of the Guys. For once, he let them see what was in his mind. He told them that the thing he hated even more than the thought of being wounded or killed was the image of his assassin, some idiot like Sirhan Sirhan, sitting there after the murder with a grin on his face and not a mark on his body, exulting in the fact that he had brought down the King! As he flashed on this image, Elvis went livid with rage. He turned to Red and, leveling his voice like a gun, he spelled out slowly and malevolently the punishment that was to be administered to his attacker. "I don't want the man to just die! I want you to gouge out his eyes. I want you to kick in his nuts. I want you to put your foot in his face! Do anything you can to waste him."

That night the agents and the Guys felt like the garrison of a fort anticipating attack. Armed men were posted at the entrance to the showroom, where they subjected the arriving guests to close scrutiny. Other men were stationed in strategic positions in the house and backstage. The nine-millimeter killer planted himself squarely before the stage, where he could scan the entire room. Before Elvis went onstage for what he feared might be his final performance, he called Priscilla and Lisa Marie. In a strangely solemn voice, he said that he loved them. Neither his wife nor the musicians knew that his life had been threatened.

All through the show that night Elvis's mind was running like films on a split screen. With one part of his consciousness, he was concentrating on giving a tight, clean, professional performance. On the other side of his head were flashing images of shadowy killers. Every few minutes Elvis would ask himself: "Is that sonovabitch really out there?" At one point in the performance, when he sang "You've Lost That Lovin' Feeling," the blocking called for Elvis to turn his back to the house as the stage lights were all extinguished save for a pin spot on the back of his head. Elvis flashed: "This is it! Now, you're a perfect target." Then, as he stared at his drummer, Ronnie Tutt, who was positioned directly behind the singer, Elvis thought: "You poor bastard—if he misses me, you're a dead man!" The lights went up again and the show went on without incident, until, suddenly, a voice rang out from the back of the room.

"Elvis!" cried a man's voice. As the house lights shot up, Elvis dropped to one knee, ready to pull his gun, ready to take his dive, ready for anything, as he struggled to see through the glare of the stage lights to the rear of the room. As every guard in the house felt his scrotum tighten and his heart start to race, the mysterious voice spoke again, saying: "Can you sing 'Don't Be Cruel'?" It was an iron-bound rule that Elvis Presley never took requests. Elvis leaped to his feet and shouted, "I'll sing anything you want!"

The next few nights were still very tense, but when nothing more was heard of the madman or the extortion plot, the anxiety ebbed away. Elvis had faced his worst fear. After a terrible ordeal, he had been spared. Now he knew exactly how it felt to have your life threatened by a dangerous lunatic. That experience was soon followed by his own deterioration into homicidal madness.

Chapter 31

Death Threats

Less THAN four months after becoming a mother, Priscilla began the ardent pursuit of the lover for whom eventually she broke up her marriage. Ironically, the occasion that inspired this fateful affair was one that had been contrived by Elvis. It was a grand karate tournament held on May 28, 1968, at Honolulu. Elvis had gone to Hawaii that week to vacation at the Ilikai Hotel. When he arrived, the media were blaring forth announcements of the event, which pitted the famous fighters of the islands against the champions from the mainland. The sponsor of this dramatic contest was a Hawaiian-born Los Angeles karate instructor whom Elvis had met years before at the Beverly Wilshire, Ed Parker.

Though it was totally out of character for Elvis Presley to appear at any public event, the prospect of seeing so many great fighters in a single night overcame his customary caution. Summoning Parker to the hotel, Elvis arranged to slip into the Honolulu International Center after the house lights were extinguished so that he could enjoy the matches under conditions of comfort and safety. Among the karate stars who appeared that night was Mike Stone.

Stone, a native Hawaiian with a Caucasian father, resembles those Afro-headed, fist-saluting black athletes

who were typical of the sixties. A cocky-looking dude with
a killer glint in his eye, Stone is your classic martial artist.
Born on the island of Oahu, he got into karate while serving a hitch in the army. Discharged in 1963, he started
training intensely for competition. Within six months he
was appearing in local matches. By 1965, he was Western
U.S. karate champion. By 1966, he was International
Grand Champion. At that point, he married and opened
a school in southern California. Though officially in re-
tirement, the prospect of a free trip to Hawaii was enough
to lure him back into the ring.

Stone struck a nerve in Priscilla Presley that was set
to vibrate. As she sat there in the dark watching the
swarthy, crudely featured athlete in the white *gi* chopping
and kicking his opponents into submission, she decided
impulsively that this was the man she really wanted.
Stone himself was later to express the most profound astonishment that any woman would wish to exchange the
great Elvis Presley for an impoverished, married and not
very handsome karate instructor. If he could have seen
himself that night through Priscilla's eyes, he might not
have been so surprised. The man she saw bore a certain
resemblance to Elvis—he wore a similar costume, was
applauded as enthusiastically and was a recognized star.
The difference was that Mike Stone was the reality of
which Elvis Presley was simply the semblance: Stone was
an authentically virile man.

Virility had become the basic issue in the Presley marriage as far as Priscilla was concerned. The moment she had
announced that she was pregnant, Elvis had stopped having
sexual relations with her. Now that the baby was born
and Priscilla was looking as lovely as ever, Elvis gave no
sign of resuming sexual relations with her—ever! This
was not so surprising, in view of the fact that Elvis had
always been averse to sex with married women and
abhorred the thought of having intercourse with a mother.
In fact, with every woman with whom he became seriously
involved, Elvis would display the same pattern. First he
would demand that she treat him as if she were his mother
by petting, pampering and baby-talking him. Then, when
he had gotten his heart's desire, he would begin to exhibit

the symptoms of what might be called the Sword in the Bed Complex.

The archetype for this behavior pattern is the scene, famous from medieval legend, in which the knight-lover, like Sir Lancelot or Sir Tristram, goes off into the forest with his queen-mistress and beds with her in a romantic woodsman's cabin. Honorable, even in the midst of Oedipally tainted adultery, the knight lays his sword, edge up, between the queen and himself. Thus is it is that they are discovered by her husband, his master, the king. Thus it is, too, that mama's boys must lie abed with their mistresses or wives, whom they are prone to call "Mommy" and toward whom they suffer soon a mysterious loss of "affect."

As a naive young woman, Priscilla could not possibly have foreseen what was in store for her when she insisted on Elvis marrying her and then immediately became pregnant. These developments destroyed whatever remained of her original relationship with Elvis, which was based entirely on the fact that she embodied not womanly maturity or maternity—God forbid!—but an angelic girlish innocence, so inviting to the hand of the Lolita lover and the eye of the sly voyeur. The celerity with which Priscilla found a new mate once she became a mother suggests that she recognized that Elvis's sexual withdrawal was permanent. It also indicates that she did not want to go on living indefinitely without romance, passion, masculine strength and authority—all the fundamental affections that had been denied her during her eight-year pajama party with Elvis.

Now Priscilla enrolled herself in Chuck Norris's karate school, knowing that sooner or later her involvement in the tight little world of karate would bring her into contact with Stone. It did. At the Long Beach International Competition, Priscilla informed the surprised Stone that she would much prefer to have him as her instructor. He pointed out that his school, at Westminster, was eighty miles from Los Angeles. Priscilla made light of the problem. The following week she appeared in the company of her close friend, Joanie Esposito, who had offered to do the driving.

Priscilla proved an adroit pupil. She was also very
charming. When Stone invited her home to meet his wife
and family, she snapped at the invitation. She became
friendly with Stone's wife and spent the evening turning
over the pages of the family's photo album. Stone was no
happier with his marriage than was Priscilla with hers.
He was ready for an affair. Priscilla, however, having
brought matters to a head, was overwhelmed now with
anxiety. She didn't trust herself to go off alone with the
man she had been pursuing. She persuaded the compliant
Joanie to join her on a double date, Joanie riding in the
front of the car with Chuck Norris, while Priscilla and
Mike snuggled in the back seat.

The first time the lovers stepped out in public, Priscilla
insisted they employ all the precautions of secret agents.
Though her anxiety proved to be highly exaggerated, it
was perfectly normal. Not only was she surrounded by a
network of domestic spies, she lived in a world in which,
she assumed, she could be easily recognized as the wife of
Elvis Presley. This latter fear was dissipated in an amusing manner on that first day.

Boarding a tourist boat bound for Catalina, Stone
walked twenty paces behind Priscilla, acting as if he didn't
know her. When they got aboard, he sat five rows behind
her. Even so separated, Priscilla acted as nervous as a
jackrabbit. Every time a tourist pointed his camera out
the window, she would cringe and pull down the long bill
of her cap over her face, which was heavily masked by
oversized sunglasses. Ironically, though no one recognized
her, many people recognized *him!* Soon Stone detected a
certain chagrin in his mistress, who found herself again
the unnoted companion of an acclaimed man.

Once the affair had become a settled relationship, Priscilla put it on a well-organized and secure basis. Whether
taking dancing or karate lessons, studying to be the ideal
wife or the ideal mistress, Priscilla Presley was efficient
and disciplined. As soon as she saw that she and Stone
were destined to spend a lot of time together on the sly,
she found the perfect love nest. It was a little beach apartment in the obscure community of Belmont Shores, thirty
miles south of Los Angeles.

Having found a place where no one was likely to recognize her, Priscilla set to work to decorate the hideaway
in accordance with her romantic fantasies. It was the day
of the hippies, the earth people. Like her counterpart,
Margaret Trudeau, Priscilla was a very stylish hippie. She
did up this little pad in earthen colors and rich natural
textures and lit it at night with numerous multicolored
candles. Beside the murmuring sea, she contrived a cave
of love.

Many nights, as Priscilla and Mickey lay in each other's
arms, he would paint for her even more romantic scenes
from his homeland in Hawaii. (It was one of the ironies
of this affair that the cuckolding of the star of *Blue Hawaii*
and *Paradise Hawaiian Style* should have been done by
a Hawaiian.) With Stone, Priscilla experienced the reality
that Elvis could at most feign on the screen. "We made
love very often," recollects Mike Stone. "It wasn't just a
desire for sex—it was love. Priscilla was starved for affection. She was warm and loose and funny. She was born
again."

What a contrast, this intensely erotic and exotic life
with her dark virile lover (whom some of the Guys claimed
later was "half nigger") with all those years of watching
Elvis nod out at dawn after a long night of Clint Eastwood
and cheeseburgers at the Memphian. What a difference
to be spending so much time with a real man instead of
a human myth. How thrilling to have a life of her own
instead of one assigned to her by her keeper. To feel the
powerful naked body of a superbly conditioned athlete next
to her instead of the alternately obese or diet-starved body,
all bundled up in pajamas, of a man who hated to bathe.
Sometimes Stone would ask her: "If anything ever went
wrong with us, would you go back to Elvis?" Priscilla
would invariably reply: "No, I could never go back. I've
finally come out in the world and started living."

Priscilla concealed her affair for three and a half years.
The great length of this subterfuge tells a lot about the
Presley marriage. Clearly, the marriage entailed so little
intimacy or even cohabitation that Priscilla was at liberty
to make what was in effect a second marriage, establish
a second home and lead another, far more engrossing life,

without disturbing the façade of her relationship with her husband. If this seems hard to believe, consider for a moment the character of this so-called marriage.

Elvis was almost invariably absent. It drove him crazy to spend more than a week or two with Priscilla so he contrived always to have some excuse to be away from home. Once he resumed touring, he made it a rule: "Wives don't go on tours." The purpose of this prohibition was well understood by all involved. When Elvis spent a month at Las Vegas, for example, he would preside every night over a party that all his courtiers anticipated with pleasure. All afternoon and evening, the Guys would cruise the lobby of the hotel lining up girls for the evening. This practice became so familiar that the girls who wished to be invited adopted the practice of seating themselves on a particular sofa where they were sure of being noticed and summoned to the royal presence. It was well understood among the girls that if they wanted to be invited back to subsequent parties and enjoy such privileges as free admission to the shows, they would have to accommodate the Guys. Naturally, many of them aspired higher.

Elvis's parties at Las Vegas were no different essentially from his parties in the old days in Bel Air. Always there was the sense of attending a court function, where the primary attraction lay in feasting your eyes on the King and gaining the opportunity to catch his eye and perhaps win his favor. Elvis would be pretty wired up after his second show; it would take him the rest of the night to calm down. His favorite way of spending this time was holding court with a circle of admiring young women.

If he were particularly inspired, he might order a karate demonstration. Working with Red or Sonny or someone else willing to play "dummy," Elvis might demonstrate how he could go up against a man carrying a pistol and disarm him with his bare hands. Nobody in his right mind would attempt such a feat, not even the greatest karate champion, but Elvis rehearsed the routine endlessly like an obsessed ballet master. Sometimes, Elvis's coordination would be so impaired by drugs that he would strike out with uncontrolled violence. On quite a few occasions he contrived to kick his dummies in the balls, and once, demonstrating with a young woman, he fractured her ankle. These little mishaps apart, Elvis's karate exhibitions were generally the high points of an evening spent in his company.

As dawn neared, Elvis would signal Joe Esposito or Hamburger James that he was ready to retire. Immediately an order would go down to the kitchen for the final meal of the day, usually a couple of cheeseburgers. At the same time, Elvis, who had made his selection among the ladies present, would suggest to the girl that she follow Joe into the bedroom and make herself comfortable. It was a fixed protocol of the court that King Elvis never retired publicly with any woman save his consort. The girls would be led into the bedroom by the majordomo, who would show them which bathroom they could use and instruct them how to prepare themselves for receiving the King. It was very important that the girls be scrupulously clean. So it might be suggested, very tactfully, of course, that they might want to brush their teeth or use the other hygienic facilities. As Elvis abhorred the sight of a naked woman, unless he was wildly aroused, pajamas and lounging robes were provided for the overnight guests. The most critical thing in any encounter with the King was, of course, that his dignity be maintained. Joe would always take pains to explain to the girls how they were expected to behave. He would make it clear how intolerable any vulgarity or unladylike behavior was to Elvis. Then, wishing them a cheery good night and a pleasant time, the majordomo would withdraw.

The next person who would appear in the royal bedchamber would be a waiter rolling a cart with Elvis's food. The waiter would place a cloth on the bed and stand by to serve Elvis when he entered the room. Elvis would don his pajamas in his bathroom and slide under the covers to eat, propped up on pillows behind his head. Then, signing to the waiter to remove the silver covers, he would gobble up his cheeseburgers. The chances of any sex act occurring before Elvis went off to sleep were small. To become aroused, Elvis would have to watch other people having intercourse in one of the other bedrooms of the suite. Then he would leave on the run to ram his charge

home into his own companion. Normally, at some point
after dawn, the King would abruptly nod. If the girl were
wise, she would take her cue and nestle peacefully under
the covers, a human teddy bear.

When Elvis was not enjoying himself with the women
he encountered at his parties, he was accompanied by one
of his steady girlfriends. During the same engagement in
the fall of 1970 which had produced a threat to his life, he
made a conquest of which he and his boys were particularly
proud: nothing less than the girlfriend of the powerful
media executive, Jim Aubrey. At that time, Aubrey was
president of MGM, which was preparing to make a documentary about Elvis. Appearing in Elvis's dressing room
after opening night to meet the star and congratulate him
on the show, Aubrey brought with him a dark, sultry and
faintly Indian-looking girl. Though it was a grave violation of the code of macho ethics to attempt to seduce another player's woman in the man's very presence, Elvis
was feeling so sure of himself that night that he began to
flirt with this beautiful girl in a manner that was obvious
to everyone in the room. When he asked her for her telephone number, she reacted with great embarrassment; but
he insisted so strongly that finally she scribbled on the
piece of paper he held surreptitiously beneath the table:
"Barbara Leigh, 213 487-9344."

When Barbara got home the next day, she found her
phone ringing. It was Elvis, begging her to turn around
and rush back to Las Vegas. She countered that she had
a date with Aubrey that weekend to go sailing on his yacht.
Elvis was so insistent that finally she agreed to break her
date and come back to the International. When she got
into the hotel, she was met by a couple of the Guys, who
rushed her to a special apartment with a big round bed
which Elvis maintained for guests who could not stay in
his suite. When Barbara asked if arrangements had been
made for her to see the show that night, the Guys acted
very alarmed and said that she would have to stay put
until they brought her to Elvis. Late that night, she was
finally admitted into the presence. Elvis explained with
much laughter that the reason he had kept her away from

the showroom was that Jim Aubrey had also returned—
with Jo Ann Pflug (of M*A*S*H).

Barbara, a model and movie actress, a southern girl
from a very poor family, became a great favorite of Elvis's.
During the next year, she traveled extensively with him
on tour, stayed with him at his homes in Memphis and
Los Angeles, slept with him in the marital beds. When,
in March 1971, Elvis was suddenly hospitalized with sec-
ondary glaucoma that could have resulted in partial blind-
ness, instead of calling Priscilla to his side, he called Barbara, who flew across the country. She held his hand at
the most critical moment, when Dr. David Meyer of Memphis inserted a hypodermic needle directly into Elvis's eye-
ball. Elvis squeezed Barbara's hand so hard he almost
broke it. Eventually, the affair faded away because Barbara believed that Elvis would never leave Priscilla. As
events were to prove, she was both right and wrong.

Even when Elvis would return to Priscilla's company,
he would hardly have his feet up on the table before he
announced that he needed to "unwind." That was the code
word for "orgy." Immediately, Joe Esposito would be on
the phone lining up the showgirls from Las Vegas and Los
Angeles. Frank Sinatra's private jet would be chartered
to fly the girls down to Palm Springs, where Elvis maintained a house with high walls. The King and his men
always had enough pills to supply a dispensary. For a big
party, somebody would go out and score four or five lids
of grass. The food would be brought into the house pre-
cooked, eliminating the need for tattletale servants. The
only time a maid ever set foot inside one of Elvis's Palm
Springs homes was when the freakout was over and it was
time to clean up the mess.

The routine was an obscene and decadent parody of the
good old days in Bel Air. Around six in the evening, everybody would turn on. Then the whole gang would get naked
and jump in the pool. The usual water games would soon
have the Guys and girls well aroused. Then the chasing
and screaming phase would commence. Soon the satyrs
would seize their prey and drag them off to the numerous
bedrooms ranged around the pool like the rooms of a motel.
Elvis himself never participated in these games, which

were too threatening to his shallowly rooted masculinity.
While the orgy whirled around him, he would be locked
up in his bedroom like a pornographic filmmaker shooting
his latest triple X-rated product. His cast would be three,
four or five splendid bodies from the best chorus lines in
Vegas. These girls were not permitted to play with the
Guys. They were "on exclusive" with Elvis. If Elvis was
lucky, he would have the star of his orgies present: a beautiful lesbian from the Sahara Tahoe, who was very adroit
at arousing the other girls and getting them to abandon
all their inhibitions. Sometimes this woman would generate so much steam that the girls would forget all about
Elvis, writhing ecstatically on his big bed with no thought
but of their own pleasure.

For a voyeur, this state of being present yet invisible
at the orgy represents the ultimate in excitement. One
night, having watched this inciting spectacle with pounding heart for nearly two hours, Elvis got so carried away
that he did something that was totally out of character.
He opened the big French windows of his bedroom and
stepped out on the patio, where he exhibited himself to
the gang around the pool. He was totally naked and had
hooked one of the Colonel's canes over his erect penis.
What an image! But what does it mean? Does it shout,
"Fuck you, Colonel Lardass!" Or is it an unconscious
confession that Elvis had lived his whole adult life with
the Colonel's hook deep in Elvis's dick?

Priscilla must have had more than an inkling of how
Elvis "unwound." She was of a highly suspicious turn of
mind; but even if she had been as innocent as a child, she
would have been wised up by the incriminating evidence
she discovered at the house during her own visits there.
In 1970, for example, after watching Elvis open at Vegas,
Priscilla and Joanie Esposito decided to spend a few days
sunning themselves in the desert. When they arrived at
the house, they checked the mailbox. Inside, they discovered a couple of thank-you notes that had been sent by the
girls who had enjoyed the last party at the house. One
little missive on colored paper was signed, "Miss Lizard
Tongue." When Priscilla found this shocking confirmation
of what she had long suspected, she flew into a rage. Seiz-

ing the phone, she called Elvis at the hotel. The moment he answered, she started denouncing him for his cheating ways. Mingled with her rage was a feverish curiosity. All through the conversation, she kept demanding, "Who is Miss Lizard Tongue?"

Elvis was a firm believer in the maxim: "The best defense is a good offense." Instead of backing up under the fury of Priscilla's attack, he brazenly informed her that the letters were just crank mail from fans whom he had never met. He hadn't the faintest idea who was Miss Lizard Tongue. She must be some crazy girl with hot pants. He then swung around to counterattack, demanding to know what right she had to upset him just before he went onstage. Didn't she realize that she might make him so nervous that he would blow the show? How did she think he earned the living that kept her in fancy clothes and cars and mansions she spent fortunes decorating? When Elvis got through with Priscilla, he had her beaten so badly that she wound up making apologies for even calling him. There you have, in miniature, the Presley marriage.

In February 1972, after years of leading a double life, Priscilla finally decided to tell Elvis the truth. She announced to the astonished Mike Stone: "I'm going to fly up to Las Vegas this week and tell him the truth. It's time we stopped hiding like this. I want everyone to know how much I love you and that I am going to live with you." This was a brave decision, a brave speech; there is no reason to assume, however, that when Priscilla walked into Elvis's dressing room that night—taking care not to arrive until the second show was over—she had any intention of confessing she had a lover. All that was necessary at first, she knew, was to say that the marriage had failed and she wanted her freedom. Or, perhaps she could just say that she felt the need to be alone for a certain time in order to come to terms with herself—or some such tripe. Alas, there was no way to exit gracefully.

No sooner did Priscilla start reciting her carefully rehearsed lines, standing alone with Elvis, now, in the bedroom of the penthouse, than he shocked her by tearing off her clothes and practically raping her. When this act of manly possession failed to weaken her resolve, he changed

his tactics abruptly and swore that he would make any
sacrifice to maintain the marriage. He would give up his
tours and remain at home. He would become the perfect
husband and father. They would start all over again and
have a new life together. Priscilla countered that he had
promised all these things many times before and nothing
had ever come of his vows. Now, it was too late. He could
not change, but she had changed. She had grown, developed, matured. She was a different person now from the
little Cilla he had reared in Graceland. As far as she was
concerned, he was free to do as he had always done. She,
however, had the right to lead her own life. Elvis had no
choice but to let her go.

A day later, Mike Stone witnessed Priscilla's arrival at
their little pad in Belmont Shores. She drove up in an old
station wagon stuffed with luggage and personal belongings. Lisa Marie was also in the car. Priscilla was ecstatically happy. With a triumphant cry, she announced that
she had left Elvis and come to live with Stone. From the
overflowing store of things at Monovale Road, she had
taken just what was most essential to her needs and abandoned the rest. Stone was astonished. It was hard for him
to believe that this woman who had everything, including
the most desired man in the world, had given it all up for
him, a poor karate instructor still burdened with a wife
and child. Priscilla was the greatest romantic since the
Duke of Windsor.

Obviously, they couldn't continue to live in their little
hideaway. It was time, once again, for Priscilla, that instinctive nest builder, to find and furnish yet another
home. This time her fancies led her to the soaring futur-
istic apartment complex at Marina Del Rey, the home of
the swinging singles. Soon Mickey, Cilla and Lisa were
established in a new two-bedroom apartment that was
short of furnishings but had a lot of "potential."

By this time, word of the separation had leaked out to
the media and the story was flashing around the world.
"Priscilla Leaves Elvis": It was, as one Hollywood film
magazine stated, "the most shocking separation in recent
years." The stories were soon identifying Mike Stone as
Priscilla's new "escort," and underscoring the interesting

coincidence that Stone was filing for divorce from his wife of many years. Some of the papers and magazines even printed pictures of this striking couple cocking their heads together and smiling like newlyweds. Elvis was mortified by this notoriety. He had hoped to restrict the news for a while to the inner circle. The day after Priscilla's departure, he had called the Guys together and told them his wife had gone off with another man. The men were profoundly embarrassed. They didn't know what to say. Finally, Red West, hoping to lessen the blow, remarked bluffly: "That's what you wanted, isn't it?" Elvis turned away, silent.

In the month that followed, the layover period between the closing at Vegas and the spring tour in April, the Guys watched with alarm as Elvis's drug consumption soared and his moods sank often to black despair. They read clearly in these signs the signals of a coming storm. Anxiously, they conferred among themselves. After all, if "E" blew it out at this point, they all would suffer. Finally, as if with one mind, it was decided that the only hope of avoiding a disaster was to pacify Elvis by finding him a new woman, ideally one who was not only a knockout but had strong maternal instincts. As soon as the April tour began, all the Guys set out to find this fabulous new creature, like medieval huntsmen seeking the unicorn. Just three days into the tour, while they were in Detroit, the man who was out on point picked up the scent that led within a month to the very thing they were seeking.

Let's call her Kit. She had a body that would make you clutch for digitalis. Extremely tall, willowy, with a waist so tiny a big man could span it with his two hands, she was a stunning dark-haired girl with a beautiful face and a flawless complexion. She was a dancer with a road company of *The Desert Song*. The funny thing about her discovery was that she was not the girl Elvis's scout picked up in the street outside the hotel in Detroit. That was Kit's roommate, who was a totally different sort of young woman, very adventurous and blasé—not at all the type for Elvis Presley. The Guys, however, usually did their recruiting by physical appearance, allowing the Boss to deal with the young ladies' spiritual qualities. This was

a task at which Elvis was highly proficient and one that
he enjoyed performing.

When Kit's roommate came back to the dressing room
of the show that evening, she told the other girls in the
line that they had all been invited to a publicity party for
Elvis Presley. She warned them that they could expect the
worst, but that if they went prepared, it might be an exciting adventure. Kit did not accept the invitation but the
other girls went along for the experience. When they arrived at Elvis's hotel and had been passed through his
security network, they arrived in an ordinary sitting room
where, instead of a party, they discovered Elvis, Vernon
and Joe Esposito watching television like the men in the
family waiting to be called in to supper. This was just the
first in a whole series of dismaying surprises that constituted the balance of the evening.

These dancers were prepared for a fast round of drinks,
snorts, tokes and then a fast proposition to repair to the
sack. Instead, they were offered nothing but soft drinks
and then subjected to hours of relentless grilling about
their careers, lives, families, religious beliefs and God
knows what else. When it was all over and Joe Esposito
had written down their phone numbers in his little black
book, the girls left Elvis feeling totally mystified. Instead
of a proposition, they felt like they had undergone a place-
ment interview. In fact, as they left, Joe said something
that sounded like, "Don't call us, we'll call you."

What these girls could not possibly have understood
was that Elvis always engaged in this sort of intense pre-
date screening to assure himself that he ran no risk of
being either rejected or "used" by the girls with whom he
engaged in intimacies. He had always been extremely
wary of women; now, as he grew older and crankier, his
caution had grown to the point of phobia. If a girl's fingernails looked a little dirty or she used an improper
expression or didn't laugh at one of his jokes, it was all
over fast! Elvis still liked to play with dolls, but he knew
that many young women today are not dolls—they just
look like dolls! Underneath those pretty faces, those firm
bodies, those trendy clothes lurked all kinds of evil animals: not just bitches but jungle cats and crazy bats! It

used to be that the big problem with girls was getting them into bed. Now that was no problem at all: The problem was getting them out of bed when you wanted to sit up all night reading religious books.

About a month later, while the girls were playing San Francisco, they got a call from Joe Esposito, who said: "I'll bet you thought you would never hear from us again, ha, ha! Well, here's Elvis—he wants to talk to you." Elvis got on the wire and after some friendly chitchat, he extended an invitation to spend the weekend at his house in Palm Springs. He assured the girls that they would be put up in their own rooms at a local hotel and that they would be treated with the greatest respect and courtesy. They agreed to join him and added to their original number one girl more—Kit.

She was a very proper young lady. A Roman Catholic, reared in accordance with very strict principles, she never swore, smoked, drank or did anything naughty. Though she was twenty-four years old, she was still a virgin. Oddly, though, she did have a steady boyfriend whom all the other girls called King Kong. This dude was a slick-haired macho who ran a beauty supply business. It was incomprehensible how such a goody-goody as Kit could be involved with such an ape. As it happened, however, just at the moment of Kit's meeting with the King, she was starting to break up with Kong.

The moment Elvis laid eyes on Kit, he was smitten. As always it was love at first sight, the perfect girl, where have you been all my life and when are we getting married? Naturally, Elvis was inspired to great heights of southern gentlemanliness, hovering attentively over Kit's every dainty gesture. When the weekend party had ended, Elvis and Kit were stuck on each other. No sooner was Kit back in her apartment in Los Angeles than the wires were burning up with calls from Elvis. Soon he was down to get her in his forty-five-thousand-dollar custom-built Stutz Blackhawk, which blew Kit's mind. Not long afterward, while motoring home one afternoon, Kit pointed at a "darling" little sports car driving past them in traffic. Elvis said nothing; but a couple hours later, Kit's roommate got a call from Elvis. "Get her out in the street," he demanded.

"Tell her the dog needs walking or something—I'm bringing her a new car!" When the great moment arrived, Kit
was out on the pavement playing her part according to the
script. Elvis drove up, shadowed by the boys, of course, in
the brand new car. Hopping nimbly out the door, he approached his beloved with the car keys in one hand and
in the other the title to the vehicle. As Kit came gurgling
and gasping to his side, Elvis bowed and said: "Your wish
is my command!"

No sooner did Kit begin to enjoy the good things in life
than out of nowhere appeared the threatening Kong. Raging with jealousy, the beast pounced on Kit and began to
lash her with the thongs of a Savonarola, falsely accusing
her of being a fallen woman, a concubine, a receiver of
harlot's gifts. As if this weren't bad enough, the monster
went to the press and told the reporters all about Elvis's
"latest affair," even providing the hungry journalists with
pictures of Kit. Instantly, the press was all over the little
apartment house where Kit lived. This was hot stuff. Elvis
Presley, separated from his wife, dating a gorgeous dancer!
Hey! How often did you get a story like this about the
King!

One afternoon, matters got so out of hand that poor Kit
picked up the phone and called Elvis. She told him that
reporters and photographers were all over the building
and that she was afraid to go out the door. One guy in
particular was so aggressive that she feared he was going
to break into her apartment, boo hoo! A call from a maiden
in distress has always been the ultimate summons for a
southern gentleman—or a comic strip hero! Elvis barked:
"Hold on! I'll be there in a minute!" Then, before you could
say—"It's a bird! It's a plane!"—it was a *Presley!* roaring
up to the door in his powerful black Stutz Blackhawk and
dressed to the nines in a black Napoleonic suit with a
white tie and a case full of police badges and a load of
expensive weapons. Hard at his heels followed the Guys.
Elvis rushed into the apartment as if he were a fire chief
and started shouting orders. "Joe, you take the stairs!
Sonny, out back! Jerry, check the roof!" In no time Elvis's
private SWAT team was swarming all over the building.
Meantime, Elvis was holding poor quaking Kit in his arms

and swearing that so long as he was alive no one would
ever harm her.

Finding a new mate for the Minotaur made the Guys
feel good. Just hip enough to be really dumb, these boys
assumed that they could placate Elvis like a baby by sticking a new doll in his hand after the first one had been
snatched away. This was a complete delusion as events
soon proved. For while Elvis was out on tour or back home
in Los Angeles or Memphis, he called Priscilla every day.
The boys assumed that this was a sign that he still missed
her and was sweet-talking her into returning. Actually,
the calls were of a very different nature. First, Elvis would
get a heavy load on and sink down into that black hole
where deeply self-pitying junkies always fall. Then, he
would start to lacerate himself with humiliating or enraging thoughts. He would see himself, the King, reduced
to a ridiculous figure, a mere cuckold, a man who couldn't
hold his own wife. Then, he would think of her seducer,
a goddamned nigger bastard with an attitude on him that
made you want to cut his nuts off. Then, he would veer
back from rage to self-pity, thinking of how sad it was that
a man who had everything couldn't look forward to coming
home and finding his wife and baby waiting for his return.
Back and forth he would crawl in his mental cave, until
he had worked himself into a murderous rage. Then, he
would call Priscilla and tell her that he was coming down
to the Marina that night. He was going to be carrying his
M-16 automatic rifle and he would have all the Guys with
him armed to the teeth. She would see what a piece of shit
she had picked to fall in love with. She would see Mike
Stone down on his knees vomiting with fear, begging for
his life. She would see what a white man does to a wife-
stealing nigger!

These threats terrified Priscilla. At first she kept them
to herself. Stone would come home and find her white with
fear. He'd ask her what was wrong, and she would make
some implausible excuse. Then, one night, when Stone was
in the apartment, the phone rang. As Priscilla talked, she
began to get hysterical. "What's wrong, honey?" asked
Stone. "It's Elvis," she said. "He says he's flying down here
from Las Vegas with the Guys, and he's going to make me

watch while he makes you get down and crawl." Stone
shouted across the room so that Elvis would hear him
distinctly, "You tell that sonovabitch that I'm not hiding
anywhere. He knows where to find me when he wants me.
I'm not afraid of him *or* his bodyguards." When Priscilla
hung up, she was shaking with fear. "You don't understand
how dangerous he can be when he gets into these black
moods," she gasped. "If he says he's going to kill you, he
might try it." Stone laughed off her fears but agreed to be
careful. Later, in Hawaii, karate friends told him that
Elvis was gunning for him. They offered to hit Elvis. Stone
rejected the idea as "ridiculous."

The death threats from Elvis did not stop. He continued
to call week after week, month after month. Sometimes
he would tell Priscilla what a fool she was to run off with
a pauper when she had a man who could give her anything
in the world. Sometimes he would pour abuse on Mike
Stone, calling him obscene names and suggesting that he
was just a pimp living off Priscilla's money. Eventually,
he would always work around to the thought that obsessed
him: the threat to kill or maim Mike Stone while Priscilla
was forced to stand by helplessly watching the hideous
scene.

As these threats continued for nearly a year and a half
and as they came very close to fulfillment on one occasion,
they cannot be discounted as a momentary aberration.
They were profoundly revealing expressions of Elvis Presley's psyche. The first thing they show is that Elvis's aim
is way off the mark. Why should he be focusing all his
rage on Mike Stone when it was Priscilla with whom he
should be angry? The obvious answer is that according to
the macho code which Elvis embraced, women are possessions that can be stolen by other men. Elvis was furious
at Stone because he was a thief. Yet it is just as apparent
that Elvis cared nothing for Priscilla as a woman or a wife.
So why should he go out of his mind when someone else
laid claim to her? Knowing the Oedipal character of Elvis's
personality, it appears much more probable that his rage
was triggered by a deeper disturbance. As a mama's boy
nothing could threaten him more or inspire greater rage
than the thought of his "little mama" being taken away

from him by another, especially by a more virile man. Surely the prolonged, profound and murderous malevolence of his reaction had to be grounded in some such serious threat to his essential well-being.

As for Stone, it's perfectly clear that he was just the "other man," the inviting blank that can be scribbled over with all the most hateful and paranoid delusions that a highly disturbed mind is capable of forming. Stone was like one of those silhouette targets that Elvis used to riddle with machine-gun rounds in the smokehouse behind Graceland. A blank "assailant," "nigger," "wife stealer," whatever Elvis's imagination caricatured him as being at any particular moment. Even so, he was not the only target at which Elvis was shooting when he made his death threats. Though the shots were aimed entirely at Stone, their greatest effect was registered by Priscilla. Elvis knew this perfectly well; in fact, it was part of his intention to punish her severely in the very act of wooing her back by scaring her out of her wits.

Though Elvis never stopped making threats, he never made good on any of his promises of retribution. This, too, is a most revealing feature of his behavior. Elvis was a man who ruled by fear and intimidation. Everyone around him was always motivated by the thought that if they crossed Elvis, he might go crazy and do something violent. He was like that anarchist in Conrad's *The Secret Agent,* who walks around with a bomb always in his pocket. At the slightest threat, he is prepared to blow up both his adversary and himself. Yet, like so many men who rule by fear, Elvis was basically chicken. He wouldn't hesitate to hit a woman or one of his henchmen because he knew there was no danger they would hit back. He was always quick to whip out a gun and threaten anybody who displeased him because he was confident that his victim wouldn't retaliate by drawing a weapon himself. When it came down to scratch, however, Elvis was terrified at the thought of answering for his violent impulses and destructive instincts. Though as Red West said, "Elvis had a need to kill," Elvis could not kill or even work off his rage in a fist fight in his later years. His only outlet for the profound anger that filled his soul was to make death threats.

By July 1972, Priscilla could bear the nightmare of her life no longer. She demanded an immediate divorce. She met with Elvis face to face, and, dealing now with the sensible Jekyll instead of the crazy Hyde, the day man instead of the night demon, she found Elvis rational, calm and perfectly willing to cooperate with her in ending the marriage. When he asked what she wanted by way of settlement, she said she wanted nothing. She would trust Elvis, she said, to provide her with enough money to live comfortably. She did not want to make any claims against his property or exploit the fact that they had been married. All she wanted was her freedom. Elvis, who had a little more sense of money and practical problems than Priscilla (who at this point was like a kid leaving home for the first time, eager to get away and oblivious of the difficulties that lay ahead) insisted on a settlement. Priscilla told him to name his own figure, whatever he thought was fair. He suggested $100,000. This figure was ridiculously low, both in view of his wealth and in terms of the standard of living to which Priscilla was accustomed. When Elvis and his lawyer, Ed Hookstratten, met with Priscilla later in the month, Hookstratten, according to his account, warned her that the proposed settlement was inadequate. She insisted that the amount was sufficient and that having computed her daily expenses, she found she could manage nicely on an alimony allotment of one thousand dollars a month— another absurdly inadequate sum. Hookstratten drew up the papers, and the marital termination agreement was filed on August 15.

The agreement stipulated that Elvis and Priscilla were to have joint custody of Lisa Marie. Elvis was to provide five hundred dollars a month for the child's support, up to the age of eighteen. Priscilla was to receive $1,000 a month for the next five years plus $100,000 in cash. For technical reasons, it was agreed that Elvis would be the one to file for divorce. One of the problems that Priscilla would have incurred if she had filed would have been a demand that she put her current address on the public record. This would have exposed her and Lisa Marie to criminal attempts. With everything agreed upon, it appeared now that the nightmare of the past nine months was over at last. Henceforth, Elvis and Priscilla would live peaceably apart, their future relations determined by a binding legal agreement.

Just as negotiations for the divorce were beginning, Elvis met Linda Thompson, the woman with whom he was to enjoy for the next four and a half years the closest and most fulfilling relationship of his life. The date was July 5, 1972. The place was the Memphian Theater, where Elvis was holding one of his all-night movie screenings. The man who made the introduction was none other than Elvis's old girl-finder, George Klein. The little banjo-eyed Klein came down the aisle to where Elvis was sitting, enthroned in front of all the other guests, and announced: "I just came from Friday's. I saw a girl there I know. I think you'll dig her." When Linda arrived about fifteen minutes later, accompanied by another girl for "protection," Klein bustled back down the aisle. "That girl's here that I told you about. Do you want me to bring her down?" Elvis, blasé about a mere local girl, replied, "No, I'll meet her in a minute." Then, when he went to the men's room, he gave the newcomer a good once-over. What he saw so pleased him that he sat right down by her side and remained sitting there through the balance of the evening.

It was natural that he should be attracted to Linda Thompson. Not only was she Miss Tennessee of 1972, she was a dead ringer for Kit. Elvis was still very much involved with his virgin dancer, but their relationship was destined to cool soon owing to all the bad publicity that King Kong was bringing down on the pair. In any case, being involved with a woman in California left lots of room for action in Tennessee. Elvis hadn't been able to cash in on his immense local fame in years owing to his marriage. Now that he was once again a bachelor, there was no reason why he shouldn't make out with the hometown belles.

Elvis and Linda hit it off very well that night and the following. He was gratified to learn that she was still a virgin, the only real evidence that Elvis could have of a woman's essential goodness. How he felt about her having attended college is not clear; in any case, it was not a problem any longer because she had dropped out before receiving her degree to pursue a career in modeling or acting. This put her squarely inside Elvis's world, where everything was comfortably familiar. No sooner had the two met, however, than Linda went off for a three-week summer vacation with her family, which took her to some remote location where there was no way she could be reached. When Elvis failed to get her at home, he set all the King's men on her trail; but they didn't fare any better. Finally, Elvis had to go back to the West Coast to start rehearsals for his August engagement at Las Vegas.

Kit was on hand during Elvis's first week; then, he received word from George Klein that Linda Thompson was back in Memphis. Instantly, Elvis was on the phone to her. "What did you do? fall off the face of the earth?" he demanded. "I told you," she said, "that I was going on vacation." "You didn't tell me that you wouldn't be able to be reached at all," he replied in that slightly hurt tone that he always had when his wishes had not been understood or anticipated. This conversation took place on a Friday. Saturday morning at 11:00 A.M., Linda stepped off the plane at Los Angeles. Elvis, who never got up till midafternoon, was at the airport, waiting nervously, like a little boy with sweaty palms. This was the sort of moment he loved: the moment when, through his great powers of attraction, he brought a new woman into his grip from some distant place.

It should be noted how Elvis demanded that women come to him rather than his going to them. Oh, there was always some rationalization for this arrangement: He was working or he had a nice place for them to visit or his security demanded that he do his dating at home. The truth is that this let-them-come-to-me pattern was another of the countless expressions of Elvis's basic insecurity: his need to have absolute control over the situation, particularly any situation involving a woman. This practiced seducer, holding every advantage conceivable, would get tense and uptight about such encounters, as if he were meeting some difficult or novel challenge and were not certain of his success. Again, his horror of rejection was so great that even a lifetime of incessant triumphs had not served to assuage it.

That night Elvis and Linda flew to Las Vegas. He could have arranged to meet her there and avoided this doubling back but that would have entailed waiting another day, an unthinkable demand on such an infantile temperament. It's interesting to observe how in the writings about Elvis Presley and in the tales told by his "boys," Elvis's intolerance of frustration is taken as a sign of his great power, his magic ability to wave a wand and get what he wanted no matter how late the hour or excessive the demand or incredible the cost. Actually, this inability to bear even momentary deprivations is a sign not of strength but of terrible weakness. It doesn't represent power or even a great appetite, like greed or lust. It's essentially a confession of lack of self-control: the incapacity to act like an adult.

Sunday and Monday, Elvis and Linda spent together in a suite on the floor below the penthouse. As they lay out on the terrace sunning themselves Monday afternoon, Elvis said to Linda: "You know what we've done?" "No," said Linda, mystified. "We've gone and fallen in love." "We *have?*" she echoed, utterly astonished. "Well, I have," replied Elvis, in a vulnerable tone that fairly begged for a reassuring response. "I love you, too," Linda replied, fulfilling instinctively his need for an immediate sign of acceptance. No sooner had she left for home, however, than Elvis was on the phone to Los Angeles, making arrangements to fly in Kit and her roommate for the show that night.

Elvis could never have enough of sweeping women off their feet and romancing them with grand gestures of gallantry. Always he had to be telling them that this was love and they would soon be walking up to the altar. His pattern with women was like his favorite amusement park ride, the roller coaster. First there was the slow, steady climb, with the questions and answers ticking off like so many turns of the cogwheels under the laboring car. Then, when he was convinced that this gorgeous girl he was quizzing was a virgin, a Christian and a naif who knew nothing of life, there would come that thrilling moment when they went over the first great peak and shot downward in a vertiginous dive of romantic ecstasy. After that, it was a much tamer climb, a less dizzying swoop, until, finally, they were both lobbed out in the tunnel of love, falling sound asleep.

Linda soon displaced Kit in Elvis's affections. Elvis told Kit that her boyfriend was causing too much turbulence in his life, that he loved her dearly but that in his current highly vulnerable situation as a man seeking a divorce, he had to be very careful. It was all phony, of course, and Kit knew it. Though she was a virgin, she wasn't an idiot. In fact, she was a very fearless young woman. Once she realized that she had been given the brush, she flew back to Vegas, marched into Elvis's dressing room and told him off, right to his face. Then she returned to the embraces of King Kong.

The reason why Linda won out over Kit is not hard to grasp. Though both girls were much alike in appearance, age, feminine temperament and moral standards, they differed in one important essential. Linda, despite her conventional small-town rearing, had the makings of an ideal mistress. She was by turns coquettish, amusing, attentive, affectionate, intelligent and faithful. For a moody, sensitive, demanding and aging male prima donna like Elvis Presley, a woman like Linda Thompson was a godsend. If Elvis wanted to play the comic-strip hero, she could transform herself instantly into the erotically enticing southern belle. If Elvis wanted to relapse into the sad, sick little boy, Linda could instantly metamorphose into the gentle, doting young mother. If Elvis were in the mood to play the zany and cutup, Linda was always ready to black out a couple of front teeth and put on funny clothes and play the clown. No matter what her lover's mood or demand, Linda had the temperament and the other resources to discern it and to satisfy it.

At first, Elvis found this new relationship so absorbing and fulfilling that for the only time in his adult life, he went for about a year without seeing any other women. Eventually, though, he found fidelity confining. He began to invent excuses to go off by himself so that he could enjoy his former pleasures. Linda recognized this demand for what it was and rose to the challenge. She told Elvis she didn't want their relationship to deteriorate into the hypocritical pretences that had characterized his marriage and, for that matter, all his relationships with women. She wanted everything to be out front. They came to an understanding that allowed him considerable freedom. They even got so chummy on this issue that Elvis would sometimes introduce his latest discovery to Linda, and all of them would go out together as a threesome. When the date was over, Elvis might discuss his new chick with Linda, soliciting her opinion of the girl's appropriateness to his needs. This was not only having your cake and eating it: It was the first and only time in Elvis's entire life that he had experienced sexual freedom without suffering from guilt. It was a startling contrast with his marriage.

In addition to being a very free and harmonious relationship, Elvis's involvement with Linda Thompson fulfilled completely his lifelong yearning to reconstitute the total trust and intimacy he had once enjoyed with his mother. Nor was it simply his relationship as an adult with his mother that he revived at this time but the even more satisfying relationship he had had with her as a little child. Nothing in Elvis's history is more astonishing than the degree to which he regressed to infancy in this period, unless it be the fact that this relapse was attended by so little shame. It's true, of course, that Elvis had always demanded that women mother him, wait on him and coddle him, conversing with him in that special baby talk he had used with Gladys. Now, however, he wasn't content to play at being a baby: He wanted to experience again the relationship of mother and child in the most literal manner.

He called Linda "Mommy" and she called him "Baby Buntin'," which comes from an old nursery rhyme, "Hush, Baby Buntin', Daddy's gone ahuntin'." "Buntin'" is, of course, the familiar word "bunting," which is used in the South for the wrappings around an infant, its swaddling clothes. So Elvis was a baby in swaddling clothes and even, sometimes, in diapers. Lying for days on end in bed, comfortably swaddled and blissfully stoned, Elvis would have Linda read to him from his favorite books or simply watch over him as he gazed bemusedly at the television screen. When it was time to eat, she would feed him by hand. When it was time for his sleeping medication, she would

administer the dose. Soon they had reconstructed the atmosphere and regimen of the nursery.

Clearly, this whole pattern of behavior was a reaction
to the trauma of discovering Priscilla's infidelity. Unmanned by sexual betrayal, Elvis reacted by regressing
to an infantile state of being. It was also the counterpoise
to that other and fearful reaction which had transformed
him into the nightmare persona of the midnight caller
threatening horrible violence and even murder. As always
with Elvis, we see the contrasting extremes between which
he was condemned perpetually to oscillate. One minute he
is the gun-wielding bad-ass; the next a mewling infant
lisping to his mommy in baby talk.

These extremes had a profoundly deleterious effect on
Elvis both psychologically and physically. This was the
period when he finally became a hopelessly addicted junkie, a delusional paranoid and a bloated, dysfunctional
and frequently sick man with a vast range of symptoms,
all of which could be ascribed to one basic disease: total
incapacity to deal with reality. The only effective remedy
for this condition, interestingly, was a rare challenge posed
to Elvis's talents as an entertainer.

The Satellite Show, *Aloha From Hawaii,* was announced by Colonel Parker and NBC at the conclusion of
Elvis's engagement in Las Vegas in the fall of 1972. At
first glance, it appeared to be the most awesome application of modern technology to show business since the
astronauts' vaudeville act on the moon. Elvis Presley was
to stand on the stage of an auditorium in Honolulu and
be televised by equipment whose signal would be bounced
off an orbiting telecommunications satellite and showered
down over half the world. For one night Marshall Mc-
Luhan's "global village" would become a literal reality.
Staring into their domestic hearths, all the villagers would
see the same shapes in the electronic fire and hear the
music of the spheres.

To make the program pay its enormous cost of about
two and a half million dollars, however, it was necessary
that it play everywhere in prime time, which necessitated
in turn that the global village be divided into marketing
areas and the program peddled country by country—

a rather less sublime image. Eventually, instead of one awesome broadcast, anticipating the world of the future, economics dictated a live show aimed at Japan, followed two days later by a taped replay in Europe, followed a couple of months later by a second rebroadcast in the States: an arrangement that points backward to the early days of network TV when programs like *Your Show of Shows* were broadcast live from New York and then relayed across the country one and two hours later by kinescope. What the great global telecast reduced to in real terms was something far less thrilling than the hype with which it was packaged. For a hustler, however, illusion is reality. As a hustle, the Satellite Show was worthy of Barnum.[1]

What most appealed to the Colonel about the satellite deal was the opportunity it provided to showcase Elvis's stock Las Vegas showroom act as a stupendous feat of performing by the World's Greatest Entertainer. Though nothing out of the ordinary was demanded, except that Elvis lose weight, though not even Elvis's schedule was disrupted because the dates for the broadcast and taping were dead time before the winter opening at the Las Vegas Hilton, Colonel felt quite secure demanding his price: one

---

[1]Though Colonel Parker has always been credited with conceiving this show, the idea was actually suggested by the President of RCA Records, Rocco Laginestra, who concedes (with a smile) that Colonel had never so much as heard of a telecommunications satellite. Elvis was paid $500,000 for his performance plus fifty percent of the net profits after a ten percent commission on the profits to Colonel Parker's All Star Shows. Colonel and All Star got $350,000 up front. After two showings, the program was owned by RCA Tours and Elvis Presley. This show is always cited as an outstanding example of Elvis's charitableness because $85,000 in ticket sales were donated to a local cancer fund. Not one dime of this money came out of Elvis's pocket. The truth is that compared with other great performers, such as Al Jolson, Bing Crosby, Bob Hope or Jerry Lewis, Elvis Presley contributed very little to charity. In a career of twenty-one years in the big time, his benefit performances were so few that they could be counted on your fingers.

million dollars plus reversion of the show to Elvis and
himself after two repeats. As for NBC, which had to pay
the cost of rigging the auditorium in Honolulu, leasing the
satellite, hiring an independent producer (Marty Pasetta,
who does the annual Oscar awards show) and clearing the
air time, it was motivated in large part by the desire to
aid its satellite company, RCA Records, which was being
strongly pressured by its foreign companies to present its
greatest star abroad, especially in Japan. So enormous was
the demand for Elvis in Japan that the broadcast was
parlayed into an Elvis Presley Week, which reached its
climax at seven-thirty Saturday night, January 12, 1973,
when Elvis's share of the viewing audience was a staggering *ninety-eight percent*.

RCA also decided to record the show and issue it as a
two-record album. Though most of the songs had been
recorded by Elvis time and again, particularly on his
wretchedly produced live concert albums, the great ballyhoo given this recording made it appear to be both a
historic document and an extraordinary performance. Another sales feature was the use of the brand new quadraphonic process. This was a ludicrous idea because conditions in the field were highly unfavorable for making
such an experiment and because virtually none of the pur-
chasers would ever be able to play it on a four-channel
system. As it turned out, last-minute engineering problems rendered this "state of the art" recording distinctly
inferior to even a mediocre stereo disc, with startling fluc-
tuations in the volume levels and bad mike balances dis-
torting the sound. Considerations of quality, however, had
never counted for anything where the Elvis public was
concerned. For years Elvis's albums, which were packaged
and even mixed under the Colonel's supervision, were
among the shlockiest products produced by any major record company. Elvis would explode in rage when he heard
the finished disc and discovered that the Colonel had ordered the engineers to raise the level of Elvis's voice far
above that of his accompaniment. As for the album jackets,
they were about as sophisticated as an old-fashioned billboard. So it is not surprising that the people who bought
all those styrofoam boaters and pink teddy bears bought

this bad album. The "package" sold an impressive two
million "units."

Everyone who recalls Elvis's appearance on the Satellite Show remembers how well he looked. He was ex-
ceptionally slender, deeply tanned, dazzlingly costumed
and utterly charming in manner. Never at any time in his
entire career had he made a better physical appearance.
Even allowing for all the arts of media illusion, the choice
of the right camera angles, lights, colors, makeup and
costume. Elvis could not have looked so well if he had not
prepared himself carefully for this occasion. For three
months he restricted himself to a diet of tiny, frozen-food
packets that added up to only five hundred calories a day.
This punishing diet he supplemented with daily injections
of vitamins and a hormone extracted from the urine of
pregnant women. As all of Elvis's subsequent life testifies
to his tendency to let himself go until he became a grotesque-looking monstrosity, it is important to recognize
how different his fate might have been if he had been
stimulated from time to time by other such challenges as
this program presented. Imagine the inspiration Elvis
would have derived from a great tour of Europe or the
Orient or a two-week stand in some vast hall in London
or Tokyo or an around-the-world tour! How much greater
his will to live and exercise his talents if instead of being
worked like a mule at Las Vegas or toured through the
sticks or shut up in paranoid seclusion at Graceland, he
could have enjoyed a royal progress that would have taken
the World's Greatest Entertainer all over the world! This
raises the vital question: Why didn't Elvis Presley ever
tour abroad?

Elvis was always eager to play in foreign countries.
From as early as 1957, he was telling the press that he
would soon be going to England, Australia or continental
Europe because demand for his appearance in those coun-
tries was so great. At the press conference after his initial
opening at Las Vegas in 1969, he spoke of going soon to
Europe. Time and again, European, Australian and Jap-
anese promoters offered fabulous sums to persuade the
Colonel to allow Elvis to leave the United States. One
English promoter was so eager to book Elvis that he offered

a million dollars for a single night's work plus transportation across the Atlantic and back on a plane with a capacity of one hundred and thirty-five passengers. Even more extravagant was the behavior of a Japanese promoter whom Alex Shoofey introduced to the Colonel.

The moment this man was ushered into the Colonel's fourth-floor suite at the International, Colonel snapped: "I want two million dollars on my desk tomorrow. I want you to make sure you cover this whole desk." The Japanese replied, "No problem." Shoofey jumped in at this point to assure the Colonel that the man, whom he knew well, had immense financial resources and the money was in American banks. His bluff called, Colonel grumbled, "Don't wanna go to Japan." Then he said: "Tell you what I would like to do. I'd like to do a picture. But you have to come up with a million dollars that's mine, for *me* alone! Understand me? I get a million right off the bat before I sign. You pay for the movie and everything, and then we'll split the distribution. Okay?" The imperturbable Japanese replied, "Okay." Exasperated, the Colonel barked, "Forget about it!" Shoofey was amazed and bewildered by this exchange because, as he puts it: "In Japan they would have paid a hundred dollars to see Elvis."

As money was the Colonel's raison d'etre, his behavior in cavalierly dismissing these golden offers seems absolutely inexplicable, until you associate it with certain other oddities in the man's conduct. Colonel Parker has always displayed a profound reluctance to cross any border where you have to show a passport. Though he was quite comfortable taking Elvis to Canada or Hawaii, he never once visited his "boy" during the fifteen months Elvis was in Germany. Jean Aberbach went to Europe, Hal Wallis went to Europe, Freddy Bienstock went to Europe but Colonel never came over for as much as a weekend. Why? At the time the Colonel told the wife of Dave Gardner, the southern good ole boy comic, that he couldn't obtain a passport because he was a "foundling." This story is an obvious fabrication, but it does underscore the most likely reason why Tom Parker never took Elvis abroad: The Colonel does not have a passport and did not wish to apply for a passport.

Apart from sheer perversity, why would Colonel Parker sacrifice millions of dollars over an issue as trifling as a passport application? Did he fear that the application might raise questions whose answers the Colonel does not wish to give? One such question might have been: "Are you an American citizen?" Colonel Parker has always maintained that he is an American citizen, citing a number of ways in which he could have become a citizen: adoption by American parents, service in the American army and marriage to an American citizen. All of these avenues toward naturalization were dependent in the old days, however, on legitimate entry into the United States. Gabe Tucker, who has been one of the Colonel's cronies since the early forties, appears to be persuaded that the Colonel did not enter the country legally. In the book he produced with Houston gossip columnist Marge Crumbaker, Tucker quotes Elvis Presley as his authority. "I just feel in my bones that the Colonel is in this country illegally," Elvis remarks at one point in *Up and Down With Elvis*. "Hell, I think the Colonel was born in Holland or Sweden somewhere. He probably got here by jumping ship, finding a job in a carnival, and making up all that stuff about being born on the road heading south." At another point in the book, Tucker remarks: "Colonel had a personal fear of walking across that American boundary line," citing instances that go back to the days when Colonel was managing Eddy Arnold. In light of these disclosures, the many peculiarities in the Colonel's life-style noted before could be seen to have arisen from the need to invent and maintain a fictitious past that would mask the Colonel's real history.

It is a sign of how taboo the notion of a foreign tour was in Colonel Parker's mind that at the very moment when he was spurning offers for millions of dollars from European and Japanese promoters, he was busy concocting a deal whose only acceptable rationale is a desperate need for money. In March 1973, the Colonel sold outright to RCA for $5.4 million (and a seven-year guarantee of $500,000 a year against royalties) Elvis Presley's entire record catalogue. The value of these more than seven hundred chart records was literally inestimable. Though,

it could be argued, the records were old merchandise that
had been issued and reissued, packaged and repackaged
a number of times, they were of immense potential value.
Particularly at this moment, with Elvis back in favor
again, wowing them at Las Vegas and on tour, profiting
from the rock 'n' roll revival and looming before millions
of people as the King, the future earnings from his immense and unique catalogue could be seen as a virtual
Golconda. It's significant of the vitality of this material
that no sooner did RCA obtain complete possession of the
records than the company began releasing a series of ret-
rospectives, titled *Elvis Presley—A Legendary Performer,*
that proved highly successful. Considering, too, that Elvis
was earning immense sums again, thanks to his recent
movie, TV, showroom and concert profits, it seems very
strange that his manager would want to close out all the
future royalties on twenty years of record-making for even
so large a sum as $5.4 million. When you add the further
fact that Elvis had no means of sheltering this huge dollop
of cash, which would simply be dumped atop his other
income, already sufficient to put him in the highest tax
bracket, the whole deal becomes preposterous as business
and clearly contrary to the artist's best interests. As it
turned out, after splitting the money with the Colonel
fifty-fifty, Elvis netted only about $750,000.[2]

If you look at the deal not from Elvis's but the Colonel's
point of view, the perspective changes radically. Elvis was
only thirty-four years of age; with any sort of luck, he
could profit from his old recordings for another twenty or
thirty years and then pass on the property, enhanced im-

---

[2]Owing to the lucrative side agreements which he attached to
the buy-out, Colonel Parker wound up with $1,550,000 *more* than
Elvis plus ten percent of the net profits of RCA Record Tours,
which was sponsoring Elvis's road shows. Elvis, for his part, got
a royalty rate that was only half that being paid at the time to
stars like the Beatles, the Rolling Stones and Elton John. He was
also stripped of the protection provided by the standard auditing
clause, which was deleted from the agreement, leaving a conspicuous blank space on the face of the contract form.

mensely by his death, to his heirs. Colonel was sixty-four
with a bad heart. His expectations were foreshortened by
age, health and indifference to the future. The Colonel's
view of the future is well expressed in a conversation he
held with Lamar Fike in 1965, when Parker was fifty-six.
"How much longer do I have to live?" asked the Colonel
rhetorically. "Ten or fifteen years, if I'm lucky. I'm gonna
live it like I wanna! I don't give a shit! I do like I want to,
I spend like I want to. I take care o' my people. Fuck it!
Talk about leave it to somebody—why should I leave it
to somebody? Ain't nobody I wanna leave it to!" What
concerned the Colonel was not the future but the present.
In that present, however, he was spending his money at
an alarming rate.

Colonel Parker's huge gambling losses at the International Hotel were secured both by his ability to pay and
by the management's gratitude toward the Colonel for
giving them Elvis Presley at a low figure and never demanding to renegotiate. This cozy arrangement was
threatened, however, in February 1972, when Kirk Kerkorian sold the hotel to the Hilton chain. At that moment,
a clean broom began to sweep through every room of the
huge establishment, including the showroom and casino.
Though Alex Shoofey remained for the time being as the
general manager, he was threatened with a loss of the
total control he had enjoyed under his former boss. Now
he had to deal not with a great venture capitalist but with
professional hotel managers who prided themselves on
their ability to keep track of every last pat of butter going
through the labyrinthine machinery of their biggest
house. Yet for all their expertise in running conventional
hotels, the Hiltons were not yet expert in managing gaming establishments. Soon the new owners and their general
manager came into conflict on the issue of how to deal
with Colonel Tom Parker.

As Shoofey recalls, Barron Hilton ordered his manager
one day to get aboard the company plane and fly down to
Palm Springs to lay down the law to the Colonel. Shoofey
objected vehemently to what he regarded as a foolish order.
"You don't go to Palm Springs and tell the Colonel anything!" he rasped. "Colonel Parker—*minus* Elvis Pres-

ley—is the best customer you ever had at this hotel. He's
good for at least one million dollars a year. You know what
you do with a million-dollar customer? You pick him up
at night, carry him to bed and kiss his goddamn ass!"
When this argument failed to persuade, Shoofey drew on
his knowledge of gambling. "There are two types of gamblers," he explained to Barron Hilton, "dangerous and nondangerous. Colonel Parker is a nondangerous gambler.
The longer he plays, the more money you get. He cannot
win! Do you know what a hotel would pay for a guy that
cannot win?" Shoofey finally carried his point; but not
much later, he resigned. At this point, the Colonel found
himself dealing with people who didn't share Alex Shoofey's
policy for dealing with big-time gamblers. Nor was this
the Colonel's only problem: at this very moment Milton
Prell dropped dead of a stroke, depriving Parker of his
closest friend in Las Vegas.

Jean Aberbach, who had developed a close relationship
with Tom Parker over the years, recalls this period vividly.
He sees it as a watershed in the Colonel's life. "Some people," he says, "are split personalities at the same moment;
others are split personalities at different moments. The
latter explains Colonel Parker. Up to the time he discovered Las Vegas, he was a loyal, wonderful human being.
But this Las Vegas thing changed his entire personality.
His gambling...he lost enormous amounts! He was forced
to deal with the people to whom he lost the money. So he
might have lost control. He was forced to do many things
that he otherwise might not have done. He was forced to
go in directions in which he otherwise might not have
gone....The Colonel sold for a flat fee all the income that
was to be made from the records. It certainly fit in with
his need to come up with money because there are certain
people to whom you cannot owe money."

The crisis in Colonel's affairs described by Jean Aberbach not only explains the shortsighted management policy implicit in the catalogue sale but also reveals on a
deeper level the astonishing similarity in temperament
between the Colonel and Elvis. Just as Elvis was accustomed to living for the moment, squandering his money
with the excuse that "you don't come back for an encore,"

so we now see Colonel Parker acting on precisely the same principle. Both men appear bent on playing their parts, strutting across their stages, without concern for future consequences. Dominated and obsessed alike by their images, their exaggerated sense of self-importance, they resemble characters in comic strips rather than real human beings. Elvis thinks that if he buys a hundred pickup trucks or herds a hundred groupies through his hotel suite or psychs his men up to risking their lives for him, he has power. In truth his acts of acquisition, seduction and authority all bespeak the same emptiness, insatiability and paranoia. The Colonel, secure in the expectation of limitless credit, stands at the crap table betting "around the horn," laying every possible wager in a pattern that insures great losses. As the same audience that has applauded Elvis in the showroom marvels at Colonel's profligacy, the old man revels in his moment of glory. He, too, had "power."

Less than two weeks after the Satellite Show, Elvis opened again at Las Vegas. The first week went smoothly, though he complained of a heavy mucous discharge that forced him constantly to turn away from the audience and cough up a glob of phlegm between each number. Diseases and disorders of the upper respiratory system had begun to plague him during the past year. A local nose and throat specialist, Dr. Sidney Bower, could not account for this particular symptom. He prescribed a nasal douche, rest and avoidance of drugs. At the same time that Dr. Bower was treating Elvis's throat and warning against drug abuse, Dr. Thomas "Flash" Newman (so called because of the dispatch with which he made his calls) was whisking into Elvis's dressing room every night to give him an injection of "B 12" before he went onstage. Dr. Newman is a small, dapper, grey-haired man who dresses like a golfer and speaks in a high, light, whispery Irish voice, always punctuating his conversation by saying, "God bless you, Joe" or "God bless you, Lamar." In addition to giving Elvis his vitamin shots, Dr. Newman was responsible for seeing that Elvis got to sleep every morning around dawn.

Insomnia had been the bane of Elvis's existence since adolescence. Beginning in 1960, with his return to Hollywood, he had begun to rely on sleeping pills as a diabetic relies upon insulin. He had grown accustomed to taking heavy doses of Placidyl, Valium, Percodan and Demerol every night. Such heavy downers often caused him to fall asleep in the middle of a sentence or even a meal. One moment he would be sitting at the table, piddling with his mashed potatoes. The next, he would be head down in the slop. Linda Thompson once left Elvis for a moment while he was eating a bowl of chicken and rice soup. When she returned, she discovered him with his face totally submerged in the dish. If she hadn't pulled his head back before it was too late, he would have earned the doubtful distinction of being the first man in history to drown in a soup bowl.

Drugs like Percodan and Demerol contain synthetic opiates that have all the dangerous properties of natural opiates. They are addictive and if used continuously must be taken in ever-increasing quantities to compensate for the tolerance that the body quickly develops. It is unclear when Elvis Presley first became addicted. Perhaps it was as far back as the early sixties, when he first began his study of the *Physicians' Desk Reference* and obtained access to a wide range of drugs. It was in the nature of things that eventually he would graduate from the lesser opiates to the most powerful of the lot, the notorious Dilaudid. There can be no question that Elvis was using Dilaudid by 1972 because a couple of the more astute Guys saw the name on the medicine bottles. What's more, we know that Dilaudid was Elvis Presley's favorite drug. Pat West, Red's wife, recalls Elvis listening to a family discussion of drugs one day and remarking, "I've tried them all and Dilaudid is the best."

Dilaudid has been called "drugstore heroin," the implication being that even though it is legal, Dilaudid is as powerful and dangerous as the proscribed drug. The truth is even more startling. Dilaudid is much stronger than heroin: 2.5 times as strong, to be exact; five times the strength of morphine. That's why it is prescribed for all the most excruciating kinds of pain: deep knife wounds, extensive burns and terminal cancer. As Dilaudid is always full strength and heroin is invariably cut, a small, cheap dose of the legal drug will produce the same effects as a couple of hundred dollars' worth of the diluted illegal drug. Why, then, it will be asked, do junkies spend immense sums of money and incur other serious risks scoring for heroin if all they need to get high is a pill sold in any big-city slum for about twenty dollars? One answer is that heroin "holds" much better than Dilaudid. Though Dilaudid is supposed to be effective for as long as six hours, it won't hold a hard addict much longer than two or three hours. As such addicts dissolve the pills in water and shoot the solution into the mainline, and as they soon begin to have a lot of trouble getting a "register" because their veins collapse from this abuse, it makes a great deal of difference whether they are using a drug that demands three or four injections each day or six or seven long sessions probing desperately for a hit.

Apart from these quantitative differences in holding power, there are qualitative differences between the effects of synthetic opiates and refined natural opiates. Junkies insist that the pleasure of the heroin high far surpasses, both in the initial flash and the subsequent head, the sensations they experience on Dilaudid. This being the case, it would seem natural for Elvis Presley—whose favorite motto was "Take it to the max!"—finally to exchange the legal for the illegal drug and become at last a regular old boot-and-shoot junkie.

Though it's possible that at some time or other Elvis tried heroin, in the manner of today's Beautiful People, by snorting it like cocaine, he never appears to have been a heroin addict or to have developed the obscene habit of the mainlining addict who, not content with simply injecting himself with the drug, insists on jacking back the blood in the chamber of the syringe and reinjecting himself a number of times in a kind of venous masturbation. Though Elvis began in 1972 to take enormous quantities of both Demerol and Dilaudid through injections, he would never use the needle on himself and he always skin-popped instead of taking the drug in the veins.

Putting all these facts together, you get the picture of a man controlled by an easily comprehended psychological taboo. Though Elvis would concede that he was deeply

dependent on drugs, he could not tolerate the image of
himself as a "junkie." Junkies were loathsome creatures
whom he would have liked to have seen rounded up by the
police and put in prisons, along with their pushers. (In
fact, on more than one occasion, Elvis hatched elaborate
plots for personally assassinating the most notorious pushers in Memphis.) No one could ever stigmatize him with
this hated label, he persuaded himself, because he did not
conform to the three-part definition of a junkie. A junkie
Elvis defined (and taught the Guys to define) as someone
who (1) uses heroin; (2) injects himself; (3) mainlines. Elvis
did none of these things: QED—Elvis was not a junkie.
How did Elvis define himself in terms of drugs? He was
a man martyred by his career and fame, who lived under
enormous and unnatural pressures that interfered with
his natural functioning and produced distressing medical
problems, like insomnia, that demanded treatment with
certain legal medications. *Medications:* That was the crucial code word for dope in Elvis's dialect of double-talk and
his exercises in double-think.

This sort of preposterous rationalizing was actually
once very common in America: back in the days before the
Harrison Act, when hundreds of thousands of neurasthenic
ladies who suffered from undiagnosable but severely de-
bilitating complaints took every day their measured doses
of those patented "elixirs" and "tonics" that were in fact
laudanum: or, in plain English, opium dissolved in alcohol.
That someone living in the midtwentieth century, especially someone as bright and hip and well-versed in drug
description as Elvis Presley, could have deluded himself
with such transparent pretenses would appear unbelievable if we had not had already such abundant evidence of
Elvis's profound capacity for self-delusion and self-escape.
Once you learn the rules of Elvis's mental game with
drugs, they make perfect sense not only in terms of their
purpose but in the larger terms supplied by his personality.
Once again you confront the essence of his being: his profoundly divided self.

On February 1, 1973, Priscilla arrived at Las Vegas
with Lisa Marie to celebrate the child's birthday. The dining room of the penthouse was decorated with balloons

and streamers. A birthday cake with five pink candles was set on the table. Priscilla had come with Joanie Esposito and one of her little daughters. Both women stayed close together and said virtually nothing to Linda Thompson, who was now established as Elvis's regular companion. While the children and the other guests ate the birthday dinner, Elvis and Priscilla withdrew to another part of the suite to have a serious discussion. When it was over, they returned to the table.

As soon as they arrived, Lisa looked up brightly and said: "Didn't you make things all right, Daddy, so that we can be back together again?" Elvis practically strangled. Priscilla told the child that they would have to leave soon for the airport because she had to be in school the next day. Spoiled little Lisa flared up instantly: "But the party just started!" she protested. "Do what your momma says, Lisa," Elvis warned in a low, forced voice. He knew that he would be blamed if the child misbehaved at this moment. Then he embraced her impulsively and lifted her clear out of her chair. "Daddy, you made me drop the piece of cake on the floor," the child complained. Elvis put her back into her chair and said softly, "I'm sorry, honey, I'll buy you another cake tomorrow."

That night, Elvis had to cancel the late show. The next night, he canceled the midnight show again. He couldn't sleep. His eyes showed great black rings. Instead of holding court with the Guys, he secluded himself in his bedroom. A storm was brewing and the Guys could feel it. Then, one night in the dressing room down under the stage, as Elvis was putting on his costume, he recounted to Hamburger James a dream he had had the night before.

In the dream he was on trial for his life. The prosecuting attorney was Colonel Parker. The chief witnesses for the prosecution were Priscilla and Red. No one would defend Elvis. All the Guys had rejected him. Among the jury, the only two who were sympathetic to his case were his Jewish jewelers in Beverly Hills, Schwartz and Ableser. The judge wore a white robe and carried a black medical bag. "What does it mean, E?" asked Hamburger James. Elvis replied, "It means the end is near."

This dream, whatever its ulterior meaning, represents

with cartoonlike clarity many of the most basic features
of Elvis's life and psyche at this critical moment. The court-
room suggests the coming divorce proceedings. The Colonel appears as the arch accuser, the prosecutor. He is the
man who told Elvis when they made their first deal—"If
you ever do anything to make me ashamed of you, you're
through!" Priscilla and Red, the two people closest to Elvis
emotionally, are both depicted as aggrieved parties, as,
indeed, they had every right to be. The notion that the
Guys had rejected Elvis is a typical expression of his oft-
repeated statement that none of them were really his
friends but that all of them were simply seeking to exploit
him. The Jewish jewelers, who had designed the TCB symbol, are a puzzle; but the "Chosen People" are always benign presences in Elvis's private mythos. The judge in the
white robe suggests, of course, Elvis in his white stage
costume. The medical bag belongs to the judge. Is he a
doctor, like Flash Newman, condemning Elvis for his addiction? Or is he Elvis, condemning himself? Whatever
meaning one infers from the dream, its ominous tone and
the resigned and hopeless air with which Elvis read it
prepare one for what happened next.

---

[3]The foregoing account of Priscilla Presley and Mike Stone's
relationship is based primarily on interviews with the latter.

Chapter 32

A New Kind of Hit

THE WEEKEND following the ominous dream, there was a violent incident on the stage of the Showroom Internationale. A group of flashily dressed men with swarthy complexions, accompanied by some of the local hookers, took places at the end of one of the long tables that run up to the edge of the stage apron. When the party had been seated, another member arrived, spectacularly costumed all in white, with a cape, hat and cane of the same color. As he greeted his friends, they applauded and received him as if he were their leader.

During the course of the performance, one of the men in this ringside party jumped up on the table and from the table hopped onto the stage. As he advanced toward Elvis with a jacket over one arm, Red West rushed up behind him. Grabbing the interloper's head in a hammerlock, Red ran him right off the stage and into the arms of a security guard who searched him immediately for concealed weapons. No sooner did this happen than another member of this same party leaped onstage to aid his comrade. He was stopped by the tall, dour-looking J. D. Sumner, who told him in his deep barrel-tone voice: "Pal, get off! You can't come up here onstage!" With that the man cocked his fist, which was covered by adhesive tape. Elvis came rushing over and assumed a karate fighting stance. Before any

607

blows were exchanged, Jerry Schilling seized the man and pushed him violently off the stage so that he fell back on his back atop a table. Now a third man came charging onto the stage, followed by 'a whole string of people who probably wanted to help Elvis. One by one, friend or foe, they were pushed back by Sonny West and Jerry Schilling, who were soon involved in a vigorous game of King of the Mountain.

During the height of the melee, Elvis kept flourishing his hands and legs karate-style, shouting, "Let 'em go! Let 'em go!" as if nothing would have pleased him better than to get a crack at these unknown assailants. When Sonny, who had been reinforced by this time by numerous security men and house detectives, looked around and saw how manic Elvis had become, he rushed over and seized Elvis in a bear hug, as would a parent trying to restrain and calm a hysterical child. "Elvis! Elvis! They're gone!" cried Sonny, trying to still the panic he saw in Elvis's face. Finally, Elvis recovered himself and resumed his position before the audience, to whom he apologized for the disturbance, complaining only that he hadn't been allowed a shot at the interlopers because he would have "kicked their asses." So far as the audience was concerned, the incident was over; but that wasn't the way Elvis felt.

The moment he came offstage, he started an investigation into the incident, which he swore was a plot against his life engineered by Mike Stone. He pointed to the fact that the men were foreign-looking and one of them had tape on his knuckles. They were Hawaiian karate killers, Elvis insisted, who had been foiled only because he and his men were so well prepared. Having recognized one of the call girls with the men, Elvis got her on the phone. (Elvis was very well acquainted with the local whores.) She told him that it was worth her life to talk about these men, who were definitely shady operators. This revelation fueled Elvis's paranoia even further. Now he was Dirty Harry, deeply involved in a dangerous case, pushing the local police to get the men's rap sheets and discover exactly who they were.

Far from being Hawaiian karate killers, they turned out to be South American porno and go-go girl hustlers

from Lima, Peru, whose heaviest rap was toting an unli-
censed weapon. They had not been armed. The bit of tape
around the one dude's fist was explained by the fact that
he had slammed his fist into a slot machine at the Landmark that didn't pay off. The more the incident was in-
vestigated, the more obvious it became that all the first
man had wanted to do was shake Elvis's hand and present
him with the jacket that he had carried onstage. Everything that followed was triggered by Red West's strongarm
tactics.

Nothing could persuade Elvis that he had not missed
death by a narrow margin as a result of Mike Stone's
supposed machinations. Till the day he died, Elvis carried
about with him the rap sheets he had obtained from the
police. He told the story of the attack countless times,
embellishing it, like Falstaff, so that the number of his
attackers constantly increased and his own heroic exer-
tions reached the point where he was standing off fifteen
men single-handed. In fact, the incident had a vastly different conclusion from that over which Elvis crowed.

When he got back to the safety of his penthouse the
night of the incident, he called up the security detail that
had taken the four men in custody. He told the guards
that when they released the men, they should tell these
guys that if they didn't get out of town instantly, they
wouldn't leave alive. The guards were so submissive to Elvis's orders that they did just what they were told. The
South Americans, who came from a world where death
threats are a serious matter, panicked and demanded an
armed escort to the airport.

Elvis was now meeting Dr. Newman before and after
every show. The moment Elvis would arrive in the dressing room, he would say, "Where's Flash?" Then, as soon
as the nattily dressed, silver-haired doctor appeared, he
and Elvis would disappear into the bathroom, where the
Doctor stuck Elvis with a hypodermic syringe. As soon as
Elvis returned to the dressing room after the show, Newman flashed on the scene again, closeting himself briefly
with Elvis in the little bathroom. Two shows a night, four
visits from the doctor. What is the logical surmise? Powerful stimulants to get Elvis up for the show. Powerful

sedatives to get him off after the show. Then another tug on the human yo-yo before the next show. Finally, late at night, perhaps four or five in the morning, the indefatigable Flash—"the speediest sixty-year-old man in the world," as the Guys called him—would pop up again in the bedroom of the penthouse to give Elvis his sleeping potion by hypodermic.

Though Elvis was being medically "managed" twenty-four hours a day, he was still like a human bomb. All it took was one minor incident to trigger off the final explosion. The cause was that perpetual source of outrage, Elvis's exacerbated relationship with Priscilla.

Priscilla was quite content to cut the domestic ties that attached her to Elvis, but she was reluctant to abandon her excellent black maid, Henrietta. An arrangement was worked out that enabled Henrietta to retain her job with Elvis and at the same time do some work for Priscilla. Naturally, this opened a conduit of information between the two households. One day while Henrietta was talking with Hamburger James, she confided that Priscilla had Lisa Marie sleeping in a crib at the foot of the bed in which Priscilla slept with Stone. The implications of this false tale are as clean or nasty, as harmless or damaging, as the mind of the man who repeats it. Hamburger James blames himself today for ever repeating this bit of gossip, but repeat it he did, to Red West. West, who as the sequel will show, appears to have had a profound antagonism to Mike Stone, relayed the story to Elvis.

Elvis, it will be recalled, had slept for many years in the same bed with his mother and father. This might have disposed him to regard such arrangements as being quite harmless. Instead it disposed him to kill. On the night of February 19, after the second show, Sonny, Red and Lamar were sitting in the living room of the penthouse drinking beer when Elvis called for them from the master bedroom. What happened next has been sensationally but accurately described in the opening pages of the West-Hebler book, *Elvis—What Happened?*

When Sonny got into the bedroom, he found Elvis dressed in his pajamas and sitting on the bed yoga-style. Linda Thompson was beside him. Elvis, who had been

looking worse every day for a week, was now a ghastly
apparition. He was drenched with sweat, stoned blind and
obviously plumbing the depths of one of his darkest, black-
est moods, the sort of annihilatory rage into which he would
work himself after days of brooding over some painful
insult or injury. Elvis commanded Sonny to come near.
Then he said, "Look into my eyes, Sonny, look into my
eyes." Sonny recognized instantly what Elvis was about:
He was trying to hypnotize Sonny just as Elvis had seen
the Colonel hypnotize Sonny on a number of occasions. As
soon as Elvis felt he had Sonny under control, he began
to fill the mind of his bodyguard with posthypnotic sug-
gestions and commands.

"The man has to die," rumbled Elvis, slurring his words
and struggling to look hypnotic. "You know the man has
to die. The sonovabitch has to go! You know it, Sonny, you
know it. There is too much pain in me and he did it! Do
you hear me? I am right. You know I am right. Mike Stone
has to die. You will do it for me. Kill the sonovabitch!
Sonny, I can count on you, I know I can!" Sonny had seen
Elvis emotionally disturbed many times. He was also very
much aware that Elvis was an actor and could feign emotions. This time there was no feigning. As Sonny looked
at Elvis, he realized that his boss meant every word he
said. This was a command.

Sonny started to reason with Elvis, to talk him out of
this mad notion. He told Elvis that though his pain was
terrible, it was wrong to talk about killing a man. The
man didn't intend to hurt Elvis, certainly not to kill him
with rage and grief. Nothing Sonny said made the slightest
impression on Elvis. He continued to sit there like a fat,
sweating Buddha, with his eyes glaring hate instead of
love, his mouth opening and repeating over and over like
a man in a malarial delirium: "Mike Stone must die, he
must die, he has no right to live."

Finally, Elvis could brook delay no longer. Rolling
clumsily out of his enormous platform bed, he staggered
to his clothes closet, rummaged inside and then turned to
confront Sonny with an M-16 automatic rifle in his hands.
At this point, Linda Thompson who had been watching
this scene with slowly mounting terror, started screaming:

"What's the matter with him? Won't somebody do something. Calm him down, for God's sake!" Elvis shoved the gun into Sonny's hands. Sonny started to retreat, walking backward toward the door, protesting at every step. Elvis, stung to fury, hurled himself onto the bed, screaming: "Doesn't anyone understand? Why can't you all understand *this man must die!*" Then, he started clawing the wall, trying to climb it. Sonny saw this as an act of insanity. He flung out of the room carrying the automatic rifle, which he hurled with disgust into a wastebasket. Now it was Red's turn to deal with Elvis.

Red was just as appalled at Elvis's madness as was Sonny. An angry man himself, he was at a loss to deal with this kind of crazed malevolence. Fortunately, Linda had her wits about her. She picked up the phone and called the house doctor, Elias Ghanem, who promised to come up immediately and give Elvis a calming shot. Meantime, Elvis continued to repeat the same demand that Mike Stone be killed. Not until the doctor's needle had squirted a powerful sedative into Elvis's veins did he stop raving. When at last he lapsed into sleep, Red consoled himself with the thought that next day everything would be different. Old E had simply blown his stack. He would be a different man in the morning.

When the next day came, however, Elvis did not relent one jot in his determination to have Mike Stone killed. The only difference was that instead of ordering Red or Sonny to do the job, he told Red to hire a hit man to do the dirty job. At first, Red did not take the order seriously; but when every day Elvis kept renewing the command, stressing that this was something that could be done and must be done and was Red's responsibility to do, Red began to feel that perhaps Elvis was right. Stone was a monster. He had destroyed a marriage. He had driven Elvis insane. Finally, Red succumbed to Elvis's demands. He got the number of a member of the Mob. Soon the Memphis Mafia was talking to the real Mafia. It took no time at all to cut the deal. The Mafia dudes said they would be honored to help out a man as great as Elvis Presley. They set a modest figure for their work; ten thousand dollars. A trifle! No more than the cost then of a new white Lincoln Mark V

Continental. Finally, Red was able to go to his master and give him the word that the hit had been contracted.

The last night of the engagement, February 23, Red knocked on the door of Elvis's dressing room twenty minutes before show time. He was admitted and Hamburger James sent out into the lounge. Red told Elvis that one word from him would send Mike Stone to his grave. Elvis pondered the idea anew. Then, he said: "Aw, hell, let's just leave it for now. Maybe it's a bit heavy. Just let's leave it for now." Red felt enormously relieved. Looking back on the event later, he realized that he must have been acting like a mindless zombie, totally subservient to Elvis's mad will. To be more precise, one could say that he had been acting as if he were simply the embodiment of Elvis's anger, which is, in fact, what his role had been for many years in Elvis's life. Only never before had it been so clear. As Elvis used to say, "Red is anger." He should have said: "Red is *my* anger."

Though Red experienced a keen sense of relief when he was released from his dreadful mission, Elvis could not share this comfort. He experienced a profound sense of depression. Rage that cannot be released through action soaks back into the mind as deep, self-destructive gloom. The very night that Elvis renounced his plans for revenge, he nearly died.

It was shortly before dawn when Linda awoke, brought to consciousness by some intimation that her "baby" was ill. The first thing she noticed about Elvis was that he wasn't breathing normally. Indeed, he appeared to be having great difficulty in merely drawing breath. His breaths were long and strangled. They subsided for so long that it seemed each time as though he wouldn't breathe again. When Linda tried to shake Elvis awake, he did not respond. Now she noticed that he was ice cold. Greatly alarmed, she called Joe Esposito, who promised to get Dr. Newman up to the room as quickly as possible.

Newman recognized Elvis's condition instantly as a drug overdose. Normally, the medical response in such a situation would be to call an ambulance and rush the patient to an emergency room. This was not a normal situation. It was vital that Elvis not become the center of a scandalous incident that might seriously damage his career and the reputation of the whole resort. Even the Mob doesn't kill in Las Vegas. So the doctor applied the standard resuscitation procedure unaided.

A Dilaudid overdose produces first a shortness of breath, a slowness of heartbeat, a lowering of blood pressure that signals a profound depression of the central nervous system. As this process continues, the patient slips into a deep coma until finally he reaches the terminal state: cardiac arrest and death. The treatment is a procedure with which Elvis himself must have been familiar because it is printed on the endpapers of his favorite book, the *Physicians' Desk Reference*. First, the physician must facilitate breathing by sticking a pipe down the patient's throat. Then, he injects a chemical antagonist to the narcotic, like naloxone hydrochloride. Next, a catheter is inserted in the penis and the bladder is drained to determine the degree of dehydration, for the shutdown of the central nervous system results also in kidney failure. Fluids are then infused intravenously in accordance with the volume of urine. How long it took to bring Elvis around and what incidents occurred during this perilous process is information known only to the two or three people who were present. The next day the Guys were told only that Elvis had taken a bit too much of his medication and had to have the doctor in the middle of the night.

After this close call, Elvis lay low for a couple of months. In April he made a brief tour of the West Coast, thirty pounds overweight and clearly suffering from drug addiction. He wound up the tour with a stand at the Sahara Tahoe. Here again he got so wiped out on his medications that the final portion of the engagement had to be canceled. The public was given the excuse that Elvis was suffering from "throat congestion" or "pneumonia." The situation appeared so threatening to those around Elvis that the boldest and most resourceful of them, Ed Hookstratten (a friend of the Colonel, who must have seconded the lawyer), decided to take matters into his own hands and attempt to save Elvis's life by means of a stratagem.

Hookstratten realized that there was no point in trying to persuade Elvis to relinquish drugs voluntarily. What the shrewd and tough attorney had in mind was an attack on the doctors who supplied the drugs. Engaging John O'Grady and another private eye named Jack Riley, Hookstratten ordered the detectives to ferret out the principal prescription writers and discover their modus operandi.

At the end of a six-week investigation, O'Grady and Riley were able to identify positively three doctors and one dentist who were major sources. (They failed to pursue the fifth culprit, Dr. George Nichopolous, because they received assurances from Vernon Presley that Dr. Nick was O.K.). Most of the prescriptions were made out to the Guys and their wives or even to Lisa Marie. They were filled in Las Vegas at the Landmark Pharmacy, directly in sight of the Hilton International, and delivered to Elvis's suite, where they all wound up in Elvis's hands.

When the two tough-talking detectives confronted the doctors with the evidence of their deeds, they made no effort to protect themselves through denials. The doctors simply said that if it were not for their work, both Elvis and the public would be much the poorer. Evidently the federal and state authorities concurred with this judgment, for when the results of the detectives' investigations were presented to the appropriate law-enforcement agencies, no action whatsoever was taken.

Elvis had so many doctors all over the country that it would have been a major undertaking to identify them all and determine what contribution each made or did not make to Elvis's constantly widening pattern of drug abuse. Like all junkies, Elvis was an adroit feigner of medical complaints. If all else failed, he would rip out a tooth filling and get a fix from a local dentist. Any doctor or dentist who appeared the least bit disposed to hero worship or financial opportunism was fair game for the insatiable Elvis. No sooner, for example, did the house doctor of the International Hotel, Elias Ghanem, display concern for the famous star, than Elvis began wooing the doctor in the most extravagant manner. Dr. Ghanem reciprocated with true Arab hospitality by providing Elvis with a haven in the doctor's home.

Slight, swarthy, with typical Lebanese features, Elias

Ghanem is a very boyish-looking forty-three. Dressed like
a swinger in tight hip-huggers and a clinging body shirt
whose open collar reveals a massive gold medallion on a
chain, he receives you in a low medical building adjacent
to the hotel. His private office is decorated like a suburban
parlor, but its walls are covered with photographs showing
the little doctor in close, often affectionate contact with
famous celebrities. As he speaks, in a low, intimate, earnest voice, he toys constantly with a lock of thick, black,
slightly greying hair. Smiling, he confides that many of
his celebrated patients have suffered from rather embarrassing complaints. One homosexual star had hideous
herpes sores all around his anus. Another middle-aged
swinger, recovering from open-heart surgery, had his
stitches ruptured by an overactive playmate. The doctor,
you learn, has two valuable specialties: He is expert at
emergency room procedures and the treatment of "Vegas
throat," a condition highly disturbing to singers, produced
by the arid and particulate-laden air of the desert.

Dr. Ghanem has amassed an extraordinary amount of
wealth in the short time he has been in practice. Seven
years after his arrival at Las Vegas, a young, unknown
and in no way remarkable practitioner, he owned his own
one-story medical building and a luxurious house on the
border of the country club, while holding a sizable interest
in a bank, a travel agency and a charter air service, Jet
Avia, that boasts one twelve-million-dollar four-engine jet,
but is best known for the crash of two Lear jets in the same
day, January 6, 1976, one of them carrying Frank Sinatra's
mother to her son's opening at Caesar's Palace.

As for Dr. Ghanem's relationship with Elvis Presley,
it was of such value that it inspired Elvis to shower the
doctor with such costly gifts as a sixteen-thousand-dollar
Mercedes and a forty-two-thousand dollar Stutz Blackhawk; on the doctor's side, it inspired him to build an
especially designed room on top of his house just to accommodate his favorite patient. One would expect this room
to be luxurious, judging from the style of the rest of the
house, which, though small, glitters with opulence and
fulfills every fantasy of desert chic, down to a cocktail table
in the conversation pit that rises and falls at the press of

a button. What the Presley room suggests, however, is not just luxury but the sort of decor and paraphernalia with which a great magnate might furnish the boudoir of his movie star mistress.

The room is carpeted to the ankles in thick shag. The bed is raised on a dais and fitted with mirrors around the top and headboard. A few steps from the foot of the bed is an erotic-looking oval Jacuzzi lined with fake onyx veined with gold and controlled with gold faucets. Beside it is an elaborate dressing table. A humidifier sits on the floor. The windows, looking out on the greens of the golf course, are heavily shuttered. Beneath them is a bookcase filled still with Elvis's spiritualist books. Opening one at random, you see the familiar underscoring beneath the words: "Should I return, you would not recognize me." It is said that Elvis would enter this soothing environment to lose weight through a remarkable Sleeping Beauty diet that allows the patient simply to snore through the unpleasant days of self-denial. Dr. Ghanem scoffs at this notion. He says that Elvis used the room to retreat from the pressures of his life, and that he often conducted with Elvis long, probing conversations. "What were they about?" you ask. He replies, "Drugs."

Dr. Ghanem admits freely that he gave Elvis injections before and after his shows at Las Vegas. What he denies heatedly is that he ever gave Elvis dangerous or addictive drugs. In fact, he insists that he worked hard to wean Elvis from the addictions engendered by the practices of other doctors. When asked whether it was true that before the show he would stuff up Elvis's nose wads of cotton soaked in liquid cocaine—a preparation a number of the Guys also enjoyed—Dr. Ghanem explains patiently that this was a drug called Lidocaine. (Lidocaine is a local anesthetic widely used to cut cocaine.) When you ask Dr. Ghanem about the story told by a couple of the Guys that they intercepted a Mason jar filled with pills sent by Dr. Ghanem to Elvis in Memphis, he says he has no recollection of the incident. According to Dr. Ghanem, most of the drugs he administered to Elvis were harmless placebos.

Elvis's most important source of drugs in his later years was Dr. George Nichopolous of Memphis. Dr. Nick, as everyone calls him, is another instance of a young, unknown and unremarkable physician who established an extraordinarily close and compelling relationship with Elvis Presley. It was early in 1967, at the time when Elvis bought the ranch in Mississippi, that these two men were brought together by chance. Elvis was suffering from saddle sores. He couldn't get in touch with his regular doctor. George Klein's wife suggested her boss, Dr. Nick. Anyone who stepped inside the charmed circle of Elvis Presley's life wanted to remain there. What's more, Elvis was often willing to give them a chance if they proved faithful. What Elvis sought in everyone was not intelligence or skill or credentials but loyalty, dependability and submission. Dr. Nick was abundantly endowed with the virtues that meant the most to Elvis. Almost immediately the young doctor, who had only begun to practice medicine seven years earlier, became Elvis's regular physician.

No sooner did Elvis come out of the hospital in the spring of 1973 than he was hit by a legal action that had scandalous overtones. Priscilla Presley had discovered in the nine months since the signing of the marital termination agreement that the amounts of money stipulated in this agreement were wholly inadequate for her lifestyle. Her combined alimony and child support payments came to only fifteen hundred dollars a month. Now Priscilla claimed that the figure should be ten times as much. What's more, she had gone into the dress designing and manufacturing business in January 1973, with Olivia Echeverria, using the name Bis and Beau, and she required more money to capitalize this endeavor. Elvis had been generous to her, after his fashion, furnishing her new apartment in the Marina Del Rey at a cost of $50,000 and giving her an expensive new Jaguar. What Priscilla was seeking now was not more gifts or special allocations but an entirely different separation agreement based on a division of their community property.

As she had signed and lived with the old agreement for so long, accepting all the monies that Elvis offered her, she had now to find some strong legal grounds for setting aside the previous settlement. Engaging a lawyer for the first time, she presented the Superior Court of the State

of California in May 1973 with a motion to set aside the
agreement on the grounds of "extrinsic fraud" (a civil not
a criminal action).

   The nature of the alleged fraud was set forth not only
by her attorney, with his various points and authorities,
but in a personal declaration that was soon to be exploited
by the movie magazines with sensational effect. To imagine the impact of the following statement, one has to bear
in mind that up to this moment hardly one word of a
scandalous character had ever appeared in print concerning Elvis Presley and very little concerning the nature of
his marriage, his wife or his decision to sue for divorce.
Now after seventeen years of silence, the following remarks were put into the public record by Priscilla Presley
and swiftly smeared all over the hitherto immaculate Presley image:

   Since I was sixteen years old I have been living
   with my husband's family and during that time I
   developed trust and confidence in my husband, his
   father and other persons associated with them. During our marriage I was never involved in my husband's business or financial affairs. I was never informed of my husband's income nor the nature and
   amount of property which we had accumulated. My
   expenses were paid through an unlimited checking
   account upon which I wrote checks. Although I
   signed federal income tax returns I never examined
   the returns and do not know what income was disclosed by him.

   In August, 1972, my husband told me that we
   should agree to a division of property.... I told him
   that I would accept $100,000 because I assumed it
   was fair.... A few days later I was called by Mr.
   Hookstratten and asked to come to his office to sign
   the papers. When I got to his office he had the papers
   prepared and he told me that it was necessary for
   a lawyer other than him to look at the papers for
   me. He told me he had made arrangements with Mr.

Robert Brock whose offices were in the same building
and that he would take me there. Mr. Hookstratten
told me Mr. Brock might ask me about my husband's
finances and start to discuss money with me but he
told me if this happened I should not pay any attention to what Mr. Brock said regarding money and
to tell Mr. Brock that Mr. Hookstratten had fully
informed me about finances and that I did not need
his help concerning that subject.

Mr. Hookstratten took me to Mr. Brock's office
and left me there. Mr. Brock already had a copy of
an agreement in his hand which he had apparently
obtained from Mr. Hookstratten. He asked me if I
knew what the paper meant. I told him that I did.
He then asked me if I knew how much money my
husband received as residuals, royalties, and other
income. I told him that Mr. Hookstratten had informed me about all these matters and that I was
fully aware of my husband's finances. Mr. Brock then
asked me to sign a letter to him stating that I had
not employed him for the purpose of advising me
about my husband's assets or income. I was in Mr.
Brock's office for about fifteen minutes. I then signed
the Property Settlement Agreement believing that
I was getting my fair share of our property and believing that in any event I would be taken care of
by my husband in the future as I had in the past.

A few days later I received a check for $50,000.
I was told by Mr. Hookstratten that I should put the
money in the bank and leave it there so that I could
have it for my future needs. After that I began receiving $750 twice a month. This money is not
enough for me to live on....I signed the Property
Settlement Agreement because both my husband
and Mr. Hookstratten told me that it was fair and
represented what I was entitled to....Had I known
that I was entitled to one-half of the community
property and adequate spousal support based upon
my husband's income and our previous style of living
and had I known that the sum of $100,000 as my
share of property and $1000 a month was not fair,

I would not have signed the Property Settlement
Agreement.

Elvis and Hookstratten responded to these charges with
independent declarations denying Priscilla's allegations
and offering their own, quite different, versions of the
story. They contended, plausibly, that Priscilla had been
informed that she could obtain a larger settlement but had
insisted that $100,000 was sufficient. Her story was
"copy," however, and theirs was not. Hookstratten disso-
ciated himself from this undesirable case and substituted
another attorney. This new attorney, Harry M. Fain, took
a deposition from Priscilla in which he forced her to admit
that she knew very well the character of her husband's
work, including the fact that he made a lot of money, and
that she had actively participated in the purchase and
furnishing of their three California houses. He could not
get her to admit that once or twice in the years when she
was signing Elvis's income tax she took a peek at the net
income line. She insisted to the end that she had no idea
of what the form in her hand said. Though the efforts of
Fain weakened Priscilla's case, they did not by any means
destroy it.

Now, Priscilla's lawyer began to demand Elvis Presley's
financial records, a demand that drove both Elvis and
Vernon to the limits of outrage but which could not be
denied. At this point, the case started to get hectic. At
issue were such questions as whether the California law,
which demands a fifty-fifty split of community property,
applies to a man whose domicile is in Tennessee, whose
law has no such provision for the division of property in
divorce. Also there were knotty questions concerning what
part of Elvis's income was his as an unincorporated business and what part was his as a private person and so on
ad infinitum.

It's not hard to imagine the effect of Priscilla's demands
on Elvis. Now, in addition to the mortal wound he had
suffered to his pride, he was facing the possibility of an
enormously costly divorce settlement. Even apart from the
financial threat, there was the enraging sensation of having his most private affairs, including his confidential fi-

nancial records, ripped open and studied by lawyers seeking ways to strip him of his property. Coming after a prolonged period of emotional stress and drug abuse, this latest crisis undermined the last supports sustaining Elvis's sanity. Now, he began acting like a lunatic.

During his customary August-September engagement in Las Vegas, everyone noticed how ill he looked and how heavily he was leaning on his drug crutch. Suffering constantly from sleeplessness, though absorbing immense quantities of narcotics and hypnotics, Elvis soon became wildly erratic in behavior. One night the maitre d' of the Italian restaurant at the hotel told Elvis a long tale of woe. The man claimed that for no good reason, he was about to be fired by the Hiltons and thrown out in the street. Elvis, whose sense of injured innocence was a lot stronger than his sense of reality, responded by promising the Italian that the problem would be swiftly solved. That night when Elvis got onstage, he stopped the performance to announce to two thousand guests in the showroom that he had just discovered that Conrad and Barron Hilton were about to perpetrate a terrible act of injustice. Then, as everyone listened in astonishment, he recited the pathetic tale of the little maitre d' and wound up the yarn by denouncing the Hiltons and demanding that they reinstate the man immediately.

Colonel Parker had just finished negotiating a new arrangement on Elvis's behalf that would reduce his engagements at the hotel from four weeks at a stretch to two. The Hiltons could have made serious objections to this cutback, but they had been very sympathetic to Elvis's complaints about the punishing effect of such long runs. Now, no sooner do they conclude the deal that lets Elvis off the hook than Elvis turns around and gives them a black eye in front of their own guests.

As soon as the show ended, Colonel Parker—who had been sitting backstage during Elvis's rap and had groaned repeatedly, "No! oh, no!"—came storming into Elvis's dressing room intent on rebuking him for this outrageous and irrational act. Elvis was in no humor to suffer a tongue lashing. As soon as the Colonel launched into his speech, Elvis turned on the old man and told him off in the most insolent manner. When Colonel Parker renewed his charges, Elvis raised the issue of the Colonel's gambling, pointing out that the reason they could not entertain the lucrative offers that were being made by other hotels, like the soon-to-be-opened MGM Grand, the biggest hotel in town, was because the Colonel had to offer Elvis to the Hiltons as payment for his gambling debts. "You can't talk to me like that!" exploded Colonel Parker. "The hell I can't!" snapped Elvis. "Then I quit!" barked the Colonel, rising to leave. "You can't quit," sneered Elvis, "because you're fired!" "I have quit," countered the Colonel, "and I'm calling a press conference tomorrow to explain the whole situation." By the time the old man was out of the dressing room and heading up the hall, Elvis stuck his head out the door and shouted: "I'm calling a press conference tonight!"

No press conference was called by either man, but the Colonel sat up till dawn drawing up an enormous bill of charges, which he claimed was money that was owing him from past operations. Having completed this tally and seen to its delivery, the Colonel and his staff decamped.[1] For the next ten days, Elvis was on the rampage. Night and day he gave orders one minute and countermanded them the next. He insisted that no one leave him at any time, even to sleep. One morning, Red West had taken a sleeping pill and was just falling to sleep, when there was a loud banging on his door and the voice of one of the Guys shouting: "Elvis is up and wants you to go to the dentist with him." The thought of getting back into his clothes and going on this nitwit mission was almost more than Red could bear. Grumbling, he got himself together and reported for duty in Elvis's suite, still grumbling. Elvis, alert always to the slightest sign of insubordination, came charging out of his bedroom and confronted Red. "If you're so goddamned sleepy," he thundered, "get your ass back

[1]Colonel always had a large sum owing him during Elvis's last years. Elvis's 1974 tax returns show that the Colonel took only twenty-five percent that year, though he was entitled to far more. When Elvis died, he owed Colonel Parker one and a half million dollars.

downstairs and go back to bed!" "No," sighed Red. "I'm here to do my job." Again, the implication was clear that only duty motivated him. Elvis was so annoyed by this attitude that he ducked back in his room and came out a moment later with his M-16, which he pointed straight at Red's chest. Responding as Sonny had years before when Elvis socked him in the jaw, Red gasped, "Elvis, after all these years, I never would have believed that you would point a gun at me!" Then, recovering his nerve, he turned mean and threw the challenge back in Elvis's face: "Go on, you bastard, pull the trigger—kill me!" At that point, Elvis put up the gun; as he turned to put it in his room, he gave Sonny, who was standing nearby, a fast wink.

Elvis also had a violent falling out with Jerry Schilling during this engagement, which commenced with Schilling keeping to his room for a couple of days and came to its climax with the two men squaring off for a fight, each one egging on the other to make the first move. At this time, Elvis seemed intent on driving his closest intimates away. Most of the Guys were making excuses to escape. Lamar left for a funeral. Red went back to his family. As soon as the engagement concluded, Joe Esposito and Jerry Schilling took off for Europe. Finally, Elvis began to calm down.

One morning early, he told Sonny to get the Colonel on the phone. Sonny rang just as the old man was walking into his office in Hollywood. Elvis spoke with the Colonel briefly, and they made up their differences. This is precisely what most of the Guys had anticipated would happen, although Lamar had insisted that Ed Hookstratten was standing in the wings ready to make his entrance as Elvis's new manager. Hookstratten, who is one of the foremost managers of showbiz and athletic talent, with a roster of clients that has included Cary Grant, Glen Campbell, David Merrick, Joseph Levine, Jim Brown, and Rowan and Martin, had discussed the possibility of taking over as Elvis's manager back in 1970, when the Colonel was so ill that it appeared he might be forced to retire. Nothing had come of the suggestion then nor did it now. (It was not until the very end of Elvis's life that any serious effort was made to terminate this famous relationship; then the initiative came not from Elvis but from the Colonel.)

When "Hell Week" finally ended, Elvis decided that it was time that he and his remaining men have a little fun. Picking up some girls, they went down to Palm Springs for a week's rest and recreation at the house on Chino Road. Elvis's date was a pretty teenager who had been since childhood a devoted fan. One night they went to bed and drank a lot of Hycodan, a blood-red, cherry-flavored cough syrup with a narcotic base. When neither Elvis nor the girl made an appearance the following morning, Sonny West entered the bedroom.

The room was freezing cold. Both Elvis and the girl were unconscious. The empty bottle of Hycodan was on the bed table. Sonny suspected an overdose immediately. "C'mon. Wake up!" he shouted. When neither of them responded, his alarm mounted. Raising the girl's eyelids, he saw the eyes were as fixed and unwavering as marbles. Listening to her breath, he heard what sounded like a death rattle. Slapping her hard across the face, he was horrified to see that she didn't move a muscle. Elvis appeared just as inert. For one second, Sonny thought that both of them were dead.

Then he scrambled around to Elvis's side of the bed and slapped his face. The blow produced a low moan. Lifting Elvis's lids, Sonny saw the sightless eyes rolling from side to side. Elvis, at least, could be saved. Sonny picked up the house phone and called their local physician, Dr. Kaplan, who said that he would be at the house in a few minutes.

Now Sonny alerted the other guys, Charlie Hodge and Hamburger James. Immediately, they fell to plotting who would take the blame if the girl were found dead. As both Sonny and James were married, the obvious choice was Charlie. He agreed to say that the girl was his date and that he had offered her the deadly syrup. Next, they began to think of the other girls in the house. They mustn't be allowed to know what was going on, or they might talk and the whole outrageous story would get into the papers. James agreed to keep the girls occupied in a room at the rear of the house and prevent them from getting out until the crisis had passed. By this time the doctor was at the door.

Dr. Kaplan took one look at the girl, who by this time

was turning blue, and picked up the phone to order an ambulance. Elvis was just getting his head up when he heard the doctor's call. "You don't have to do that," Elvis said. "Just give her a shot of Ritalin [a central nervous system stimulant] and she'll come around." The doctor explained that the girl was near death and would have a chance of recovery only if she were rushed to an intensive care unit. As the argument mounted, the ambulance, warned not to use its siren, arrived. The girl was put on a stretcher and borne out of the house. As soon as she was removed, Elvis got on the phone and called the Colonel, a man who had extensive influence in Palm Springs.

That night the girl began to come out of the coma. Sonny, who was deeply concerned about her condition, had gone to the hospital. The doctor told him that he was very worried about possible brain damage produced by prolonged deprivation of oxygen. Sonny sat down beside the bed and began to call the girl softly by name. Suddenly, her eyes popped open. She turned and glared at Sonny. Then, she sprang out of bed, hissing like a wildcat. Sonny was stunned. "What's the matter with her?" he gasped. "She doesn't know where she is," replied the doctor, leading the girl back to bed. "Will she be all right?" persisted Sonny. "We don't know how long her brain was deprived of oxygen. We'll just hope for the best," answered Dr. Kaplan.

Eventually, the girl recovered sufficiently to leave the hospital and return home. The Colonel had done his hush work well. Not a word about the incident leaked to the press. Another Presley skeleton had been neatly locked in its closet. Just to make doubly sure that there were no dangerous grievances, the Colonel offered the family money. The girl's mother—who was a great fan of Elvis's—refused to take even a penny. Elvis never visited the girl or called her, save for once when she was long out of danger. He told her, "Honey, when you're feeling better, I'm gonna take you on tour with me." He never took her anywhere nor did anything for her. He wiped her off his mental slate. Sonny saw the girl a year later at a show. She struck him as being a different person. Instead of an easy laugh and an open demeanor, she seemed unnaturally quiet and withdrawn. She told Sonny that she held no grudge against Elvis. She regarded the whole incident as entirely her own fault.

The long postponed divorce was granted on October 9, 1973. Elvis and Priscilla appeared at the court in Santa Monica: When they left the judge's chambers, they posed, smiling, for the photographers, giving the impression that, as always, they were the best of friends. Under the new settlement, Priscilla received far more money than she had under the original agreement. She obtained in cash $750,000, with a commitment to receive another $1,250,000 in monthly payments of $6,000. Her alimony was increased to $1,200 a month but reduced from five years to one. The child support figure was raised from five hundred dollars a month to four thousand. Priscilla was also granted half the proceeds from the sale of the house on Monovale Road, valued with its furnishings at half a million dollars, plus five percent of the stock in two of Elvis's publishing companies: Elvis Presley Music and Whitehaven Music. As before, Lisa Marie was to live with her mother but her custody was to be shared by Elvis and Priscilla. Considering the fact that during this period Elvis's annual income rose to seven million dollars, this settlement is not notable for its generosity. On the other hand, its cost to Elvis in mental turmoil and emotional anguish was incalculable.

All of Elvis's intimates agree that the fatal decline that ended in his death began during the period of his conflict with Priscilla over her affair with Mike Stone. Up to the day when he was forced to recognize that his wife had rejected him for another man, Elvis Presley was riding high. He may have betrayed his talent or developed a soul-shriveling life-style or planted the seeds of self-destruction with his dependency on drugs, but the man's basic strength was still intact and capable of revival. Once he suffered the castrating blow of Priscilla's infidelity, he was like Sampson, shorn of his locks by Delilah. He could rage and bellow and threaten to shake down the world, but in truth he was the broken column. It took a few years before this blow registered its full and fell effect. Meantime, he was still free to swagger and posture and lord it as the King of Rock. In truth, however, he was like Eliot's Fisher King: a man who has suffered a crippling wound and is presiding over an emotional wasteland. Never again could he convince himself that he was what he had once been: a man who had never known defeat.

Had Elvis Presley been made of better stuff than comic-book fantasy and Hollywood heroics, the disaster of his divorce might have straightened him out instead of reducing him to a helpless infant. The strengthening that suffering confers on men, however, is contingent on their learning the truth about themselves and the world. No narcissist can ever afford to learn the truth about himself. That is the meaning of the ancient myth in which Eros goes to Tiresias to complain of his rejection by Narcissus and demand some appropriate punishment. Tiresias warns: "If he learns the truth about himself, he will die." Elvis Presley made sure that he would never have to face the truth about himself. He escaped into a cloud of unknowing called narcosis. Drifting back into a fetal Eden, he experienced that sensation of "oceanic" bliss that enables a man to imagine himself a god even as he is sinking into a condition more pitiful than that of any beast.

Elvis's decline into infantilism and drug invalidism had no effect on his popularity as an entertainer or his status as the King. One of the bizarre ironies of his career, always characterized by the incongruity between his limited talents and his limitless fame, was the way his myth imposed itself on the world in later years, mounting to ever greater peaks of popularity and power, while the man who was the object of all this adulation was steadily declining to the condition of a hapless wretch. Ultimately, the only way to account for this awesome disparity between cause and effect, between the moribund star and his immensely vital image, is to invoke concepts like royalty or divinity that explain how even a man so far gone that he can barely mount a stage can compel the admiration of millions of people the world around because they believe that in his grotesque body and deadened mind there lies some wondrous essence that gives joy to their own humdrum existence.

Chapter 33

Easy Come, Easy Go!

BY THE AGE of forty, Elvis Presley had earned a hundred million dollars—and was broke! The explanation for this astounding state of affairs is found in the deadly combination of profligacy and stupidity. Elvis operated always on the principle that "you don't come back for an encore." This great truth inspired him to become the world's foremost impulse buyer. The tale of his spontaneous extravagances is as long as it is bizarre. The fourteen Cadillacs that he bought in one night at Memphis, winding up the performance by inviting an old Negro woman who happened to be passing by to pick out any machine she fancied; the sudden mania to acquire airplanes—after a lifetime of being afraid to fly—which made him soon the master of a fleet of four multiengine aircraft; the disposition to set his favorites up in new houses, an impulse that was extended in the case of Linda Thompson to include not only a house for her but a house for her parents and a house for her brother—this kind of spending, though suitable to a prince, could only reduce him in the end to a pauper.

Spending money was something that Elvis did in a progressively more reckless and self-destructive fashion as he grew older, exactly as he increased the number and potency of his drugs. When he was young, as we've seen, he

was tight with a buck, like his father. Then, when he got
religion in the midsixties, he began to obsess about texts
like, "It shall be harder for a rich man to enter heaven
than for a camel to pass through the eye of the needle."
At that point, he started to indulge himself both in fantastic spending sprees and in spontaneous gift offerings
to the Guys. What characterized the final phase of his
money madness was the act of throwing money away.
Though Elvis never quite got to the final symptom of this
disease, the flinging of bills into the street, he came pretty
close. Consider two acts of extravagance from his final
years. The first is of the old self-indulgent variety, but
carried to insane lengths. The second is a perfect specimen
of spending as a self-destructive stunt.

On Lisa Marie's eighth birthday, February 1, 1976,
Elvis was entertaining at Graceland two of his favorite
law-enforcement officers: Ron Pietrafeso, an undercover
narc who was head of the Organized Strike Force Against
Crime of the State of Colorado, and Captain Jerry Kennedy
of the Denver police. Early in the evening, Elvis began to
describe to his men the fantastic peanut butter and jelly
sandwiches that he had enjoyed at a restaurant called the
Colorado Mine Company in the Denver suburb of Glendale. The sandwiches were fit for a king: a whole loaf of
French bread sliced twice from end to end, plastered with
rich peanut butter and oozing jelly and further larded with
no less than a pound of bacon. The most remarkable feature of the sandwiches was their price, $49.95, which is
why they were named, Fool's Gold.

As Elvis evoked these mouth-watering concoctions, one
of the Guys unthinkingly remarked, "Boy, I wish I had me
one of them now!" Instantly, a bell rang in Elvis's head.
It was like the fairy tale of the three wishes. You couldn't
voice a desire for anything in the palace of the rock king
without having your wish fulfilled. No matter how trivial
your desire or how great the cost of obtaining it, your wish
was the King's command. Leveling a heavy-lidded stare
at his subject, Elvis barked, "Let's go get 'em!" Next thing
the Guys knew, they were aboard the *Lisa Marie* heading
out toward the Rockies.

The owner of the restaurant was notified that the King

was arriving with a party of nineteen. Twenty-two massive sandwiches were prepared and carried out to the airport by the owner, his wife and one of their employees. A case of champagne and a case of Perrier were also brought along to wash down the sticky treat. Elvis's plane pulled up before a private aviation hangar at 1:40 in the morning and the food was carried aboard. For two hours the royal party munched peanut better and jelly sandwiches inside the royal coach, while Elvis showed off his guns, his belts and his jewelry. Then, the order was given, the mighty jet fired up its engines, roared down the runway, lifted into the night air and headed back to Memphis, a thousand miles distant. According to the reckoning of the pilot, Milo High, that mess of peanut better and jelly sandwiches cost the King sixteen thousand dollars.

During the same or the following year, Elvis found himself one night working a little town in North Carolina. He hated working such places, but as he deteriorated under the influence of drugs and began to draw a drumfire of savage criticism from the local press, his bloated appearance compelled Colonel Parker to carry his freak further and further away from the major population centers so as to expose him only to those people who wouldn't have cared if Elvis had come onstage trundling his belly in a wheelbarrow. The trouble with these good folk was that, though Elvis worked to them like a traveling evangelist, holding up his right hand as if "testifying" and bawling out spirituals, there were nights when they reacted much as had the very first audiences Elvis faced when he was just a lad touring the Bible Belt with Bob Neal. By this point Elvis was not like other entertainers, who must work harder when they encounter resistance in the audience. Elvis was the King. The King doesn't have to work to win an audience. Hell, it's the King's role to give audiences! So on this particular night, looking out into the house and seeing that he wasn't getting the proper adulatory reaction, Elvis suddenly called a halt to the show.

As everyone onstage looked on incredulously, the King waved in from the wings the royal goldsmith, a nondescript little jeweler from Memphis named Lowell Hays, who, like everyone else around Elvis, had gotten his foot in the door and found himself like a man with a winning lottery ticket. Elvis had commanded Hays to accompany his King on all tours, carrying with him at all times—on pain of banishment!—a box filled with gaudy but costly female jewelry. Whenever the spirit moved him, the King would beckon to his jeweler, survey the treasures in the box and make an appropriate selection for his favorite of the moment. In this manner in a few years, Hays sold Elvis $800,000 worth of jewelry.

Once the goldsmith had come out onstage with his box, an incongruous, almost invisible figure when standing next to his huge master, opulently attired like a great white carnival reveler from Rio, Elvis ordered the box opened, hovered over it a moment with his own richly jeweled hand and finally settled on a brilliant. "Lowell, whass' this I got heah in mah hand?" asks Elvis like a TV interviewer, tipping the royal mike toward the stage-frightened jeweler. "Elvis, that theah is a star sapphire with six baguettes in a white gold settin'." "What's it worth, Lowell?" asks the interviewer. "That one goes for thutty-five hundred dollahs, Elvis." With that Elvis turns around, a big grin on his huge egg-shaped face, and squinting into the stage lights, he pins a little old granny in gingham in the front row. Walking over, holding the ring before him like a butterfly, he leans over gallantly and, speaking into the mike, he offers the gem to the old woman: "Grandmah, I want you to have this now 'cause you remind me 'zactly of my own gran', Dodger, back theah in Memphis." With that, he hands the ring to the astonished woman—and the whole auditorium explodes in cheers, whistles, screams and applause. Now he's got 'em!

Another man would figure that he'd made his point. Not Elvis. The Monarch of Momentum, His Supremest Extremist, Elvis can't stop with just one spectacular gift. He has to go on and on, until he has emptied the jeweler's box—then, he has to give a royal command to fill the box again for further giving. At least $35,000 worth of jewelry was distributed that night to the first couple rows before Elvis would resume the show. Poor old Vernon, fresh out of the hospital because of a heart attack, had to be supported to the dressing room after witnessing his son's ultimate act of folly. It's easy to imagine what effect this story had on Colonel Parker; the old man must have chewed the tip off his cigar thinking what should be done before Elvis went completely crazy and gave away Graceland.

Though it probably wouldn't have made the slightest difference in the final reckoning if Elvis had earned ten times one hundred million dollars, the fact is that he earned far less than he would have if he had managed his money sensibly. If he had sheltered his income from the taxman and invested it intelligently, Elvis Presley could have become as wealthy as Bob Hope. That Elvis never had a tax shelter or an investment portfolio or even a pension plan can be laid squarely to the account of Colonel Parker, who dreaded the thought of some shrewd money manager sticking his nose into the Colonel's dealings with Elvis. So instead of making his money work for him, Elvis followed the advice and example of his manager and flung it all away. This infantile behavior he justified by insisting that any time he chose he could earn immense sums simply by stepping on a public stage. This was no idle boast, as Elvis demonstrated time and again during the seventies.

At the end of 1975, for example, the Presley finances were so depleted that the Colonel said their only hope lay in playing a long shot. Though never once in twenty years had they worked on New Year's Eve, this year they would do the unprecedented. The easiest shot would have been the Hilton at Las Vegas, which made them a handsome offer; but the Colonel was looking for megabucks. He found them way out in the sticks in Pontiac, Michigan, where there was a promoter eager to play Elvis in the arctic immensity of the 80,000-seat Silver Dome sports arena. Trying to fill such a house on New Year's Eve was an extremely dangerous maneuver: a bad break in the weather and the whole event would turn into an enormous fiasco. The ole Colonel was nothing if not a gambling man. He decided to take the chance. Gallantly, he led his forces into the far north, arriving in town early to direct personally the preliminary publicity barrage.

When the great night came and Elvis, fresh from buying everyone diamond jewelry for Christmas or giving himself some well-deserved gift, like a new four-engine plane, turned up in his Prince Valiant costume, the atmosphere was not exactly soulful. The Silver Dome is an immense color-coded, deep-freeze tank, with a flying saucer ceiling high enough to accommodate a fifteen-story building and acoustics comparable to the Carlsbad Caverns. When Elvis walked out onstage, he couldn't find his band. Casting frantic glances to right and left, he located the players finally, huddled a couple of stories below him on a platform so drafty that they were all wearing overcoats. As Elvis threw himself into his first numbers, standing all alone atop the towering stage, like an obese go-go girl, he experienced suddenly not that lovin' feelin' but the shame and terror of feeling a cold draft blow up his ass where his pants had split. Fighting gallantly to protect his endangered rear, he went on with the show, until the last volley of trumpets and drums. Then, he reeled offstage, practically screaming for his "medication." The following week, it was announced in all the trades that Elvis Presley had broken the record for "single date by single attraction" by grossing on New Year's Eve $816,000.

Such enormous earning power may appear to justify even the most reckless life-style. Its true effect was simply to draw Elvis even deeper into debt. In 1974, for example, he played the staggering total of 152 shows. Two-thirds of these performances were one-night stands, which meant that for most of the year Elvis was cut off from the comforts of home and condemned to live in the hotels and motels found in towns like Monroe, Louisiana; Auburn, Alabama; Hampton Roads, Virginia; and Murfreesboro, Tennessee. Considering the condition of Elvis's mind and body, this was a heroic effort. Nor did it go unrewarded. Elvis earned in this one year the stupendous sum of seven million dollars. A king's ransom! Yet it was not enough to allow Elvis to break even. At year's end, he was forced to tap his bank account for $700,000 just to pay his bills.

Where did all the money go? Precisely where it always went. High operating costs, including $1.7 million for the services of Colonel Thomas Andrew Parker, gobbled up four million dollars. Of the remaining three million, fifty percent went for taxes. Elvis's net income was a paltry

$1.5 million. Still, many men could scrape by on that sum. Not Elvis. In addition to his heavy nut, his basic living costs, he had incurred such extra expenses as his father's quarter-million-dollar divorce settlement, the cost of buying several multiengine airplanes and the sizable expense entailed in hiring a private gospel group (in addition to the one he used onstage) that would follow him around the country, adding its three voices to his in impromptu all-night sings. The bill for this extravagance was ten thousand dollars a month plus all expenses. Among the hidden costs of living like a king was an estimated half-million dollars poured out on the purchase of drugs and their transportation by an endless series of couriers from the Landmark Pharmacy in Las Vegas to wherever Elvis might be at the moment out on the road. Though Elvis bought his drugs dirt cheap at standard retail prices, his doctors were not so inexpensive.

All of Elvis's money problems reduced ultimately to his attitude: that stubborn and sometimes violent refusal to recognize that there were any limits to what he could spend. Elvis was confirmed in his contempt for reality by the Colonel. Like characters in an allegory, Elvis and the Colonel had become hypostatized ideas: Elvis the emblem of self-gratification, the infinitely indulged, endlessly spoiled child, who spends his life stuffing himself with goodies; the Colonel the grim, military personification of wordly power, hard-fisted manipulation of money and relentless day-and-night work. So caricatured did these identities become over a period of twenty years that Elvis and Colonel became like characters in an animated cartoon.

To the very end of the relationship, however, people in show business were saying that Elvis and the Colonel were the perfect combination. The Colonel had freed Elvis of all the time-consuming, bewildering and exasperating problems of business so that he could devote himself entirely to his art. Yet, when you're a commercial artist, as was Elvis, it's questionable whether there really is any difference between art and money because the art is done for the money and the money is the measure of the art. Though Colonel Parker insisted that he never interfered in any way with Elvis's art, the truth is that by managing Elvis's business as he did, the Colonel exercised a profound and decisive effect on Elvis as artist. Though he didn't tell the singer what songs to sing, he set him up in the music business in such a way that Elvis could not sing any song that was not offered to him by his publishers, who, in turn, confined Elvis to the kinds of music that they could obtain on their terms and actively discouraged him from reaching out for better music from sources that the publishers could not control. Likewise, though the Colonel never told Elvis how to read even one line in all his movies, by working out the formula for the Presley picture and by confining Elvis to such pictures throughout his film career, the Colonel destroyed Elvis as a film star. The division between art and business proved in practice, therefore, an unreal distinction.

Allowing Colonel Parker to take complete control of his career was not only ruinous to Elvis as an artist: It was just as destructive to him financially. For though the Colonel was highly ingenious in his schemes for making money, in order to maintain the control on which his own wealth depended, the Colonel had to keep Elvis perpetually in the position of the donkey plodding after the carrot. An Elvis Presley who had learned to make his money work for him or an Elvis Presley who had learned to live within his means would not have been an Elvis Presley whose life was in the hands of Tom Parker. Ultimately, therefore, Colonel's management of Elvis was self-serving, for the enrichment of the Colonel and his grateful business partners.

Like all hustlers, the Colonel distrusted everyone instinctively and assumed that everyone was on the make. Yet when the question of his own dealings was raised, the Colonel would climb up in the pulpit and start sermonizing about the sacred value of trust and how impossible it is to do business on any other basis than one of absolute trust. He would insist that his word was his bond. His handshake was as good as any contract, blah, blah, blah. This line of malarkey never impressed, one can be sure, such shrewd operators as Hal Wallis, Jean and Julian Aberbach, Hank Saperstein, Abe Lastfogel or any of the successful businessmen with whom the Colonel traded.

They recognized the Colonel for what he was and acted accordingly. The only person fool enough to swallow the Colonel's bunkum was Elvis.

Though he had every reason to be distrustful of a man like Tom Parker, especially in his later years when Colonel's addiction to gambling became obvious, never once in twenty-two years of professional association entailing hundreds of millions of dollars did Elvis Presley demand any general accounting from Colonel Parker. Undoubtedly, the mere suggestion of an audit would have produced a tremendous explosion of emotional fireworks by the Colonel, who would have retaliated by making all sorts of counterthreats, including the ultimate threat—and bluff—to quit. As Elvis was not the sort to suffer any sort of pain or embarrassment over a mere matter of money, he never made any such demands. Nor were his contracts, all of them personally authored by the Colonel, designed to provide for such a contingency. The first five-year contract with RCA had contained the standard clause stating that if no objection to the accounting were raised in one year, the matter could no longer be opened. The second contract, for seven years, executed after Elvis came out of the army, contained no audit provision whatsoever (though it did contain sizable payments to the Colonel for unspecified services). Ultimately, therefore, Elvis had to take everything on trust. Or to put it differently, Elvis got what Colonel gave him.

All that Elvis ever knew about his business was that every week or ten days a note would come from the Colonel's office reporting a sum or sums received from one or more of the great number of companies that sent remittances regularly to Elvis Presley. Numbers would appear, tagged with cryptic notations. Sums would be deducted for this or that reason. All Star Shows (Colonel Parker) would deduct its twenty-five percent or fifty percent—and that would be that! An accountant in Memphis would collect these statements every month, tote them up on an adding machine and use them to prepare tax returns. Oh, saintly simplicity!

After Elvis's death, the truth about the Colonel's management began to come to the surface, bit by bit. One day

in Nashville, for example, Joe Mascheo, who had worked
with Elvis for years as a singer in the Imperials but who
now held a desk job with BMI, took it into his head to
punch out Elvis's account on the computer. He was curious
to learn how many hundreds of thousands of dollars his
former boss had earned over the years in performance
royalties on the famous songs for which he had cut-in
deals. Imagine Mascheo's astonishment when the computer returned a list of twenty-seven songs, for which Elvis
was credited as coauthor, with the notation: "Not affiliated." Unable to believe his own eyes, Mascheo punched
the data back into the computer again. Once more the
startling line came sputtering out: "Not affiliated." Assuming that he had made a mistake, Mascheo now
punched in the code for ASCAP, the other major royalty
collecting agency. Once again the computer responded:
"Not affiliated."

This was amazing! Here was a man who owned a one-
third interest in many of the most popular songs of the
twentieth century, who had his name on the sheet music
and record labels of immense hits like "Heartbreak Hotel,"
"Don't Be Cruel," "Love Me Tender"—and he never received a nickel in composer broadcast royalties! Where
had all this money gone?

When the Colonel saw that Elvis was starting to break
down from heavy drug abuse, he determined to protect his
interests in every way possible. After all, the old man
hadn't spent a lifetime in show business without learning
what happens to pig junkies. He must sometimes have
been reminded of the fate of his old crony, Oscar Davis,
who booked Hank Williams for a New Year's show and
received delivery of a corpse. Oscar ended his days broke,
after having earned and gambled away vast sums of
money. For years before Davis died, Colonel used to put
a little check for his fellow player in the mail every month.
It was like a paper caput mortuum.

Two devices of self-protection lay in the Colonel's hands.
First, he could demand a bigger share of Elvis's earnings;
second, he could sell his interest in Elvis to another party.
The principal source of Elvis's income in the seventies was
his concert tours. In February 1972, Colonel had gotten

Elvis to give him a one-third commission on the profits of
these tours: "In consideration of the rendition of our complete organizing of tours, handling all transportation...tour
supervision, etc." In fact, what Colonel did was put the
tours in the hands of the well-known promoter, Jerry
Weintraub, who engaged Concerts West to do the real work
of running the tours. Colonel Parker's labors consisted in
little more than checking out the locations in advance and
increasing the number of radio spots if the concert was not
a sellout. Now, on January 22, 1976, he demanded for
these meager services a further increase in commission to
a flat fifty percent of the net profits for all tours, TV specials, merchandising arrangements, etc. By this point,
Colonel was close to the goal prophesied by the "overages"
agreement of 1967: a down-the-middle division of everything Elvis earned. As for Elvis, he was now sustaining
rank after rank of managers, agents, merchandisers and
promoters, like one of those circus strongmen with a pyramid of other men piled on his shoulders.

Now that the end was near, all of Elvis's jockeys were
maneuvering for a bigger share of the stakes. In 1974,
Colonel Parker set up a corporation entitled Boxcar Productions, which appears to have been designed partly with
the idea of giving his old guard a final bonus. To Boxcar
were transferred all the merchandising rights in the name
and image of Elvis Presley. The stock was divided as follows: Tom Parker, forty percent; Tom Diskin, fifteen percent; George Parkhill, fifteen percent; Freddy Bienstock,
fifteen percent; Elvis Presley—fifteen percent! How's that
for a deal? Not only did Colonel and his cronies take eighty-
five percent of the stock, but they also took substantial
annual salaries and bonuses. The Colonel's salary in 1976
was $36,000. Tom Diskin's salary as president was
$46,448. Don't get the wrong idea, though—Elvis got a
salary, too. He received $10,500.

Dumping Elvis proved a much more difficult and disturbing task than cutting deeper into his earnings. Inevitably, the Colonel's overtures leaked out, producing a rash
of stories in the press. An item in the *Nashville Banner*
was particularly disturbing because it quoted sources close
to the Colonel as saying that the old man needed cash to

pay his gambling debts (one million dollars in December 1976 alone), being no longer able to discharge these debts as he had in the past by trading off Elvis's services at the International. The Colonel threatened the paper's editor with a suit for defamation if he did not print a full retraction. The editor told the Colonel to go right ahead with his suit but to be prepared to see all his gambling records subpoenaed as evidence at the trial. That prospect silenced the Colonel. As matters turned out, Colonel discovered that his fears about Elvis's death depriving him of income were like the reports of Mark Twain's demise, "highly exaggerated." Elvis would die soon, but the event would only improve the Colonel's business.

Cutting into the dying King became the major preoccupation of every member of the royal court in the final years. One of the most successful petitioners for financial favors was the court physician, Dr. George Nichopolous. Elvis, it appears, could not deny his doctor any more than his doctor could deny Elvis. First, the doctor received the customary gift of a home, but it was a home on a much grander scale than was ever given to any other royal favorite, including Vernon. Three hundred fifty thousand dollars was the price of the doctor's new house, which in Memphis in the midseventies was a very expensive residence. Then, the doctor decided to join a medical group that built a $5.5 million medical center equipped with all the latest and most costly equipment. Again, it is likely he found support in his principal patient. The greatest boon the doctor craved, however, was something that had nothing to do with his personal comfort or professional practice. A skillful racquetball player, Dr. Nichopolous fancied himself as the man who would popularize this sport on a large scale in America and in the process reap the vast profits that belong to the owner of a successful franchise operation.

Presley Center Courts was conceived as a chain of fifty racquetball installations all across the country, with the pilot facilities being built in Memphis and Nashville. Associated with Dr. Nick in the project were a Memphis bond salesman named Jim McMahon, who was the only businessman in the deal, and Joe Esposito, who was cut in for a share of the business as a reward for his indispensable services to Elvis. The arrangement was that a contractor would build two courts for about a million dollars and rent them back to the corporation for $12,000 a month each. The basis of the whole undertaking was a commitment by Elvis to underwrite the project to the tune of $1.3 million in exchange for a twenty-five percent share of the stock.

The first problem arose when the Colonel got wind of the scheme and went crazy at the thought of Elvis lending his name to a commercial enterprise without a license being granted through Boxcar Productions. The real problem arose, though, when the corporation, which was badly undercapitalized, began to go broke during its first year of operations. As soon as the contractor began to get excuses instead of cash from the Courts, he went after Elvis. Boiling with rage, Elvis found that he had no recourse but to honor his commitment. He was forced to borrow $1.3 million from the National Bank of Commerce in Memphis, putting up Graceland as collateral. Joe Esposito claimed to have disassociated himself from the project, but the Guys learned that he had simply given his shares to Dr. Nick after signing a secret covenant that would assure him of his share of the profits if the enterprise were ever successful.

When the word got out that Joe Esposito was cutting himself a slice of the pie, the Guys got very upset. Joe made a lot more money than did Elvis's other men, and he enjoyed every sort of privilege and perquisite that went with being Elvis's right-hand man. Everyone was accustomed to this arrangement and accepted it because Joe was working much harder than any other man in the organization. Being underwritten in a business, however, was another matter entirely. This sort of provision raised the whole issue of what should be done for Elvis's other veterans, some of whom had been with him twenty years.

Money was not a major issue among the Guys until the final years. Elvis never paid any real wages, but it didn't matter when you were young, single, carefree, provided with hotel or house accommodations and free meals, driving around in one of the Boss's fancy cars and going to a party every night where there were ten times as many girls as there were Guys. Once the Guys became husbands

and fathers, however, matters took a different turn. The
salaries grew larger: Instead of something ridiculous, like
thirty-five dollars a week, which is what Elvis was paying
in 1960, he would give you in 1970 $170 and by 1976 $350,
tops. Still, with all the additional weight you had to carry,
it wasn't a very good deal. Okay, once every three years,
Elvis might drop a fancy car on you; but you had to go out
and sell the goddamned thing because on the money you
were making, you couldn't afford to run a Cadillac or a
Mercedes. Eventually, if you were really in good with the
Boss, you might score for a loan to buy a house or pay off
your bills. That was a once in a lifetime proposition, and
you wouldn't ever be allowed to forget it. There were bonuses at the end of tours and at Christmastime, but they
were always preceded by a period of extreme anxiety because if Elvis called the shot, you might get a couple thousand dollars for the holidays; whereas if Vernon, who hated
the Guys, cut the checks, you wouldn't get a week's salary.

It's extremely difficult to balance the accounts between
Elvis and his Guys because, on the one hand, the service
he demanded was so excessive, running even to the risk
of their lives, while, on the other hand, the generosity of
some of his gifts was so breathtaking that anybody who
complained would appear to be a monster of ingratitude.
Put it this way: The whole arrangement was a perfect
demonstration of how not to Take Care of Business. By
reducing everything to the language of love and personal
loyalty, while, at the same time, baiting his hook constantly with lavish material rewards, Elvis succeeded in
screwing up everybody's mind so badly that it would have
taken a professional labor relations mediator to strike a
proper balance between the equities. The only imaginable
parallel would be Howard Hughes and his Mormons.
Hughes paid his men about four times what the Guys got.

The greatest occupational hazard in being one of the
Guys was the continual stress it placed upon your relationship with your wife. All of the "wives," as they were
collectively known, knew that after they had been flown
out for opening night at Las Vegas or given a week in
Hawaii or been invited to a dull party on New Year's Eve
at Graceland, their basic job was to get lost. "Wives don't

go on tours": that so-called "rule" admitted of only one interpretation. Elvis was still intent on leading a bachelor life and sleeping around. The Guys were urged to do the same. The wives hated the system, and they hated the man who created and sustained it, Elvis Presley. The Guys were caught in the middle: They were the rope in the perpetual tug of war between Elvis and the wives.

Getting the Guys away from their women was one of Elvis's deepest, though least acknowledged, desires. Elvis was accustomed to being the obsessive focus of attention among his men. Any deflection or defection of sentiment was quickly detected and punished. Not that Elvis objected to his men marrying. Quite the contrary: He would pay for the wedding, stand for best man and even urge the couple to move in and live with him, as they might with their parents. But one thing is sure: No matter what feelings the man had about the woman he married, he still belonged to Elvis. That's why, as the years wore on, virtually every marriage in the Presley circle broke up, sometimes with dismaying consequences.

Alan Fortas's marriage was one of the first to crack. The problems were largely owing to the fact that Alan was always leaving home and staying away for weeks on end with Elvis. When his wife left him, Alan tried to commit suicide and was saved only by being rushed to a hospital in Los Angeles. Soon the other marriages were perishing of the same causes. Jerry Schilling was divorced. Lamar Fike's wife left him, receiving custody of his three children. Joe Esposito's wife, Joanie, went off on her own. Sonny and Judy West were separated for years. What a massacre! Yet what else could you expect? The kind of women the Guys were drawn to—ex-showgirls, actresses, dancers, etc.—were not the kind to sit back forever hearing endless rumors of the wild parties and capers in which their husbands were indulging at Las Vegas, Palm Springs, or wherever the party was that night out on the road. Even Vernon's marriage with Dee was a casualty of his prolonged absences with Elvis.

Eventually, Elvis decided to give all the Guys a slice of the pie. He gathered them together one evening and told them that he was preparing to make a karate film in

which they would all have parts and shares of the profits.
He also told them, individually, that they were provided
for in his will or by means of his insurance policies. Most
of the Guys at this point would have given anything to get
off the road and settle down with some little piece of income
property: a parking lot, a 7–11. The only one who had
managed his money shrewdly was Red West. He had a
little farm outside Memphis and a good working relationship with Bob Conrad, in whose TV series, *Ba Ba Black-
sheep,* Red performed with great humor and conviction as
the tough, redneck plane mechanic—thus demonstrating
that he was a much better actor than Elvis. Sonny West
had starring roles in a couple of biker movies, in one of
which he incurred very severe injuries. It wouldn't have
hurt Elvis to have exerted himself a little to advance these
men's careers after all the years they devoted to his service. Instead he resented their independence, revealed extreme jealousy at their relations with other stars or men
of influence and exerted himself only to get them back
under his thumb. Then, he fired them and threw them out
in one of the craziest and most self-destructive acts of his
final years.

The presumed cause of these abrupt dismissals, in July
1976, was the mounting number of lawsuits that were
being brought against Elvis by people who charged that
they had been injured by Presley bodyguards. In the most
notorious case, a California real estate man sued Elvis and
the Sahara Tahoe for six million dollars. He alleged that
after paying sixty dollars to a member of the entourage
to be admitted to a party in Elvis's suite, he had been
turned away at the door. Enraged, he had switched off all
the lights on the floor. That brought Elvis and his men
pouring out of his suite. According to the complaint, while
David Stanley and Dick Grob (one of Elvis's bodyguards)
held the man, Red West and Elvis beat him badly, causing
"severe laceration of his lips, loosened teeth, possible fractured jaw, injury to the left ear, brain concussion, etc."
Elvis eventually settled out of court for a sizable sum.

The irony of firing his bodyguards over an incident like
this one is obvious. For years Elvis had been seeking to
forestall attempts on his life by inculcating in his men a

passion for fast and violent action. He had armed them, deputized them and exhorted them to stop at nothing in their efforts to safeguard him. Once their zeal began to produce lawsuits, he swung the other way and started denouncing Red and Sonny for their violence. Ambivalence toward violence, alternately lusting after it and retreating from it, was characteristic of Elvis always. Now, in the last year of his life, Elvis decided impulsively that for his own protection he had to fire his protectors.

The firing of Red and Sonny (and Dave Hebler, a former karate instructor) signified the end of the Guys, the vital personal institution that for twenty years had been synonymous with Elvis and his life-style. The departure of the bodyguards had been preceded by the resignation or dismissal of Richard Davis, Alan Fortas, Gene Smith, Lamar Fike, Marty Lacker and all the others, save for Charlie Hodge, Billy Smith, and Joe Esposito, Elvis's factotum. The new men around Elvis were either his kid stepbrothers—Billy, Rickey and David Stanley—or his new bodyguards, Sam Thompson (Linda's brother), Dick Grob (a former Palm Springs police sergeant) and Al Strada (a former Los Angeles security officer). Now, the King's men were no longer brothers in arms but kids and rent-a-cops.[1]

Firing Red, Sonny and Dave Hebler without notice and just a week's severance pay (Vernon wielded the hatchet and said afterward that it was "one of the happiest moments of my life") was not only an act of injustice but an

---

[1]Elvis's treatment of his stepbrothers is one of the most shameful chapters of his life. Instead of treating these boys, all of whom adored him, as a father surrogate, insisting that they go to college or prepare themselves in some other way for the future, Elvis took them out on the road at an early age and systematically corrupted them. He employed Rickey Stanley as his connection for illegal drugs, a course that eventually led to Rickey's arrest for forging a prescription. Billy Stanley's marriage broke up after he discovered that Elvis had seduced his wife. David was encouraged to become a bad-assed hitter, a substitute for Red and Sonny. So deadly was Elvis's effect on his brothers that David was inspired to remark: "Rickey and I would have died if Elvis hadn't died first."

act that invited retaliation. In short order, the men made
a deal with *The National Star* to expose Elvis in a paperback book. They were promptly assigned a hotshot Rupert
Murdoch reporter named Steve Dunleavy, who concentrated on giving his exposé a sensational air. When Elvis
got wind of this deal, he began to get uncomfortable. He
offered to buy off the bodyguards for a hundred thousand
dollars. They stuck to their guns—in every sense of the
word. They were so concerned about the possibility that
Elvis would order them killed that they put in a safe de-
posit box a lengthy statement identifying their likely assassins and some highly damaging photographs and other
documents. Instead of hiring a killer, Elvis worked himself
into a murderous rage one night in Los Angeles and tried
to persuade David Stanley to go out gunning for Red and
Sonny. David, a tough, salty kid, ridiculed Elvis's macho
rhetoric and told him that Lisa Marie would be more
ashamed of a father who was a murderer than one who
was exposed as a drug addict. Elvis simmered down.

Elvis's prolonged relationship with Linda Thompson
also concluded in 1976. Linda had been everything to Elvis
that a woman could be for four and a half years: mistress,
mother, wife, sister, daughter and concubine. She had
demonstrated an extraordinary capacity to adapt herself
to Elvis's bizarre way of living and his extremely demanding and exasperating temperament. Inevitably, during this long and trying relationship, her attitude toward
Elvis had changed drastically.

Originally, Linda had been a stagestruck young woman
in love with a great star. She loved the touring, the elaborate and luxurious travel arrangements, the trappings
of the royal progress. Most of all, she loved her proximity
to the throne. Apropos of this period, she quotes the phrase:
"Power is the greatest aphrodisiac." If Elvis was like Jack
Kennedy riding about in *Air Force One,* Linda was
Jackie—and had the mountain of luggage to prove it! She
would come out in front of the stage at a concert for the
express purpose of signing autographs. She was in showbiz
heaven.

When, after the first year or eighteen months, Linda
had lived through her initial infatuation, she began to see

Elvis in a different light. She realized now that he was a drug addict, the most compulsive womanizer imaginable, a supreme narcissist and a man who was profoundly averse to marriage. She had also by this time established a friendly relationship with David Briggs, a tall, ordinary-looking Nashville studio musician who worked in Elvis's road band as a keyboard player. David offered Linda some of the attention that she was obliged to pour out day and night on Elvis. Gradually, Linda began to alter her relationship with Elvis to make it conform with the old formula: "romance equals finance."

Over the next few years, she acquired everything that she needed to make a fresh start. Elvis bought her an ugly new brick ranch house in a development near Graceland, and gave her $75,000 with which to furnish the place. She filled it with bright green shag carpeting and white garden furniture, including a white piano, giving the whole establishment the look of a California leisure house focused on a large outdoor pool. Linda accumulated a quarter of a million dollars in jewelry and had an extensive wardrobe of the kind of stagy clothes that Elvis loved, purchased at Giorgio's in Beverly Hills or Suzie Cream Cheese at Las Vegas. When Vernon beefed at her spending ten thousand dollars at a shot in a dress shop, she countered by protesting good-humoredly that she never had a chance to go shopping because of Elvis's schedule: The size of the bill reflected not her extravagance but the rarity of the occasion.

During her last year with Elvis, Linda obtained an apartment in Los Angeles and began to put out feelers for film and TV work. She was represented by Ed Hookstratten, and eventually, after the breakup of her relationship with Elvis, landed a steady job as a sexy comedienne on Hee-Haw. The best-educated person ever to survive in Elvis's company (Elvis once told a reporter: "I'm afraid of intellectuals—they bring dissension and envy and jealousy") and one of the most cheerful, Linda won the good will of everybody in the Presley family and entourage. She saved Elvis's life on more than one occasion and made extraordinary efforts to accommodate herself to his needs. Ultimately, however, the only relationship that any woman

could sustain with Elvis Presley was that of an infinitely
loving mother with her very sick and cranky child. Linda
played this role to the hilt, entering the hospital with Elvis
when he was drying out from drugs and lying by his side
night after night as they watched the babies in the nursery
on closed circuit TV. Even in the hospital, however, Elvis
always had someone who would smuggle him in some
drugs. Eventually, Linda realized that if she wanted to
have a life of her own she would have to break free of
Elvis's morbid grasp.

The termination of the relationship was not totally am-
icable. Elvis called up John O'Grady one night and told
him to throw everybody out of the house on Monovale
Road, including Linda. She, for her part, blew $25,000 in
a final shopping spree and then held Elvis to a promise
to send her on vacation to Europe. Taking along a girlfriend to keep her company, she went through another
$25,000 abroad. Alluding with a laugh to her $50,000 kiss-
off, she slaps one impressive hip and quips, "I hit him
where it hurts the most—right here!"

Chapter 34

So Shall It Be in the End

WHEN AN interviewer asked Ginger Alden, the woman Elvis was engaged to marry at the time of his death, what she felt on meeting the great star for the first time, she exclaimed: "Well, you expected trumpets or something!" It was true. By the end of his life, Elvis Presley was hallowed by fame and ringed with the nimbus of the superstar. Though the man was moribund, the Myth was vibrantly alive. Elvis could have echoed that Caesar who murmured at his expiration, "I feel myself becoming a god!"

Especially was the King awesome to a twenty-year-old girl like Ginger, who had grown up in Memphis. Almost as soon as she could walk, her mother had taken her to Graceland, where they stood outside the fence waiting to catch a glimpse of Elvis riding his big Palomino down the hill to the Music Gate to sign autographs for the fans. When Ginger was five, her mother brought her to the Fairgrounds on one of those nights when Elvis had rented the whole park. Elvis patted little Ginger on the head and took her with him on the roller coaster. It's not hard to imagine how overwhelmed she felt the first time she was

summoned to the King's palace. She went in the company
of her two sisters, one of whom, Terry, was the new Miss
Tennessee, and therefore a prime candidate to succeed the
old Miss Tennessee, Linda Thompson.

At the time, Ginger looked rather like Rita Hayworth
before she was transformed by the Hollywood image-mak-
ers: a voluptuous heart-shaped face with big sloe eyes, full
lips, a slightly cleft chin and a widow's peak: a sensuous
but slightly coarse beauty combined with a figure a trifle
too ample for current taste. When the King exercised his
right to the pick of the litter, he surprised everyone by
choosing Ginger instead of Terry. Doubtless he was impelled by her obvious innocence and naivete, qualities that
he prized above all in women. Having chosen such a young
and simple sweetheart, he prepared now to enjoy the kind
of pleasure that a rich, powerful and thoroughly jaded
older man can have with a silly little girl. No, he wasn't
thinking about taking her virginity or introducing her to
anything kinky in the way of sex or drugs; he just wanted
the thrill of "blowin' that child's ever-lovin' mind!"

On their first date, they took a spin out to the airport
in the Stutz Blackhawk. When they arrived at the gate
of Memphis Aero, Elvis inquired casually if Gingerbread,
as he had dubbed her, would care to go for a little hop
aboard his Jet Star. Naturally, she agreed. As they
boarded the big plane, they met Elvis's favorite cousin,
Patsy Gambill, Uncle Vester's daughter, and her husband,
Elvis's former valet, Gee Gee, as well as some other guests.
Just as they were about to take off, Elvis announced that
their destination was Las Vegas. Ginger was startled. "I
have to call my mother!" she gasped. "You can call your
mother as soon as you get there," replied Elvis smoothly,
while fastening his safety belt. Glancing anxiously about
her, Ginger observed that everyone else was laughing and
chattering as if they were about to go on one of the fun
rides at the Fairgrounds. Meekly, she submitted to her
fate.

Seated face to face with Elvis, Ginger noticed during
the course of the long flight that Elvis was examining her
on the sly. He'd sneak a peek, then turn to stare out the
window with a little smile on his lips. Puffing on a skinny

cigar, he seemed very much at ease. Sandwiches were
served. The plane purred along. Finally, the King called
for his makeup kit.

When he received the battered box, he rummaged in
one of the drawers until he found a little plastic cross.
Motioning for Ginger to bend forward, he looped it around
her neck. It was a worthless trifle that he had picked up
somewhere or perhaps been given by a well-wisher. Then,
groping inside another drawer, he withdrew a solid gold
bracelet and slipped it on Ginger's wrist. When she turned
it around, she saw that on its surface, picked out in glittering little diamonds, was the word "Elvis." Looking up,
she found herself staring directly into Elvis's blue eyes.
His sensuous lips opened, his famous voice murmured,
"This will show everybody that you belong to me." Ginger
was thunderstruck. She didn't dare to reply except to say
in her clear, musical voice, "Thank you."

When they arrived at dawn at Hughes Air Terminal,
they were met by a couple of limousines and rushed to the
Hilton. The next thing Ginger knew, she was alone in a
hotel room with Elvis, who gave every indication of being
about to retire to bed. At this instant, all the doubts and
fears that had been gathering for hours at the back of
Ginger's mind suddenly burst forth in a flood of anxious
questions and images. "Will he expect me to sleep with
him? Did he bring me out here just for *that?* What will
happen when I say, 'No'?" She postponed the confrontation
briefly by picking up the phone and calling her mother.
When she explained that instead of being in Memphis she
was now in a hotel in Las Vegas with Elvis, she anticipated
an outburst of anger at the other end of the line. Oddly,
her mother, after registering surprise, made no outcry at
all. When Ginger put down the phone, however, she was
trembling.

Elvis offered her a pair of pajamas and suggested that
she go in the ladies' bathroom and change. She noticed
that it contained an odd-looking fixture, which she sur-
mised must be a bidet. When she emerged, feeling very
vulnerable and uncomfortable, she found Elvis already in
bed wearing an identical pair of pajamas. He beckoned her
to his side. She slipped under the covers and lay there

rigidly. He extended his hand. She clasped it. She waited for his words, his touch. Finally, she heard an odd sound. Turning to gaze at him, she discovered that he had dozed off and was snoring, his hand still in hers.

That evening, they arose, dressed, ate a meal in the room and left again for the airport. Without going anywhere or doing anything or even popping a coin in a slot machine, they boarded the plane and flew back to Memphis. The next day, Elvis was scheduled to leave on tour. Ginger contemplated her strange experience as if it had been a dream. Now it was over, she thought. He had been "a perfect gentleman." She had been "honored by his presence and everything." She would never see him again. What else was she to think?

Just a week later, however, she received another call from Elvis. This time he was in San Francisco. He was dying to see her. She must come and see his show. He would send his plane to pick her up. Could she leave the next morning? Hastily assembling a few things and borrowing a "dressy" dress from Terry, Ginger suffered herself to be picked up in a big car, carried to the airport, put aboard the Jet Star and flown across country to Elvis. When she arrived at the hotel in San Francisco, she was shown to her room by one of the Guys. Unpacking was the work of a moment. She freshened up her makeup. Then, she didn't know what to do.

Through the entire afternoon and evening she sat in her room without so much as receiving a phone call. Finally, as the evening wore on, she began to get very hungry. She hadn't eaten anything since breakfast. Now she was starving. She knew she could order food from room service, but she was reluctant to incur the expense or charge anything to Elvis. She kept debating what to do until it got so late that she had to go to bed. Next morning, when she awoke, there was still no sign of Elvis. Now, she was starting to feel very uneasy. She wanted to go home. Where was she? What was going on?

Had Ginger known the answers to these questions, she would have been astonished. In fact, she might even have relinquished the idea that Elvis was "a perfect gentleman." What had happened was really quite embarrassing.

It was one of those *Box and Cox* farces in which every inveterate womanizer must some day play the foolish starring role. Though Elvis and Linda Thompson had concluded their relationship, Linda had turned up in San Francisco and spent a couple of days with Elvis. He knew she was leaving and was so certain of the day that he had arranged to have Ginger fly out on the same day in a revolving door arrangement that would protect him from even a moment's loneliness. When the time came for Linda to depart on the Jet Star, she insisted on spending another night in San Francisco. Elvis did not want to provoke a scene because he couldn't tolerate hassling. So there was nothing for it but to keep Ginger stashed below stairs in her holding pen until his penthouse suite was cleared of Linda. Someone should have been constantly checking on Ginger's condition, chatting her up, making sure she was fed, offering her excuses for the delay. Alas, there had been an outrageous failure to TCB. Hence, Ginger's weird welcome.

The morning after Ginger arrived, Linda took off with her baggage train. Her room, adjoining Elvis's, was given a fast but thorough going-over. Then, Jerry Schilling came knocking at the perplexed Ginger's door, telling her: "We're going to move you." She should have picked up the nearest heavy object and saluted him with a deadly blow. Being a nice obedient belle, about a hundred fathoms out of her depth, she followed her guide up to the floor where the group was quartered. Ushered at last into Elvis's room, she discovered him sitting at breakfast clad in a blue robe with a monk's hood and wearing sunglasses. He got up and greeted her warmly. He asked her about her flight, as if she had just stepped off the plane. Naturally, Ginger said nothing about the depersonalizing experience she had undergone during the past twenty-four hours, sitting alone in a hotel room without the faintest idea of what was happening. She must also have eyed Elvis's burnt bacon and Spanish omelette with greedy eyes.

That night Elvis was playing at Anaheim. He took Ginger with him in the limousine, but then he left her backstage while he put on his costume and makeup. As she wandered about, watching all the activity prior to the show, she felt again as though no one would come near her. No one would, in fact, until her status had been clearly defined. If she proved to be just a one-night stand, she would become fair game for the Guys. If, on the other hand, Elvis showed a real interest in the girl, she would become strictly taboo. When Elvis reappeared, he ordered a chair placed for Ginger at the edge of the stage, where she would have a perfect view of his performance. The Guy who brought the chair offered her a bit of advice: He told her that when Elvis went into "Can't Help Falling in Love," she should duck off and head for the limousine at the stage door.

Never once during the whole show did Ginger stop worrying about her cue. When Elvis finally went into his closing theme, she got down on hands and knees and started crawling offstage so as to present the lowest possible profile. As she was making her escape in this rather undignified posture, she was suddenly struck by the sound of Elvis's voice booming over the auditorium's sound system, commanding—*"Stay!"* Looking over her shoulder like a startled cat, she realized that he was hollering at *her!* It was another of those shocks that were now defining the rhythm of her existence. "I couldn't believe," she explains, still astonished, "that right in the middle of a big hit song he would say, real loud, 'Stay!'" The whole thing was so confusing to her that the moment Elvis turned his back, she slipped away and ran to the car. When Elvis joined her a little later, with a towel around his neck and his whole body steaming like a horse hot from a race, he was very annoyed. He chewed out the Guys, complaining that they hadn't kept Ginger onstage for the very last moments of the show when he did all his spectacular karate kicks and chops. Because they fucked up, she had missed the best part—and he had lost the chance of impressing her with his prowess!

There were other ways, of course, to "blow her everlovin' mind"; for example, the magic wand routine. A few days later, in Las Vegas, he decided to give Ginger the knockout blow. Picking up the phone at four in the morning, he called Gerald Peters. He told the imperturbable Englishman, long since accustomed to receiving bizarre

and oddly timed commands, that he must go forth at once
and procure for immediate delivery, that very day in fact,
a white Mark V Lincoln Continental.

Peters discovered the moment he set out to purchase
the car that the machine could not be obtained. Ford was
six months behind in its delivery schedule. Every deal-
ership on the West Coast had lone since been cleaned out.
As no true Elfan could ever abandon a mission on behalf
of his King, Peters got in touch with Ford in Detroit. He
threaded the office labyrinth and discovered the secretary
who was conversant with the delivery schedule for the car.
He begged her to tell him whether there were any dealers
in California who had just received white Mark Vs. She
told him that the information was confidential. He offered
her fifty dollars. She still seemed reluctant. Finally, he
pronounced the magic words—"Elvis Presley." Instantly,
she revealed the whereabouts of the cars. Peters located
quickly the last unsold car. Rushing to the showroom, he
wrote out his own check for $17,000 and drove the big
bomb off the floor and straight to the Hilton Hotel in Las
Vegas. Thus is served a king!

The punch line of the story is that after Peters had
driven the Mark V across country to Memphis the following week, he discovered that Elvis had already bought
Ginger another car. She had complained the Lincoln was
too big for her, so Elvis gave her instead a nifty little
Cadillac Seville, his favorite lady's model. What had Ginger been driving prior to receiving these biggies? Giving
you her blankest Candy look, she confides: "I had a three-
speed bike."

Even in Las Vegas, after having known Ginger for less
than two weeks, Elvis was hinting broadly at marriage.
He would say that when he closed his eyes, he could en-
vision Ginger in a white bridal gown. Ginger was startled
by these remarks. At first she thought, "Wait a minute,
this isn't right!" Once she got close to Elvis, her attitude
changed. Now she thought, "Hey, I really care for this
person!" Soon, she was studying ways to accommodate
herself to Elvis's strange life-style and make him happy.

She would read him to sleep in the morning or watch
closely while he made his preparations to go onstage. He

was very keen on having her study him. He would insist that she be present while he had his hair washed or as he prepared his throat gargles. Once he said to her: "I want you to watch carefully the way I walk." Then, he paced back and forth across the room. "Do you see anything special?" he demanded. Ginger didn't see anything remarkable about the way Elvis walked, so, just as a joke, she answered: "One leg is shorter than the other." Elvis threw a fit. He was outraged. Finally, he calmed down and explained to her that his walk was *"catlike."* Poor thing, she would never have guessed the secret word in a hundred years. In fact, to this day she describes the whole experience of living with Elvis by repeating constantly the same phrase: "I was in a daze."

Nine weeks after meeting Ginger Alden, Elvis decided that he wanted to marry her. Consulting the indispensable *Cheiro's Book of Numbers,* he discovered that the ideal moment for the engagement would be that very day, January 26, 1977. Clearly, some fast action was necessary because an engagement means an engagement ring and the ring that a king offers his bride is no ordinary ring. Around one in the morning, the King called the royal goldsmith to give him the order. As was so often the case, the royal command could not be filled in the allotted time. Elvis wanted a ring the size of the one he wore, which was eleven and a half karats, delivered to his house that very night. When Lowell Hays told the King that it was impossible to get such a big stone out of a jeweler's safe in the middle of the night, Elvis took the objection as a stinging challenge. After hours spent in terse, urgent calls of the sort you would make if your mother were dying and there was just one chance left in the world to save her but it demanded a coast-to-coast flight in an Air Force fighter with the serum in a special box that had to be kept at all times at absolute zero—after playing this game of phony crisis and long-shot triumphing over enormous odds—Elvis agreed finally to the sensible (and amusing) suggestion that he surrender his own stone and have it set as an engagement ring. Early the next day, he had the precious ring, which the jeweler told him was now worth about $70,000.

Having taken such pains to obtain the ring, Elvis offered it now in the most romantic setting imaginable—his bathroom. (Bear in mind that for Elvis, as for any junkie, the bathroom was the seat of countless blissful fantasies, like this one of getting engaged.) When the great moment arrived, Elvis played his part to the hilt. He seated Ginger in his black leather and chrome reading chair next to the toilet. Then he sank down onto his knees on the thick red shag carpeting. His speech was more touching than any he had ever delivered in his many movies. Never, he said, had he thought he would find someone so beautiful in his own backyard. Now, for the first time in his entire life, he realized what it meant to be truly in love. Other times, when he had been in love, he had been forty percent happy or even sixty percent happy; but this time he was one hundred percent happy. As he spoke, Ginger started crying. When he said, "Will you marry me?" she said but one word, "Yes."

Elvis reached into his pocket and pulled out the ring. Carefully, he fitted it on her finger. When he rose to his feet, he took her by the hand and led her out of the bathroom into the bedroom. There she found Charlie Hodge with Rickey and David Stanley. They all knew about the engagement. They offered congratulations and embraced the happy pair. Elvis was ecstatic. Ginger found that every time she raised her hand to look at her ring, the hand trembled uncontrollably.

No date was set for the marriage, but many plans were made. Among the changes that were destined to take place was another total renovation of Graceland. Elvis had already made some significant changes. Ginger had noticed that when she first visited Elvis, everywhere she looked in his rooms, there were pictures of Linda. Then she discovered that there was a small bathroom off the upstairs office that had obviously been Linda's dressing room. After Ginger returned from Las Vegas, all the pictures were gone and the bathroom had been repainted in Ginger's favorite colors. When she remarked on the changes, Elvis told her that Linda had put up all the pictures of herself while he was off on tour. He spoke of Linda as one aggrieved, complaining especially of the fact that she had asked him repeatedly to marry her. "I thought the man was supposed to do the asking," he grumbled. Now that he had the right sort of woman, his sweet Gingerbread, he wanted to proclaim her presence by constructing an art studio behind the house (Ginger dabbled in painting), as well as a movie theater that would have a dais with two thrones: one for the King and one for his Queen.

Ginger, for her part, was well pleased to become Elvis's queen. She says: "I came to feel that maybe that's why I was put on earth. If I could make Elvis happy, I would have served my purpose. He wanted a son. He wanted me with him night and day." This last desire was a demand that Elvis had made always of everyone who was close to him. Now for the first time in his life, it began to create problems. When Elvis asked Ginger to leave home and move in with him, she flatly refused. She justified her refusal on both moral and practical grounds. To her moral objections, Elvis had no real rejoinders; after all, he was the "perfect gentleman." When she argued that her constant attendance on him was unnecessary because he was surrounded by other people who could attend to his needs, he flared up angrily and barked: "Ginger, those people are not my friends! Do you think that if it wasn't for their paychecks that they would be around?" This statement shocked Ginger, who assumed, as did everyone, that Elvis regarded his men as bosom buddies. She refused to alter her stance, however, insisting that she had to spend time with her family and continue living at home.

This resistance might not have angered Elvis if she had not enlarged it to include refusals to travel with him on his tours or to his recording sessions. It was just after the happy time of their engagement that the first such disagreement occurred. Elvis was scheduled to go to Nashville to cut some records. It was an important date because RCA was clamoring for fresh material. Elvis made all the arrangements on the assumption that Ginger would accompany him. When she said that she hated Nashville and didn't want to go there, he left without her. By this point in his life, the prospect of recording disgusted him, which is why RCA could never get any new "product" out of its superstar. If Elvis couldn't sweeten the experience in some

way, he couldn't bring himself to make the effort. He
stalled the sessions for three days. Each day a large number of musicians and singers would gather and wait patiently for him, running up a good-sized bill for the company. Elvis remained sulking at his hotel, alternately
pleading with Ginger to join him or getting so whacked
out on drugs that he couldn't rise from his bed. Finally,
at the end of three days, he turned around and went back
to Ginger.

It was a pattern that repeated until Elvis's death. Time
and again this simple, modest, conventional girl brought
the King to his knees by refusing to do his bidding. At the
age of forty-two, Elvis was getting rejections from a
twenty-year-old girl who was his fiancée! The situation
enraged him so much that one night when she left the
house, he ran down the stairs after her brandishing a
pistol, which he actually fired over her head as a warning
of what would happen if she did not return. That night,
he got her back. On another occasion, when he saw that
she was getting ready to leave, he told David Stanley to
let all the air out of her tires. When she came back into
the house to demand an explanation, she found him hiding
under the bed and shaking with laughter. Asked to sum
up Elvis in one word, Ginger replies unhesitatingly:
"Headstrong!"

Not only did Ginger refuse to oblige Elvis on numerous
occasions—she even challenged his right to behave ca-
priciously at other people's expense! Just a week before he
died, in August 1977, Elvis announced that he was taking
all the kids in the entourage to Libertyland, the renamed
and refurbished Fairgrounds. When the great night arrived, Lisa Marie was visiting her father and there were
a number of other children present, including Ginger's
niece, Amber. Ginger and the little girls had worked themselves up to quite a pitch of expectation, when suddenly
it was announced that Elvis had canceled the plan. This
was the sort of killjoy trick that Elvis had been playing
all his life on the Guys. They had long since learned that
if you showed too keen a relish for a certain project, you
were courting a last-minute cop-out by Elvis. Anything
the Guys were eager to get, they kept at a very low heat.

Ginger, innocent of such wiles, couldn't understand what had happened. She marched into Elvis's bedroom and demanded an explanation. "Why aren't we going," she asked, quite reasonably. Elvis replied, "We can go another night." This was not a satisfactory answer—but when had the King been obliged to answer to anyone? Ginger, in an act of unprecedented *lèse majesté,* refused to take no for an answer. "Everyone's dying to go.... They're all ready.... Why can't we go tonight?" Now, Elvis was forced to offer an excuse. "Everyone out there has gone home already," he explained lamely. Ginger looked at Elvis in astonishment and said, "Elvis, I thought you once told me you could do *anything!*" After that challenge, there was nothing for Elvis to do but pick up the phone and order everyone rounded up again so that the canceled visit could be made that very night.

In July 1977, the first copies of the West-Hebler book, *Elvis—What Happened?,* started appearing in the jobbers' racks of drugstores, supermarkets and airports all over the country. For the first time in his long and carefully guarded career, Elvis was going to have his covers pulled. It was an ominous moment. Elvis was at his wits' end. One night he received a call from Frank Sinatra, who offered to use his "influence" to have the book quashed. Elvis had hated Sinatra all his life. Even in his moment of greatest need, he could not accept his rival's help. He declined the proffered aid. Meantime, he read the book in fits and starts, suffering agonies when he reached the parts about his reckless use of drugs. There had been rumors for the past few years that the federal drug authorities were going to investigate Elvis's doctors. In Denver, for example, some police officers with whom Elvis was hobnobbing picked up a prescription for Dilaudid in his hotel room and recognized that their honorary captain was a hardcore junkie. They offered to slip him into a sanitorium. Elvis left town like a bandit. Now, with this stuff coming out, how was he going to hold on to his connections? Night and day, he wracked his brain for some scam to take off the heat. Then, one night, he found the answer.

Chapter 35

One Last
Night of Fun

On AUGUST 15, 1977, Elvis Presley was preparing to depart on a twelve-day tour that would begin at Portland, Maine, and take him to Utica, Syracuse, and Uniondale, New York; Hartford, Connecticut; Lexington, Kentucky; Roanoke, Virginia; Fayetteville and Asheville, North Carolina; and home to Memphis for two final shows. Elvis awoke about four in the afternoon and called for his extra-strong, almost syrupy coffee. He ate no solid food because he was fasting to reduce his weight. As always his awakening was a slow and difficult process, a laborious reversing of the physical and mental machinery slowed virtually to a stop by massive doses of barbiturates and opiates. Eventually, he got out of bed and went into the bathroom to make that long and elaborate toilet that was designed to restore him, like a man taking rejuvenation treatments, to the image of youthful beauty and vigor.

By early evening, he had gone so far as to step out of doors, a thing he did rarely in his last years, where he watched Lisa Marie riding merrily about the back of the house in the specially built electric golf cart that was her favorite toy. The child had been sent to Graceland for a long visit by Priscilla, who was eager to cheer up Elvis and distract him from his worries about the book. For this last night at home, Elvis had planned one of his favorite treats: He had ordered that the Ridgeway Theater be reserved after the last show and that a print be obtained of his favorite recent movie, *MacArthur*. Doubtless he looked forward to the scene in which the great general, brought home in disgrace from Korea, stands up in the American Senate and delivers his eloquent farewell address, a speech that Elvis had memorized twenty years before and recited so many times since. Yes, Elvis was perfectly capable of seeing now a parallel between his own fate and that of his hero, MacArthur. They had both served their country with genius and devotion; they had both been acclaimed the greatest heroes of their time; and now Elvis, like MacArthur, was being humiliated unjustly by people who owed their lives to him. No wonder he was calling for this film again at this moment. It spoke to his condition.

As it turned out, Elvis was deprived of this last night at the movies. The projectionist said he could not work late, and no one else could be found to take his place. Casting about for something else to do, Elvis decided abruptly to see his dentist, Dr. Lester Hofman. Calling the dentist at his home after supper, Elvis explained that he was about to leave on tour and needed some last-minute treatment. Dr. Hofman, who had known Elvis for years and who drove a Cadillac that he had received from Elvis, made light of the inconvenience. He agreed to open his office for an appointment that night at ten-thirty.

Though Dr. Hofman did fill, according to his own account, an upper right first bicuspid and an upper left molar that evening, it is doubtful that Elvis's motive in suddenly seeing the dentist was purely medical. As the prescription records compiled after Elvis's death indicate, on this day Dr. George Nichopolous prescribed for his famous patient the following drugs:

Amytal: 100 three-gram capsules and 12 half-gram ampules. Amytal is a barbiturate which in high doses has a pronounced hypnotic effect. As it is not manufactured in ampules, the compiler of this record may have confused Amytal with Amytal Sodium, which *is* packaged in half-gram ampules and sold in boxes of six. Amytal Sodium is a very powerful drug whose proper medical application is in the treatment of grave disorders, such as convulsions, meningitis, tetanus or strychnine poisoning.

Quāāludes: 150 300-milligram tablets. Ludes are one of the most widely abused drugs in the world. Called "wall bangers" by the kids, they produce the slurred speech and loss of muscular control that were such conspicuous features of Elvis Presley's behavior in later years.

Dexedrine: 100 five-milligram tablets. These little golden "hearts" are the most familiar form of speed.

Biphetamine: 100 twenty-milligram spansules. This is the familiar "Black Beauty," a powerful amphetamine that is surpassed in effect only by the injectable varieties of speed, like Methedrine.

Percodan: 100 tablets. Percodan is another drug that has been used by heads for many years. Unlike the other preparations on this list, Percodan is a compound of five different drugs that act in concert to relieve pain. The principal ingredient, oxycodone, is a narcotic with effects similar to morphine.

Dilaudid: Fifty four-milligram tablets and twenty ccs of two-milligram solution. Elvis was furnished with the drug in both oral and injectable form. The solution was provided in a multiple-dose vial rather than in a fixed-dose ampule, thus allowing him to inject far more than the normal dosage.

Stockpiling drugs in this manner on the eve of a tour was standard practice with Dr. Nichopolous. The reason was simply that doctors cannot write prescriptions in any state but the one in which they are licensed to practice medicine. As this tour was of less than two weeks duration, the list indicates clearly not only what drugs Elvis was taking but the rate at which he was consuming them under Dr. Ni-

chopolous's supervision.[1] Actually, of course, Elvis had
access to drugs from many other sources, as no junkie ever
recognizes the concept, enough. Hence, the sudden inspiration to go to the dentist this night, otherwise a rather
odd substitute for an evening at the movies.

Elvis left Graceland for his dental appointment about
ten in the evening. He was wearing a blue jogging suit
with the letters DEA (Drug Enforcement Administration)
blazoned across the back. He was accompanied by Ginger,
Charlie Hodge and Billy Smith. As he drove out of the
Music Gate for the last time behind the wheel of his Stutz
Blackhawk, he was hailed by a handful of fans. One of
them snapped a picture that shows an obese and gross-
looking Elvis wearing his trademark shades and with the
hood of his suit pulled over his head.

Arriving at Dr. Hofman's office on Estate Drive in a prosperous neighborhood in East Memphis, Elvis appreared to
be in high spirits. "Isn't this an ugly girl here?" he jested as
he introduced the beautiful Ginger to Dr. Hofman. Then,
as she sat in the waiting room and the two Guys trailed
off somewhere, Elvis closeted himself with the dentist.

Dr. Hofman recalled later that Elvis inquired about the
dentist's wife, Sterling, and boasted of his new Ferrari.
When the session ended, Dr. Hofman made a request.
"Listen," he said, "next time you're going out to California,
I'd like to come. It would be a nice surprise if I could drop
in on my daughter out there." "Sure," answered Elvis,
"there's always room on the plane—you know that!"

When Elvis got back to Graceland, it was nearly twelve-
thirty. A small crowd of fans was still hovering around
the gate. One of them was Robert Call from Pierceton,
Indiana, who had come to Memphis with his wife and four-
year-old daughter, Abby, expressly for the purpose of taking pictures of the family against the backdrop of Graceland. As Elvis pulled up to the gate, Mrs. Call had the

---

[1]Dr. Nichopolous argued at a medical board hearing after Elvis's death that these drugs were intended for the whole touring
group but were prescribed for Elvis so that he would receive the
bill.

little girl in her arms. She raised the child to Elvis's car
window. Automatically he grinned and waved his hand.
At that instant, Robert Call, using a twenty-dollar Insta-
matic with a flash cube, snapped the last picture of all the
millions of pictures that were taken of Elvis Presley.

Back at the house, Elvis showed unwonted energy in
calling the men on duty up to his room and making inquiries about the arrangements for the tour. He was told
that every concert was sold out. The Colonel was already
at Portland, Maine, with the advance party. The musicians
were leaving after dark from Los Angeles on the Jet Star,
which would by captained by Milo High. Everything was
in order, as always. Everybody was taking care of business.
Elvis, for his part, had come up with a list of five or six
new songs that he wanted to try out on this tour. He asked
Dick Grob, the former Palm Springs cop who was now
working the security detail, to see if he could find the lead
sheets for the songs. As Elvis and Grob continued their
conversation, the topic of the recent press reports concerning Elvis's health and the shocking revelations in
Elvis—What Happened? came up.

Elvis was going to face the public for the first time on
this tour knowing that many of them had read this book
and were examining him for signs of drug addiction. He
certainly didn't look very well. Though he had been fasting
for the past two days, he weighed 255 pounds. His weight
troubled him so much that he had even told Ginger that
they should go to a fat farm, an idea that would never
even have crossed his mind in the old days. Still, he was
confident he could deal with the public. The trick was
simply to give them the kind of show that would make all
the ugly rumors look ridiculous. "Dick," Elvis said, winding up the conversation, "we'll just show them how wrong
they are. We'll make this one the best ever."

At two-thirty in the morning, Elvis called Tish Henley—Dr. Nichopolous's head nurse, who lived with her
husband in a trailer behind Graceland—and told her that
Ginger was suffering from menstrual pain. Nurse Henley
testified at a hearing after Elvis's death that she dispensed
one tablet of Dilaudid. Ginger recollects nothing about
suffering menstrual cramps on this evening or receiving

any medication. The little white pill went straight down
the throat of Elvis Presley. Scoring had such a good effect
upon him that he was inspired once more to take up his
favorite theme: his forthcoming wedding to Ginger.

Calling her into his office, where he had been watching
TV, he started building chapels in the air. He said they
should be married in a church of pyramidal design. (Charlie Hodge had gotten on a pyramid kick and persuaded
Elvis that such spaces concentrated precious spiritual
energies.) Though the wedding was going to be Elvis's
production, he said that he wanted the occasion to reflect
Ginger's tastes as well. For example, he wanted to know
what color she preferred for the limousines. Before she
could answer, he told her that he had some original ideas
about organizing the security forces so that they wouldn't
mar the appearance of the event. Then, at last, he came
around to the theme that obsessed him most of all: Ginger's
bridal gown.

Priscilla had offended Elvis with her gown. Impelled
by her crazy pinch-penny attitude toward money, she had
bought an inexpensive gown and fitted it with a train
herself. Elvis wanted Ginger to have the most magnificent
gown imaginable. There were certain features he described with such vividness that Ginger has never been
able to forget them. He told her: "Your dress is already
being made. I want you to have small rosebuds with gold
sparkles that will shine in the light. I want you to wear
glass slippers, like Cinderella. I..." "But, Elvis!" broke in
Ginger (who, as we have seen, was of a commonsensical
turn of mind), "they don't even have my measurements!"
Elvis smiled knowingly at this remark. "Well," he said,
"they'll just have to come here and give you a fitting." Oh,
he was high that night!

Finally, he disclosed the most thrilling idea of them all.
He was considering announcing their engagement from
the stage here in Memphis on August 27, the last night
of the tour. Ginger was breathless when she heard these
words. As she listened for further revelations, she was
surprised to see Elvis leap up and pace excitedly back and
forth in the room. Now he started explaining who was
going to be present at the ceremony. There would be many

famous people and public officials: mayors, governors, congressmen. Unlike the last time when he had been married by a judge of the Nevada State Supreme Court, this time he was determined to be married by a judge of the national Supreme Court. As that image flashed through his hopped-up brain, he exclaimed—"God! *It's gonna blow all this stuff sideways!*" Ginger couldn't imagine to what he was alluding, though he repeated the statement several times, like a man relishing a marvelous thought. Obviously what he had in mind was the ultimate riposte to the West-Hebler book.

Here these guys were saying that he's a junkie freak, an evil dude who lays around stoned out of his gourd blasting away at TV sets with pistols. *Then,* he steps out in front of his own people in his own hometown and tells them: "I'm getting married! Here's my fiancée!" Wow! Elvis Presley getting married! That announcement would blow any story in the world off the front page and set every woman in the country blithering and gossiping and crying like a baby. Then, as the capper to the whole scam, he would be surrounded at the wedding by public officials and police officials and all the straightest, strictest, law 'n' order ole daddies in the country, with a Supreme Court judge standing up there like Judge Stone pronouncing the vows. After a snow job like that one, who would ever believe that he was a junkie? Ha! Elvis hadn't spent a quarter of a century with Colonel Parker without learning a thing or two about manipulating public opinion.

As Elvis raved on that night, probably feeling the tongue-loosening effects of those big Black Beauties, he thrilled Ginger time and again with the sweet and sentimental things that he said. Just the other day, he told her, he had been talking with his father. Poor Vernon! He was so ill. Nowadays, the doctor didn't allow Vernon to walk more than fifty feet at a time. His health was very precarious. Yet, he was so happy with his new companion, a former nurse named Sandy Miller. Elvis and Vernon had been talking about Elvis's relationship with Ginger. "Does she do little things for you, son?" Vernon had asked. Elvis assured him that Ginger did. Then, they had drifted to the differences in age between Elvis and Ginger: Elvis was old enough to be his fiancée's father. Vernon had assured Elvis that this was no problem; in fact, if anything, the shoe was on the other foot. "What could a thirty-year-old woman do for you?" asked Vernon, adding before Elvis could reply, "What could a sixty-year-old woman do for me?" Gladys would have been sixty-three now, if she had lived; but Elvis let the remark pass. Then, his father had looked at Elvis and said something that when Elvis repeated it to Ginger thrilled her more than anything else he had ever said since the day he proposed. "You know what my father said to me?" Elvis confided with a radiant smile. "He said he had never seen me so happy as a man. I looked so happy to him, he said, that I reminded him now of that little boy he put overalls on back in Tupelo."

After this long and ebullient conversation, which had been practically a monologue by Elvis, he was certainly in no mood to walk in the next room and fall to sleep. In fact, he felt like going out and blowing off steam! Though it was four in the morning, the night was still young for Elvis. He picked up a phone and called Billy Smith at his mobile home out in the backyard. He told Billy to wake up his wife, Jo, and join him at once at the racquetball court; they would all play for an hour and have some fun. As soon as Elvis hung up, he started changing into his exercise suit and urging Ginger to do the same.

The racquetball court behind the house at Graceland is a monument to Elvis's last and most costly folly. Originally, he was interested in the game by Dr. Nichopolous, who urged Elvis to take it up as a means of conditioning his body. The spectacle of the physician encouraging his patient to exercise and then in the same breath agreeing to give him enough drugs to stun an elephant is one of many ironies implicit in this grotesque doctor-patient relationship. The building, a windowless cast-concrete structure of severe modern design, resembles from the outside an industrial structure or a coastal defense bunker. On the inside, it is a two-story gym. The approach is from the rear door of the house by means of a curved and covered walkway. Entering the building, you find yourself in a large space that resembles a lounge, with a bar to the right and to the left a piano, pinball machine, jukebox and sofa.

At the rear of this chamber is a sunken observation area with a long sofa that permits visitors to view the action on the court through a glass wall. Up the curving stairs that rise beside the bar is a second floor that suggests a health club, with a Jacuzzi whirlpool, steam room, showers and dressing rooms. A balcony at the back of this floor offers an overhead view of the action below on the court.

It was about four in the morning when Elvis emerged from the house, wearing a striped exercise suit and accompanied by Ginger, who was similarly dressed. Pointing off in the distance, he indicated where her future painting studio would stand. Then, entering the new building, he walked out on the court and began to play with Billy. As Ginger and Jo sat in the downstairs observation pit, Elvis and Billy banged the ball around the court. Elvis was still in high good humor, performing trick shots and showing off for Ginger's benefit. Every time he made an eccentric move, he would turn around to see if Ginger were watching; then, he would do something even more nonsensical. Unfortunately, the ludes, which he had taken a little earlier, were showing their effect; soon his coordination began to deteriorate. Finally, he took a mighty swing at a ball and struck himself painfully in the shin. At that point, he limped off the court and came back behind the glass wall to sit beside Ginger.

Once Elvis had recovered himself, he got up and went to the piano, where he started playing and singing an old country weeper, revived by Willie Nelson, "Blue Eyes Crying in the Rain." Then he mounted an electric exercycle. By the time the foursome left the building, it was about six and the sun was rising. Elvis and Ginger went upstairs, but he was still extremely restless. He had ordered the bed turned down much earlier in the evening. Mary Jenkins had removed the spread and laid back the sheet invitingly. Ginger threw herself on the bed at once, without even troubling to get out of her clothes. Elvis changed into a pair of blue pajamas and switched on the big TV facing the bed. He picked up a book on psychic energy but found that he was still not inclined to sleep. At six-thirty he called downstairs for his sleeping medication, and Rickey Stanley brought upstairs some Dilau-

did that he had obtained the day before by presenting one
of Dr. Nick's prescriptions to the pharmacist at the Baptist
Memorial Hospital.

Around eight in the morning, Ginger was awakened by
Elvis calling downstairs for more sleeping medication. She
assumed that he was nervous about the tour, as he often
was on the day of departure. Rickey brought up a standard
packet of sleeping pills that included Quaaludes, Seconal,
Tuinal, Amytal, Valium and a couple of Demerol tablets:
eight pills in all, a fatal dose for a normal human being
but precisely what Elvis took every morning before retir-
ing.

This morning, apparently, he feared that he would not
experience the desired effect because just fifteen minutes
after Rickey left his room, Elvis was on the phone to Dr.
Nick's office, where he found Nurse Henley. He explained
that he was going to have a trying day, what with Lisa
going back to California and his own departure imminent:
It was vital that he receive some extra sleeping medication
so that he would be equal to the day's demands. She agreed
to help him.

She called her husband, who was still at home, and
instructed him to take from the bag of medications that
was kept in the trailer two Valmid tablets and a "Placidyl
placebo." Valmid is a nonbarbiturate hypnotic, and two
of these elongated pale blue pulvules are a standard prescription for insomnia. Placidyl is another sleeping pill.
Dr. Nichopolous dispensed this drug in staggering quantities to anyone in the Presley organization who complained of sleeplessness. (Marty Lacker has testified that
between January 1971 and October 1976, he received from
Dr. Nick 6,464 doses of Placidyl, plus numerous other
drugs.) The drugs were given to Aunt Delta, who brought
them up to the bedroom and handed them to Elvis. Receiving these pills was the last act anyone in the group
witnessed Elvis perform, save for Ginger.

Groggy and nearly asleep, she saw Elvis pick up another book, this one on the interesting topic of the Shroud
of Turin, and start to go into the bathroom. "Precious, I'm
gonna go in the bathroom and read for a while," he ex-

plained. "Okay," she sighed, "but don't fall asleep." He
smiled at her and answered, "I won't."

What happened during the next six hours can only be
inferred from the position of Elvis's body when it was found
and from the results of the post-mortem examination. According to Dr. Norman Weissman, a pathologist at Bio-
Science Laboratory at Van Nuys, California, Elvis's body
contained at death fourteen different drugs, three of which
may have been produced by metabolism or interaction
among the other eleven. The drugs found and their sources
are as follows:

Codeine—(at a concentration ten times higher than
the toxic level)
Morphine—possible matabolite of codeine
Methaqualone—Quaalude (above toxic level)
Diazepam, diazepam metabolite—Valium
Ethinamate—Valmid
Ethchlorvynol—Placidyl
Amobarbital—Amytal
Pentobarbital—Nembutal
Phenobarbital—Carbrital
Meperidine—Demerol
Amitriptyline—Elavil (antidepressant)
Nortriptyline—Aventyl (antidepressant)
Phenyltoloxamine—Sinutab (decongestant)

This list suggests a pretty busy night. If one were not
familiar with Elvis's astonishing pattern of drug abuse,
the simultaneous consumption of so many drugs would
suggest a grave crisis or a bad breakdown. Actually, the
volume was probably only a little greater than was customary for Elvis. The enormous quantity of codeine, for
example, is easily accounted for by the enormous tolerance
of opiates which Elvis had developed after so many years
of addiction. Far from seeing these drugs as evidence of
suicidal despair, one should regard them as evidence of
reckless overconfidence. If Elvis's last night were any different from other nights that preceded it, the difference
would have to be ascribed to higher not lower spirits. Elvis

died as he had lived, pleasuring himself bountifully and anticipating future triumphs.

Around two in the afternoon, Ginger awoke in the big bed, still wearing her exercise suit. It didn't surprise her that Elvis was not at her side. For all she knew, he had gone downstairs or even left the house. The only thing that occupied her mind was the thought that within a matter of hours she would be leaving to go on the tour. Suddenly, it occurred to her to call up David Stanley's girlfriend, Cindy Mies, and find out if she were going, too. The girls chatted briefly, and Ginger learned that Cindy had been invited to make the trip. That pleased Ginger because she would have another young woman to keep her company. Then, she called her mother to say that she was coming home directly. Only after she had been on the phone for a quarter of an hour did it occur to her that Elvis might still be in the bathroom.

Getting out of bed she crossed the room and knocked on the door. "Elvis?" she called. Getting no response, she knocked again and again. Unlike Linda Thompson, who would have barged right in to check on Elvis, Ginger was reluctant to violate his privacy. Finally, she opened the door and peeped inside. What she saw was Elvis doubled up face down on the floor, with his buttocks elevated, in the fetal position. Clearly, he had been sitting in the black leather and chrome chair reading and had toppled forward onto the floor. The book was still lying on the chair. In falling, his head had struck a hair dryer that someone had left on the floor. If it had been anyone else Ginger had found in this condition, she might have been alarmed. With Elvis, this kind of thing was normal. He was always dropping off abruptly from the effects of his sleeping potions and landing head first in the most unlikely places. Ginger hated to see him in these grotesque positions, but there wasn't any reason to panic.

Walking over to him, Ginger called, "Elvis!" Then, suddenly, she began to feel alarmed. The thought crossed her mind that he might have struck his head in the fall and injured himself. She reached down and touched him. He was as cold as ice. Again, this was typical. Sleeping for hours without stirring in a room whose temperature had

been forced down twenty degrees by a powerful air con-
ditioner, Elvis often felt icy to the touch. Finally, Ginger
knelt down and turned Elvis's head around so she could
see his face. Now, for the first time, she was gripped by
terror. Elvis's face had become a grotesque mask, purple
with engorged blood, his teeth set in his lolling tongue.
Trembling, she raised one of his closed eyelids. The eye
was blood red and motionless. The thought that Elvis was
dead never once entered Ginger's mind. She was certain
that he had collapsed from the medication and struck his
head on the floor. He had injured himself. But he was
certainly still alive.

Standing up again, she reached for the phone next to
the toilet. She pressed the button for the kitchen and heard
the voice of the cook, Pauline. "Who's on duty?" Ginger
asked anxiously. When she heard it was Al Strada, she
said, "Would you tell Al to come up here really quick?"
Then, she started out of the room to meet Al coming up
the stairs.

Now she was convinced that something was terribly
wrong, but the thought of death had still not forced itself
into her mind. Al came running up the steps, where Ginger
met him as she came down. "I think something's really
wrong with Elvis!" she blurted out. "Come and look at
him!" Al didn't speak a word. He took one look at Elvis;
then he said, "Let me get Joe up here." Picking up the
phone, he called downstairs. Joe had just arrived at the
house to supervise the departure for the tour. He charged
up the stairs and came hustling into the bathroom.

Having been through this business so many times before, Joe knew exactly what to do. First, he turned Elvis
over on his back. As he did so, he heard a sighing sound
that convinced him that Elvis was still breathing. Turning
the body over, however, produced a grotesque sight. The
legs remained rigidly flexed at the knees. It looked as
though Elvis were trying to touch his chin with his kneecaps. Ginger had never heard of rigor mortis. She stood
there marveling at the odd position of her lover's legs. Joe
reacted very differently. He leaped up and grabbed the
phone. Punching into an outside line, he tapped out the
emergency number. Talking rapidly to the dispatcher, he

explained that someone was having great difficulty
breathing at 3764 Elvis Presley Boulevard. He told the
dispatcher to tell the ambulance driver to come straight
through the gates and drive up to the front door of the
house. The name of the victim was never mentioned.

A minute later, Unit Six of the Memphis fire department emergency division got the call. Charles Crosby and
Ulysses Jones started racing toward Graceland at 2:33 P.M.
Though all they had was the address, they knew it was
Graceland. In fact, they had an idea who it was they were
supposed to succor. Once before they had been summoned
to the house to rescue Vernon Presley, who was succumb-
ing to a heart attack. They had rushed the old man to the
hospital and saved his life. Trained paramedics, the men
were prepared to find the same situation and apply the
same remedy: CPR (cardiopulmonary resuscitation).

Meantime, at the house, Joe was down on his knees
giving Elvis mouth to mouth resuscitation or, alternately,
pounding on his chest, while Al Strada stood at the phone
making call after call for help. The first person called was
Dr. Nick, who was at Doctors' Hospital, five miles distant.
The operator informed Strada that she would page the
doctor by beeper. She advised him to keep a phone line
open. Then Strada called Dr. Perry Holmes, a local physician in Whitehaven, whom they used sometimes for minor complaints. Learning that Dr. Holmes was also out of
the office, Strada slammed down the phone. Moments
later, Dr. Holmes's associate, Dr. James Campbell, was
told of the call by his receptionist. He called Graceland
and got Aunt Delta. She told him that her nephew was
experiencing some difficulty breathing. She asked the doctor if he could come to the house immediately. He suggested that they bring Elvis to his office.

By this time, everyone at Graceland was crowding into
the bathroom in a vain effort to save Elvis. Charlie Hodge
arrived and started shouting, "Breathe, Elvis, breathe!"
Aunt Delta fell on her knees to continue the mouth-to-
mouth resuscitation. Then Vernon, desperately infirm and
barely able to climb the stairs, came gasping into the room.
At the first sight of Elvis, he started wailing: "Son, don't
die! Son, don't leave!" Ginger was wandering around in a

daze when she heard Lisa's voice, as the child climbed the stairs to the second floor. As Ginger rushed to the bedroom door to intercept her, Lisa yelled, "What's wrong?" "Nothing!" cried Ginger, reaching down to seize the child. "Something's wrong with Daddy and I'm going to find out!" shouted the little girl. Then she darted around the other end of the landing to enter the bathroom from the opposite side. "Al!" shouted Ginger, "Lisa's trying to get in!" Strada swiftly threw the lock on the bathroom door.

Suddenly, the two paramedics burst upon the scene, having dashed up the stairs unheard by the people in the bathroom. Pushing away the dozen people who had squeezed into the room, the firemen looked down and saw a man who was so disfigured that neither of them recognized the most famous man in Memphis. Ulysses Jones recalls that this totally unfamiliar-looking man was "clothed in pajamas—a yellow top and blue bottoms. From his shoulders up, his skin was dark blue. Around his neck, which seemed fat and bloated, was a very large gold medallion. His sideburns were grey. I knelt down and checked the pulse and shined a light in his eyes. There was no reaction. No pulse. No flicker from the eyes. He was cold, unusually cold. The people around me were weeping. 'Is there anything you can do?' they cried. I couldn't give them an answer. Suddenly a young man [David Stanley] blurted out, 'I think he ODed.' It was the second time that an overdose was mentioned. The first time was at the door of the house where a guard had said, 'He's upstairs and I think it's an OD.' I inserted an airway tube into his throat and gave the nearest man a squeeze bag for pumping air into his lungs." The other paramedic, Charles Crosby, recalls: "It took five of us to lift him onto a stretcher. He must have weighed two hundred fifty pounds. The pajama top was unbuttoned all the way down, and I could see the great big rolls of fat on his belly. It looked like he had been dead for at least an hour."

As the men jockeyed the stretcher around the corners and down the stairs, feeble, emaciated old Vernon tried to follow, crying and calling: "Son, I'm coming.... I'll be there.... I'll be meetin' you there!" Two of the Guys had to forcibly restrain Vernon, who could have dropped dead of a heart attack at any moment.

Just as the ambulance was preparing to roll down the driveway, Dr. Nick came racing up to the house. He had spoken to Joe just after the paramedics had arrived and been told that Elvis was still breathing. Now, he climbed into the ambulance and started massaging Elvis's heart. At 2:48 the ambulance cleared the gates of Graceland and took off at speeds that reached eighty m.p.h. for Baptist Memorial Hospital. All through the incredibly swift seven-minute trip, Nichopolous kept shouting: "Breathe, Elvis ... come on, breathe for me!" Said Jones: "All the way to the hospital, the doctor had this look of sheer disbelief that this could have happened to Elvis."

At the hospital's communications center, a call was received now from the speeding ambulance: "Have a white male, approximately forty, under CPR, no response." Immediately, a summons sounded from every loudspeaker in the building: "Harvey Team report to E.R. [Emergency Room]...Harvey Team report to E.R....Harvey Team report to E.R." Harvey Teams are groups of emergency specialists who literally come running the moment the arrival of a critically injured or dying patient is announced.

Elvis was borne into Trauma Room Number One, a small operating theater, and laid out naked on a surgical table. Instantly, his body was covered with monitoring electrodes, as the doctors and technicians struggled to revive him with oxygen, mechanical respiration and injections of powerful stimulants. For nearly half an hour they worked on him but all their labors were in vain. Finally, they abandoned the effort and classified the case as a DOA: dead on arrival.

All this while, Joe Esposito, David Stanley and Maurice Elliott, the vice president of the hospital and its principal public relations officer, waited for word in an adjoining emergency room. Finally, at three P.M., the door to Room Number One opened and out came Dr. Nick, with his head hanging. Looking up at Joe Esposito, the white-haired Nichopolous said, "There is nothing we can do . . . we tried." Then, as his eyes began to water, he herded everyone out of the room, turning to close it behind him as if he were sealing up a tomb. Ten minutes later a nurse emerged carrying a bag which contained Elvis's necklace, rings, bracelet and pajamas. She gave the bag to Nichopolous. Now, it was his painful duty to break the news to the family. This was not just a task that was hard to perform for emotional reasons: There was a distinct possibility that the news might kill Vernon Presley. Nichopolous persuaded the two paramedics who brought Elvis into the hospital to drive him back to Graceland and stand by until it was clear that Vernon would survive the shock of his son's death.

Once the ambulance had left Graceland, Vernon, Sandy, Aunt Delta, Aunt Nashville, and some members of the staff drifted into Minnie Mae's room where they began to pray for Elvis. Ginger had felt she should ride in the ambulance with Elvis to the hospital, but before she could gather up her resolution to go, the door slammed shut. Suddenly, she felt that she had been shut out of his life. "I never felt so alone in my life," she recalls. Then Aunt Nashville put her arms around Ginger and sought to comfort her. "He's going to be all right," she soothed. "He's got so much to live for." Ginger felt so much better at this moment that she was impelled to comfort someone else. She thought of Lisa and went upstairs to find the child. Entering the little girl's room, Ginger said, "Lisa, your daddy's gonna be okay." Lisa was easily persuaded that there was nothing to fear. Soon she was chasing merrily from room to room, playing with Amber.

Now Ginger went downstairs and while she was standing in the parlor, Dr. Nick walked into the house flanked by the two paramedics. He didn't say a thing. The moment Vernon, who was seated in a chair, caught sight of the bag in the doctor's hand, he fell backward, crying, "Oh, no, no! I know he's gone!" Nichopolous was virtually speechless. "I'm sorry," he murmured, but his words were drowned out by the wail that went up from everyone in the house. Screams, cries, moans and curses filled the air. Suddenly, people started running aimlessly in every direction. Little Lisa was beside herself, crying, "My daddy is gone! I can't believe my daddy is gone!" Before anyone could reach her, she dashed halfway up the stairs toward her room. Then she darted back down again and ran into the kitchen. A second later she came tearing back into the drawing room. Vernon was sobbing and shaking in every limb. Nichopolous got the old man to his feet and led him slowly into the kitchen. Ginger recalls staring out the back window toward the pasture. "It was like all the leaves were dying," she recalls. "It was weird...like everything died." She kept saying to herself, "No, no!" Finally, Dr. Nick came back into the parlor and signed to the paramedics that they could leave. Then, he picked up a phone and called Maurice Elliott. It was time that the announcement be made to the public.

By the time Maurice Elliott got the go-ahead from Dr. Nichopolous, the hospital had been laid under siege by the press corps. Word of the crisis had spread from the reporters who routinely monitor police and fire emergency calls. Then the rumors had begun to fly. Elliott had stalled the press, saying that Elvis was having difficulty breathing. Now, at last, he could disclose the truth. Joe Esposito, who had been closeted during this time in Elliott's office, making calls to the Colonel and Tom Huelett of Concerts West, was asked if he would like to make the announcement. He said he couldn't face the press. It now became Maurice Elliott's duty. He called in the reporters and told them that Elvis had been pronounced dead at three-thirty, apparently from heart failure. He stressed, however, that nothing official would be forthcoming until that evening, when a press conference would be called to release the results of an autopsy.

The autopsy is a traditional ritual of royalty. At the French court, whenever a member of the ruling family died, the other members would assemble in the bedchamber, just as they would for a birth, to witness the court physician dissect the body, each organ being plopped into a fine silver bowl. The reason for this practice lay in the fear of poisoning, which, strange to say, was precisely what Vernon Presley believed was the cause of Elvis's death. Actually, Vernon knew as well as anyone in the inner circle that his son was a confirmed drug addict. The staff of Baptist Memorial Hospital knew a great deal about

Elvis's addiction because he had gone there several times to kick his habit, his most recent stay being in April. Their knowledge was shared undoubtedly by the Memphis Medical Examiner, Dr. Jerry Francisco, whose responsibility it was now to establish the cause of this sudden death in a relatively young man.

Within an hour of Elvis's death, his body was brought into the hospital morgue, where an unusually large number of people were present, including as many as eight pathologists. Though autopsies are usually conducted by one forensic pathologist and an assistant, in this case the combination of curiosity coupled with the desire to have every detail witnessed and verified as a protection against charges of carelessness or unprofessional conduct produced an extraordinary multiplication of medical men, as it did also of laboratory reports and independent analyses of the findings. It is one of the great ironies of Elvis Presley's life that his death, which was the subject of intense scientific scrutiny, should have been enveloped in the same cloud of mystery that long enshrouded his birth.

Elvis's body was laid out on a stainless steel table, equipped with a sink and drains, under a battery of powerful lights similar to those used in operating rooms. The autopsy was conducted by Dr. Eric Muirhead, chief of the department of pathology. Dressed in a gown with a plastic protective apron and flanked by his assistant, notebook in hand, the pathologist commenced the process by examining carefully the surface of the body, which he would have found pitted with countless needle marks. Under the skin he would have found traces of the hematomas produced by earlier injections. Once every detail of the surface had been noted, the internal examination commenced.

The procedure is to make a Y incision: two long cuts from the shoulders down to the belly button and then a single incision down the abdomen to the pubis. The skin is then lifted back and secured so that the pathologist can examine the underlying tissues and muscles. Next the rib cage is cut with a saw so that the chest plate can be removed, exposing the heart and lungs. Each major organ is examined, removed and weighed. Slices of the liver and kidneys are taken and put into bottles filled with pre-

servatives for microscopic examination and chemical analysis in the toxicology laboratory: Elvis's heart was found
to be enlarged, his arteries somewhat clogged and his
liver—the organ most affected by drug abuse—so diseased that it looked exactly like pâté de foie gras.

After opening the stomach and examining its contents
(which would normally have included some half-dissolved
pills[2]) samples are taken of the blood, blood serum, urine,
spinal fluid and bowel contents. The final task is the examination of the brain. The scalp is cut and pulled both
backward over the nape of the neck and forward over the
face to expose the surface of the skull. The entire top of
the head is then cut off with a power saw, which sends
puffs of dust into the atmosphere, against which the operators protect themselves by donning face masks. When
the top of the skull is lifted off like a bowl, the brain
beneath is examined and then scooped out for sampling
and sectioning.

When every part and organ of the body has been exhaustively examined, the three-hour procedure terminates
with the remains of the brain being put back inside the
skull and the internal organs gathered in a bag and stuffed
back inside the body cavity, which is then stitched up.
Encased in a paper shroud, the corpse of Elvis Presley was
now ready for the embalmer and the cosmetician.

At the same time that Elvis was being cut up in Memphis, he was being repackaged in New York. Colonel Parker received Joe Esposito's announcement that Elvis was
dead in his hotel suite at Portland, Maine. After a brief
conversation, the Colonel slumped for a few minutes in
his chair. Then he called Vernon Presley at Graceland.
Colonel told Vernon that it was vital they act immediately
to protect their own and Lisa Marie's interests. What concerned the Colonel especially was the prospect of a wild
exploitation of Elvis's name and image by a horde of un-

[2]The gut-paralyzing effect of opiates greatly retards digestion,
which is one of the reasons why drugs ingested by mouth are so
slow to produce their effects in addicts.

authorized souvenir and paraphernalia manufacturers and merchants.

As soon as the Colonel received Vernon's permission to carry on, the canny old man put into effect a long-meditated plan. Getting in touch that very afternoon with Harry "The Bear" Geissler, president of Factors, Inc., a merchandising company whose hottest item was a Farrah Fawcett-Majors T-shirt, the Colonel commenced the negotiations that concluded two weeks later with Factors obtaining exclusive rights to the Presley merchandising in exchange for a $150,000 guarantee and a sizable royalty on every item sold. Colonel chose Geissler, it has been said, because Factors had once been forced to pay one hundred thousand dollars in damages as a merchandising bootlegger. Operating on the principle that it takes one to know one, the Colonel reasoned that Geissler, whose contract obliged him to prosecute bootleggers, would be the ideal man to police the Presley market.[3]

It is highly significant that the contract with Factors was negotiated by Colonel Parker not on behalf of the Presley Estate but with his company, Boxcar, Inc. The deal Colonel made with Vernon Presley provided for two fifty-fifty splits: half of the income received by Boxcar would be paid to Colonel Parker as manager; the other half would be divided equally between Boxcar and the Estate. The upshot of this arrangement was that Colonel and his men obtained *seventy-five percent* of the merchandising income. Another oddity of the deal was the ten percent off-the-top commission given to William Morris, an immense sum of money that Colonel characterized later as a "finder's fee."

At eight o'clock the night of Elvis's death, the medical examiner and Dr. Nichopolous held a press conference to disclose the gross findings of the autopsy. Dr. Francisco said that the death appeared to have been caused by "car-

---

[3]Two months after Colonel signed with Geissler, the FBI received a tip that Factors had defrauded three of its licensors of a substantial sum in royalties. The company pled guilty to three counts of mail fraud.

diac arrythmia," or, in plain English, an erratic heartbeat. Asked to elaborate, the coroner averred: "There was severe cardiovascular disease present. He had a history of mild hypertension and some coronary artery disease. These two diseases may be responsible for cardiac arrhythmia, but the precise cause was not determined. Basically, it was a natural death. It may take several days, it may take several weeks to determine the cause of death. The precise cause of death may never be discovered." Strike "discovered" and substitute "disclosed," and this statement becomes a prophetic utterance.

Chapter 36

Sixteen Coaches Long

LESS THAN an hour after the announcement that Elvis was dead, a thousand people had gathered at the Music Gate. An hour later, the crowd had swollen to three thousand. By the following afternoon, when the gates were opened to allow mourners to view the body, twenty thousand souls had lined up along Elvis Presley Boulevard. The great stationary parade stretched back for nearly a mile. As it began to shuffle forward, fresh arrivals appeared at the end of the line. No matter how many people passed through the gates and mounted the driveway and entered the house, there were just as many who arrived at that moment a mile distant to take their places. When the gates were finally forced shut at six-thirty that evening, eighty thousand men, women and children had come to pay their respects to the King.

Many of these people came from afar. The newsmen arrived first, pouring off the planes at Memphis Airport, dressed in khakis and toting their gear like combat troops going into action. They were followed by waves of fans, who took off from all over the world in a wild lemming rush to Memphis. Some of the faithful were so distraught that they abandoned their most vital duties. One young mother from Illinois was charged with child neglect when it was discovered that she had left a two-, a four- and a

five-year-old child in the care of a twelve-year-old baby-
sitter so that she could fly to Graceland.

When the fans arrived, or even before they left home,
they ordered flowers. The customary floral offerings did
not suffice. They demanded the symbols of their cult. From
all over the world, orders poured into the florists of Memphis for guitars, hound dogs, teddy bears, broken hearts,
bibles and, above all, crowns. Hundreds of floral crowns
had to be fashioned with inscriptions that read "The King,"
"To Our King," "The Only King." The symbolic and ritualistic mania that had always characterized the faithful
now reached its final frenzy. Soon the supply of flowers in
Memphis was exhausted. Orders were dispatched to other
cities. Their supplies were also quickly depleted. Eventually, two great airlifts were organized, which brought
in from California and Colorado an emergency supply of
five tons of flowers.

One hundred vans were pressed into service to deliver
the flowers on a round-the-clock basis. The first displays
were brought to the house and set up in the drawing room,
where the body was to be laid out. As more flowers were
received, the music room, the dining room, the trophy
room, the den were swiftly filled. Still the flood of flowers
poured in, increasing rather than diminishing in volume,
until there was no alternative but to start setting out the
largest pieces before the house. Soon the entire length of
Graceland was staked out in floral displays that threatened eventually to inundate the property. As the mourners
began to form their great line during the night following
Elvis's death, taking their positions in the dark like those
first crowds twenty-one years before in Times Square, the
sickly sweet odor of funeral flowers came wafting down
the hill from the house.

Eventually, the floral flood overwhelmed the property.
When the number of tributes had reached three thousand,
orders were given for the flowers to be transported to Forest Hill Cemetery. If the period of mourning had been
protracted for just two more days, Elvis's fans would have
poured enough flowers into Memphis to line the highway
to the cemetery. The funeral cortege would have resembled
those oriental religious processions in which priests and

potentates proceed to the shrines upon elephants that
tread ponderously on carpets of blossoms.

At six minutes past noon on the second day, as the
oppressive heat of August was made even more unbearable
by a smoggy mist, the waiting crowds were electrified by
the appearance of a motorcade advancing along the boulevard with flashing dome lights and the low moan of
muted sirens. It was the hearse bearing the body to Graceland. The Music Gate was swung wide by two details of
police, six men to each wing. Then they were forced shut
against the protesting fans, as the big white hearse as-
cended the curving driveway. Elvis came home for the last
time encased in a nine-hundred-pound seamless copper
casket. No undertaker in Memphis possessed such a costly
casket. It had been flown in overnight from the manufacturer in Oklahoma City.

When the massive lid was raised, Elvis's intimates were
horrified by his appearance. The embalmers had not succeeded in restoring the mutilated corpse. The fat face swollen with engorged blood had proven an insurmountable
obstacle to the local morticians. Elvis appeared to have a
swelled head. Larry Geller was on hand to style the hair
for the last time. He did the best he could; but at one point
in the afternoon, a sideburn came loose and had to be glued
on afresh.

Elvis was costumed for his final appearance in a white
suit that he had received from Vernon as a Christmas gift.
He wore a light blue shirt and a pale gold tie. On his hand
shone his gold and diamond TCB ring with its two lightning bolts. As he looked so deformed, a strict ban on pictures was imposed. Nonetheless, one of Elvis's poor relations, Bobby Mann, smuggled a Minox camera into the
house and took the shot that was published in *The En-
quirer*. The picture shows the face in profile buried deep
in the satin lining of the coffin. The facial configuration
and particularly the dark shadowing around the eyes made
Elvis in death resemble Gladys.

As the day wore on, the late summer heat became ever
more oppressive. The sufferings of the devoted reached
alarming proportions. The local Red Cross had stationed
its canteen in the midst of the mourners and had erected

first-aid stations in tents on the lawns of Graceland. As
one mourner after another fainted, cries of "Medic! Medic!"
resounded up and down the line, as on a battlefield. At the
same time, the mood of the crowd began to change.

When the first crowds had gathered at Graceland, their
demeanor had been that of people who had just received
some crushing blow, like a sentence to prison. They were
limp, broken, glassy-eyed. They would slump down on the
curb to bury their faces in their hands and cry. By the
afternoon of the second day, the mood had shifted to one
of seething hysteria. There were outcries and scuffles. Wild
rumors ran up and down the lines. Frenzied speculations
were exchanged. There was a feeling that now anything
could happen. The police were apprehensive. At all times,
two helicopters were overhead, searching the crowds for
signs of incipient violence. On the ground, the detail assigned to Graceland was never less than 150 uniformed
men. As a special precaution, a National Guard unit was
called out and military sentries posted before the house.

When the gates were thrown open at three in the afternoon to the mourners, the mood changed yet again, this
time to an attitude of anxious anticipation. It was obvious
to everyone that it would be impossible for all those who
had lined up to enter and leave the house in the two hours
allotted for this purpose. The question now became: Would
they get in? After making such great efforts to see Elvis
one last time, would they reach their goal? When the hour
of five arrived, only a fraction of those who had come had
been admitted to the house. Though they were rushed past
the coffin with the greatest speed commensurate with dignity, there was no admitting them all. Vernon Presley,
vulnerable as always to such appeals, authorized the extension of the viewing period another hour and a half,
until six-thirty. By that time, about twenty thousand had
filed before the casket. Finally, orders were given that no
more were to be admitted.

Police officers, using bullhorns, announced that the
gates were going to be closed. There was a tremendous
uproar, as the people cried, "No! No!" or "Just a half hour
more!" For one dreadful moment, it was feared there might
be a riot. Would the fans stampede through the gates and

dash up the driveway to the house, like a rock 'n' roll crowd charging the stage? The officials commanding the police and the troops massed all their men behind the gates. Prepared to call for immediate reinforcements, they gave the order to close the entrance. When the patrolmen started pushing the gates shut, the people gave ground. The point of danger was past. Soon the crowds were melting away. They would mass again the following afternoon, when they came to see the funeral procession.

On the morning of the third day, at four A.M., there were still many people standing outside the stone fence of Graceland under the yellow sodium vapor lights. Suddenly a white Ford racing up the boulevard swerved in and out of the crowd, knocking down several people and causing a frantic outcry. The driver was arrested just a block away: He was a nineteen-year-old lad named Treatise Wheeler. With him were a couple of teenaged girls and a number of cans of beer, some full, some empty. As the arrest was being made, the paramedics rushed to the aid of the people who had been hit. All three of them were teenaged girls. Two of them were dead. The third was critically injured. The moment the crowd realized what had happened, it came charging down the street to seize the driver. Cries of "Lynch him!" "String him up!" were heard. The police threw their man and his companions into a squad car and left the scene hurriedly.

This third day, August 18, was declared by the governor of Mississippi, Cliff Finch, a day of mourning. Governor Ray Blanton of Tennessee also ordered all flags in that state lowered to half mast. President Carter issued a statement at the White House, asserting that "Elvis Presley's death deprives our country of a part of itself," and concluding that "he was a symbol to the people the world over of the vitality, rebelliousness and good humor of this country." From countless other sources all around the world came tributes and recollections and statements of regret and loss.

On the day of the funeral, at nine o'clock in the morning, a fleet of vans began to pour in and out of the gates of Graceland, carting off the thousands of floral displays, which were being conveyed to the cemetery. The mood of the crowd, which had shifted so many times, suggested now the atmosphere before one of Elvis's out-of-town shows. Souvenir hawkers worked the long lines, peddling Elvis T-shirts or selling postcards of Graceland or serving soft drinks and ice cream. The fans were engrossed now in comparing their collections of memorabilia or boasting of how many years they went back with the King or how many miles they had traveled to this sacred spot. As the time for the funeral neared and the special guests began to arrive, including a couple of indubitable celebrities such as Ann-Margret and George Hamilton, speculation and rumors began to build about who else would appear or who had actually gained entrance unnoticed. It was widely rumored, for example, that Burt Reynolds had slipped into Graceland riding in the back of a bread truck.

Bread had been the primary thought in Colonel Parker's mind when he had arrived that morning, dressed in a loud aloha shirt and wearing an admiral's cap. He had spent the previous day in New York firming up his deal with Factors, Inc. Now it was vital that the Colonel get "Mr. Vernon's" signature on the dotted line. Sitting down at the dining room table, clearly within sight of Elvis in his casket, the Colonel explained his proposition to the doddering father and collected the desired endorsement.

The funeral service was a hopelessly inadequate ceremony. The arrangements were improvised by half a dozen competing people, all of whom were eager to assert their authority, but none of whom had the remotest idea of what was appropriate or how to achieve the goal. Elvis would have wanted a funeral comparable to the grandiose wedding ceremony that he had spent his last night imagining. He would have relished the thought of a grand ritual conducted in the Auditorium and witnessed by all the highest government officials and showbiz celebrities and carried by the media all over the country like the obsequies for Jack Kennedy. A believer that all religions were one, Elvis would have welcomed a service in which ministers and rabbis, priests and yogis, took turns at the altar. (In his last years Elvis wore habitually about his neck a cross and a Star of David, explaining, "I wouldn't want to be kept out of heaven on a technicality.") The King demanded the

service of a king, but what he got was about right for some
cornball country yodeler destined for the Hall of Fame in
Nashville.

Colonel Parker invited Elvis's warm-up act, the comedian Jackie Kahane, to deliver the eulogy. The old Jewish joker did the best he could. As he stood before two
hundred guests squeezed into the drawing and dining
rooms, with the musicians behind a screen in the music
room, he began: "When Colonel Parker hired me, he said,
'Keep it clean.' Elvis Presley always stood for clean entertainment." The next speaker was a local minister of no
distinction, who was supposed to be Vernon's minister,
although none of the Presleys ever went to church or had
any dealings with ministers—a breed toward whom Elvis
was always very sarcastic. This poor man delivered himself of an address that could have come off the back of one
of Elvis's shlocky record albums: "Elvis never lost his desire to stay in close touch with humanity"—this of a man
who was the most notorious recluse in the history of the
entertainment business. The third and briefest speaker
was the TV evangelist Rex Humbard, whose association
with Elvis consisted of one brief backstage meeting, in the
course of which Elvis suggested that the Second Coming
might be nigh. Had it not been for the efforts of the gospel
singers behind the screen—Jake Hess, James Blackwood
and J. D. Sumner with their groups and Kathy West-
moreland with her high "heavenly" voice—the ceremony
would have been an utter fiasco.

Finally, the moment came for which everyone was longing. The enormously heavy casket was shouldered by Elvis's pallbearers: Lamar Fike, Charlie Hodge, Gene Smith,
George Klein, Joe Esposito, Billy Smith, Jerry Schilling
and Dr. Nichopolous. As they were carrying the coffin
through the house door, there was a loud cracking overhead and a dead limb fell from one of the oak trees. Lamar
recalled Elvis saying many times: "Wherever I am, if there
is a way to communicate with you—I'll find it!"

The finest and most appropriate part of the funeral was
the motor cortege. Automobiles had been Elvis's lifelong
passion. Nothing would have pleased him better than some
signal display of car consciousness. As if in recognition of

this unvoiced demand, the funeral director decreed that all the vehicles bearing the official party, as well as the hearse, should be white! It was a perfect stroke. White had become Elvis's color ever since his revival at Las Vegas. White accorded best with the spirit of a performer who was received as a pop messiah. As the Music Gate swung open for Elvis for the final time, he emerged onto Elvis Presley Boulevard as mighty as a king, borne along in a massive white Cadillac hearse, preceded by a glittering silver Cadillac limousine and trailed by sixteen white Cadillac limousines. Elvis had boarded at last that mystery train—"sixteen coaches long."

As the motorcade began its slow mournful progress toward the cemetery, it was swelled by fifty more vehicles carrying the guests who could not be accommodated in the big cars as well as the press. Numerous motorcycle flankers patrolled beside the procession, which was viewed silently by thousands of people lined up on both sides of the highway along the three-mile route. Overhead, taking pictures of the event, were a half dozen helicopters, whose thut-thut-thutting rotors sounded in the silent air like muffled drums.

So slowly did the cortege move that it was an hour before it entered the gates of the cemetery. Finally, the procession reached its goal: a grim-looking granite mausoleum shaped like a little Greek temple with four Doric columns. As the family and guests stood to one side in a semicircle, the pallbearers shouldered the coffin again and carried it to the crypt. The rest of the party followed and bowed their heads in prayer. Then, they were dismissed. Only Vernon lingered behind.

As he stood there watching, five workmen entered the space with a wheelbarrow full of sand, a five-gallon bucket of water, a bag of cement and a box of tools. Setting to work, they sealed the crypt first with a double slab of concrete, then with an outer slab of marble. No ghoul was going to have an easy time snatching the body of the King.

Though the obsequies were concluded, the fans were still not satisfied. They required something more before they could turn away from this riveting event. So it was decided that on the morning following the interment, twenty florists would come to the cemetery and strip the floral displays so that every fan could have a flower as a memento. By nine that morning, a thousand people were standing at the gates of the cemetery. As this was the first time that unlimited access was being offered to Elvis, tens of thousands of people decided to seize the opportunity that they had hitherto been denied. That day proved as great a demonstration of Elvis's popularity as any of the preceding days.

By midafternoon, traffic was strung out, bumper-to-bumper, all the way from Graceland to the cemetery and a half mile beyond. Cars crammed with the curious converged from every direction. The exhaust fumes and heat on this August afternoon were almost unbearable. Inside the cemetery, the police pleaded with the crowds through bullhorns to keep off the graves and to leave as soon as they had taken their pictures and received their token flower. By the end of the day, the superintendent of Forest Hill estimated that fifty thousand visitors had passed through the gates. Not only had every precious flower been taken, but even the leaves, ribbons and styrofoam backings had been eagerly snatched. Everything the fans had bestowed, they had now reclaimed.

Epilogue:
Always Elvis

WHEN THE WORD that Elvis Presley had died was received in Hollywood, one cynical showbiz kibitzer cracked: "Good career move!" He was right, of course. Elvis live was a problem. Elvis dead was a property. In fact, in the year after his death, he became the hottest property in the business. The explanation for this bizarre phenomenon lies in an ancient, seemingly remote theory about the connection between royalty and divinity.

During the Middle Ages, when everyone from the simplest peasant to the most sophisticated theologian believed, in Shakespeare's words, "There is a divinity that doth hedge a king," an elaborate doctrine and practice was developed for distinguishing between the king as man and the king as god. At royal funerals, for instance, the wasted or bloated corpse of the king was conveyed through the streets in a coffin surmounted by an exact replica of the king as he appeared in his prime, dressed in his coronation robes and bearing in his waxen hands the orb and scepter, symbols of his dominion over the world. The effigy signified the king's immortality, his "body politic": a body devoid of "Defects and Imbecilities," which, though manmade, was imperishable, as opposed to his natural body,

693

which, though made by God, was corruptible. Now let us
apply this theory to the death of the King.

The moment Elvis was pronounced dead, his immortal
body, which we call today his "image," was released from
the encumbrances of his mortal frame, with its all-too-
obvious defects and imbecilities. The result was an instant
resurrection. Overnight, the King sprang up again with
all the force that belongs to an immortal. The first sign
of his revitalization was the ubiquity of his image. Everywhere you turned you saw his face and heard his voice.
RCA's pressing plant labored around the clock struggling
to satisfy the overwhelming demand for his records; eventually the company was to announce that its total sales
of Presley products had reached the awesome total of *one
billion units*. At the same time, TV stations all around the
world began to run Elvis festivals that put all his films
back into circulation. The paraphernalia industry discovered in Elvis such a Golconda that soon whole stores or
even, as across the highway from Graceland, an entire
shopping center filled up with souvenirs—two hundred
million dollars' worth in the first year alone! Sheer numbers, the awesome scale of his success, its unimaginable
immensity, had always been a vital element in the Elvis
mystique. Never during his life, however, had the King's
visible presence ever swelled to such colossal proportions.
Only by dying could Elvis live up to his Barnumesque
ballyhoo, as "The World's Greatest Entertainer."

This final burgeoning of the King could be dismissed
as simply an illusion, the product of the customary posthumous reprise of a great entertainer's works and days.
To view Elvis Posthumous in this light, however, would
be to miss the point entirely; for what was asserting itself
after his death was not simply nostalgia or the compulsion
to rerun his career. Quite the contrary, Elvis's death
marked the beginning of a second life in which he both
grew enormously as a man and asserted himself through
important new dimensions as a performer.

Elvis had been so totally concealed and controlled during his lifetime that only after his death did the public
begin to get even the most rudimentary idea of what sort
of person he was. Commencing with the West-Hebler book,

Elvis—What Happened?, which sold an astounding three
and one-half million copies, every member of the Presley
entourage, right down to his hospital nurse and his household cook, struggled to let the Cat out of the bag. Most of
these people knew so little about Elvis and were so fearful
of saying what they did know that the net effect of this
vast outpouring of books was simply to heighten the curiosity and increase the perplexity that had always been
the lot of the public. Nonetheless, some of the books offered
solid information. Soon the vaporous outline of the mythic
Elvis began to fill with jarring facts and shocking revelations.

At the same time that the King's literary image was
undergoing a radical transformation, his physical image
was likewise being altered by the appearance of hundreds
of candid photos that offered a very different picture of
Elvis from all those carefully posed shots that had poured
for a quarter of a century from the Colonel's publicity mill.
Especially revealing were the photographs by Alfred
Wertheimer, who had dogged Elvis in the spring and summer of his most memorable year, 1956, catching him in
the act of thrusting his fat tongue into the mouth of a
backstage groupie or taking a fresh pair of Jockey briefs
from the hand of his doting mother or hunkering on the
globular, nubby-textured, dowel-legged furniture of the
house on Audubon, listening to his own records, while
showing a bare back spotted and pitted with acne and a
sullen, sensual and self-absorbed face, like the face of a
young George Wallace.

Even more penetrating were the photos snapped by a
Munich nightclub photographer, Rudolf Paulini. What
these pictures documented was the blank, listless, half-
stoned yokel that Elvis became when he was separated
from his showbiz persona. A big baby-faced boy with short
unruly hair, dressed in ugly, ill-fitting civilian clothes, he
allows himself to be taken with every ugly hussy in torn
net stockings and sleazy sateen leotard. As the dancers
and hookers of this upholstered sewer entwine themselves
about him, flashing manic grins revealing those bad European teeth in those old-fashioned horse gums, Elvis offers himself up like a life-sized dummy.

Not just the man but the performer continued to emerge
after his death. Though RCA had nothing better to offer
than gleanings from its soon exhausted archives, the record
bootleggers, those great friends of the fans, cut the legal
knots that had long restrained the release of Elvis's most
significant live sessions. The legendary Elvis of the *Louisiana Hayride,* the Dorsey Brothers shows and the
Hawaiian benefits appeared. All the jams from the Singer
Special were offered in two beautifully packaged albums
from California that far surpassed both in interest and in
appearance any legitimate offerings of Victor. In yet another illicit release came at last the most sought-after tape
in the history of rock 'n' roll: the fabled "Million Dollar
Quartet," an impromptu sing in the Sun Studio around
Christmas 1956, by the three greatest heroes of rockabilly:
Elvis, Jerry Lee Lewis and Carl Perkins (minus the anticipated fourth voice, Johnny Cash). Though in this instance
the reality of the recording hardly matched the glamour of
its legend, the value of the disc as a document was enormous. At last you were inside the Sun Studio listening attentively as Sam Phillips's greatest singers did what they
most enjoyed doing: pickin' and singin' their favorite rock
songs and hymns.

Death also made more visible the magical and religious
powers of the King. The immense and inexhaustible appetite for Elvis souvenirs and memorabilia provided an
awesome demonstration of *mana:* the supernatural force
that is believed to lodge in certain beings and which can
be transferred from their bodies to other bodies by means
of physical contact. The Veronica, the replica of the cloth
that St. Veronica pressed against the face of Jesus as he
bore the cross, thereby capturing his likeness, is the classic
example of mana in the West. Now a similar transfer was
effected from the face of the star who so often identified
himself with Jesus to the bodies of his fans through the
medium of the celebrity T-shirt.

As for the notion of the King's divinity, it was exempli-
fied in a manner that far surpassed the symbolism of the
medieval monarchs. Instead of a mere wax dummy, Elvis
had for his emblem of perpetuity a whole legion of living
effigies: the Elvis impersonators. These strange figures

sprang out of the soul of the Elvis cult, which had always
entailed flagrant mimicry, as had the celebration of Elvis's
only rival for the title "World's Greatest Entertainer,"
Charlie Chaplin. Like the Little Tramp, the Hillbilly Cat
inspired his admirers, all those hungry souls desperate to
participate in his being and exercise his magic, to make the
most extravagant gestures of identification.

What one saw after Elvis's death, however, was not just
emulation but replication: the rite according to St. Xerox.
Like those mythical soldiers sprung from dragon's teeth,
there appeared overnight a new class of entertainers who
were not so much mimics, impersonators or impressionists
as Elvis clones. Some of these human effigies were so fantastically dedicated to their assumed identity that, like
transsexuals, they submitted their bodies to plastic surgery so that their natural resemblance might be height-
ened to virtual indistinguishability. Their only problem
lay in the fact that Elvis's image had changed so much
over the years, from the skinny Hillbilly Cat to the obese
showroom stud, that what they really needed was not so
much plastic surgery as some pneumatic device that would
allow them to inflate and deflate at will like balloon dolls.

Even as the Elvis clones started to appear on the nightclub stage and the TV screen (some of them making as
much as $45,000 a week at Las Vegas, where the real
Elvis had bombed during his last engagement), the latest
development in American popular culture became the New
Wave—Punk phenomenon. One of the most striking features of this new fad was the fashion look it inspired: punks
togged out in the bop clothes and greasy hairstyles, as
they struck the rough trade poses, that comprised the image of the original Elvis. The result was that not only the
King's men but the King's people were transformed into
Elvis clones. At a New Wave club in the late seventies,
you could see a horde of Elvis lookalikes thrilling to the
performance of an Elvis epigone, like Elvis Costello, whose
music was directly inspired by Elvis's first rockabilly recordings. What a coming together!

The customary interpretation of such surrealistic hall-
of-mirrors scenes is that they are products of nostalgia, a
much-abused term whose meaning has now been stretched

beyond its tolerable limits in the effort to avoid recognizing how inadequate is this concept for explaining current sensibility. Nostalgia in its conventional sense means the longing for some treasured moment in one's past. Such a yearning could hardly be the inspiration for the Punk Generation because its members were not yet born when Elvis the Pelvis was at the peak of his fame. Not recollection but infatuation is the key to Punk: infatuation with a pop myth, a hipper, harder version of *Happy Days*, an idealized epoch that the current generation did not experience but which it feels it should have experienced because it was the last moment that offered the bliss of unself-conscious adolescent joy. Punk, American style, is pop culture's counterpart to the romantic's infatuation with the Middle Ages or the eighteenth-century cult of antiquity.

All the bizarre phenomena that followed upon Elvis's death can be interpreted as expressions of the fundamental conviction that the King was not dead but alive. It is not surprising, therefore, that the more fanatical Elfans should have labored to prove that he was not dead, or, at least, that he had not died of natural causes. Thus, it was often said among the fans that Elvis had staged his death. What was more interesting than this familiar fantasy was the reason given for the hoax. It was widely believed that Elvis had removed himself from the world in order to escape the fans![1] A more sophisticated version of this pipe dream had Elvis checking into some mysterious West

---

[1] The most frequently cited cause for Elvis's death in the six hundred interviews conducted for this book was persecution by his fans. No one but his intimates realized that Elvis exulted in his public's extravagant behavior and often sought to provoke it. Elvis's real attitude toward the fans is neatly conveyed in an anecdote told by Gerald Peters, his limousine driver. On the first occasion Peters drove for Elvis, the fans started to chase the car. Peters executed a brilliant maneuver and eluded his pursuers. Instead of praise, however, he received a rebuke. Elvis warned him never again to flee the fans. The proper procedure, he explained, was to drive along as if they were unobserved; in other words, to offer themselves to their voyeuristic public with the unconcern of professional exhibitionists.

Coast clinic the moment he learns he is dying so that from healthy cells removed from his diseased body he can be regenerated as a clone. *Official UFO* magazine offered a one-hundred-thousand-dollar reward for any information concerning this spooky creature.

Even if a fan couldn't swallow the crazy notion that Elvis was still alive, he didn't have to accept the fact that the King's death had been inevitable. After all, who was to say what—or *who*—had killed Elvis Presley? The idea that the King had not died a natural death was voiced on ABC's *20/20* by Geraldo Rivera. The aggressive TV reporter, a former lawyer, thrust the finger of accusation squarely at Dr. George Nichopolous, Dr. Elias Ghanem and Dr. Max Shapiro, a Los Angeles dentist with whom Elvis had been very friendly. Rivera's most impressive offering was a copy of the confidential report by Bioscience Laboratory analyzing the specimens obtained through the post-mortem. A battery of eminent forensic pathologists was shown the report, and they all agreed that the cause of Elvis's death was *polypharmacy,* the lethal interaction of a number of drugs taken concurrently.

Rivera also denounced Dr. Jerry Francisco for covering up the true cause of Elvis's death. The case against the coroner was built on uncontradicted assertions that the contents of Elvis's stomach had been destroyed before the autopsy; that the police had closed the case the night of the death—long before the full findings of the autopsy were available—and that the supervising pathologist and his assistant had not concurred with Dr. Francisco's final pronouncement, that there was "no evidence of drug abuse." Efforts by ABC to set the matter to rest once and for all by obtaining a copy of the autopsy were foiled when a Memphis court ruled that the autopsy, having been requested by the deceased's family, not the county, was protected by the privacy rule for fifty years.

The charge that the King had been "murdered" was lodged by John Lennon just before he was murdered. In an interview in *Newsweek,* Lennon drew on his closely parallel experience as a superstar and long-time drug user to locate the ultimate cause of Elvis's death in his lifestyle, which consisted in being surrounded by people who would do anything to satisfy their master in order to protect their own favored positions. As Lennon grimly quipped: "It's the courtiers that kill the king."

The man who knew best what killed Elvis was also the man most determined to act as if Elvis had never died. Not more than a few minutes after he received the news of Elvis's death, Colonel Parker told Lamar Fike: "Nothing has changed. This won't change anything." Soon the old man demonstrated exactly what he meant. Shifting into high gear, the Colonel started cutting deals and laying out cards so fast that in the first year of his posthumous career Elvis Presley made far more money than he had during any year of his life. Colonel had always had the nerve to ask for the top price; now his bluff reached overweening proportions. When NBC wanted to use five minutes from an old Elvis special for the company's fiftieth anniversary program, Colonel demanded five hundred thousand dollars. When he started peddling the rights to an Elvis documentary that would employ all the stuff in Elvis's private film stash, the asking price was ten million dollars.

So carried away did Colonel become with the idea that he was still representing "The World's Greatest Entertainer" that he tried to play Elvis one last time at Las Vegas. Taking a leaf from the great Barnum's book—the Barnum who rallied from the news that Jumbo the Elephant had been killed by ordering the huge beast stuffed and put on exhibit—Colonel Parker staged a festival titled "Always Elvis" at the Hilton International in September 1979, substituting for his 255-pound "boy" a 450-pound, $150,000 bronze statue that resembled an enormous souvenir paperweight. The suckers were inveigled into paying the customary admission price for an Elvis show, fifteen dollars, to be admitted to an exhibition room that contained, like a gyp show at the carnival, nothing better than a few old costumes on dummies that were too small for the sleeves and an endless array of paraphernalia displays presided over by peddlers who had paid the Colonel a good price for the privilege of displaying their wares in such a prime location.

Colonel's next brainstorm was bottling Elvis. He authorized the Frontenac Vineyards at Paw Paw, Michigan, to offer 120,000 bottles of a white wine with a picture of Elvis on the front of the bottle and on the back a commemorative poem by the Colonel. The poem earned the Colonel over $28,000 in royalties, making him, line for line, the best-paid poet in the world.

The first three years after Elvis's death were the Colonel's glorious Indian summer. Though the grosses tapered off after the incredible first year, the operating expenses were virtually nil. What's more, the Colonel was no longer troubled by the defects and imbecilities of an aging and drug-addicted star. He had finally found the perfect client: one who never talked back or made trouble, one who was forever young and sexy. Elvis earned twenty million dollars in this period. No living entertainer could match that figure. The Colonel took the lion's share, and the estate, which after Vernon's death in June 1979 devolved on Lisa Marie, received about half as much.

Then, just as everything was going so nicely, the good ship Hustler struck a submerged mine. On September 29, 1980, the probate court at Memphis received a fifty-two-page report on the management of the Elvis Presley Estate prepared by a court-appointed attorney, Blanchard E. Tual. The occasion for his appointment had been the presentation of a petition by the executors of the estate—Priscilla Presley, Joe A. Hanks (Elvis's former accountant) and the National Bank of Memphis (Elvis's former bank)— for approval of all the financial transactions they had made with Colonel Parker on behalf of the estate. Once this approval was granted, the executors intended to put the wealth of the estate into a trust fund, which might remove it from any further public scrutiny. When Judge Joseph W. Evans read the petition, he was troubled by the enormous commissions the Colonel was charging the estate. Instead of giving his approval, he appointed a guardian ad litem, or temporary guardian, for Lisa Marie, charging him with the duty of representing and defending the child's interests.

Blanchard E. Tual could have discharged the responsibility with a relatively narrow inquiry focusing simply on the final compensation agreement; instead, he chose to investigate the entire field of the Colonel's dealings with

Elvis, which soon entailed an extensive and unprecedented
inquiry into the hitherto carefully guarded network of relationships between Colonel Parker and RCA Records, Hill
and Range, William Morris, Factors, Inc., and a host of
other major entertainment companies. Proceeding with
skill and address, Tual was able in six months to report
in impressive detail on what amounted to a quarter century of financial transactions entailing billions of dollars
of gross earnings. What he discovered added up to a searing indictment of Colonel Parker's management of Elvis
from first to last.

The report revealed the exorbitant commissions the
Colonel had charged Elvis; the deals and arrangements
that were contrary to the star's best interests; the failures
of fiduciary responsibility; and, in a crowning irony, the
extreme impropriety of the Colonel's continuing to act
after Elvis's death precisely as he had when his client was
alive. For the conviction that "nothing has changed" had
passed out of Colonel Parker and into Vernon Presley and
the trustees with such force that it had hypnotized them
all into acting in a manner that was not only unjust to
Lisa Marie but arguably illegal. For as the guardian ad
litem demonstrated, the enabling agreements were simply
updated versions of the same contracts that Colonel had
drawn with Elvis when he was alive; therefore, they continued to rest on the basic assumption that both parties
were alive! The Colonel's supreme creation, the Elvis
Myth, now suddenly boomeranged and came back to strike
the old man down in the act of exploiting his creature.

Even more ironic was what happened next. Not long
after the report was filed, newspapers and magazines all
over the country began running stories about how Colonel
had taken fifty percent of Elvis. These stories threatened
the Colonel's reputation nearly as much as the stories
about drug addiction had damaged Elvis before his death.
Naturally, they deeply disturbed the old man. One night
while leaving his office in the RCA building in Hollywood,
the Colonel slipped and fell on the threshold of an elevator.
Stunned by the fall and burdened by his enormous weight,
he found himself unable to rise. The elevator door, which
had recoiled after the first impact, now rolled back again

like a rubber-edged guillotine and struck the Colonel's recumbent body. Over and over again, the door buffeted the old man, until he was rescued. He could hardly have been beaten worse if he had been set upon by the King's immortal body, chopping and kicking his lifetime persecutor with the full power of a karate killer. Colonel's injuries included a permanent disability in his right shoulder.

The Colonel remained undaunted. When people would inquire about his arm, suspended in a sling like a wounded soldier's, he would reply: "Doctors say I may never get full use of it again, but..." here he would make a Fagin-like gesture, rubbing together thumb and forefinger—"I can still grab ahold on them big checks."

On July 31, 1981, the guardian ad litem filed a final report that was far more damaging than his original statement. This document revealed several private financial agreements between Colonel Parker and, respectively, RCA, the Hilton International, and Jerry Weintraub's Management III: an arrangement that the guardian stigmatized as a "textbook-type conflict of interest." When these agreements, of which Elvis had no knowledge, are added to all the side agreements Colonel contrived for his own benefit after Elvis's death, without the knowledge of the Estate, the picture of Parker and RCA that emerges is one of possible conspiracy and fraud. Parker appears a conman who enriches himself by selling his client short or allowing Elvis or his heirs to be cheated. Drawing his conclusion from a mountain of evidence, the guardian concluded his report by denouncing Colonel Parker and RCA for "collusion, conspiracy, fraud, misrepresentation, bad faith, and overreaching."

Once the dirty little secret of Elvis's management was out of the bag, matters swiftly took their course. On August 14, the probate court ordered the Presley Estate to sue Colonel Parker within forty-five days. The Court requested further information concerning the deals with RCA Records within ninety days before ruling on the possibility of litigation. The Court also ordered audits of accountings from Factors, Inc., and Chappell Music, which manages Elvis's publishing companies. At the same moment, the news broke that IRS had raised its assessment

of the Presley Estate in light of the guardian's disclosures
to twenty-five million dollars. The resulting demand for
fourteen million six hundred thousand dollars in additional taxes presented the Estate with the grave threat of
bankruptcy. Though Colonel was quick to deny any wrong-
doing, it was suddenly obvious to millions of people the
world around that the world's most celebrated artist-man-
ager relationship had finally, after twenty-six years of
uninterrupted success, exploded in scandal.

In October, 1981, Dr. Nichopolous was brought to trial
at Memphis on fourteen counts of illegally prescribing
drugs. The list of patients included Jerry Lee Lewis as
well as Elvis Presley. Testimony at the trial revealed that
in the last thirty-one and a half months of Elvis's life, he
had received from Dr. Nick more than 19,000 doses of
various drugs, including a great number of addictive and
dangerous drugs. Dr. Nick's defense rested on two basic
arguments: 1) that Elvis could not have survived without
drugs; 2) that Dr. Nick sought to wean Elvis from drugs
by substituting placebos for real drugs. Lawyers who re-
viewed the trial, which resulted in Nichopolous's acquittal,
attributed the result in large measure to the superiority
of the defense attorney, James Neal (the Watergate prosecutor) to the local prosecutor. At one point, for example,
the prosecutor had five local doctors ready to testify that
Nichopolous's prescribing practices were out of line with
community standards. Neal persuaded the prosecutor to
present only one of the five doctors, stipulating that the
others would have supported his position—a rather feeble
substitute for the effect of having all the doctors testify
before the jury. It was also felt at Memphis that the whole
emphasis of the trial was allowed to fall on Elvis Presley's
culpability, which was not an issue before the court and
which aroused the powerful protective instinct which has
asserted itself everywhere and every time Elvis has been
depicted in a bad light.

Colonel Parker was not prosecuted until January, 1982,
at which time he became the target of a complaint filed
by the executors and trustees of the Presley Estate before
the California State Labor Commission. California has a

unique and rarely invoked law that obliges everyone who acts as an agent or manager to register with the Labor Commission. Failure to register is punishable by a fine equivalent in amount to every dollar the agent has earned representing his client. (The fine is awarded to the client.) Parker was charged with not registering. As this book goes to press, a hearing on the matter is pending.

Though Colonel may end his days enmired in exasperating litigation, while all his Presley income lies frozen in escrow, he did succeed in promulgating his final version of the Elvis Myth. In April 1981, at Memphis, Colonel's long-heralded documentary on Elvis had its premiere. If the filmmakers, headed by David Wolper, had set out to sound simultaneously every note of the King's posthumous career in one profoundly ambiguous chord, they could not have succeeded better.

The notion that the King is still alive is proclaimed by the very title, *This Is Elvis*, which sounds like an urgent introduction to a hot new star, or, at least, one at the peak of his popularity. The basic form, a biography, narrated primarily by an Elvis impersonator, suggests you are getting the story straight from the King's own lips as he watches his life flash before him in his Howard Hughes hideout. His existential status is complicated even further by the constant intercutting of authentic documentary footage with episodes of "docudrama" (filmed with a slightly misted filter) that star Elvis clones playing opposite actors who represent friends and relations who may appear elsewhere in the documentary sections in their own persons. The grand effect is that of a spooky spectacle in the illusion tent at the carnival, or, better, a heart-tugging (and purse-emptying) séance conducted by Madame Blavatsky with her life-sized puppets. The greatest puppet of all is Elvis, who is finally reduced to spouting all those ideas about his life which Colonel Parker put into the mind of the scriptwriter: an oblique but compelling form of ventriloquism.

Paradoxically, however, at the same time that Elvis is being reduced to the status of a dummy, he is released at last to give the greatest performance of his career by being permitted to play in scene after scene (extracted from old kines and TV outtakes) the only hero he could have ever impersonated successfully: himself. His greatest scene is a tour de force of histrionics.

You see Elvis at the end of his life standing onstage, looking like a great white clown. He is smiling but sweating so profusely that his face appears to be bathed in tears. Going up on a line in one of those talking bridges he always had trouble negotiating, he comes down in a kooky, free-associative monologue that summons up the image of the dope-crazed Lenny Bruce or the mind-fuguing Jonathan Winters. For thirty or forty seconds of mental free-fall, you are up in that padded cell atop Graceland watching Elvis blither with tightly shut eyes as he voices all the crazy ideas that come thronging into his dope-sprung mind.

The effect of this startling soliloquy, embarrassing at first, is ultimately exhilarating. The whited sepulchre of the World's Greatest Entertainer falls apart before your eyes and out of the plaster shards comes flaring the soul of the King, gibbering Monty Python nonsense patter and sneering hipster obscenities. Suddenly, you snap to the fact that Elvis ended his life not entirely defeated or demented but fighting to the last, with crack-brained audacity, to break free of his imprisoning image.

Index

CONGO

The National Bestseller by

MICHAEL CRICHTON

Author of THE ANDROMEDA STRAIN

"Darkest Africa. Strangling vines. Rain forest. Pygmies. Clouds of mosquitoes. Rampaging hippos. Roaring gorillas. Killer natives. Gorges. Rapids. Erupting volcanoes. An abandoned city full of diamonds, lost in the jungle. Maybe a new animal species, a weird cross between man and ape, but unheard of in 20th-century anthropology. Zaire. Congo. Michael Crichton's newest thriller. And of course: technology, which is what it's all about today, isn't it? Zoom!"

The Boston Globe

"A gem of a thriller!"

Playboy

"Oh, is this ever a good one!"

Detroit News

"The master of very tall tales plunges into the heart of darkness. . . . A dazzling example of how to combine science and adventure writing."

People

"What entertainment! . . . Crichton has created in Amy a 'talking gorilla' of enough charm to enshrine her in pop culture as firmly as R2D2."

Saturday Review

AVON Paperback   56176 • $2.95
Congo 10-81

The National Bestseller by
GARY JENNINGS

"A blockbuster historical novel. . . . From the start of
this epic, the reader is caught up in the sweep and
grandeur, the richness and humanity of this fictive
unfolding of life in Mexico before the Spanish
conquest. . . . Anyone who lusts for adventure, or that
book you can't put down, will glory in AZTEC!"

The Los Angeles Times

"A dazzling and hypnotic historical novel. . . . AZTEC has
everything that makes a story appealing . . . both
ecstasy and appalling tragedy . . . sex . . . violence . . .
and the story is filled with revenge. . . . Mr. Jennings
is an absolutely marvelous yarnspinner. . . .
A book to get lost in!"

The New York Times

"Sumptuously detailed. . . . AZTEC falls into the same
genre of historical novel as SHOGUN."

Chicago Tribune

"Unforgettable images. . . . Jennings is a master at
graphic description. . . . The book is so vivid that this
reviewer had the novel experience of dreaming of the
Aztec world, in technicolor, for several nights in
a row . . . so real that the tragedy of the
Spanish conquest is truly felt."

Chicago Sun Times

AV☉N Paperback   55889 . . . $3.95

Available wherever paperbacks are sold, or directly from the publisher. Include 50¢ per copy for postage and handling: allow 6-8
weeks for delivery. Avon Books, Mail Order Dept., 224 West 57th
St., N.Y., N.Y. 10019.

Aztec 1-82